The Jewish Bund in Russia

From Its Origins to 1905

The Jewish Bund in Russia
From Its Origins to 1905

Henry J. Tobias

Stanford University Press, Stanford, California   1972

Stanford University Press
Stanford, California
© 1972 by the Board of Trustees of the
Leland Stanford Junior University
Printed in the United States of America
ISBN 0-8047-0764-2
LC 75-153820

To Dora, Itche, and Shime,
who provided the early background

Preface

Historical importance cannot always be measured in terms of political success. Victors do not exist without losers and cannot be understood without them. The study of even a relatively small movement can provide valuable insight into man's condition simply by presenting a unique point of view. The fullness of historical knowledge, like the fullness of life itself, resides in an awareness of the depth of man's imagination and of the experiences he has borne in confronting his problems. Such considerations alone could justify the study of the Bund.

But there is another important reason for studying the Bund. Its history is the record of a search and a struggle for justice, dignity, and identity. And that struggle plainly has great relevance today. Indeed, the search for justice and dignity can never be treated lightly as long as the study of history remains a humanistic enterprise.

I concern myself here with the growth of the Bund itself and of the relationships that were important to its development. Obviously, some of those relationships were more important than others. Establishing ties with the Russian Social Democrats, for example, was a greater Bundist concern than relations with the Polish socialists in the period under study. Accordingly, I have tried to weight the narrative in favor of the larger concerns of the Bundists themselves, and some areas of lesser importance may appear neglected. The definitive history is, in any case, a pipe dream. In the end, one can only work toward that goal in the hope of filling in a few of the blanks—and perhaps creating new interest in filling in those that remain.

As with most acknowledgments, mine are made in the painful knowledge that all the help I received from colleagues, teachers, and friends, and from various institutions cannot be adequately recognized here. I want to thank particularly Professor Charles E. Woodhouse, of the Department of Sociology at the University of New Mexico, for his enormous patience, high standards, and untiring loyalty. My mentor, Anatole G. Mazour, must also be given special mention, for it was his recognition that there was a job to be done on the history of the Bund that prompted me to the task in the first place. And I owe a special debt of gratitude to Mrs. Jeanne Bonnette, who so beautifully rendered the Bund hymn for me.

In the way of institutions, I wish to thank especially the Faculty Research Committee and the Alumni Faculty Grants Committee of the University of New Mexico for their constant support; and the American Philosophical Society for help at particularly crucial moments. The New York Public Library (Slavonic and Jewish divisions), the YIVO Library in New York, and the Zimmerman Library at the University of New Mexico have all served me well.

Above all, I must mention the Bund Archives in New York, without whose existence this work would have been impossible. The natural interest of the staff in my project does not account for the extraordinary sympathy, understanding, and encouragement they gave me. They did considerably more than supply the materials I requested; they sought out much information I would not otherwise have found. The dedication of Hillel Kempinski and Mrs. Lola Szafran and the valuable critical advice of J. S. Hertz literally allowed this volume to become a reality.

Finally, a word of appreciation to my family, who lived with the creation of a work that doubtless affected the fabric of their lives no less than it did mine. To my wife, Haven, I offer a spiritual coauthorship.

Norman, Oklahoma   H.J.T.

Author's Note

Yiddish, the folk idiom of most East European Jews before World War I and the principal language used in Bund publications, is closely related to German, though it has Slavic and Hebrew elements and is written with the Hebrew alphabet. Since its written form was still highly erratic in the period under study, transliteration is something of a problem. I have not attempted to follow the Germanic spelling but have instead relied on the phonetic qualities of the Hebrew alphabet for transliteration. Where dialect differences have produced a variety of spellings, however, I have chosen to hold to a single spelling in violation of the phonetic rule, in order to avoid confusion. There are no capital letters in Hebrew, but because doing away with them altogether could be disturbing to some readers, I have adopted a limited use of capitalization, e.g., *Di Arbeter Shtime*.

The difference between the Russian calendar in use during the Tsarist era and the Western calendar also creates problems. The sources published in Russia are in old style. So are the reports from Russia to the journals published in the West, which themselves employed the Western calendar. Memoir literature is usually vague on dates at best, but tends to rely on the Russian calendar. I have routinely employed (or assumed) the Russian style date unless otherwise noted.

Contents

THE BUND HYMN

THE OATH

Brothers and sisters of work and need,
All who are scattered like far-flung seed—
Together! Together! The flag is high,
Straining with anger, red with blood,
So swear together to live or die!

REFRAIN

Earth with its heaven hears.
Witness: the bright stars,
And our oath of blood and tears.
We swear. We swear.

I

We swear to strive for freedom and right
Against the tyrant and his knave,
To best the forces of the night,
Or fall in battle, proud and brave.

II

We swear our stalwart hate persists,
Of those who rob and kill the poor:
The Tsar, the Masters, Capitalists.
Our vengeance will be swift and sure.

III

To wage the holy war we vow,
Until right triumphs over wrong.
No Midas, Master, Noble now—
The humble equal to the strong.

IV

To the Bund, our hope and faith, we swear
Devotedly to set men free.
Its flag, bright scarlet, waves up there,
Sustaining us in loyalty.

Shlomo Zanvil Rappoport (Sh. An-sky), 1902

Introduction

The "General Jewish Workers' Union in Lithuania, Poland, and Russia," or the Bund as it is commonly known, was founded in Vilna in October 1897 by a group of Jewish Social Democrats representing five cities in the Pale of Settlement. The Bund's history, however, properly begins in the late 1880's, when the founding pioneers first became committed to Marxism and the cause of transforming the Empire into a socialist society. The pioneers, products of a Russian school system that opened their eyes to new enchantments, began their revolutionary careers as cosmopolites whose primary interest and goal was an Empire-wide revolution. Though they never abandoned that position, their emphasis shifted markedly over the years as they became more and more absorbed with the human material around them, the downtrodden and largely passive Jewish working class. By the time the Bund was founded these Jewish Social Democrats had set themselves the task of generating a new spirit in the Jewish proletariat, a sense of national pride and personal worth that would allow the Jewish workers to participate with other proletarians in the struggle for a new society.

Convinced of the correctness of the Russian vision of Marxism, with its heavy emphasis on political action and the attainment of political freedom, and faced with the problem of converting the proletariat of a small and distinct minority into an organized force capable of joining in a common struggle toward that end, the Bundists were led to undertake a series of closely interwoven operations, each amounting to a separate but necessary revolution. The first of these, the building of a socialist society, was at once the most farreaching and far-removed, in their eyes. Like many of their contemporaries, the Bundists chose to devote their energies to a more practical assignment—the destruction of the Tsarist regime, the omnipresent symbol of oppression and the major obstacle to the progress of the revolutionary movement.

But though the end was clear, the means of achieving it were not. The Bundists and their revolutionary cohorts had to make some difficult decisions. How were they to organize the working masses into an instrument for the overthrow of the regime? What appeals should they make to the masses they hoped to lead, and how should they make them? Theory and life mixed here. Answers had to be found that would both accommodate the ideology providing the outlines for the revolution and fit the circumstances of the human material assigned to its execution.

Even the overthrow of the regime, however, was a comparatively remote objective during most of the period studied here. Before the revolutionaries could assume their efforts in earnest the working masses of Russia had to be welded into a single, mighty force. To bring about the necessary class solidarity the Bundists had to undertake yet another revolution—a social and psychological change in the attitude of the Jewish workers. It was an enormous undertaking, this breaking down of a deeply rooted tradition of religious and cultural isolation reinforced by a long history of legal discrimination. And yet, as leaders of a small minority, the Bundists could not dream of achieving victory alone, and perforce had to pin their hopes on an aroused class consciousness and sense of common purpose among all workers. That in turn supposed an end to the mutual distrust and hostility between non-Jew and Jew, in which effort the Bund could do little more than cooperate with parties working among the non-Jewish masses.

The welding of class unity involved a third revolution. Marxist theory postulated an economic struggle as well as a political struggle, a conflict that was bound to develop out of the natural antagonism between worker and master. Since most Jewish workers were employed by coreligionists, the Bund in effect had to call for class warfare in the historically united Jewish community.

Further, both the second and the third revolution had their non-Marxian complexities. The Bundists had no wish to destroy the cultural heritage of the Jewish workers altogether; indeed, they eventually came to consider Jewish cultural development a positive goal. Consequently, they had to face the classic dilemma of many a minority group committed to a universalist movement: how to perform the delicate surgery of separating the group member from his environment and urging him into a new consciousness of the world around him without destroying what he treasures and wishes to retain of his cultural life. In upholding the right of the Jewish workers to exist as Jews, the Bundists were forced to devise a formula that would maintain a balance between assimilation and exclusiveness—and that would, at the same time, be compatible with their Marxist beliefs.

If the Bundists did not realize all their aims, theirs was not a negligible effort. By 1905 the Bund had become a spiritual home for thousands of workers, men and women who firmly believed in its creed of Jewish particularism and Marxist internationalism. It is the development of that creed, the growth of the Jewish movement, and the cycle of revolutions the Bund sought to bring about that I study here.

A brief word about the compass of this work. For reasons that I shall touch on below and that I hope will become even clearer in the course of this study, I have elected to end my narrative with the October days of the Revolution of 1905—to begin, that is, with a few young men and women protesting conditions they found intolerable and groping for ways to correct them, and to end with a mature revolutionary organization engaged in a battle to overthrow its declared enemy, the Tsarist regime. In short, I want to present the evolution of a revolutionary movement, the transformation of isolated, secret, purely local groups into a cohesive, highly motivated party that gained the respect, albeit grudging at times, of the whole of politically minded Russia.

In the period studied the Bund established the major features of its program, narrowing its view of its revolutionary tasks, if not its vision of the revolutionary future. After it moved from a doctrine of general freedom to a specific political and cultural program, it changed very little. Moreover, throughout this period it was the dominant radical force among the Jewish workers in the Empire, indeed often the only force attempting to improve the lot of the Jewish proletariat there. After 1905 it was forced to compete with other radical groups for the allegiance of the Jewish workers. Finally, the period up to 1905 stands apart for psychological reasons. The novelty of a Jewish revolutionary organization that dared to challenge the seemingly all-powerful Tsarist tyranny, the lure of underground work, the idealism of a cause and the strength gained from suffering for that cause—all combined to make this an era of romance and heroism for those who participated in it and for those who came after. Contemporary and later generations of Bundists, and their admirers, remained awed by the trials and successes of the pre-Revolutionary period. The decline of revolutionary fervor after 1905, as well as new conditions brought on by changing circumstances, only enhanced the image of the earlier time. For many Bundists, the days before the Revolution were glorious days, the days of their youth, their time of bright hopes and pristine thoughts.

The Jewish Bund in Russia

From Its Origins to 1905

The Pale of Settlement in 1905
All of the cities shown except Moscow and St. Petersburg were important Bund centers

1. The Historical Background

Toward the end of the eighteenth century, the Tsars were led by their military and diplomatic successes to occupy lands heavily settled by peoples radically different in their cultural and religious life from the Great Russian core of the Empire. Through the Partitions of Poland, a series of dramatic advances in the westward expansion of the Russian frontier, the largest Jewish community in the world became the subjects of Orthodox Christian Tsars. For these Jews this was no wandering into new territory as so many times previously in the Diaspora, but a forcible incorporation into an alien Empire.

The inclusion of heterodox populations within the Empire raised problems for the Tsars that were not readily solved. Policies they had formerly employed against foreign political enemies and alien infidel groups now had to be reconsidered in the light of internal political processes. Rapid assimilation or complete subjugation of such large numbers of newcomers proved impossible, and the problems of a multinational Empire remained a matter of great concern to the regime until its fall. Within the framework of a generally unsatisfactory state of affairs among the national minorities, the Jewish question occupied a unique and important niche.

In the century that elapsed between the last Partition of Poland, in 1795, and the creation of the Bund in 1897, the Tsars set policies for their Jewish subjects that had a remarkable uniformity of purpose. The most general, persistent, and bitterest of the policies was the confinement of the Jews in the Pale of Settlement. The Pale was a ghetto; only a few Jews, by virtue of wealth, education, occupation, or military service, were allowed to live outside it. Moreover, even inside the Pale, the Jews had restricted dwelling rights, which the government altered from time to time. Although the boundaries of the Pale did not remain constant, during the history of the Bund it included the tier of northwestern, southwestern, and southern provinces stretching from the Black Sea to the Baltic coast. Jews also continued to live in the Polish provinces.*

* At the time of the Bund's founding the Pale of Settlement comprised the northwestern provinces (*gubernii*) of Vilna, Kovno, Grodno, Minsk, Vitebsk, and Mogilev, the south-

The preconditions for the creation of the Pale resided in the age-old differences between Jew and Russian, not only in religion but also in culture, civil status, and occupational practice (with the added element of economic competition). The regime stated its attitude toward the Jews in the baldest terms. In 1835 the majority of Tsar Nicholas I's Council of State, discussing the right of Jewish merchants to reside in the interior, agreed that such an intrusion "would produce a very unpleasant impression upon our people, which, on account of its religious notions and its general estimate of the moral peculiarities of the Jews, has become accustomed to keep aloof from them and to despise them." Nicholas concurred, noting: "This question has been determined by Peter the Great. I dare not change it."[1] The twin pillars of faith and tradition provided him with justification for keeping Jew and Russian separate: maintenance of the Pale was a sacred trust.

The Tsars devised legislation that also differentiated the Jews from other non-Russians in the Empire—even those who lived alongside them in the Pale. They levied special taxes on Jews; barred them from certain occupations and limited their access to others; at times restricted their educational opportunities; and periodically expelled them from the rural areas in which they lived within the Pale. These circumstances heightened the mutual awareness of difference between the Jews and their closest neighbors, the Russians, Belorussians, Lithuanians, Poles, and Ukrainians.

Paradoxically, even as the state made great efforts to separate Jew and Russian, it sought to break down the traditional identity of the Jews. Tsars Alexander I (1801–25) and Nicholas I (1825–55), for instance, sought to draw Jews into new occupations and out of the Pale by creating agricultural colonies on the new frontiers in southern Russia and even in Siberia. Other policies were aimed at bringing about a degree of external assimilation. Under Nicholas I, Jewish dress and hair styles came under attack—an action reminiscent of Peter the Great's policies toward the Old Believers. Perhaps the most brutal instrument used to reduce the distinctiveness of the Jewish community was that devised by Nicholas I: recruitment of boys below the age of eighteen and as young as twelve into the army in order to wean them from the faith and customs of their fathers. In 1844, in an effort to break the autonomy of the Jews, Nicholas abolished the Kahal, the traditional Jewish communal governing institution, which had retained some legal functions under Russian rule. Alexander II (1855–81), with a considerably lighter touch, thought to push assimilation by opening Russian schools to Jews and by permitting those with higher education to enter government employment. The Tsars applied this array of mechanisms in a sporadic and arbitrary manner, legislating, rescind-

---

western provinces of Volynia, Podolia, Kiev, Chernigov, and Poltava, the southern provinces of Bessarabia, Kherson, Ekaterinoslav, and Tauride, and the ten Polish provinces.

ing, modifying, and intensifying their acts in ways that at times bewildered both the bureaucracy and the general population, as well as the Jews themselves.

The outlines of the government's thinking and actions emerge from the facts. Jewry, with its religious practices, social institutions, and economic way of life, was regarded as a generally harmful quantity within the Russian Empire. This conclusion led officialdom to uphold the special stamp it placed on its Jewish population, hardening the lines that set the Jews apart from the other peoples of the Empire. It saw them as a religio-cultural-economic group, without claims to national real estate in the Empire like those of the Poles or the Finns. The Jews were considered a rootless people—vulnerable yet stubborn intruders. Uncertain how to deal with them, the regime, at its most benevolent, permitted a carefully selected few to live in the interior of Russia, to attend Russian schools, to receive minor posts in the government, and to assimilate peacefully. At its most perverse, it condoned and abetted violence, practiced libel and discrimination, and foisted on the Jews every disadvantage to which an unwanted but helpless guest could be subjected.

The Jewish community responded to the Russian state out of the resources of its own historical tradition. The vast majority of Jews, from the time they found themselves in Russia until the downfall of the Romanovs in 1917, preserved their cultural identity, thereby thwarting the objectives of the regime. Those among them who sought no change retained a considerable amount of control over their home lives and their educational system. Their well-knit community gave them internal defenses and resources independent of the outside environment. The regime could not breach these arrangements without resorting to extreme force or offering some inducement that would supersede the value of the traditional faith and culture in the eyes of its most ardent practitioners. The state would not take the first course, and had no satisfactory substitute for the second.

At the same time the Jews needed to participate in the general economic life of the country and perforce had to reach beyond their own communal environment. Here they fared far worse than they did in their own religious and cultural setting because of the restrictions forced on them by the state. They had no power to alter the political conditions that constricted their economic welfare, and the means at hand with which to resist the official barriers were few and weak. The petition for redress of grievance frequently proved ineffective, and the bribe an expensive and degrading expedient. True, a number of individual Jews escaped; but the burdensome restrictions continued to bind the vast majority until the fall of the Romanovs. The desires of most of the Jews and the Tsarist government were, therefore, at odds most of the time: what the Jews sought to maintain of their indigenous way of life, the regime wished to destroy; when the Jews had to reach outside the limits of their community, the regime hampered them by limiting the range of their opportunities.

The histories of the Jews and their Christian neighbors within the Empire differed sharply. Bearing the mark of their wanderings, the Jews had no historical territory in Europe and lost no independent territorial status when they became subjects of the Tsars. Unlike the Poles and Finns, who sought to be masters in their own national houses, they were not tied together by bonds of territorial nationalism. Religious practice gave them unique customs, dietary habits, holidays, and educational traditions, even a unique Sabbath. On top of these distinctions lay the use of different languages. In the areas of heavy Jewish concentration, the Jews spoke Yiddish, the heritage of their centuries in Germanic Europe. To be sure, they used the tongue of the people among whom they lived when necessary—Polish or Russian. All the same, the linguistic barrier was yet another wall insulating them from their non-Jewish neighbors.

Extensive cultural differences did not, however, prevent the Jew and the Christian from significantly shaping each other's economic and social lives. In daily contact they depended on each other for goods and services. At times this interdependence even proved strong enough to stay the hand of the state against the Jews. Nicholas I discovered on one occasion that it would be impossible to remove the Jews from a fifty-*verst* strip along the frontier without serious harm to whole cities and to his treasury.[2] In another instance, Prince M. S. Vorontsov, the governor-general of Novorossiia, defended the Jews against the frequently brought charge of parasitism. "One cannot help wondering how these numerous tradesmen can be regarded as useless," he declared, "if one bears in mind that by their petty and frequently maligned pursuits they promote not only rural but commercial life." It was his conclusion that "there is no possibility, and for a long time there will be none, of replacing them."[3] Still, this interdependence did not prevent each group from enjoying separate existences far removed from the purview of the other. Their interaction ordinarily occurred only in the marketplace or in the street, not in the home.

The Jews also differed markedly from their neighbors in the economic structure of their community, and most notably in their relationship to the land. Virtually no Jews farmed for a living—the result of legislation as well as custom—and their concentration in towns was consequently high in proportion to the other peoples of the Empire. In a country where the soil and those who worked or owned it held high esteem and a major place in the economy, the Jews were a world apart; at best they could play only a subsidiary role.

Up to the founding of the Bund, the landowner and the peasant still represented the chief socioeconomic estates of the Empire, and the Jews remained outside both groups. They were instead, as the Grand Duke Nicholas, the future Nicholas I, noted in 1816 in his diary, "everything here [Belorussia], merchants, contractors, saloon-keepers, mill owners, ferry-holders, artisans."[4] (Coming from Nicholas's pen, this remark may be taken as a complaint. But complaint or not, he has given us an idea of just how extensive the concentration of Jews in commerce and small manufacture was.) Although the Jews lost the right to engage in some of these occupations and moved into new ones during the century, their overall pattern of employment remained essentially the same throughout. Table 1 shows the occupational distribution of the Jewish population as compared with the total population of Russia in 1897, the year the Bund was founded.

In general, the Jews faced greater hazards in their economic endeavors than the Christians, both because of legal constraints and because of their insecure status as an alien minority. Where Jewish and Christian merchant, manufacturer, and artisan met, the element of competition frequently came into play—usually to the disadvantage of the Jew. The Christians invoked, and often received, the support of the state. Indeed, the Pale of Settlement itself appears to have been established at least in part because of the complaints of Russian competitors in Smolensk and Moscow, who petitioned the state to confine Jewish residency to areas already inhabited by Jews.[5]

The hostility fostered by economic competition did not end the list of Jewish-Christian problems. The hard-put Russian peasant at times made the local Jewish trader or innkeeper, and even the entire local Jewish population, the target of his wrath. In the last decades of the Empire particularly, officials, confirmed anti-Semites, and even members of the revolutionary community on occasion justified the wholesale violence of the pogroms on the grounds that the Jews were exploiters and to blame for the woes of the population.

In sum, the Jewish community lay in an uneasy relationship to the socio-cultural environment that surrounded it. Bound by the dominant structure

Table 1. Occupational Distribution of the Jewish Population and the Total Population of Russia in 1897
(per cent)

Occupation	Jews	Total population	Occupation	Jews	Total population
Trade	38.65%	3.77%	Free professions, government, etc.	5.22%	2.04%
Manufacture	35.43	10.25	Transport	3.98	1.55
Day labor, servants, etc.	6.61	4.61	Agriculture	3.55	74.31
Indefinite	5.49	2.48	Army	1.07	0.99

SOURCE: B. D. Brutskus, Part 2, p. 11.

and yet distinct from it, the Jews could appear either necessary or harmful in the eyes of the non-Jews, depending on the general conditions outside the Jewish community. To the Jews, the surrounding groups could also be seen as necessary or hostile, or even, as the overwhelming majority, potentially dangerous.

The Jewish community maintained historical continuity through its indigenous social structure. The main criteria of differentiation within the community were wealth, religious learning, and *yikhus* (status acquired chiefly through ancestral wealth and learning).[6] Political power, to the extent that it existed, resided in the hands of the rich and the learned, who were in a better position to gain the ear of local officials than the less-educated or the poor. The power the Jewish leaders exercised over the community was great enough when backed by the state; but they were able to stand only as supplicants before the neighboring non-Jews or the ruling establishment.

The social integration of the Jewish community was a much more powerful force than the political control exercised by the Jewish leaders. The Jews maintained a network of institutions covering religious, welfare, economic, and charitable functions that operated independently of the non-Jewish environment. The *khevrat*, associations based on occupation that bore some resemblance to medieval guilds, were the instruments that carried out these functions.[7] The khevrat exemplify the cohesiveness of large portions of the Jewish community.

The three dimensions that formed the matrix from which the Bund developed—the state, the Jewish community, and the neighboring non-Jewish population—did not in and of themselves create the Bund. The necessary catalyst was provided when developments in Russia caused the old relationships to break down, forcing a search for new responses and opening new horizons in the process.

One of the most important and far-reaching of these developments was industrialization. The irrepressible dynamism of modern industrial civilization, which had already changed the face of Western Europe, began to impress itself in every quarter and on every level of the Empire in the second half of the nineteenth century. Social changes of a cataclysmic nature accompanied the economic changes. In 1861 Tsar Alexander II abolished serfdom, thus setting in motion what was to amount to a social upheaval. This act and the accompanying reform legislation make the 1860's a watershed in Russian history, defining the beginning of the modern era in the social, economic, and legal sense.

These social and economic changes acted as a powerful corrosive on the Empire's old institutions while inducing the creation of new ones. The modern industrial tools, with their incredible efficiency, gradually shunted aside the artisan-craftsmen (depressing but not displacing the class), and the increased production capacity of the machines forced manufacturers to seek broader markets. Businesses that were able to adapt to the changing situation or to adopt the new tools found new wealth and power; the rest limped along or closed their doors. As a modern, urban, industrial working class began to emerge, relations between labor and capital changed—but in ways that went deeper than mere work habits; expectations changed as well. Finally, the end of serfdom dissolved the traditional relationship between nobleman and peasant, and this led to dislocations among the Jews who lived in the small towns or served as agents of the noblemen.

By and large, these economic and social changes did not take place simply through the force of circumstance. The state was in a position to initiate, hasten, or impede developments to the detriment or benefit of given portions of society. From the 1860's on, its actions had great effects on the Jewish population. The measures of Alexander II, of all the Tsars the mildest in his Jewish policies, did not permit a mass adjustment to the fundamental alterations taking place in society, but they did provide increased economic and social opportunities to a limited number of Jews by lifting some of the barriers to education and easing residential restrictions for selected groups.

However restricted the Jewish program of Alexander II, it was liberal compared with that of his successor, Alexander III (1881-94), whose harsh policies fell heavily on almost every Jew in Russia. Under the Temporary Rules of 1882, which were installed after the wave of pogroms that followed his accession to the throne, Jews were forbidden to settle outside of cities and towns, even in the Pale of Settlement. These laws became more inclusive in subsequent years, culminating in the expulsion of all Jews from Moscow in 1891. Early in the reign of the last Tsar, Nicholas II, the state established a monopoly on liquor, thereby depriving several hundred thousand Jews of their livelihood. Moreover, Nicholas, like Alexander III before him, tightened the restrictions on the number of Jews who could enter certain occupations and institutions of higher education.

These repressive measures occurred against a background of population and urban growth. Between 1847 and 1897 natural increase alone caused the Jewish population to triple. Even between 1881 and 1897, when the harsh legislation led to a wave of emigration, the net population increase was 22 per cent.[8] This population growth coincided with a strong general movement toward towns and cities. The number of city dwellers in the Empire nearly doubled between 1863 and 1897, accounting for about 13 per cent of the total population in 1897. Although data are sketchy, in Poland, where roughly one-fourth of the Jewish population of Imperial Russia lived, about 11 per cent of the Jews lived in communities of ten thousand persons or more in the period 1855-60; by the late 1890's this figure had risen to 24 per cent. Similarly, whereas in the years 1855–60 only 6.5 per cent of the Polish Jews lived in communities of twenty thousand or more inhabitants, by the late 1890's over 20 per cent of them lived in cities of this size.[9] Thus, almost half of Poland's Jews had become urban residents by the time the Bund held its founding congress.

But even these figures do not reflect the full extent of the problems of a rapidly growing Jewish urban population and the ill effects of overcrowded cities. For a truer picture, one must consider the distribution of the Jewish population within the Pale. In the most thinly settled area, the southern provinces (Bessarabia, Kherson, Ekaterinoslav, and Tauride), the Jews made up only 26.3 per cent of the urban population in 1897. In the more thickly populated southwestern provinces (Volynia, Podolia, Kiev, Chernigov, and Poltava), however, the figure rose to 38.1 per cent; and in the area of densest population, the northwestern provinces (Vilna, Grodno, Minsk, Vitebsk, Kovno, and Mogilev), which were, along with Poland, the areas of the Bund's greatest successes, the concentration of Jews in the cities was extremely high, the Jews representing 57.9 per cent of the urban population.[10] This at a time when Jews made up only 4 to 5 per cent of the total population of the Empire. Under the circumstances it cannot be argued that state measures alone produced all the economic woes of the Jews. The government did, however, make the already serious problems accompanying industrialization even worse. Moreover, the regime alienated for good an entire generation by the drastic manner in which it imposed its policies.

The economic and social changes also affected the relationship between the Jews and their Christian neighbors. Christians too began to migrate to the cities in increasing numbers in the last two decades of the nineteenth century, and to move into the new factories and workshops. Although members of the Christian and Jewish middle classes had met before as competitors, and continued to do so now, new segments of both communities began to approach each other on a partially altered basis: as members of one group, the working class. The Jewish urban workers, mostly artisans, continued to dominate in such traditional occupational pursuits as tailoring, shoemaking, and baking. But they also moved into the factories, into cigarette making, tanning, brushmaking, and weaving. At the same time, non-Jewish workers began to move in increasing numbers into the larger and more modern factories. The two labor forces remained largely isolated from each other, but now at least they shared the pace of city life. The gulf between town and country, between peasant and artisan, was bridged. What remained was the isolation of differing cultures, occupational traditions, and places of employment.

Still, the very changes that drew segments of the Jewish and Christian populations together made competition between the two groups possible as well. The Jews, their life especially disrupted in this period of rapid urban and industrial growth, were forced to look to the new mills for employment. Here they faced discrimination from employers and workers alike. Many employers considered Jews ill-suited for the work; many Christian workers were simply unwilling to accept them as co-workers. Collisions inevitably took place between the workers of the two communities, though not on a large scale.

The internal cohesion of the Jewish community also frayed under the pressures of broad environmental change. Indeed, even before the effects of rapid modernization were felt in Russia, a modernist movement had arisen within the community. This was the Haskalah, or Enlightenment, movement, which had made its appearance in Western Europe in the eighteenth century with Moses Mendelssohn as its main spokesman.[11]

Haskalah thought found adherents among the Russian Jews in the mid-nineteenth century, but its advocates did not have an easy path. They were strongly resisted, not only by the traditionalists but also by the Hassidim, with their heavy emphasis on mysticism and emotion, faith and joy.[12] What Haskalah's opponents objected to primarily was the attention to currents outside the community. Such concerns, the Hassidim charged, would lead to heresy and conversion.[13] The charge was not unfounded, for Haskalah did indeed develop secular tendencies and assimilatory characteristics, a major new fact of Jewish life in the European world of the nineteenth century.

Alexander II's relatively liberal policies thus came at a crucial time: the opening of doors to the outside world fit in neatly with the modernizing tendencies of the Haskalah movement. Gratified by the opportunity to carry their ideas into practice, some followers of Haskalah entered Russian schools and joined the larger society. Even though the vast majority of Jews remained unaffected by these dramatic changes, the meeting of Haskalah and Russian modernization formed a bridge that spanned the chasm separating the Jewish and Russian worlds; once built, it could not be destroyed.

More and more young Jews began to aspire to a secular education and a place in the general society, only to be faced with new repression under Alexander III. It was in this atmosphere of rising expectations and dashed hopes that the first generation of Bundists was born and raised. That segment of Jewish youth bent on breaking down the barriers now found itself confronting not only the traditional forces within the Jewish community, but the state as well.

Meanwhile, the great social and economic changes in Russia were having profound effects on the Jewish community. The rapid urban growth forced those seeking employment into an unhealthy competition. The Palen Commission, which was set up to examine the legislation governing Jewish life, reported to the Council of State in 1888 that "about 90 per cent of the whole Jewish population ... come near being a proletariat."[14] Pauperization, estimated by the number of families that sought public assistance at Passover, increased rapidly. By the late 1890's about 20 per cent of the Jewish popula-

tion had reached such straits.[15] Economic strangulation led to desperate measures, and emigration on a grand scale became a permanent feature of life,
though the departures did not keep pace with the misery.

The internal social order of the Jewish community began to be transformed.
Up to this time most Jewish workers had been employed in the shops of their
co-religionists, both because of external restrictions and because of their own
customs. The fact that the Jewish Sabbath fell on Saturday, for instance, kept
many workers inside Jewish-owned establishments. Most of these enterprises
were small, and there was little social or economic differentiation between employer and employee. Indeed, as often as not, the workers regarded their condition as temporary and expected eventually to own their own shops. As industrialization proceeded, however, this traditional patriarchal relationship tended
to break down, especially in the larger cities and in those industries requiring
complex and expensive machinery. The social distance between employer and
employee increased, and the Jewish worker's thoughts of independence faded.
Once his position took on permanence, new tensions replaced the older harmony, paving the way for labor conflict within the Jewish community. The
old institutions began to give way to new ones more expressive of the developing class system.

The disruptive conditions in Russia, particularly after 1881, forced the Jews
to reconsider their fate. The pressures reinforced and accelerated existing tendencies. Insecurity of life and property, and feelings of hopelessness about the
future, produced the well-known mass emigration to the West. Other Jews
also looked beyond the frontiers of Russia, but they saw a Jewish homeland,
not the West, as the solution for their woes and the only hope for their regeneration. The great majority of Jews, however, remained where they were and
sought to adapt themselves as best they could. But among those who gave no
thought to leaving, and particularly among the young Jews ready to break
with tradition, a spirit of resistance began to grow up. It was this spirit that
was to create the Bund.

2. Early Social and Ideological Elements

The first of the "pioneers" (a term applied to all those who participated in the movement that led to the creation of the Bund) were intellectuals: young Jews who had acquired some degree of higher secular education in Russian schools and who, around 1890, formally organized the Jewish Social Democratic Group, also called the Vilna Group, the direct antecedent of the Bund. This nucleus in Vilna, the most important center of early Bund activity, included Arkady Kremer, the acknowledged "Father of the Bund"; his future wife, Matle Srednitsky (Pati); Isaiah Izenshtat, a merchant's son who had already tasted imprisonment for radical activity at the Juridical Lyceum in Yaroslav; Liuba Levinson, later Izenshtat's wife; Tsemakh Kopelson (Timofei, Grishin), a Vilna gymnasiast; Samuel Gozhansky (Lonu), a graduate of the Vilna Teachers Institute; and Joseph Mill (John), a polytechnical, or Real school, student.[1]

Within the next few years the Group expanded to include the taciturn young ideologue Vladimir Kosovsky (real name, Nahum Levinson), Abram Mutnikovich (Gleb, Mutnik), Noah Portnoy, Pinai Rosenthal (Pavel, An-man), all of whom were students; Anna Heller, Rosenthal's future wife; and Pavel Berman, a friend of Mill's from Real school days. The significance of the Vilna Group to the Bundist movement is immeasurable: the Group included the major organizers, editors, and polemicists of the "first generation" of Bundists, and six of its members served on the Central Committee of the Bund at one time or another before 1905.

The similarity in the lives and background of the first pioneer-intellectuals is striking.[2] All of them came from middle- or lower-middle-class families; all were strongly influenced by the Haskalah movement, that intellectual bridge for adaptation to modern life; and all were educated in secular Russian schools. The future Bundists received, at most, a smattering of teaching in traditional Jewish subjects, so minimal in fact that only a few of them were able to write Yiddish readily in the early 1890's. Even Gozhansky, the most competent of them at the time, modestly confessed to a poor command of the written language in these years.[3]

All of the Vilna pioneer-intellectuals were born between 1865 and 1873. They grew up in the northwest provinces and so did not experience the pogroms of the early 1880's directly. They were not unaware, however, of the strong anti-Jewish sentiment in Russia, or of its official expression in decrees and legislation throughout the decade of their adolescence and early adulthood. Mill recalls the unofficial quotas for admittance to Real school and the scornful exclamation of "empty fantasies" from his lower school director when he learned of the lad's desire to attend;[4] and Pati Kremer describes her father-in-law's intense hatred of the state, an emotion his son Arkady soon took to heart.[5] Pavel Rosenthal, too, felt the weight of the anti-Jewish decrees blocking the path to higher education, though he was fortunate enough to go on in the field of medicine.[6] Even those who were not directly affected were only too aware of the difficulties others encountered; there was virtually no way a Jewish youngster could escape appreciating the civil liabilities of his Jewishness or avoid a sense of outrage. Undoubtedly, the responses of the young people to these painful episodes account in no small way for their concern with social problems and revolutionary change.*

Estranged from their traditional religious environment, these young Jews were ready for new intellectual challenges. They eagerly explored the vistas opened to them by the Russian printed word, their curiosity and training carrying them even further from the old ways than their fathers before them. Enchanted by their Russian books, they glorified and romanticized a world beyond the Pale in which a brilliant nineteenth-century Russian culture thrived and the aspiration for freedom vibrated. Not untypical was Mutnikovich, who describes how he was intoxicated by the very thought of Mother Russia: "Russia, the wonderful country. . . . Russia, which gave mankind such a poet of genius as Pushkin. The land of Tolstoy. . . . The country with such a heroic student youth."[7]

The future Bundists became increasingly aware of alternatives to their limitations through their exposure to Russian culture. But the Russia of the 1880's was not the Russia of the 1860's. Where their fathers had sought to adapt themselves to the existing order peacefully and to remain Jews, the new generation felt that their situation warranted more radical answers. The optimism of the 1860's, the hopes that had rested in the benevolence of Alexander II's regime, had disappeared. Moreover, the new Jewish youth now perceived the problems they faced as problems of the whole of Russian society, if not of

---

* Franz Kursky, an early Bundist who knew the pioneer-intellectuals well (and who later, as director of the Bund Archives, became the leading bibliographer of the Bund), felt that the pioneers' revolutionary attitudes hardened in 1887, when the government imposed a *numerus clausus* on Jewish students (*Gezamelte*, p. 142). See also Shulman, "Pionern-period," p. 356. Shulman, also a Bund pioneer but of a somewhat later era, knew a great many of the early pioneers over a long period of time.

mankind in general, and argued that solutions were not to be found within the existing political and social order.

At the secondary schools and universities, the young pioneer-intellectuals were attracted to radical circles, where forbidden literature was read and discussed. A number of them paid a price for these activities. Izenshtat, Srednitsky, and Kremer all had their first experience with Tsarist jails while still students, and at least six of the thirteen members of the Vilna Group were temporarily expelled, thanks to their illegal activities. Mill attributes his failure to be admitted to higher schools to an essay he wrote lauding the radicals Dmitri Pisarev and Nicholas Dobroliubov, which fell into the hands of a school inspector; after he was closely questioned by the authorities, his application for entry was returned without comment.[8] Most of the Group were blocked in their attempts to study for the professions, the most likely careers for persons of their background and aspirations. Only Gozhansky, Portnoy, and Rosenthal were able to complete their studies and practice their intended specialties in the early years. (Many of the others resumed their formal education in later years.) In these circumstances, the young men and women had ample time and opportunity to make radical activity their main preoccupation.

The main form of Russian radical organization in the 1880's was the circle, a small reading and discussion group made up of interested and trusted intellectuals, and sometimes including a few workers as well. The circle was by no means a new phenomenon in Russian intellectual and social history; it had long been the standard instrument for radical dialogue wherever young intellectuals settled in any number, despite a tradition of shortlivedness and transient membership, the result of exposure and exile, as well as student vacations.

Many of the pioneers had amassed considerable experience in the techniques of circle operation prior to 1890. Kopelson was a veteran of Vilna circles that dated from the mid-1880's. He attended the Real school in Ponevezh (where he first met Mill while living with Mill's grandparents) and organized his own circle there. Kremer's activities in Riga, Srednitsky's in St. Petersburg, and Izenshtat's in Vilna and Yaroslav testify both to the proliferation of the circle movement in Russia and to the accumulated knowledge the pioneers could bring to bear on their work in Vilna.

Two major forces shaped the radical ideology of the mid-1880's: Populism (*narodnichestvo*), a movement that had undergone a considerable evolution in the preceding decade, and, more immediately, the People's Will (Narodnaia Volia), a revolutionary group. Populism contributed a ready hatred of the Tsarist regime and its injustices, and sought the regeneration of society through socialism. Its emphasis was largely agrarian. Insisting on the perfectibility of man, the Populists placed strong reliance on education as a means of reforming society; and self-improvement through study and the obligation to teach others remained powerful themes in the intellectual circles of the 1880's.

The People's Will was more a political organization than a broad movement as such. An outgrowth of Populism, it was formed in part in reaction to the Populists' failure to achieve concrete gains. Its adherents advocated direct political action to achieve a social revolution, and both justified and practiced terror. The high point of their activities was the assassination of Alexander II in 1881. Like the Populists, the members of the People's Will insisted on the importance of education, but with the significant difference that they addressed themselves to the public at large instead of arguing for a special role for the peasantry.

The circles of the mid-1880's were eclectic, reflecting both of these currents; and though all the participants in the circles of Vilna and Minsk (a second center of early significance in the development of the Bund) considered themselves *narodovoltsy*, or followers of the People's Will, no single dimension can cover the richness of the texture of circle development in this period. The level of individual achievement in study and the role of individual temperament left room for considerable differences between circles. The student circle Kopelson formed in Ponevezh, whose members simply read illegal literature, cannot be compared with the revolutionary Minsk circles of the mid-1880's, which had a well-developed curriculum. And these in turn were far from being as activist as the Vilna circles, which included outright advocates of terror and even participants in an abortive plot on the life of Alexander III in 1887.

Despite an admiration for the members of the People's Will, whose daring roused romantic dreams of heroism and sacrifice, the pioneers leaned heavily toward the role of teachers and students. In fact, only relatively late in their revolutionary careers did they engage in practical work—procuring and distributing illegal literature, establishing underground libraries—thus making their circles something more than private salons. When they drew together in 1890, they were still heavily influenced in their actions by their own background and training.

The pioneers were still young, the eldest barely twenty, when a new *Weltanschauung*—Marxism—gained currency in Russia. Their growth to political maturity thus coincided with the popular advance of the doctrine they would soon claim as their own. This advance began quite soon after G. V. Plekhanov, the commonly designated "Father of Russian Marxism" and a former Populist, reinterpreted Marxism to explain Russian conditions in the early 1880's. Emil Abramovich, possibly the first herald of Plekhanov's ideas in Jewish Russia, came to Minsk from Paris in 1884. There he organized circles and devoted his summers to propounding the new doctrine. It was he who introduced Plekhanov's work *Nashi raznoglasiia* (Our Differences) into Minsk and later, in 1886 or 1887, into Vilna.[9]

The major tenets of Marxism contradicted some of the conceptions and methods of the older Russian doctrines, notably in predicating itself on the historical development of an industrialized, urban society in Russia. It was not the peasantry, as the Populists supposed, but the urban factory proletariat, the inevitable outgrowth of capitalist industrialization, that would bring about revolution. Placing the future in the hands of masses of workers ("The revolutionary movement in Russia will triumph only as a movement of the workers," in Plekhanov's oft-repeated maxim), the Marxists saw terrorism as a heroic but unscientific and essentially futile form of activity that could seriously harm the movement.[10] Far more significant for the success of the revolution was the role of the revolutionary teacher, the intellectual who understood the course of historical development and could show the workers their place in the historical process. The duty of the revolutionary intelligentsia was to instill consciousness in the workers and pave the way for their self-liberation.

A number of factors drew the pioneer-intellectuals to Marxism. Though they admired the heroes of the People's Will and the dedication and democratic spirit of the Populists, they did not necessarily adore the Russian masses or glorify the peasants. The peasantry, after all, had remained unpersuaded by the blandishments of the Populists. The oldest of the pioneer-intellectuals, Evgeniia (Zhenia) Gurvich, who worked in Minsk and whose career extended back to the late 1870's, implicitly expressed her disillusion with the peasants in noting that the city worker was "easier to organize and would yield more readily to agitation and propaganda."[11] Marxism lay close to the life and habits of the city, and the pioneer-intellectuals were urban denizens. Moreover, it was more cosmopolitan than the older Russian doctrines, a great virtue in the eyes of the pioneers. Marxism assigned no special merits either to Russian peasant institutions or to the Russian people; it offered equality on the basis of class alone and provided the pioneers with an opportunity to accept and support a doctrine that bore no national content, a doctrine that did not require them to denounce their own past and settle for a narrowly Russian national future.

The scientific cast and claims of Marxism also appealed to the pioneers. Science had a powerful attraction for young radicals eagerly seeking certainty in a rapidly changing world. The circles of the 1880's stressed the study of natural science, and many of the pioneer-intellectuals were formally educated in one or another of the scientific disciplines. Eight of the thirteen pioneers who formed the nucleus of the Bund leadership pursued some form of advanced technological or scientific study.

Despite heated exchanges among the country's leading spokesmen for the various revolutionary doctrines, the ideological lines were not drawn sharply in Minsk and Vilna. Indeed, many of the revolutionaries there embraced both the new and the old. Zhenia Gurvich confesses that the Marxism of her circle in Minsk in 1885 contained "a strong dose of Populism." Her brother Isaac expresses much the same sentiment, writing that in those years his Marxism "still had a strong Populist scent."[12] As late as 1887 Zhenia still regarded the countryside as the center of revolutionary gravity. Even the question of terror as a tactic did not become a seriously divisive issue.[13]

The situation in Vilna was much the same, though there the argument over tactics was fiercer. The narodovoltsy sought to attract promising circle members to their views on the efficacy of terror, the Marxists to persuade them that this tactic would lead to the neglect of agitation and propaganda and to a disregard for the value of mass action by the working class.[14] Nevertheless, the conflict remained muted enough to permit continued joint revolutionary activity. In any case, the major issue—the role of the peasantry—meant little in this urban milieu, and theoretical differences had few practical consequences.[15] Until the late 1880's, the Minsk and Vilna circles operated in virtual isolation from the society around them. The need for secrecy kept them small, and the educational program remained their major form of work.

The influence of the terrorist school of thought began to wane soon after the introduction of Marxism. The discovery of the plot to kill Alexander III in 1887 led to the arrest of the oldest and most experienced adherents of terror in Vilna, Isaac Dembo and Anton Gnatovsky. Not all of the new arrivals among the revolutionary youth in Vilna were Marxists, of course; nor did the work in the circles suddenly take a new direction as a result of the arrests. Nevertheless, with the decimation of the terrorist ranks, the field was left open for the Marxists as never before.

One of the major concerns of the intellectuals was to propagate socialism among the workers. The circle was their major link to society, the means by which they attracted others to the new faith. The self-imposed obligation to champion the rights of the downtrodden had a long history among Russian intellectuals, many of whom no doubt felt, along with Isaac Gurvich, that they owed "a 'historical debt' to the people."[16] But there was more to the process than simply recruiting new members to the cause: once initiated, the neophytes were expected to carry the message to their fellow workers.[17] In this sense, the intellectuals had by this time gone beyond the realm of theory into the field of practical work, and were beginning to project their ideas outside the limits of their own small circles.

The intellectuals confined their recruitment efforts among the masses to those who seemed to have the proper prerequisites for study. In Minsk the worker-initiates passed through three stages of instruction. They first had to learn to read and write Russian, then to study natural science. Only after they had completed these courses were they allowed to turn to socialist studies. Even then, their investigation of socialism was limited to an analysis of the economic basis of capitalism and an outline of socialist ideals; political matters received scarcely any attention.[18]

The program of study was much the same in Kopelson's circle. As in Minsk, the emphasis in Vilna was on natural science and the origins of capitalist society. Lev Jogiches, the leading figure in this circle in the late 1880's (and later an important leader of the Polish-German Social Democrats), even offered lectures on anatomy—complete with skeleton. Here, too, the highest stage of study was given over to scientific socialism and the history of the Russian revolutionary movement.[19]

Up to the late 1880's the intellectuals' thoughts were all for the Russian society whose culture had so greatly influenced them. "Our task then," Kopelson states, "was developing cadres for the Russian revolutionary movement, associating them with Russian culture."[20] On the same subject, Kremer writes: "The first founders of workers' circles in Vilna . . . wanted only to educate individual, more developed workers, lead them to socialist consciousness and train them as agitators for Russia—for the industrial centers, for the Russian working class."[21] In short, the russified intellectuals of the time ignored the social and political problems of their immediate surroundings.

But the Minsk-Vilna intellectuals ran into unexpected difficulties in their attempt to organize the working classes. In their own studies and radical activities, they had usually worked among similarly disposed gentiles.[22] Both in Russia and abroad, the crossing of religious and national lines by students was common. In recruiting workers for the circles, however, the intellectuals found the traditional cleavages between nationalities being carried over into their groups. Since local custom dictated segregation by nationality among the workers in the northwest provinces, Jewish workers had to be taught by Jewish intellectuals. Language differences helped to impose this arrangement on all parties.

Still, the presence of Jewish workers in the circles did not prompt any specific interest in Jewish problems among the intellectuals. Whenever questions of this nature arose, says Zhenia Gurvich, "we entrusted all our hopes to the future revolution which dares all and solves all problems."[23] And in 1886 we find a People's Will writer stating: "The Russian revolution alone can give to the Jews the civil rights that would equalize them in their civil relationship with all other elements of the Russian population. . . . The Russian revolution, as the embodiment of the true progressive aspirations of society, bears within itself all the conditions for the salvation of the Jews."[24] Indeed, Izenshtat still took this position in a discussion with Zionists in the early 1890's.

As for the question of the future of the Jewish people, there was a considerable range of opinion among Jewish revolutionaries in the late 1880's. The dominant viewpoint reflected an estrangement from the mother culture. Lev Deutsch, a Jew and an older revolutionary whose career went back as far as the 1870's, describes his early attitude to things Jewish: "We wanted the Jewish masses to assimilate as quickly as possible; everything that smelled of Jewishness called forth among many of us a feeling of contempt, if not more. . . . We all deeply believed that as soon as Jews began to speak Russian, they would, just as we had, become 'people in general,' 'cosmopolites.' "[25] Some of the intellectuals had even gone so far as to convert to Christianity.[26]

To be sure, the idea that Jews should be drawn into the movement as Jews had its advocates, though they were neither numerous nor successful. The best known of these advocates was Aaron Liberman, a student in the Vilna Rabbinical Institute in the mid-1870's, who used Hebrew to reach yeshiva students.[27] (Deutsch referred to him, somewhat inappropriately, as "the first Bundist."[28]) Standing on the same side was the so-called Group of Socialist-Jews, an organization formed in 1880 under the influence of a Ukrainian nationalist, M. P. Dragomanov.[29] The Group issued a statement criticizing Jewish socialists for not working among their own people and pointing out that Yiddish was the proper language for propaganda among the Jews.[30] Little came of any of these efforts.[31]

The pioneer-intellectuals stood somewhere between Deutsch and Dragomanov in their views. They clearly exhibited assimilative tendencies; and their upbringing and schooling ensured their use of Russian among themselves. Some were even still insisting in the late 1880's that their efforts in the Pale were temporary, "a sort of preparation for the coming 'true' revolutionary work among the Russian masses."[32] "In practice," says Kopelson, "almost all of us were declared *assimilationists*."[33] Nevertheless, the pioneers were far from espousing the deliberate assimilation proposed by Deutsch. The fact that they had crossed certain boundaries did not prevent them from working among Jewish workers in their circles, nor did they find living in the Pale particularly abhorrent. They did not see Vilna as a temporary stopping place, as a number of other assimilated Jewish revolutionaries did.[34] Moreover, when they taught Russian to Jewish workers, they did so only out of necessity: Russian was simply an educational medium. Isaac Gurvich maintains that the use of Russian in his circle "was definitely not an 'assimilatory' or russificatory tendency, as was later claimed, but a necessity to give the future worker-propagandists access to socialist literature"; he is supported in this by his sister Zhenia.[35] Kopelson, significantly, did not find it unseemly to react quite emotionally to the arrival of the first Yiddish pamphlets in Vilna: "I became enthusiastic looking at them," he is quoted as saying, "and kissed them as something holy."[36] Thus, unlike Deutsch, the pioneers were not led by their own experience to press for assimilation as a solution to the Jewish question. Rather, they sought merely to draw individuals into the revolutionary movement. At most, assimilation was simply a byproduct of their revolutionary ideas. Indeed, the very fact that they did not have strong *a priori* answers for the problems of the Jewish community may have enabled them to see special problems and seek different solutions for the Jewish workers.

Under the impact of industrialization, the institutions that had met the occupational, welfare, and even religious needs of the Jewish workers began to disintegrate. As noted, the traditional khevrat, the artisan associations, began to lose their social cohesion as economic differentiation grew between employer and employee. In earlier times masters and workmen had often joined together in single associations, but now, with the establishment of large and heavily capitalized enterprises, class lines became more sharply drawn, particularly in the larger towns. Owners of enterprises no longer wanted to be in the same organizations as their employees; and the workers, for their part, objected to their employers dominating the khevrat.[37] By the middle of the nineteenth century, workers were forming their own organizations, attempting to establish themselves as a socially and economically distinct group without forfeiting the benefits they had enjoyed in the old associations. Despite a certain continuity with tradition, these early attempts at differentiation clearly represented a step on the path toward labor consciousness.

In the 1870's conflicts between workers and employers increased. Labor found a new weapon, the strike, one of the earliest of which took place in 1870 in Belostok.[38] However, traditional means for settling disputes continued to be important—we find a rabbi mediating a strike in Warsaw in the late 1870's, for example—and older channels of protest were still used.[39] The practice of workers refusing to allow the Torah to be read in the synagogue until their grievances received a public airing not only persisted, but with certain adaptations was used in later years by the Bund.[40]

The textile and tobacco industries in particular seem to have had considerable labor consciousness by the 1880's. Thanks to the custom of levying dues, a matter of long practice in the khevrat, workers were able to carry on sustained battles. There is also evidence that strikers received aid from outside sympathizers, and that they struck only a few factories at a time, so that those still working might help those on strike.[41] From all of this it is clear that traditions of mutual aid were being carried over into the newer forms of labor action.

But to say that the Jewish workers were relatively class-conscious by the 1880's is not to suggest there was a broad or highly organized labor movement. The fact is, economically the Pale of Settlement witnessed the coexistence of the old paternalism and the new militancy. Moreover, the developing labor movement made little real impression on the circle intellectuals for a number of years. The Minsk and Vilna circles were certainly aware of the strike activity around them, but even as late as the mid-1880's the intellectuals as a group did not become directly involved in strikes, or indeed show much interest in them, though on occasion they did donate money to the cause.[42] The largely self-contained environment of the circle, with its security problems, its narrow educational tasks dedicated to individual achievement, its theoretical emphasis, its primarily Russian orientation, and its cultural alienation from the Jewish masses, contrived to isolate the intellectuals from the infant labor movement.

Nevertheless, it was the circle that forged the first ties between the intellectuals and the Jewish workers.[43] The all-important links were the worker-recruits. The earliest of these did not become Bundists, but they shared some of the same characteristics. For many, the old faith no longer sufficed. "I never met a single religious worker," Zhenia Gurvich declares, writing of her experiences in that period.[44] The circle not only offered the worker-members unique opportunities, but also exposed them to new beliefs that often proved more satisfying than the old. By the 1880's Haskalah thought, which had had such impact on the middle class, began to filter down to the working class—with similar effect. For those converted to the new faith, or at least for those uncertain of the old one, the circle offered the opportunity to escape the confines of tradition and to study the world in scientific and secular terms.

The revolutionary career of Hillel Katz-Blum, one of the earliest of the Bund's worker-pioneers, provides almost a case study of the transition from traditional worker to circle member (though his case is an anachronism, since he did not join the circles in Vilna until the early 1890's).[45] Blum was born in Kovno in 1868. His father, a tailor, was a deeply religious man, and the boy received a traditional education, reaching the yeshiva, the highest rung of the Jewish educational system. Here he began to read the Haskalah authors secretly. "The bacillus of doubt was already infecting me," he tells us, "and that brought me many uneasy days and nights."[46] Rejecting his father's wish that he become a religious teacher, Blum dreamed of taking up some kind of craft. The poverty around him prompted him to leave home as soon as possible, that he might cease to be a burden on his parents.

In 1892, after completing his military service, Blum went to Vilna, where co-workers interested him in the circles. At first he saw the instruction he received as "a kind of liberalism or philanthropy: young students devoting themselves to teaching poor workers how to read and write Russian."[47] But later, when his teachers led him to studies dealing with the concerns of workers, he was delighted; for all his previous study, he had still not found any solutions for the problems of the poor.

Blum's new education cost him most of his spare time—the Sabbath and the few hours he could manage after a twelve-hour workday. Finding the formal study of Russian too time-consuming, he chose to attend lectures on political economy and natural science, and to work at his Russian on his own.

His literary tastes were eclectic, ranging from Hugo and Turgenev to Dmitri Pisarev, Henry Thomas Buckle, Darwin, and Plekhanov.[48] What he learned of systematic study came from his first teacher in the circles, Arkady Kremer.

Blum's studies eventually led him to socialism, where at last he found "a strong foundation," as he put it. All of a sudden "it was worthwhile to live and suffer, to fight and die for an idea, for a liberation movement."[49] He experienced something very much like a religious conversion, a depth of feeling that he saw as typical of hundreds of workers in those years, and willingly accepted the new obligations that came with the new faith. "One felt a duty to learn, to study the new ideas in order to avoid making errors in social work, much as a conscientious doctor [takes care] because he is dealing with living, feeling persons."[50] Blum remained in the movement for many years.

But not all the workers fit so successfully into the circle environment, especially those in the skilled trades. Education sometimes led to isolation from former friends and fellows, and even to disdain for the uninitiated; and the newfound opportunities were often seen simply as a way to improve one's personal position.[51] In short, the workers did not always accept the obligation to teach as they had been taught. This was to lead to a serious conflict with the intellectuals in the 1890's.

Still, many of the circle-educated workers did play their assigned role, and increasingly so toward the end of the 1880's. One of their major activities was strengthening and expanding the *kases*, organizations that had been established in the early years of the decade to provide strike funds.[52] Stretching further into the ranks of the workers than the craft-associated khevrat, the kases were in fact embryonic trade unions. By the end of the decade, they were highly organized and firmly entrenched in Vilna.[53]

In the organization of the kases, workers, worker-propagandists, and intellectuals came together in a meaningful way for the first time. But this is not to suggest that the Jewish intellectuals and the Jewish workers were truly united at this point; in fact, contact between the two groups was still limited. The circle and its work were still the intellectuals' chief concern, and there language continued to be a barrier between the two groups. In addition, the need to maintain secrecy kept circle membership small and recruitment to a minimum.

Nevertheless, at the end of the decade the main elements in what was to become a mass movement were clearly beginning to come together. To be sure, the intellectual-pioneers had not yet begun to identify themselves closely with either the labor agitators or the Jewish masses. But they had succeeded in drawing a number of workers into their circles; and that success was beginning to arouse their own interest in the labor movement as a field of battle. A spark of awareness had been lit on both sides that was to lead to a new search for unity in the 1890's.

3. The Path to the Mass Movement, 1890-1894

The Jewish Social Democratic Group, more commonly known as the Vilna Group, was the immediate forerunner of the Bund. We do not know precisely when it was founded—possibly as early as 1889, though 1890 seems more likely.[1] What we do know is that it was the organizational home of the pioneer-intellectuals and workers who created the Bund, that it brought to the revolutionary movement a previously unknown formality and discipline, and that it set the tactical course for many years to come. The Group was disbanded in 1897, with the formal establishment of the Bund.

Our lack of precise information on the founding date suggests the unexceptional nature of the event. This was not the first attempt at organization. Thanks to Kopelson, we know that there were at least two groups organized earlier, in 1887. One, a society complete with rules, program, and party duties, was formed in August; it scarcely got off the ground, since it included a number of students who had to return to school soon after. The other fared little better. This was the Vilna Central Organization, which was headed by Lev Jogiches, with Kopelson as his second. Given the personal relationship between the two leaders (they did not get along well) and the close atmosphere required for successful circle work, one is hard put to believe that any kind of disciplined organization emerged from this collaboration. In any event, the Vilna Central Organization was dissolved in mid-1888, and Jogiches left Vilna a year later.[2]

There were other important differences between the earlier organizations and the Vilna Group. For one thing, the faces were new. Kopelson was the lone holdover among the intellectuals. The other key personnel—Mill, Kremer, Izenshtat, Srednitsky, Gozhansky, and Liuba Levinson—all came to Vilna at about the same time, certainly a happy coincidence of time and place so far as the Bund was concerned. But there was an even greater difference: a spirit of cooperation and activism that had been lacking before. Kremer's skill as a leader is indisputable; but it was the combined performance of the Group that is striking. Mill catches the moment that was so dear (almost holy) to him in his memoirs:

It seemed as if new forces had gathered imperceptibly, slowly, and had fallen from heaven. . . . The potential material had existed, but an organized, disciplined, centralized collective, capable of giving this material a form, a content, and a well-worked-out and considered direction had been lacking. It is for this reason that an outsider could not even guess that the material was present.[3]

The significance of Vilna itself as a factor in the Group's durability should not be overlooked. Sometimes called "The Jerusalem of Lithuania," Vilna was an important cultural center for the Jews in the northwest provinces. Although it no longer had a university at this time, a number of gymnasia and trade schools, a Real school, and the Vilna Teachers' Institute were located there. (The last, a school that prepared Jewish students to teach in the state school system, had a long history of radical activity.) In attracting young people to Vilna, these educational institutions were the channel through which numbers of students found their way into the revolutionary movement. Six of the thirteen pioneer-intellectuals were natives of the city and at least eight of the thirteen attended its schools. The practice of the Tsarist police of banishing minor political offenders to towns without universities or large industries added to the richness of the young radical forces in Vilna.[4]

Geographic location also played a role in making the city a center for revolutionary work. Situated on rail lines to St. Petersburg and the West, Vilna was an important crossroads of the revolutionary movement for several student generations—a stopping-off place for students en route to and from Russia, a place where ties with fellow students were maintained and contacts with other radicals made. Thanks to these comings and goings, Vilna was no isolated provincial town, but a cosmopolitan center that remained abreast of events in the world.* The Vilna Group thus benefited from a particularly fortunate set of circumstances.[5]

The first years of the decade were a time of adjustment for the new organization. Though virtually all of the pioneer-intellectuals had considered themselves Marxists in the late 1880's, there had been little to distinguish their activities from those of their non-Marxist rivals. Adherence to Marxism did not automatically tell them where and how to proceed, and neither their perception of the world about them nor their habits changed quickly. As the pio-

---

* Nor was the city without significance for other revolutionary movements. The Poles, for instance, considered the city a major center of activity. As early as 1883 we find K. P. Pobedonostsev, Tsar Alexander III's mentor, writing to D. A. Tolstoy, the Minister of the Interior: "Many are convinced, and not without reason in my opinion, that it is Vilna and not Warsaw that is the true center of Polishness" (C. Pobedonostsev, *L'Autocratie Russe*, p. 262).

neers plunged deeper and deeper into the Marxist literature, however, Plekhanov's works began to have an ever-greater influence on their thinking. Gozhansky, who played an important part in designing the Group's tactics in the early years, considered Plekhanov the major ideological source for the intellectuals' practical work. And, indeed, there is no mistaking the direct relationship between Plekhanov's ideas and the emergence of the concept of the mass movement, which was to become a fundamental of the Group's belief and practice: his *Our Differences* had convinced the activists of the 1880's that they needed to create educated workers' groups to lead the future revolutionary movement; when he shifted direction in 1892 in *Concerning the Tasks of the Socialists in the Struggle Against Famine in Russia (O zadachakh sotsialistov v bor'be s golodom v Rossii)* and called instead for agitation among the masses, the Group heeded his words.[6]

Though Russian Marxist thought unquestionably supplied the major ideological thrust for the intellectuals, the ideas and work of the Polish revolutionaries were an important influence. The revolutionary movement among the Poles was an old one—and despite serious setbacks, a vital one. And one whose impact was readily acknowledged by the pioneer-intellectuals. Mill, whose ties with the Poles dated from his school days, writes: "In the Lithuanian-Polish radical intelligentsia of Ponevezh [near Vilna] I found not only support in my search for the truth, not only comrades-in-arms, but also something that no other national-radical group could have given—an understanding of the special Polish approach to contemporary political problems and goals."[7]

To what degree the pioneers imitated the work of the Polish revolutionaries is difficult to determine. The activities of such organizations as the Union of Polish Workers (Zwiazek Polskich Robotnikow), which in the late 1880's and early 1890's sought to incite and finance strikes, undoubtedly affected their views.[8] They learned the importance of practicality. Gozhansky put it neatly many years later: "Our acquaintance with the Polish workers' movement showed us that a real revolutionary movement must have its roots . . . in its own environment."[9] As an object lesson, this was among the most important the pioneers would ever learn. What is not clear is how much of this lesson was learned from the Polish experience and how much from the indigenous khevrat of the Jewish workers and earlier instances of mutual aid.

In any case, the Polish movement and the Marxist ideology between them pushed the Group into an increasing concern with the situation of the workers around them. Marxism did more than give the pioneer-intellectuals an opportunity to escape a narrow Russian populist orientation; it allowed them to see what was before their eyes. They began to find substance for the classic Marxist view of class antagonisms and the control of the means of production in the economic life of their own community. Furthermore, the ideology contained no intrinsic obstacle to the growth of a proletarian movement among the Jews.

As the work of the Group became more and more organized, the revolutionary movement became highly structured, with a tight-knit band at the center and a "periphery" of intellectuals who taught, obtained literature, and collected money for the movement at the bidding of the center. (Some of those on the periphery would later become important figures in the Bund; they were simply too concerned with other affairs to be included in the center.) In time, a separate central body of workers was set up as well, primarily for security reasons. The pioneer-intellectuals met weekly, but the two core groups got together only when important matters arose, for it was difficult for workers and intellectuals to meet without attracting attention.[10]

Membership figures from this period attest to the vitality of the new organization. In 1889, according to Kopelson, only some fifty to sixty persons attended a meeting in Vilna to commemorate the death of a comrade; by the early 1890's, by his estimate, there were not only some sixty to seventy intellectuals but at least 150 workers in the circles.[11] Within a few short years the activities in Vilna were showing promise of an interesting future.

By 1892 the Jewish worker had become the central preoccupation of the Vilna movement, and the kase and the strike the most important instruments of radical activity. To be sure, the intellectuals of the late 1880's had made a start in this direction. Jogiches, for instance, had attempted to stir the workers to protest against their employers and the government.[12] But as some of the kases developed into permanent workers' organizations, dedicated primarily to the economic struggle and specifically to the strike as a means of carrying on that struggle, the intellectuals gradually became aware of the revolutionary potential of the workers' movement. (To Kopelson, the change seemed scarcely noticeable over the years.[13]) Moreover, from 1888 on, the intellectuals were in direct contact with a number of kases, notably those among the stocking-makers, printers, locksmiths, and tailors, via the workers in the circles.[14]

The kase proved to be the magnet that drew the intellectuals and the workers they educated to the masses, the instrument that linked up strike-conscious workers' organizations and Marxist intellectuals anxious to translate theory into action. "No matter how primitive this movement was," one pioneer asserts, "it had to attract the attention of the revolutionary and especially of the Marxist intelligentsia and bring them closer to earth, to the real life of the Jewish worker."[15] The kase also offered the circles a fresh field of action, one that had not existed when study was the major form of expression and when theory had suggested the Russian population centers as the focus of revolutionary activity.

It is from Mill that we learn how the Group maintained its links with the workers in these early years:

I led several workers' circles of about eight to ten persons each. Only one was uniform, being made up exclusively of seamstresses; the rest brought together male and female workers of various trades. This made it easier to find out what was happening in individual shops and factories, and provided opportunities to discuss the workers' conditions in order to discover ways and means to improve them. Theoretical propaganda and education, in this manner, went hand in hand with preparations for practical worker politics.[16]

Contrast this description with the Gurvichs's reports of their activities in the mid-1880's, and the evolution of the movement becomes quite clear. The intellectuals in Vilna were being drawn ever closer to the daily concerns of the worker, and the emphasis was becoming one of improving the conditions of his life. Still, they had not yet abandoned their earlier orientation of bringing the worker into their own milieu, and circle members continued recruiting and educating workers.

The Group and its supporters also tried to heighten the workers' political consciousness by promoting the idea of an international workers' movement. The commemoration of revolutionary holidays was an old custom in the circles (the Decembrist revolt of 1825, the assassination of Alexander II, the French Revolution, and the revolutions of 1848 were among the events that received attention); but the proposal that May Day be celebrated to express the solidarity of working people, which originated with the First Congress of the Second International in 1889, particularly caught the fancy of the Russian Marxists. The holiday was celebrated in Warsaw the following year and in St. Petersburg the year after; by 1892 the tradition had spread to Lodz, Tula, and Vilna.[17] For the first observance in Vilna, about 100 workers were invited to join two intellectuals from the Group (security considerations militated against sending more) at a secret meeting in the woods. Once assembled, the gathering was first addressed by the Group members, Kremer and Mill, then by four workers, who spoke to their audience in Yiddish and Russian.[18]

The very fact that the intellectuals gave the workers a voice on a political holiday indicated their trust and pride in their charges. Delighted with the performance of their pupils, the leaders pushed for the publication of the May Day speeches. Jogiches, who was living abroad at the time, took on the task, and in due course a pamphlet containing both the speeches and an introduction (probably written by Boris Krichevsky, an important Social Democrat) appeared. These speeches tell us much about the impact of Marxist propaganda on the workers to that date. We find in them not only the urge to identify with workers everywhere and considerable interest in the improvement of the workingman's lot, but also a faith in the ultimate victory of the working class. More to the point, we see the workers' recognition of the immediate tasks before them: to propagandize and agitate among their fellows.[19]

The intellectuals' increased awareness of the labor conflict around them began to produce practical results in 1892. Gozhansky discovered a law dating back to the reign of Catherine II that fixed the maximum workday (including mealtimes) at twelve hours—this at a time when a sixteen-hour workday was common.[20] It was a valuable find. Here was an issue that could at once rally the workers to fight their employers and teach them an important political lesson. Moreover, the workers would be given direct evidence of the advantages of having the intellectuals on their side.

And indeed the intellectuals had chosen their issue well. As a result of this, their first agitation among the workers, strikes gained a new impetus and direction that pleased them—and reinforced their conviction that agitation among the workers on the basis of their daily needs was a necessary part of the Group's program.[21]

The May Day event of 1892 and the call for a twelve-hour workday represent a watershed in the tactics of the pioneer-intellectuals. In the next two years mass agitation among the Jewish workers began in earnest. However, it was not until early 1894, and only after considerable and hot discussion, that the change in tactics was formally spelled out. In that year two short works appeared: *A Letter to Agitators* (*A briv tsu agitatorn*), written by Gozhansky, and *On Agitation* (*Ob agitatsii*), written by Kremer with the help of Julius Martov, the future Menshevik leader, who had chosen to live in Vilna during a term of administrative exile.* These works had enormous influence, particularly *On Agitation*, whose impact was felt in the greatest centers of revolutionary activity in Russia. Together, they summed up the experiences of the early 1890's, formulated the theoretical justification for the new developments, and pointed the way to the future.

Gozhansky's *Letter* (which addressed itself specifically to the Vilna scene, but which in time had meaning for a number of other cities in the Pale) sought to resolve the severe conflict within the movement over the decision to change work methods. That the success of the movement was conditional on the existence of revolutionary and class consciousness was accepted *a priori* by all concerned. But how to go about producing that consciousness in the

---

* Franz Kursky believes that most of the work Martov did related to matters of style (*Arkady*, pp. 77–78). See also Martov, *Zapiski*, p. 233. Gozhansky claims that he originally wrote *A Letter* in Yiddish ("Yevreiskoe," p. 91), but Cherikover, a close student of Yiddish literature, feels Gozhansky may be mistaken ("Onhaibn," p. 584). It seems quite possible that Gozhansky did indeed err. As he himself admits, he relied on memory to describe events that had occurred some forty years earlier ("Yevreiskoe," p. 81). In any case, the handwritten copy in the Bund Archives is in Russian.

working masses was a hotly debated issue. Gozhansky argued that Jewish workers could not by themselves achieve rights that were lacking throughout the entire Empire; consequently, it was up to the local Social Democratic organization to raise the political level of the Jewish workers, so they might join in the general struggle for political freedom.

The way to reach the worker, said Gozhansky, was to relate the struggle to his direct experience. The worker had to be shown how to get what he needed —a process he barely understood at this point. The revolutionaries had to become involved in the workers' day-to-day affairs—to show them what to do and how to do it, and indeed to teach them where the ultimate struggle was to take place. Theoretical studies would not make the workers feel the necessity of change as much as practical involvement. "The masses can only understand those theoretical principles with which they have direct contact," Gozhansky asserted, "and, as we know, their lives depend entirely upon their economic condition."[22]

The difference between Gozhansky's *Letter* and Kremer's *On Agitation* was more a matter of form than content. Kremer intended his work for a wider audience, as a kind of Social Democratic strategy paper, and so made his points all-encompassing. Taking as his text Plekhanov's assertion that "the attainment of political power is the main task of the struggling proletariat," Kremer insisted that it was only through the economic struggle that the proletariat could be made to see the necessity of the political struggle. The worker would see "the impossibility of improving his lot under existing political conditions," and once in a direct confrontation with the regime, "the struggle would be transformed into a conscious political struggle."[23]

Many of the circle members had already recognized that in maintaining the small, secret circle and making the education of individual workers their goal, they had not succeeded in reaching the masses, as the Poles had done and as Plekhanov recommended.[24] But now, with the appearance of the Kremer and Gozhansky papers, the circle procedures came under critical scrutiny and attack. The reformers charged that the old methods had kept the movement isolated, and that the training of workers in the circles was a costly and inept way to reach the masses, which was now the principal concern.

A new objective meant a new approach. The Group began to call on worker-agitators, men who were in direct and daily contact with the masses, to work for the development of a genuine class consciousness. To them fell the two-fold task of organizing meetings where the workers could discuss the improvements they considered necessary, and determining which of these might become a successful rallying point. The intellectuals did not deny the value of theoretical studies, but they now insisted that "the *main* content of the Saturday meetings must be the *question of agitation.*" And they laid down a new dictum: "*Agitation is the basis of the Social Democratic program.*"[25] To those who disagreed, the response was unequivocal—they were simply not members of the Social Democratic Group. The Vilna Group had crossed a tactical and strategic Rubicon on the path to the mass movement.

One immediate consequence of the change in tactics was a turnabout in the circle training program. Not only was there a shift away from the study of Russian and theoretical education, but Yiddish, to this point used only as an expedient, was now to be used as a matter of principle. The new goal, after all, was to go directly to the Jewish masses, the new purpose of the training program to prepare leaders for the workers' organizations. The trainees were not to look on their instruction as a preparation for joining the intelligentsia or for work in a foreign, i.e., Russian, environment. In a word, where once the emphasis had been on an individual and relatively passive type of program, the thrust was now heavily toward mass action.

The worker-agitator program led to a whole new set of problems, however. The question of agitation was not a new one, to be sure; but in 1893 there were so many strikes that employers were prompted to join together to fire the suspected ringleaders.[26] Opposition to the change of tactics developed within the circles, notably among the worker-members, many of whom resisted the innovations. In the end, most of them came around—because, according to Blum (who sided with the opposition for a time), as they delved deeper into Social Democratic literature and recognized the "objectivity" of the view that socialism would evolve out of economic necessity, they were drawn back to the Group and into the worker organizations.[27]

Real as were the worker-members' fears of reprisal, their opposition to the plans of the intellectuals was based on something much more fundamental. The circle, as constituted, gave them a chance to move up the social ladder, even to earn a place among the intelligentsia, a group with a very special status in Jewish and Russian society. Some workers in the circles even tried to copy the dress and manners of the intellectuals. To ambitious but intellectually cramped workingmen like Blum (who describes his satisfaction upon reading a volume stamped "For intellectuals" at being counted a member of that elite group), simply being in contact with the intellectuals was worthwhile.[28]

To appreciate how difficult it was for Jewish workers to improve their social and economic position, one need only look at their limited opportunities for a secular education. Bad at best, the chances of a Jewish child of the working class going on to secondary school were considerably worse after 1887, when the Jewish quota was reduced. Thus, where the period 1882–86 had seen a Jewish enrollment in the Vilna school district of 1,378, the following period, 1887–91, saw the figure fall to 798, a decline of 42 per cent.[29] Under the circumstances, it is all too clear why the worker looked on the circle as a way out of his situation.[30]

Under the leadership of a Vilna circle worker named Abram Gordon (Rezchik), the challenge to the intellectuals became so determined and widespread that it came to be called simply the Opposition. Gordon, a man of undisputed intelligence, had been voicing his complaints since 1891 (and even before, for he was known to be dissatisfied when he belonged to one of Jogiches's circles in the 1880's).[31] But it was in 1892 that his views became well known: at the first May Day celebration in Vilna he produced, in Mill's words, "a sensation—a negative one" when he gave an unscheduled speech attacking the intellectuals and their propaganda and agitation tactics.[32] By 1893 Gordon's point of view had become a significant issue that consumed no small portion of the energies of both intellectuals and worker-propagandists. A majority of the worker-intellectuals—the "worker-aristocrats," as Mill called them—sided with Gordon.[33] Indeed, so highly did they regard him, that when he faced arrest in January 1893 workers gathered around his house and threatened the police—an almost unheard-of action and a testament to his popularity.[34]

Gordon's major concern was to define the relationship between the intellectual and the worker. The true role of the intellectual, he contended, was to help the worker achieve freedom through education. Or as he stated it in 1892: the intellectuals must "lead the movement in such a way as to enable [the workers] to become conscious and independent in the course of things, for only then will they be able to develop great strength."[35] By introducing the tactics of mass agitation, which did not even require a worker to have a basic education, the intellectuals were acting just like leaders of other movements who had misled the people, Gordon claimed. They were tearing the worker from one milieu, and then, before he was ready, insisting he act at the intelligentsia's bidding, accepting the intelligentsia's decision on what was necessary and what was not. Thanks to the "revolutionary poetry" of the movement and the intellectuals' understanding of the workers' interests, the workers idolized the intellectuals, and in adopting the new tactic the Group was doing nothing to prevent this.[36] What it came down to in the end, Gordon asserted, was that the intellectuals considered themselves above the workers. There was just one solution in his eyes: the workers must become educated, which is to say, the old circles had to continue to operate as before. Gordon took as his slogan: "The liberation of the worker is the independent and conscious business of the worker alone."[37]

The arguments of the Opposition reflected the still existing social chasm in the movement. Gordon's supporters were passionately partisan, displaying a fervor born of accumulated years of social injustice. The intellectuals, it seemed to them, were taking the movement away from the workers and worker-leaders, to whom it rightfully belonged. The Opposition had its Populist elements—but with a social inversion. Now it was the worker-oppositionists who insisted on the importance of education; now it was the worker-oppositionists asserting the obligations of the intelligentsia. Instead of the intellectuals going "to the people," the Opposition wanted to go "to the intellectuals," whose duty it was to serve the masses.

Whatever its merits, Gordon's program was doomed to almost certain defeat. It was fragmentary, isolating, a call for individual work at a time when the masses were prepared to make open economic demands and to accept revolutionary slogans. The movement had proceeded too far to allow the use of the circle in the old way. Gordon was caught in a dilemma: how were the workers to be both conscious and independent, if consciousness was conditional on an education that the intellectuals alone could provide? Gordon needed the intellectuals, yet wanted to deny them a leadership role. He had succeeded in joining the issue of the relationship between leader and masses; but to censure the intellectuals was not to resolve the issue. Yet the intellectuals only won a battle in 1894; they did not win the war. The conflict over tactics spread and repeated itself in many forms, both within the Pale and outside it.

To be fair, ultimate failure of the Opposition was not entirely due to the ideological shortcomings of Gordon's position. The Vilna movement's ability to adapt to changing circumstances provided a solid basis for victory. Experience had convinced the intellectuals that the growth of a mass movement needed more than the development of "critically thinking individuals," the model Gordon adopted from the Russian populist ideologues Peter Lavrov and Nicholas Mikhailovsky.[38] The most valuable lesson the pioneer-intellectuals had learned was that there was a field for active work at hand, and that new approaches promised to be more effective than the old. They had also recognized that if they were to enter this field and reach the masses, Yiddish would have to be their medium of communication. Victory rested on the support of worker-cadres who could lead the movement.

Just when the Vilna pioneer-intellectuals began to concern themselves with the Jewish worker as such is difficult to pinpoint, but this much is clear: by the year 1894 the issue had been decided. The first sign we have of the pioneers' awareness and acceptance of a Jewish identity is in their choice of a name for their organization—the Jewish Social Democratic Group. But there is nothing to suggest that there was any conscious concern with creating a Jewish mass movement at the outset. Before coming to Vilna, the pioneers had worked in non-Jewish or mixed environments. They may have decided to include the word Jewish only to differentiate themselves from other ethnic revolutionary groups. More probably, they did so in deference to the ethnic composition of the population in their new surroundings. Such an identification was bound to be important to their work, for it was still a fact of Vilna life that Jewish intellectuals would work among Jewish workers. The various nationalities there continued to be "partitioned by an impenetrable wall; each nationality lived a separate life and had absolutely no contact with the other."[39]

For most intellectuals, adoption of the term Jewish implied nothing more than a commitment to work on the scene. But for at least one of the pioneers, it meant more. From the start, Mill believed the Jewish workers deserved attention not simply because they filled the local landscape, but because they had value in and of themselves. He felt that a number of persons close to the Group shared his concern, to the point where "they used to regard with heartfelt pain every instance of one activist or another leaving the Jewish labor environment to settle among the Russians to work."[40]

The question of Jewish identity came into sharper focus at the May Day celebration of 1892. As one would expect, the speakers' main theme was the unity of the workers' cause everywhere; but several speakers took up the problems of the Jewish worker as well. One worker-speaker, taking a negative view, maintained that the Jewish workers should renounce their own holidays and rely on the truths of science rather than the myth of a Messiah.[41] But a second speaker was not content merely to identify the cause of the Jewish worker with that of all workers; Jews should take pride in their own heritage as well. To be sure, Jewish workers had a common goal with all workers, namely liberation from exploitation. But, he said, "for us Jews there is no reason to be discouraged or ashamed that we belong to the 'dishonored' Jewish race. The history of the Jews gives us this right."[42] By 1892, then, ethnic identification had proceeded to the point where one could claim to fight as a Jew along with other nationalities without apology—and the intellectuals were willing to accept that proposition.

Once the decision was taken to make Yiddish the language of agitation and propaganda, it became apparent that the lack of printed materials would be a serious problem. Communication with the Jewish workers had long been a problem for the russified pioneer-intellectuals in any case. In the 1880's, according to Kopelson, they had had to fall back on "Yiddish-Russian" or "Russian-Yiddish"; and Russian works had to be translated into Yiddish in the lower circles.[43] It was not until 1889 that the first illegal works in Yiddish began arriving in Vilna. The earliest was probably S. Dikshtein's popular pamphlet *Who Lives by What?* (*Kto z czego źyje*), a translation of a work replete with Marxist economic terminology.[44]

Apart from the acute shortage of Yiddish literature, there was another obstacle that slowed the pace of the intellectuals' new program. The simple fact was that many workers in the circles wanted to learn Russian, which was, after all, the language of emancipation from the ghetto. One need only recall how bitterly the Opposition fought the use of Yiddish, even after it was formally adopted as the language of agitation. In Mill's opinion, the lack of a body of Yiddish literature in 1893 and 1894 strengthened the Opposition's case for staying with the Russian language.[45]

The Group searched for solutions to the problem. One answer was to recruit new members with fluency in Yiddish and enough writing skill to produce materials that could be easily understood by the average worker. Here,
the intellectuals were fortunate in having an unusually rich source to draw
on: the large number of yeshiva students and ex-students in Vilna. Other recruits were drawn from the ranks of the self-educated (autodidakten). All of
these new members were given the title half-intellectuals, a name apparently
concocted by the intellectuals.[46] Apart from language ability, the half-intellectual also had to know and move easily around in the working-class environment, for he was, ultimately, the direct cultural channel between the intellectuals and the masses.

The half-intellectuals were a very special breed, at once translators, speakers, and writers. And special among them in these years were A. Litvak (real
name Khaim Yankel Helfand); and Sendor Zeldov (Nemansky) and his wife,
née Taibechke Oshmiansky. Litvak, the archetype of the half-intellectual, entered the movement in the winter of 1893. His first contact was made through
friends, who told him that the intellectuals wanted to meet young people with
a good knowledge of Yiddish. His training consisted of reading certain books,
discussing their contents with the intellectuals, and then writing on assigned
subjects under the supervision of his mentors.[47]

The Group's purposes were well served by the half-intellectuals, but there
were distinct drawbacks to the program, for the new recruits brought with
them attitudes that were often alien, if not inimical, to the ideas of the pioneer-
intellectuals. Litvak's love of Yiddish, for example, led him to encourage its
use far beyond the point envisioned by the intellectuals, for whom Yiddish
was simply a propaganda medium. He established libraries of Yiddish books
and attempted to introduce Jewish workers to the rich literature of the late
nineteenth century,[48] especially to works of social protest and to writers like
Yitskhok Laibush Peretz and David Pinsky, who began to make Jewish workers the subjects of their stories.[49] Litvak felt that the intellectuals probably
discounted the importance of such "proletarian" literature, seeing it as simply
"one of the means to be used for their great aims," whereas he and the other
young half-intellectuals, "soaked through with Jewishness," considered the
names of Peretz and Pinsky holy.[50] From Litvak's point of view, there was
no way to separate Yiddish literature and language from the problems of the
Jewish workers; it was a question of cultural ties, not tactical necessity. The
use of the half-intellectual thus introduced an emotional tie that was to go
to the very fibre of the movement, a pride in the Yiddish folk culture that
was, to say the least, muted among the russified intelligentsia. The intellectuals could not possibly have foreseen the enormous consequences of their decision to make Yiddish the revolutionary language: that the need for Yiddish
would open the way for tendrils of activity to grow far beyond the narrow
area they had staked out, and that, in the long run, their movement not only

would have a broader social base but also would find new emotional and literary attachments.

The events of 1893–94 point up how much the movement had changed in the span of a few short years. The fight against the Opposition alone indicates the new level of discipline and organization achieved in the early 1890's, for how else explain the containment of that conflict and the eventual success of the pioneer-intellectuals? These years saw the Group take two momentous decisions. First came the commitment to work among the human resources at hand, spelling the end of the earlier inner-directed orientation. Then came the decision to go directly to the masses, a policy of immense significance for both the future of the Jewish labor movement and the future of the Bund.

At the same time, these decisions had considerable impact on the intellectuals themselves. With each adjustment they made to their environment they moved further from a concern with the Russian movement and closer to a concern with the fate of the Jewish workers around them. As could be expected, this meant a partial turning from their earlier preoccupation with sweeping and theoretical issues to a search for solutions to the knotty and very real problems of the working class.

The Vilna movement was clearly growing. But far from solidly unified. It was still made up of separate elements: intellectual circles, worker-propagandists, half-intellectuals, and small but mass-type workers' kases. Those elements were fusing, but there were still difficulties—problems of bringing the kases under firm discipline, problems among the workers themselves. And as yet there had been no explicit recognition of Jewish problems as such. Nevertheless, the major tactical path—to reach the masses—was set by 1894. The drive to achieve a more complete transition to mass work would not lag far behind.

4. The Rise of the Mass Movement, 1894-1897

Between 1894 and 1897 the number of labor conscious Jewish workers grew rapidly, and Jewish Social Democratic organizations spread throughout the Pale. As the movement expanded there developed a more or less formal organizational arrangement linking the Jewish Social Democrats and the workers. At the bottom of this vertical arrangement stood the strike kase. Organized originally simply to provide strike funds, the kases became increasingly active in the 1890's in the struggle for workers' rights. A reading of kase rules of 1894 shows the labor leaders had a keen appreciation of the meaning of class struggle by this time. The kases continued to be organized along trade lines, though they accepted other workers until they could form their own organizations.[1]

Above the kase stood the *skhodka*, a board made up of representatives of the kases and agitators that was the real intermediary between the Social Democrats at the top and the kases at the bottom. The skhodka was designed to present and argue the workers' case, though many rank-and-file kase members were only vaguely aware of its existence.[2] The skhodka also organized circles and distributed literature.[3]

Blum describes how the skhodka in Vilna was linked to the top level of the hierarchy, the Committee, i.e. the Vilna Group:

The meetings were held in three separate parts of the city, with 10–12 persons in each place. The participants in these meetings, some 30 agitators and trade delegates, were the core of the movement. . . . No minutes were kept. . . . All three boards met jointly for special reasons or when the secret Committee had to be elected. These meetings were kept secret from the rest of the movement, and the Committee was elected by secret vote. It [the Committee] was a kind of holy of holies of the movement. Officially, no one knew who it included. Only one person was the official contact between the meetings and the Committee—that was Alexander [Kremer]. The duties of the Committee were to provide propagandists for the workers' circles, supply literature, establish links with other cities and also foreign countries, and procure funds. It had the right to co-opt anyone it found suitable without the permission of the skhodka.[4]

What Blum is talking about is only one operation in one city, of course. Nevertheless, his description can be taken as fairly typical of the system that functioned in the mid-1890's wherever the Jewish Social Democrats were sufficiently organized.

There were those in the movement who were not particularly happy with the new hierarchical form of the organization. The heavy predominance of intellectuals at the top, a heritage of Russian social and revolutionary history, was more a matter of circumstance than design; but this did not make intellectual direction any more palatable to those who insisted on strict adherence to Marxist ideology: it was the worker, not the intellectual, who was the bearer of the future. On various occasions workers in Minsk, Kovno, and even Vilna, challenged the "despotism" of the intellectuals in the name of organizational democracy and in terms of the intellectuals' obligation to educate the working class.[5]

Nor were these views necessarily considered mistaken by all intellectuals. Kremer, for one, demanded greater representation on committees. After all, it was the worker-agitators who had "to hold the pulse of the crowd."[6] It was equally clear to Kopelson that theory put the central workers' organization at the head of the movement; it was only because the intellectuals had organized first that they directed the work.[7] In any case, over the years more and more workers held committee seats and other responsible positions in the movement.

Several groups and individuals outside the organizational structure supplemented its activities. Private libraries like Litvak's had long been maintained for the education of workers and half-intellectuals;[8] and many kases also had established libraries for their members. When the Yiddish works of Peretz, Pinsky, and other proletarian-oriented writers began to appear, however, the movement had to devise new transmission techniques. Often marginally legal, such literature had to be distributed quickly. This became the task of certain groups of workers, who personally handled the publicity and distribution instead of relying on book peddlers.[9]

One of the best known of these peripheral organizations was the Jargon Committee (Jargonishe Komitet), which was formed in Vilna in 1895 "to spread good literature among the Jewish workers, to found workers' libraries for Jews in the provinces, and to put out popular scientific books and literary works in Yiddish."[10] The committee had branches in Minsk, Belostok, and other towns. Some of the most important pioneers participated in its activities, among them Rosenthal, Kremer, Izenshtat, Kopelson, and Tsila Klis (who later became Gozhansky's wife). Litvak and other half-intellectuals also took part. One of the committee's major undertakings was the publication of legal books. Initially, these were printed in Warsaw on a press owned by Abraham Kotik, a long-time socialist. Later, some of the press work was done in Berlin. The Jargon Committee performed an important function in the movement until 1898, when the Social Democrats found a better way to achieve the same goals.[11] In addition, it helped to create an independent environment for the movement.

The pioneers' decision to join the economic struggle was a happy one for the growth and development of the Bund. Thereafter the interests of the workers and the interests of the revolutionary movement were seen as one and the same. The stress was now on the practical and immediate needs of the workers. Gozhansky's *Letter to Agitators* had already singled out those demands the workers would most readily understand: shorter hours, higher pay, prompt and full payment of wages, more hygienic working conditions, heated shops in the winter, better lighting, higher pay for night work, better food for apprentices, and civil treatment by employers.[12] A call for small gains would be the most effective course, Gozhansky suggested.[13] The workers knew what was wrong with their working conditions even if they were incapable of articulating their grievances, and would regard agitation for small improvements as reasonable. The beauty of the demand for a twelve-hour day, which had so roused the workers in Vilna (and, subsequently, those in other cities), was its very legality; it did not require of the workers a traumatic break with their traditional penchant for obeying the law. Moreover, there seemed to be little risk to the individual worker in asking for something already established in law. And, finally, if nothing else, failure to have the law enforced would teach the workers a useful lesson—the mutuality of interests of the government and the employers.

Largely on the basis of such piecemeal demands, the organized Jewish labor movement grew steadily in the years 1894–97. The most dramatic gains were posted in Vilna and Minsk, where Social Democracy made the greatest inroads among the Jewish workers before the founding of the Bund. Though our figures for those cities are far from complete, we do have some data on the rapid growth of the kases there (see Table 2).

Table 2. Growth of the Organized Workers' Movement in Vilna and Minsk,
1894–1897

	Vilna		Minsk	
Year	Number of trades organized	Number of workers organized	Number of trades organized	Number of workers organized
1894	11	—	4	220
1895	16	500	15	870
1896	27	962	21	912
1897	—	1,500	—	1,000

SOURCE: Vilna. Mutnikovich, "Materialy"; *Arkady*, p. 159. Minsk. Agursky, *Sotsialistishe literatur; Rabotnik* (Geneva), 3–4 (1897): 61–63.

The organized labor movement under Social Democratic leadership also made gains elsewhere, less substantial to be sure, but nonetheless real. According to statistics presented at the International Socialist Congress in London in 1896, Warsaw and Smorgon also saw a notable organizational growth; the four Jewish groups together claimed some 3,000 members.[14] The first congress of the Bund a year later included delegates from Belostok and Vitebsk, and their organizations were considered important ones.

The Jewish Social Democrats were particularly successful in organizing workers in the bristle-making and tanning shops, most of which were small-scale enterprises with fewer than fifty workers. Towns like Volkovyshki, Krinki, Kreslavka, and Smorgon, where these industries thrived, became centers of Social Democratic activity in the mid-1890's. The organizational effort in these towns tended to be industry-wide rather than on a factory-to-factory basis, as in the larger cities.[15]

Withal, the growth of labor activity cannot be credited exclusively to the efforts of the Social Democrats. In Belostok, for example, Jewish workers in factories had fought their employers long before there were any Social Democratic organizations in the city. A case in point: some 3,000 Jews had joined thousands of other textile workers in a strike in 1895;[16] yet by Mill's estimate there were still only about 1,000 persons in the organized movement in Belostok two years later.[17] In this case it was the workers who spurred the Social Democrats to action, rather than the other way around. Nor was this a unique development. In the tanning and bristle industries, the labor movement was created largely by the workers themselves.[18]

The strike continued to be the workers' major weapon in the economic struggle. In the organized trades, as soon as a kase became strong enough the workers presented their demands to their employers and walked out if the demands were ignored. By the middle of the decade strikes were occurring in significant numbers. Between 1894 and 1897 there were at least 54 strikes in Minsk.[19] Vilna saw even greater labor conflict, witnessing 56 strikes over a two-year period (1895–96).[20] There were also numerous strikes in the towns where bristle-making was an important industry.[21] Despite occasional periods of labor peace, the number of strikes increased throughout the three-year period.

The mass movement proved highly successful in achieving economic gains. By 1896 the working day in some trades had been cut by one to three hours in Vilna and Minsk.[22] Wage rates rose sharply between 1894 and 1897, often doubling in the three-year period.[23] Most of the strikes were in demand of shorter hours and higher wages, but the workers were willing to go out for lesser grievances, such as insulting and violent behavior by employers and unhygienic conditions. Our data on the number of strikes actually undertaken in these years are incomplete, but from what we know the Jewish workers seem to have won about 75 per cent of their strikes.[24] These gains were not all permanent, however; in many cases the hard-won benefits did not survive later hard times.

In this atmosphere of growing labor unrest the workers became increasingly aware of their common problems and needs, and by the mid-1890's the mass movement began to appear as something more than a theoretical formula. The Social Democratic groups played a significant role in promoting the growing sense of solidarity among the workers. In Minsk, for example, where the most conscious workers formed the central skhodka, agitators were assigned to still-unorganized trades to help in the drive for unity.[25] Wherever possible organizations helped each other, both within towns and between them. In Vilna roughly half of the 500 rubles the kases spent on strikes in 1895–96 was in support of strikes outside their own trades.[26] In 1897 strikers in Krinki asked for, and received, help from the organization in Belostok.[27]

When workers in Minsk and Vilna struck on behalf of fellow employees fired for belonging to kases or for leading strikes, they were expressing their awareness of the meaning of united effort and their willingness to think beyond their own immediate benefit.[28] It took discipline and conviction to strike, for most workers lived near the subsistence level, and even at best the kases could not compensate them for wages lost during strikes.[29]

Encouraged by the success of their efforts, the Vilna Social Democrats decided to extend their work outside the city and its environs. To be sure, the movement was already spreading as workers relocated in other cities. But now movement members were to be sent to other areas in a deliberate attempt to spread the revolutionary message.

This decision was taken at an August 1894 meeting of the most important activists in the Group, which concluded that "closer cooperation with Jewish workers' organizations in other cities" was the "next logical step."[30] Soon after, a number of Vilna pioneers, both workers and intellectuals, set out to found new Social Democratic organizations among the Jewish workers, a process that became known as "colonization." Mill, Tsivia Hurvich (a dedicated worker), and Leon Goldman (a member of a whole family of revolutionaries) went to Warsaw and became leading figures in the local group there.[31] It was Vilna activists who founded the Jewish Social Democratic organization in Belostok, among them Gozhansky and Blum. Other Vilna workers who took part in the Belostok organizing effort were Abraham Baskin, Albert Zalkind, and Shaine Raizel Segal.[32] Pavel Berman helped to revitalize the movement in Minsk, where revolutionary activity had died down in the early 1890's.[33] Many other towns and cities could also count newcomers from Vilna as important additions to their revolutionary activity in the years 1894–96. Colonization established the Vilna organization as the de facto leader of Jewish Social Democracy in the northwest provinces of the Pale and Poland. No other organization had the Group's advantages: personal contacts and a common understanding of the work to be done.

In June 1895 delegates from the Minsk and Vilna organizations met in Minsk, and there took the first step toward establishing a mutual policy on the problems at hand and how to settle them. This meeting, known as the Minsk Conference, was one of the earliest indications of the new thinking on expand-ing the movement and of the role the Vilna colonizers played in that effort. Though the Minsk activists initiated the meeting simply to discuss strike-breaking activities in their city,[34] the talks were by no means restricted to so narrow a topic. Pavel Berman, by this time one of the leading Social Demo-crats in Minsk, was a member of that city's delegation at the conference.

The attempt to work out a unified approach to the mass movement is note-worthy in two respects: first because it was the earliest step in that direction, and second because coordination was achieved not through a centralized offi-cial administrative procedure or authority but through a common viewpoint. The Vilna Group was well on the way toward creating a widespread network of Social Democratic nuclei that would work well together because they were led by men and women who knew and trusted one another. To understand the character and vitality of the Bund, one cannot overlook the importance of this intermediary step.

Just as the Jewish labor movement grew stronger in the 1890's, so did the opposition to it. The activities of the new organizations heightened existing social strains in the Jewish community and created new ones. Not only did the workers' groups meet strong resistance from the established powers of the community; many workers were hostile to them as well. The state, too, showed more and more concern as the movement became increasingly visible.

The Jewish Social Democrats introduced a new set of beliefs to the Jewish workers. The aggressive tone, secular content, and socioeconomic aims of their Marxism represented a challenge to the foundations of the Jewish community —religious, social, and intellectual. To be sure, the old Jewish institutions had already been severely shaken in the past few decades, and the Jewish way of life was clearly changing. But the erosion was far from complete in the 1890's, and there were many who wanted no further erosion. Even those prepared to accept tradition-based modifications were unalterably opposed to the radical solutions of the Social Democrats.

The changing economic relationship between Jewish employer and worker made the framework of traditional justice difficult to maintain. The workers now fought their employers with an intensity, with weapons, and on a scale previously unknown to the community. From an economic point of view alone, the new methods and aims of the organized movement made the con-tinued social unity of the Jews impossible. The employers began to look to the state to intervene in their behalf or sought to have religious leaders exhort and condemn the workers for their supposed errors. Where once there had been only occasional rifts in the community, there was now an increasingly sharp cleavage along class lines.

Bent on arousing revolutionary class consciousness in the workers, the Social Democrats did what they could to deepen these divisions. Inevitably, their doctrine of class struggle collided with the dogma of the rabbinate, the very repository of the established order. The Social Democrats challenged the authority of the religious leaders, charging that they supported the class enemies of the workers, the employers.

A famous incident illustrates the open clash between the new leaders and the old. The trouble began with a strike at a Vilna tobacco factory in 1895. The police, apparently seeking a peaceful end to the affair, urged a preacher to speak to the strikers. He obliged—but instead of smoothing things over, he made matters worse by openly criticizing the workers in the synagogue. Not only were they breaking the law, he told them; they were doing serious harm to the Jewish people as a whole. Thanks to them, the government would now look on all Jews as seditious. If they would return to their jobs, he concluded, he could promise that they would not be fired.[35] To say that the workers did not take kindly to the sermon is putting it mildly: they responded by hooting the preacher down, an unheard-of occurrence that produced great excitement in the city.

The Vilna Group considered this incident so important that it mustered its meager resources to publish a special pamphlet on the event—*The Town Preacher (Der shtot magid)*.* As the Group saw the event, the religious leaders had invited such disrespect. It was "a humiliation for the temple" that it let itself plead the cause of the employers. Moreover,

if it is right for those chosen by the community to bring the struggle of the capitalists against the workers into the temple for the benefit of the owners, then should the workers be silent? ... There is no longer any single Jewish people.... The great Jewish people are divided into two classes whose enmity is so great that it does not stop for the holiness of the temple ... not even for the strength and cruelty of the all-powerful Russian police.[36]

Clearly, the old social structure was no longer secure.

Gradually the Jewish community at large began to take notice of the move-

---

* The original pamphlet was hectographed. A printed version was published two years later, in 1897. Agursky believes *Der shtot magid* is the work of Martov, who wrote an article at the time on the same strike (Agursky, *Sotsialistishe literatur*, p. 131). But I side with Cherikover, who feels the language and subject matter leave little doubt the author was Gozhansky; he knew the Yiddish language and culture, Martov did not. Cherikover also believes that all but a few passages were worked from Yiddish to Russian ("Onhaibn," p. 591).

ment, and to react to it. Judging by the nomenclature used—"the philosophers" in Vilna, "the weaver patriots" in Belostok, "the compassionate ones" in Brest—the general attitude toward the activists was one of mildly mocking condescension. But there were harsher critics and less friendly nicknames, like "roughnecks."[37] In some instances, the reaction went far beyond mere name-calling. In one town, for example, some of the local activists who were late for the Sabbath because of a meeting outside their city were stoned by angry townsmen.[38]

The employers responded to the new labor militancy by firing striking workers, who were easily replaced in those days of heavy migration to the cities. Should the local labor supply be exhausted, they had only to turn to sources outside the area. The employers also developed their own kind of cooperative effort, helping each other financially, sharing information on troublemakers, and blacklisting known leaders.[39] But they had even more powerful weapons at their disposal: official support and official violence in the person of the local police. On occasion they even resorted to the use of terror, hiring gangs to attack the workers.[40]

Meanwhile, the government attitude toward the growing economic conflict was changing. At first the workers sought to achieve their aims through legal means, as when they petitioned the authorities to enforce the law establishing the twelve-hour day.[41] More often than not, such petitions fell on deaf ears, though some officials were sympathetic. The Grodno police, for example, issued a report in 1897 that pointed out the plight of the Jewish workers, and that went so far as to criticize the employers for giving every protest against exploitation a political coloration.[42] But even when the authorities did intervene on the workers' behalf, such relief as they obtained was neither substantial nor lasting.[43] In any case, police intervention was more likely to be against the workers than the employers, even in the early days of the movement. Threats of arrest or actual detention of strikers for short periods of time were common. A more serious punishment was the banishment of workers to their birthplaces.

As the strike movement grew in size and began to reflect Social Democratic influence and organization, the opposition of the local police and factory inspectors stiffened. By 1895 each and every strike in Minsk was being investigated.[44] In 1896 and 1897 the number of arrests climbed sharply. The use of spies in ferreting out agitators and important members of the movement became standard practice. Indeed, the police spies were often recognized as such by the worker-activists. One spy in Vitebsk was known to members of the movement there as "a professional thief [who] specialized in stealing horses."[45] In contrast to an earlier day, when labor unrest provoked only sporadic official firmness, the regime now saw strikes as something more than simple economic disputes of concern only to workers and employers.

Police reports on areas where the Bund pioneers operated indicate the government had become aware of the existence of an organized movement. From Vilna, Minsk, Grodno, and other provinces came descriptions of the structure of the revolutionary groups and their tactics. The police did not miss the change from individual strikes, "called independently of each other," to the collective efforts evident in the use of agitators and leaflets, in the threats to employers, and in the attempts to organize hitherto untouched trades.[46] From Grodno, Governor Batiushkov was prompted to remark, "I am compelled to say that disorders among the factory workers are especially prevalent among the Jews."[47] The state could not be expected to watch these developments with equanimity.

By 1897 the strike movement in the Pale, as in all Russia, had attracted the attention of the highest levels of the government. The Minister of Internal Affairs, I. L. Goremykin, now saw in the spread and new discipline of strikes the work of "secret revolutionary societies."[48] A ministerial circular issued on August 12 of that year described the movement and recommended that the police and other arms of the government work together closely wherever there was evidence of labor unrest. Special attention, the circular noted, should be paid to any intellectuals in contact with the workers.[49] The state, appreciating that it faced a growing and disciplined movement, began to prepare a coordinated assault against the new threat.

The young Jewish revolutionaries adopted a new life style to fit their new aspirations. The result was further strains in the community structure. Family ties weakened, and the established occupational hierarchy, once a key to status in the community, crumbled. The break with tradition was not total, however; just as the khevrah had played a role in the evolution of the kase, so the old religious and social traditions found new forms of expression in the revolutionary movement, forms that came as much from the masses as from the intellectuals.

Unlike the pioneer-intellectuals, with their thirst for knowledge, many Jews, especially in the lower educational and economic brackets, had no interest in secular learning. For them the traditional education, leading if possible to the prestigious role of tutor, teacher, even rabbi, was prized above all else. Here the desire to discover the outside world met heavy parental resistance. The generational tugging and pulling often caused great heartache—for children and parents alike. Blum's case was fairly typical. When he told his parents that he wanted to take up a trade instead of becoming a *melamed* (religious teacher) as they had planned, his father retorted bitterly, "You want to be a tailor? Some other place, not in my house!"[50] What seemed a tragedy to one generation, however, seemed to spell liberation to another.

An even more dramatic departure from tradition was the involvement of women in the movement. Women formed a substantial segment of both the intelligentsia and the kase-organized working force.[51] In a society where parental authority was great in any case, women led far more restricted and regulated lives than men. It was not unusual by now for the daughters of the assimilated bourgeoisie to attend state schools and universities. But among lower-class Jewish families the very idea of educating women, beyond the minimum needed for prayer, was out of the question.[52] In these families the break with the older generation was excruciating. It is easy to imagine the shock of parents on learning that their daughters had attended secret meetings late at night or on the Sabbath. Home life was likely to prove bitter indeed for a young woman who joined the movement. Arguments, if not beatings, were sure to follow, once her affiliation was discovered.[53] The gradual move toward the emancipation of women shook the very foundation of Jewish social life.

Alienated from their own homes, the young revolutionaries found a new home in the movement itself. Comradeship made up for the loss of family love, new beliefs for the loss of the old ones. Sympathetic older women in the movement comforted newcomers, lending them strength and at times financial help.[54]

A special morality developed among the activists. Young women sought equality in the revolutionary community. Many came to regard references to their physical appearance as out of place and frivolous, and security considerations as more important than personal emotional considerations.[55] The idealism of the initiated and the almost religious mood in which they approached their work bred a kind of purity—in speech and body as well as in personal relationships.[56] Many worker-activists saw love and marriage as weaknesses that hindered the revolutionary movement. "When [a member] married," says Blum, "he was regarded as an ex-revolutionary."[57] The intellectuals had no such qualms; marriages among comrades were common and caused little concern.

The sense of belonging was reinforced by the use of a special form of address—*bekante* (acquaintance) in the early years, *khaver* (comrade) in later times.[58] At May Day celebrations the young revolutionaries began to use the distinctive color of revolution, proudly flaunting their red blouses, red flowers, and red flags.

Still, with all the changes, there were many elements of traditional Jewish life in the revolutionary mix. The calendar of Jewish holidays, for example, remained in use into the Bund period. Song, an ancient part of Jewish religious ritual, became an important ceremonial rite in the mass movement as well. In 1896 the half-intellectuals created what is considered the first modern Jewish revolutionary hymn, "The Oath." The more famous Bund hymn, also entitled "The Oath,"* was composed in 1902 by Sh. An-sky (real name, Shlomo

---

* A translated version appears on p. xiii above.

Zanvil Rappoport), a Russian-Jewish writer who was once Peter Lavrov's sec-retary.[59] The old revolutionary circles had had their songs, of course; but now the singing of "The Oath" was a ceremonial act, more akin to the Jewish re-ligious ritual. The act itself was an important symbol of internal discipline in a society largely lacking external enforcement. To the workers, singing the hymn was a solemn affair, to be performed with joined hands and even at times with the sacred scroll of the law or the prayer shawl.[60] For them, a simple description of class struggle did not suffice as a declaration of faith.

As might be expected, the new and old did not always mix easily, particu-larly at the bottom of the movement. The old attitudes died hard in the kases. Men did not wish to meet with women, for economic as well as social reasons. Indeed, the whole range of shop relations had to be taken into account with the rise of the strike kase. Conditions in the small shops were diverse and com-plex. Not only were there such questions as apprentices, piecework, seasonal work, work within the home, competition among workers, and the financial situation of employers, says Kremer; "there was also the problem of the women workers in the tailor shops where women's clothes were made—women were assistants to men in those shops, and relations between the two groups were bad."[61] These problems of economic competition and status retreated slowly even where the movement made headway.

The intellectuals meant to do more than simply improve the workers' lot, of course; they meant to convert the workers to their own Marxist view of the world. But it soon became clear to them that their efforts to educate the masses would be hampered by the lack of propaganda materials in Yiddish. Producing such materials became a major preoccupation. At first the Group depended largely on the growing quantity of literature from the pens of serious Yiddish authors and the efforts of a handful of half-intellectuals and intellectuals. The early literature was didactic and down-to-earth; it dealt solely with problems the worker would immediately recognize as a personal concern. Gozhansky, in an early work entitled "A Dispute About Fortune" ("A vikuakh vegn mazel"), struck at the psychological barrier of resignation that led to the pas-sivity of the Jewish workers. Gozhansky's hero counters the argument of the fatalist ("We are poor people, and we will remain poor people.... He who has luck needs no skill and, conversely, he who is destined to have bad luck can do nothing about it") with an explanation of economic cause and effect, and insists on the power of the worker to change his life.[62] In another work, "Memoirs of a Cigarette Maker" ("Erinerungen fun a papirosen-makherke"), Gozhansky dealt in story form with factory conditions and such thorny prob-lems as strikebreaking. The genres the Social Democrats used to get their message across became as varied as literature itself.

Because of the urgent need for literature, the Social Democrats were forced to fall back on non-Marxian and non-movement sources, thereby drawing the workers into the mainstream of Yiddish literary activity. Books like the *Holiday Leaves* (*Yomtov bletlakh*) of Peretz gave the Jewish workers at least some sense of their situation. The Yiddish literary works were highly popular and represented an important source of propaganda material (despite certain reservations on the part of the pioneer-intellectuals about Peretz's socialism, which they found to be too vague and too far from their own).[63]

It was not long before the Vilna Group began to consider establishing newspapers and a printing press. The delegates at the Minsk Conference of 1895 discussed the possibility of exchanging local publications and the need for a printed organ—that very important sign of a going revolutionary concern.[64] However, a projected follow-up conference was never convened. The first feeble attempt at regular news dissemination in Vilna came in 1894, when a handwritten sheet entitled *Naies fun Rusland* (News of Russia) appeared briefly. The project seems to have been abandoned with the fifth issue. A more substantial effort was the *Arbeter Bletl* (The Workers' Sheet) of Minsk, a hectographed paper that appeared in 1897; nine issues were published in runs of fifty to eighty copies.[65] Though not particularly successful, these early efforts gave the activists a certain know-how that ultimately led to greater achievements.

The Vilna Group began issuing printed pamphlets in 1895. Through Joseph Pilsudski, the future head of the Polish state, the Vilna activists made contact with Galician Jewish Social Democrats in Lemberg[66] and arranged to have some of their earliest material printed there. Other material was printed in Switzerland and Germany through the good offices of Russian Social Democrats in those countries. Once these arrangements were made, a significant number of pamphlets, both translations and original works, began to flow into the Pale.

In December 1896 the first issue of *Der Yidisher Arbeter* (The Jewish Worker) appeared. Printed abroad in quantities of 1,000 copies, it was written in Vilna and distributed from there. Vladimir Kosovsky did much of the editing and writing in the first few years. The journal became the organ of the Foreign Committee of the Bund two years later and was published until 1904.

The appearance of *Der Yidisher Arbeter* marked the beginning of a highly coordinated organization by Russian revolutionary standards. As the editorial introduction made clear, the Vilna Social Democrats now recognized that the movement had to spread beyond the local level and the needs of a few isolated groups. They meant to educate the workers, the editors asserted; to show them that the kases were a source of proletarian strength and to explain the political needs and duties of the movement—all this against the day, fast-approaching, "when the individual, separate, struggling groups of the Jewish proletariat will unite in one workers' socialist organization."[67]

One of the most notable achievements in these years was the creation of *Di Arbeter Shtime* (The Workers' Voice) in August 1897. The handiwork of workers and half-intellectuals, the paper demonstrated not only their great enthusiasm for the cause but their ingenuity as well, for it was printed in Russia, under the noses of the unsuspecting pioneer-intellectuals, on a secret press built by a worker, Israel Mikhel Kaplinsky.* The intellectuals soon took over the paper, making it the official organ of the Central Committee at the founding congress of the Bund; it retained that status until 1905, when it was discontinued.

By 1897 the mass movement was no longer just a dream of the intellectuals; it was a force to be reckoned with. Thousands of Jewish workers had either joined kases or come to sympathize with them. Thousands of others had at least become aware of class issues through strikes and movement literature. A sense of discipline and labor consciousness had clearly taken root.

But if the mass movement was complete in an economic sense, it was still largely unharnessed and unorganized. Secrecy continued to be important and kase membership restricted. Nevertheless, the organization, such as it was, was effective for the time. The movement could look forward to continued growth —to recruiting more workers into kases, to organizing more trades, to achieving more economic gains through tested methods or finding new ways to meet new conditions in other cities and towns.

Certainly the pioneer-intellectuals had every reason to be well satisfied with their new tactic. They had succeeded in capturing the imagination of thousands of workers and alerting them to the possibility of change. But for the Jewish Social Democrats this was only a beginning. Their vision went beyond immediate economic gains; this movement they had created was only a stage and a vehicle for broader political achievement and eventual revolutionary victory.

Of all the important developments in the years 1894–97, the most significant for the history of the Bund was the consolidation of the intellectual-worker alliance. The spirit of solidarity among the organized workers and the direction, education, and increased sensitivity of the intellectuals to the workers' needs and traditions had created something altogether new: masses of workers willing to fight not only for the improvement of their own condition but for the recognition and rights due them as a class. The intellectuals were satisfied that they now had a solid basis for expansion.

---

* Sendor Zeldov, who later described the founding of *Di Arbeter Shtime* (*Di Hofnung*, Sept. 25, 1907, p. 3), wrote most of the first issue himself. Kaplinsky later acted for the Tsarist secret police and became the most notorious provocateur in the Bund's history. During the period under study, he built a number of secret presses, both for the Bund and for other organizations.

Reminiscing on the state's attitude in the late 1880's, Shmuel Rabinovich declared that if he had told the police himself about his translation of the work *Who Lives by What?* into Yiddish, "they simply would have laughed at my imagination."[68] We can be sure that after 1895 the government was not amused by the movement among the Jews. Nor was the Jewish community any longer taking the new current in its midst lightly. The social and political forces of the northwest region of the Pale had finally awakened to the presence of the revolutionary newcomers.

5. The Early Stage of the Political Movement

Political mobilization within the Pale proceeded much more slowly than economic mobilization. Necessarily so, for in political work there was no buffer between the revolutionaries and the state. Political action meant direct confrontation; no convenient instrument like the legitimate demand for a twelve-hour work day was available to shield those advocating political revolution. Thus, at a time when economic action was public and indulged in by increasing numbers of workers, political work was secret and was largely confined to the kind of study and education practiced in the circles of the late 1880's. The annual May Day celebrations were certainly political acts, but they were still secret and open only to the most trusted members of the movement. In any case, the early May Day celebrations were the mildest of political acts, offering no open challenge to the regime.

In the view of the Jewish Social Democrats, circumstances required that political action be left in the background. Despite Kremer's assertion in *On Agitation* that "the attainment of political power is the main task of the fighting proletariat,"[1] the intellectuals believed the proletariat first had to be taught what it was to fight for. Since the movement belonged to the workers, they had to be made to see the political struggle as vital to their interests. Such awareness would develop naturally, according to Kremer: "The ideas of socialism can work themselves out only on the soil of the capitalist structure and only at a certain level of development."[2] The workers were beginning to understand the economic struggle, and that struggle would inevitably bring them into conflict with the state, for sooner or later the state would back the employers, demonstrating its hostility to labor. In a word, *On Agitation* simply asserted that given the immature capitalism of the time and the relatively low consciousness of the workers, this was not the historical moment to make the political struggle "the main task."

Nevertheless, the Jewish Social Democrats could not simply stop thinking about political tasks and political theory. After all, the leaders saw their long-term role as a political one, and their ultimate task as educating and organizing the workers for the day when they would be drawn into the political struggle.[3] Moreover, the period was one of political ferment throughout the Empire, a time in which the revolutionary and intellectual communities hummed with new concepts and ideas about Russia's political future. Yet in considering that future, the purely Russian circles were not especially concerned about the problems of the Empire's diverse ethnic groups. It was for the pioneer-intellectuals to single out the special problems of their community, to seek solutions for them, and to explain them to the Jewish workers.

In the early 1890's the Vilna Social Democrats were internationalists; their political allegiance was not to the Jewish community as such, but to Marxism in general and to Russian Marxism in particular. When they turned their attention to the Jewish worker, it was to persuade him that his interests were those of all other proletarians. "We Jews renounce our holidays and fantasies, which are useless to human society," one of the speakers proclaimed at the 1892 May Day celebration. "We are joining the ranks of the socialists and we stand for their holiday."[4] The introduction to the published speeches praised the Jewish workers for putting the unity of the class struggle above race and creed.[5] Belief in that unity and in its significance for the political struggle remained a cornerstone in the ideology of the Jewish Social Democrats.

Despite this universalism, however, the question of Jewish identification had to be considered. Specifically, what role was the Jewish worker to play in the general struggle? This was clearly a question that some of the worker-speakers wanted answered that first May Day. One asked: "If the struggle is imminent for the Jewish worker as well as for all other workers, who will fight for him if he will not fight for himself?"[6] In insisting on the class unity of all workers, the Jewish Social Democrats inevitably had to deal with another issue as well: the patently inferior social and legal position of the Jews. The pioneers thus simply could not avoid the subject of Jewish political rights. They did, however, try to play it down, to emphasize instead common economic rights and related class political problems. The "national-Jewish political struggle," Gozhansky wrote in his *Letter to Agitators*, was not an exclusively Jewish struggle but a general struggle of all workers in the course of which the Jews would gain their rights.[7]

Gozhansky's view seems to have been shared by most of the pioneer-intellectuals, though they took no theoretical position on the national issue. Indeed, discussion of the point was rare. We can surmise, though, that Izenshtat expressed the feelings of most of the Group in an exchange with local Zionists in 1892, when he countered their arguments for a national rebirth and renaissance with those of Il'iashevich, outlined a few years earlier in a well-known article.[8]

"The essence of contemporary history," Il'iashevich had asserted, "is not the *national*, but the *class struggle*." It was the economic system in Russia and the regime preserving it that were responsible for the unhappy condition of the Jewish worker. The fate of the Jewish worker was tied to the Russian revolution; a victory there would be his victory. It was thus the task of Jewish youth to organize the movement among the Jews and to prepare them for a fight against a government that was so ready to sacrifice them to the angry mob to save itself. The revolutionary youth had to educate the Jews, so they would not be confused by the "hostile demonstrations" of the Russian mob or the narrow national prejudices of some intellectuals.[9]

The cosmopolitanism of the Jewish Social Democratic leaders did not go unchallenged. It was inevitable, given the concentration of Jews in Poland and Lithuania, that the question of political relations with the Polish revolutionaries would arise, and with it the issue of nationality. The Poles, far into the fight for national rights and eager to press others into their cause, made every attempt to influence the Jewish Social Democrats. The questions they raised were difficult—and embarrassing. Gozhansky, for instance, tells us how he was hard put for an answer when two Polish comrades asked him to reconcile the teaching of Russian with the organization of Jewish workers. Why, they wanted to know, did Jewish workers need Russian?[10] As it was, he was uncomfortable with a theory that insisted on an international workers' movement and a reality that confined Jewish workers to a national milieu.[11] The Poles exploited this uneasiness among their Vilna colleagues and with their questions probed at the gap between the Group's cosmopolitanism and the Jewish workers' cultural separateness.

Polish revolutionary thought, at least as it was expressed in the program of the Polish Socialist Party (Polska Partja Socjalistyczna or PPS, which was formed in 1892), was first and foremost nationalist. An independent and democratic Polish republic was one of the party's major planks.[12] Proceeding from their own views and assumptions, the Poles saw the Jewish revolutionaries as misguided at best. One of the most outspoken critics was Joseph Pilsudski, a major figure in the PPS. Pilsudski deplored the tendency of the Jewish proletariat "to avoid political questions in general and the policies of the Polish-Lithuanian socialist movement in particular." This was a grave error in any case but even worse because of conditions in the Russian Empire. In following a policy of russification, the Jewish Social Democrats completely isolated their movement from other local movements, making cooperation difficult. In a country where the russification policies of the state caused such pain, where oppression and restricted opportunity were used to uphold the state's prerogatives, no socialist had the right to remain neutral; "he should in no way, even indirectly, support the reactionary aspirations of the administration."[13] The conscious russification of the Jewish movement, which Pilsudski took as typical of the entire Jewish community, gave aid and comfort to the enemy.

It was shortly after this attack, which was made in April 1893, that the Vilna

Group decided to switch to Yiddish for its propaganda. Nevertheless, the assumptions on which Pilsudski based his criticism were to trouble relations between the PPS and the Jewish movement for many years. In his view, any inhabitant of Poland who could look with equanimity on the treatment the Poles had endured at the hands of the Russians was, if not an enemy, at least to be despised. The Tsars' russification program in Poland was not only political but cultural as well, and any person in Polish territory who in any way associated himself with Russian culture betrayed both his homeland and the revolutionary movement.

The Jewish Social Democrats, products of the Russian educational system and, more significantly, of the Russian revolutionary movement, saw the matter quite differently, however. Many of them, especially the Vilna intellectuals, had been led away from their narrow Jewish environment toward the larger Russian society. To be sure, their view of Russian culture was in international, not national terms. But they easily fit Russian culture into this cosmopolitan view, for unlike the PPS they did not see Russian culture as an extension and instrument of Tsarist national policy; rather, they saw it as providing easy access to the world in general. Mill, who was in closer personal contact with the Polish revolutionaries than any of the other early pioneer-intellectuals, says of the relationship between the two groups:

Our relations with the PPS were negative from the start. Not so much because of their plank on the independence of Poland as because of the motives that prompted it. We who regarded the common struggle of all socialist and revolutionary organizations against Tsarism as the most important thing ... could not easily swallow the PPS's mistrust of the Russian socialists, their unfounded doubts about the possibility of a revolution in Russia, [and] their chauvinistic language, so alien to revolutionary circles until then.[14]

In short, the Jewish Social Democrats considered the PPS attitude divisive and nationalistic. Ever the universalists, they wanted no part of a new parochialism. Were they not the first generation to break out of one of the tightest religio-national communities known to man? Were they, they asked, to give up everything they had gained for a new national doctrine, whatever its democratic and socialist trappings?

There was, of course, some justification for Pilsudski's charge that the Jewish movement's neutrality on the Polish question indicated a lack of political orientation. In relying on a cosmopolitan Russian revolutionary movement, the Jewish Social Democrats ignored the ethnic composition of Poland and the northwest provinces of the Pale. The simple fact is, however, that having broken with one kind of confining national feeling, the Vilna pioneers could scarcely turn to the Poles. Accepting the Polish view raised even more difficult questions. Why was a demand for an independent Poland better for the Jewish proletariat than the demand for independence and equality for all inhabitants of the Russian Empire? What effect would the separation of Poland from the Empire have on the Jewish proletariat scattered over the provinces of the Russian Pale? Above all, could or should a Polish program become the major feature of a movement based on the Jewish proletariat? In the end, Mill's answer was the Group's answer: liberation of the Jewish masses did not rest in a Polish victory, but only in "the victory of the united revolutionary and socialist forces of all Russia, including Poland."[15]

Social Democracy was just one of the ways the Russian Jews responded to the pogroms and restrictive legislation of the early 1880's. Many were convinced that they could never live in peace and dignity in any "alien" country. As Leo Pinsker put it in 1882, the Jews were "guests everywhere and *at home* nowhere." Since other nations never had to deal with a Jewish *nation*, only with mere Jews, he declared, the solution was to "seek our honor and our salvation ... in the restoration of a national bond of union. [We] must determine ... what country is accessible to us and also capable of offering the Jews of all lands a ... secure and unquestioned refuge."[16] In the mid-1890's Asher Ginzberg (Ahad Haam), a leading essayist of the new Hebrew literature, stressed the need for a Jewish spiritual regeneration as a preparation for a Jewish state.[17]

To the Jewish Social Democrats, the Zionists, with their national independence without socialism, appeared to be even further from the path to true freedom than the PPS. At least the Poles were fellow revolutionaries, bent on toppling the Tsarist regime. In the view of the class-oriented pioneers, a bourgeois Palestine could be expected to exploit the Jewish worker just as Russia did.[18] Though there were occasional arguments between the two groups, the Zionists' goals seemed so utopian and so far from those of the Social Democrats, there was little ground for discussion, and mutual repudiation was simple.* Moreover, since the Zionists and the Social Democrats did not really compete at this time—the Zionists did not actively court the masses and had little influence among the workers—there seems to have been little open polemic between them.[19]

Yet the Jewish Social Democrats could hardly miss the implications of the nationalism that led to the spread of Zionism, the growth of the PPS, and the formation of a Lithuanian Social Democratic Party in 1893. Nationality was

---

* A number of Jewish intellectuals turned from Zionism to Social Democracy in the 1880's and 1890's, among them Pavel Rosenthal's wife, Anna, one of the first pioneer-intellectuals in Vilna. Other pioneers who made the same transition were Bainish Mikhalevich, Victor Shulman, and Ben-tsion Hofman. (A. Rosenthal, "Bletlakh," p. 429; Mikhalevich, *Zikhroinos*, 1: 16; Shulman, "Baginen," p. 51; Hofman, "Vi azoi," pp. 59–61.) Except for Anna Rosenthal, none of these converts played a leading role at the outset. Nevertheless, their importance to the early movement should not be discounted, for it is fair to assume that they awoke at least some of the Vilna pioneers to the problems around them.

becoming an important political factor in the western provinces. This fact became even clearer as they moved out into the community, where the same kind of forces were at work. Inevitably, if slowly, they had to cope with the new reality and to formulate specifically Jewish aims. Early pioneers like Kremer, Gozhansky, and Kopelson had in fact already changed their views on the role of the Jewish worker several times. First they had seen the Jewish circle recruit merely as a member of the proletariat to be prepared for participation in an Empire-wide revolution.[20] Implicit in this view is the denial of a purely Jewish role[21] (not wholly unexpected, given the background of the pioneers who held it, i.e., their departure from the Jewish community and their identification with an international workers' movement).

The first change in viewpoint came when the Vilna pioneers shifted their attention to their immediate surroundings. It was only a short step from recognition that the Jewish worker could be mobilized in the pursuit of economic goals (a recognition that was reflected in the new tactic of mass agitation) to recognition that he might be mobilized politically as well. Indeed, *On Agitation* had indicated as much. So had Gozhansky in his *Letter to Agitators* when he asserted that the Jewish workers must organize themselves in order to take part in the political struggle. Some years later Vladimir Kosovsky faulted Gozhansky for not being explicit on this subject. "*In what form*," Kosovsky asked, was the Jewish proletariat to build this force.[22] That question was not even being considered in early 1894.

By mid-year, however, the Social Democrats had begun to examine this issue. In two half-day sessions in August 1894, the Vilna leaders met to discuss political tactics. It was the first time, says Mill, that the Group had so clearly and "with the fullest resolve" declared its position on the national question: that the Jewish workers suffered not only as workers, but also as Jews; that in its work the Group must emphasize all forms of national oppression; and that one of the immediate tasks must be the struggle for equal civil rights, a struggle that was best led by the Jewish worker himself.[23] Self-recognition was plainly beginning to stir the Group deeply.

One lone dissenting voice was heard at the meeting. Leon Goldman (Akim) feared a harmful national mood would develop among the workers that would isolate them from the Russian masses and weaken the general political struggle.* Kosovsky, then a relative newcomer to the Group, answered him: on the contrary, national considerations would aid the work of the Social Democrats enormously by bringing new members into the ranks.[24] No one else joined the debate. Both opponent and proponent were concerned with the question only as a matter of tactics, not as a matter of ideology.

---

* Goldman later worked with the Russian Social Democrats. His younger brother Mikhel, better known as Mark Liber, was one of the most important Bund leaders in the early twentieth century.

There were important political implications in the stress on equal rights for Jews, a point on which the vast majority of the Vilna Social Democrats were agreed. Making a distinction between equal rights for all and equal rights for Jews implicitly carried with it the whole issue of national culture, and more: the very future of the Jews. In arguing that the political problem was one of national versus international (or at least imperial) interests, Goldman made the same either-or distinction that plagued the Bund in later years.

Having decided that they could no more ignore the importance of Jewishness in the political struggle than they could avoid the use of Yiddish in the economic struggle, the pioneers now sought practical means to put their new program into action. One important answer had been suggested at the August 1894 meeting, namely, that closer ties be established with other Jewish workers' organizations.[25] The pioneers were moving ever closer to the formation of the Bund; they had now accepted the idea of establishing a purely Jewish political organization and were prepared to recognize the Jewish workers not only as a specific group, but as a group equal in all respects to every other group in the revolutionary movement.

The clearest statement of the new policy we have is in a speech Martov made at a post–May Day meeting of leaders and agitators in Vilna in 1895. The movement had become more democratic and practical, Martov began; its work had grown beyond the restricted intellectual achievements of small groups. Formerly, Jewish intellectuals had seen the salvation of the Jewish workers in the triumph of Russian workers. They had considered the Jewish movement "*a secondary matter*"; indeed, they had seldom really noticed the Jewish workers' plight. But all this had changed; the movement had adapted itself to the realities of the Jewish condition. "Although tied to the Russian movement," he said, "the Jewish proletariat must not await liberation ... either from the Russian movement or from the Polish movement." The Jewish workers could not win alone, but neither could they risk hanging back. The Russian working class, still weak, would be facing its own difficult struggle. It would be concerned primarily with its own needs and might be willing to sacrifice those demands of concern only to the Jews, such as religious freedom or equal rights. Then came the dramatic challenge that was to become a rallying cry: "That class which cannot fight its own way to freedom," Martov declared, "does not deserve to have that freedom."[26]

How was the Jewish working class to fight for its freedom? By "openly and clearly" stating "that our aim, the aim of the Jewish Social Democrats who are active among the Jews, is to build a special Jewish workers' organization that will educate the Jewish proletariat and lead it in the struggle for economic, civil, and political rights." Such an organization would have limited use, to be sure. The struggle was, after all, an international one. But, Martov insisted, so long as the world was divided into states, "the pressing task is winning for every nation, if not political independence, then at least full equal rights." The national indifference of a people without civil rights impeded the development of international socialism. Consequently, it was the task of the socialists to assure all people of their rights. This was in no way incompatible with the ultimate goal, for the movement was socialist, even if it had a national character.[27]

In later years both opponents and supporters of the Bund looked back on this speech as a kind of watershed in the history of the movement. Moishe Rafes, a one-time Bundist who turned to the Communist Party, sees in the speech the very foundation of the Bund's "nationalistic ideology": Martov had set forth "independent" tasks for the Jewish workers and had "pushed" them onto the path to an independent political party.[28] To Mill the speech was of "first-class historical significance," "a turning point" in the history of the Jewish workers' movement that established its future organizational form.[29] In 1900, when the speech was published, the title of the Russian version was *The Turning Point in the History of the Jewish Workers' Movement* (*Povorotnyi punkt v istorii yevreiskago rabochago dvizheniia*). Mill's turn of phrase thus came from an early addition to the Bund vocabulary.

Much, then, has been read into Martov's speech. But it is important to note that it was not regarded as a "turning point" at the time Martov gave it. Consider, for example, its original modest title—"On the Theoretical and Practical Successes of the Movement During the Past Year."* As Martov himself later admitted, he hit on the idea of a special Jewish workers' organization "purely empirically," simply because the Jewish Social Democrats were being hampered in their efforts to form close organizational ties with the Social Democrats of Moscow and St. Petersburg by the weakness of the local Russian movement, and at the same time were having some success in establishing ties between groups working among the Jewish proletariat.[30] In fact, Martov was merely summing up the results of a year's discussion.

To assert that the Jewish workers ought to seek civil rights through their own organization was simply to give voice to a movement that was already under way. By May 1895 the effectiveness of organized activity for economic purposes was well recognized. Far from being an abrupt departure (which might be inferred, since only this one key document has been preserved), the Martov speech reflects a gradual change of emphasis that took place as the workers showed themselves ready and able to join in a struggle. The Jewish Social Democrats' willingness to shift the initiative to the Jewish workers thus grew out of a new psychology, not a new ideology. Confidence in the Jewish workers and certainty that Jewish national feeling could be channeled into the revolutionary movement gave rise to a new self-consciousness. Moreover,

---

* "O teoreticheskikh i prakticheskikh uspekhakh dvizheniia za poslednii god." The Yiddish version, which like the Russian version was published in 1900, bore the title *Di naie epokhe in der yidisher arbeter bevegung* (The New Period in the Jewish Workers' Movement).

the Social Democrats could not help measuring the gains of the Jewish movement against those of the Russian movement; and by this yardstick the Jewish
movement had done well indeed.

The fact is there was not one new ideological precept in the speech. The call
for equal civil rights lay squarely within the ideological framework of Russian
Social Democracy. The real change was the new positive meaning of "equal
civil rights." More was at stake now than the elimination of legal discrimination; the Jewish Social Democrats had begun to think in terms of the Jewish
worker's right to personal dignity—his right to equality not only as a worker
but as a Jew.

Perhaps the one really new point expressed in the speech was the suggestion
that the Russian workers might not be as aware of the needs of the Jewish
workers as the Jews themselves were. There is at least an implication here that
the Russian workers, like the Poles, might be guided by group interests and
might work for their own ends rather than for a general revolution in Russia.
But Martov may have been stating only the obvious: that since the Russian
and Jewish worker populations were rigidly divided, the Russians could not
possibly know all the ins and outs of the local situation. At most, all one can
say of the speech is that it tells us the Jewish Social Democrats began to insist
"officially" in 1895 on the right to organize and fight as a Jewish movement
within the larger Social Democratic movement.

If Martov's speech did indeed chart the way to the national program of the
Bund and the creation of an independent political party, those developments
were certainly not foreseen in 1895. As a matter of fact, Martov himself was
soon worrying about the vulgarization of his ideas among the working-class.[31]
But the Jewish Social Democrats could neither ignore nor resist the tide of
national consciousness sweeping the Jewish community; they had to respond
to the new sentiment. In Minsk Abraham Liesin, a persuasive young Jewish
socialist who sympathized with the Social Democrats in principle but who
did not formally join their ranks, argued that their work had as little meaning
for the Jewish workers as the Populists' work had had for the Russian peasants. Liesin's views attracted considerable attention. In late 1894 or early 1895,
after he discussed the problem of working out a program of national aims with
Kremer, he came away with the impression that Kremer scarcely understood
what he was after.[32] Liesin, no Zionist but a firm supporter of Jewish national
goals, was still very far from the point of view expressed in Martov's speech.

To the Social Democrats Liesin seemed heretical for merely suggesting a
positive national program.[33] Yet as he admitted he himself could not formulate
its aims at this time.* How much less prepared, then, were the Social Democrats to initiate such a program?

---

* Liesin moved to New York City in the late 1890's. He earned a considerable reputation
in the United States as a poet and as the editor of *Di Zukunft*.

For all their brave words, the Social Democrats' political work did not just lag behind their economic work; it did not even begin in any practical sense. Until such time as the political relations between the Tsarist state and its subjects changed, the call for equal rights was an empty slogan. Only a broad-based political movement could effect so fundamental a change. The Social Democrats could be reasonably effective on the local level when it came to economic matters; they could do virtually nothing at the local level to accomplish their political aims. The only way the government could have been forced on the issue of rights was by armed revolt; there was no revolutionary organization, or combination of organizations, capable of such an undertaking in the mid-1890's.

Under the circumstances, the political effort continued to be largely educational, the technical work largely a matter of distributing political propaganda. Though many of the politically conscious intellectuals preferred to remain aloof from the economic organizations and to insist on the theoretical distinction between economic and political tasks, there was little to distinguish their political work from the economic work of the other activists. Below the top level, however, political organization was beginning to take place among the rank-and-file members of the movement—both at the middle level, in the skhodkas, and at the lowest level, in the kases. In fact, some of the more politically conscious workers began forming political kases. Special study, celebrating holidays, helping arrested comrades, disseminating propaganda and illegal literature—these were the main kinds of political activity in the mid-1890's.[34]

One sign of the growing political consciousness was the increased attendance at the still-secret May Day meetings. Whereas only some 100 persons had marked the holiday in Vilna in 1892, better than twice that number attended the 1895 meeting; and in the next year the figure doubled again, to 550.[35] There is evidence of increasing politicization, too, in the wide acceptance of the symbols of revolution. The first red banner flew at the 1895 Vilna meeting;[36] within a few short years red flags and revolutionary slogans were part of the ceremony. By 1897 the meetings had attracted official attention. When May Day came around the worried authorities surrounded the city of Vilna with troops, sealing off the routes to the woods and forcing the cancellation of the meeting.[37]

The attitudes expressed in the Martov speech soon came to represent the prevailing political mood within the movement. We find, for example, national overtones in the lead article of the first issue of *Der Yidisher Arbeter*, which appeared a little over a year later. Though the proletariat's struggle against the state was of course the first concern of all conscious workers, said *Der Yidisher*

Arbeter, the truly conscious worker did not forget to include on his banner the demand for equality for the Jews.[38] It was clear that a balance had been struck between Marxist universalism and Jewish national expression. Next to come was a program that would give purpose and direction to that national consciousness.

6. The Founding of the Bund

By the time the 1890's passed the midway mark the need to build a united organization had become generally recognized among Russian Social Democrats. This was not a new idea, of course. The Russian émigrés in Plekhanov's
Group had long been insisting that organizational ties ought to be formed
among the Social Democratic groups scattered throughout the Empire; and
in the early 1890's they themselves had had "significant contact" with their
comrades in Russia.[1] But with the proliferation of Social Democratic groups
it soon became clear that some kind of coordination was needed to make their
work effective. Plekhanov was only giving voice to the general sentiment
when he asserted at the London Congress of the Socialist International in 1896
that the building of a united organization must be the chief aim of the Russian
Social Democrats in the immediate future.[2]

The Jewish Social Democrats were close to these developments. When a
group of Russian Social Democrats in Europe formed the Union of Russian
Social Democrats Abroad in late 1894 to arrange for the printing of materials
for mass agitation, the Jewish organizations soon established ties with them.
In early 1895 Kopelson participated in a meeting in St. Petersburg at which
delegates from various centers endorsed the decision of a Moscow group to
work closely with both the Union and its collaborator, the Liberation of Labor
Group.[3] He became the link between the Union Abroad and the Jewish Social
Democrats when he went to Western Europe later that year. The Union's own
publications, *Rabotnik* (The Worker) and *Listok "Rabotnika"* ("The Worker's" Leaflet), both of which began publication in 1896, frequently carried
articles on the Jewish movement.

The first serious efforts to bring some unity to the Social Democratic movement were made in 1895 by Russian groups in Moscow and St. Petersburg.
They were forced to give up the attempt when police arrested some of those
involved.[4] From 1896 on the Vilna Group (through Kremer) and Social
Democrats in St. Petersburg and Kiev attempted to come to an agreement on
unification.

Meanwhile, within the Jewish movement itself groups were being drawn together through their own activities. The Minsk Conference of June 1895, which followed hard on the heels of Martov's May Day speech, saw the first tentative move toward an organizational link between local groups with the proposal to establish a common organ.[5] However, the delegates left the matter to a second conference with other Jewish Social Democratic organizations,[6] which apparently was never convened.

Mutnikovich indicates that there was a three-day conference in Vilna in 1895 at which delegates from various towns exchanged views and agreed on the need for a special Jewish Social Democratic organization to develop the political and social consciousness of the Jewish workers.[7] It is not clear whether this conference preceded or followed the Minsk Conference. He may have been referring to the extensive discussions described by Moshe Dushkan (a member of Martov's circle who later worked in Russian organizations), which were held in early 1895 and which took up the question of the need for unity and centralized leadership.[8] At all events the concern for broader organization among the Jewish Social Democrats is clear.

The Jewish Social Democrats were far better prepared to weld their groups into a single organization than their Russian compatriots. Their energetic work and solid achievements were widely recognized. The report of the Russian delegation to the 1896 Congress of the International, which Plekhanov himself delivered, praised their activities, pointing with "special satisfaction" to the "successes of Social Democratic propaganda among the Jews."

These pariahs ... who do not even have the paltry rights the Christian inhabitants possess, have shown so much staunchness in the struggle with their exploiters and such keenness in understanding the sociopolitical tasks of the contemporary workers' movement that in some respects they may be considered the avant garde of the workers' army in Russia.[9]

The handling of routine activities led toward unification in practice. From technical coordination it was but a step to common work. In creating *Der Yidisher Arbeter* the pioneer-intellectuals created a focal point, an enterprise that drew intellectuals and half-intellectuals together into an integral working arrangement.[10] Even more significant was the Vilna Group's role as a de facto center. The ties the Group had established through "colonization" and personal contact, as well as the talented personnel it had at hand, made it a practical and functioning core, something the Russian Social Democrats were still groping for.

Part of the peculiar strength of the Jewish Social Democrats lay in the uniqueness of their situation. Having chosen to make Yiddish their medium of communication, they were bound to work together; there was nowhere else to go for revolutionary literature. It was a special need that encouraged independence—and more. The Jewish Social Democrats may have wanted to establish ties with other Social Democratic organizations in Russia or abroad; they were forced to seek ties with each other.

Despite the favorable climate for unification, over two years elapsed between the Minsk Conference and the formal creation of the Bund. The leaders of the Vilna Group were cautious. Indeed they were notorious for their security precautions. They had been frankly shocked, for instance, at Martov's openness with them when they first met him on his arrival in Vilna.[11] After Lenin stopped in Vilna on a brief visit in 1895 he commented on the cautiousness in the provinces; apparently the Vilna Social Democrats suspected him of being a provocateur for a time.[12] Such wariness was more than justified. Only a few months after the Minsk Conference a wave of arrests swept Russia. Some of the movement's most effective and oldest activists were caught. Hardest-hit was Belostok, where Gozhansky, Liuba Izenshtat, and Dushkan were among those arrested. Gozhansky received the longest sentence—five years exile in eastern Siberia.[13] Other arrests and searches took place in Vilna, Warsaw, Kovno, and Lodz, and in some of the smaller towns as well. With the Tsarist police increasingly vigilant, meetings were extremely dangerous. So cautious did Kremer become that he almost called off the founding congress of the Bund even as delegates were arriving because of Pati Srednitsky's arrest at that time. It took a determined stand by Mill to change Kremer's mind.[14]

Still, there was no reason why the Jewish Social Democrats could not have formally united the existing groups long before 1897 with a fairly high chance of success. Apart from the fact that the specific dates, October 7–9 (N.S.) were chosen to coincide with the Jewish high holidays so the delegates could travel under cover of going home to be with family and friends, there was nothing exceptional about the early fall of 1897.[15] It was, as we shall see, the press of events that pushed the leaders into convoking the first congress.

Despite the practical benefits that a special Jewish workers' organization could provide, this was not the main reason the pioneers were promoting the idea. The purpose of such an organization was the purpose of the revolutionary movement itself—the attainment of freedom.

By the mid-1890's the Jewish Social Democrats had come to view their organizational task as a dual one. As always they were bent on teaching the worker his class role in preparation for the general struggle of the proletariat. But now they also took into account the Jewish worker's identity as a Jew and his own struggle for freedom; and they set out to provide the organizational means for carrying on that struggle.

Although the leaders' specific aims did not go beyond the general aims of Social Democracy, in both statement and performance they informed the revolutionary community that they wanted—and expected—the Jewish workers to be recognized as full partners in the movement. When it became clear to them that the formation of other Social Democratic groupings was imminent, they began to regard the need for a Jewish workers' organization as urgent.

Until mid-1897, however, the unification efforts of the Russian Social Democrats had not been crowned with success. In fact, they had even had some difficulty organizing workers in the major Russian centers. When the great strike of 1896 occurred in St. Petersburg, *Der Yidisher Arbeter* observed that the Russian workers had "finally" joined the "great struggle for liberation from the yoke of capitalism, which the Polish and Jewish workers were already waging."[16] The Jewish leaders were more impressed with the potential of the Russian workers' movement than with its achievements.

The comparatively slow growth of Russian organization had much to do with the reluctance of the Jewish Social Democrats to push ahead. In the mid-1890's the Jewish leaders were still bound by their early training; they continued to believe that freedom would come through the efforts of the whole working class in Russia, and that their fate was tied to that of the Russian Social Democrats. The pioneers worked hard for the general movement. Vilna transported illegal literature, supplied printing materials, and helped get people in and out of the country.[17] The Jewish Social Democrats were wary of moving ahead too fast. A special organization could create its own dangers; it could lead to excessive national consciousness.[18] The leaders were willing to wait. In its first issue, *Der Yidisher Arbeter* stated unequivocally that the Jewish workers' organization would join the future general party; it remained for the Russian-led forces to ready themselves.[19]

The interconnection of Russian and Jewish Social Democratic affairs in the formation of the Bund is confirmed by Kremer's description of the steps taken toward the founding congress. He made a special trip to Western Europe in May 1897 on behalf of the Vilna Group and the St. Petersburg Union of Struggle for the Liberation of Labor. One of his missions was to discuss with Plekhanov's Group the question of official representation abroad for the Russian Social Democratic movement. The Plekhanovites asked him, "How can we represent you if you yourselves are not united? As yet there is nothing to represent formally." The question made a "strong impression" on Kremer. When he returned home in August he discussed the matter with Mill in Warsaw and with the inner circles in Vilna. A congress of the Jewish Social Democratic groups was then agreed on and was set up in a matter of weeks.[20]

Kremer's account is too simple, perhaps. Both Mill and Kursky, for example, insist that Kremer made his trip in 1896, not 1897.* Other critics point out that since there had been numerous meetings and discussions among the Jewish

---

* *Arkady*, pp. 86, 156–57. Elsewhere, however, Mill recalls that he and Kremer attended a congress in Zurich, which was convened to discuss the legal position of workers (*Pionern*, 1: 258–59). Such a congress was in fact held in August 1897; Kremer wrote an article about it for the November 1897 issue of *Der Yidisher Arbeter* (No. 4–5).

Social Democrats on the subject of a Jewish organization since 1895, the notion could scarcely have occurred to Kremer for the first time in the summer of 1897.[21] The difference is no doubt a matter of semantics. Kremer surely meant he was struck with the idea of acting on the notion of formally organizing rather than with the idea of an organization itself.

In any case there is some evidence that a decision to unite the Jewish organizations was made before Kremer returned from Switzerland. In the spring of 1897, when asked why a report to the Union of Russian Social Democrats Abroad could not serve as a report for all the Jewish organizations, Kremer replied: "The question of the creation of a general party, not only a Jewish one, is being considered at the present time, and will be decided in the near future."[22] Further, Mutnikovich feels that a plan to unite all the Social Democratic organizations, which was circulated in Vilna by the Kievan group after its conference in March 1897, prodded the pioneers into calling a meeting "as soon as possible."[23] If this is so, then Kremer's return in fact only marked the final stage in the decision to call a congress.[24] Given the Jewish leaders' long, cautious discussion of the whole question and the short span of time between Kremer's return and the convocation of the congress, it seems likely that only the formal arrangements for a meeting remained to be worked out.

The major reason for the choice of dates, then, was the progress being made toward a united Russian party. Kremer certainly knew of the steps being taken. While abroad he saw the first issue of *Rabochaia gazeta* (The Workers' Newspaper), which the Kievan Social Democrats had established in the hope it could be made the organ of a united party. Unification was clearly becoming a serious possibility, and the juxtaposition of this possibility to the call for a special Jewish organization is unmistakable.

To a limited extent the founding of the Bund also came about because of the growth of Social Democratic groups in Poland. This was particularly true of Warsaw, where the "colonists" had been working two years in an atmosphere of competition and steadily growing animosity on the part of the PPS.[25] The PPS had made only a limited effort to gain Jewish support. In 1894 the Polish socialists brought a total of 23,776 pieces of illegal literature into the country; only 778 of these were in Yiddish. By 1895 the overall percentage of Yiddish literature was considerably higher—1,253 pieces out of a total of 12,777 —but the quantity was still small.[26] At the end of 1895 Jewish PPS members complained to their Central Committee about the party's efforts in the Jewish community. The cause could be hurt by the party's neglect of matters affecting the Jews, they warned, pointing to the danger from the Social Democrats, and they appealed to the committee to take a position on the Jewish question.[27] Unlike the PPS in Vilna, which took Jewish matters seriously and tried to make gains in the face of a well-developed Social Democratic movement, the powerful Warsaw party neglected the opportunity of outdistancing its weak Social Democratic competition.

In 1896 the Jewish Social Democrats in Warsaw began posting some gains, and relations between them and the PPS took a bad turn. Differences over Polish independence, the unification of Jewish organizations, relations with the weak Polish Social Democrats—the natural ideological partners of the Social Democratic Jews—grew sharper. In October the Jewish PPS members in Warsaw held a meeting at which they reiterated the fears expressed to the Central Committee and complained that none of their requests had been fulfilled. They pointed out that the new Social Democratic competitors, with their printed matter, were threatening to take over the trades. To combat them effectively, the PPS members wanted funds, propaganda materials, and articles about Jewish problems in the party journals.[28]

Despite the fears of the Jewish section of the PPS, the Warsaw Jewish Social Democrats considered themselves weak, particularly since they were working with what amounted to only a small segment of the total worker population. The picture changed in early 1897, when several groups in Poland, including the Jewish PPS members, combined to form a Jewish Workers' Union (Bund). Agitation and strikes soon followed, and in May the new organization produced a leaflet in Yiddish. However, with the growth of political activity by the Social Democratic contingent, the PPS members withdrew, leaving an organization with a strongly Social Democratic character.[29]

Still, this was only a beginning. The new group needed the support of a party that would take a stand on the basic issues raised by the PPS. To activists like Mill, who was working in Warsaw at the time, it seemed evident that only with help from the outside was there any chance of success. "No other group was then as interested in the founding of the party as the Jewish workers in Warsaw," he tells us.[30] Mill worked as hard as any man for the fulfillment of that goal.

The founding congress of the Bund was characteristically modest in its actions, reflecting the pragmatism that had governed the work of the Jewish Social Democrats to that point. Indeed, the very mechanics of the congress show the same deliberate, cautious approach the Jewish leaders had used throughout the years of mass agitation and organization. This was to be a secret meeting of insiders, not a constituent assembly. The Vilna hosts issued formal invitations only to the groups in Warsaw, Minsk, and Belostok. Mill, who had already discussed the conference with Kremer in Warsaw, was given the time and place in a coded message in a newspaper article; the Minsk organization was invited by mail and the Belostok organization by a message relayed from Warsaw. Vitebsk was apparently represented only because an important member of the group there happened to be in Vilna at the time.

Security, always an important consideration, was the main reason there was no attempt to make the congress broadly inclusive. The invited groups met two requirements: they had achieved considerable success and their members

were known to the Vilna Group.[31] The need for security governed the physical arrangements as well. The sessions took place far from the center of town,
the delegates going singly to the modest house taken for the occasion. At no
time did all the delegates meet at once; and after the first session the Vilna
center group was represented by only two persons at a time. No official records
were kept, though at Kremer's request Kosovsky took notes for a report for
Di Arbeter Shtime. The delegates representing the paper alternated in their
attendance, accounting in part for the poor records we have of the proceedings.[32]

Foreknowledge of the agenda, outside of Vilna at least, was scanty. In Warsaw Mill drilled his fellow Social Democrats in preparation, trying to foresee
what questions might arise on the subject of unification.[33] The Minsk delegate,
Pavel Berman, who was invited so late as to miss the first session (probably
because of Pati Srednitsky's arrest), had no time to discuss the meeting with
his group and remained silent throughout the congress.[34]

The Vilna Group dominated the proceedings. Three of its members—the
pioneer-intellectuals Kremer, Mutnikovich, and Kosovsky—attended. They
were joined by three Vilna workers: David Katz, Israel Kaplinsky, and Hirsh
Soroka. Katz represented the workers, Kaplinsky and Soroka *Di Arbeter
Shtime*.[35] The other participants were Berman (Minsk); Leon Goldman,
Marya Zhaludsky, and Mill (Warsaw); Rosa Greenblat and Hillel Katz-Blum
(Belostok); and Yidel Abramov (Vitebsk). Ten of the 13 delegates were
Vilna-trained.*

Kremer's opening statement set the direction of the meeting. He began by
pointing out that in a practical sense all the cities were now bound together.
They all based their tasks on the immediate needs of the workers, and they
all held similar views on the relation between the economic struggle and the
political struggle, leading to a common strategic view. In addition, material
needs had drawn them together and did so increasingly as the movement
developed. The exchange of personnel, literature, and financial aid had been
going on for a long time. "We see," said Kremer, "that the cities are already
tied together in fact, and that it remains only to pour this existing unity into a
mold so that it will have a definite form."[36]

Turning to the present, Kremer stressed the urgency of uniting. The government was attacking the Jewish workers and their leaders with such intensity
as to endanger the bonds between the cities. A central organization linking the
cities would prevent them from becoming isolated. It could operate without
dealing directly with the masses, thereby avoiding police persecution, and at

---

* Two sources (*25 yor*, p. 31, and Mutnikovich, "Ershter," p. 3, col. 1) name only 11
participants. However, Mill, who wrote the article in *25 yor*, later changed the figure
to 13 (*Pionern*, 1: 272). That figure accords with the accounts of Kremer and Katz
(Kremer, in *Arkady*, p. 361; D. Katz, "Pervyi s"ezd," p. 139).

the same time maintain contacts between the local groups. Moreover, the government was bound to be more impressed by a joint stand than it would be by the demands of a single local group.

A central organization was not proposed merely to legitimize the existing relationship, however. The movement among the Jews had become strong, and the time had come to step forth with the whole proletariat of Russia for political rights and for equal rights for Jews. These issues had to be pressed more systematically and more vigorously than in the past. Moreover, said Kremer, there was the question of a general Russian party. The day was drawing near when that dream would be realized. The Jewish proletariat would certainly participate in that development—but "it could not enter the party divided into separate, independent groups."[37]

There were no debates on Kremer's statement or indeed on the general subject of program and tactics.[38] In fact, no program was worked out. The practical tasks necessary for the formation of a united organization were accepted without question.[39] The congress resolved that the new organization would enter the Russian party when it was formed as an autonomous section, with the right to make decisions in all Jewish matters.[40] (Since this point would prove to be a fateful one for the Bund, it is unfortunate that we do not have the precise wording of the resolution. For security reasons all discussion of joining the Russian party was omitted from the published report.)

Future relations with other revolutionary groups were given some attention. The congress formalized the existing arrangements with the Union Abroad, which was to print and procure literature in Western Europe for the new organization and continue to spread news of the Jewish movement in the Union publications.[41] A general resolution advocating closer ties with Russian groups was adopted, but no published resolution emerged from the delegates' discussions on the PPS.[42] Despite the Warsaw organization's difficulties with the Polish party and the PPS's expected displeasure at this new development, the new organization was to try to link up with Jewish groups in Poland.

As Kremer had proposed, the congress created a Central Committee that could direct the organization without becoming involved in local work and its attendant dangers. The committee's composition was never in doubt: the selection of the de facto center of the Vilna Group, Kremer, Kosovsky, and Mutnikovich, was a matter of course. Besides directing the operations of the organization, they were to publish its official journals and literature.[43] One of their first acts was to take precautions against discovery. Anticipating that the committee would be the target of police activity and aware that Vilna had been the scene of recent arrests, they decided to leave the city.[44]

One of the liveliest discussions concerned the name of the new organization. Mill proposed "The Union of Jewish Social Democratic Groups," Kremer the name "The General Jewish Workers' Union in Russia."[45] Those opposing

Mill's proposal objeced to the reference to Social Democracy, contending that properly speaking only the small group that led the workers were Social Democrats. Such terminology might make some workers uncomfortable, when the object should be to make every worker feel at home in the organization. Mill conceded that there might be some validity to this argument in the case of smaller towns, where the term Social Democracy might arouse fear, but he rejected it in the case of Warsaw and other large cities, where the political mass struggle had already begun and the word socialism frightened no one.* He was unable to carry the day. Kremer's entry pleased the majority of delegates because it suggested that the door was open to every worker "who adhered to the struggle for the better life, which the proletariat is leading."[46] His suggestion was adopted with one amendment: at Mill's request the words "and Poland" were added after "Russia" to avoid any misunderstanding. Still, a concession was made to the minority opinion: the local committees could use Social Democratic in their own names and could carry that name on local publications along with the name of the parent organization.[47] Thus the name "The General Jewish Workers' Union in Russia and Poland" came into being. The term Bund, meaning union or league in Yiddish, caught the popular fancy and became the name by which the organization was commonly known. It has been transliterated into other languages rather than translated.

The designation of central organs proceeded smoothly. Both of the existing newspapers received official status. *Di Arbeter Shtime* was to be printed in Russia as the organ of the Central Committee; *Der Yidisher Arbeter* would continue to be printed abroad, though it would not appear regularly.[48] The Central Committee soon took over the printing press in Russia, and beginning with issue No. 6, *Di Arbeter Shtime* bore the Bund name.

No decision was made on the type of literature the new organization would publish. Rosa Greenblat, the delegate from Belostok, proposed that the Bund publish basic philosophical studies, such as the works of Engels and Feuerbach, rather than propaganda materials. She argued that in places like Belostok where the Social Democratic movement was relatively new, self-education circles had never been established, so that these works would fill a gap. The other delegates apparently did not consider the matter important enough to settle at the time. In subsequent years both types of literature were published.

The founding congress of the Bund formally punctuated a process that had been spelling itself out throughout the 1890's. The congress signified the existence of a bond between Jewish workers and Jewish Social Democrats, a bond that had already been organizationally fused to a large degree and that was now to become a weapon in the search for justice for the Jews of Russia. At

* Mill, *Pionern*, 1: 276. The Bund's failure to use the designation Social Democratic has been sharply criticized by Soviet commentators on revolutionary history. They regard the Bund as an economic organization. See Agursky, *Revoliutsionere*, p. 62.

the same time, the Bundists reiterated their need and determination to be a part of the general Social Democratic movement in Russia.

The degree to which the workers and the intelligentsia had come together is apparent in the personnel of the First Congress. Unlike the old inner core of the early 1890's, it included workers who had heeded the words of the intellectuals and intellectuals who had heeded the complaints and actions of the workers. The congress was almost equally divided between workers and intellectuals, a sign that both groups had recognized their mutual dependence and integration. Tasks, aims, and personnel had been woven into a voice that could legitimately claim to speak to the society it hoped to represent; for however new its message, it sprang from that society. This is not to say that the Bund's founding congress delivered a finished ideology and organization. The First Congress merely acknowledged that the Jewish proletariat was now capable of taking an active hand in its own future, and that it had the means to work in its own behalf along with the other workers of the Empire.

At the outset, then, the Bund was both a central political organization with a number of cadres and a mass movement geared to economic and political goals. It had established a Jewish and socialist identity that would govern all future relations with other organizations; and it had established a degree of permissiveness in local initiative that would make growth and development possible. All in all, the founders had good cause to be both pleased with their handiwork and optimistic about the future.

7. The First Central Committee

The first Central Committee of the Bund presided over the affairs of the new organization until July 1898. In the ten short months of its existence it saw the Bund through as difficult a baptism of fire as any young organization could endure and remain viable. As spokesman for the new union it faced the major task of establishing relations with the outside world, while internally, it had to work out its duties as an official center and its procedures with local organizations. Events provided no time for leisurely deliberations.

Despite the long years of collaboration between the local groups, the structural reorganization could not help affecting their relationships. As de facto leader the well-established Vilna Group had felt morally committed, both by principle and by personal ties, to bring its technical resources to the aid of newer and weaker groups. A Central Committee, however, meant specified duties, formal lines of communication, and discipline. For the sake of security, the focal point was no longer to be attached to a place but to a unit; the committee was to become the agency to carry on the organization's educational and technical tasks while disappearing as a local presence—to make its voice heard and its body unseen.

From the very start the members of the Central Committee isolated themselves. When the committee moved to Minsk after the founding congress, few people knew it was there. Even Bund members in Minsk were unaware of its presence so completely did the committee divorce itself from the local organizations. Kosovsky, who remained in Vilna until March 1898 to phase out the network of contacts built up over the years, tried to keep aloof from the Vilna Committee.[1] Some of the other local committees did not even deal directly with the Central Committee but instead maintained contact by mail or through a third party. One such intermediary was a merchant, Boris Banevur, whose business trips made him an ideal link between far-flung groups and an important distributor of illegal literature. Amid all the problems of relocating and a rapidly growing list of duties, the committee members had to provide for their livelihood. Kosovsky and Mutnikovich were able to support themselves; Kremer, with only a few pupils to tutor, had to rely on the meager means of the organization.[2] Their new role placed heavy personal burdens on them.

The scope of the committee's work, if not its character, was new. The emphasis shifted from the production and distribution of propaganda materials to political problems and the development of political consciousness. *Di Arbeter Shtime* had to be made a central organ. Kosovsky enlarged his role as political writer and official editor. Kremer dealt with outside organizations and traveled extensively. He and Mutnikovich established the operating procedures.

The committee spent an enormous amount of time on purely technical problems. As the literary and publishing center for the Bund it had to arrange for the procurement, writing, printing, and distribution of literature. During its short tenure the committee published four issues of *Di Arbeter Shtime* (Nos. 6 through 9–10), as well as a number of leaflets and pamphlets. In addition, it printed material for local committees unable to make other arrangements. Despite its best efforts, however, the Central Committee could not keep pace with the growing demand for printed material within the organization, and John Mill's proposal that a press be established in Geneva was a welcome one.[3]

The secret press, the heart of the new committee, made particularly heavy demands on the members. Security demanded that the press be moved twice, first from Vilna to Minsk, then some 80 miles farther southeast to Bobruisk.[4] Kremer himself handled the contacts with the press; he worried constantly about its heavy printing schedule and security.

Another facet of the committee's technical work was the creation of a reliable system for the transmission of illegal literature printed abroad. A series of transfer points stretching from Western Europe to Russia was arranged. In the main, the committee depended on dedicated revolutionaries to perform this service, but it also hired professional smugglers to bring shipments across the borders. Mutnikovich assumes the smugglers would have charged considerably more if they had known what kind of contraband they were handling.[5] The organized bristle workers, who were located in the border areas, rendered valuable service in the importation of books and pamphlets, as did students returning to Russia, in the time-honored tradition of the Russian revolutionary movement.[6]

A start was made on drawing the jurisdictional lines between the Central Committee and the local organizations. But the strict discipline that was a Bund trademark in later years came about only over a period of time. David Katz asserts that Kremer was not even able to impose his point of view on the Vilna Committee when it decided to publish a local paper. Since Kremer phrased his objections to what he considered an excessively ambitious project in such a way as to only discourage the action,[7] it is uncertain how far he could have pressed his authority if he had chosen to do so. The fact that the new center was financed by the local organizations certainly weakened its position to some extent.[8]

At the same time, the local groups clearly began to feel the constraints of central direction. They were not allowed to make ties with other cities freely or to print leaflets at will.[9] All things considered, however, the Central Committee probably had more trouble working itself into the new structure than the local organizations did.

The committee's most significant political work arose out of the establishment of the Bund itself. The new organization soon attracted the attention of the non-Jewish revolutionary world. The PPS reacted quickly, branding the move harmful at its Fourth Congress, which convened in Warsaw in November 1897. In a spirit reminiscent of Pilsudski's arguments of 1893, the PPS found that the Bund's announced aim of seeking solidarity with the Russians was "the denial of solidarity with the Polish and Lithuanian proletariat in their struggle for liberation from the Tsarist invader." The Jewish proletariat, a party resolution contended, could have common tasks only with the proletariat of the country in which they lived.[10]

In the next several months the PPS followed up its attack. In April its central organ, *Przedświt* (Dawn), noted with ironic astonishment the attention the Bund was receiving in the foreign press: Europe, apparently, heard of every last, small strike; one would think all socialists had gone over to Judaism and joined the Bund. Without denying the energy of the Bund's leaders, the article charged that the Bund was the child of the Jewish bourgeoisie, the very group that historically had striven to separate the Jews from the surrounding population and had helped prevent the natural partnership of the Jewish and Christian workers. The PPS predicted that an open dislike of the Jew and political anti-Semitism would result from the Bund's course. Moreover, the continuing close tie between the Russians and the Bund irritated the Poles. They insisted that even those who understood and rejected anti-Semitism would be brought to a dislike of Jews who were partners of the Russian occupiers. The PPS gave notice that it felt compelled to fight against the catchwords of pan-Russianism in an organization that strove to represent the whole Jewish proletariat. It hoped the policy would not continue.[11]

The pioneers now had the wherewithal to answer the PPS, the editorial ability and printing facilities they had lacked in the early 1890's. Rebuttal came in a pamphlet that displayed, for the first time, the slashing style and sarcastic pen of Vladimir Kosovsky. Indeed, Kosovsky's language was shocking to old hands like Tsivia Hurvich, who was angry at the tone he took.[12] The pamphlet also contained a statement of aims prepared by the Central Committee.*

* The title of the pamphlet was *Di milkhoma fun der Poilisher Partai gegn dem Yidishn Arbeter Bund*. It was published in July 1898, by which time the Bund had joined

The major thrust of Kosovsky's argument was the Jewish proletariat's legitimate need for the Bund. Did the Bund really harm relations between the Christian and Jewish proletariats? That might be the case if the demands of the Jewish workers were inimical to those of other workers. But was the call for equal Jewish civil rights in fact harmful to other workers? Obviously not; equality could only strengthen the proletariat as a whole.[13]

Kosovsky struck back at the PPS, using the right of equality as his weapon. The Polish party had criticized the Lithuanian Social Democrats for organizing Polish-speaking workers in Lithuania on the grounds that those workers belonged to the Polish proletariat. If the Poles found the linguistic distinction reason enough to justify their control over Polish workers in Lithuania, why not an organization to serve the Jewish workers, who had their own language?[14] By arguing that the Jewish workers could only have tasks in common with the proletariats of other peoples around them, the PPS implied that Jewish workers could be divided among, say, Poles and Lithuanians. It differentiated Jewish workers from others. The Poles claimed their right to unity regardless of territorial boundaries. To deny the Jews the same right was patently unfair.

The Central Committee dealt with the charge of bourgeois inspiration in its general statement. Admittedly, it declared, the bourgeoisie might benefit from the drive for equal civil rights; but then the same held true of all national struggles for equality. Would not the Russian bourgeoisie profit from the Russian workers' demand for political rights? A goal did not become bourgeois simply because the bourgeoisie also benefited in its attainment; political rights had not yet been divided into capitalist and proletarian categories.[15]

Kosovsky took up the second part of the charge, that of separatism and its alleged historical bourgeois basis. He was blunt. The PPS suffered from confusion. In arguing that the concept of Jewish national unity was soaked through with bourgeois ideas, to the point where a separate Jewish workers' organization would lead to unification "not only against the Jewish bourgeoisie but also against the proletariats among whom they live," the Poles mixed the separativeness of a nation with the organization of a social class that had its own independent program.[16] The same argument applied to the charge that the separatism of the Jewish worker benefited the Russian regime. In fact, the Bund's aims were in full accord with those of the international proletariat. The only distinction was the call for equal civil rights for Jews. If independence could be regarded as a proletarian demand when it was a question of Polish workers under Russian rule, why could the Bund not make the same claim? If a separate Jewish workers' organization hurt the general cause of the work-

the newly formed all-Russian party. The committee's statement, "Unzere tsielen," was reprinted in *Di Arbeter Shtime*, first in issue No. 9–10 (which was confiscated by the police), then in issue No. 11, dated December 1898.

ing class, why was the PPS not guilty of the same offense? The PPS greeted the efforts of other national workers' organizations with joy; why was the Jewish proletariat treated differently?[17]

It appeared to the Bundists that the arguments against them were contradictory: they were charged with separatism and assimilation in the same breath. On the one hand the Bund was accused of building a wall between the Christian and Jewish workers; on the other it was branded a russifier. But the special meaning the PPS gave to the word russification was not the Bund's. The Poles, Kosovsky maintained, carried over their enmity toward the Russian autocracy "to everything Russian"; even spreading the ideas of leading Russian socialists was russification.[18] The Bund's desire for an all-Russian cohesion of workers implied neither a partnership with the Tsarist regime nor any judgment on the question of Poland's separation from Russia.

Having made the Bund's case, Kosovsky had a few questions of his own. What had the PPS done for the Jewish workers in areas where they were a weak minority? What had it done to raise the Jewish workers' consciousness or to dissuade the Polish workers from their enmity toward the Jews? It was true, was it not, that if there were no Bund, the PPS would not consider doing work in Yiddish?

Finally, Kosovsky came to one of the most vicious points in the PPS attack. In raising threats of political anti-Semitism and insisting on the Jewish position as one of a state within a state, the leaders of the Polish party exposed their own anti-Semitism, he suggested. Their references to the socialists joining the Jews sounded suspiciously like the voice of the notoriously anti-Semitic paper *Novoe vremia* (New Times), which held that the Jews had taken over the Russian revolutionary movement. The PPS had adopted these views and had simply couched them in socialist terminology.[19]

The Central Committee concluded its statement on a no less forceful note: the Bund could work freely within the all-Russian party, which did not brag that it would take care of "the Jewish question." It left "the role of the bird who ... wanted to swallow the ocean" to the PPS.[20]

The arrest of the Central Committee in July effectively ended the controversy with the PPS for the time being. The PPS's stand made no strong ideological impression on the Bundists. On the contrary, the nationalist-minded Poles, with their desire to keep revolutionary activity in Poland concentrated in their hands, only reconfirmed for the Bund leaders the correctness of their own national and international goals. They could, after all, support their position with one of the most fundamental tenets in the Marxist catalogue—their connection with the new all-Russian party was an example of international class cooperation in contrast to the narrow national view of the PPS. The Bundists saw no need to alter their ideological synthesis.

Nor did the PPS challenge change the Bund leaders' view of the rights of their proletarian constituents. The demand that the Jewish workers sacrifice their own interests to the Polish movement appeared to them to limit the Jews' right to equality; they were to be treated as outsiders or, at best, as supporters of the Polish struggle, to be rewarded as the new Polish nation saw fit. The Bund leaders pounded at this theme in their counterattack, content that it effectively answered the PPS arguments. They had to do no more than stand on their established position of equal civil rights to point out the reactionary nature of the policy the Poles were advocating. The Central Committee publicly rejected the PPS claim to leadership and reiterated its own position: an all-Russian emphasis in general revolutionary policy and organizational independence in Jewish matters.

For the Jewish Social Democratic groups, and particularly for the Vilna pioneers, an all-Russian party was a must. They had accepted that notion when they had first started their work and reached the conclusion that their own success rested on the success of such an organization. The importance they placed on a united party can be seen in the yeoman service they rendered to build it. All the same they had a definite view of what their place should be in the party and were determined to make their position clear to the Russians. One way to accomplish this was to establish their own organization before the unification meeting took place. It was to this end that they founded the Bund.

After the St. Petersburg Social Democrats failed in their efforts to bring about unity, the initiative passed to the Kievans. Under the leadership of B. L. Eidelman, the Kievans worked energetically in the spring and summer of 1897 to draw the various groups in Russia together. They set up a meeting in their city in March, inaugurated *Rabochaia gazeta* in August in the hope of making it a party organ, and expended considerable effort over the next few months in working out an agenda for a party congress.

These efforts brought the Kievans into closer contact with the Vilna Group, which had been participating in the debate on the problems of unification for the past year. In general Vilna had stronger ties with St. Petersburg than with Kiev; Kiev received some literature and news about the Social Democrats abroad through Vilna.[21] The Vilna Group's desire to have its point of view represented had its effects on the new efforts of the Kiev comrades. When a Kievan group, the Workers' Cause (Rabochee delo), started a newspaper in January 1897, the Vilna Group was against accepting it as a common organ, arguing that with so narrow a base it could not pretend to speak for all Social Democrats in Russia.[22] This rejection made the Kievans start thinking about a general Russian newspaper.[23]

Kremer wanted to consult with Plekhanov and the old guard abroad on the discussions that had taken place between Kiev, St. Petersburg, and Vilna in late 1896. However, he was not able to get away until spring. In the interim the Kievans called their meeting. Though the Vilna Group accepted Eidelman's invitation, no one from Vilna attended the conference.

Different reasons have been suggested for the absence of a Vilna representative. Eidelman, who organized the meeting, believes the Group did not receive the letter announcing the time and place of the meeting.[24] V. P. Akimov, who spent considerable time talking to the participants in the next several years, believes the absence was deliberate, noting that the meeting could only have been disruptive from Vilna's point of view. The Vilna Group was bound to find it premature, both because of the conversations still to take place abroad and because of its own indecision on the uniting of the Jewish groups.[25]

Akimov's argument is persuasive, especially in view of the Vilna Group's open dissatisfaction with the Kievans' earlier publishing effort. It is possible that the Kievans were operating too independently to suit the Vilna Group. There had been other indications of that independence; the most important was the Kievans' refusal to let Kremer represent them abroad, an assignment the St. Petersburg group was willing to grant him.[26] Under the circumstances Vilna was probably pleased that the Kiev meeting ended up a colloquium pure and simple.

Whether or not Vilna representatives deliberately boycotted the meeting, their absence almost certainly slowed the impetus of unification. But only temporarily. In the summer and fall of 1897 the preparatory work toward unification accelerated. After the Bund congress, Kremer visited St. Petersburg and Kiev, where the future meeting was discussed.[27] At that time he undoubtedly conveyed the Bund's conditions for joining the general party. It was also then that technical arrangements were made for the meeting, which the Bund agreed to host.

Largely for security reasons, Minsk was made the site of the meeting. Not only did the level of police activity there make the city itself safer than others, but the delegates could travel to Minsk at reasonable risk, thanks to the Bund's extensive network of contacts.[28] Eidelman willingly deferred to the Bund in security matters, for "only the Bund counted older and more experienced workers in its ranks than the [Kievan] Group Rabochaia Gazeta."[29] The Bund also contributed machinery and type for the press of the designated central organ of the party, *Rabochaia gazeta*.

The founding congress of the Russian Social Democratic Workers' Party (RSDWP) met from March 1, the anniversary of the assassination of Alexander II, through March 3, 1898.* Nine delegates representing four cities and

---

* Soviet historians, particularly those writing from the 1930's on, have found this first congress a touchy subject. They have difficulty accepting it as the founding of the Russian Communist Party for three reasons: only one of the delegates became a "true" Bolshevik; Peter Struve wrote the party manifesto; and Lenin had virtually no influence on

the Bund attended. There were three delegates from Kiev, one sent by the Kiev Union of Struggle and two representing *Rabochaia gazeta*; three Bund delegates, Kremer, Mutnikovich, and Samuel Katz, the only worker who attended (not to be confused with David Katz, who attended the first Bund congress); and one delegate each from Moscow, Ekaterinoslav, and St. Petersburg. The size of the delegations was not supposed to be a factor, since each unit was to receive only one vote; as it turned out, the voting did not work out this way. As at the Bund congress, no minutes of the proceedings were kept, and only the resolutions that were adopted were recorded.[30]

The agenda, prepared by Eidelman and circulated prior to the meeting, concentrated on such practical matters as the name of the new organization, the selection of a Central Committee, the relation of the Central Committee to local groups and other parties, and the problems of illegal literature and education. The invited organizations had been asked to provide their delegates with definite positions on all these points.[31]

This practical approach indicated the modest immediate goals of the founders. It was, in fact, simply an extension of their attitude toward their own work. The congress had neither the personnel nor the time to work out a theoretical program. All of the delegates accepted the achievement of socialism as the final or maximum goal and the methods of scientific socialism as the proper guide to reaching that objective. It was the immediate tasks—the struggle with the Tsarist regime and the organization of a party on the basis of existing capabilities—that preoccupied the founding congress.[32]

These were on the whole the same tasks that had preoccupied the founding congress of the Bund. The concern with organization and with the establishment of a network geared to immediate service rather than an ideological center reflects the similarity of operational concepts among many of the Social Democratic groups in Russia. There was an important difference, however, in the relationships of the groups convened. Whereas the Vilna Group had already had many of the attributes of a central core, no single delegation held a similar position at Minsk in March 1898. At the general party congress the situation was one of negotiations among equals having widely diverse interests and comparatively weak personal ties.

In some respects the delegates' responses to the agendas at both congresses were also alike. In both cases, for instance, the opening statement on the necessity of creating a unified organization passed without debate. And at the party congress, as at the Bund congress, the choice of a name provoked con-

---

the proceedings. In addition, the Bund's role has made the congress suspect for the Communists. Nevertheless, Lenin accepted the assembly as the first party congress, as did succeeding congresses, and both the Bundists and the Bolsheviks used it as a legal reference point for discussion and maneuver. See Medesh, "The First Party Congress"; and Tobias, "The Bund and the First Congress."

siderable discussion. The Bund delegates advocated using Rossiiskaia (All-Russian) instead of the narrower ethno-cultural Russkaia (Russian), in order to distinguish the entire proletariat of the Empire from the Russian-speaking workers alone.* After P. L. Tuchapsky, one of the Kiev delegates, supported the Bundists, their choice was accepted.[33]

The ideological designation for the new party—Social Democratic—passed without dispute. Apparently the Bundists were willing to accept a description they had previously rejected for their own organization as too narrow in its implications. Whatever their reasoning in this case, their organization kept both its own identification and direct control of the Jewish workers it had mobilized, leaving the new party at least one step removed from the workers.

The use of the word Workers was also argued.† Opponents insisted that the term would be a fiction, that few workers would belong to the party. The Bund delegates apparently favored using the word, projecting their own experience with workers to the party at large. After some debate the suggestion lost by one vote.[34] (The word was inserted later, with Kremer's support.) The final word, Party, was accepted without discussion. The name Russian Social Democratic Workers' Party was one of the lasting landmarks of the party founders.

The major work of the congress involved organization. The bulk of the deliberations were concerned with creating a central guiding institution and establishing its relation to local units. Closely connected with this inquiry was the question of the Bund's status. Indeed, the two matters were handled in succession.[35] The party had need of a center for the same reasons the Bund did: to gain a degree of security unattainable at the local level, to maintain the contacts between local groups that they were unable to maintain themselves, and to produce literature to inform and educate the workers.[36]

In the end the Central Committee as constituted had only limited authority over the local groups. Eidelman favored a strong center at the time but felt, on reflection, that the degree of control given was consistent with the realities of the moment. He hoped that in the course of work the center would be strengthened, particularism weakened, and a party spirit (*partiinost'*) developed.

In any event, even before the congress the younger organizations were known to favor latitude for their own work, and they were expected to resist any "interference."[37] The resolution accepted by the congress, without ap-

---

* In the English translation the adjective Russian is usually used. I follow that practice unless it seems necessary to make a fine distinction.

† Both "Labor" and "Workers" are used in English. I prefer the latter as more appropriate to what the founders had in mind, the workingman and his relation to the party. For me the term labor has a trade union connotation that does not reflect the thinking of the Social Democrats at the time.

parent bitterness, granted local committees the right to refuse to carry out the orders of the Central Committee in exceptional cases and gave them a free hand in local affairs within the framework of the program. The delegate from Ekaterinoslav, K. A. Petrusevich, led the fight to restrict the power of the Central Committee.[38]

Given the wide powers granted to simple local committees, there could be little argument over the Bund's insistence on autonomy within the party. In fact, its distinctive problems of language and geography could scarcely have been handled any other way at the time. Both in organization and in coping with problems related specifically to Jewish workers, the Bund was granted full autonomy.

In later years the Russian Social Democrats would argue that the Bund's position was unexceptional. "In essence," Eidelman wrote in 1921, "this autonomy did not differ from the autonomy of the other committees as it was understood at the congress." Nor, he said, was the Bund representative on the Central Committee, Kremer, in any way distinguished from the other members.[39] These protestations notwithstanding, the fact is that there were considerable differences between the Bund and the Russian local committees as organizations. The separate consideration of the subject of the Bund's autonomy, as well as the nature of the questions asked in the attempt to establish its special relationship to the Central Committee, indicate the congress fully appreciated that the Bund was a special case. The delegates simply avoided delving into the nature of the differences in their desire to preserve unity; it was easier to emphasize the similarities in work and ultimate goals.

Nevertheless, the Bund had only a limited freedom and, indeed, it wanted no more at the time. Compared with the demands made by the other ethnic groups that might have participated, the Poles and the Lithuanians, the Bund's conditions for joining were merely technical. Assigned the task of inviting the Lithuanian Social Democrats to the meeting, the Bund asked Kosovsky to handle the negotiations. Ultimately, they refused to attend. "It was not enough for them to be an autonomous part of the general party," Kremer relates; "they demanded that the whole party be structured as a federation."* This demand was far more radical than the Bund's national claims in 1898.

The PPS received considerable attention at the meeting, although it was not represented at the congress either. According to Tuchapsky, the PPS had demanded recognition of an independent Poland and exclusive control over all the party branches in Lithuania and Poland. These conditions were unaccept-

---

* *Arkady*, p. 364. Akimov-Makhnovets asserts that the Lithuanian Social Democratic Party could not attend the congress because arrests in the fall of 1897 had decimated its ranks (p. 141). But Kremer believes the Lithuanians were determined to have the party recognize their territorial autonomy. He can probably be believed, since he either participated in the talks or was in close contact with those who did.

able.[40] Although the PPS was not invited to the meeting, the congress discussed the national question (the only matter of principle it formally passed on) and adopted a resolution favoring self-determination for each nationality.[41] The issue emerged, it should be emphasized, not from conditions set by the Bund, but from the discussions of the PPS.

The Bund was thus given the status it wanted by the general party it had worked so hard to create. Moreover, its success did not come at the expense of the other member groups or the Central Committee.[42] All of the congress's important decisions were arrived at amicably and had even been agreed on in advance in their basic outlines by the leading groups. Agreement was plainly quite close, and the participants were well satisfied with the results at the time.

The first congress of the RSDWP had scarcely concluded when a wave of arrests crushed first the infant party, destroying it in all but name, and then the Central Committee of the Bund. The trail that led to the arrest of the Bund leaders in July 1898 began with the preparations for the party congress. Agents of S. V. Zubatov, head of the Moscow secret police, had been keeping an eye on Eidelman and managed to follow his movements as he made his way to Minsk. In a report dated February 28, the day after Eidelman arrived, the police assigned the code name Chernyi (Black) to a Jewish intellectual— Abram Mutnikovich.[43] The secret police had hit on one of the key members of the Bund.

There is little doubt that the congress at Minsk introduced the Bund to Zubatov's agents. Minsk, it will be recalled, was chosen as the congress site because of its comparative lack of police activity. That activity picked up markedly after the congress, says Kremer. We also have the statement of Leonid Menshchikov, an agent of the Okhrana (the notorious "Third Section" or secret police of the Tsarist state), that the police had no information on the Bund at the time.[44] The clearest evidence of all comes from the police files themselves. In the wave of arrests that swept a number of Russian cities a week after the congress, pulling in several of the delegates including Eidelman, not one Bund member or participant in the whole of the northwest region was touched.

As the police carried out this action the Central Committee of the Bund was hard at work on certain RSDWP assignments. The party congress had accepted the suggestion of S. I. Radchenko of St. Petersburg, who along with Eidelman and Kremer sat on the party's Central Committee, that the new organization announce itself in a manifesto, since it had not undertaken to write a program. Radchenko handed the task to P. B. Struve, a leading intellectual and Marxist of St. Petersburg. Struve's draft took Kremer to the capital for consultation in late March. Eidelman had been arrested by then.

In the draft Struve took what he considered to be an orthodox Marxist line. By this time he was no longer in complete agreement with that viewpoint, but he did his best to keep his personal views out of the declaration.[45] The draft did not please Kremer "either in spirit or in tone," but Radchenko sided with Struve and the document remained essentially unchanged.* It was at this time that the word Workers was added to the party name.[46] Despite Kremer's continuing dissatisfaction with the manifesto, the Bund undertook to print it. There was nothing suitable to replace it or any other way to get it printed since the arrests in southern Russia had led to the discovery of the *Rabochaia gazeta* press. In light of the police repression, it seemed imperative to have the manifesto appear as soon as possible. It was printed at the Bund's press at Bobruisk in both Yiddish and Russian.

The Bund did its best to meet the needs of the party and its own local committees after the arrests in the south. It printed several leaflets at Bobruisk for various committees as well as a May 1 leaflet for the party. But it soon became apparent that the existing press facilities could not turn out the work of both organizations, and the Bund decided to make special arrangements for Russian publications. A printer named Sherman obtained type and set up a press in Minsk.[47] Bund members apparently made a concerted effort to get Russian type and supplies for the new press, for the authorities seized a considerable quantity of these materials in the raids of July.

All of the Bundists' efforts on behalf of the RSDWP were unavailing. They had neither the literary nor the technical resources to keep both the Bund and the party going. For the RSDWP, already seriously wounded by the March arrests, the seizure of the top Bundists in July was a deathblow. No other Social Democratic group was strong enough to keep the party alive.

Once Zubatov got a line on the Bund, the zeal of the Central Committee and its agents ensured his continued interest. A measure of the seriousness with which he regarded the find is the amount of money he spent in pursuit. About 20 agents were assigned to the investigation at a cost of something under 10,000 rubles, well over half of the 18,515 rubles he was allowed for agents in the first half of 1898.[48] Five months elapsed from the time his men first began to trail the Bundists until their arrests. Zubatov went about his work calmly, holding off making arrests while information flowed into his Moscow office.

The police investigation itself reveals one of the flaws of an isolated, clandestine, center-directed form of organization.[49] Precisely because the Central Committee was highly secret, small, and aloof, police work was made easier. Mutnikovich, the first Bundist to be spotted, led agents to Kremer. The trails of the two Central Committee members, who between them held the most

---

* *Arkady*, pp. 365, 383. It seemed to Akimov that the Bund's Central Committee disliked the manifesto even more than Kremer did (Akimov-Makhnovets, p. 160). Kremer is not specific about what he found objectionable. Struve believes it was the manifesto's emphasis on political liberties ("My Contacts with Lenin," p. 75), but Akimov believes Kremer was unhappy about the slighting of the political role of the proletariat, not about the political emphasis as such (p. 162).

important threads of organization, diverged at that point—but only to come together in a kind of circle. In Minsk Kremer's trail led to Kosovsky, the third member of the Central Committee, as well as to such important local figures as Zhenia Gurvich. Meanwhile Mutnikovich went to Lodz, exposing local contacts along the way. One of these was the merchant Boris Banevur; a search of his hotel room on May 6 yielded a tiny scrap of paper torn from an illegal publication. Another was John Mill, who met Mutnikovich in Lodz on May 11 to pick up some packages of illegal literature to take back to Warsaw. From Warsaw Mill went to Vilna; surveillance of his movements exposed contacts in Belostok and St. Petersburg. Banevur also returned to Vilna, his permanent residence, where the authorities established his identity. When he went to Minsk and was seen with Kremer, Kosovsky, and Zhenia Gurvich, the circle closed.

The Bund press at Bobruisk was another casualty. At first agents thought the work there was the effort of a small, isolated group. However, they soon learned different, for Kaplinsky, who ran the press, met Kremer in Minsk several times in June. When, on July 23, the Bundists began transferring furniture from the press quarters to Vilna and Grodno, the police got ready to act. The period of observation was over; the suppression of the Bund was about to begin.

The intensive police activity inevitably attracted the attention of the security-conscious Bundists. Kosovsky, like Kremer, noted the increase of spies in Minsk after the RSDWP congress.[50] Amazingly enough, the police did not focus on the congress itself. Though agents had followed several delegates to Minsk, they had no idea of what the meeting was and did not pursue the matter further. Even after the March arrests, official information on the RSDWP was fragmentary. Later knowledge of what had taken place caused the police some discomfiture, despite their obvious accomplishments.[51] Aware of the March roundup and the danger closing in on them, the Bund leaders expected to be arrested before the May Day holiday, which was certain to bring greater police activity than ever before, judging from the experience of previous years.[52] But Zubatov was not ready to move then. Kaplinsky testified after his arrest that he had been informed in June about his own precarious position.[53] By that time the Central Committee was so aroused that it issued a circular, warning of "a band of spies ... close to thirty," which had been operating in Poland and Lithuania for the past two months or so. The circular listed the spies' stations, physical descriptions, and known abodes, and in one case gave an agent's name and hotel room number, clear evidence of counterespionage.[54] Such countermeasures were probably superfluous by June, however, for the government agents had become so bold that they sat at the same tables as the Bundists in restaurants.[55] It was at this point that the Central Committee finally decided to act.

The decision came too late. For three months the Central Committee had been aware of its peril, yet had done little to protect itself. Only in late June or early July did it decide to leave Minsk and Bobruisk for Grodno. The committee undoubtedly decided to proceed at its own risk after weighing the danger against its obligations and its estimate of the enemy's capabilities. It had fulfilled its duties to the RSDWP before the extent of the investigation became apparent. But it still had pressing problems to handle for its own organization. "It was impossible [to] stop the work," Kremer writes. *"Di Arbeter Shtime* had to appear, and we had to answer the PPS's sharp attack against the Bund."[56] The Central Committee would not even consider interrupting its work until these goals were accomplished. From Kremer's priorities it is clear how little the committee sensed itself to be an indispensable elite and how much it felt itself to be a service organization for the Bund.

Over the years the leaders had learned to size up the local police in the areas where they worked. But this time they badly miscalculated their ability to deal with the forces deployed against them. Boris Frumkin, a veteran of the circles, felt that the movement had not met really serious opposition from the government before Zubatov entered the battle. Moreover, as the movement grew, local authorities were unable to control the situation.[57] Their helplessness led to a reorganization of the investigations in the provinces in the spring of 1897.[58] Meanwhile, the Bund leaders were lulled by their own strength and experience into continuing their activities instead of moving at the first sign of danger. "We felt ourselves strong enough to resist Zubatov's attack," Kremer notes.* If the Bund leaders' error was costly, their steadfastness goes a long way toward explaining the awe in which they were held even at the time.

The main raids and arrests took place on July 26, 1898: all three members of the Central Committee were caught; that most important instrument, the Bobruisk press, was confiscated, as was the small press in Minsk; and many of the organization's important links were taken.† With this stroke the reign of the first Central Committee ended.

---

* *Arkady*, p. 390. Although the police won the first round against the Bund, both had much to learn. On the one side, investigation was extremely difficult for agents who knew neither the city nor the local language and customs. Moreover, the new, well-dressed, blond agents were easily spotted, and Bund members were alerted to look out for them. On the other side, many Bundists did not fully understand the workings of the secret police and were not as careful as they might have been. (Men'shchikov, 2: 108, 186.) Kremer attributes this lack of caution to a desire to speed up the work (*Arkady*, p. 386).

† Sources disagree on the arrest figures. In fact, one of them, Bukhbinder, presents contradictory numbers. In an appendix note to a report from Goremykin to the Tsar, Bukhbinder says 90 persons were arrested, of whom 67 were brought to trial ("Razgrom," p. 159). In the body of the same article he says 55 were arrested in the first wave and 12 in the next (pp. 149–50). Men'shchikov uses the figure 55 in connection with the first and largest wave (*Okhrana*, 2: 112). Various Bundists cite the figure 70, notably Mill (*Pionern*, 1: 300) and B. Frumkin ("Zubatovshchina," p. 199).

In the captured contraband of the Bobruisk press lay the newly printed issue No. 9–10 of *Di Arbeter Shtime* containing the Central Committee's statement of aims—its final statement, as it turned out. In it the Bund leaders attempted to explain why the RSDWP was founded, the meaning of the PPS attacks, and the Bund's position on both developments.

For the Central Committee the creation of the RSDWP was an organizational and political capstone. The party provided the international superstructure that underlay all the plans and hopes of the Jewish Social Democrats. It would bring order and unity into the economic and political struggle of the all-Russian proletariat, advancing the main struggle—"to overthrow the yoke of Tsarist autocracy and gain political freedom."[59]

Having explained this framework, the committee next turned to defend the Bund's right to exist. It was the exceptional legal position of the Jewish worker, the famous "double yoke" of his suffering as worker and as Jew, that made the Bund necessary. The Bund, with its special knowledge of the Jewish condition, would perform a dual function. It would mobilize the Jewish workers from within, and it would advance the cause of class solidarity by making the non-Jewish workers aware of the situation of their brothers. No general organization could cope with the specific problems besetting the Jewish proletariat; consequently, the Bund's success would benefit the whole proletariat of Russia. The Bund paraded its new position within the party as the result of a correct understanding of its special tasks and status. Indeed, as we have seen, it used its autonomy as a club against the PPS, contrasting the RSDWP and the Polish party. The Bund would stand up for the interests of the Jewish worker because, at the decisive moment, the party would not be able to stand for the special interests of the Jewish masses with enough energy as it worked for the general interests of the whole Russian proletariat. "Only a special Jewish workers' organization can muster enough strength and means to lead a successful struggle of the Jewish proletariat."[60] All the same, the Bund was not asking for special treatment for the Jews; it sought only to bring them closer to the other workers of the Empire.

In the few short months of its existence, the Central Committee brought nothing new to the movement in a theoretical sense. It did, however, advance the movement a step further in its organizational development. That organization had been seriously damaged, to be sure. But not irreparably so. The Bund was far from a dead issue, and new leaders would soon come forward to begin the task of rebuilding.

8. The Rebuilding of the Center

The havoc wrought by Zubatov's hurricane was impressive. Not only had he caught the entire Bund Central Committee and closed down its two presses, but he also had taken a large number of the chief activists, that invaluable second level of workers who carried out the committee's routine duties. Among these were the press operators Kaplinsky and Sherman, the courier Banevur, and such hard-working members of local groups as Zhenia Gurvich and Hirsh Soroka. The list of those captured reads like a *Who's Who* of the pioneer period, containing the names of some of the most experienced, trustworthy, and devoted members of the movement. The best source indicates that five were arrested in Bobruisk, seventeen in Minsk, seven in Vilna, ten each in Warsaw and Lodz, three in Baranovichi, and one each in Odessa, Grodno, and Briansk.[1]

Ironically, it was the arm of the organization designed to provide the greatest possible security that took the brunt of the arrests. At the same time, because the Central Committee had maintained restricted contacts the local groups escaped almost unscathed. The local organizations found themselves in novel circumstances. If there was to be a regeneration of the Bund, it would have to come from the activists close to the top who remained free and from those engaged primarily in local work.

The emotional impact of the collapse was enormous on those left untouched. Mikhalevich, who was active in Belostok at the time, recalls: "At first we were all paralyzed ... and did not know where to begin. The central leaders were not there, we had no press, and we had to lie low. The main thing was the press. That had been like a flag to an army in battle for us. Without a press we would cease to be a party. We would become dumb; there would be no Bund."[2]

Mikhalevich's sense of shock was only momentary, however. The movement had existed long enough and had been successful enough to create a considerable reserve of agitators, organizers, and technicians who had had at least some connection with the hub of activity over the years. Within days of the catastrophe David Katz, a member of the Vilna Committee, set out to reestablish contacts and start up the routine work. Within two months a new Bund congress convened; within three, illegal literature bearing the stamp of the Bund began circulating; within five, *Di Arbeter Shtime* reappeared. The years of intensive revolutionary work were reaping their first rewards.

The quick recovery of the Bund revealed the organization's strong roots in the social soil of the Jewish community. For all practical purposes the entire Russian-educated Jewish intellectual element inside the Empire had been eliminated. That element had provided a unique leadership for the Jewish movement for almost a decade. The new leaders who emerged from the shadows were of a very different social stripe. David Katz, Leon Bernstein, Sendor Zeldov, Bainish Mikhalevich, Tsivia Hurvich, and Marya Zhaludsky, who led the movement in Russia for a year and a half after the arrests, all had their basic training in the pioneer period. All were tough, experienced agitators; one of them, Zeldov, had helped found *Di Arbeter Shtime*. These were not the Russian-oriented graduates of the state educational system but the intellectual-tutored pupils of the circles or the self-taught. Moreover, their revolutionary education had an 1890's cast: these leaders found it natural to look on the masses at hand as the proper focus of activity. On the average the new leaders were about five years younger than their predecessors. Katz was unquestionably the driving force between the arrests and the Bund's Third Congress, when some of the older movement members renewed their activities; he was only twenty-two in 1898, a full 11 years younger than Kremer.

The practical training and skills of the rebuilders were just what the crippled Bund needed at the outset. Organizational tasks were the immediate concern, and the new leaders turned to this work with determination. With the aid of Leon Goldman, who was visiting Vilna at the time, Katz reopened the communication channels by reestablishing contact addresses and codes. Katz himself went to many of the places where breaks had occurred. By the time he got to Kovno, where he discussed the reorganizing effort with Leon Bernstein, he had visited Vitebsk, Dvinsk, and possibly Warsaw.[3]

An important step in the regeneration of the Bund was the calling of the Second Congress. The need for such a meeting was obvious in light of the physical and psychological damage wrought by the arrests. Indeed, the psychological factor may have weighed quite heavily in the decision to call a meeting. In any event the new leaders felt that a new Central Committee had to be appointed to take up the formal duties of office.

Kovno, which had been untouched by the events of July, was chosen as the site. The activists there were so much a part of the Jewish artisan population that the movement did not attract any special attention. The meeting was scheduled for September, just a year after the First Congress. Bernstein's quarters served as the meeting place even though he was on police probation.[4]

Six towns, Vilna, Minsk, Warsaw, Belostok, Lodz, and Kovno, were represented, two more than were represented at the founding congress. In addition, the Bristle Workers' Union, now a formally constituted trade organization, sent a representative. The arrests ensured that most of the faces would be new;* only Zhaludsky and Katz had attended the First Congress. The majority of delegates were workers and were Yiddish-speaking.

Despite these changes, the Second Congress strongly resembled its predecessor in style. Security was even tighter. In fact, public revelation of the meeting was delayed several months lest premature announcement of the resolutions jeopardize the arrested comrades, whose status was still uncertain in the fall of 1898.

The congress lasted three days. In its deliberations it took up local conditions, the economic struggle, illegal literature, aid for arrested comrades, and relations with other revolutionary parties; and it named a new Central Committee. The published report admitted the direct relation of the Second Congress to the arrests, indicating that it had been called to adapt the Bund to the conditions resulting from the government's destructive policy and to report on the steps taken to date.[5] But the report also endorsed the notion of frequent meetings to consider problems as they arose.

The picture that emerged at the congress was not as disheartening as the Bundists had first supposed. The local reports revealed that the arrests had not disrupted the functioning of the local organizations. Indeed, the local groups were even optimistic: the number of Jewish workers reading illegal literature was growing, so much so that the supply would have to be doubled or maybe tripled to meet the demand; organizations were appearing in new areas and the established ones were expanding, especially in Lodz and Warsaw; and political consciousness was continuing to develop among the Jewish workers, witness the Bund's growing ties and increasing prestige in factories. As the local organizations saw it, their greatest problems were the lack of intellectual propagandists and the lack of literature for the workers.[6]

Whereas the First Congress had occupied itself almost exclusively with organization, the Second, despite its primary task of reorganizing, also had to deal with the lessons of a year's experience. In large part this meant assessing the progress of the economic struggle. The delegates noted that though strikes

---

* Neither the names of the delegates nor their numbers are certain. Katz and Bernstein, probably the most reliable sources, list 12 between them. They agree on Zeldov and Katz (representing Vilna), Tsivia Hurvich and Zhaludsky (Warsaw), Liza Epstein and Bernstein (Kovno), and Wolf Aleksandrisky (the Bristle Workers' Union). Katz adds the names of A. Bernadik (Vilna), M. Munvez (Belostok), Shaine Raizel Segal (Lodz), and possibly B. Levin (Minsk). Bernstein includes on his list Mikhalevich, who confirms that he was there. (D. Katz, "Mezhdu," p. 163; Bernstein, *Ershte*, pp. 122–23; Mikhalevich, *Zikhroinos*, 1: 56–57.)

were spreading among the working masses, fewer of the strikers were formally organized in kases. In fact, the number of non-kase strikers was on the rise and was threatening to surpass the number of kase strikers. This development, the congress found, tended to lessen the importance of the kase as an instrument of unification. Once the kase ceased to be the only agency for the organization and education of the workers, its structural deficiencies became evident. Secrecy prevented worker participation in any numbers; yet at the same time, employer and government reaction ensured the continuation of secrecy and so of limited membership.[7] While noting both the happy new fact of growing labor unrest and the deficiencies of the kases, the congress was unable to solve the problem. In the end the delegates decided only that the non-kase workers must be told of the need for a struggle for political as well as economic rights, and of the intimate connection between the two. Illegal literature, especially leaflets, could reach these masses where the kases could not.[8] This was an astute analysis for second-line leaders thrust so precipitately into positions of leadership, and the attempt to tie the Bund into the growing labor movement was a noteworthy, if modest, move. There was no debate on these matters.

Some aspects of the workers' behavior troubled the delegates. A downswing in the Russian economy, resulting in mass layoffs and reduced wages, had led some workers to resort to violence and terrorism. According to Katz, the delegates were unanimously opposed to such tactics, despite the difficult time the workers were having. Moreover, the congress felt that in light of the current crisis the local organizations ought to exercise restraint in the use of the strike.[9]

The question of disseminating major socialist works, a proposal that had not been warmly received by the First Congress, arose again. This body of delegates, dominated by self-educated workers and half-intellectuals, eagerly accepted the notion—a dim echo, perhaps, of the old desire to make higher education available to the workers at large. The congress recommended the publication of several important works, including the *Communist Manifesto* and Karl Kautsky's *Erfurt Program*.[10]

The need to continue the regular organs of the Bund was beyond debate. Some delegates did, however, deplore the repetitive content of *Der Yidisher Arbeter*, which the congress decided should henceforth include informative articles on foreign lands, life in Russia, scientific socialism, and past struggles.[11] *Di Arbeter Shtime* was to continue its established pattern. Aware of their slim resources, the delegates discussed using socialist materials from the United States despite their unsuitability to the Russian scene.

The serious shortage of literature encouraged a trend that had already begun to appear before the arrests. The Vilna Committee had released the first issue of its local journal, *Der Klasen-Kamf* (The Class Struggle), on the eve of the

Second Congress. Wolf Aleksandrisky proposed that the Bristle Workers' Union also publish its own organ, arguing that the relative isolation of the bristle-processing towns and the general backwardness of the workers justified the effort. The content of *Di Arbeter Shtime*, he felt, was too general for specialized trades. Furthermore, a regional paper would help fill the demand for literature. In any case a Union meeting had already decided on this course.[12] The congress not only accepted his proposal, but adopted a resolution favoring local organs in general and commending to the committees the example of the Vilna paper. Within a year Minsk, Warsaw, and Belostok took up this practice. The appearance of five local sheets, even in limited quantities, undoubtedly helped ease the shortage of literature.*

The endorsement of local organs reflected the emergency. Kremer had considered such efforts too costly. But with no literature forthcoming from the center, the decision was altogether reasonable. At the same time, the congress's approval indicated how much the congress accommodated itself to local concerns and how little it feared for the health of the central institutions. The mass character of the Bund tolerated the heavy emphasis on local work. Further, because of the homogeneity of tactics the organs could flourish without prejudice to the center, being largely agitational in nature. It was a question of complementing the more ideologically-oriented central organ rather than competing with it.[13] As long as there was no argument on basic tactics, the local organs could do a useful job.

At the time the congress convened, the echoes of the exchange with the PPS were still reverberating. For most of the delegates, such conflict within the movement was a new matter; and most were shocked by the sharp language used in the Central Committee's pamphlet as a form of address between revolutionary comrades. Katz felt that few delegates understood the PPS's position on the Bund.[14] The congress finally decided that as a member organization of the RSDWP the Bund should wait and see what stand the party took on the PPS.[15]

On those questions that went beyond the limits of purely Bundist concern the congress acted quite cautiously in political matters and somewhat more boldly in economic matters. It proposed that the RSDWP move closer to organizations with similar goals, such as the *Rabochaia znamia* (Workers' Flag) group in Belostok. Since the RSDWP was all but defunct, this meant in effect that the Bund would take no action. In response to a discussion of effective strike tactics the delegates decided to put out leaflets in Polish as well as Yiddish where appropriate. They also decided to organize societies, together with other revolutionary groups, to aid prisoners and exiles "regardless of nationality and

* The other four papers were *Der Veker* (Bristle Workers), *Ainikait* (Minsk), *Der Varshaver Arbeter* (Warsaw), and *Der Belostoker Arbeter* (Belostok).

party."* The arrests of 1898 were a vivid reminder of the plight of such victims, for those detained had been sent to Moscow, where they lived in want. These were positive steps, to be sure, but all were neutral in their political content.

The last act of the congress was to reconstitute the Central Committee. Unlike the First Congress, the Second elected the committee members: Katz, Tsivia Hurvich, and Zeldov.[16] The committee could if necessary co-opt other Bundists to help it carry out its duties.

The Second Congress accomplished its modest purpose. It demonstrated the viability of the Bund and began the work of mending the breaks in activity and contacts. It avoided problems of principle and rejected major organizational change. The delegates displayed a strong practicality that enabled the forms and instruments of organization to remain intact. Fortunately for the new leaders, the situation in the fall of 1898 did not demand more.

In the first few months following the congress the Central Committee was hard put to continue its labors. The money to produce and distribute literature was simply not available. True, the first Central Committee had had its share of financial difficulties, but it had been able to count on its connections with middle-class intellectuals. Smugglers had to be paid, literature from the United States purchased, and the families of arrested comrades aided. Somehow the paralysis resulting from insufficient funds had to be broken.[17]

The purely technical production of literature was another major obstacle to be overcome. The problems of finding a press and literate and capable workers were not solved quickly. The second echelon of propagandized workers and half-intellectuals, the same solid stratum that had given the first Central Committee its press and organ, made it possible for the top level to recommence printing operations. The press of the Vilna Committee took on the additional load of working for the Central Committee. In December the first issue of *Di Arbeter Shtime* completed since the arrests saw the light of day. Local leaflets continued to appear throughout the entire period, both in printed and in hectographed form.

The dearth of literary talent was a serious handicap. Only Zeldov, who had been one of the founders of *Di Arbeter Shtime*, stayed in Vilna. Max Tobias, a half-intellectual from pioneer days, helped him for a time but later moved to Warsaw. The other Central Committee members, like their predecessors, decided dispersion afforded the most security and left for Dvinsk. Mikhalevich and Zalkind also participated in the literary effort, attempting to acquire written materials. But even this proved difficult.

Frustrated by their slow headway, the Bund leaders called a special conference in Dvinsk in January 1899. There they took some decisive steps to im-

---

* *Di Arbeter Shtime*, 11 (December 1898): 2. The Society of the Red Cross was formed in 1881 to this end.

prove conditions. They commandeered the Vilna press for the use of the Central Committee. (As far as is known, there was no serious objection to this move from the local organization, thanks no doubt to the long association of both Katz and Zeldov with local work in Vilna.) The committee relocated the press in Warsaw, choosing the large city as a safe place to concentrate their strength. The editorship went to Zeldov, with the former staff staying on to aid him. Katz was to concentrate on maintaining contacts with the local organizations.[18] Despite the enormous difficulties, four more issues of *Di Arbeter Shtime* appeared prior to the Third Congress of the Bund.

The contacts for procuring literature from abroad coalesced slowly. Once again the bristle workers in the border areas played an important role in the effort; and the Lithuanian Social Democrats were helpful in providing smuggling contacts.[19] Aid began to arrive at an accelerating pace from outside Russia in 1899, though it was late in the year before Katz began receiving effective co-workers.

In the months between the arrests and the Second Congress there was no official executive for the Bund. The most likely substitutes for the arrested comrades were Mill, who had departed for Western Europe just prior to Zubatov's move, and Pavel Berman, who was living in Ponevezh. Berman was invited to the Second Congress and to serve on the committee, but he rejected both offers for personal reasons.[20] Though Leon Goldman had worked hard to save the Bund in the first critical days after the arrest, he apparently was not considered for a committee seat. In any case he was not willing to take the necessary risks. Both he and Katz were due to go into military service shortly. Katz decided not to go, thereby putting himself beyond the law in order to carry on his work. But Goldman felt he could not subject his family to a 300-ruble fine, though he considered reporting for duty and deserting later.[21] At all events it was Katz who assumed the burden of leadership.

Although Katz and his co-workers were neither as educated nor as assured as the members of the first committee, they were every bit as dedicated. And they gradually gained confidence and experience. The assumption of illegal civil status was a relatively new phenomenon and a dangerous one. It meant acquiring false documents, such as a passport and a draft exemption ticket, and abandoning the qualms felt by earlier leaders and even by Zeldov about living on party funds. It was during the tenure of the second Central Committee that the concept of professional revolutionary was accepted.

Katz retained his respect for the older pioneer-intellectuals, particularly Mill, but he kept his own counsel. When Mill suggested that the Central Committee enlist the aid of Pati Srednitsky, then in administrative exile, in its literary work, Katz did not oppose the idea; however, he maintained that she should flout the law by breaking her exile if necessary.[22] Katz kept as strong a hold on the reins as he could. Despite Mill's slightly condescending tone and perhaps excessive zeal, relations between the old pioneer-intellectuals abroad and the Central Committee were good.

Although Katz was cautious about the general progress of rebuilding, the Bund's recovery received distinct recognition from outsiders. Katz undoubtedly would have been enormously gratified if he had heard the words of praise Vera Zasulich had for the Bund in a letter to Plekhanov:

The Jewish Bund is a pure marvel of balance [*van'ka-stan'ka*]. Two of their presses were taken and a crowd of people ... but they have already succeeded in putting out a small issue of a newspaper in jargon [i.e. Yiddish] in Russia. And the path across the border is again in working order. It is annoying that it is they who are so businesslike and not the Russians; all the same one must do them justice.[23]

As Katz and his hard-working colleagues began rebuilding the Bund in Russia, John Mill undertook the task of aiding the harassed organization from the outside. Fortunately for him he had departed for Western Europe just prior to the July arrests to set up a press in Geneva and arrange for the transmission of illegal literature.[24] Though he and the other leaders had expected to be taken at any moment, the news of the arrests burst on him like a bombshell. With his strong attachment to the old pioneer-intellectuals with whom he had worked so many years, he perhaps more than the worker activists in Russia found it hard to believe that the organization could continue without the old generation.[25] It was "one inspiring surprise after another" when communications began arriving, he recalled in later years. It was "simply indescribable and unbelievable; after the great catastrophe the Bund lives and will live."[26] He lost no time in attempting to carry out his assignments.

Mill carried the burden of the work in the West. Kopelson, who was working with the Union Abroad as the Bund's liaison man, supported his old comrade when Mill arrived in Zurich and gave him money. In contrast Berman, who had refused a leadership role after the arrests because of his decision to marry and study abroad, gave Mill virtually no help from his residence in Darmstadt. In those days, Mill tells us, he worked 16 to 18 hours a day for the organization.[27]

Mill's first task was to inventory the available resources in the Polish-Jewish and Russian-Jewish student colonies and in the Jewish immigrant populations of Western Europe and the United States. These temporary and permanent expatriates, victims of revolutionary behavior, Tsarist educational restrictions, or economic conditions in the Pale, lived in the university centers and great capitals. Mill had some success in enlisting them into associations for the support of the Bund, and within a very few months he had funds flowing back to Russia.[28]

During the last months of 1898 Mill fashioned a formal structure for his activities. After discussing the matter with Katz, he set up a Foreign Committee of the Bund, which began functioning in December 1898 as a semiofficial arm of the home organization.[29] The Bund needed such an organization badly. The type of activities Mill engaged in demanded more than individuals speaking personally for the Bund. As an official representative the Foreign Committee would be able to perform its literary and technical tasks with authority—it would be regarded as part of the Central Committee—and the network of organizations being created would operate smoothly.[30] The creation of the Foreign Committee was formally announced in a leaflet in January 1899, which was reprinted in March in *Der Yidisher Arbeter*. After the Third Congress the committee became the official representative of the Bund abroad, replacing the Union Abroad in that capacity.

In contrast to the second Central Committee, which carefully followed the pattern of work set by its predecessor, the Foreign Committee pioneered. Not only did it have impressive literary and organizational talent to draw on, but residence abroad gave its members a freedom of operation and perspective that soon had its impact on the more parochial home organization. The milieu of the revolutionary was vastly different abroad. There were more students and intellectuals than workers in the colonies, and more time spent in ideological debate and discussion than in Russia, where routine agitation and organizational work drained almost all the Bund's energies. Even the practical-minded Mill was impressed by the tone of these discussions; and when he began editing *Der Yidisher Arbeter* in 1899 he did his best to convey their essence to the home organization. The result was an increasing emphasis in the movement on ideological issues, above all, on the national question.

Within a few months of his arrival abroad Mill established a press in Geneva, obtaining type through German Social Democratic sources in Berlin, where he spent some time helping to reorganize the transport of literature to Russia.[31] The expenses of operating the press consumed more than half of the foreign operation's income. Of a total of 3,011 Swiss francs spent between July 1, 1898, and March 10, 1899, 1,634 went to the press.[32] Mill received 1,000 rubles from a Polish aristocrat, a close friend, to defray the cost of the press itself.[33]

The literary output of the Foreign Committee grew apace. *Der Yidisher Arbeter* now became the official organ of the committee, to be published in its name.[34] More like journals than newspapers, with over 50 pages each, the sixth and seventh issues appeared in 1899. Some of the articles and ideas came from persons Mill had recruited among the Jewish intellectuals living abroad. Many translations were used, in keeping with the decision of the Second Congress to make the journal informative.

The Foreign Committee also began to issue pamphlets in some quantity. Jewish students in Berne helped in this effort, notably I. Blumstein, who translated the *Communist Manifesto* into Yiddish and published it with a special foreword by Karl Kautsky. Although Blumstein was praised for this attempt, his translation was regarded as a poor one.[35] Other Marxist classics, including the works of Kautsky and Ferdinand Lassalle, also appeared in Yiddish. The Bund report to the International Congress at Paris in 1900 attested to the excellent progress of Mill and his colleagues. Between July 1898 and December 1899 they printed 79 different leaflets for the Bund. By July 1900 they had printed a total of 62,900 leaflets. Of the 22 pamphlets printed by the Bund during the period, 14 came from the European press, totaling some 52,000 copies.[36] The output abroad was decisive in meeting the needs of the Bund in Russia.

Mill was equally successful in arranging the shipment of material back to Russia. Vorwärts, the publishing house of the German Social Democrats, became one of the major transshipment centers on the route between Switzerland and Russia. There smugglers and travelers were given false-bottomed suitcases to carry the literature across the frontier.[37] The quantities moved in this manner averaged 144 pounds per month in the period August 1898–September 1900; the Bund report estimated that this came to about 200,000 pages.[38]

The Foreign Committee became a central point for disbursing funds to political prisoners in Russia or their families. Between July 1898 and December 1899, 1,760 Swiss francs were either collected by Mill for this purpose or passed on through him to the recipients. The committee also made special allotments, such as the 879 francs it sent to support a strike in Dvinsk. The bulk of its funds, however, went to the press and to cover the expenses of getting literature to Russia.[39]

Finally, it was during these early days of activity that the Foreign Committee moved toward the formal establishment of a Bund archive. In an announcement in Der Yidisher Arbeter, it requested copies of materials on the Jewish workers' movement in Russia and Poland. It asked to be sent no fewer than three copies of all new leaflets, newspapers, and pamphlets issued in Russia; and it hoped the local organizations would send it semiannual reports.[40] The residence of the Foreign Committee henceforth afforded an ideal opportunity to maintain a permanent record of the Bund.

The Bund thus not only reestablished itself after Zubatov's blow, but even strengthened itself with a new arm abroad. As an active and secure base the Foreign Committee began to serve as a crucial source of supply. Far from destroying the Bund, the arrests revealed the depth of its personnel, its vitality and capacity for continued growth, and the spirit and dedication that placed it at the forefront of the Social Democratic organizations of the Empire.

9. The Local Organizations, 1897-1899

The response of local groups to the formation of the Bund was mixed. Among those closely tied to Vilna, generally the colonized organizations of Minsk, Warsaw, and Belostok, the step was loudly applauded. Indeed, the reaction in Warsaw led Mill to assume that there was a general enthusiasm for the Bund.[1] But the enthusiasm was hardly general. For one thing, many kases probably did not know of the Bund's existence for a time.[2] For another, some groups were clearly dubious about the whole enterprise, and others were openly hostile. Kremer felt that of all his tasks, attracting organizations to the Bund was the most difficult. Occasionally he was forced into all-night arguments on the question of whether the Jewish worker in fact needed a special central organization.[3]

The most notable rebuffs to the Bund came in the cities of Gomel and Grodno. Gomel did not join the Bund until 1900, mostly because the local Social Democrats were not convinced of the need for such an organization.[4] In Grodno the challenge was more serious. There a group of intellectuals actively opposed the Bund, objecting to the concentration on strikes, the change to agitation, and what some regarded as the organized isolation of the Jewish movement.[5] This led to a split in revolutionary ranks, with many intellectuals joining the PPS and a group of workers forming a Bund group within months of the founding congress.

In other areas the formal establishment of the Bund stimulated and gave direction to the growth of organization among the workers and intellectuals. In Riga the appearance of Bund newspapers split the loosely organized Zionist socialist groups, with one wing becoming Bundist.[6] Similarly, a loose "Group" in Lodz was replaced by a fully organized Bund committee.[7] Many smaller towns also developed organizations, a few of which grew to some importance later.

The creation of the Bund did not initiate a period of new activity for the local committees. Many were composed of the same people who had served in the Vilna-led pioneer groups, and these continued to work as before. The

major difference now was in the association with the center and the new responsibilities and privileges that association entailed: financial support for the
Central Committee (recognized but not always honored in the beginning),
systematic exchange of information and literature, and adherence to the rules
laid down at the Bund congresses.

The local committees worked relatively free of pressure from the center in
the Bund's first two years. In part this was because their activities were largely
governed by local circumstances, and in part simply because the Central Committee was so preoccupied with its own difficulties at the start. In any event,
the highly secret and isolated committee was neither designed nor equipped
to exercise tight central control in this period; it was a resource and guidance
center, not a command post.

Instances of the center exerting real pressure on the local bodies are rare,
though on occasion the weak Central Committee of mid-1899 attempted to
make its wishes felt on matters of general tactics. It intervened in Minsk, for
example, when the circle–mass agitation argument that had plagued the Social Democrats a few years earlier began anew in the local committee. Albert
Zalkind, the Central Committee's representative, used his control of incoming
illegal literature to force the dissidents to accept the policy of mass agitation.
However, when a meeting of workers challenged the Bund position and
threatened to overthrow the local committee, it yielded, despite Zalkind's objections. He felt that "perhaps the workers should know also that the world
turns," i.e., that others might know more than they. Zalkind persevered and
managed to maintain the line. The opposition did not die, however, and the
continuing debate was to lead to a significant chapter of local conflict in the
history of the workers' movement among the Jews.[8] The Central Committee
stuck to its guns even at the heavy price of division.

That the center adopted any kind of a hard line at all is surprising, given
the attitude of the local organizations toward its financial needs. At the Third
Congress the Central Committee complained that their failure to aid the Bund
was circumscribing its activity.[9] The initiative rested with the local unit, and
the center had to get along as best it could.

The activities of the local committees were essentially the same as those the
various groups had pursued before the founding of the Bund: attempting to
organize workers, supporting the strike movement wherever possible, distributing literature, arranging demonstrations to emphasize worker solidarity
or to register political protests under suitable conditions. To carry out these
duties, activists had to have not only organizational talent and the ability to
deal with emergencies, but also precise knowledge of local conditions and a
realistic grasp of what was possible and what was not. Because of the great
local differences in the territory within the Bund compass, the general pronouncements of Bund congresses could not deal with all local contingencies.

Still, no small portion of the agendas for the congresses of 1898 and 1899 was devoted to local problems warranting general attention.

The interpretation of local events was a major concern of the activists, and the increasing number of local organs testify to their energy in this regard. The Third Congress of the Bund reaffirmed the approval of the Second on the publication of separate organs and appeared generally satisfied with the efforts of the local groups to bring consciousness to the workers.[10] The organs were all pretty much of a piece. Written in a popular vein, their dominant themes were the solidarity of the working class, the state as the workers' enemy, and the local strike movement. Local people, both in and out of the movement, were prevailed on to help with the writing.

The leaflet became an increasingly popular form in 1898 and 1899. Usually a single sheet, it could be composed quickly in swift response to some local event. Leaflets were particularly useful as the movement grew and it was no longer possible to reach all workers personally.[11] The Bundists took advantage of every opportunity to gain maximum exposure. They posted leaflets on synagogue walls on Friday nights, for example, where they were bound to remain through the Sabbath unless a Christian could be found to remove them.[12]

The local committees encouraged mass meetings as a matter of policy. But they also made a point of avoiding any direct involvement as a group; after the arrests of July 1898 the local organizations observed even tighter security measures than before.[13] Yet individual committee members could and did participate directly in such rallies (except for the intellectuals, who continued to find it prudent not to attract attention by attending workers' meetings).[14] Important agitators from the kases often made the necessary arrangements. The format varied: meetings were called to introduce important works, to formulate strike demands, even on occasion to present a play. When the weather permitted, they took place in the woods; otherwise, the workers met in smaller groups in town.

Gatherings of a political nature became more frequent as time passed. The open demonstration, a sign of considerable spirit, size, and discipline, was a common phenomenon by 1899. May 1 demonstrations took place in Warsaw in 1898 and 1899 in which both Christian and Jewish workers participated. The Vilna May Day demonstration of 1899 (involving only Jewish workers) seems to have been the first open independent political manifestation of the Jewish movement.[15] Other cities with Bund committees also saw more and more political activity. The arrest of workers or their recruitment into military service, the movement of political prisoners through or from town, even funerals—all served as occasions for open protest.[16]

The growing variety of local actions reveals the flowering of the movement at its base. The Central Committee could prompt, could supply literature, could offer aid—but it could not itself rally the working masses in these years.

Even in the celebration of May Day, the most universal form of political expression in 1897–99, the decision rested with the local committees and their evaluation of specific conditions, rather than the decree of the Central Committee. It was the local groups that bore the brunt of growth and reprisal; and to them fell the responsibility of responding to every contingency of revolutionary life.

The committees had to contend with a bewildering array of problems as they plunged ahead with the task of organizing and guiding the economic struggle. Urban growth continued unabated, demanding constant agitation to attract new workers and maintain discipline. Relations between Jewish and Christian workers remained touchy. The financial situation of the employers had to be considered. What worked in small towns did not work in large cities. What worked in one type of industry did not work in another. Some factories were easily entered by organizers and agitators, others proved virtually inaccessible. Workers could be highly receptive or openly hostile or just indifferent.

Without complete data it is impossible to know precisely to what extent the Bund penetrated the ranks of the Jewish proletariat in these first few years. Nevertheless, we can make a fair guess on the basis of the available figures, which include the Bund's report to the Paris meeting of the Socialist International in 1900 (see Table 3).

Other sources indicate there were about 200 organized workers in Grodno and some 400 in Vitebsk in 1898; by 1899, the Vitebsk movement alone had gained about 100 members.[17] In addition there were unknown numbers of workers loosely organized in circles. Recalling the Jewish Social Democrats' claim of 3,000 adherents in 1896 (and even without data for Lodz and Warsaw), one must regard the Bund's growth as impressive; by the turn of the century it had 5,600 members at the very least.

Our information on the chief instrument of economic action, the strike, is also fragmentary, but the picture that emerges is one of general success: of 237

Table 3. Bund Estimate of Worker Organization in 1900

City or organization	Number of workers organized in kases	Per cent of Jewish workers in organized areas
Belostok	1,000	20%
Vilna	1,400	24
Minsk	1,000	35–40
Leather workers	700	—
Bristle workers	800	60

SOURCE: *Istoriia*, 1901 (Bund biblio.), p. 83.

strikes undertaken by Jewish workers, 180 ended in a clear victory, 27 in a defeat, and 30 in some form of compromise.* The workers thus won about three of every four strikes for the entire period.

The vast majority of strike demands concerned pay and hours. In that regard, the Jewish strike movement up to 1900 was highly successful. Cuts of two to four hours in the workday and wage increases of one to two rubles a week were common. Other grievances—indiscriminate fines levied by employers, late and inaccurate payments of wages, abusiveness on the part of employers, and the firing of co-workers or "troublemakers"—all achieved some degree of redress. The demand that fired workers be rehired, an important indicator of labor solidarity, was an issue in almost 10 per cent of the strikes.†

Statistics alone say little, of course, of the strain of these strikes, of the hardship of workers who barely earned a living and yet managed to remain off the job for some time—an average of three weeks in 1898 and of 17 plus days the next year.[18] And this, moreover, in the face of increasing resistance by employers and police and a developing economic crisis.

The very success of the strikes revealed the weaknesses in the economic structure of Jewish life that had caught the attention of the Second Congress in 1898. There were limits to how much the (mostly small) Jewish-owned enterprises, virtually the only employers of Jewish labor, could bear in terms of increased labor costs. Many were having difficulty competing with the newer, mechanized plants, and some already had little choice but to die or sell out to the modernized industries. Economic crisis disclosed the precariousness of their position and, consequently, the precariousness of that of their employees. To be sure, new kinds of businesses were replacing the failing ones, many of them employing far more workers, and these were well able to meet the strikers' demands. But to deal with the larger firms, the movement needed new workers' organizations. The kase worked well only for small strikes. The longer the strike and the larger the number of strikers, the greater the problem of resources and discipline. Unemployment broke the spirit and discipline of all but the most dedicated workers. Desperate for work, men would take any job. If nothing was available, they would move on, flooding the labor market elsewhere or emigrating.

The Second Congress's concern about the calling of strikes in times of eco-

---

* Borokhov, p. 66. Though the Bund's report to the International in 1900 deals with a slightly different time span, it generally bears out Borokhov's findings. It states that of 262 strikes between the end of 1897 and the summer of 1900, 239 were successful (Bund biblio.: *Istoriia*, 1901, pp. 95–97).

† Bund biblio.: *Istoriia*, 1901, pp. 98–99, 102. The factories tended to strike for pay raises, the handicraft shops for a reduced workday. In Gomel some 30 shoemakers, working an 18-hour day, went on strike for a 13-hour day. A similar reduction was sought by tailors in Vitebsk, who were working 17 hours and demanded a 14-hour day.

nomic decline had some effect. The Bristle Workers' Union set up a controlled strike-fund system, forcing local units to check with a regional center
before they could strike and receive funds from the regional body.[19] The most
union-like organization in the Bund, the Bristle Workers' Union displayed
considerable ability to adjust to economic conditions.

The Bund committees played a substantial role in many of the strikes, do-
nating money, helping to formulate demands, leafleting, and in general drum-
ming up support for the strikers and their aims.[20] Where the kases and skhodkas were exceptionally strong, however, the committees did not take a direct
hand. This was the case in Belostok, where strike leadership came directly
from the workers' ranks. In other instances, notably where strikes were frequent and many, the committees could neither lead all of them nor resolve
all the disputes.[21] It was largely in areas where the strike movement was young
that committees did the major part of the organizing work and were the most
active.[22]

In any case, the Bund committees could exercise only a degree of control
over the strike movement. Economic hard times often broke the back of a
strike, though many continued even after all prospects of winning were gone.
Violence on the part of the workers became an increasingly serious problem
as time passed. The Bund, as a Social Democratic organization, disavowed
terror, though the Bundists understood the provocation that prompted it.
Following the dictates of the Second Congress, *Di Arbeter Shtime* noted in
August 1899 that "both political and industrial terror *as a policy* are completely
contrary to our tactics."[23] But abhorrence of such practices in the abstract did
not stop the workers from resorting to violence during strikes. The beating of
strikebreakers, police spies, and employers who called in the police was common.

All other methods the strikers fell back on were acceptable to the committees. The boycott, an established tactic before the Bund was founded, was often
used against businesses engaged in local or regional trade. On one occasion,
a boycott was called against a cigarette factory, after which rumors were circulated that the strikebreakers who had been employed had syphilis. The local
committees often endorsed such actions and participated in them.[24]

Differences between the workers and the committees over the organization
of the movement continued to be a divisive issue. The views expressed by the
Vilna Opposition of the early 1890's cropped up again and again. Indeed, the
Bund itself, with its secret committees and policy of mass agitation, represented
the kind of organization that led to these persistent protests against the intellectuals. As the labor consciousness of the Jewish proletariat grew, so did the
demands for organizational democracy. In a few cases there were some attempts at accommodation. In Minsk, for instance, when the higher echelons
of agitators objected to the absence of elections for committee members, the

committee compromised: the agitators were allowed to choose the committee by secret vote and to have one liaison man who knew the identity of the committee's members.[25] Minsk, with its long traditions of propaganda and agitation, proved to be a particularly difficult town for the Bund leadership, despite substantial membership gains. There, committees of workers represented each trade, and at times the local Bund committee was little more than an administrative unit, a kind of "cabinet of ministers." The Minsk case was but an illustration of a general rule: where the worker-led labor movement was strongest, the opposition to the Bund's policies was the strongest.[26] In Dvinsk, where terror was widespread and indiscriminately applied, intellectuals in the movement were even physically attacked by workers.[27]

The *birzhe*, a sort of street labor market where workers in certain trades gathered hoping to find employment, became an important outlet for the committees' political work. In the street crowds, news and orders were easily spread by word of mouth, and the agitators and distributors of literature could work at their best. The birzhe allowed the movement to advance a stage beyond the kase, bringing the worker into the open street where political issues could be tied into economic discussions. There, convinced workers could corner and exhort potential recruits, propagating and encouraging a sense of organization and solidarity. In a sense the birzhe was the frontier of the mass movement. It allowed the committees to turn the workers' attention gradually from purely economic matters to political matters, and so spread their own influence deep into the non-Bund working community. The birzhe also served as a form of resistance, "a permanent demonstration" against the authorities.[28] Seemingly innocent and difficult to disperse except by stringent measures, it became increasingly important to the Bund over the years.

The fact that local control was a problem for the committees indicates the Jewish labor movement was not the creature of the Bund. This is not to detract from the role of the Bund and the groups that preceded it as the first and the most successful organizations to engage in the systematic mobilization and political education of the Jewish workers, only to emphasize that the Bund and the workers' movement were not synonymous. Indeed, the Bundists themselves recognized—and were concerned about—the independent growth of the labor movement. At the same time, it is important to note that where the Bund committees did not exert some degree of influence, the Jewish labor movement of 1897–99 consisted largely of sporadic and local responses with no general aim and no real direction.

From the committees' point of view, the most ominous development in these years was the close collaboration of their traditional enemies, the employers and the police. The state, awakening from the comparative lethargy of the mid-1890's, now intervened frequently and forcibly in strikes. In some instances the police went so far as to forbid employers to accede to workers' demands.[29] In the two and a half years after the Bund's founding between 733 and 1,000 intellectuals and workers were arrested.[30]

Employers now not only blacklisted known troublemakers, but often refused to hire anyone suspected of belonging to the Bund; and not only fired suspected strike leaders, but frequently turned them over to the police.[31] At times the employers worked together to thwart strikes, though not as often as they might have under the circumstances. At times the police used direct pressure on the workers to accept terms.

Nevertheless, the employer-police combination failed on two accounts. First, it was ineffective: in 1899, a year of heavy reprisals on workers as well as of general economic crisis, the Jewish workers won 72 per cent of their strikes (many of which, it should be remarked, were of a defensive nature, seeking only to keep gains already achieved).[32] Second, the combination failed because it gave the local organizations an ideal opportunity to press home their message on the political struggle, a textbook illustration, if you will, of one of the central themes of *On Agitation*: the collusion of state and employer.

The Jewish employers occasionally resorted to one measure that had important implications for the Bund's relations with the non-Jewish world: the hiring of Christians as strikebreakers. This practice created a dilemma for the local committees. When Jewish strikebreakers were used, strong methods could be used to convince them of the error of their ways. Christians, however, had to be dealt with more gingerly lest manhandling be regarded as a religious act. In the circumstances, the fear of an outbreak of virulent anti-Semitism easily took precedence over the economic struggle. Since strikebreakers almost by definition lacked class consciousness, misinterpretation was all the more likely. Thus, a violent response to Christian strikebreakers might even threaten the dream of international labor solidarity itself.

The essential unfairness of a double standard for Christian and Jewish strikebreakers was not lost on the Jewish workers, and their responses to the situation varied. Mostly they followed the generally accepted policy of trying education and persuasion, but abiding by the "rules" was to admit defeat, and inevitably there were clashes—to say nothing of lost strikes and jobs—because of this maneuver by the employers.[33] There was no easy way to thwart the employers on this score, and the tactic of using non-Jewish strikebreakers continued to be a persistent if minor threat to the movement.

We get some inkling of what the Bund faced in trying to weld the Jewish and Christian workers together from Leon Bernstein's report of a discussion he had with the Pole Feliks Dzierżyński. The future head of the Cheka (the Bolshevik counterintelligence organization), Dzierżyński was at this time working with the Polish Social Democrats and in close touch with the Bundists. Wanting to make contact with local Bundists in Kovno, he called on

Bernstein for help, and a meeting was arranged with Liza Epstein and her husband, Alter. As Bernstein and Dzierżyński left the Epsteins' house, Dzierżyński remarked that for his part he would not have been able to introduce Bernstein into the home of even his most faithful Christian worker, for the best of them had not mastered their anti-Semitism. Yes, he answered Bernstein, he was working against that sentiment, but "it is a difficult and almost thankless task. To succeed in our mass agitation, we have to avoid certain questions."* The distance between the Jewish and Polish masses was still very great.

Still, there were hopeful signs that this gap was closing. The late 1890's saw joint workers' demonstrations and strikes in Warsaw, as well as Polish support for Jewish workers.[34] And the PPS, stung by the appearance of the Bund, finally began to take the Jewish workers around them seriously, so seriously in fact as to put out a newspaper in Yiddish, *Der Arbeter* (The Worker), the first issue of which appeared in December 1898. Withal, these were bare beginnings; the estrangement of Pole and Jew was still almost complete.

The local organizations remained close to the masses and strove mightily to broaden the base of the movement's membership; and leaders well suited to the tasks of local organization continued to emerge from the circles and the ranks of labor agitators. But progress was not always smooth. Older workers, religious workers, family men often proved difficult to recruit. Feeling their beliefs or the security of their families threatened, many workers were antagonistic, sometimes going so far as to identify organizers for the police. Employers usually tried hard to keep such workers on, and to rid themselves of the less conservative elements, including, at times, even non-religious employees.[35] The small-town workers were particularly conservative, not only because the old customs and ways were followed more closely outside of the large centers (even the sight of books and newspapers in the hands of common people sometimes offended employers), but also because the police there had tighter control and beat workers more readily than in the larger cities.[36]

Up to the end of 1899 the Bund and its local groups showed little division in their economic and political organization. The local organs and leaflets continued to tie the economic struggle closely to the movement's political goals; and the local groups themselves had no "specialists" of theory or practice.[37] But if the development of political consciousness seems slow, it is best measured against the whole picture: the fact is, except for the rather feeble efforts of the PPS, the Bund was the only organization operating among the Jewish

* Bernstein, *Ershte*, pp. 85–86. The Comintern leader Karl Radek found it amusing that though the Polish Social Democratic leadership included several Jews, only Dzierżyński, a Pole, could read Yiddish (*Portraits*, p. 100).

workers doing the kind of practical economic and political work that could be carried out in Russia at the time. Workers who did not follow the Bund simply had no other organizational framework for concerted action. To a large extent the local committees in the years 1897–99 were the whole of the Bund, and thus the whole of the Jewish revolutionary movement.

10. The National Question and Economism

In 1898 and 1899 the Bundists operated on a relatively narrow level, confining their work to technical matters and the practical problems of keeping the movement alive. Nevertheless, questions of a broader and more theoretical nature began to cry out for answers. One was the still largely unspoken question of the concept of the Jewish worker as Jew, which in turn raised the question of the Bund's role as a leader of the Jewish workers. The pressure from within the movement to resolve these questions became greater and greater, especially when other national movements began to attempt to define themselves. However reluctantly, the Bund finally was forced to face the problem of cultural identity and its own relationship to the revolutionary movement.

The Bundists, like the rest of the Russian Social Democrats, also gradually began reconsidering the major forms of their revolutionary activity in these years. Specifically, the question of whether the strike was in fact the most effective revolutionary instrument became of increasing concern. With the emergence of these two issues—the question of identity and the question of tactics—the Bund turned in a new direction.

The Bund's Third Congress, held in December 1899, provided the opportunity for a formal discussion of the new issues.* Representatives from 12 cities and organizations, including the Central Committee and the new Foreign Committee, participated. As in the case of the Second Congress, the exact number of delegates is not known; there were at least 15 and perhaps as many as 20.[1] The composition of the assembly points up the recovery and growth of the Bund since the arrests of 1898. New cities were represented, and new, young participants joined such familiar pioneer figures as John Mill and Pavel Rosenthal at the three-day meeting. (Rosenthal, now a doctor, had taken up practice in Belostok after completing his studies at the University of Kharkov.)

---

* The date of the Third Congress was deliberately falsified in the reports carried in *Di Arbeter Shtime* and *Der Yidisher Arbeter* in order to confuse the police (P. Rosenthal, "Bialystoker," p. 53). The date given in both journals is January 1900.

The old pioneers, with their spirit and experience, were a heartening sight for the rest of the delegates, especially for the veterans David Katz and Zeldov, who had sustained the movement in its dark days.

The new issues did not come up simply in the course of debate at the congress. The national question was specifically put on the agenda because of an open argument within the Bund and Mill's insistence that the matter be discussed. As editor of *Der Yidisher Arbeter*, Mill had consistently included materials relating to the national question from the beginning of his stewardship. One article in particular had drawn angry reaction. This was a piece by Chaim Zhitlovsky, which appeared in the March 1899 issue.[2] In it Zhitlovsky, a well-known Jewish socialist intellectual who had written on socialism and the Jews in both Russian and Yiddish for years, asserted that the socialist goal should be not only civil rights for Jews but also national rights. Attacking Zionism as a false path, he called for the strengthening of Jewish national culture through the use of Yiddish, and even predicted that the future would see a system of schools and universities taught exclusively in Yiddish. Jewish national culture, he maintained, would in no way hinder the path to socialism; on the contrary it would have positive effects, for the Jewish workers would be freed from a reliance on their own bourgeoisie.[3]

The fact that Mill published this article did not mean he was prepared to endorse all these views. Indeed, he added a footnote to the passage dealing with the development of Yiddish educational institutions, challenging it as purely conjectural.[4] Mill simply believed it was important to retain the passage for the sake of discussion, and it was discussion that he hoped to raise among his comrades in Russia.

Publication of this article particularly incensed Aaron Weinstein, a young intellectual in Warsaw. He distributed that issue of *Der Yidisher Arbeter* in his area with a notice attached stating his disagreement with the author and criticizing the journal for its emphasis on Jewish questions. This outburst led David Katz to go abroad in mid-1899 to discuss the matter with Mill. The two agreed that a delegate should be sent to the Third Congress to raise the issue, a duty the old pioneer decided to take on himself.[5]

The debate on the national question became the high point of the Third Congress. Mill (called Comrade A in the report of the proceedings) proposed that the Jewish proletariat should demand equal national rights as well as equal civil rights. Civil equality was not enough, he said; witness the Poles in Germany who had civil rights but had to speak German at meetings. What good was the right to meet if Jews had to speak Russian? Moreover, there was the future to think of. The Bund was not a short-term proposition; thus it was the Bund's duty to demand rights that would be needed by the Jewish proletariat at a later date, just as other parties did.[6]

Mill's proposal met strong opposition. The Social Democrats in Russia, opponents insisted, had to avoid making demands that could divert the attention of the proletariat from class interests to national interests. The immediate tasks were those affecting the Russian proletariat as a whole—winning political freedom, for instance—and their fulfillment required a concerted effort. National demands could fritter away energy, making more difficult the *sine qua non* of political freedom, the destruction of the Autocracy. Mill's opponents, uncertain in their own minds about the future of the Jews, were consequently doubtful about the necessity of dealing with the question of national rights.[7]

On the whole, the major objections to Mill's proposal were based on tactical considerations.[8] What concerned most of his opponents was the harmful effect a demand for equal national rights could have on working-class solidarity, not the right or wrong of the question itself. Many did concede, however, that a search for a socialist solution to the national condition of the Jews was in order.[9]

At the conclusion of the debate, the congress adopted the following resolution: "The Bund, among its political demands, puts forth only equal civil rights, not national rights." Nevertheless, Bund members were to be given a chance to present their views on the national question; *Der Yidisher Arbeter* would set aside a section for discussion on the understanding that no editorial endorsement was to be attached to the opinions expressed therein.[10] Mill did not win the day, but his stand opened the door to further study.

The inability to discuss this issue intelligently probably caused many of the delegates some discomfort. According to Katz, the Bund organizations in Russia had only the barest knowledge of the pros and cons, and Mill alone had delved into the subject.[11] Mill was undoubtedly much closer to the national issue than any of the others because of his work with the Polish socialists. He himself says that the inadequacy of the call for equal civil rights had gnawed at him throughout the course of the debate with the PPS in 1898. He was convinced that the Polish position had not been examined thoroughly enough.[12] Mill's major opponents at the Congress were Rosenthal, Weinstein, and Katz.

Though some of the Bundists in Russia took the position that this "leap to nationalism" was a new issue, in hindsight its introduction appears less dramatic than its opponents suggested.[13] The Bund had long since adopted a civil rights plank, and the RSDWP had gone still further, recognizing the right of nations to self-determination. Thus the right of a Jew to claim his cultural heritage was a logical, if unexpressed, step beyond previously accepted positions.

Mill's desire to raise the national question reflected the broadening effect of his years in Warsaw and his residence abroad. He had been particularly affected by his close contacts with the intellectual émigré communities of Western Europe and came to share their preoccupation with theoretical problems at a time when his comrades in Russia were still absorbed with purely technical matters. He sought to transmit this new interest to his fellows by publishing articles like Zhitlovsky's, whose main target in fact was Zionism, the Bund's major competitor for the allegiance of Russian-Jewish students abroad.[14] Similarly, he ran a major article by the prominent German Social Democrat Karl Kautsky, again trying to communicate to the movement back home a deepening concern of the Western Social Democratic parties: the national problem in general and the nationalities problem in the Austrian Empire in particular.

It is difficult to determine how far Zionism pushed the Bundists into considering the national question. The publication of Theodore Herzl's *Judenstaat* in 1896 and the meeting of the first Zionist Congress at Basel in 1897 undoubtedly raised interest in the subject to a new level. Indeed, Mill says as much:

Before Herzl came out with his *Judenstaat*, the Zionist . . . movement had no roots in Jewish life in Russia and Poland.

This movement remained absolutely dead among the Jewish *workers*. It is significant that at all three congresses of the Bund the question of Zionism did not appear on the agenda.

After *Judenstaat* appeared and the idea of a Jewish state in Palestine began to spread gradually . . . it became clear that the Bund could no longer ignore the new movement. If not today, then tomorrow [Zionism] would appear among the Jewish masses in socialist dress to express the new aspirations among the Jewish petit bourgeoisie.[15]

It was the potential of Zionism fitting itself into a socialist framework that influenced Mill's decision to publish Zhitlovsky. But he did so simply to keep his comrades informed of the growing appeal of Zionism in the West. The Bund faced little competition from this quarter in the northwest provinces, and the discussion of the national question at the Third Congress centered around the deleterious effects a national emphasis could have on international socialist solidarity, not on the threat of a competing ideology. Withal, Zionism cannot be discounted as a factor in Mill's decision to press the issue.

The Kautsky article had impressed Mill while he was still in Poland. Kautsky regarded the national question as a critical issue, important not only to the bourgeoisie but to all classes and peoples. He felt that national feeling among small nations developed as the level of education increased, and that this trend would continue. And properly so, in his view: "The proletariat is not only not an enemy of such national movements," he argued; "it is very much interested in having such movements continue to develop."[16] Kautsky did not believe that the cultural development of ethnic groups living in one land had to lead to conflict; Switzerland was a living example of diverse cultural groups dwelling together in peace. Judging by the problems besetting the Austrian Empire, the difficulty lay in the impossibility of the various nationalities achieving their goals, i.e., acquiring territory. The way out of the dilemma was simply to recognize the autonomy of a people on a linguistic basis without granting them territorial independence. This issue could not be avoided, Kautsky concluded. A correct answer to the national question was necessary so the proletarian could lead his class struggle correctly. "Although the proletarian stands on the principle of internationalism," he asserted, "this does not mean that he rejects national identity; it means he seeks the freedom and equality of all peoples."[17]

The very name of Kautsky made discussion of the national issue important. The Russian Social Democrats were great admirers of their German confreres, and few German socialists had more prestige than Kautsky in this period. His words lent an air of authority to the debate that was extremely welcome to the Marxists of those days; and all the more so in this case because, absent Marx's views on the subject, the Jewish Social Democrats had been led to expend much of their early efforts in fighting national identifications.

The objections raised at the Third Congress show that the majority of delegates feared the national issue as a threat to working-class solidarity. Moreover, to their minds the future of the Jewish workers was in any case uncertain. In short, the Third Congress was unwilling to define its worker constituency as anything more than a separate class with certain economic rights and with full rights of citizenship. The fact that the delegates decided to allow general discussion, however, reveals certain doubts about their position.

The Third Congress was the last to reflect the intimacy of the underground movement of the 1890's. To this point every major decision on tactics and principle had been adopted only after long discussion. The change to mass agitation, the call for equal civil rights, the demand for a Jewish workers' organization, even the creation of the Bund itself—all had been the result of consensus rather than individual innovation. The documents and actions of the pioneer period were formal expressions of prevailing attitudes, not new theoretical formulations put forward for debate. But with the establishment of the Bund came a new formality, which together with the increased difficulties of communication after 1898 altered the decision-making pattern of the earlier day, the informal techniques by which agreement was reached among intimates in Vilna. The first time the Bundists had to consider an issue they had not had a chance to discuss and agree on came precisely at a point when the personal element of the Vilna days was missing. The group that took up the national question had neither the cohesion of the old circles nor the same opportunity to study and discuss a major issue in advance.

The decision to open the door to further discussion of the national question was to have enormous consequences for the future of the Bund, for the search for ethnic definition within Marxism implied a shift to new areas of struggle;

indeed, it promised to affect every premise except the necessity of the struggle against the government. It is fair to say that this quesion was the knottiest issue of principle the Bund had to deal with in the next several years.

In the late 1890's the ranks of Russian Social Democracy were shaken by a debate over the direction in which the movement was heading. The argument paralleled in part a similar development in the West, where Marx's views on the necessity of a violent overthrow of capitalism had been challenged by a new interpretation known as Revisionism. The challengers, led by the German socialist Eduard Bernstein, held that the working class had made great gains since Marx's day through the development of trade unions and democratic parliamentarism, and that consequently socialism could be achieved by peaceful evolution. These views had gained many adherents by the late 1890's.

There were important differences between the Revisionism of the West and what the Russians called Economism, notably in the legal political element. The use of political parties and parliamentary tactics to achieve socialism was clearly impossible in Russia at the time. But some Russian Social Democrats believed the achievement of narrow economic gains through a mass workers' movement could lead to the strong trade unionism that made parliamentary tactics work in the West.[18]

The Plekhanovites would have none of it. They stood on the side of Marxist orthodoxy and recognized only too clearly the danger to revolutionary Marxism inherent in the new school of thought. That the old guard would defend itself against "revisionist" tendencies like those in the West was inevitable.

In fact, there had been constant friction between the Russian revolutionaries in the West and those at home since the mid-1890's, when the Union of Russian Social Democrats Abroad began sending home materials suitable for mass agitation. They were aided in this by the Liberation of Labor Group, but the Plekhanovites were never at ease in the enterprise, and the relations between the two organizations had become increasingly strained. Personality, status, and age differences contributed to the mutual mistrust between the Plekhanovites and the young comrades of the Union Abroad.[19]

The pioneer Jewish Social Democrats had been close to the Union from the beginning. Not only were there personal ties between the pioneers and the young Unionists, but their perceptions of work were the same. As the differences between the old guard and the younger comrades over the needs of the mass movement sharpened, the Jewish Social Democrats moved closer and closer to the Union and further and further from the Liberation of Labor Group.[20]

Kopelson, the old pioneer and sometime secretary of the Union Abroad, was a key personal link between the Bund and the Union. However, his years abroad began to affect his ties with his comrades in Russia. At times he acted as if his primary obligation was to the Union Abroad rather than the Bund, which he officially represented; and on occasion he even categorically refused to carry out some duties that were vital to the Bund. For example, when certain problems developed in Berlin over the transshipment of literature, he insisted on remaining in Switzerland. Mill, who was in danger of being picked up and deported by the German police, had to go in his stead.[21]

The pioneer-intellectuals had had no personal contact with the Plekhanovites until Mill's trip abroad in 1894, when he delivered a report on the activities in Vilna to the old guard. At that time, his reception had been decidedly cool. Akselrod alone had shown any cordiality, and Plekhanov and Vera Zasulich had displayed little enthusiasm for the work of the Jewish Social Democrats.[22] Nor did subsequent contacts do much to improve the personal relations between the two groups. In a meeting between Kremer and Plekhanov in 1897, the two men exchanged sharp words over the kind of literature needed in Russia, with Kremer clearly unwilling to defer to the judgment of the old guard. Despite Kremer's effort to get On Agitation published, the arrangements dragged on for two and a half years; the pamphlet was not issued until the end of 1897, four years after the work had first appeared. Nevertheless, Kremer's admiration for the Liberation of Labor Group remained high.

Akselrod's postscript to On Agitation reveals some of the dissatisfaction of the Plekhanovites with the work of the Social Democratic organizations back home. Conceding that the essay had been valuable in the mid-1890's when the movement needed broadening and deepening, Akselrod asserted that Kremer's message had outlived its usefulness; these lessons had already been absorbed into the Social Democratic consciousness. The younger Marxists were ignoring the broader issue, he charged. Raising numbers and preparing organizations for struggle were not sufficient in themselves; the movement had to further the interests of all classes if the struggle was to be successful. The proletariat needed allies and sympathy from other portions of the population; political isolation had to be avoided.[23]

The Akselrod critique was impersonal. He did not single Kremer out for blame, nor did he attack the work as a uniquely Jewish Social Democratic document, even though it was based largely on the Jewish experience. Indeed, as he pointed out, some of Plekhanov's statements had presaged the same kind of practical work the Jewish Social Democrats had undertaken.[24] Plekhanov soon had his own criticism to level. In a letter to the editors of Rabochaia gazeta criticizing the newspaper, he remarked that the Russian comrades did not always remember "that every class struggle is a political struggle" and recommended Akselrod's postscript to On Agitation to them.[25]

In fact, the Bund was largely at the periphery of the growing disagreements between the Unionists and the Plekhanovites, both of whom were preoccupied with activities in the West in 1896–97. This allowed the Bund virtually a free hand in its own area of interest—its base in Russia. The Bundists in the West concentrated on helping the mother organization at home; and with the establishment of the Foreign Committee, the Bund became even more independent. Equipped with its own press, its own shipping system, and its own Yiddish materials, it could easily avoid the conflicts over press and editorial controls and policies that raged among the Russians. Indeed, at the end of 1898, the Union Abroad permitted the Bund's Foreign Committee to have its own treasury, editors, and administration.[26] When the Third Congress officially recognized the Foreign Committee as the Bund's representative in the Union,[27] the committee in effect achieved the same autonomy inside the Union the Bund had gained within the RSDWP.

Strictly speaking, Economism was not a real issue among the Russian Social Democrats until the late 1890's. Even the critics of *On Agitation* recognized the value of the mass agitation tactic, and the decision to print Kremer's work in late 1897, despite all the grumbling, indicates that no ideological principle was involved at the time. The disagreement was only over tactics. In any case Kremer never intended to suggest that economic gain was the final goal of the workers' movement. For that matter, Lenin, who fought Economism with every weapon at his command from the late 1890's on, noted in his major work on the subject in 1902 that "the leading Social Democrats of that period [the early 1890's] *zealously carried on economic agitation* (being guided by the really useful instructions in *On Agitation* ...), but they did not regard this as their sole task."[28]

The first strong initiative for a workers' movement in Russia based primarily on economic aims emerged in St. Petersburg.[29] It began with the appearance in late 1897 of an illegal newspaper, *Rabochaia mysl'* (Workers' Thought), which protested the intellectuals' control of the movement and argued for democratically run mass unions. So long as the movement remained an instrument to assuage the guilt of repentant intellectuals, the editors said, it must perforce be alien to the worker. Politics followed economics, and the strike movement alone tied the workers together to give them a better life. Accordingly, kases were "dearer to the movement than a hundred other organizations. Let the workers lead the struggle, knowing that they are fighting not for some future generations, but for themselves and their children."[30]

The clearest ideological expression of Economism came in a work entitled "Credo" by Ekaterina Kuskova, who, with her husband, S. N. Prokopovich, had been close to both the Union Abroad and the Liberation of Labor Group. Her manuscript, published without authorization by Lenin, appeared along with his strong protest in *Rabochee delo* in 1899.* Kuskova denied the efficacy

---

* "Protest Rossiiskikh sotsial-demokratov," *Rabochee delo*, 4-5 (September-December 1899). Kuskova later claimed that the manuscript was never meant for publication: it contained her private views, which she had formulated at the request of certain "orthodox" Marxists ("Istoricheskaia bibliografiia," pp. 325-26).

of political struggle in Russia: the political circumstances made it too difficult, there were no practical means of carrying it on, and the masses were neither ideologically nor organizationally ready for it. Instead the workers should continue to pursue the economic struggle and learn to organize, pushing the labor movement beyond its present embryonic stage. The proper task of the Russian Marxist was to find a Marxism based on the national condition; this meant, not the creation of an independent workers' political party, but participation with the liberal forces striving for legal change.[31] These arguments flew directly in the face of the Liberation of Labor Group's position.

But Kuskova's work received no support from the Union Abroad. Quite the contrary; Lenin's protest against her views received the blessing of the editors of *Rabochee delo*, who felt compelled to add their own criticism in a postscript to the Lenin article.[32] In late 1899 the Union did not regard its own work as Economist in any sense of the word.

In 1898 and 1899 the Bundists took no theoretical stand on the relative merits of economic and political activity. Since the first of the decade the Jewish Social Democrats had assumed an intimate relation between the two: political work would develop as the economic struggle proceeded, would supersede economic work, and ultimately would lead to the attainment of socialism. The Bundists did not cross swords on ideological matters with the Plekhanovites. (Indeed, they had no one capable of doing so after the arrests of July 1898 even if they had wished to enter into an argument.) From the start the Bund had considered itself an organization for the masses. If it had anything like an intellectual elite at the top, this developed more for reasons of trust and friendship than for reasons of theoretical brilliance. The leaders had never wavered in their position that the organization should belong to the workers, and had shown no desire to maintain power in their own hands as some kind of brain trust. Between July 1898 and December 1899 the half-intellectuals and workers played a particularly strong role in the Bund. In light of the growing Economist controversy, the issue, then, was whether the Bund's tactics, notably its economic work, were subverting the deep revolutionary elements of Marxism.

In fact, the doctrines of Economism made little impression on the Bund in Russia. According to David Katz, there were few theoretical differences at the Second Congress and no theoretical debates.[33] Information on the developing controversy was not even readily available locally. When the first issue of *Rabochaia mysl'* finally arrived in Minsk early in 1898, it was barely legible and was circulated only to the top people.[34]

By 1899 the subject was important enough to be raised at the Third Congress of the Bund, though by all accounts the discussions revealed no deeply thought-out positions. The Congress certainly made no claim to having solved the problem.[35] The question clearly did have some impact, though, for the Congress attempted to modify slightly the view implied to some activists, namely that the economic struggle was an overriding consideration. After considerable debate, the delegates adopted a resolution that carefully spoke of economic struggle as "one" means of developing political and class consciousness among the laboring masses.[36] They apparently hoped that they could clarify the Bund position on the economic struggle without upsetting the work that had served the organization so well. The ideological issue that was beginning to tear Russian Social Democracy apart had little practical meaning for the Bund at this point. The Congress confirmed and justified existing practices, citing the use of propaganda, agitation, and circles as proper means for raising political consciousness; it was content merely to warn Bund members against putting undue emphasis on the economic struggle. The Bund leaders did not have the same deep concern about tactics as the Russian ideologues abroad.

Though the national question and Economism were still far from burning issues, these early discussions heralded the end of a narrow and local economic focus. The Bund would soon reach a level of concern that demanded more than mere technical tasks, more than cautious approaches to the working masses, and more than the relatively simple political concepts of the 1890's.

II. A Period of Transition, 1900-1901

By the time the Bund held its Fourth Congress, in May 1901, it had matured politically. By that time too it had seen a remarkable growth. The tensions that arose as a result of this rapid development drove it to reappraise itself as both an organization and a movement. That reappraisal was many-sided. Expansion forced the Bund to define its relationship to other revolutionary organizations and to the Jewish workers within its new boundaries; the quickening of political life in Russia, as well as its own growth, led it to lay increasing emphasis on its own political activity; and challenges from both Zionism and the state prompted it to examine its membership goals and its aims as a Jewish revolutionary organization. The emergence of strong leaders among the Russian Social Democrats further sharpened the Bundists' self-awareness. Consciously and unconsciously, the Bund altered its tactics, form, and content in response to each of these developments.

In 1900 the Bund began to recover from the effects of the arrests of 1896 and 1898. A number of the pioneers returned and reassumed positions of leadership in the movement. Among them was Noah Portnoy, who escaped from exile in eastern Siberia and rejoined his comrades in the spring of 1900. He was immediately co-opted to the Central Committee by Katz, who had been reelected to the committee at the Third Congress. Portnoy soon became the single most important figure in running the Bund machinery in Russia, a position he maintained for many years. Rosenthal was also invited to join the Central Committee in the summer of 1900, after having refused to join it at the Third Congress. The Central Committee thus moved back into the hands of the old pioneer-intellectuals for whom, it appeared in retrospect, Katz had been holding it in trust.*

The Foreign Committee received an even greater influx of old hands. Krem-

---

* Zeldov and an unidentified third person were elected to the Central Committee at the Third Congress. But Zeldov soon went to St. Petersburg, leaving Katz to run the organization in Russia virtually singlehandedly. Mill, *Pionern*, 2: 63–64; P. Rosenthal, "Bialystoker," p. 54.

er, Kosovsky, and Mutnikovich, released pending sentencing in 1900, fled Russia in the summer and late fall of that year. The entire first Central Committee moved into action again, this time from a distant outpost—Switzerland.

Between the First and Third congresses, the Bund added only seven organizations, a reflection of the dangerous situation and also of a deliberately restrictive policy of representation. The years 1900 and 1901, however, saw a proliferation of new committees and an expansion into regions far from the Bund's original bases in Belorussia, Lithuania, and Poland. In the summer of 1900 some of the Social Democrats of Gomel, one of the areas where initial resistance to the Bund had been strongest, joined the Bund. The decision was not taken without dissension, but finally Victor Shulman led a group into the Bund, and by mid-1900 the Central Committee was requesting reports for publication from the fledgling organization.[1] Gomel, scarcely a southern city, represented the Bund's southernmost expansion to that time. In less than a year two cities lying squarely in the southwestern provinces—Berdichev and Zhitomir—were represented at the Fourth Congress.

Though the Bund did not make any fundamental changes in its structure or operations to accommodate the new southern units, it did have to take into account the lower proportion of Jews in the southern populations, a proportion that dropped the farther south one moved. In 1897 Jews formed 57.9 per cent of the urban population in the northwest region, 38.1 per cent in the southwestern provinces (Zhitomir had a Jewish population of 45.9 per cent), and only 26.3 per cent in the southernmost areas.[2] The differences between areas were even greater when it came to the respective labor forces. In the northwest Jews made up 43 per cent of the labor force, whereas in the southwest they formed only 8.8 per cent and in the south only 2.7 per cent.[3] Yet it was the south where the Jewish population was increasing most rapidly, rising 60.9 per cent between 1881 and 1897 as compared with a 13.4 per cent increase in the northwest and a 16.7 per cent increase in the southwest.[4] In part this rapid increase was the result of migration from the north in search of employment.

Migration brought to the south a number of Jewish workers who had been tied to the pioneer Social Democratic groups. They played an important role in organizing the southern workers, in some cases even initiating a workers' movement. Jewish workers from Lithuania organized the first trades in Berdichev in 1897 and introduced the Bund's Yiddish literature into that area. "Can you imagine now," one worker recalled, "with what thirst, with what fire our workers began to swallow these simple, easily understood books?"[5] In essence, this process was merely a continuation of the earlier northern colonization.

In Kiev the Bund began to attract members of the student societies at the university, particularly those in the Social Democratic groups, which were heavily Jewish. By the turn of the century Jewish students had formed an organization specifically to defend their own interests. In the summer of 1900 some of these students decided to form Bund organizations among the Jewish workers in Kiev. One of them, David Zaslavsky, an important contributor to *Pravda* after the Bolshevik Revolution, later remembered: "We did not just respect the [Bund]; we believed in it."[6] For him and his Social Democratic comrades, the Bund was at once an answer to their Zionist opponents and the perfect wedding of their ideology and their feelings of Jewishness.

Some of the northern Jewish activists moved south and began working among mixed groups of Russian and Jewish Social Democrats. In Odessa, where the conditions were much the same as in the northwest, the first Social Democratic organizing was done in part by Jewish workers with Bund training. They did not, however, try to form Bund organizations. Rather, as P. A. Garvi, a prominent Social Democrat who worked in that city, notes, "these organizers *par excellence*" created the mass basis for the Odessa RSDWP organization, from which all Odessa revolutionary organizations subsequently grew.[7] Similarly, it was activists reared in the tradition of the Bund who helped establish the movement among the Russian workers of Ekaterinoslav.[8]

Of all areas, the south provided the Jewish activist the best opportunity to find a place in the mainstream of the revolutionary movement, that is, among the Russian workers. The old desire to serve the Russian movement had never died. Men like Leon Goldman, Moshe Dushkan, and Abraham Ginzburg (Naumov) were able to become deeply involved in the creation of a Russian workers' movement without breaking their ties with the Bundists, at least for a time. Dushkan, who had been in Martov's circle, felt that it was up to those who spoke Russian well to bind the work of the Russian and Jewish masses.[9]

The comparative lack of ethnic homogeneity in the movement in the south led the Bund to formulate certain guidelines on expansion. In contrast to the northwest, where the Bundists originated the Social Democratic movement among the Jews and were even at times the only group in a position to organize workers, many of the southern cities had Social Democratic organizations before the Bundists arrived on the scene. In such cases the Bund had to decide, first, what its own role should be and, second, what policy to adopt on Jewish workers belonging to other circles.

These questions were taken up by the Fourth Congress in May 1901. It decided that wherever Jewish workers had formed separate groups, this development should be encouraged to some degree; that the Central Committee could help form local committees where purely Jewish groups existed; and that Jewish activists belonging to Russian Social Democratic groups could remain in the Russian organizations but could receive the Bund's Yiddish literature. The congress also resolved that where a separate Jewish movement might prove harmful to the Russian movement, Bund committees should not be established.[10]

These decisions merely formalized what had already been accomplished. The Bund, working in virtual isolation, had no higher authority to turn to on the question of expanding into areas already served by Social Democratic organizations. The founding congress of the RSDWP put no geographical limit on the activities of the Jewish Social Democrats, or any other limit on the Bund's power to deal with problems affecting either the Jewish worker or its own internal organization.[11] With the exception that once the Bund moved into the south, where ethnic distinctions could be made between itself and the Russian Social Democrats, the southward advance was essentially a continuation of an accepted pattern of work.

The Fourth Congress was in fact notably cautious in its resolutions on this point, no doubt fearing to overstep the bounds of propriety in its attempt to help the Jewish workers. The Central Committee was clearly reluctant to accept groups until it was satisfied that they understood what the Bund was. In discussing the activities in Kiev in 1900, Portnoy, by then the Bund's chief organizer, referred to the Kievans as "Bundists who were not yet acquainted with the Bund."[12] The Kievan Bundists were not officially accepted as a group until 1903.

Implicit in the Bund's growth was the issue of its relationship to the proletariat of the whole Empire. Its continued expansion and success and its isolation contributed to a feeling that the Bund was more than an offshoot of the abstract and indeed nonexistent RSDWP. Where the Bundists had always referred to the Bund as the organization in the past, many now began referring to it as the party, a term that had been reserved for the RSDWP.[13] However complex and subtle the reasons for this shift in nomenclature, the Bund began establishing a pattern in 1900 and early 1901 that was to make it a good deal more than the founding fathers had in mind in 1897 and 1898.

One of the first evidences of the reinvigorated Bund leadership was a new emphasis on creating political consciousness among the Jewish workers. Portnoy's hand is to be seen in small ways and large in *Di Arbeter Shtime* from the first issue he had anything to do with, that of April 1900, which was timed for early May and printed on red paper. Taking his cue from the Third Congress, Portnoy sounded the keynote of political struggle soon after. In the July issue he pointed out the limited nature of economic activity, necessary as it had been in the past, and stressed that the state's role as the enemy of the working class had never been as well understood as now. Indeed, he wrote, the movement had once even been able to use the law to gain its demands, for instance in shortening the workday. The growth of the movement and the government's response, however, proved that the workers had to depend on their own efforts, and with that knowledge their political education began. The government had shown itself to be the workers' greatest enemy, and the time had come to meeet its attacks. "To gain political freedom—that is the task which our time puts before us and which must be accomplished."[14]

In the same article Portnoy attempted to call the workers' attention to the fact that there were others in Russian society besides the workers who opposed the government. The liberal intelligentsia could prove useful, for instance, at least to the extent that their demands agreed with the movement's political aims. Without denying the usefulness of past practices, Portnoy singled out the political demonstration as a particularly valuable tool. Through political demonstrations the liberals would learn the true state of the workers' struggle and derive courage from it. If the state resorted to violence and brutality, hatred of the regime would grow. Further, demonstrations would inform uninvolved workers of the movement and its aims. Strikes and demonstrations, especially the latter, were the best means of struggle while the open political struggle was still in its first stages. New methods would arise later. Meanwhile, persecution by the state would be of no avail; the work would go on.[15]

Statements echoing Portnoy's became common in the Bund literature. In April 1901 the editors of *Di Arbeter Shtime*, commenting on the year's work, stressed their increasing interest in political struggle and expressed delight with the results so far. In their exuberance, they changed the name of the column that carried news of Russia from "Di finstere velt" (The Dark World) to "Di likhtige velt" (The Bright World).[16]

The new emphasis on political demonstrations soon brought results. Gatherings of predominantly Jewish workers began to reach significant size. On May 1, 1900, 700 workers in Vitebsk stayed away from work, and over 1,000 met in Vilna. In Minsk tempers flared at a meeting, a spy and several policemen were beaten, and troops were called in to disperse the crowd. The funeral of a Belostok bristle worker in 1901 brought out some 3,000 workers who sang revolutionary songs and wore red bands. The secret gatherings of the mid-1890's, with their handfuls of workers, had become secondary; now the demonstrations were open, large, and militant enough to lead to scuffles with the police.

All this is not to suggest, however, that the Central Committee advocated open fighting. On the contrary, the committee distributed leaflets in Vilna in advance of the May Day celebration of 1900 urging the workers to remain peaceful; and it criticized the violence in Minsk. However legitimate the workers' anger, the committee declared, they should refrain from violence "because fighting is useful *only* to the government and the capitalists, who can then represent our worker demonstrations as brawls."[17] The Bund, looking beyond its own membership, was beginning to consider its public image. In their caution, the Bundists viewed the political struggle in terms of practical advantage. Thus, it was "only little by little, taking one position after another from our masters," that they would attain their goal.[18] For now the policy was gradualism; violence was premature.

Just as the Bund began emphasizing political activity, it met a calculated attack against its very existence from the Tsarist police. The police had more in mind than destroying the Bund by jailing its leaders and suppressing its work; they were bent on splintering the entire revolutionary movement by divorcing the economic struggle from the political struggle. To this end they were prepared to help the workers in their economic battles. This tactic proved quite successful in some quarters, presenting the Bundists with the serious problem of retaining their hold on the masses as they pushed for a deeper political struggle.

The driving force behind the new attack was the Bund's old nemesis, Zubatov. A one-time radical and circle member, Zubatov had turned informer and had risen in the ranks of the secret police to become chief of the Moscow Secret Police Department. His scheme to defeat the revolutionaries by helping the workers was backed wholeheartedly by such powerful figures as his superior, Moscow Police Chief D. F. Trepov, and the Grand Duke Sergei Aleksandrovich;[19] it was given its first test in Moscow.

Zubatov's program to destroy the revolutionary movement involved a number of ploys. To divert the strike movement from a revolutionary political path, he hoped to drive a wedge between the intellectuals and the workers. To satisfy the workers, he argued for the development of a legal trade union movement as in Western Europe.[20] At the same time, he planned to pursue routine police methods, above all infiltration, in the hope of destroying the revolutionary organizations from within.

A number of conditions helped further Zubatov's ambitions. The intensified strike movement fit admirably into his plans to promote trade unionism. The doctrines of Revisionism gave him an ideological lever with which to counter the prevailing revolutionary Marxist doctrine. And the internal problems of the Jewish movement itself, specifically the differences between workers and intellectuals over leadership, immediate goals, and tactics, played into the hands of the resourceful police official. He exploited each opportunity.

Zubatov was now going far beyond the simple police action he had taken in his original encounter with the Bund. Convinced that "the movement grew numb with terror and sank" after his coup of July 1898,[21] he had been quite proud of his work. Indeed, reports on the liquidation of the organization had been sent to the Tsar himself, and Minister of Justice N. V. Muraviev came to see the prisoners when they were moved to Moscow.[22] Unhappily for Zubatov, the arrests did not have the intended results.

Nevertheless, the captured materials and agents' reports were a rich source of information on the Bund, enough to make the police conclude that a serious political organization had developed from what had once been a movement centering around circles designed only to provide economic support.[23] Realizing that he had become entangled with an important, well-disciplined organization, Zubatov became convinced that the Bund was largely based on economic interests, and that he might use its member groups to create a labor movement devoid of revolutionary content.[24]

The catch of July 1898 was disappointing on the whole. Zubatov learned nothing new from his conversations with Kremer and Kosovsky. Indeed, all of his prisoners showed such great discipline that he was led to remark, "The Jewish movement produced an impression of some kind of mighty, almost unassailable force."[25] The old hands were too experienced to be misled by Zubatov's low-keyed approach and pretended omniscience about the Bund, or to be deceived into breaking their silence on the chance of helping their fellow prisoners.[26]

Zubatov was apparently undaunted by the rebuffs from the "generals" of the Bund, for he seems to have continued to hope to convert them to his point of view. After Kremer was released in April 1900 pending sentencing, Zubatov wired him asking him to come to Moscow to discuss the possible sentences that could be meted out for the 1898 arrests. In mid-1900 he was still trying to persuade the Bund leaders of his reasonableness by suggesting that Kremer could influence the fate of his comrades.* To Zubatov's chagrin Kremer fled the country at that point, ending any notion of swaying the Bund leadership.

Zubatov approached the nonintellectuals on a somewhat different tack. In the case of Kaplinsky, the best known worker arrested in 1898, Zubatov pointed out the merits of improving the workers' economic condition without pursuing unnecessary political goals. Kaplinsky promised to think the matter over but in the end dismissed the argument. Nevertheless, he was drawn into Zubatov's net and later became a notorious provocateur.[27]

Minsk was one of the main centers of Zubatov's interest, primarily because it was there that the Bund first came to his attention. Besides being the site of the congress of the RSDWP and the seat of the Bund's Central Committee, Minsk had been an important center of revolutionary and labor activity for years. It became the focal point of Zubatov's attempts to subvert the revolutionary workers' movement among the Jews, rivaling for a time at least Moscow and Odessa as centers of police concern.

In early 1900 Zubatov's agents began a new campaign in Minsk. Operating independently of the local police, they scooped up prisoners indiscriminately

---

* B. Frumkin, "Zubatovshchina," p. 207; Mikhalevich, *Zikhroinos*, 2: 10; Zaslavsky, "Zubatov," p. 103. Soon after the arrests, Kremer pleaded with Zubatov to release those who were innocent (even Zubatov granted that some had been arrested wrongly). The police chief cynically asked Kremer to point them out. In reply, Kremer suggested Zubatov use the information he had gathered in his investigations. *Arkady*, p. 391.

and sent them to Moscow where Zubatov could argue his own case to them.[28] This plan had some success, for the police net caught many young and inexperienced radicals who were susceptible to Zubatov's blandishments. Alexander Chemerisky, arrested in May, was one of them. Later an important opponent of the Bund (which he subsequently rejoined), Chemerisky was given books to read, including a work of Sidney Webb's, and discussed the movement once with Zubatov in a highly emotional interview. Afterwards, Zubatov used Chemerisky's name in discussions with other prisoners.[29] Others arrested in this wave report that Zubatov offered them works by Eduard Bernstein, invited them to join an independent movement, dwelt on the harmful role of the intellectual, attempted to provoke heated argument in the hope of gleaning information in unguarded moments, and tried to recruit agents to spy on Russian émigrés in Western Europe.[30]

This series of arrests brought Zubatov a far richer harvest than he had reaped in 1898. The issues he raised were the very ones that underlay the conflict dividing the activists in Minsk, and they proved to be highly exploitable points. Many of the arrestees seemed ready to listen to Zubatov's ideas. Convinced of his progress among the prisoners, the wily policeman released his captives in short order.* He wished to see the practical results of his work.

Through Boris Frumkin, a Minsk activist, we learn of the effectiveness of Zubatov's splintering maneuver. On their return the released prisoners split into four groups: those remaining loyal to the Bund, who at once pointed out the seriousness of the threat; those who had testified about their activities and who, though still convinced of the need to fight, had become so demoralized that they could not bring themselves to continue their participation in the organization; those who had maintained silence out of a sense of honor, but who, having been persuaded to the Zubatov view, at once severed their ties with the organization; and those who now began to oppose the Bund actively, criticizing its underground activities and calling for a legal workers' movement.[31]

The times were on Zubatov's side. His views coincided with and reinforced existing tendencies within the movement in Minsk, creating a serious crisis for the Bund. General economic conditions at the turn of the century were difficult, and improvements through strikes attainable only through hard fighting. Zubatov's suggestion that the legal path was the best path for the workers, since it eliminated the state as an enemy, appeared eminently reasonable to some. Police support for strikers or even police neutrality struck directly at the Bund's political program, which rested on the call for revolutionary action against the state. Moreover, since it was primarily the intellectuals who advo-

---

* Shulman was paroled after three months, and Chemerisky was held only ten weeks (Shulman, "Baginen," p. 55; Chemerisky et al., p. 316).

cated a political struggle, Zubatov's theories appealed to workers who felt the movement was run undemocratically, as well as those who still insisted on the need for education—in the tradition of the earlier Opposition movement.

The Bund's response to Zubatov's challenge evolved over a period of months. Even during the period of the Central Committee's weakest leadership, before the Third Congress, it had attempted to alert the workers to the dangers of the new police line. In December 1899 *Di Arbeter Shtime* warned of Trepov's statements on the possibility of legalizing the workers' economic organizations. The workers should not be taken in by such small concessions, the committee argued. In fact any talk of concession by the state was evidence the workers were winning their battle. Russian laws continued to be obstacles in the workers' struggle, and had to be fought.[32]

The reappearance of the Minsk arrestees served as the starting point for the fight against Zubatov's methods in the Jewish movement. Among those who returned were Chemerisky and Yehuda Volin. They and other former members of the local organization began agitating in the kases in the summer of 1900, deploring the Bund's lack of democracy and arguing for a legal labor movement.[33]

The Bund reacted to the activities of the defectors immediately in its pronouncements, but it was somewhat slower in adopting effective countermeasures. The first clear signals of resistance to the events in Minsk came in the summer of 1900. The Central Committee distributed a leaflet warning the workers against Zubatov's tactics.[34] Written by Portnoy, it analyzed Zubatov the secret police official, not Zubatov the ideologist. In a tone dripping with venom and scorn, Portnoy pointed to the disparity between Zubatov's attempt to pose as a friend of the workers and the state's record of mass arrests since 1898. No true revolutionary could "have dealings with such scum," he wrote. All who did so only hurt the workers' cause and lost the right to call themselves revolutionaries. Portnoy ended on an even harsher note: "No member of our [Bund] . . . has the right to have any connections with Zubatov or with other Tsarist spies. Any member who does not obey this injunction will be considered a traitor and a provocateur, and his name will be revealed in our [newspapers]."[35] The stand adopted was a tough one, and the punishment decreed the severest the Bund could officially hand out.

The Central Committee soon followed up its leaflet with an article in *Di Arbeter Shtime*.[36] The article took much the same line as the leaflet, but it hurled its anathema in a somewhat altered form. The Bund would "exclude from our ranks everyone who for any reason whatsoever has ties with Zubatov without the knowledge of the organization to which he belongs, declare such a person a provocateur, and print his name in our papers." Arrested comrades were instructed to deny all evidence and acquaintanceships under interrogation, even when the police confronted them with accurate information.[37]

In the same issue the Bund leaders reasserted their own political position. They admitted that it would take time to destroy the existing social and political order, and that consequently their present aim was to improve the condition of the working class to the point where it would be capable of further struggle. Their ultimate goal, however, could be achieved only through political power. It was this goal that terrified the state and led it to adopt any means to stop the movement. But would the state allow workers to meet and discuss what had to be done in a strike? Could it guarantee that it would allow the worker to fight freely to improve his economic condition? Economic struggle meant political struggle, the leaders declared, adding: "As part of the fighting proletariat in Russia we cannot reject political struggle, we cannot cease to be Social Democrats."[38]

It is clear from both statements that the Central Committee understood the threat to the organization; it is also clear, especially from the language of the article, that the committee foresaw difficulties in meeting that threat. Where the leaflet explicitly denounced anyone having a tie of any kind with the Zubatovites, the article took a somewhat more relaxed stand, tacitly recognizing that some communication might be unavoidable. Even in the leaflet the leaders had made a distinction between a member who dealt with the police out of ignorance and a member who did so out of conviction. The one was of course "no longer our brother," but the other, by implication, was salvageable.[39] The article demanded that the organization be informed of any connection between its members and the police. The problem of security was the uppermost concern and the chief reason for fighting Zubatov.

The issue of economic versus political activity promised to be even more difficult to solve. The Central Committee sought to link the two, maintaining the need for a political struggle and still admitting the necessity and benefit of the economic struggle. Zubatov's design was to sharpen the conflict over the two tactics by denying any connection between them. Given the historical development of the Bund, the solution had to come in organizational and tactical terms rather than ideological ones.

But dealing with those attracted to the Zubatov line was not as easy as the Central Committee had suggested. They operated at the local level, agitating among the workers in the economic organizations, which were purposely cut off from the center. In the skhodkas, and even more in the kases, the screening of prospective members was not rigorous. The desire to attract recruits and the relatively democratic procedures in use led to a different set of controls in these organizations from those governing the Bund's secret leadership units.

How could the Central Committee's rules be applied? The charge of provocation was to be leveled only against those plainly working with the police. Since the main reason for excluding a worker was security, what was to be done about those who agreed with Zubatov, not because they had been converted but because they had come to the same conclusions on their own? Clearly, simple opposition to the Bund's policies was not grounds enough for exclusion from a kase. Nor could all those who had been in Zubatov's clutches be expelled automatically. How were the local committees to determine who was and who was not in contact with the police? It was virtually impossible to know for certain whether a released prisoner was in communication with his former captor. The committees could only suppose that those who cried loudest for a legal labor movement were agents. But this was a dubious judgment at best, for arguments about tactics had long been the bill of fare in Minsk, and the Bund, which was still in the early stages of defining itself as a political party, did not find legal economic activity negative or harmful. Indeed, the use of legal channels to obtain a twelve-hour day was not so far in the past, nor the 1897 legislation on working hours so distant as to lose all meaning for the workers.[40] The simple fact is, it was no easy matter to draw a line between provocation and ideological or tactical conviction.

The reason Zubatov could raise a problem so serious as to cause internal disruption and structural change in the Bund was largely due to the peculiar stage of development the Bund had reached by 1900. Although it was the only effective mass organization among the Jewish workers at this time, its outlines were far from complete. Only at the top levels was it beginning to be called a party; no such concept had taken hold at the lower levels. Vladimir Medem, then working in Minsk, says, "I was a member of the Bund, that is, a Bundist (although we did not use that term at the time)," but adds he had no clear notion of what the Bund was as a Jewish organization.[41] If a young intellectual of some standing in the local organization had so doubtful an understanding of the Bund's demarcation lines, how much more confusing this point must have been to a worker who had heard the theme of class solidarity sounded over and over again. As late as December 1900, the official organ *Der Minsker Arbeter* (The Minsk Worker) was insisting that there ought not to be any hostility between Social Democratic workers and Zionist workers, since the Zionists also participated in the economic struggle.[42] The logic of class conflict still overrode ideological differences, weakening the definition of party membership.

The structure of the Jewish movement also contributed to the Bund's difficulties. Unprepared to alter its institutions at a stroke, the Bund groped for ways to counter Zubatov's move to drive a wedge between the economic organizations and the politically oriented ones. The Minsk Committee had to fight to retain its leadership over the economic organizations and to regain control where it was slipping even as it continued to push for a political struggle and to deemphasize the value of the economic struggle. The old conflicts in Minsk, however, had not prevented contact between workers of differing views before, and the desire to convince and keep open access to those who did not accept the Bund point of view made the use of blanket condemnation inadvisable. The Central Committee could lay down principles, but the local committee had to choose its weapons carefully.

Then, too, Zubatov's plans and strategy were not immediately clear. It did not occur to the Bundists, for instance, that the short sentences given the Minsk group were part of a carefully thought-out program.[43] In any case, it is doubtful that foreknowledge would have helped much. Zubatov was certainly not going to give his plan away by releasing only those he had recruited, thus making it possible to identify the new enemies immediately.

Despite all these difficulties of organization and inexperience, the Bund's counterattack against the first phases of the Zubatovite movement was partially effective. Mania Vilbushevich, one of the most outspoken of the Zubatovite leaders, admitted in her correspondence with Zubatov that the Central Committee's leaflet of August 1900 had made a strong impression on the workers.[44] Nevertheless, the economic organizations began to split soon after, gradually clarifying the Bund's internal situation but also creating a new opposition on the outside. Chemerisky tells of siding with the carpenters in a fight with the local committee in mid-1900 for worker democracy and for renewed emphasis on the economic struggle.[45] Loyal Bundists fought the advocates of independent economic activity in late 1900 and early 1901, but the battle was still stalemated when the Fourth Congress met. The fact that the local committee made as much headway as it did under difficult circumstances, that it was able to force the Zubatovite leaders out of the organization and still hope to gain the loyalty of the workers, attests to the determination of the Minsk Bundists.* The Zubatov offensive was a life and death matter for the Bundists, and they fought it as hard as they could.

Though Minsk was Zubatov's main concern at this time, he did not ignore developments elsewhere. He made what use he could of prisoners from other towns, including Belostok, Vitebsk, Grodno, and Kovno. However, all of these efforts seem minor in comparison with the Minsk attack, both in their intensity and in their success. Zubatov made a somewhat more serious attempt to win over the bristle workers. He spoke to bristle worker prisoners about legalizing their union; and though he denies it, some say he even offered them 20,000 rubles for that purpose and to support *Der Veker* (The Wakener), the union organ, as a legal journal.[46] Whatever the truth, Zubatov's aim to get

---

* Solomon Schwarz asserts that the Bund took a conciliatory attitude toward the Zubatovites (*The Russian Revolution of 1905*, pp. 285–300), a view that has brought strenuous objections from J. S. Hertz and others. On the contrary, says Hertz, the Bund uncompromisingly opposed Zubatov from the outset ("A farshvartster ponem"). I think Hertz is closer to the truth, though the word "uncompromising" is perhaps misleading, at least with respect to the situation in Minsk.

a foothold in the powerful organization failed. At the union's Tenth Congress, in October 1900, a resolution was passed declaring that all legal activity had to cease, and that those who participated in such work had as good as left the organization.[47]

Zubatov's campaign accelerated the growth of the already rapidly rising political consciousness of the Bundists. The Bund had to reexamine its organization in relation to the developing political-economic controversy. If the beginnings of the debate over Economism helped awaken the Bund to a threat to political Social Democracy, Zubatov's program forced it to look again at its own character as an economic and political tool. The Bundists had to be wary of the economic struggle at a time when economic activity was being turned to a clearly trade unionist direction to the detriment of the revolutionary ideology on which they had been nurtured. First of all political animals, the Bundists were prepared to respond to the attack with organizational changes, however drastic and complex these might be.

The Bund also had to contend with a new political reality in this period— the inroads Zionism was making in the Jewish working class. A minor issue in Russia before 1900, Zionism began to worry the Bundists deeply after the turn of the century. The Fourth Congress of the Bund, the first to discuss Zionism, recognized its growing importance and expressed its concern over the fact that "in the past year attempts by the Zionists to intensify propaganda among the workers were noted in some cities."[48]

The Bund continued to regard Zionism as an ideological enemy, a bourgeois concept and a tool with which the Jewish capitalists hoped to divert the workers from their true class interests to a national point of view. In a flood of articles and news items the Bundists denounced the rival ideology as an attempt to divide the Jewish workers from their brother proletarians, and the proposed Zionist state as a country of the bourgeoisie.[49] Denying there was unity among the Jews as the Zionists claimed, the Bundists pointed to the existence of class interests and to the suffering of Jewish workers at the hands of their Jewish employers. The bourgeoisie was attempting "to lead Jewish workers astray with national melodies" even as it fought them with the aid of the Russian government.[50] These charges were repeatedly and regularly leveled at the Zionists between 1897 and 1901.

About the turn of the century Zionism began to take on a new ideological and social coloration. A growing interest in socialism, the very point that had worried Mill before the Third Congress, served to sharpen the Zionist-Bundist conflict. In fact the linking of Zionism and socialism had begun at least as early as 1898. Nachman Syrkin, a major contributor to this ideological development, wrote on this theme from abroad in that year; Zhitlovsky had touched on the same subject in his article in *Der Yidisher Arbeter*.[51] In Russia, however, this transformation came about virtually spontaneously, developing independently in several areas. According to Ber Borokhov, another important organizer and formulator of labor Zionism in Russia, there were groups moving in this direction in 1900 and 1901 in a number of cities, including Odessa, Warsaw, and Vilna.[52] They were then only in their first stages of organization.

One impetus for the growth of a labor conscious Zionism was the Zionist workers' uneasiness in belonging to the same organizations as their social and economic superiors. Moishe Gutman, a Zionist worker in Vilna, describes his discomfort when he sat at a table with his employers. Moreover, his high expectations for the first Zionist congress had been dashed. The Zionists at Basel had "completely ignored 'present work,' that is the improvement of conditions here in the Diaspora. If radical salvation was at hand, it was hardly worthwhile devoting oneself to patching up the Diaspora garment!"[53] Jewish workers attracted by Zionism were certainly influenced by the Bund, says Gutman, but "they did not want to go to the Bund because of its half-assimilationist character."[54] Social distinctions, daily needs, and the example of the Bund—all combined to divide the Zionists. Out of that fragmentation a new mix grew, offering Jewish workers other answers to their problems. However insignificant labor Zionism may have been at first, it provided the Jewish worker an alternative to the Bund where none had existed before.

The Bundists had frequent contacts with the Zionists at the end of the 1890's. As yet not competing for control of masses of workers, the two forces had at least raised the level of discussion by this time. The debate went on everywhere: between brothers, in university circles, in coffee houses.[55] It was a particularly frustrating situation for the Bundists, one in which they often had to refuse their opponents' invitations to debate or at least to limit their arguments out of fear of the police.[56]

The Bundists' concern with the Zionists took up more and more of their time, and by the beginning of 1901 Zionism was occupying a major place in Bundist literature. The Fourth Zionist Congress, held in August 1900 in London, rated an article in Di Arbeter Shtime. Challenging the Zionists' claim to represent all Jews, it raised the all-important question for the Bund: what were the Zionists prepared to do for the Jewish worker? Though this issue had been raised by some of the delegates, the article declared, the bourgeois congress feared the word class, had shown itself to be indifferent to the economic condition of the proletariat, and had been unable to deal with the question.[57] The Bundists remained satisfied that they were still safe on ideological grounds, despite the increased momentum of the Zionist movement.

Meanwhile events in Minsk took an extraordinary turn. The Minsk case had always been a special one for the Bund. It was a city that had harbored many movements since the 1880's; revolutionary socialism had still been in its embryonic stages when a circle had been organized there; similarly, one of the earliest Zionist worker groups in Russia was formed in Minsk.[58] It was there too that a strongly national worker opposition had developed in the mid-1890's under the leadership of Abraham Liesin, the young intellectual who had taken the Jewish Social Democrats to task for their lack of a national program.[59] The Zionist workers of Minsk opposed the Bund on both national and economic grounds. They kept their eyes riveted on economic improvement and ignored political matters. When they confronted the Bund at this key moment in the debate over economic and political tactics, a clash was inevitable.

The Minsk Committee recognized the new threat by the end of 1900. As in the case of Zubatov, the Bund faced the problem of drawing a line between its adherents and other workers. It was not ready to abandon workers wholesale simply because of their ideological views, particularly since the Zionists were still weak. Accordingly it took the position that so long as workers of Zionist bent participated in the economic struggle with Social Democratic workers, there could be no hostility between the two groups. The keynote was persuasion: "We must convince them of the correctness of our aspirations," the committee advised, "but in no way come out against them with hostility or hinder them by force in their activity."[60] Nevertheless, the committee still made clear that it disapproved of Zionism and would continue to fight it with all honorable means.

Mania Vilbushevich and other Zubatov supporters in Minsk saw the potential value of the Zionists in the fight against the Bund. In a letter to Zubatov she predicted great success for his economic program because of the Zionists. Zionism could be a useful instrument, she pointed out: its advocates abstained from political activity; moreover, it was clearly beginning to appeal to many workers, as witness the Bund's growing resistance to it.[61] Vilbushevich served as Zubatov's key link to the Zionists and was perfectly willing to play the role of police spy, a fact that did not go unnoticed for long.[62] The police helped strikers in Minsk frequently from late 1900 on, and the Bundists' suspicions and abhorrence of the connection grew proportionately.[63] The greater and more obvious the aid given by the police to non-Bundists, the further apart the Bundists and the Zionists moved and the more certain a complete rupture became. The Fourth Congress of the Bund finally drew the line, resolving that "under no circumstances" were Zionists to be allowed "into either our economic or our political organizations."[64]

The definition of Bund membership thus proceeded one more step. Not just those having ties with Zubatov, but all Zionists were now excluded from the organization. It was more than a question of security now; it was a question of political ideology as well. Minsk was the only area in the Empire where Zionism became a significant issue for the Bund before the Fourth Congress; what ideological argument there was was largely carried on abroad. But the threat was there, and it was taken seriously. The Bund's response was to demarcate its membership—not just in Minsk but everywhere.

The Bund experience abroad paralleled developments in Russia to some extent. There, as in Russia, the Bund grew both in numbers and in the geographical extent of its activities, reaching even into the United States. The Foreign Committee continued actively pursuing every avenue of possible aid for its varied activities in this period—with notable success. Student and émigré groups dedicated to the Bund's support began to dot the Western European landscape. Also as in Russia conflicts, splits, and new ideological turnings led to the quest for self-definition.

The Bund's diligent search for support eventually brought it into conflict with other revolutionary organizations abroad, especially the Liberation of Labor Group. The growing controversy among Russian Social Democrats over what type of literature to use, popular or theoretical, and over the new Economist line led to another controversy, this one over financing. The Liberation of Labor Group had been receiving substantial funds from the United States for a number of years. But when the conflict developed in Europe, the sympathizers of the Russian Social Democrats in New York split. The Bund probably did not receive any money from the United States for its own use before 1900. In 1899 Abraham Kisin, a Bund pioneer who had worked in Mogilev and Gomel, solicited support in the United States for the Union Abroad. Convinced of the value of popular literature, he was aware of the Bund's role in transporting such materials to Russia. Kisin returned to Europe in late 1900. His successor in the United States, Isaiah Golovchiner, did even more to popularize the Bund. Golovchiner initiated *landsmanshaften*, immigrant mutual-aid organizations, which were often sympathetic to the Bund, and established ties that would last beyond the Bund's final hour.[65]

The Liberation of Labor Group, already unhappy with the Bund because of its stand with the Union Abroad against the Group, began to feel the direct pinch of the Bund's efforts in the United States. The old guard fumed over the new competition. In February 1901 Pavel Akselrod complained to Lenin about the small amounts coming in from Dr. V. S. Ingerman, a leading and long-time supporter in the United States, who had informed the Plekhanovites of the growing conflict there over the Union Abroad and its ally, the Bund.[66] By July of that year Akselrod was complaining even more bitterly. "Hold your pockets when you have business with [the Bund]," he wrote, "or something will be stolen."[67] The Bund's drive for support gained it new enemies but also new friends and a reliable base of material resources of inestimable value to the organization.

Certain of the Bund's decisions give further evidence of its effort to sharpen its organizational outlines and establish its own position within the Russian Social Democratic movement. The Third Congress not only officially recognized its new arm, the Foreign Committee, but also instructed it to send delegates to the forthcoming Congress of the Socialist International in Paris.[68] In the words of the Foreign Committee, the Bund now felt that it had become "a force that played no minor role in the Russian revolutionary movement. We have the right to be represented by a large delegation, which would reflect our strength, our work, and our real significance. . . . We must not fall behind the others; we must make use of our right and fulfill our duty."[69] Again it was Mill who was pushing the Bund to recognize its real role and to take what he considered its rightful place as the leader of the Jewish workers' movement.

The presence of 11 Bund delegates at the Paris Congress, which met in September 1900, contrasted sharply with the previous meeting of that august body: in 1896 the Plekhanovites had been mandated to represent the Social Democratic organizations of the Pale. The Bund had the largest single contingent in the Russian delegation and twice as many votes (12) as the Liberation of Labor Group.[70] The Bundists worked hard to gather materials for a report, which they considered essential "since at earlier congresses there were no reports concerning the Jewish workers' movement, and International Social Democracy is, in any case, little acquainted with the conditions and struggle of the Jewish proletariat."[71] Recalling Plekhanov's words of 1896 declaring that the Jewish workers were "the avant garde of the workers' army of Russia," the report noted that the events of the past four years justified that characterization. "Along with the Polish proletariat," it declared, "the Jewish proletariat is the most advanced in Russia in both class and political consciousness."[72] The Bundists' self-confidence and pride in their achievements differed markedly from the Jewish Social Democrats' hesitations and deference to the Russian Social Democrats in the pioneer period.

The Liberation of Labor Group was as irritated by the Bund's representation at the International Congress as it was by the Bund's success at fund raising. Akselrod, writing to Lenin in November 1900, decried "the ludicrous and pathetic spectacle our delegation of 30 presented, four-fifths of which consisted of Bundists abroad, among them simple Vilna Philistines there only in flight from compulsory military service."[73] He exaggerates, of course; it was the Bundists *and* the Union Abroad that formed a majority of the Russian delegation. Together they voted in a compromise on the hot issue of whether a socialist should accept a ministerial post in a bourgeois government over the opposition of the Plekhanovites and their sympathizers.* The Bund was proving a running sore to the old guard.

The conflict between the Liberation of Labor Group and the Union Abroad

---

* The Bundists' inexperience in such meetings caused them some embarrassment. They lost an opportunity to include the treatment of the Jews in Russia in a resolution of sympathy to the Poles, Finns, and Boers. This led the Zionists to attack the Bund's "treason" to the Jewish people. Mill, *Pionern*, 2: 90–92.

became more and more bitter as the century drew to a close. In November 1898 the Group gave up its editorial functions in the common newspaper *Rabotnik*, which ceased publication. It was soon replaced by *Rabochee delo*, edited by three Union members, B. N. Krichevsky, V. P. Ivan'shin, and P. F. Teplov. Increasingly dismayed at what they considered the growing Economism of the Union, the Plekhanovites finally attacked it openly in March 1900.[74]

The Bund remained silent in the conflict despite its close ties with the Union, and it was not included in the Group's attack. Privately, however, many Group members felt the Bund was the moving power behind the Union. In September 1899 Zasulich informed Lev Deutsch that the Group had parted company with the Union, whose main contingent were "the patriots of the Minsk-Vilna fatherland," an obvious reference to the Bund.[75] The Bund's technical strength, as evidenced in its fund-raising success in New York and its network for transporting illegal literature (which "held the frontier"), convinced some of the Bund's predominant role in the Union.[76]

If the Bundists did not openly side with the Union, they did react publicly to the Group's actions. Plekhanov's *Vademecum*, the vehicle for the attack on the Union's ideological "deviation," drew the fire of *Der Yidisher Arbeter*, which criticized Plekhanov for airing what was in effect an inner organizational matter. Further, said the paper, the old Marxist had used uncomradely methods; he had published the private letters of Kopelson, a Bundist, and was "throwing mud" at him. It was Plekhanov who was guilty of breaking discipline and introducing anarchy into the party.[77] This article was run not as a political statement, but as a news note with commentary.

The reference to broken discipline and party anarchy stemmed from an incident that had been reported in the New York newspapers. Plekhanov and Akselrod had indeed showed themselves to be a good deal less than comradely, according to the news item in *Der Yidisher Arbeter*. It seems that Dr. Ingerman had made public a letter he received from the two Social Democrats asking for aid against "the Minsk and Vilna *yidlekh*,"* who were bringing disputes into the Union. Not so, retorted *Der Yidisher Arbeter*; "the Minsk and Vilna yidlekh" were "the first in the Union to stand for peace, for unity, for discipline and centralization."[78]

The Bundists, conscious of their own experience and tradition as a single mass organization, found no matter of principle involved in the conflict, a point of view the Plekhanovites did not accept. The Group believed that its principles were being eroded and saw the conflict with the Union as an ideological one. But for the Bund, the economic struggle was part of the Jewish movement and as such an organizational and tactical problem, except where Zubatov came into the picture. Since, openly at any rate, the conflict between

* A diminutive of the Yiddish for Jews, which is sometimes used pejoratively.

the Plekhanovites and the Union Abroad was essentially an ideological dispute, the Bund's attitude remained a side issue. The Group's jibes and sneers at the Bundists were private. It found the Bund irksome but did not make it an open target. Kopelson was drawn into the argument as a member of the Union Abroad, not as a member of the Bund.

In the midst of this internecine warfare, a new factor appeared on the scene. A number of experienced and articulate Russian Social Democrats returned from Siberian exile ready to try out their own ideas of revolutionary action and organization. The chief figures among them, Lenin, Martov, and A. N. Potresov, had watched the developments in Social Democracy from afar and had given serious thought to their own roles in achieving its aims. Dismayed at the disintegration of the RSDWP, they had strongly attacked Economist tendencies in the famous *Protest* of 1899 while still in exile. Before their exile ended, they had decided to join forces as a "Triumvirate" to alter the deplorable state in the party.[79]

Lenin began detailing the results of his thoughts in 1899. In a series of articles, unpublished at the time, he outlined the requirements for a revolutionary uplifting of Social Democracy in Russia. Reaffirming the traditional Marxian tenet of a conquest of political power by the proletariat followed by the building of a socialist society, he put first priority on the attainment of political freedom.[80] To accomplish that goal, what was needed was a disciplined revolutionary machine, along with a central party organ to make the workers in the movement conscious of the importance of their work in the party.[81] Hence, the immediate task of the Russian Social Democrats was to unite. They needed organization to carry out their duties and a discipline based on responsibility.[82]

Upon their return the three leaders dedicated themselves to this task. In a draft declaration written in the spring of 1900, Lenin noted that their efforts had the blessing of several Social Democratic organizations and groups, including the Liberation of Labor Group, as well as that of many individuals of no small importance in the movement.[83] The first need, as they saw it, was creating a body of literature consistent in principle and capable of uniting revolutionary Social Democracy. Only after an organ had been established and the necessary machinery created to arrange contacts, supply information about the movement, and distribute the journal and other material should party activity be resumed. "Before we can unite," Lenin wrote in a declaration for the editorial board, "and in order that we may unite, we must first draw firm and definite lines of demarcation."[84] The newcomers thus showed themselves to be publicists like their ideological fathers, the Plekhanovites. The important difference was their determined and energetic attention to organizational matters.

Until September 1900, when Lenin made the editorial board's declaration, the newcomers busied themselves with meetings to gain support for their plans. These were months of fact-finding and probing. Lenin cautiously suggested that the fight over Economism might not mean a definitive break and invited Social Democrats of all views to engage in open discussion ("comradely polemics") of their differences in the forthcoming organ, *Iskra* (The Spark).[85]

Meanwhile, the Triumvirate displayed a keen sense of practical maneuver. Their arrival in European Russia coincided with an attempt by the Ekaterinoslav Social Democrats, the Union Abroad, and the Bund to reestablish the RSDWP's Central Committee.[86] The returnees rejected this move as premature, but they had no wish to alienate the powerful organizations involved, and hoping to influence them, they agreed to a meeting to discuss the matter. The Triumvirate was even offered the editorship of a new party organ. Lenin and his colleagues saw the possibility of gaining a ready-made organization. Moreover, even if they failed to dissuade the others from their course, they might be persuaded to postpone their activity, giving the Triumvirate time to create their own organ and carry through their own plans, thus retaining the initiative.[87] At whatever cost, the Triumvirate was bent on forestalling any independent move toward rebuilding the party without their strong presence. As it happened, the planned meeting did not take place.

While still in Siberia, the exiles had agreed to work with the Liberation of Labor Group. In the spring of 1900, they and the Plekhanovites, who had broken completely with the Union Abroad by this time, worked out plans to publish two organs, a newspaper for workers (the future *Iskra*) and a high level political journal, *Zaria* (Dawn).[88]

In some respects the Triumvirate took as independent a stand with the Plekhanovites as they did with the Social Democrats in Russia. Despite an ideological affinity, the returnees' organizational bias, along with differences of temperament and experience, led to arguments and strained feelings.[89] Lenin became convinced that if the new paper was to retain its independence, it must be located away from the direct weight of Plekhanov's hand.[90]

Contacts between the Bund and the Triumvirate were limited. Martov, of course, was well known to the Bundists. He and the members of the first Central Committee of the Bund were especially close; it was to him that they had turned with an appeal for literature to publish during the trying months of 1898, when the Bund was struggling to maintain the vestiges of the RSDWP.[91] The Bund's independence and silence in the ideological debate and the Triumvirate's own caution allowed relations between the two to remain correct. When Plekhanov launched a tirade against the Bund at a conference in August 1900, first characterizing it as "an organization of exploiters who exploit the Russians and not a Social Democratic organization," then asking the conference to resolve that one of the aims of the new organization should be "to throw this Bund out of the party," Lenin and others objected to such "indecent speeches." Although Plekhanov did not change his stand, the conference adopted no resolution on the Bund.[92] The behavior of the returnees was quite proper and certainly not inimical to the Bund at this stage.

When the first issue of *Iskra* appeared in December 1900, good relations were still evident. Martov commended the Jewish movement, which had withstood Zubatov's attack in 1898 and had since "taken an open political character." Predicting that the Zubatovite corruption would not affect the core of the Jewish movement, he declared that the Bund had already passed the point where the police could destroy it with ordinary measures of force and espionage, which were still effective against Russian workers.[93] Plekhanov objected to such "glorification of the Bund" and wanted the article replaced rather than print "advertisements" for the Bund.[94] He was overruled.

In Russia relations between the Iskraites and the Bundists also remained correct, if somewhat touchier in this period. While Lenin was abroad arranging the publication of the new organ, Martov was in Poltava attempting to establish the technical machinery to distribute it. By late 1900 he and his followers were working hard to attract both individuals and local organizations to their cause.[95] Their chief efforts lay in the south and in Moscow and St. Petersburg. In the hope of making use of the Bund's distribution system, S. O. Tsederbaum, Martov's brother, went to Vilna in 1901 to discuss the matter. Martov had told him that the Bund had promised its cooperation. But the trip was a disappointment. Tsederbaum felt that only the top Bundists in Vilna were seeing *Iskra*, and despite affirmations of support, he saw no particular sympathy for the publication there.[96] To him, relations seemed less than satisfactory.

From the Bund's point of view, the *Iskra* position was confusing. The Central Committee received a letter from Martov criticizing the Bund's recent work: the concentration on the economic struggle and neglect of political and socialist agitation, the propensity to work in its own circle instead of working for the all-Russian masses. Martov also criticized the Bund's *kustarnichestvo*, the petty narrow attitude that allowed the publication of local newspapers.[97] The Martov and Tsederbaum opinions were only private to be sure, but Portnoy, the Bund's chief organizer in Russia, was alarmed and remained cautious in his approach to the new *Iskra* Group. "They [the Bund leaders] feared the position it would take concerning the Bund," notes Central Committee member Rosenthal.[98] Kosovsky, who was abroad at this time, confirms the uneasiness of the Bundists. However agreeable the political orientation of the new organ, the Iskraites' agenda seemed to him to have dictatorial possibilities.[99] Kosovsky's view may contain a dose of *ex post facto* experience, though the correct, rather than friendly, relations between the Bund and the Iskraites as compared with the Triumvirate's closeness to Plekhanov perhaps gave him pause. Matters stood at this point when the Fourth Congress of the Bund took place.

The national question received quiet direction in the period between the Third and Fourth congresses. The Bundists sought answers to the future of the community they wished to influence and began to search for a suitable program. Several articles printed in 1899 contained possible solutions. One of these was the Zhitlovsky article, with its commitment to Yiddish as the instrument of Jewish culture.[100] Another was an article on the Brünn Congress of the Austrian Social Democratic Party, where the national question had received a full dress review.[101] Those discussions were far too little known, according to Mill, to influence the debate at the Third Congress. By the Fourth Congress, however, the proceedings at Brünn, which resulted in resolutions or debates on the desirability of the Austrian Empire becoming a democratic union of nations, on the granting of equal status to languages, and on the recognition of an independent national existence regardless of territory, were familiar enough to the delegates to permit meaningful discussion.[102] Though the Austrians had not concerned themselves with the position of the Jews in their talks, Mill and his fellow Bundists drew inferences from these debates. The weakening of the territorial principle of identification among the Austrians and the emphasis on culture became important keys in defining a solution to the national question; the equality of national cultures promised an end to the eternal guesthood problem of the Jews.

Despite the Third Congress's decision to open the issue of national rights to discussion in the Bund's organs, articles on the subject did not begin appearing until about the time of the Fourth Congress.[103] Even then, they were not considered important.[104] None of the old leaders, either in Russia or abroad, said anything publicly. Yet when the Fourth Congress convened and the national question came before the assembly, the Bund was ready to accept the idea of national autonomy in principle.

Thus, positive principles with enormous implications for the future of the Jews were quietly adopted during this transition period. The pioneers, with their strong sense of security and cohesion and their habit of working out matters of internal concern among themselves, were not prepared to engage in public discussion on such an important issue. Indeed, the Third Congress, with its debate on the national question, was the first exception. At the same time, many of these same pioneers had no difficulty in moving the distance from equal civil rights to national autonomy between the Third Congress and the Fourth without further open discussion. Although Mill may exaggerate the ease with which the change took place, his remarks in this respect carry some weight: "One could feel and see that the new tendencies had already won, and that the Bund was for a change in its program in the area of the

Jewish question. What point was there in losing words, in convincing the Bundists of something of which they were already convinced."[105] The condition of the Jews in Russia, their aspirations, and their relations with their proletarian neighbors were more convincing, Mill concludes, than any discussion.[106] Kremer himself apparently did not attend the Fourth Congress, assuming that its resolutions would merely reflect the previous discussion between the Central Committee and the local committees.[107]

At all events the leaders were clearly interested in the national aspects of Jewish life, even if they did not choose to publish on the subject. Kremer, writing to Leon Bernstein from Geneva in 1900, declared that "it would be very important to write about Yiddish schools." Ten years earlier he probably could not have even conceived of his taking such a cultural position;[108] Yiddish schools meant nothing less than accepting the Jews as a nationality with a future. Rosenthal, Portnoy, and sometimes Zeldov, though not always in agreement, were quite aware of the changing mood on the national question and accepted that the Bund had to take a stand on the issue in its program.[109]

More than the veterans, a number of newcomers, an incipient second generation of Bundists, were concerned with this issue. Among them was Bentsion Hofman, by his own admission not a full Bundist until 1901, who wrote one of the few early articles on the question in *Der Yidisher Arbeter*.[110] Another was Leon Goldman's younger brother Mikhel (Mark Liber), who took to the debate platform in Berne in 1900 on the subject.[111] At the Fourth Congress a year later he was one of the strongest advocates of national rights.

The Jewish students abroad, especially those in the so-called Berne Group, reflected the growing importance of Yiddish and Jewish considerations. After the fall of 1900 Mill had increasing help on *Der Yidisher Arbeter* from the Berne students. Attracted to the Bund and enlisted to write and translate articles in Yiddish, they gradually awakened to the problems of Jewish life and the Jewish movement.[112] It was the very growth of the Bund's activities in Russia that made numbers of Russian Jewish students abroad conscious of the problems of their community back home.

The impulse to identify the Bund as a national party was stronger abroad than in Russia. The emphasis on ideological identification and debate among the émigrés forced lines to be drawn sharply as political positions were formulated, leaving fewer political no-man's-lands. The Bund's Foreign Committee continued to differ substantially from other Russian revolutionary groups abroad in making aid to the parent organization its main concern. No other group could perform the logistical tasks the Bund performed for itself. Its keen sense of self-sufficiency contributed to an isolation that the heightening ideological conflict abroad only sharpened. Writing to Leon Bernstein in Paris in November 1900, Kremer remarked: "Here [abroad] exist the most extreme nationalists and Zionists on the one hand and russified Jews

on the other, neither wishing to hear about the Bund and even hostile to it."
Kremer appealed to Bernstein for help, chiding him for devoting too much
time to the affairs of the Union Abroad and not enough to the Bund.[113]

Without intention, for the Bund cooperated with Social Democratic groups
all through these years, the distinction between the Bund and other organizations grew. As Kursky puts it: "In the Party [the RSDWP] there was a bitter
conflict between tendencies, between groups pretending to leadership. It was
in this atmosphere that the isolation of the Bund was created.... We actually
became a separate party. We became accustomed to this, and a we-they psychology developed."[114] The practical isolation of the Bund's cultural work and
the separation of the nationalities in Russia were being matched by the sharpening ideological and organizational isolation abroad. It was a process that
affected the entire revolutionary community in Russia, not just the Bund.

Faced with the fact of its virtual independence and separate tasks, the Foreign Committee played an important role in rousing the home organization
to the need of further definition. But conflict in Russia also pressed the Bund
in this direction. The Bund was becoming at once increasingly political, increasingly complex, and increasingly self-sufficient. As it began defining itself
more precisely in ideological and organizational terms, it moved ever closer
to becoming a full-fledged Jewish workers' party.

12. The Politicization of the Bund

The economic woes of the Jews weighed ever more heavily on the Bund in the early years of the twentieth century. Small shops continued to suffer as more and more factories mechanized, and some employers simply could not improve working conditions. In such circumstances, the economic struggle was bound to be ineffective. The problem of how to improve the workers' economic lot without jeopardizing their jobs plagued the Bund, as indeed it had since the Second Congress.

The Fourth Congress, like the Second, found that in some trades "economic improvement . . . can go no further under present conditions of production." It sought to reassess the value of an economic struggle that required great energy and effort yet produced negligible results. It was decided that strikes should be curtailed where gains were no longer possible and fostered in industries still unaffected by the movement. Strikes were to be encouraged and supported at all costs where previous gains were threatened.[1]

In terms of tactical principle, the changes the congress made were mild. The strike as such was not condemned. "No one doubted," the delegates declared in their report, "the enormous significance of strikes for the improvement of the economic condition of the workers and for their class consciousness and education."[2] Nevertheless, in differentiating between useful and non-useful strikes, the congress removed the aura of universal value the strike had had since the mid-1890's, and still had for some workers. The congress's resolution went even further, suggesting that in some instances strikes had already achieved their purpose: arousing class and political consciousness and drawing workers into the movement.[3]

The strike movement followed this new direction in the months following the congress. The economic struggle grew in virgin areas. Local workers supported by cadres from nearby large centers prepared the assault in small towns. The Jewish workers of the Baltic region, though outside the Pale and under the threat of expulsion, began to stir. In areas where the movement was well established, defensive strikes became frequent.[4]

Even with all the difficulties posed by the adverse economic situation and the breaking of new ground, the strike movement continued to register victories. The Bund's report to the Second Congress of the RSDWP (held in July-August 1903) showed solid achievements in the two-year period between the Fourth and Fifth Bund congresses. By June 1903, 172 strikes had been recorded, 95 with known results. Of these, 80 were reported as victories, 12 as failures, and the remaining three as partial successes.[5] The success rate was high—almost 90 per cent. On the other side was the sobering fact that fewer than 7,000 workers were involved: 4,745 in the 80 successful strikes and 1,760 in the 12 unsuccessful ones.[6] The picture thus presented was fairly somber considering that the Bund, which had numbered only around 5,600 in 1900, had some 30,000 members in mid-1903.[7] The Bund had not been wholly successful in involving workers in strikes.

The limits placed on the economic struggle had their effect on the Bund's organization. The Second Congress had concerned itself, however indecisively, with the limitations of the kase; and the Third Congress had pursued the matter, debating the value of an institution that on the one hand drew members together, and on the other set them apart from non-kase workers. But in the end the Third Congress was no more prepared to take a stand than the Second. It could not "adopt a general agreement on fight kases for all trades and cities."[8]

The Fourth Congress did not consider the problem of strike kases specifically. With the economic struggle promising to be of reduced effectiveness, it sought to turn the movement to political action.[9] In practice the attempt to separate the economic and political struggles was not a radical step. The economic struggle was still considered a legitimate tactic to attract the masses to the movement. What the congress did in effect is dissociate itself from a strict interpretation of the revolutionary path advanced in *On Agitation* (which in any case had not been a rigorous or universal guide to development in the Bund). Its resolution on the political struggle asserted that "there is no necessity to lead political agitation from the very beginning exclusively on the basis of economic agitation."[10]

The congress made further changes to this end, not only by setting political criteria for Bund membership but also by resolving "to devote attention to the greater development of political kases."[11] Tactical emphases were changed to accommodate political action: demonstrations were designated as the premier manifestation of political action; agitation, both oral and written, was to center on political themes; and local organs were to treat events politically when suitable. Finally, all members were to study governmental and social institutions and their shortcomings.[12]

Another development in this period quickened the Bund's transformation to a political party. This was the creation of the Jewish Independent Workers'

Party (Yidisher Unabhengike Arbeter Partai, YUAP or Independents) in Minsk in July 1901. The new organization offered a rallying point for various elements inimical to the Bund.

It was clear to the Minsk Committee that the movement was being torn apart by the arguments over tactics and the issue of democratic organization. In June, on the eve of the final split, *Der Minsker Arbeter* warned the workers of the dangers facing them and tried to expose the state's hand in the disintegration of the economic movement in the city. It concentrated in particular on the actions of the chief of the Minsk police, Colonel Vasiliev, who, following a meeting with Zubatov in April 1900, began assuming the role of friend to the Jewish worker. Already he had allowed clerks to meet openly and to form a committee; more, he had addressed one of their meetings, depicting himself as their protector. All this, the Bund organ insisted, only proved the state so feared the revolutionary movement that it was ready to turn to soft tactics to destroy it. But the state's image of protector was not credible; the regime as constituted would always be the enemy of the workers and would, if allowed, destroy everything that the workers had fought for.[13] For the Bund, the YUAP suggested a close tie between the government and those advocating exclusive emphasis on economic struggle.

The YUAP leaders were Zubatov's ex-prisoners and others who had reached the same conclusions on their own: Vilbushevich, Chemerisky, Volin, and Joseph Goldberg, a labor Zionist. It was Goldberg who wrote the party's statement of principles, which was distributed as a hectographed handbill.

The Independents took the position that the Minsk movement had serious shortcomings. No theory was so indisputably correct, said their statement, that it could lead the workers to goals they did not understand. What the Jewish masses wanted was bread and knowledge; it was criminal to risk these goals in the pursuit of political goals that were alien to the masses. The Jewish worker had a right to defend his economic and cultural interests without reference to political issues, and that would be the sole end of the new organization.[14]

From these assumptions and the further assumption that the Bund was a political party, the Independents concluded that the Bund's economic organizations were an anomaly. The Bund used economic action for one purpose, to radicalize the masses, and thus ignored many activities that could benefit the workers. It closed its doors to workers who did not hold the same views and scared off others because of its reputation as a political organization.[15] Admittedly the Bund had played an important role in developing a spirit of dissatisfaction among the masses. Nevertheless, its ideological grip stifled the workers, and its political grip made economic and cultural activity impossible, the Independents argued.[16]

The YUAP had other goals. It would devote itself to raising the material and cultural level of the Jewish proletariat, and to this end would create unions and clubs, legal where possible, illegal where necessary. It would concern itself with political questions only insofar as they touched the workers' daily interests. It would draw workers together regardless of their political opinions and would govern itself democratically.[17]

Both the Minsk Committee and the Central Committee responded to the new challenge. The Central Committee insisted that the YUAP's program and the tactics of the Zubatov-Vasiliev forces were virtually syonymous, though it did not go so far as to claim the YUAP had direct connections with the secret police. Besides, said the Central Committee, there was a serious omission in the YUAP program: the Independents did not criticize the capitalist order that gave rise to the misery of the working class. Further, the committee warned, police permission for cultural work ultimately meant police control of culture. What kind of party was this, it asked, that tried to answer problems hand in hand with the Autocracy?[18]

The Minsk Committee in turn questioned the goal of achieving economic gains without political aims. Every step in the economic struggle had been treated as a political crime. Were the Independents tying themselves to the government, whose interests were the opposite of their own? Did the workers need Vasiliev? As for the complaint that the Bund wanted all its members to be Social Democrats, did the YUAP expect the Bund to make its members Zionists? What would the YUAP do if persons of various political convictions joined its ranks and tried to win it over to their own views? The YUAP's program simply would not do, the Bundists concluded. Only the overthrow of the despotic state could bring true liberation. Then the socialist society, the highest ideal, would be realized.[19]

For those who disagreed fundamentally with political revolution or socialism, the Bund's arguments were meaningless.[20] The YUAP gained a substantial following, and may even have had more members in Minsk than the Bund at times.[21] But if the Bund's opponents could not be shaken by ideological arguments, they were still open to attack on practical grounds. The YUAP's success depended on its ability to produce results. Would the government really countenance legal unions and strikes? If it did not, would not the inevitable state reprisal of economic protest reveal the validity of the Bund's contention? Zubatov's policies were matters of complicated negotiation and uneven application, and the Independents could not influence them. In fact, the YUAP was basically "dependent" on those policies. If Zubatov failed, the YUAP would be in a difficult and largely untenable position.

The Independents were also open to attack on moral grounds. Why was Zubatov so interested in the Jewish workers in particular? Working with the police against fellow workers was often a cause of anguish, even for those who were bitterly opposed to the Bund, and many drew the line at serving as provocateurs or informants.* The Independents' willingness to indulge in such practices as baiting the Bund and provocation laid them open to attack. The Bundists hammered at this point in their agitation among the workers, making the most of their limited weapons.[22]

The government never legally sanctioned the YUAP. The Minsk police gave the party permission to hold meetings and to organize discussion clubs. Guest speakers were also allowed though they were forbidden to mention politics. These lectures were well attended in 1901 and 1902.[23] Colonel Vasiliev himself joined these gatherings from time to time; and the obvious police support occasioned a number of strikes. Employers, aware of Vasiliev's changed attitude, sometimes found themselves forced to make concessions they might not have considered otherwise.[24]

The conflict in Minsk sharpened with the passage of time. By October 1901 one of Zubatov's more optimistic correspondents was noting the Bund's efforts to spy on the Independents and discover what they were up to. Another reported some of the Bundists' disruptive techniques: destroying tickets for YUAP celebrations, spreading rumors that the ticket takers were police agents, and calling meetings to coincide with those of the YUAP. The Bundists had even attempted to attack him physically, he added.[25]

Relations between the two organizations reached their nadir in 1902. Arrests of Bundists brought the issue of provocation to the fore. Independents were accused of having loose tongues about members of the Bund, and the Bundists were warned to maintain better security.[26] In March the Minsk Committee issued a handbill condemning all relations with the Independents. Noting the "atmosphere of political depravity" created by the YUAP, the Bund asked "all respectable people" to break with them. For Bund members the instructions in the handbill were "unconditionally binding"; infringement would mean "immediate exclusion from the ranks of our organization."[27] Other revolutionary groups in Minsk officially endorsed the Bund's stand.

Satisfied with their success in Minsk, the YUAP leaders decided to try to establish a branch in Vilna. Organizing the workers there would improve the chances of official recognition, they felt; they would be in a position to present the government with a *fait accompli*. The state understood their need for legitimacy, and a few organized workers in a large center like Vilna would be more impressive than many workers organized in smaller towns.[28]

The YUAP initiative in Vilna came in the summer of 1902, just after a series of harrowing events that culminated in an attempt on the governor's life and the execution of the would-be assassin, Hirsh Lekert. The Bund and indeed the entire city were in an uproar. The YUAP, seeing a chance to capi-

---

* Chemerisky, for one, felt that he was using the state for his own purposes. After the YUAP collapsed, the remorseful party leader was accepted back into the Bund fold (Chemerisky et al., pp. 318, 322; Blekhman, pp. 179–85).

talize on these developments, presented itself as a refuge for workers willing to organize but unwilling to take on the government. Fighting the state, the newcomers held, could have only one result, failure; their path, the economic struggle, would show the government that the time had come when workers' demands had to be heeded.[29] Thus it was not only the YUAP's previous success, but also its assessment of a demoralized state of affairs in the revolutionary movement that prompted it to move into Vilna.

But the YUAP found the workers of Vilna considerably more resistant to its program than the workers of Minsk. Although the same grievances divided intellectuals and workers in Vilna, these had been largely offset by the Bund's success over the years, leaving the ground less fertile for the YUAP's growth. (For that matter, the Zionists, too, were making less headway in Vilna than in Minsk at this time.)

The Minsk experience was not lost on the Vilna Bundists, who sprang to the attack immediately. In the anguish of the moment the Bundists invoked appeals based on local events at every turn. In one handbill they accused the YUAP of timing its intrusion to take advantage of the situation while the ground was still soaked with blood. The Independents were not to be treated as ideological enemies, as were the Zionists and the Liberals; their relations with the police stripped them of all right to be regarded as honorable opponents. The keynote of the handbill was boycott, and the charge of "political prostitution" the justification for that action.[30]

The Independents continued to work successfully in Minsk throughout 1902 and in the first months of 1903, but they found the going increasingly rough in Vilna. In a report to Zubatov on developments there, Vilbushevich observed that thanks to the state's repressiveness, which had heightened the revolutionary mood, YUAP followers were attacking the organization at its meetings.[31] Chemerisky, who went to Vilna to lead the YUAP effort, noted the strength of the Bund's boycott. Even the Zionists were less cooperative than elsewhere, he remarked, apparently regarding the YUAP as a competitor.[32]

Conditions in Vilna and the efforts of the Bund prevailed against the YUAP. In February 1903 it abandoned its efforts to organize, announcing the decision in a handbill. Ordinarily, the Independents noted, the Bund's insults and lies would not frighten them, but the general state of ignorance and conservatism in the city left them no choice. The Bund had convinced the masses to fear the YUAP and had thrown so much mud at the organization that it was forced to devote all its energies to defending itself. Since the YUAP's purpose was to fulfill its program, not to fight the Bund, it had decided to end its work in Vilna for the time being so as to make better use of its strength elsewhere, where it could do more for the working class.[33]

The Independents' position in Minsk also began to erode in 1903. A year earlier the Bund reported a drop in attendance at YUAP meetings, but its optimism was premature.[34] The YUAP was not so easily dislodged; its death was slow and was brought about more by other problems than by the Bund's hand. For one thing, the tacit support of the police had its limits. Zubatov's policies were not universally accepted within the government, and various higher officials began opposing some of Vasiliev's actions as a threat to their own status. In this opposition employers found a handy weapon with which to resist the Independents.[35] In addition widespread unemployment in 1902 and 1903 led to defections in the YUAP, as it did in the Bund's kases. The YUAP, however, was much more seriously affected than the Bund because of its heavy emphasis on economic factors. Attractive in a period of high employment to older workers and those seeking better conditions without the risk of jail sentence,[36] the YUAP had little of a positive nature to offer those workers in times of unemployment, and many fled its ranks.

The final blows to the YUAP's hopes came in the spring and summer of 1903. A dreadful pogrom in Kishinev in April raised anti-governmental feeling and self-awareness among the Jews to new heights. Soon after, Zubatov, still pursuing the dream of legal unions and strikes, saw his position destroyed when agitation and strikes in Odessa, fostered by the Independents and supported by him, got out of hand. For Minister of the Interior V. K. Plehve this was the last straw, and police support for the YUAP ended.

With the government's change in attitude, the YUAP was deprived of its one great advantage. Its hopes of legalization dashed, the party abdicated. In July 1903 the YUAP issued a statement notifying the public that it had decided to halt its work because it could no longer operate as an open movement. Since it was impossible to use even half-legal "freedoms" under the present conditions, the YUAP would be forced to fall back on conspiratorial methods, which would make distinction between the YUAP's activities and those of the revolutionaries very difficult indeed. The YUAP statement also touched on the government's persecution of all Jewish social movements, observing that use of conspiratorial methods would simply allow the state to hurl further charges of Jewish "heresies."[37] The government itself had dashed all hopes for an improvement of the workers' condition.

The Bund greeted the fall of its enemies joyfully. It marked the occasion in leaflet and article, commenting on the aptness of "suicide" as a form of death for the YUAP. The Bundists insisted on claiming some credit for the YUAP's demise, contrasting their own increasing strength with the defections from the YUAP, which had grown weaker despite the support of the police. Social Democracy, the Bund maintained, had won out among the Jewish workers, for it was alive whereas the movement that had based itself on the existing political order was dead, sentenced to a social death from its inception.[38]

The end of the YUAP was clearly a victory for the Bund, even if there were other important factors contributing to the party's failure. The YUAP's

successes had never been enormous, though the Bundists had plainly been
worried about the new organization, particularly in Minsk. The Independents'
poor showing in Vilna was topped by even more fruitless efforts in Grodno,
Ekaterinoslav, and Kiev.[39]

For all its ultimate failure, the YUAP was of some importance in shaping
the Bund's history. Its actions, along with those of the police, accelerated the
Bund's push toward political explanation and organization, under way since
the Fourth Congress. Moreover, for a large portion of the Jewish working
masses the failure of the Independents was the failure of trade unionism "pure
and simple." Many workers now moved into a political camp, either Bundist
or Zionist, and the line between economic and political activity became
sharper, to the advantage of the latter. The political path was open and the
Bund ready to embark on its new political tasks.

There was another element in the conflict with the YUAP, especially in
Minsk, that had political significance for the Bund: the sympathy of some
labor Zionists for the YUAP cause. Zubatov had quickly recognized that
Zionism might suit his purposes. In 1900 he confided to his superiors that
many Jews, seeing nothing to be gained for themselves in political revolution,
were abandoning politics in Russia for a national ideal. This ferment inside
the Jewish community was useful to the secret police, he suggested. Excessive
outside interference, such as police repression, would only aid the revolutionaries.[40] A coincidence of aims brought labor Zionism and Zubatov into a tri-
angular relationship with the YUAP.

In 1901 labor Zionism was still represented in the Bund strongholds by only
a few scattered circles. In November of that year its adherents held a meeting
in Minsk, which served as the leading labor Zionist center for Bobruisk,
Grodno, Belostok, Borisov, and, to a degree, Vilna.[41] Enmity to the Bund
was one topic discussed at the gathering. "Congratulate me with a great victory I did not expect so soon," Mania Vilbushevich (who was probably responsible for the few reports we have on the meeting) chortled afterward in
a letter to Zubatov. "The Congress of Zionists has decided to fight the Bund."
"Now," she went on, "all the Zionists are our assistants. It only remains to
discover how to make use of their services."[42]

In Minsk labor Zionism found an easy ideological accommodation with the
YUAP. The Zionists did not oppose the aim of improving economic conditions as long as their own goals were not lost in the process. Early in 1903 a
Minsk labor Zionist publication noted: "We do not demand that anyone sacrifice his daily interests; everyone is entitled to his own views about religion
and other subjects. We only demand the unity of the Jewish working masses
in helping to carry out the great holy Zionist idea."[43] The new breed of Zionists did not need to disavow the YUAP even if some of them regarded the
economic struggle as a weak palliative for the ills of the Jewish workers.[44]

When the YUAP disbanded, many of the Independents turned to labor Zionism, an indication of the strong affinity between the two groups and of their common reluctance to engage in political activity in Russia.[45]

The Zionists' accommodation with Zubatov is more difficult to establish. The Bundists correctly assessed Zubatov's intention to make use of the Zionists and worked hard to make this ploy public knowledge. After the labor Zionist meeting of November 1901, the Bund labeled them bourgeois friends of the workers and pointed up their ties with the Independents.[46] In the summer of 1902 Mania Vilbushevich used her influence to persuade the authorities to let the Russian Zionists (of all stripes) hold a congress in Minsk. Thereupon the Bund began to tar the Zionists with the same brush as the YUAP, decrying their dishonor and the tie between the YUAP leader Vilbushevich and the police.[47] Eventually some of the Zionists refused to have anything to do with the YUAP or with a police-sponsored activity.[48]

The labor Zionists' dismissal of political goals in Russia and (in Minsk at least) partial support of the YUAP pushed the Bundists to greater political concern. To compete with an apolitical labor Zionism, they had to assert the promise of a socialist future in present political action. This was no less important to their cause than asserting the necessity of political activity in general to counter the YUAP's claims.

Yet another factor induced the Bund to greater political effort. Violence, on the part of both the workers and the state, became a major problem—calling, in the Bund's view, for political solutions. The use of terror by workers, though long criticized by the Bund, had never been eradicated. The Fourth Congress accepted without dispute the view that such tactics weakened Social Democratic consciousness; but how to combat them was not so easily agreed on. Some held that the Bund should oppose economic terror openly; others maintained the organization should remain passive, arguing that without these tactics some strikes would be lost, and that in any case the workers themselves considered terror necessary. The congress finally resolved to reject terror unequivocally as a tactic.[49]

The Fourth Congress also took up the use of force by the police. This was a very sensitive issue, for it went to the heart of the Bund's *raison d'être*. Over the years the Bund had labored mightily—and with some success—to instill a sense of dignity and human worth in the downtrodden Jewish worker, that he might be induced to stand up for himself. As a consequence, a number of the rank and file in the local organizations felt retaliation was the only way to restore the honor of comrades who had been beaten by the police. Once aroused, these workers were not to be persuaded in the name of a higher Social Democratic consciousness and principle; they were not ready to submit to a restrictive discipline that tied their hands now in the hope of future gains.

This question apparently generated some heat at the Fourth Congress, with certain delegates insisting that violence had to be repaid in kind. Their position was not endorsed.[50] In its final resolution on the subject the congress recommended that brutality be met with legal means. Lodging complaints against the police would put the onus squarely on a regime that did not enforce its own laws and would teach the workers their rights. The congress also recommended using the established forms of protest—agitation at every opportunity and demonstrations in certain instances—to express the indignation of the revolutionaries and to arouse society.[51]

The question of political terror as a tactic arose during the congress's examination of the political struggle. Three points of view were expressed. Some delegates unequivocally rejected any kind of terror as harmful to the movement; it could only increase repression and slow the movement's growth. Others argued that terror did not violate Social Democratic principles but should be practiced only by special groups acting on their own. Still others accepted terror used in self-defense, against provocateurs, for instance, as distinct from systematic political terror aimed at forcing concessions from the government. Unlike political terror, defensive terror did not require permanent organization and could even be carried on by individuals at their own risk. In the end the congress resolved that "It is not the business of the *organizations* to resort to defensive terror." Aggressive political terror was rejected as inopportune.[52]

While formally maintaining the position adopted by earlier congresses, the Fourth Congress showed some reluctance to prohibit absolutely all use of force by everyone in the Bund. The resolution's emphasis on the word organizations appears to have been designed to accommodate those delegates who felt strongly that defending one's honor was a legitimate reason for violence. By implication the resolution freed the Bund of official responsibility for acts of violence, leaving the decision in private hands.

The subject of violence also came up in the deliberations on demonstrations. In advocating demonstrations, the congress recognized that this form of protest challenged the regime far more directly than strikes, inviting an immediate police response, and attempted to ensure discipline by resolving that the organizations should initiate demonstrations. Yet the delegates also recognized that the Bund could not easily disown spontaneous action on the part of workers and declared further that "local organizations should always support demonstrations arising spontaneously out of the masses."[53] Still somewhat uncertain of the effects of this tactical instrument, the congress held that demonstrations should include the Christian revolutionary organizations as well as the Bund. Only in special circumstances, say the funeral of a Jewish worker, were the Bundists to demonstrate independently and even then Christian workers were to be invited.[54] Plainly aware of the danger of mob action and of bringing the various nationalities together in mass action, the delegates were not sure how far to push this tactic.

The importance of the demonstration and the meeting as forms of political action increased after the Fourth Congress: the crowds got larger, the gatherings more frequent. In a two-year period, according to the Bund's report to the Second Congress of the RSDWP (dated October 1903), there were 30 street demonstrations, 25 of them involving a total of some 7,500 persons. Manifestations occurred at theaters and schools. Meetings at which speakers discussed virtually every urgent problem of Russian and Jewish life became almost commonplace. The Bund reported 260 such gatherings, with a total audience of 36,900 at 224 of them; the largest drew some 3,000 people. There were 74 meetings attended by 50 to 100 persons, and 72 with up to 500. These figures did not include May Day demonstrations and meetings.[55]

The heightened visibility that accompanied the increasing use of the political demonstration forced the Bund to develop new organizational techniques and tactics. Practical solutions were harder to come by in the political movement than in the strike movement, where organization was accomplished relatively early. By 1901 cossacks and other military units were being called on to supplement the increasingly ineffectual local police forces to quell mass demonstrations.[56] In the weeks prior to a demonstration the authorities often carried out arrests and raids to head off the expected disturbances. *Di Arbeter Shtime* carried reports of constant military patrols in Belostok, Vitebsk, and many other centers.[57] The Bund, drawing on the resources of a small minority, could hardly contemplate engaging such forces alone.

The Bund committees thus faced a dilemma. They felt obligated as revolutionaries to express their aims and show their protest, especially on the international workers' holiday; at the same time they well appreciated the possible cost of their actions. As a result, local circumstances dictated their response to the Fourth Congress's advocacy of demonstrations. Some organizations continued the old practice of meeting secretly in the woods. Others, more sure of their strength, were quicker to challenge the regime by calling open demonstrations, though they often went to great lengths to avoid contact with the state's armed forces by shifting the date or time of the demonstration—a half-step between complete evasion and confrontation. Still others demonstrated by refusing to work. The choice of tactics was uneven, illustrating the local and relatively weak state of the political wing of the movement.

The level of unrest among workers and students rose all over Russia in 1901, pushing the state to tougher positions. Late in the year the government introduced a series of measures in a number of provinces, including those in the west, aimed specifically at thwarting the revolutionaries. Among other things, it strengthened its laws against public meetings, requiring landlords to account for their tenants' whereabouts at night; permitted secret trials in military courts; and allowed local police to detain for three months anyone suspected of belonging to a secret organization.[58] In the opinion of one Vilna Bundist, the government had opened "a new era in the history of the Vilna workers' movement."[59]

About the time these rules were established a new governor was appointed in Vilna—General Viktor von Wahl. Wahl regarded all political prisoners as ordinary criminals and was bent on the strictest possible interpretation of the law. He "could not be called a tenderhearted man," writes a former colleague.[60] Wahl immediately made his position known, warning leading members of the Jewish community that if they did not root out the revolutionary spirit among the Jews, every Jew would feel the might of the regime.[61] But the day had long since passed when the old leaders of the Jewish community could dictate policy.

For the Bund the climax to the state's new rigidity and its own political activism came in the spring of 1902. To celebrate May Day, demonstrations were staged in the streets and in a theater. The governor called in troops to break them up, and a number of workers were arrested. The next day 20 Jewish prisoners and six Polish prisoners were whipped, receiving 20 or 30 lashes (the reports vary) while the other prisoners were forced to look on.[62]

The Bundists were shocked and anguished as never before. Of all the events up to October 1905, only the Kishinev pogrom, the withdrawal from the RSDWP, and the Revolution itself had a deeper emotional impact than these beatings and their aftermath. The blow struck precisely at that exposed nerve of pride the Bund had fostered among the Jewish workers, that search for dignity leading them to stand together and fight.

A year earlier the Vilna Committee had taken a strong stand against terrorist tactics, maintaining in a special document that "the murder of individuals ... apart from the fact that it does not achieve its ultimate goal, is harmful, for it gives a government the opportunity to strengthen its police powers."[63] Now, however, the committee stopped just short of justifying political assassination, adding its name to those of the Polish, Lithuanian, and Russian Social Democratic organizations of Vilna on a leaflet that flamed: "We fight with peaceful means ... but patience has its limits. It will not be our fault if popular vengeance, hatred, and resentment take on violent forms—Wahl himself has pointed out the path." Listing the names of the major officials involved in the affair, the leaflet concluded on a ringing, apocalyptic note: "Vengeance shall fall on each of you, and your names will be damned."[64]

The next step came almost as a fulfillment of prophecy. On May 18 (N.S.) a young Bundist named Hirsh Lekert fired a revolver twice at Wahl, inflicting superficial wounds. The police caught Lekert immediately and a few days later handed him over to a military court (which alone could mete out capital punishment); after a short investigation cloaked in secrecy he was sentenced to death. He was hanged on May 28.[65]

Lekert's act of retaliation and subsequent execution attracted attention far beyond the boundaries of the Bund. He became a folk hero, a martyr, and the spirit incarnate of the militant Jewish worker, in poem, song, and drama. The Bundists and their Social Democratic comrades in Vilna characterized him as one "who in his moral qualities, civic courage, and heroic fearlessness stood a full head taller than the people around him. He fulfilled what had become our social need, accomplishing that which many dared to think and dream but not to do."[66] In an organization where anonymity prevailed, Lekert became a symbol and his death an occasion for yearly commemoration by his comrades, the same distinction accorded the heroes of the People's Will.[67]

To the Bundists it seemed that Lekert had been singled out as a worker and a Jew. His act came in the early phase of one of the most active periods of political assassination since the early 1880's. In receiving the death sentence, he was given the same punishment as Stefan Balmashev, a Socialist Revolutionary who had killed Minister of the Interior D. S. Sipiagin just a few weeks earlier. Since, "to the great chagrin of all," Lekert had wounded a mere governor, and only superficially at that, his punishment seemed unduly harsh. The Bundists reasoned: "Lekert is a Jew, Lekert came from the ranks of the workers, Lekert performed his deed in Lithuania, which is under exceptional laws, and his punishment, therefore, had to be exceptionally severe...; *for light wounds he had to pay with his head*."[68] The passions of the moment scarcely permitted a simple Social Democratic critique of Lekert's act. All the threads leading from the tactic of demonstrations, the issue of how to deal with brutality, and the general use of terror were suddenly fused in an atmosphere that approached hysteria.

The Central Committee lost some of its usual composure. It expressed pride in the moral development of the Jewish worker, who now stood ready to defend his honor. But it feared that Lekert's deed would not teach the regime a lesson, for the brutal use of the whip was not confined to Vilna: Bundists in Minsk had been beaten for demonstrating in a theater a few days later. To the Central Committee the similarity of the two cases indicated that some higher authority had initiated a new level of oppression. This, the committee said, was not the first time in Russian revolutionary history that an attack on human dignity had provoked such a response. Vera Zasulich herself, one of the outstanding women in the revolutionary movement and a close associate of Plekhanov's, had once fired a shot for an affront of this kind. One thing was certain: "our human dignity must be defended to our last drop of blood." This was only their duty as revolutionaries, the committee declared.[69]

Yet the Bund leaders still felt constrained to take into account the principles expressed at the Fourth Congress, even if the congress had not foreseen the lengths to which the state would go to stop the movement. Caught between honor and principle, the committee sought to maintain both by distinguishing force as an answer to force from political terror as a means of struggle. Thus the use of terror held great dangers for the Bund, which was fighting an entire social order and not individuals, but an action like Lekert's was a justifiable response, for the Jewish workers were not slaves.[70] The committee was uncomfortably straddling the question, condoning violence in the name of self-defense and revolutionary honor on the one hand and condemning violence against individuals on the other. The distinction could be made in logic, but the acts themselves and their consequences were more difficult to separate. The committee insisted that its analysis in no way contradicted the resolutions of the Fourth Congress; it merely brought into the open the principle of defense-by-terror that was implicit in those resolutions.[71]

Inevitably, the whole question of demonstrations was reexamined. In view of the increasingly bitter struggle between the state and the movement, the committee wondered whether the old methods were still useful. Small demonstrations and even clandestine meetings were becoming difficult to arrange, yet large demonstrations could not be prepared without the authorities' knowledge and could be broken up.

The Bundists recognized that they bore a responsibility for the demonstrators they called into the streets. Indeed, one dedicated worker in Vilna left the movement, feeling she had no right to call people to the struggle, given the possible consequences.[72] This was a time of transition, the committee concluded: "We are not yet strong enough to put an end to the Autocracy *immediately*, but neither are we so weak as to bear passively all its wild acts of violence. We must show ... that *we are capable of resistance*."[73] It was not a matter of attacking the police, but of protecting workers during the demonstrations. For instance, since police usually attacked the flag bearer, a cordon of demonstrators should surround and protect him; others should prevent anyone from being arrested. Such protective measures would require a systematic and organized effort, with members given specific assignments.[74] What had once been the informal work of small groups acting on their own initiative— Lekert himself had participated in such work—was now proposed as a formal duty. Here was the beginning of sanctioned paramilitary operations.

Top-level consideration of the crisis continued into the summer. In August 1902 the Fifth Bund Conference was held in Berdichev.* The great majority

* Mikhalevich, *Zikhroinos*, 1: 147. Contemporary documents use September, the new style date. See, for example, *Posledniia izvestiia*, 88 (Oct. 4, 1902): 1. Bund conferences were advisory gatherings called by the Central Committee to discuss important issues. In contrast to the congresses, the conference delegates were selected by the Central Committee. The Fifth Conference is the first to have so clear-cut a character. The Fourth Confer-

of those present upheld the justice of retaliation for insults to the honor of the party. This was not, the conference declared in its report, the same thing as advocating terror:

It would be a mistake to think that this kind of revenge has any relation to terror. . . . The aim of such acts is only to wash away the stain on the party, to take vengeance for a shameful insult. In an organized party that stands fast on a firm basis of principle and tactics, there will always be enough strength to see to it that individual acts of revenge do not turn into systematic terror.[75]

Like the Central Committee, the conference moved beyond the Fourth Congress on the question of violence. But it went a step further, in effect charging the party with the task of organizing acts of reprisal so as to "not allow the deeds their natural path." Only in this way would terror be avoided. Before all else, however, strong resistance had to be shown by those on the scene. Revenge made sense only when the revolutionaries defended their own honor.[76]

The mood for resistance was strengthened when the conference turned to discuss demonstrations. The group saw that in a situation of deepening conflict with the state the revolutionaries could not afford to act weakly. A demonstration that gave an impression of weakness was apt to do more damage than good. Having added the ingredient of resistance to the tactic of open demonstration, the Bund was now compelled to place some limits on that tactic. Where it appeared that a demonstration might not be able to defend itself, the conference concluded, it would be better not to have one.[77]

For the Bund leaders in Russia, the public demonstration was an intermediary step between the old techniques of propaganda and education and the expected open conflict of the future. It was a militant way to show the state the forces arrayed against it and to present the demands of the disaffected. The Berdichev conference recognized the difference between a demonstration and a revolt, however. Demonstrations dispersed whether demands were met or not; they were not an attempt to seize power. The object of defending them was to protect those involved, to produce a favorable impression, and to show the moral fiber of the demonstrators.[78] As the Bundists noted hopefully in June 1902, the demonstrators of today would be "the builders of our future street barricades."[79]

The whole tone of the discussions at the conference displayed a growth of confidence and strength since 1901. The Fourth Congress had emphasized the importance of cooperating with the Christian movements, but by the summer

---

ence, for instance, was merely a continuation of discussion after the formal adjournment of the Fourth Congress. Earlier conferences were too informal to leave much trace. The Second took place in Minsk in April 1899 and the Third in Warsaw in April 1900. I have never heard mention of a first conference. It is not clear at what point the Bundists began to account formally for gatherings of this sort; most likely they were numbered retrospectively after the Fourth Conference.

of 1902 the Bundists were plainly in a mood to push ahead without them if necessary. As long as the Jewish masses wanted a demonstration, *Di Arbeter Shtime* declared, it could be held without the support of the Christians.[80]

The position taken by the majority at Berdichev and endorsed by a number of local committees opened a major debate within the Bund.* The heat of the moment carried the Bundists in Russia to positions far beyond those held by their co-workers abroad. In a rare display of open difference, the Foreign Committee challenged the wisdom of resolutions that upheld organized revenge as a proper course for the Bund to follow. It was the Bund's leading polemicist, Kosovsky, who was the chief critic. Kosovsky refused to recognize any real distinction between organized revenge and organized terror. Since both involved killing police or state officials, they were merely different symptoms of the same dangerous syndrome. What started as simple revenge against a despot would sooner or later become a weapon for threatening the government and finally an accepted means of attaining political goals. The organization would not be able to contain terror, which would feed upon itself. When the police became more repressive, as was inevitable, the workers would repay them in kind, finding sanction for their actions in the organization's adoption of these methods. Ultimately, the organization would acquire terrorist elements, and the level of work would be thrown back to the days of economic terror.[81]

Kosovsky also challenged the equating of party honor and personal honor. For the Bund, an independent organism with its own rules and goals, honor meant upholding party principles and striving to fulfill party tasks. Its answer to insult lay in the struggle to liberate the masses. If a mass response was not possible, then the party had to make it possible. As for individuals, they had to defend their own honor, and it was the party's duty to radicalize them so they would do so. When they accepted humiliation, it was a sign that the party had not sufficiently developed the feeling of human dignity within them. If there had been no mass protest so far, it was because of the backward condition of the masses, an inadequate adjustment to the government's new tactics, the inertia of the Christian workers, and the isolation of the Jewish workers. Kosovsky saw in the turn to terror a lack of confidence in Social Democratic methods; Social Democratic work had to be deepened to destroy the psychological basis of the terrorist feelings.[82]

The differences between the home organizations and the Foreign Committee were not easily settled. Indeed, in an article on the Berdichev conference the Foreign Committee reminded its readers that the conference was "a private gathering" whose "resolutions are not binding."[83] There was a hot ex-

---

* According to J. L. H. Keep, 14 Bund committees publicly supported terrorism (*The Rise of Social Democracy*, p. 79).

change between the Minsk Committee and the Foreign Committee. When the Foreign Committee heard that a Bund speaker in Minsk had expressed regret because "the local tyrants had not yet found their Lekert," it was prompted to express its own regrets about such remarks.[84] Rushing to the defense of its speaker, the Minsk Committee argued from a legalistic position, insisting that the views of the Central Committee alone were authoritative.[85] In fact, the stands of the Central Committee and the Berdichev conference were close enough to be considered the official position of the Bund, leaving the Foreign Committee open to criticism on disciplinary grounds. But the views of the prestigious contingent abroad could scarcely be dismissed altogether. The debate was not officially settled until June 1903, when the Fifth Congress reconsidered the Berdichev resolution on organized revenge and rejected it without debate.[86] The whole affair revealed the depth of emotion of the Bundists in Russia as compared with the colder, more rigidly logical stand of their foreign comrades, who continued to insist on unwavering adherence to Social Democratic principles.

Given the stormy nature of the times, the Foreign Committee's out-and-out rejection of terror and the Central Committee's less than wholehearted approval of it dissatisfied certain activists. Caught up in the growing spirit of militancy and open struggle, some found terror an irresistible weapon and defected from the Bund. Frume Frumkin, an agitator who left the Bund to become a terrorist (and died on the gallows) found it impossible to understand the Foreign Committee's coldness toward the honor of insulted comrades.[87] Others, less ready to act individually, were still disenchanted with the inadequacy of the Social Democrats' response to state violence. A number of workers in Belostok, for instance, disappointed at the Bund's reluctance to undertake direct action, withdrew from the organization.[88] Though these defections did not seriously weaken the Bund, the question of violence remained a wound that never healed completely.

The Lekert affair and the issue of terror also involved the Bund in debates with other revolutionary groups. The Socialist Revolutionary Party (PSR or SR), established in late 1901, accepted terror as a weapon in its tactical arsenal against the Tsarist regime. The SR's applauded Lekert's deed and awarded him a place in their galaxy of revolutionary heroes.[89] As a matter of fact, they had already slated Wahl for assassination by their own terrorists.[90]

The SR's found the outrage and initial reaction of the Bundists in Russia commendable. They hailed the Berdichev conference's resolve to avenge acts of dishonor as "the only correct and deeply vital" answer to the regime.[91] In turn, a number of Bundists were attracted by the SR's hearty endorsement of terror—to the point where in early 1903 Kosovsky felt compelled to write a pamphlet criticizing such tactics in detail. He appealed to readers to recall that "a revolutionary is above all a member of a party, and that his energies belong to it and to it alone."[92] There was no possibility of either party convincing the other, and both continued to insist on their own view.

The Iskraites also crossed swords with the Bund on this question. The arguments between the two groups were more irritating than serious at this point, but they were indicative of a complicated and changing situation within the Social Democratic camp. In the opinion of the Iskraites, the effort of the Bund's Central Committee to reconcile "a nonterrorist system of political murder with the principles of Social Democracy and the resolution of the Bund's [Fourth] Congress, which repudiates terror," was unconvincing.[93] This was, in fact, essentially the same criticism the Foreign Committee had leveled; the difference was that the Iskraites adopted a harsh tone, making no allowance for the heightened emotions of the moment, where the Foreign Committee tried to cool the atmosphere and let reason prevail. Yet even two of the Iskraites, Martov and Vera Zasulich, wavered temporarily in the Lekert case. Lenin wrote to Plekhanov of an argument he had with his two colleagues in which both took the view that terror as an act of revenge was unavoidable.[94]

The events of the spring and summer of 1902 persuaded the leaders of the Bund in Russia that changes in organization and institutions were urgently needed. The reforms sought by the Fourth Congress had merely touched the surface, said *Di Arbeter Shtime* in August.[95] The kases had outlived their usefulness and were hindering further revolutionary work. Too often members confused the kases with the masses, forgetting that they represented only a part of the real masses of society. The kase had been created to perform narrower tasks and was unsuited to the new revolutionary demands of the times. What was needed now, the paper argued, was "broad political agitation *among all the masses*" and "support of every protest against the present political order." The Bund had to assume the leadership of the struggle for freedom "in all its modes and forms." Its immediate task, therefore, was "*to free our revolutionary institutions* from their old foundation—from the *professional* [union or kase] movement." The organizations had to be independent; and unlike the kases, which elected their members, they should be open to all. ("Revolutionaries are not chosen; they develop independently.") Finally, it was the duty of the organizations "not to adjust themselves to the demands of the masses . . . but to bring into the true masses their own revolutionary spirit and ideas."[96]

This was no rejection of the economic struggle, only the assertion that revolutionary organizations were needed to fulfill the political tasks facing the Bund. They would go hand in hand with the mass movement and give it a more revolutionary character. The Bund, as a revolutionary organization, had to be differentiated from the mass movement.[97]

Di Arbeter Shtime next turned to the role of the masses. The new organizations had to be developed in every city where broad masses could be united to act politically, just as they had been united to act in economic matters. Lodz and Warsaw already had such organizations. The journal expected that the masses would sympathize with the Bund's program but did not expect them to be revolutionaries. The Bund itself was the home of the revolutionaries.[98]

The Berdichev conference passed a resolution endorsing all the suggestions laid out in this article. It also requested the Central Committee to work out specific rules for consideration at the next congress.[99] But when it came to executing this new program, the leaders encountered both practical difficulties and opposition. A notable example was Vilna, where the entire workers' organization was dismantled and rebuilt on new political foundations in the summer of 1902. Soon after, the radical changes had to be curtailed, for the Independents, who were then attempting to establish themselves in that city, were profiting from the splitting of the economic and political organizations.[100] The Foreign Committee saw dangerous possibilities in the Berdichev conference's proposals on organization, asserting that

this evolution [terrorism] is made significantly easier by the projected changes in organization. . . . The new principle of organization leads to some weakening of contact between the leading circles and the masses; it can be made fruitful only under the strictest observance of the principles and tactics of Social Democracy.[101]

In time, the fears of the Foreign Committee were assuaged and the excessive zeal in Vilna curbed. As the Bund leaders found out, even with the best of revolutionary intentions, making massive changes in a functioning and well-established movement was a complicated business that was not to be accomplished overnight by design.

Other cities found the shift to political organization less traumatic. In Pinsk, which had a much younger organization than Vilna, the changes began soon after the visit in late 1901 of a representative of the Central Committee, Mark Liber. He was followed, in early 1902, by two party professionals dispatched by the committee—Ephraim Ashpiz and Barukh Kahan (Virgili).[102] Ashpiz and Kahan formed a new workers' committee by co-opting the most conscious and revolutionary workers in town and soon had both the economic and the political work reorganized. They created a birzhe to permit constant agitation and successfully cut through some of the old kase loyalties. Though the new committee encountered its share of opposition from within, particularly from a fiery former Zionist named Kolie Teper, the party professionals accomplished their purpose. They stayed in Pinsk a little over a year, the maximum time the party let its agents remain in any one city.[103]

Belostok's political organization grew out of the highest workers' institutions. There the local committee placed the most class conscious workers in agitator collectives, which were allowed to co-opt other workers as they saw fit. These collectives then formed cells or skhodkas, which operated in various trades.[104] In large centers where economic problems were severe, the politicization of kases occurred naturally as the workers became more receptive to the idea of political action.[105]

When the Fifth Congress met in June 1903, the local situation was still in flux. The congress accepted the thoughts expressed at Berdichev and gave them legal force. It upheld the power of the Central Committee to suspend the actions of local committees, to name and exclude local committee members, to name all members of the Foreign Committee, and to demand reports from the committees. The Central Committee was also given the right to add delegates to Bund congresses and to control publications. The committees had only one avenue in the event of disagreement with the Central Committee: a congress had to be called if two-thirds of all the Bund committees requested one.[106]

The Central Committee was now assured of the power to make whatever organizational changes it deemed necessary. But it rarely used its power to bludgeon local organizations into party conformity. As a Central Committee member suggested to Vladimir Akimov (who studied the structure of the Bund in 1904), though the committee had the right to issue orders, it was obeyed on other grounds ("Our basic principle is conducting business by mutual trust and by force of moral influence"). Indeed, this informant did not take Akimov's studies on the structure of the Bund seriously, considering the picture he drew too bureaucratic.[107] The strong internal ties of the Bundists outweighed differences of opinion, and the Central Committee was usually able to persuade the local committees to its view in the course of time.

The increased power of the Central Committee went hand in hand with the Bund's increased attention to political issues. The new structure allowed a more sensitive and direct transmission of the committee's will throughout the entire organization. Further, control over personnel allowed the committee to manipulate its skilled revolutionary forces effectively. It could insert its special agents into committees as the need arose with far less opportunity for the kind of rank-and-file opposition that had occurred at times in earlier days.

One unmistakable sign of centralization and greater politicization was the fact that many of the local journals fell by the wayside in 1902–3 while the publications of the Central and Foreign committees grew substantially, both in quality and in circulation. As always, these central organs had a far heavier political content than the local publications. The local committees began to rely increasingly on handbills, which were directed to an ever-wider audience —Polish and Russian as well as Jewish. From the spring of 1898 to the fall of 1900 the Bund put out 43 leaflets, totaling 74,750 copies; between the Fourth and Fifth congresses, just over two years, it issued 101 handbills, totaling 347,-150 copies.[108] The May 1 leaflets of the Central Committee alone grew from editions of 20,000 in 1902 to 70,000 in 1903.[109]

The Bund also broadened its political horizons in the years 1901–3. It sought not only to strengthen its ties with other revolutionary parties, but also to attract broad support from the Jewish community at large. The Bundists were especially anxious to gain the support of the Jewish intelligentsia, and here arguments based largely on political problems and goals, national as well as social and international, were necessarily more appealing than a simple call for economic struggle. In an appeal specifically directed to the Jewish intellectuals, Pavel Rosenthal, then a member of the Central Committee, chided them for their estrangement from their own masses and revolutionary movement. Despite the Bund's long history, he declared, they were no better informed on the Bund's activities or even its aims than they were on the Boxers in China, an unfortunate state of affairs that had been brought about in part by the class character of the movement and the use of Yiddish.[110] Rosenthal stressed the scope of the Bund's goals: political freedom, self-determination of nationalities, and, in the future, the creation of a socialist order. In an obvious attempt to blunt the appeal of the Zionists, who also looked for support in the intellectual community, he contrasted the Bund's fighting spirit with the timidity of the bourgeois Jews, who feared to stand up against oppression. Rosenthal rejected out of hand the charge of russification leveled by the Poles, the charge of narrow nationalism made by some assimilated intellectuals, and the charge of cosmopolitanism brought by the Zionists. The Bund, he declared, was national without infringing on the principles of international Social Democracy. Pointing to the progress the Jewish workers had made in improving their condition and breaking out of the exclusiveness and isolation that had bound them, he asked: "Will our intelligentsia continue to be an indifferent, cold, even hostile spectator to the struggle boiling up around it?"[111]

Finally, the Bund also made an attempt to inform Russian readers about the Bund and the revolutionary movement in general. In the spring of 1901 the Foreign Committee began publishing *Posledniia izvestiia* (The Latest News) expressly for this purpose. It carried news items from all over the Empire and aired controversies both in the Bund and between the Bund and other parties.* The Bund also issued special publications in Polish to call attention to unusual events, such as the Fourth Congress and the appearance of the twenty-fifth number of *Di Arbeter Shtime* (a remarkable achievement for an underground publication).

Thus, together the local committees and the Central Committee worked diligently in the early years of the twentieth century to shape the political character of the Bund, deepening political consciousness where it existed, trying to implant it where it did not. Yet at the same time they were careful not to move so far ahead of the rank and file that large numbers of workers lost touch with the formal organizations. When estrangement threatened, the Bundists were willing to change their pace—though never their goals.

* In all, 256 issues were published, the last appearing in January 1906.

13. The Reassessment of the National Question

The Fourth Congress was a major landmark in the history of the Bund, the point at which new answers to the national question propelled the organization into a different relationship with the Jewish workers and the RSDWP. In its arrangements, the congress served as a monument to underground organization and skill. Successfully holding a meeting of 24 delegates (representing 12 cities or organizations) in Russia amid Zubatov's strenuous efforts to destroy the Bund was no mean achievement. The well-worked-out agenda, orderly debates, press and publication arrangements (there was a full report in Russian plus newspaper accounts in Yiddish) all reveal a smooth-functioning operation.[1]

The composition of the congress reflected the mood of the home organization. The Foreign Committee was not represented. Numbers of worker-activists attended, but it was the intellectuals who dominated the proceedings, broadening both the range and the scope of the discussions as compared with the Second and Third congresses. The size of the gathering and the nature of the issues discussed produced a new formality, as befitted a large organization representing more than one point of view.

The delegates approached their deliberations with a strong awareness of the importance of the problems at hand, especially the national question, which the delegates' report termed "undoubtedly the central point in the list of problems submitted to the Congress for consideration."[2] For 15 months the local committees had had the opportunity to discuss and work out answers to this question. The congress devoted over 12 hours to the subject, with almost all those present taking part.

The delegates agreed unanimously on certain assumptions. They all accepted as a major premise that

each nationality, apart from its aspirations for economic, civil, and political freedom and full rights, also has *national* aspirations based on characteristics dear and peculiar to it—language, customs, way of life, culture in general—which ought to have full freedom of development.[3]

All agreed that the right of self-determination for each nationality as proclaimed by the RSDWP in 1898 "demands a more detailed explanation." The only solution for a multinational country like Russia, they felt, was the principle discussed at the Brünn Congress of the Austrian Social Democrats: a federation in which each nationality had full autonomy to deal with its own concerns. There was no question from any quarter that the concept of nationality applied fully to the Jewish people.[4]

The delegates rejected categorically any solution of the nationalities problem based on territory. In the words of the report, that answer "had no defenders at the Congress." Dividing the Russian Empire into historical units would involve insoluble problems in areas of mixed ethnic populations. Besides, what was historical territory? "Should Poland be as it was 110 years ago, or 200, or 300?" It was not the business of Social Democrats to change state borders and carve new states out of old, the delegates agreed. "We stand for full freedom and equal rights, and as for *national* equal rights, the only guarantee we see for them is in national autonomy."[5]

Once over the theoretical hurdle, however, agreement ceased. When it came to the matter of practical application of these principles, opinion ranged from a call for immediate and full implementation to absolute refusal to consider any positive step. Since the various positions expressed at the congress were to be reiterated time and again and consume considerable energy in the coming years, it is worth examining them at some length here.

The strongest stand for immediate steps was taken by Mark Liber (identified as Comrade X in the report of the congress), who held that

once we recognize the right to national freedom and autonomy for each nationality and once we accept the Jews as a people, the Bund, which specifically defends the interests of the Jewish proletariat, should without fail display national autonomy for the Jews on its banner and by no means be satisfied, as up to now, with demands for civil and political equal rights.[6]

In Liber's view, the Jews might attain civil and political rights, and still suffer as a people. He recognized the impossibility of achieving all these goals under the present regime, but felt that socialism was perhaps not so remote an ideal, and the demand for national rights should be advanced by the Bund in the meantime. "As an immediate minimum goal," he declared, "one can be satisfied with civil and political equal rights, but as a maximum it is necessary to add Jewish national autonomy."

Mere open pronouncement of this aim was not enough for Liber. He also wanted practical work to begin at once.

Our task, which has long been maturing but, unfortunately, kept in the shadows up to now, is to *prepare* the Jewish proletariat for national autonomy, to develop national self-consciousness in it. To a significant degree we have been cosmopolites until now. We ought to become national. There is nothing to fear in this word. *National* is not *nationalist*. When a class recognizes that it belongs to a given nationality, it becomes national (consider, for example, the Belgian National Social Democratic Party); nationalist signifies the sum total of all classes or the domination of one nationality over another.

Liber demanded that the Bund step up its agitation on the national question, laying particular emphasis on the special oppressed condition of the Jewish people; that it protest loudly all manifestations of oppression; and that it acquaint itself with the national struggle in the West. In short, along with agitation based on economic and political issues, he insisted that the Bund must begin a massive agitation campaign based on the national question. This effort would raise political consciousness without harming class consciousness by encouraging exclusiveness and isolation, Liber maintained.[7]

Other speakers, among them Portnoy and Aaron Weinstein, took a softer position.[8] The conditions in Russia that prompted both the Zionist movement and the many nationally oriented socialist parties sooner or later had to raise the Jewish national question inside the Bund, they contended. The problem was no alien one brought to the masses from the outside. If anything, the masses were too nationalistically inclined. The Social Democrats had to explain to them "that true nationalism is not chauvinism and national exclusiveness." The Jewish worker suffered from the dual yoke of being a proletarian and a Jew. He would throw off the yoke of national oppression when he understood the reasons for it. "It is our direct obligation," they said, "to further the working out of this consciousness, of *national consciousness*," which was

the consciousness of the Jewish working class of belonging to a given nationality, the consciousness of oppression that stems from it, and the conscious aspiration to destroy [that oppression] and to attain those political rights that would permit the full development of the Jewish proletariat.

The delegates in this camp agreed with Liber that such national self-consciousness would not harm Social Democratic consciousness, though caution was necessary:

In this form, the development of such national consciousness is not in contradiction with Social Democratic consciousness in general. On the contrary, the latter is unthinkable without the former; and in working for the dissemination of Social Democratic ideas and protesting against national oppression as one aspect of that oppression in contemporary bourgeois society, we are at the same time working for the development of national self-consciousness. But we cannot and should not do more in this direction unless we really want to become nationalists.

As for current activities,

As a practical party, the Bund should not put forth demands that have no chance of being realized in the immediate future. We are referring to such demands as national autonomy for the Jews. For this reason it follows that we should limit ourselves to the demand for civil and political equality at present; to wit the purely negative demand of *the abolition of all exceptional laws against the Jews*.[9]

Portnoy and his supporters held the middle-of-the-road position at the congress. They accepted as inherent the relationship between the national question and the Jewish proletariat, and so accepted the legitimacy of national consciousness. Unlike Liber, however, they rejected as dangerous any national demands beyond those already upheld by the Bund.

Pavel Rosenthal, along with a number of delegates, took a position that was poles apart from Liber's and substantially different from Portnoy's.[10] They denied that the national question arose naturally from the Jewish masses, maintaining that, on the contrary, "the attempts to tie a national structure to the Jewish workers' movement originate abroad, where the question is heated and timely." In the Bund's case, the question was "alien to the masses *at the present time* and the desire to stimulate it artificially and prematurely can bring nothing but harm."[11] The Rosenthal position argued that the Jewish worker was taught early to regard Christians with hostility for mainly economic reasons, and that only recently had he begun to rid himself of views acquired in childhood. "Social Democratic propaganda draws [the Jewish workers] from the path of national isolation and accustoms them to believe and feel that all proletarians are brothers regardless of origin or religion." It was this point of view that saved Jewish workers from the pessimism of the Zionists, whereas the proposal of Liber could only bring discord.[12]

Moreover, said the third group, there was a very real danger posed by the subtleties of terminology. Could the masses discriminate between the "national self-consciousness" suggested by earlier speakers and garden-variety "bourgeois" nationalism? The Jewish nationalists included in their definition such things as the spirit of the Jewish people, their history, and their special mission. The term "national self-consciousness" as used at the congress was inadequate; it led only to consciousness of national oppression. If it was wrong for dominant nations to be nationally conscious, then such feeling also ought to be wrong among the Jews after their persecution ceased. Rosenthal and his colleagues saw this issue as an "inclined plane" on which it would be difficult to maintain one's Social Democratic balance. A positive stand could "impart to the Bund a completely undesirable character of self-sufficiency, exclusiveness, and isolation at a time . . . when the most friendly cooperation with the Christian proletariat and parties is necessary."[13]

In the end, the congress accepted a series of resolutions embodying all points on which the assembly agreed unanimously, plus a few compromises. It declared the inadmissibility not only of class and state oppression, "but also of dominance of one nationality over another, the rule of one language over another"; and recognized that "a state such as Russia, consisting of a great number of disparate nationalities, should be reorganized in the future into a federation of nationalities with full national autonomy for each, independently of the territory inhabited by them."* Another clause made it clear that "the concept of 'nationality' applied to the Jewish people." These principles of national interest and identification had not been enunciated by previous Bund congresses.

The resolutions did not go beyond the traditional stand of the Bund as far as immediate propaganda tasks were concerned. The congress judged that the time was not right for demanding national cultural autonomy for the Jews. It was enough for now to fight against existing exceptional legislation and to protest each instance of oppression of the Jews as a nationality. Even this struggle had to be carried on without exaggerating national feelings, which would only cloud the class consciousness of the proletariat and lead to chauvinism.[14] The congress thus adopted a view close to Portnoy's position. Liber stood quite alone.

The very arrangement of the report reflects the Central Committee's awareness of the connection between the national question and other issues. In it, the discussions were placed ("for the convenience of the reader") not according to the order in which they were pursued, but "according to their internal connection."[15] Hence, immediately after the report on the national question comes an account of the Bund's name change, then a summary of the discussions on Zionism and the RSDWP.

As noted, this was the first time the subject of Zionism was placed on a congress agenda, a response to the stepped-up Zionist activities among the workers. The congress reiterated the Bund position: Zionism was simply a bourgeois reaction to anti-Semitism. If, in its avowed goal of providing territory for the Jewish people, Zionism thought to help a small number of the total community, it was an unimportant movement; if it pretended to take in all or even a significant portion of the population, it was plainly utopian. In either case its national agitation was harmful for class consciousness.[16]

Reexamining the Bund's relationship to the RSDWP in terms of the national question, the delegates found that the autonomy granted the Bund at the First Congress of the RSDWP had created problems at times. In view of these difficulties, plus the possibility of further complications arising with the entrance into the party of other national organizations on a federative basis, the congress wondered whether the Bund ought not to be given federative status rather than its present autonomy. It seemed to the delegates that a resolution on federation logically succeeded the one already accepted on the national

* The term "full autonomy" was used in error in the body of the congress's report. The language was corrected on the last page of the pamphlet to read "full national autonomy" (Bund biblio.: *Chetvertyi s"ezd*, pp. 14, 18).

question and would simplify the relations of the RSDWP with other national organizations. Accordingly they resolved:

Conceiving the Russian Social Democratic Workers' Party to be a federated Social Democratic party uniting all ethnic groups residing in the Russian state, the Congress resolves that the Bund, as a representative of the Jewish proletariat, should enter it as a federated part and directs the Central Committee of the Bund to implement this decision.[17]

The First Congress of the RSDWP had granted the Bund a vague autonomy in matters concerning the Jewish workers, some numbers of whom the Bund had organized and given ideological direction. Now the Bund was seeking recognition virtually as a national party within Social Democracy. The call for reorganization of the RSDWP contrasted with the suggested abstention from the use of national propaganda and caution on implementing principles about the future of the nationalities. The failure to reconcile these apparent contradictions was to plague the Bund for years.

The congress's resolution to expand the Bund's work into southern Russia merely reflected the Bund's desire to represent the Jewish proletariat fully. The same desire prompted the congress to change the name of the organization to include Lithuania. Henceforth the Bund's formal name was "The General Jewish Workers' Union in Lithuania, Poland, and Russia." The congress also decided to add other geographical names as needed. It was not ready, however, to add the south to its title; and it rejected the use of the word Russia alone, fearing to give a false impression of the Bund's work in Poland.[18]

If the Fourth Congress's resolutions on organization and nationalities were not totally new to the Bundists, who had long been discussing them among themselves, they seemed an abrupt departure as far as outsiders were concerned, even within the ranks of Russian Social Democracy. The congress articulated a position that was both more readily defended and more readily attacked than the broad and vague generalizations about self-determination and equal rights adopted in earlier years. Yet in tactical terms the congress soundly rejected any immediate new stand among the Jewish workers. The Bundists in Russia found themselves in the awkward position of at once fearing and being pushed by events to find a solution to the problem of Jewish identity in Russia. Their answer was a peculiar mixture of reluctance and insistence.

The national question took up the energies of the best minds in the Bund in the years after the Fourth Congress. In large part this meant the foreign contingent, for as always the necessity of dealing with immediate problems left the Bundists in Russia little time for open debates or public elaboration of principles. *Di Arbeter Shtime* did not concern itself with nationality disputes until late summer 1902, and even then it merely answered specific charges from other parties.

The Bund groups abroad, which had been growing since the turn of the century, were by no means united in their reaction to the new resolutions. Some Bundists were uneasy and unsure of their meaning; many found them altogether distasteful, some because they felt the congress had gone too far in support of the national position, others because they felt the congress had not gone far enough. To clear the air the Foreign Committee called a congress of Bund groups abroad, hoping at the same time to strengthen their sense of belonging to the Bund. This congress, which opened officially on January 2, 1902, formed a new united body, the Foreign Organizations of the Bund, with a Central Bureau directly linked to the Foreign Committee. The new group remained in existence until 1917.[19]

Kosovsky's keynote speech to the congress was published in February 1902 under the imprint of the Central Committee; it is the Bund's first publication specifically on the national question.[20] Kosovsky had little to add to what had been taken up at the Fourth Congress, but he grounded the arguments more firmly for the public and the Bundists abroad. He began by asking a practical question: why had the national issue been raised at all? "If the Bund were an organization of Great Russian workers and active somewhere in the province of Yaroslav," he suggested ironically, "the national question would not have come up even at a tenth congress." It arose because "the absence of a definite view on the national question in the Bund made itself felt at every step." The programs and demands of other nationalities around them captured the imagination of the Jewish workers. Moreover, their support was being solicited by a bourgeois party with nationalist ideals. Under the circumstances, said Kosovsky, it was doubtful that a simple call for self-determination sufficed to attract the workers to the Bund.[21] The motive for raising the national question thus appeared as both a social need and a defensive response to the actions of other parties. If the Bund would not consider the problem, Kosovsky declared, then others would. Once posed, the question demanded the best possible answer the Bund and Social Democracy could give.

In Kosovsky's view the national question required a two-pronged answer from the Bund, a solution to the problem of nationality in general and another specifically applicable to the Jews. He answered the general question by first answering the specific one. Like the Austrian Social Democrats, the Bund had found the concept of "national organisms" rather than the notion of national-territorial units a suitable solution. Further, it viewed the Jews as a national group, upheld their right to exist as such, and sought means of ensuring their continued existence through cultural and civil equality. The Jews could continue their national life by maintaining their educational, linguistic, and artistic individuality while participating in civil functions such as taxation and communications on the same basis as all other citizens.[22] In this arrangement lay the heart of national cultural autonomy.

Kosovsky's thoughts were at least as much a defense of the Bund's right to hold a national point of view as a detailed examination of the problem itself. However, his effort to spell out the national position satisfied the Congress of Foreign Organizations. Many of the vaguer points in the resolutions of the Fourth Congress had now been made clear enough to soothe most opposition, though some of the most nationally minded members abroad tried unsuccessfully to push through strong resolutions of their own.[23] The uncertainty about the precise relation of socialism to the national question was by no means completely dissipated.

Between the Fourth and Fifth congresses the majority of the intellectuals abroad, notably the old pioneers, Kosovsky, Kremer, and Mill, and the new young lights, Liber, Medem, and a later arrival, Raphael Abramovich (later famous as a Menshevik as well as a Bundist), strongly backed the national approach. At a meeting of selected Bundists convened in May 1903 in Geneva to prepare resolutions for the forthcoming Fifth Congress, Abramovich's proposal that this view be endorsed was adopted almost unanimously.[24] With Abramovich's help Medem drafted a resolution to that effect for the forthcoming congress.[25]

But the balance of opinion was considerably different at the Fifth Congress, which met in Zurich in June 1903. Present among the 30 delegates were the most important leaders from Russia as well as Western Europe: Portnoy, Izenshtat, Kopelson, Kremer, Kosovsky, Katz, Weinstein, and Medem (who sat as a special delegate to deliver the resolution). As a result the congress was a far less harmonious gathering than the preparatory conference at Geneva.[26]

The exact wording of the resolution Medem presented is not known, for no copy of it has survived. However, his major ideas can be reconstructed from the summaries of the discussions at the congress.[27] Like Kosovsky and Mill, Medem maintained that Social Democracy had to provide an answer for the national question just as it did for all other questions. He saw three possible solutions. Two of these—the nationalist and the assimilationist—he dismissed out of hand, the nationalist view because it fostered particularism, the assimilationist view because it deliberately erased all qualities of uniqueness. The third solution—the Social Democratic one—was neutral.

To Medem neutrality meant "that each given group can solve the problem in its own way." A people's particular path of development, its national identity (*angeherikait* in Yiddish), was not important "for itself alone." What mattered in the Social Democratic way was the positive aim of defending oppressed nationalities from enforced assimilation.[28] Medem's position, which became known as Neutralism, made Social Democracy no more than a means through which all nationalities could be guaranteed the freedom to seek their own path. Neutralism was one of the few new elaborations produced after the Fourth Congress, though its influence was short-lived.

The rest of Medem's argument concerned national cultural autonomy, which he saw as the proper solution for the plight of the Jews. In his view there was a Jewish national culture now, and there would continue to be one in the future. "It is impossible to imagine," he remarked in reply to an opponent, "that the Jewish masses will lose their specific identity."[29] The Bund's activity fitted well with this conception: "All are agreed that the Bund is necessary, that for the Jewish masses an official agitation and propaganda are necessary."[30]

Many of the delegates did not share the view that Social Democracy and the goal of national cultural autonomy were compatible. Some insisted that the future of the Jews lay in assimilation rather than rebirth. Kopelson, the major opponent abroad of the national point of view, felt that the most cultured Jews were becoming assimilated, leaving the rest of the Jewish population to fall into a low cultural and spiritual state; he saw this as a serious threat both to the health of the Jewish people and to the cause of the proletariat.[31] Kopelson defended assimilation in principle, invoking the authority of Marx, who had suggested this solution for small ethnic groups. "Assimilation means that the intelligentsia adopts Russian culture (because it is higher than Jewish culture)," Kopelson declared; "accepting international culture in a Russian form, the intelligentsia becomes assimilated."[32] Jews in England and the United States were undergoing this process, and the continuing growth of capitalism would draw the Jews further into this stream.

Other opponents, though not endorsing the Kopelson view, questioned the necessity of Medem's resolution rather than its correctness. To Sholom Levin, a dedicated worker active for years in the operation of various secret Bund presses, the essential problem was the Jewish worker's lack of freedom to assimilate. In his opinion the autonomy Medem proposed could be realized only in a democratic republic. "But then," Levin suggested, "it will not be needed in Russia because all freedoms will be guaranteed." Why was the resolution necessary then? Jews had helped advance Spanish culture in Spain; they would help advance Russian culture in Russia. Autonomy would make no difference.[33] On the whole Levin preferred to let the future determine itself, though he was inclined, at least implicitly, to favor a strong cultural rapprochement between the nationalities.

Another of Medem's critics was Izenshtat (who because of his early arrest and exile was attending his first Bund Congress). He wondered how calls for autonomy and neutrality could be raised simultaneously. Insisting on the fundamental relationship between means and ends, Izenshtat found the two issues contradictory and an invitation to national aspirations. Though he made no flat-out statement to that effect, he believed Social Democracy required submission to class discipline, and that what was important was not a national program but achieving a proletarian viewpoint within the national context.[34]

In all these debates no one seriously questioned the usefulness of the Bund at the moment. But there was a considerable difference of opinion on its future role. Kopelson saw no reason for the Bund after the Jewish workers achieved full civil equality. Once their exceptional legal status disappeared, allowing them to take their place in the international community of workers, the Bund too would disappear.[35] Joining him in this position was Yoina Koigan, an activist from the southern provinces, who asserted that "the Bund exists only insofar as the Jewish proletariat aspires to eliminate exceptional laws and insofar as it does not use Russian." He denied the Bund's claim to continue as a national party once equal rights were acquired and the Jews learned Russian. He differed slightly from Kopelson in not rejecting cultural autonomy altogether, believing that if national aspirations developed among the Jews, cultural autonomy would be necessary. At the moment, however, he saw no need to press for it.[36] His position at least offered the possibility of an on-going organization. Levin, for his part, continued to deny the value of autonomy; yet at one point he observed that the Bund actually took the place of autonomy.[37] In this seeming ambiguity he may have been seeking to affirm his opposition to a formal national position without dismissing the notion of a living social phenomenon.

The proponents of the national position saw national culture developing strongly in the present and insisted that it be guaranteed a place in the future democratic Russia. Kosovsky linked the growth of Jewish culture with the Jewish labor movement: "If one does not want the development of national culture, then one should come forth against the Jewish labor movement." He maintained that the Bund was playing a direct role in national development and was fostering national autonomy by its activities. National culture sprang from the masses and had to be ensured full freedom.[38] The Bund was an instrument for the development of national culture, the crucial link between means and goals. Frumkin considered Kosovsky's stand Zionistic.[39]

In the end the call for Neutralism and the active pursuit of national cultural autonomy did not find enough support to pass. The Fifth Congress upheld the decision of the Fourth. But the vote was evenly split, indicating a clear shift toward acceptance as compared with the Fourth Congress. This outcome was hardly surprising in view of the presence at the Fifth Congress of a strong contingent from abroad, including the firmest supporters of the resolution, and in view of the fact that many of those attending the Fourth Congress had known little or nothing about the subject.

Altered attitudes since the turn of the century also contributed to the new mood. David Katz, who had opposed Mill at the Third Congress, now defended Yiddish culture and its future;[40] and Portnoy, who had rejected active national work in 1901, also softened his position. He felt that, troublesome as it was to determine the Bund's future course, neutrality was not the answer. Like Kosovsky, he saw national development as a positive rather than a destructive process in the class development of the Jews, and Yiddish as a form of cultural growth. There was no assurance that the bourgeois democratic order, the next stage of political development, would guarantee the rights to which national cultures were entitled. On these grounds agitation for autonomy was necessary now, just as autonomy itself was essential in the future.

Emotional intensity was very high at the Fifth Congress. It was but two months since the savage Kishinev pogrom, and the image of dead, wounded, shamed, and impoverished Jews was fresh in the minds of all. Moreover, the congress faced the task of preparing for a forthcoming RSDWP congress, which meant confronting the vigorous new *Iskra* forces. Under these pressures, equanimity was not always possible. "Among some of the adherents of 'national cultural autonomy,' " Levin records, "the rejection of any resolution was so tragic that they accepted it with tears in their eyes."[41]

The Fourth Congress's resolutions on the national question were severely criticized by both the Iskraites and the Zionists. Of the two, the criticism that interested the Bund the most, because of the source's deep commitment to Social Democracy, was that of the Iskraites. It was Martov, the old comrade of pioneer days in Vilna, who drew the first blood in an article in the August 1901 issue of *Iskra*.[42] Martov approached the national question with caution. Skirting the issue of the future of the Jews, he asked, with rhetorical displeasure, if there were to be "self-ruling communes" wherever the Jewish population formed a majority? In a more serious vein, he deplored "the development of nationalism" among the Jewish Social Democrats of Western Russia and Poland since the Bund's Third Congress. The Bund's desire "to squeeze the Jewish workers' movement into a narrow channel of nationalism" was artificial and a great political error "when the main evil choking the Jewish masses in Russia is government policy, which restrains their rapprochement with the surrounding population."[43] In Martov's judgment, by moving toward nationalism the Bund had weakened its ties with the general workers' movement.

The Bund's Central Committee hastened to reply. In a letter to *Iskra* that coupled explanation with rebuke, the committee rejected Martov's comment on "self-ruling communes" and maintained that its own sketch of the future was sufficiently clear; language, education, and art had been specifically mentioned as areas for autonomous existence; nothing had been said about territorial independence, as Martov implied. The committee also justified its attention to national rights on the ground that the question, once having been raised, could not be ignored. "Can a nationality, aware of itself as such, not acknowledge itself openly," the committee inquired, "and acknowledging itself, renounce what it considers just for all nationalities?"[44] The committee admitted that the force of circumstances had pressed it to deal with the national question, but argued that the problem had to be dealt with in principle in any case. Besides, the committee insisted, the resolutions did not go beyond the policies of earlier congresses.

How *Iskra* felt about the national question did not come through clearly from this exchange. Martov confined himself to branding the appearance of the issue harmful. Though he lauded those Jews who worked with the Russians, he carefully avoided all reference to the Jews as a national group. He accepted, along with the Bund, the goal of abolishing exceptional laws. But what was to happen to the Jews once that was accomplished? Martov's answer was vague in the extreme: rapprochement. His own rapprochement was his cultural assimilation. Did he believe that all Jews should take that course? His sharp criticism of the Bundists for retarding rapprochement certainly implied that he did.

As chance would have it, just ahead of the Martov criticism *Iskra* printed a news item on the Polish Social Democrats that reported their adoption of a resolution proposing "full national autonomy for the Finns, Poles, Lithuanians, and all other peoples who reside in Russia," along with another calling for the organization of the Social Democratic Party of Russia on a federative basis."[45] *Iskra* did not comment on the report.

After this preliminary indecisive skirmish, the Iskraites rested their case for almost a year. Then in August 1902 they published a lengthy article on the Bund's national stand in their theoretical journal, *Zaria*, which was edited by the Liberation of Labor Group.[46] The author, Eliyahu Davidson (K. K.) had helped write Yiddish educational publications and had been close to the Bund circles in Berlin, where he had worked for *Der Yidisher Arbeter*. He had joined the Iskraites shortly after *Zaria* was founded.[47]

Davidson's whole case was based on the contention that nationality could not be defined in cultural terms as the Bund suggested. "In fact," he asserted, "the Jews have no national culture (if one does not count religion and some social customs tied to it)."[48] Davidson was willing to recognize the need for autonomy under certain conditions: it was important "insofar as it liberates a people from its enslaved condition." But a nationality had the right to autonomy only "when its working classes need it." The real question then was, did the Jews qualify as a nationality? Davidson insisted they failed to do so on many counts: how could those "who do not compose a compact mass of the population anywhere but find themselves in a minority everywhere, who have not had political independence, who long ago lost their national culture and suffer unbearably from the fact that the autocratic government does not allow them access to Russian culture" merit such a rank? Only the Zionists, who hoped for a rebirth of the Jews' ancient culture and the reestablishment of Jewish political independence could recognize the Jews as a nationality.[49]

In the main the Iskraites and the Bundists were arguing the question of the future. Davidson recognized existing cultural differences, but he refused to acknowledge that the present differences justified self-determination in the future—as recognized in the party manifesto of 1898. Insofar as the Iskraites dealt with the future of the Jews, they implied that assimilation was the answer. They proposed that path, however, simply as a desirable tendency, not as an avowed goal. The Bund attempted to wed the democratic features of Social Democracy to a people's right to maintain its distinctiveness if it so chose. The support of the principle of cultural autonomy at the Fourth Congress was based as much on the principle of democracy as on national considerations. The congress did not assume that the Jews had to maintain their culture at all costs—that question was left open even at the Fifth Congress. In sum, the Bund felt that in principle the Jews ought to be allowed whatever institutions they needed for the continuation of their culture, whereas the Iskraites in essence rejected the notion of the Jews as a separate (national) culture, though they conceded that certain distinctions existed presently. There was an overlap in these positions, but the differences outweighed the points of coincidence.

The Iskraites were not particularly concerned with the general question of nationality in the first half of 1903. The issue seems to have been forced on them, and *Iskra*'s articles to have been counterthrusts to events. Commenting briefly on a manifesto heralding the appearance of the League of Armenian Social Democrats, Lenin reduced the matter of the Armenians' call for a future republic in a federated Russia to a call for equal rights and self-determination. He hoped to return to the question in the future.[50]

In this period Lenin, like Davidson, held that self-determination was conditional. Responding to an attack by the PPS in mid-July, Lenin asked: "Does recognition of the *right* of nations to self-determination imply *support* of every demand by every people for self-determination?" His answer was that it did not. The struggle of the proletariat required "that we *subordinate* the demand for national self-determination. It is this that makes all the difference between our approach to the national question and the bourgeois-democratic approach."[51] Lenin stood for unity now and self-determination in the future— for those who deserved it. The Iskraites were not willing to examine the national question thoroughly or to allow what they considered a harmful issue to interfere with their plans to construct a united party under their direction.

It was inevitable that the Zionists, too, would confront the Bundists. Zionism continued to produce socialist and labor variants between 1901 and 1903. The Bund and the labor Zionists differed substantially both in their estimation of the present and in their picture of the future. The Bundists assumed the eventual achievement of full democracy for Jewish workers in Russia, a possibility the Zionists firmly denied. The Bund based its belief on the Marxian class ideal of proletarian unity and the assumption that the atmosphere of economic, social, and political justice inherent in democracy and socialism would be hospitable to national differences. The leading exponents of Zionism, socialist or otherwise, believed that the Jewish masses could not achieve true freedom anywhere save in a land of their own.

One of the most outspoken labor Zionists was Nachman Syrkin. In an appeal to Jewish youth—which appeared during the very month the Fourth Congress convened—Syrkin offered his own view of the correct path and pointed out what he took to be his opponents' errors. His harshest criticism was directed at the traditional Zionists, who had made Zionism "a 'Utopia' of slavery" and deprived it of its vitality through their bourgeois, reactionary vision of the ideal.[52] According to Syrkin, Zionism sprang from the awareness of the Jewish masses that they had no economic position in the lands of others, and that they would continue to suffer poverty and injustice until such time as they found a homeland where they could live their national life under a socialist order.[53] To be sure, realization of this ideal would not come easily or quickly. In the meantime the socialist Zionist must engage in the fight for dignity and material improvement—never, however, losing sight of his ultimate goal.[54]

As for Jewish socialists who were indifferent to the Zionist cause, Syrkin saw them as victims of a misapprehension based on their social heritage, as the sons of the Jewish bourgeoisie that developed after the freeing of the serfs. They had rejected their own national being for alien cultures and were antinational. It was their duty to come forth and oppose reactionary Zionism for the sake of the socialist Zionist concept of the future.[55]

In another article Syrkin attacked the Bund's doctrine of cultural autonomy as grossly inadequate for any national minority worthy of the name. A grouping of citizens without territory in a state in which each nationality had equal rights seemed to him a poor substitute for real national autonomy. Without territory there was no foundation for political and civil laws; and the Jews' own history taught that a people without their own laws had no claim to autonomy. Under the Bund's system the law would remain an alien institution. Further, the Jews of Russia were not prepared for national autonomy. They had no tradition of Jewish courts and self-administration to draw on: "How could one ask that life be led on the basis of the old Jewish law?" The Bund, Syrkin contended, childishly attempted to use a rule of autonomy devised for Austria because it had not thought through how unsuitable it was for the Jews. Even the Russian Jewish culture was not a matter of choice. What told the Bund, Syrkin asked, that Jews wanted to put up signs in jargon (Yiddish) on their businesses and shops? Indeed, if the government allowed such a practice, the Jews would feel persecuted. The rise of Zionism indicated the Jews' felt need for independent nationhood; and it was the Hebrew language, so closely tied to Jewish history, that should become the tool for informing the Jews of the outside world and their own condition. The Bund's national autonomy was foolishness, a reactionary stupidity that no one took seriously. Syrkin asked:

How does the Bund then really answer the Jewish question, that is, the question about the historical development of the masses to productive work, to socialism, to culture, to freedom, to our national creativity? It is incapable of answering because it is the enemy of the historical development of the Jews, of Zionism.[56]

For Syrkin's Zionists the Bund's answer placed it squarely in the heritage of the reactionary Jewish bourgeoisie, which sought assimilation for its own purposes, not for the benefit of the Jewish masses.

The labor Zionists agreed with their fellow Zionists in a strong contempt for the existing culture of the Jews in Russia. Although some Bundists regarded Yiddish culture with a jaundiced eye, considering it at best as a temporary nuisance, most favored work in Yiddish, and many of the most important Bundists saw a bright future for the language of the masses. But Syrkin and his fellows saw in Yiddish a heritage of degradation, which had to be overcome: "Since jargon is not the national Jewish language, but only one of the unfortunate populist forms of Jewish life, cultural work includes substituting Hebrew and European languages for this language in folk life."[57] The Zionist Asher Ginzberg (Ahad Haam) was undoubtedly referring to the Bundists when he told a Zionist Congress in Minsk in 1902 that "there is now among us a party which would raise this jargon to the dignity of a national language." Asserting further that "there is not a single nation, alive or dead, of which we can say that it existed before its national language," he declared: "The jargon, like all other languages which the Jews have employed at different times, never has been and never will be regarded by the [Jewish people] as anything but an external and temporary medium of intercourse."[58] As far as the Zionists were concerned, Yiddish was a doomed tongue. It was a transitory medium that could only open the way to assimilation.

The developing socioeconomic status of the Jew also provided grounds for deep-seated differences between the Bundists and the Zionists. In the Bund's historical conception the fate of the Jewish worker in Russia was linked to the development of capitalism. The growth of capitalism introduced class divisions into the Jewish community; and these would inevitably lead the Jewish workers to join their proletarian brothers in the class struggle. For now the Jewish workers' fight against capital was primarily a fight against Jewish employers. But in an expanding capitalist environment, coupled with a rise of democracy, the Jewish workers would gain access to the employment opportunities available to all workers in an industrialized democratic society.

The Zionists attacked the Bund on the basis of the gap between its hopes and the existing realities. Rejecting the Marxist framework that allowed the Bundists to predict the development of the entire Empire, including the Jewish population, the Zionists countered by analyzing the economic life of the Jews against a background of anti-Semitism and legal restrictions. The difficulty the Jewish worker had selling his labor was a major concern of early labor Zionist literature. One call to the workers in Minsk read: "Brothers, can we improve our economic conditions under these circumstances with a *gilden* a week raise, with the hour's less work we get out of the boss?" And though the economic struggle had to be continued: "We must not forget that we won't get far with it. . . . We must fight for every crumb because we have little bread, and for all this we have to thank the bitter Diaspora." There was no point in waiting for democracy, for the time when people would become good, because they would remain bad.[59] The Bund's hopes for proletarian brotherhood were impossible. Only by possessing their own land could Jewish workers develop a full, productive life—and even take up agriculture, if they so chose, thus forever freeing themselves of the stigma of "parasite."

The Bund fought back, insisting that the Jewish workers' difficulties were due to shortcomings in the existing society, which would be rectified when the Bund's goals were realized. Where the Zionists saw a still-undeveloped working class composed of backward artisans, the Bund saw a rapidly developing Jewish proletariat. Where the Zionists saw the exclusion of Jewish workers from modern industry as a function of national hatred, the Bundists saw the workings of a set of legal restrictions that would be eliminated in the future. Where the Zionists saw enmity between Christian and Jew as a bar to joint employment and as a permanent condition, the Bund saw merely the lack of the necessary class consciousness, especially on the part of the Christians, who participated more fully in the bourgeois society. Where the Zionists saw anti-Semitism as a factor operating against employment of Jewish workers, the Bundists saw residential restrictions that barred Jews from working in the new industrial areas outside the Pale, as well as a strong class consciousness that made the Jewish worker troublesome to employers. (The last point was intended to dig deep, for as the Bundists pointed out, Jewish employers, some of them Zionists, fired Jewish workers for this very reason.) A democratic republic would solve many of these differences and inequities. In the long run, it was only the Russian government that shut out the Jewish workers from modern industry. In a democratic republic, the Bundists noted with sarcasm, the Jewish worker would have the good fortune to be exploited with all other workers—and the possibility as well of ending his exploitation.[60]

By mid-1903 the general outlines of the Bund's national position, and that of the parties most intimately related to it by ideology and historical circumstance, were clear. The Bundists did not make great theoretical advances between 1901 and 1903. Only Neutralism, which made Social Democracy a possible tool in the attainment of a national future, was brought forth for discussion. With only the barebones outline provided by the Fourth Congress and Kosovsky's explanation to work with, the Bund was unable to go further in spelling out its vision of a Jewish future. But however vague the Bund's position, its stand on the national issue placed it in a crossfire. Despite the ideological gulf between the Zionists and the Iskraites, they shared the view that the expressions of Jewish life in Russia were poor specimens of true nationality. It is perhaps significant, in this respect, that Davidson and Syrkin knew each other well and were even close for a time in Berlin before Davidson went over to the Iskraites.[61] For those Bundists who advocated a national course for their organization, the future rested on the development of the existing culture. For their opponents, the future spelled the end of the existing culture—in probable assimilation, according to the Iskraites, in national independence without the heritage of Yiddish and the Diaspora, according to the Zionists.

The Bund thus faced attack from two directions. To its Zionist critics it seemed assimilationist—whether consciously or unconsciously—and therefore anti-national. To its Iskraite critics it appeared Zionist or nationalist, the one as much a breach of the international principles of Marxism as the other. The Bund's middle road, the attempt to fit a Jewish national consciousness into a broader, Russian framework, found no easy acceptance—either inside or outside the organization.

14. The Bund and 'Iskra': The First Clashes

The Bund's evolution toward full partyhood occurred simultaneously with the Iskraites' aspirations to build and lead a united Russian Social Democratic party. Although it was not immediately apparent how serious the differences between the two organizations were, by February 1903, when the Bundists joined the Iskraite Organization Committee to set up the Second Congress of the RSDWP, both groups were jockeying for position, and it was all too clear that they were following separate paths.

Martov found more to criticize in the work of the Bund's Fourth Congress than the resolution on the national question. In the same article in *Iskra* (August 1901) he expressed his displeasure at the Bund's decision to work in the south, which he saw as a tactical elaboration of its national errors. He pointed out that in the south "the Jewish proletarians work hand in hand, as is well known, with the Russians on behalf of the common demands of the Russian proletariat" and would not respond favorably to the Bund's "national passion."[1] He also challenged the Bund's resolution to alter its official relationship with the RSDWP. So fundamental a change could not be made unilaterally, Martov said, for the whole party would be affected. It seemed to him that the language adopted—"the Bund . . . should enter [the party] as a federated part"—indicated an attempt to present the party with a *fait accompli*, and thus the Bund's action was clearly illegal.[2]

Replying to this last charge, the Bund's Central Committee accused Martov of creating misunderstanding and of patent inaccuracies: he had not quoted the resolution in full; if he had filled in the blanks, the whole question of party organization would never have arisen. The sense of the omitted words, the committee insisted, was that the Bund meant "to raise a motion at the next party congress" about federation.[3] Admittedly, if the Bund had attempted to federalize the party on its own, it would have been acting illegally. As it was, the only instance in which the Bund might consider an alteration in this direction was in the relationship between its Foreign Committee and the Russian Social Democratic organizations abroad.

If all this was little more than bickering over words, the Central Committee still found *Iskra*'s tone disturbing. Snappishly it reminded the Russians that the Bund reported only to the party's Central Committee or to party congresses, not to member organizations—"and even less to groups whose party membership . . . does not yet exist outside of the masthead on its publication."[4] *Iskra* had no right to serve as the Bund's prosecutor, the committee held.

Behind the sparring lay the issue of party organization. The Iskraites, with their own agenda and timetable, had made it plain as early as 1900 that they opposed any independent steps toward party reunification. They feared the Bund's resolutions on the same grounds. The structural change proposed by the Bund raised the possibility of fragmentation and dimmed the prospects for the type of unity they considered necessary for success. The issue was also a crucial one for the Bund. Since it was already carrying on most of the activities it wanted to see incorporated in the party's structure, essentially what it was asking for was official recognition of a de facto situation and the extension of the same rights to the entire camp of Social Democracy.

The Bund's explanations and Martov's reply temporarily calmed the ruffled feelings on both sides. Martov expressed his pleasure with some of the explanations. He was not wholly satisfied on the organization question, however. Reiterating his fear of unilateral action, he pointed to the Bund's arrangements on federation with the Union Abroad as an example of how the Bund might take advantage of the party's weakness to alter its position; here, certainly, was justification for censure.[5]

The first round of recrimination ended on this note. Neither of the parties had plans to organize that would have precipitated a head-on battle. The only possible field of friction was in southern Russia, where both organizations were attempting to build a following. Abroad, the Russian Social Democratic camp was in an uproar and in no condition to take firm steps toward unity. Nevertheless, the skirmish over organization was a portent of future battles between *Iskra* and the Bund, and it was in this exchange that the battlelines began to be drawn.

To be sure, this was not clear at the time. Despite their word jousts, the two organizations gave little time and attention to the question of their relations. Each followed its own path in the Russian Social Democratic movement. A much greater preoccupation was the row between the major Russian factions in Western Europe—the Union Abroad and Plekhanov's Russian Revolutionary Organization "Social Democrat," a new group created in May 1900 after the bitter feud at the Union's Second Congress. Early in 1901 a group of Social Democrats in Paris, among them D. B. Riazanov and I. M. Steklov, attempted to mediate the differences, calling for a meeting as a preliminary step toward reestablishing unity.

The Iskraites moved cautiously, weighing the pros and cons of the proposal

They were still far from having a solid machine. As late as May 1901 Lenin found the organization in a deplorably weak state.[6] And the next month Akselrod described the Iskraites as "a talented literary group . . . devoid of the slightest following or operational basis abroad." He contrasted the *Iskra* group with the Bund, for which he had little love, but which he was forced to admit was "an active organization abroad and in Russia." Musing over the problem of finances, he saw the Bundists as "nimble dealers . . . who quietly make arrangements."[7] Next to *Iskra*, the Bund appeared a polished organization.

Under the circumstances, the Iskraites had no wish to alienate potentially friendly groups like the Parisians or to give up hope of gaining the support of the Bund. Lenin commented to Akselrod in April 1901 that the Parisians were unhappy about the attacks on the Union Abroad.[8] Since one of the Iskraites' main themes was the necessity of combining all forces, they could ill-afford to have it said they had refused to attend a meeting designed to improve relations with fellow Social Democrats. Accordingly, they agreed to the meeting, reacting as they had the year before to the invitation to meet in Smolensk. They felt safe enough in any case, for they assumed the meeting had little chance of success.[9]

An exploratory conference took place in Geneva in June 1901, a few months before the war of words between Martov and the Central Committee. The Iskraites were careful with the Bund. They considered challenging its presence at the meeting on the grounds that it was an autonomous organization only insofar as Jewish affairs were concerned, and so not entitled to sit in on these discussions. They finally decided, however, not to make the matter a "casus belli."[10]

The Iskraites had been following the maneuverings among the various Social Democratic groups abroad with great interest. Akselrod, for instance, felt it worthwhile to point out to his comrades in Munich in late May 1901 that the Bund's new Russian-language paper, *Posledniia izvestiia*, was published in the Bund's name, not the Union's, and to speculate that this might indicate the weakness of the Union.[11] At about the same time Martov wrote to his old friend Kremer in an attempt to persuade him of the correctness of the *Iskra* line. He recognized, with a touch of sadness, that they were no longer in the same camp but hoped they would continue to communicate.[12] Kremer, Mill, and Kosovsky attended the Geneva meeting. To Kosovsky, Martov seemed more distant than before, not friendly but always correct and even formal.[13] *Iskra* still had hopes of winning the Bund over, despite their gradually deteriorating relations.

The Geneva conference produced an agreement for a formal meeting in the fall. But there was a sudden new development shortly before the so-called Unification Congress took place. Meeting just a few days before the projected assembly, the Third Congress of the Union Abroad altered the draft agreement made at Geneva; at the same time *Rabochee delo* carried certain articles that the Iskraites took as a rejection of the Geneva principles. The Iskraites had reserved the right to propose their own changes in the June document, and the Union's actions encouraged them to use this loophole.

Perhaps the most significant cause of the worsening relations between the Union Abroad and *Iskra* was the growing popularity of the latter. After a trip to Russia in mid-1901 K. I. Tsederbaum, Martov's sister, returned to Europe to report that the new organ had gained the sympathetic interest of a number of organizations.[14] In the opinion of Steklov, one of the would-be mediators, by October, when the Unification Congress met in Zurich, Lenin had received indications that *Iskra* was doing well and thus saw no need for unification with the Union.[15]

At the Union's Third Congress the Bund's Foreign Committee and the Union, without discussion of principle, established a new working arrangement in accordance with the resolution of the Bund's Fourth Congress. The agreement was conditional, subject to the ratification of both sides. The two groups chose a council in which each had equal voice and agreed not to enter into any separate federation with other Russian socialist organizations abroad. These arrangements were designed to last only three months.[16] The Foreign Committee was intent on establishing its position wherever possible.

The Iskraites did not react to this change. Indeed, at the Zurich meeting, as at the Geneva meeting, they made little effort to solicit the Bund's support. This fits with the suggestion Martov made in a letter in mid-July to the effect that *Iskra* did not demand support from the Bund.[17] The Bundists attended Zurich as observers and took no part in the discussions. Seemingly, the Iskraites would have been satisfied to neutralize the Bund by tearing it away from the Union.

The Iskraites finally broke with the Union Abroad at the Unification Congress and formed a new organization, the League of Russian Revolutionary Social Democracy Abroad. How little Lenin and Martov were worried about the new Bund-Union partnership is apparent in a private conversation they had with the Bund representatives. The day after the Iskraites' dramatic departure from the meeting, an event that made a painful impression on the Bundists, Lenin and Martov visited the Bund delegation. Lenin acted as spokesman. Expressing his amazement that the Bund could have remained so long tied to the Union, which had played such a harmful role in the socialist movement, he asked where the Bundists now stood in light of recent events. It seemed to him the Bund would compromise itself if it remained within the Union. Answering for the Bundists, Kremer reminded the Iskraites that the Union was still the official representative of the RSDWP and indicated that the Bund would remain in it until a party congress decided otherwise. There was no further discussion.[18]

The relations between the Bund and *Iskra* also deteriorated in Russia, but less obviously so than in Europe. The Iskraites' attitude toward the resolutions of the Fourth Congress strained the already uneasy bonds between the two groups. S. O. Tsederbaum had continued to negotiate with Portnoy for help in transporting literature, but the talks came to a standstill after the clash in *Iskra* when both insisted on their own point of view. The Iskraites demanded that the Bund follow their lead in breaking with the Union Abroad and support *Iskra* as the general organ of Social Democracy.[19] The Bundists refused, and nothing came of the Tsederbaum-Portnoy negotiations.

But personal ties were not so easily broken. In fact, both before and after, organizational differentiation was sometimes vague. Says Osip Piatnitsky:

> If some one had asked me to which Social Democratic organization I belonged, I would not have been able to say precisely.... In the summer of 1901, when I was already strongly tied to the *Iskra* organization and in fact on a trip to Kovno on *Iskra* business, the local Bundists asked me to take part in organizing and leading a strike of workers.... I agreed, of course.[20]

In many instances, relatives and friends managed to live with the ideological differences. The Goldman brothers, for instance, followed different revolutionary paths without a family split. When B. I. Goldman leaned toward the Iskraites on his return from exile in 1901, his younger brother Mark Liber merely sought to persuade him not to fight the Bund if he joined them. Later, in 1903, Goldman would try to effect a compromise between the two organizations.[21]

The Bundists abroad, meanwhile, were feeling increasingly isolated. In the autumn of 1901 Kremer glumly wrote Leon Bernstein: "Our affairs are weak enough in general; we have little means and even less strength."[22] After this complaint (a common enough one among revolutionaries, surely), he shed even more gloom:

> You know *Iskra* has come out against us openly; others will probably follow it, perhaps even the Union.
> I have not the least idea of Russian affairs. The Union does not write to me. Whether there will be a Union congress or a conference of all groups I do not know, and the comrades do not know either.

The fact that *Rabochee delo* no longer published news of the Jewish movement disturbed him greatly. "It is characteristic that suddenly there is no more room for such a report where once there was always room. A sign of the times. Is this not a second 'historical turning point'?"[23]

Kremer's words emphasize the leaders' conception of the Bund as a self-limiting organization, one that wanted to maintain a separate identity yet desired and needed to work within the broader framework of a general party. Though the Bund sought to protect and advance its own position by proposing federated status, it still needed and wanted a general movement and a party representing the entire proletariat. In contrast, the Iskraites seemed satisfied to solicit the Bund's support, and, failing that, to shunt aside this ally of their most important Russian competitors.

Despite the fiasco at Zurich, practical revolutionary needs and the obvious importance of cooperating overrode or muted disagreements among the Social Democrats in Russia. Moreover, to the Bundists, unification now appeared even more desirable, not only as a good in itself but also as a means of resolving differences—an attitude the Iskraites found regrettable.

The Bundists' hopes for a reunified RSDWP did not die with the failure of Smolensk in 1900, or even after other unsuccessful efforts. It is of some interest in respect to the development of the Bund as a party to note that the Bundists were willing in 1900 and early 1901 to participate in unification ventures with a regional emphasis, a popular idea at the time.[24] In the end the Bund undertook to arrange a congress of the RSDWP on its own.[25] As Rosenthal explains:

The success of the Fourth Congress of the Bund had enthused us, and we believed we would be able to call the congress.... We thought that if we could succeed in carrying out this work, which no one had been able to effect until then, [and that] if the congress would conduct itself peacefully and choose a unifying center of leadership—an authoritative Central Committee—it would perhaps be possible to create a united Social Democratic front, and the inimical tendencies and atmosphere of factional dispute would end.[26]

The Central Committee decided the meeting should be held in Belostok so it could oversee the technical arrangements, a matter of great importance in light of the dismal experience of the First RSDWP Congress.

Though the Bund's own problems made it keenly aware of an isolation that only a unified party could dispel, its reasons for this new attempt were the same as in 1898: the Bundists still believed wholeheartedly that real unity would come only through cooperative, practical work. Furthermore, in view of the recent disappointment at Zurich, we can suppose the Bund was also interested, again as in 1898, in ensuring its position within the party. The Bundists were aware of the difficulties their project entailed, and expected the Iskraites to resist the proposal, just as they had resisted all previous attempts to call congresses.[27]

The Central Committee began making firm arrangements for the meeting in late 1901. Shortly after, in January 1902, Portnoy went to the southern provinces and Zeldov to those in the north to extend invitations. Meanwhile Rosenthal made the local arrangements, finding a trusted couple to move into the new quarters that were rented, complete with furniture, for the meeting. Some organizations donated money to help offset the Bund's expenses.

The Foreign Committee and the Union Abroad made the necessary contacts in the West. As expected, the Iskraites regarded the proposed meeting with distaste. Nadezhda Krupskaia (Lenin's wife) wrote that "no one was taking the Bund's attempt to convoke a congress in Belostok seriously."[28] Elsewhere she dismissed the Bund's move as an attempt to gain the advantage over *Iskra*, whose position was sure to improve with time.[29] Plekhanov regarded the whole affair as pure intrigue.[30]

Lenin's attitude, preparations, and dispatch of a representative to the meeting belie Krupskaia's disparaging words. He worked hard to prepare for the event. In his report to the meeting he called the effort premature and pointed to an agenda that showed traces of Economism and lacked principle. But ever the realist, Lenin saw that he could not stop the meeting. Accordingly, he threw in a new suggestion: that the meeting be made merely a conference to prepare for a full-scale party congress a few months later and to appoint an organization committee to make the necessary arrangements.[31] Despite substantial gains, *Iskra* was still unprepared to build a party on its own and too weak to forestall efforts initiated by others.

In the end only a handful of delegates from widely scattered areas attended the Belostok meeting in April 1902. Present were Rosenthal and Portnoy, hosting for the Bund's Central Committee; Kremer representing the Foreign Committee; V. P. Krasnukha and Zeldov (a Bundist) of the St. Petersburg RSDWP Committee; A. O. Yermansky of the Union of Southern Committees; F. I. Shipulinsky of the Ekaterinoslav Committee; M. G. Kogan of the Union Abroad; and Fedor Dan of *Iskra*. A delegate from Nizhni-Novgorod, A. I. Piskunov, attended but left early and apparently took no part in the voting.[32]

The meeting was peaceful enough. The Iskraites accomplished their principal purpose, having the meeting designated a conference, without much difficulty; too few committees were represented to warrant calling the gathering a congress. Eventually the delegates unanimously bowed to the decision.[33] With this change most of the agenda was abandoned. The delegates confined themselves to issuing a statement of principle, formulating a May Day proclamation, and creating an Organization Committee (O.C.) for the future congress.

The mood of the delegates reflected the stresses within Social Democracy, though the desire for unity was also evident. When Dan proposed a statement of principle that strongly stressed revolutionary political goals, the Bundists balked, as did all the other delegates save the Ekaterinoslav representative, who abstained. But when the Southern Union countered with a proposal heavily slanted toward mass economic action, all the other delegates moved to the opposite side of the balance. The conference then temporarily agreed on a version presented by the Bund's Central Committee, which emphasized militant party organization and political struggle but left room for all types of revolutionary activity. The Southern Union and the Union Abroad succeeded in softening the Bund's formulation by amendment, leaving a statement that dissatisfied both the Bund and *Iskra*. Ultimately Dan refused to accept the resolution in its new form.

In general the Bund stood closest to *Iskra* in the positions adopted at the conference. In the balloting on ten proposals, the Central and Foreign committees of the Bund voted with *Iskra* six times, and abstained or opposed it on four. Even the two Bund delegations agreed on only seven of these votes, though they avoided opposing each other directly by abstentions. (Similarly, when the two delegates of the Central Committee disagreed, the committee vote was withheld altogether.) Dan wrote to *Iskra* immediately after the conference to report that "Aleksander [Kremer] supported me most of all in the question of principle and the Central Committee of the Bund sometimes."[34] But this did not imply any warm friendship.

The Bund's was the closest to a compromise position at the conference. The Bundists were willing to advocate militancy and unified political action, reflecting their own sharpening inclination toward political struggle, yet upheld all means of struggle. But compromise in general was in the air. Even Dan did not appear as extreme as his Iskraite comrades abroad. He was probably satisfied to attain his major goal—the heading off of a full congress—and felt he could then afford to relax.

After agreeing to publish a May 1 leaflet in the name of the party, the conference chose the O.C.: Dan, Yermansky, and Portnoy.[35] Both extremes (*Iskra* and the Southern Union) and the middle (the Bund) thus received representation.

The conference had a fateful end. In a virtual duplication of the events of March 1898, police agents tracked a number of the delegates to Belostok and arrested them shortly after the meeting dispersed. Among them were Rosenthal and several local Bund activists who had worked to set up the meeting, as well as two of the three members of the O.C., Dan and Yermansky. The remaining member, Portnoy, managed to escape.

But the conference had foreseen the possibility of police detection and disruption of the work of the O.C., deciding that if the committee should be captured "its reestablishment should be the business of all the members of the conference."[36] It was this slim reed, arising from a preliminary conference of a small number of Social Democrats, that supplied the thread to the second party congress.

The fate of the O.C. after the Belostok meeting had great significance for the Bund's relations with *Iskra* and the history of Russian Social Democracy.[37] The Iskraites learned of the proceedings through Dan, who was able to send a report before his arrest. When Kremer returned to Europe with the documents of the conference, he offered to give the Iskraites a personal report as well, but they declined.[38] Instead, they asked him for information on members of the O.C. and how to communicate with them.[39]

Convinced of the necessity of rebuilding the RSDWP on their own terms, the Iskraites realized that the Bund posed a major stumbling block to their plans. Not only had it played an important role at Belostok, but Portnoy, its representative on the O.C., was still at large. Unable to avoid the Bund, the Iskraites could only stall and sidetrack it temporarily. Aware of the rules agreed on at the conference, they chose a course of action calculated to re-establish the O.C. on a new basis more favorable to themselves. To accomplish this, they had to work quietly, seeking to gain leverage among the various Russian committees before contacting the rest of the legitimate participants.

The relatively peaceful relations between the Bund and *Iskra* at Belostok may have played into Lenin's hands. Kremer's courtesy and the information he supplied gave the Iskraites an edge in time and effort, and they took full advantage of it. On May 23 Krupskaia wrote to a colleague in Samara, F. V. Lengnik, that the Bundist member of the O.C. had escaped arrest and would be directed to him. "You will have to devote yourself to preparing the congress with him," she declared, "but it is necessary to be diplomatic with him and not to reveal all your cards."[40] Lenin added a note, revealing his own purpose all too clearly:

Your task is to form a committee of *yourselves* to prepare the Congress, to take the Bundist into this committee (sizing him up *from all sides*, NB!), to slip our people into as many [local] committees as possible, guarding yourself and our people [from arrest] like the apple of your eye until the Congress....

Be wise as serpents and gentle as doves (with the committees, the Bund, and St. Petersburg).[41]

The Iskraites were not above trickery. On June 22 Lenin suggested to I. I. Radchenko, one of his agents in St. Petersburg, that he give Zeldov a false impression. "It might be convenient to say that you have already organized this committee [the O.C.] and would be happy to have the participation of the Bund." At the same time, Lenin cautioned Radchenko to be careful not to arouse criticism.[42] A month later he gave Radchenko more specific instructions: "With the Bund, be extremely careful and firm. Don't show your cards; leave it to manage its own affairs and *don't allow* it to *poke its nose* into Russian affairs. Remember that it is an unreliable friend (*if not an enemy*)." Lenin's ideal O.C. was an all-Russian one, consisting of G. M. Krzhizhanovsky from Samara, one of "our people" from the south, and Radchenko.[43]

Meanwhile the organizations abroad were attempting to create a foreign section of the O.C., as authorized by the Belostok conference. At the initiative of the Union Abroad, a meeting was held in Paris in July 1902 to this end. Martov represented *Iskra*, N. N. Lokhov the Union, and Kremer the Bund. Upon receiving the proposals made at the meeting, Lenin rejected all those that seemed likely to endanger *Iskra*'s efforts in Russia. More specifically, he was unwilling to let a foreign section of the O.C. have anything to do with the composition of the future congress or the problems to be discussed there.[44] A foreign section that included his opponents, with power to make substantive arrangements, could scarcely be to Lenin's liking. His answer was to withdraw *Iskra*'s representatives from the discussions in early August on the grounds that the St. Petersburg Committee and the Russian organization of *Iskra* had asked that nothing be done until an O.C. had been formed in Russia.[45] The Iskraites in Russia were in fact just on the point of achieving that goal, for which they had been feverishly working for the past several months. When the O.C. was finally formed in November, Lenin instructed his agent P. A. Krasikov to see to it that the O.C.'s work abroad remained unimportant.[46] Later, at the Second Congress of the RSDWP, the Union Abroad's spokesman, Vladimir Akimov, pointed out that the effort to create a foreign section had not been supported by the "Russian comrades."[47] Those comrades, firmly linked to *Iskra*, vetoed any significant role for the foreign section.

While the Iskraites worked to create an O.C. loyal to their cause, the Bund in Russia fell into a period of temporary hardship. Of the Central Committee, Portnoy alone was free, and he had to flee Belostok, the seat of the committee. Moreover, it was in this same year, 1902, that the Zubatov movement reached its peak and labor Zionism began making great headway. The growing propensity for terror in the Bundist ranks, the weighty problems of internal reorganization, and the continuing concern over the national question, together with the press of routine business, so occupied the Bund's leaders as to preclude their taking the initiative in rebuilding the O.C. In any case, most of that work had to be done outside the Pale of Settlement.

How much actual contact there was between the Bund and the Iskraites after April is difficult to establish. Zeldov and Portnoy were the two persons best qualified to pursue the matter of the O.C., since both had been present at the Belostok conference. While abroad in June 1902 Zeldov was directed by Lenin to meet Radchenko in St. Petersburg.[48] Whether they ever met is problematical; given the absence of references to any meeting, it seems likely they did not. In any event Zeldov was arrested in October. Portnoy did not join the O.C. until after it was formed.

The Iskraites' preliminary arrangements to reestablish the O.C. began on August 15, when several delegates from Iskraite organizations met in London with Lenin. Said Krupskaia in a letter to I. I. Radchenko in St. Petersburg: "Representatives from Bori [the Bund] and from the south should join this committee eventually; but that is later. For the time being the O.C. will be considered as not established, and no one but us knows about it. It consists exclusively of our people."[49]

The formal meeting to reconstitute the O.C. took place in early November in Pskov. This assembly was of an entirely different complexion from the Belostok conference. Only three of the seven organizations present at the first conference participated in the second. Two of the three—the Southern Worker Group and the St. Petersburg organization—had declared for *Iskra* prior to the meeting; the third was *Iskra* itself. Delegates came from Samara, Kiev, and the Northern Union, none of which had been represented at Belostok. No foreign groups were represented. Needless to say, the result of a representation with an exclusively Iskraite point of view was complete harmony. As P. Lepeshinsky puts it: "Thanks to the absence of the 'opposition' (the Bund representative would surely have held up the business at every step), the conference solved the most important questions in one day."[50]

The calling of the Pskov conference paved the way for a new and more serious round of recrimination between the Bund and *Iskra*. In fact, the Iskraites had no intention of keeping the Bund out of the O.C. permanently; they were simply bent on controlling its composition and form. They adopted the instrument of co-optation, for instance, to ensure the proper result. The Pskov conferees agreed to inform the Bund of the conference and to invite it to join. But what seemed the apparently simple matter of issuing an invitation proved to be a Pandora's box. Reporting to Lenin on the proceedings, E. Ia. Levin of Samara, a member of the new O.C., noted that there had been no representation of the Bund at the meeting, which continued without it. He thus implied an invitation had been extended to the Bund before the meeting.[51] Whatever the truth of the matter, the O.C. formed at Pskov certainly invited the Bund to join it, assigning Krasikov to discuss the matter with Portnoy. Later, the O.C.'s official report to the Second Congress of the RSDWP noted that the Bund had expressed its desire to join, asking only that it be permitted to participate in the editing and signing of the declaration heralding the reestablishment of the O.C. as compensation for its absence from Pskov. Krasikov had accepted these conditions.[52] The O.C. did not follow through, however, and the Bund had no hand in the announcement, which was made in *Iskra* in January 1903. Stating that the Bund had been approached to attend the meeting "but for reasons unknown to us" had not appeared, the declaration added that the O.C. hoped this absence was a chance one and that the Bund would soon send a representative.[53]

When the Pskov conference and the formation of a new O.C. became public knowledge, the Bund reacted angrily. It challenged both the version of events presented in the declaration and the Iskraites' motives. The Central Committee, while admitting the possibility of a mix-up in communications, laid the blame squarely on the Iskraite rump committee's inadequate attempts to inform the Bundists of its plans. The Foreign Committee, in a separate statement, hinted darkly that the O.C. knew the reason for the Bund's absence but was trying to create the impression that the Bund was indifferent to the reestablishment of the party. In light of the confusion surrounding the invitation to Pskov, it found publication of the declaration particularly reprehensible. As the Central Committee noted, the question of the announcement had been discussed with a delegate from the O.C., who furthermore had not presented himself until close to a month after the meeting. Despite all this, the Central Committee stated, it was ready to join the new O.C.[54]

Both *Iskra* and its agent Krasikov defended themselves. *Iskra* insisted that the announcement was made in all innocence; and Krasikov asserted that the Bund knew it might not receive the text before publication and had not regarded the matter as a *sine qua non*.[55] Open discussion of the O.C. affair stopped at this point.

A representative of the Central Committee, probably Portnoy, sent a letter to *Iskra*, which was not published. In it, the committee asserted Krasikov's explanation was untrue and a pure fantasy.[56] In a word, the letter suggested the Bund had been cheated. It is worth noting that even some of the Iskraites felt Krasikov had behaved badly—to the point where Lenin was forced into the awkward position of both defending his agent and admitting his shortcomings.[57]

The Bund leaders decided, at a meeting in Dvinsk, to affiliate with the O.C., and did so when the O.C. next met, at Orel in February 1903.[58] There things were smoothed over: Portnoy dropped the implication of a premeditated snub, and both Krasikov and the initiators of the Pskov meeting accepted a share of the blame for the misunderstanding.[59] The O.C.'s report to the Second Congress, an official explanation of the events formally accepted by the Bund, ascribed to pure accident both the Bund's failure to receive an invitation to Pskov and the publication of the declaration without its participation.[60] Acceptance of that explanation did not necessarily signify satisfaction. The Bundists simply recognized nothing could undo what had been done at Pskov.

Once the Bund entered the O.C. every effort was made to end the dispute, though this did not rule out debates between the Iskraites and the Bundists on other matters. The official conclusion to the affair came in a declaration on March 13, 1903, in which the O.C. blamed the whole incident on misunderstanding. The O.C. did not wish to keep the Bund from participating, and the Bund did not wish to hinder the activity of the O.C. All organizations were asked to refrain from further statements on O.C. affairs. Portnoy, now an O.C. member, added his agreement and noted that the Bund would not reply to O.C. statements published in *Iskra*. With this the matter was closed.[61]

The end of the O.C. affair also ended the first phase of preparation for the Second Congress of the RSDWP. The failure to create a congress and an O.C. broadly representative of Social Democratic views revealed the Bund's limitations within the changing stage of Russian Social Democracy. The problems of 1902 had turned the attention of the leading Bundists inward on the Bund.

Further, in a period of general growth of revolutionary forces in Russia, it was in a poor position to influence greatly the state of affairs outside the Pale. The Bund thus lost any initiative it once had in organizing a second party congress. From this point on, until the Second Congress of the RSDWP, no matter how strong the Bund was within its own milieu, it was thrown increasingly on the defensive within the general camp of Russian Social Democracy. What's more, where control of the party had belonged to no single group either at Minsk in 1898 or at Belostok in 1902, *Iskra* now had every prospect of a clear field ahead.

15. The Bund and 'Iskra': Party Organization

With the Organization Committee unmistakably in the Iskraite camp, Lenin and his colleagues were in a position to exercise enormous influence in shaping the forthcoming party congress. To counter this advantage, the Bundists sought to make the congress as broadly representative as possible, a move that might bring them support for the change to federation. Commenting on the observation in the O.C.'s declaration that the first attempt to form the party had not been a success, the Bund's Central Committee urged that the new congress be of a constituent nature. Only by opening the meeting to all Social Democratic organizations in the Empire, including the national groups, could the O.C. gain the "one centralized disciplined army" it so desired.[1]

Lenin responded to the Central Committee's commentary as if stung. This, the issuing of a special statement against the O.C., was a flagrant violation of the most elementary rules of mutual work and an unseemly display of un-comradeliness, he charged. The Bund took this action so as to put its relations with the party on a new footing. It sought "not to *affiliate* with the Russian Social Democratic Workers' Party on the basis of the Rules of 1898, but to enter into a *federative* alliance with it."[2] Lenin accused the Bund of seeking support for its views from outsiders rather than discussing them inside the O.C., to which it had been invited.

Lenin saw the Bund's most recent actions and assumptions as part of a long string of mistaken views and conclusions. Addressing himself specifically to the Jewish workers, he charged that "the present leaders of the Bund are making a serious political error, which no doubt time will correct."[3] The Bund had erred in the past by supporting Economism and terrorism, and these views had been eradicated; in time its present "nationalist passion" would also disappear. The Jewish workers certainly understood the importance of effecting the "closest unity" with their Russian comrades and the folly of deciding in advance how the Jewish people were to develop in a free Russia. They understood "that the Bund ought not to go beyond the demand (in the Russian Social Democratic Workers' Party) for complete autonomy in matters concerning the Jewish proletariat," the formula recognized by the Congress of 1898 and never denied by anyone. The immediate task was "to cement and unite a basic nucleus." The Bund's invitation to all nationalities was desirable, of course; but, Lenin declared, "we can think of expanding the nucleus . . . *only after* [its] *formation has been completed* (or at the very least, after there is no doubt about its stability)."[4] There was no mistaking the Iskraites' intent: they were determined to control access to the congress in order to push through their views on organization.

Kosovsky was quick to reply. What right had *Iskra* to prosecute the Bund and to give the impression that the O.C. was an official body of the party? he asked. In fact, the O.C. declaration had stressed the committee's private status, binding only on those groups that had authorized it.[5] *Iskra* was demagogic in trying to suggest that the Bund was fighting the party; the Bund had every right to criticize a private group in print.[6] Nor was the Bund separatist in any way. On the contrary, it had been quite clear ever since Belostok that the Iskraites, rather than the Bund, "wanted to come out separately," "wanted their *own* O.C." Why? Because, Kosovsky asserted,

You are striving not only for theoretical, but also for organizational hegemony. The Bund is hampering you by its separate existence, by its independence, and for this reason you fight it. . . . You are leading the revolutionaries who heed you to such a state that the following deeply significant words escape from their mouths: "the task of the Second Party Congress is to destroy the Bund." Yes, gentlemen, this is a fact; there are revolutionaries in Russia, and not a few, who have fallen into this delirium.[7]

As for the attack on the Bund's past, *Iskra* was rewriting history. If the Bund was guilty of Economism and of siding with the Union Abroad, Kosovsky wondered why *Iskra* had not challenged it at the time. Furthermore, what had *Iskra* contributed to the Bund's fight against terrorism that could match the Bund's own fight against it? That *Iskra* raised such matters could be explained in only one way: "You want at all costs to drum into the heads of your readers that you are 'the navel of the earth.' "[8] Kosovsky's language, like Lenin's, was harsh.

Kosovsky also defended open discussion of federation and the national question. Only through prior consideration in the press could there be satisfactory discussion of these issues at the congress. *Iskra*'s reference to the "nationalist passion" of the Bund, moreover, was mere tactical sniping. Did the Iskraites not permit the Armenian Social Democrats the same degree of national cultural autonomy, the Bund asked for?[9] To Kosovsky, these distinctions between the Bund and other national Social Democratic groups were no doubt reminiscent of his fight with the PPS in 1898.

Kosovsky also argued the importance of the national question for the future. Lenin's claim that it was premature to discuss the development of the Jewish people begged the question. Jewry "in slave Russia" was already evolving along a different course from Western Europe; "for this reason a force has risen among the Jews in Russia that is unknown to those in Western Europe: this force is the Jewish workers' movement."[10] By ignoring such facts, *Iskra*, it seemed to him, still had a great deal to learn.

Given the tensions of the moment, it is not surprising that nothing slipped by either of the antagonists without rejoinder. But the discussions grew even wider and more acrimonious as the Bundists sought to assert their leadership over the whole of the Jewish proletariat. In January 1903 the Foreign Committee of the Bund sharply criticized a leaflet the RSDWP Committee of Ekaterinoslav had directed to the city's Jewish workers.[11] In it the Russian comrades had attacked the strong influence of the Zionists and their emphasis on the unity of the Jewish people by pointing to the miserable conditions that existed wherever Jewish workers labored.[12] But why, asked the Foreign Committee, was nothing said of the Jewish workers' struggle against the government, the employers, and the bourgeois tendencies in Judaism? That omission exposed the weakness of the Ekaterinoslav enterprise, the effort to show that Jewish and non-Jewish workers had the same interests. The Russian comrades did not understand that the Jewish workers had to wage a special battle and needed separate organization; thus, their attempts to keep the Bund's existence secret were absurd.

The Foreign Committee also challenged the Ekaterinoslav Committee on its handling of anti-Semitism. In telling the Jewish workers that anti-Semitism was an exclusively bourgeois phenomenon, the Russian comrades were as guilty of deception as those who insisted on the unity of the Jewish people. Anti-Semitism was in fact equally evident in proletarian ranks, witness the Czestochowa pogrom of 1902 and the boasts of Christian workers who replaced striking Jewish workers that they would massacre the Jews. It was the task of the Social Democrats to conquer this evil. One way to do that was to spread the news of the Jewish proletariat's struggle and of its "inalienable organ"—the Bund.[13] The Bundists were piqued because the committee failed to mention the shortcomings of the Russian workers. Surely the anti-Semitic acts described indicated that the Russian workers had something to learn, too.

Lenin answered the Foreign Committee in an article entitled "Does the Jewish Proletariat Need an Independent Political Party?"[14] If the Bund was indeed "an independent political party"—the description was the Foreign Committee's, not his—it was news to him, said Lenin. But the pretense was a logical consequence of the call for federation. It was "that reduction to absurdity of your fundamental error in the national question that will inescapably . . . be the starting point of change in the views of the Jewish proletariat and of the Jewish Social Democrats in general."[15] The autonomy granted by the Rules of 1898 were enough for the Bund, Lenin asserted. Anything more was destructive of the unity necessary for proletarian struggle. Even the Fourth Congress had urged restraint in areas where Bund organizing had not begun. "We must not weaken the strength of our offensive by breaking up into numerous independent political parties," Lenin insisted; "we must not introduce estrangement and isolation and then have to heal an artificially implanted disease with the aid of these notorious 'federation' plasters."[16] Lenin was contemptuous of what he considered the Bund's narrow views. He argued that since the Bund had no organization in Ekaterinoslav, the Russian group there was under no obligation to mention it. Further, anti-Semitism was quite correctly treated as a matter of bourgeois self-interest in broad Social Democratic terms, rather than as a sometime practice among ignorant Russian workers. As for their violence, it was a small matter: "The editors of *Posledniia izvestiia* are so accustomed to dealing with large strikes involving five or ten workers that the behavior of twelve ignorant Zhitomir workers is dragged out as evidence of the link between international anti-Semitism and one 'section' or another 'of the population.'" In persisting in its course the Bund was blunting the class consciousness of the Jewish workers.[17]

It is plain from this exchange just how great a chasm there was between the two camps on the basic question of whether the Bund was even necessary. The Bund's complaints to the Ekaterinoslav Committee were based on its profound belief in a Jewish identity, and hence in the need for a revolutionary organization specifically for the Jewish workers. It was this need, as the Bundists saw it, that explained the success of Zionism in Ekaterinoslav and convinced them that the chosen path of their Russian comrades was bound to fail. The Iskraites, for their part, saw the Bund's insistence on a Jewish nationality and a federated status as an obstacle to proletarian unity. The development that had carried the Bund to the threshold of demanding recognition as the legitimate representative of all Jewish workers within the Social Democratic camp was simply unfortunate in Lenin's view, for in that course lay fragmentation.

Where the Bund aimed at broad accommodation of the national question, the Iskraites sought to avoid the issue altogether. And where the Bund sought to focus attention on anti-Semitism as a current and extremely painful problem, the Iskraites took a broad, more diffuse view, dismissing the evidence as trifling and reducing the solution to the hoped-for class unity. In effect Lenin suggested that Jewish workers ought to overlook a little violence committed against them now on the promise of a brighter future.

Again the Foreign Committee replied, this time arguing the historical reality behind the Bund's position. The Bund had grown up "as a *completely independent organization*."[18] No one had asked about the interests of the Jewish proletariat as the Bund was developing into a party. Once it had become one, the Iskraites pretended surprise and sought to curtail its further growth on the basis of rules established in 1898, which had never been more than a paper arrangement. For that matter, what about *Iskra*'s use of rules? Did it ask anyone when it became first a local organization and then a general one, or when it "built a 'new party' bedecking itself with the title of the old one?"[19] *Iskra*'s confusion, the Foreign Committee explained, arose in its inability to distinguish between the Rules of 1898 and the party. The situation had changed for the party, but the rules remained the same.

Iskra's tone and style seriously concerned the Foreign Committee. It viewed the use of grammatical devices like exclamation marks, as in the "forces (!!) of the Jewish proletariat," as evidence of the Iskraites' scorn for the Jewish workers.[20] *Iskra* regarded the Jewish proletariat as an auxiliary force, subordinate to others. The committee also accused the Iskraites of attempting to sow discord within the Bund by asking whether the Foreign Committee spoke for the organization as a whole.[21] The fact that there were certain differences between the Bundists abroad and those in Russia was enough to set the Bundists aquiver at *Iskra*'s interference.

It was Martov who next took up the Iskraite cudgel. He chose to plead the cause of the movement's present needs.[22] If the Bund could claim independent development, he argued, so could others. But there were no general answers to be found in so narrow a development. A separate party was not necessary for the Jewish workers "just as it is not necessary for the workers of the Ural or Siberian regions." Work of a purely local character reflected petty interests, parochiality; the party had to end such *kustarnichestvo*. Admittedly, *Iskra* was striving for hegemony, but to only one end: the unification of Russian Social Democracy. Once that was accomplished, the *Iskra* group itself would no longer be necessary. Life demanded that revolutionaries lead the way; this was what prompted *Iskra*'s so-called imperialism. The Bund should accept this fact. Had it already become so isolated that it could not understand the motives for this hegemony? Those who asked for control were not enemies of the Bund and the Jewish movement; they asked only that the Bund abandon its parochialism and join the common ranks.[23]

Kosovsky had the last words on the subject for the Foreign Committee in a pamphlet published in April 1903.[24] He proudly upheld the Bund's qualifications as a party of revolutionaries. Taking issue with Lenin's comment that the Bund had learned what it meant to be a revolutionary organization from the Iskraites, Kosovsky suggested that it was the other way around: "Lenin came to the thought of 'an organization of revolutionaries' looking at Bund activity."[25] Contrary to the Iskraites' contentions, national organizations would not weaken the movement; the development of a class-conscious proletariat in any nationality, regardless of numbers, strengthened the whole. It was only a question of how much strength, never a question of weakness. *Iskra*'s attitude, Kosovsky insisted, was a continuation of the traditional view that the Jewish masses were incapable of activism, the supposed result of their centuries-long isolation. But that medieval way of life, the ghetto psychology and readiness to endure passively, were gone. If there were still vestiges of that tradition among some intellectuals, the further growth of the Jewish proletarian movement would erase them.[26]

Part of the problem, in Kosovsky's view, was that *Iskra* saw the Bund as a regional organization. This was clear from Martov's comparison of the Jewish workers with the "Uralians." The issue, however, was not that the Bund had arisen in certain places, but whether the interests of Jewish workers could be served outside of it. Having accepted the special task of developing class consciousness among the Jewish workers, the Bund was obliged to satisfy their needs wherever and whenever they arose.[27]

And what of the argument that the Bund drew off strength from the "general Russian organization"? It had no validity whatsoever, Kosovsky declared. On the contrary, the more the Bund grew, the more new workers were drawn into the movement. How could this be considered a disruptive tendency? Indeed, if the Bund continued to attract workers, did that not prove it was serving their needs better than the Russian committees?[28]

The so-called opposition of the Bund, Kosovsky felt, resulted from a different view of the relation of national proletariats to the general movement. He saw behind the Iskraite plea for unity the assumption that victory hinged on the revolutionary awakening of the largest proletariat of the Empire, the Russian proletariat. Accordingly, *Iskra* concluded that the Jewish Social Democrats had to devote their energies to a Russian (Russkii) proletariat as being one and the same as the general Russian (Rossiiskii) proletariat. The interests of the part, in this case the Jewish workers, had to be sacrificed to the interests of the whole. The logical outcome of such reasoning would be the nullification of the Bund and assimilation dressed to suit the revolutionary movement. The Jewish Social Democrats, it seemed, were to work everywhere but among their own masses.[29]

In Kosovsky's view the concept that all other workers' movements should be subordinate to the Russian movement was harmful, since a purely Russian thrust was not in fact to be equated with the general Russian movement. All movements, including that of the Russians, served the general cause. In order to ensure the movement the greatest amount of revolutionary energy, every national Social Democratic organization had to have equal rights. An outsider was incapable of comprehending, for instance, the significance the Jewish movement had for Jews: "The Bund," Kosovsky declared, "does not exist for the 'general Russian' movement but for the Jewish proletariat"; it could only have arisen "because it has its own goals."[30] The areas of autonomy *Iskra* considered proper under the Rules of the First Congress—the right to use Yiddish for propaganda, agitation, and literature, to hold congresses, to advance separate demands consistent with the Social Democratic program, to meet local needs peculiar to Jewish life—all these could be handled by a technical organization.[31] At all events, *Iskra*'s interpretation of the rules was considerably narrower than the Bund's, Kosovsky insisted. The party had given the Bund autonomy in all questions dealing with the Jewish proletariat; it had made no mention of regions.[32] As an organization of the Jewish workers, the Bund had the right to act broadly in their behalf. It could publish literature in languages other than Yiddish in an attempt to draw Jewish intellectuals to the cause, since their support was essential if the Bund was to succeed among the Jewish workers. And it could have its own national program as well. What did *Iskra* mean when it spoke of the "nationalist aspirations" of the Bund? The Bund had merely undertaken to clear up the ambiguities surrounding some questions. All these steps were entirely permissible in an organization that wanted to give equal rights to all national Social Democratic groups, i.e., in a federation.[33]

Finally Kosovsky turned to the idea that a party core should be formed, which would then tie other organizations to it. "On *what conditions* should it be built?" he wanted to know. The Bund's principle of federation permitted an all-Russian Social Democratic movement that included national organizations. The major difference between *Iskra* and the Bund lay in what each felt the Bund to be—a regional organization or the class organization of an entire people. If it was a regional organization, autonomy was better; if it was the party of a distinct nationality, as Kosovsky believed, federation was better. Uniting Russian organizations would lead only to a Russian party, not an all-Russian one. Indeed, without the Bund there could be no all-Russian party.[34]

While the Bund and *Iskra* carried on their debate, arrangements for the Second Congress moved apace. As a potential obstacle to the desired centralization, the Bund was given careful attention by the Iskraites. Indeed, Lenin put the Bund at the head of the list of problems for consideration before it even joined the O.C., which was advised that if the Bund would accept only federation to "depart at once and meet separately. It is necessary to prepare everyone for this."[35] The desire to settle the Bund question before working out a party program remained uppermost in Lenin's mind throughout; and the issue was given top priority at the Second Congress: the Bund was to accept unity before regular business began.

Lenin was pleased to have the Bund join the O.C. in February 1903, for as a non-Iskraite organization and constituent of the first O.C. it added fullness and a degree of legitimacy to the successor. At the same time he feared the possibility of compromise and fought the Bund continually, both inside and outside the O.C. In March, in a confidential letter to the editors of *Iuzhnyi*

rabochii (The Southern Worker), he wrote: "We want you privately to prepare everywhere and everyone for a fight with the Bund at the Congress. The
Bund will not give up its position without a stubborn struggle, and we can
never accept its position. Only the firmest resolve on our part to see this
through, even to the expulsion of the Bund from the Party, will force it to
yield."[36] In a similar vein, in late May he told one of his supporters on the
O.C., E. M. Aleksandrova, to be "correct and loyal to the Bund formally (no
open kick in the teeth), but at the same time quite cold" and to "press them
mercilessly and hourly on a legal basis without fear of going to the limit."
And then a last piece of advice: "Let the Bundists leave if they want to, but
we must not give them the slightest excuse ... to make a split."[37]

This approach to the Bund, at once legalistic and very hard, worried some
in the *Iskra* camp. Plekhanov, who only a few years before had shocked
Lenin with the ferocity of his attack on the Bund, now warned Lenin that
"the public must see the difference between our polemic with the SR's and
our polemic with the Social Democrats, be they Bundist or otherwise."[38] There
were doubts in the O.C. as well—about the treatment of the Bund in general
and about the actions of Krasikov in particular.[39] Krupskaia found it necessary to criticize certain Iskraite comrades for assuming good will on the part
of the Bund.[40]

In early 1903 B. I. Goldman, both Iskraite and friend of many prominent
Bundists, attempted to compromise the differences between the Bund and
Iskra.[41] He worked out clauses for *Iskra*'s draft party program that recognized
the equality of languages, granted national minorities full rights, and gave
each minority the maximum autonomy within the party acceptable to Lenin,
hoping thus to make national programs superfluous for the minorities that
did not wish to separate from Russia.[42]

Goldman proposed that the Bund retain its autonomy in Jewish questions
but confine its activities to its current boundaries; and that it keep all its own
institutions and effective organizational control, its resolutions alone being
subject to the approval of party congresses. He also wanted a member of the
party Central Committee, approved by the Bund, to sit on the Bund's Central
Committee. There was to be no automatic Bund representation on the Central Committee of the RSDWP, though this did not preclude a Bundist serving on that august body simply as a party member. Explicit Bund representation on the party Central Committee smacked of federation, he explained.
On the local level, Goldman proposed that Bund groups be incorporated
routinely into existing Russian organizations. In such cases, the Bund organizations could form "subcommittees for Jewish work (or more simply the
committees could also include Jews to lead agitation among the Jewish workers)." The Foreign Committee of the Bund was to become an autonomous
part of the Foreign League (Zagranichnaia Liga), a body formed by the

Iskraites after the split at Zurich in October 1901. Finally, every Bund member was to consider himself an RSDWP member in any kind of all-Russian matter.[43]

The effort to work out a compromise failed. The national guarantees Goldman offered were more than offset by the external elements he wanted to introduce into the Bund, elements that bid fair to undermine the organization from within. Skeptical of the outcome, Lenin nevertheless let Goldman present his proposals as a semiofficial offer. It was flatly rejected. The Bundists interpreted the terms of the compromise as a mockery of their demands. At this point Lenin felt a split at the congress was certain.[44] In refusing to accept the Goldman compromise the Bundists may have alienated some of the more sympathetic Iskraites; but at best there were few real Bundist sympathizers in the *Iskra* camp, and virtually none when it came to substantive differences between the two groups.

The rules for the Second Congress were formally established at Orel in February 1903. The Bund fought hard to protect its interests against the Iskraite majority, but with little success. Portnoy proposed that the congress be declared constituent, and that all Social Democratic organizations in Russia be invited; he lost on both counts.[45] He fought another losing battle on the question of "imperative mandates," i.e., binding instructions on delegates in support of a given position. The Iskraites argued that delegates might have a change of heart after hearing all sides of an issue, and that a preset position would hinder the business of the assembly; the first obligation of the delegates was, after all, to the party, not to their own organization.[46] Under this rule it was illegal for a Bund congress to instruct its delegates how to vote. The Bundists saw such an arrangement as a threat to the unity of the Jewish Social Democrats and felt it could downgrade the importance of their organization.

Portnoy's lone success was in amending the original plan for representation. As first submitted, the Iskraite plan was to bar all organizations that formed part of a union from independent representation and to grant each organization the same number of voting delegates,[47] meaning that a local committee of the RSDWP and the entire Bund had equal weight, with two votes each. Portnoy declared categorically that he could not accept those terms,[48] and even the *Iskra*-dominated meeting had to give way on so patently unfair an arrangement. In the end the O.C. reported to the congress that, "taking into account the quite exceptional dimensions and influence of this organization, the O.C. considers it just to give the Bund three votes at the Congress (along with two votes for the Foreign Committee of the Bund)."[49] The Iskraites could well afford this concession. Considering the size of the Bund, they came out well ahead.

The Bund Central Committee did not see its efforts in the O.C. as altogether hopeless. Despite the strains in the weeks preceding Orel and the kinds of problems that arose there, Portnoy could still report that the O.C. was composed of "serious people," who could be expected "to do much." In his judgment, though the enmity of the Iskraites toward the Bund was unmistakable, they treated it with respect—at least as long as they feared it. He advised that relations between the Bund and the O.C. be carefully maintained.[50]

Portnoy and his fellow O.C. member Izenshtat did their best to steer the Bund's Central Committee clear of troubled waters as the preparations for the congress went forward. While the Foreign Committee, with Kosovsky's sharp-tipped pen at the ready, jousted round after round with Lenin and Martov, Portnoy earned the grudging respect of the other O.C. members. One of them, Krzhizhanovsky, remarked to the editors of *Iskra* in March: "Boris Portnoy has been very 'decent' and has conducted himself quite correctly. He is a sensible fellow with great self-control and a good understanding of party discipline."[51] It was worth noting, Krzhizhanovsky felt, that Portnoy dissociated himself from the tone of the Foreign Committee, which he treated "with some irony."[52] In May 1903 Portnoy still maintained that the Central Committee was not responsible for the actions of the Foreign Committee, a view the Iskraites wanted to see in print.[53] Portnoy avoided polemics about principle. When pressed to say whether the Bund would choose autonomy or federation and nationalism, he simply replied the matter would not be decided before the congress.[54] At the height of the slugfest between the Foreign Committee and *Iskra*, the Central Committee called on the O.C. "to put an end to this harmful polemic of the foreign organs."[55] Portnoy did not even intervene when the Iskraites, by their own confession, abused their power by trying to pressure committees to their cause through the O.C. "We do this," Aleksandrova admitted, "and the Bundist knows all about it and remains silent, not daring to open his mouth." She felt the Bund would endure a great deal in order to stay in the O.C., "but not everything."[56]

One asks what persuaded the Bund to remain in the O.C. under such unfavorable circumstances. In Aleksandrova's opinion, Portnoy's forbearance was easily explained: the Bund had to curb its own rebellious organizations by demonstrating through its O.C. membership that it was not isolated from the Russians.[57] In a letter to Akselrod in April Martov speaks of an increasing sympathy for *Iskra* among the bristle workers.[58] But these reports were on the whole mere wishful thinking, as the Iskraites were to discover when the Bund left the party. The plain fact is the Bund had never ceased to emphasize the universal nature of the revolutionary venture in Russia. Its own success as an independent force did not alter its fundamental belief in the principle of working-class solidarity. The Bundists never deceived themselves that the Jewish workers might make the revolution on their own. For the Bund to cut itself off from the official Social Democratic family it had helped found at a moment when unity seemed at hand would have been countenanced only on the most extreme provocation.

The Bundists' most pressing problem before the Second RSDWP Congress was to decide their stand on the Bund's position in the party. The Fourth Congress's endorsement of federation had received the firm and continuing support of the Foreign and Central committees. By early 1903 the process of partyhood had advanced to the point where many of the Bund's leaders agreed with the contention expressed during the Ekaterinoslav debate that the Bund was the "inalienable organ" of the Jewish workers.[59] In the first Yiddish article on the new principle, *Di Arbeter Shtime* also held up "national independence and international solidarity" as the proper basis for uniting the organizations of the RSDWP.[60]

Still, several Bundists disagreed with the wisdom of federation, notably Anna and Pavel Rosenthal, Sendor Zeldov, and David Katz, who in early 1903 sent a joint letter to the Central Committee to that effect.[61] The Jewish proletariat did not need federation as long as the Autocracy existed, they contended. They saw neither a present threat from the Russian comrades that justified such a demand nor future tactical differences based on national interests. Further, the Bund's demand for equality with the Russians was a mistake. Only the Russians had a real industrial proletariat, and it was far larger than the Jewish artisan class. Moreover, its revolutionary consciousness was growing and becoming relatively more important in comparison with the Jewish proletariat, a development that was being helped along by increasing peasant unrest. In any case, they concluded, the Bund knew the Russians too little.[62] Their objections were voiced in vain.

Although the Bund's Fifth Congress originally was scheduled to convene in Russia, Liber succeeded in getting the site changed to Zurich.[63] Security was an important consideration in this decision, though probably not the only one. Concerned that the tense state of affairs in Russia would not permit the necessary unhurried and deliberate study of the issues before they reached the congress, Liber also won approval for his proposal of a preliminary conference in Geneva.[64]

All the matters discussed at Geneva in June were based on the belief that nationality was a strongly unifying force in the proletarian movement. The conferees held that, in order to exist and develop, national Social Democratic organizations had to formulate their own programs expressing the specific needs of their constituents. It was only in having unique problems that these organizations differed from other Social Democratic organizations, but they needed the greatest possible independence to deal with those problems. The task of the party, as the unifier of these national Social Democratic parties, was to coordinate their activity; it was to this end that the various parties subordinated themselves to the central institutions.[65] As for the Bund, its sole task was to free the Jewish proletariat. As a regional organization, it would fail in this endeavor, for then it would be unable to represent all Jewish workers. Furthermore, the conference agreed, the Bund must be the only representative of the Jewish proletariat as such.

What did this mean with respect to the RSDWP? The Geneva meeting suggested there were only two pure principles of organization: at one end, the fusion of independent and equal parts, i.e., a federation; at the other, complete centralization without any representation of the component parts, i.e., imperialism. Between these two organizational forms was partial fusion, or autonomy, which was but a milder form of imperialism. The delegates concluded that federation was the only suitable form for the Bund and other national Social Democratic parties, whose *raison d'être* was precisely the specific demands they upheld in addition to the general demands of the party. Entering the party without safeguarding the right to push these special demands was "an act of suicide" for any national party.[66]

The Geneva meeting suggested three variants of federation for the Fifth Congress's consideration. The first conceived the party as a federation of national Social Democratic organizations, a broad formula intended to accommodate the Polish Social Democrats and other national parties that might be represented at the congress. The second conceived the party as a federation of national Social Democratic organizations "and other united SD organizations that enter the Party," a formula designed to serve the Bund's interests without committing others to the same course. The third conceived the party as a federation "of the Bund and other united SD organizations that enter the Party." Presumably this last formula was devised in the knowledge that the congress would be essentially anti-national.[67]

With some minor adjustments, the Geneva proposals on organization were laid out for discussion at the Fifth Congress.[68] The result was a 12-point resolution, whose major provisions were as follows:

1. The Bund is a federated part of the RSDWP.

2. The Bund is a Social Democratic organization of the Jewish proletariat, unrestricted in its activity by any regional framework, and enters the Party as the sole representative of the Jewish proletariat; moreover, any activity in the name of the whole proletariat in an area where the Bund, as well as other Party organizations, is active, is permissible only with the participation of the Bund.

3. The Bund elects its own representatives to the Central Committee, the Foreign Committee, and the congresses of the Party.... The method of representation must be based on principles that are alike for all contracting sides.[69]

The congress accepted the party program as its own but hoped to supplement it with special points raised by "the specific conditions of the Jewish proletariat in Russia." The Bund was to retain all its present prerogatives: the right to hold congresses, to have its own executive institutions, to maintain internal controls, to publish in any language, and to enter into temporary agreements with revolutionary organizations outside the party. Where the workers of a given area were of mutual interest to the Bund and other revolutionary groups, each party's rights were to be safeguarded by establishing channels authorized to specify courses of action. All these points were presented "as a basis for discussion of the question of the Bund's position in the Party."[70]

The various provisions on organization did not go undebated, though the differences were mild in comparison with the debate on the national question. Many important points, such as the claim that the Bund was sole representative of the Jewish proletariat and consequently entitled to operate where it perceived a need, won universal approval.[71]

One point that was hotly contested was the clause declaring that the Bund was to be allowed to participate with other party organizations where activity in a given area was carried on in the name of the proletariat as a whole. Opponents argued that this, the second half of Paragraph 2, was not only repetitive but harmful, in that it placed "explicit limitations on the power of other parts of the Party," which were already implicit in the first half of the paragraph.[72] They saw this language as a search for guarantees against "unpleasantness" resulting from "the abnormal structure of the Party," which left relations between Social Democratic groups undefined. This provision asked that the Bund represent a whole territory. But consider the situation in Poland, for example. How could the Bund make a direct appeal to the proletariat in Polish territory, given the existence of the Polish Social Democratic Party? Neither party could work alone. Only together could they pretend to represent the whole. The opponents of the provision insisted that friction would cease with unity, and that therefore the rules had to rest on the "normal order of things" implied in that unity.

Those who wanted both points included contended that the party program was being worked out "in conformity with various aspects of Party activity," and that without such elaboration the provision would be reduced to a mere introductory principle. The Bund could not count on the normality that was to come with unification. "We cannot *proceed* from this normal order," they insisted; "we must *go toward* it." Rather than a supposed future normality they saw a current abnormality, which no mere principle could solve. "It is necessary to destroy these abnormalities by direct struggle," they argued, "to get rid of them step by step."[73]

The differences over Paragraph 2 rested more on mood and tone than principle. The opponents of elaboration worried about future sensitivities and arguments; they did not question the first half. When the provision was put to a vote, 22 delegates favored retaining the second half, three opposed it, and four abstained.[74]

In Paragraph 3, which dealt with the Bund's relationship to the highest institutions of the party, most of the delegates opted for equality with all other parts of the party. The majority also insisted that at international socialist congresses the Bund representatives should vote as a national unit when the interests of the Jewish proletariat were concerned, that is to say, in the Bund's normal area of control, but as individual members of the all-Russian party in all other matters. The vote was 22 for and one against, with six abstentions.[75]

Opinion was somewhat more divided on the question of the Bund's status as an organization with respect to other, similar organizations. The majority of the delegates held that the Bund was "Jewish Social Democracy" and equal to all other organizations, including the Russian ones. They were not insisting here on numerical equality but simply demanding that if Russian representation was to be by number of committees, the Bund's representation should be reckoned on the same basis. The vote on this point was 18 in favor and two opposed, with nine abstentions.[76]

Paragraph 4, on the Bund's right to have its own goals as long as they did not contradict the general program, was unopposed, though there were two abstentions. Paragraph 5, the Bund's right to decide questions touching the Jewish proletariat, proved one of the more difficult issues. Opponents argued that all such questions were closely and automatically linked with "the totality of other questions" and thus became of "general significance."[77] The supporters based their position on what they considered present realities. Though they admitted the difficulty of categorizing problems so neatly in theory, they argued that once a united party existed situations would arise in which problems of importance for the Jewish workers would be only details to the party. A line had to be drawn, for it was the Bund's province to deal with Jewish problems. Sixteen delegates agreed; five voted no on this point and eight abstained.[78]

Paragraphs 7, 8, 10, and 11 dealt with the formal structure of the Bund-party relationship. They provided the Bund with a considerable degree of independence. Paragraph 8, for example, specified the Bund's absolute right to publish in all languages. These paragraphs also limited the right of party organizations to turn to a given nationality without the agreement of the organization serving that nationality; declared that no organization could appeal to the proletariat as a whole without the express permission of the party's Central Committee; and stated that no appeals could be made to the Jewish proletariat without the agreement of the Bund's Central Committee. Some delegates objected to this last point, arguing that as in the case of the second paragraph it was superfluous and harmful. The second half of Paragraph 8, which strongly emphasized the Bund as a federated part of a whole, had wide support, with a vote of 19 for and only six against;[79] and the eleventh paragraph, which provided that the party could address itself to Bund groups only through the Bund's Central Committee, received unanimous support.[80] The congress insisted on the organization retaining sharp lines of identity and operation.

The most debated issue was Paragraph 1—the Bund's formal relationship to the party. This central point was discussed last. Izenshtat, perhaps the most consistent opponent of the Bund's plans for the Second RSDWP Congress, argued against the formal demand for a federalized party on tactical grounds: it could hinder the passage of concrete demands desired by the Bund. He also contended, with the support of David Katz, that unification in a centralized party was of greater importance than federation.[81] The federationists, for their part, insisted on equality with other groups in the party, specifically the Russians, who must not be equated with the all-Russian party. Neither did they want to cloak the resolution's language in order to avoid difficulties. "We must not play blindman's buff," Portnoy insisted. "We must name our statute one thing or the other."[82]

The definition finally adopted by the Fifth Congress was more limited than that adopted by the Geneva meeting and the Fourth Congress, both of which had declared their desire to see the RSDWP a party built on federative foundations. The Fifth Congress only mentioned the Bund as a federated part, thus avoiding the issue of the status of other parts of the party or of the party as a whole. "This principle," the official report explained, "will serve us in our further work both as an initial position and as a guiding directive that points out our road in the struggle."[83] The congress accepted the first paragraph by a vote of 20 to seven, with two abstentions.

The delegates, keenly aware of the difficulties they would face at the party congress, considered a series of substitute points that might prove acceptable to the Iskraites without compromising the Bund's principles. These rules, which became known as the minimum or ultimate points, were to serve as a *sine qua non* for the Bund's affiliation with the party and, as their supporters saw it, for the Bund's very existence. The minimum statutes took into account, in some part, the arguments that had been overridden during the debate. They provided for the dropping of the first paragraph, which the majority had so firmly demanded. The specific designation "federated part" was not essential as long as the structure was federative in spirit. The official report added, however, that no formulation carrying the spirit of autonomy would be acceptable.[84] Also, the Bund was prepared to drop the contested second half of Paragraph 2, but there was no question of eliminating the provision naming the Bund as the sole and unrestricted representative of the Jewish proletariat. The minimum rules, ten in all, merely cut out much of the detailed description of the powers and limitations of the Bund and the party. As provided, the Bund remained substantially independent.

Several alternatives were proposed in the event the Bund's minimum stand proved unacceptable to the party congress. The southern organizer Koigan and Rosa Levit, a delegate from Warsaw, led the minority in arguing against an ultimatum that involved leaving the party congress immediately. Koigan proposed that a special Bund conference be held directly after the party congress, and that the Bund hold off any action until the next RSDWP congress. Levit also pleaded for delay, though she suggested the Bund might leave right after the unification of the party, lest its later actions set the new unity back. But Liber and Medem strongly resisted delaying measures. Said Liber: "We proceed from the fact that the general Party is dear to us, but if our interests are likewise dear to the Party, it should satisfy our basic demands." Medem took a legalistic view: "A conference cannot solve the question of the Bund's existence in the RSDWP, and a conditional ultimatum is therefore superfluous." The congress voted 19 to six to make the ten rules an absolute minimum; there were two abstentions.[85]

In an attempt to present a face of total unity at the party congress, the Bund tried to erase all evidence of the internal debate and arrangements for compromise at the Fifth Congress. The national question, which had so sharply divided the congress, was not mentioned in any of the contemporary reports, and the delegates maintained the strictest secrecy on the subject.* It was also not disclosed until after the party congress that there was a set of minimum rules. In point of fact, these amounted to binding instructions, and as such were illegal under the rules established at Orel.

When Lenin learned of the minimum rules after the party congress he wrote an outraged article in *Iskra* entitled "Maximum Brazenness and Minimum Logic."[86] Furious, he accused the Bund of haggling and asked sarcastically whether the minimum points were really the Bund's last. "Perhaps you've got a minimal minimum in another pocket? Perhaps in another month or so we shall be seeing that?"[87] But the votes of the Bundists at the Fifth Congress and later, at the party congress, undercut Lenin's sarcasm. Fewer than one-third of the Bundists at the Fifth Congress seriously disagreed with the resolutions on party organization. In later accounts, Bund participants, even those who rejected national cultural autonomy and had strong feelings for unity, insisted the opposition on the organizational question was minor.[88] On the whole the Bundists were largely united in their determination to maintain the Bund as a strong entity.

As a final piece of business the Fifth Congress chose the five delegates to the party congress. Kosovsky and Medem were the Foreign Committee's representatives, Kremer waiving his right to sit as a voting delegate in order to take advantage of the oratorical talents of Medem. (As a member of the first

---

* In fact, the debates were not published until 1927 and 1928, when they were carried in *Unzer tsait* of Warsaw.

RSDWP Central Committee, Kremer could and would attend as an honorary delegate with an advisory voice.) The Central Committee chose two of its own members, Portnoy and Izenshtat, and added Liber as the third delegate.[89] The Bund was thus to be represented by the two young firebrands Liber and Medem, the loudest voices for national cultural autonomy and a firm stand on organizational matters, members of a new generation of Bundists that was ready, even eager, to fight for the Bund's existence in the face of the grave challenge. For the old campaigner Izenshtat, who leaned closest to the Iskraite view, the Second Congress of the RSDWP would prove an eyeopener.

16. The Second RSDWP Congress

The Second Congress of the RSDWP, which convened in Brussels in July 1903, was a crucial turning point in the history of Russian Social Democracy. Designed by its Iskraite organizers to create a unified party under their auspices, the congress instead revealed the Iskraites as hopelessly divided among themselves. The resulting split into two camps, the Bolsheviks and the Mensheviks, was permanent—and of enormous consequence for the Social Democratic movement in Russia. The congress was a historical landmark for the Bund as well. Its differences with the Iskraites were too great, and the determination of both sides too firm, for reconciliation and compromise. The congress saw the Bund's withdrawal from the RSDWP.

The Bundists arrived at the congress with an established line of retreat: the minimum rules laid down by the Fifth Congress. But they were determined to expose, if they could, the mistakenness of the Iskraite view before retreating to their final position. Given the character and intent of the congress, it did not take long for the clashes to start. Indeed, they began with the agenda itself. From first to last, each draft agenda constructed by the Iskraites made the Bund's place in the party the first order of business.[1] It was clear to Lenin that the Bund's desire for federation threatened the Iskraites' organizational design for the party and the control or at least guidance of central party institutions by Martov and himself. Determined to stop the Bund, the Iskraites had led the O.C. to declare the forthcoming congress a successive one, thus ensuring that the statutes of the First Congress would be in force. The Iskraites held that in calling for federation the Bund exceeded the autonomy it had been granted in 1898, and both Lenin and Plekhanov argued for the agenda as a necessary legal step: the Bund had to divest itself of its views before other business could begin.[2]

The Iskraites also defended their agenda on moral grounds. According to Lenin, many of the organizations attending the congress disagreed sharply with the Bund, suggesting the possibility of disruptive arguments. "It is impossible," he declared, "for the Congress to begin harmonious work until these differences have been settled."[3] Leon Trotsky, then a young Iskraite, added that the matter of the Bund had to be settled prior to other party business precisely because it was of such great significance.[4]

Liber, whose voice became a familiar one at the congress, spoke for the Bundists. The Bund too accepted the congress as a successive one, he said; and it too recognized its position within the party as autonomous. Since its party membership was not in question, its desire to alter the principle of organization did not require a special place on the agenda, but rather belonged in the regular discussion on organization. Under the Iskraite agenda, Liber charged, the Bund's views were being prejudged.[5]

In fact, the Iskraites stood on rather shaky legal grounds. Since 1901 the argument had centered on what the autonomy granted the Bund by the First Congress meant. Did it simply represent a technical expansion of the powers given the local committees, as the Iskraites claimed, or did it carry a vague but implicit promise of federation, as suggested by the Bundists? The truth is the question of national organization did not come up at all in 1898, and the First Congress made only the most rudimentary start on setting out organizational principles. Failing a clear definition there, both sides were free to supply their own interpretations of the statutes. Neither side showed any confidence in the congress's organizational arrangements. Lenin's efforts to design a centralized party in the years 1901 to 1903 plainly undermined the seriousness of any legal argument based on the rules of the First Congress. Falling back on the congress was simply a convenient device, the means by which the Iskraite congress thought to impose its own will on the Bund.

Be that as it may, the Iskraites had their way. By a vote of 30 to ten the delegates upheld the order of the agenda, demonstrating the solidity of *Iskra*'s preparatory work on the issue. The vote bore out Lenin's estimate before the congress of 26 sure votes against 19 in doubt or opposed.[6]

The Bundists now had to swallow the recipe prepared for them by the Iskraites. The discussion on "The Place of the Bund in the Russian Social Democratic Workers' Party" came up at the fourth session. Liber presented the Bund's by now well-known stand. Stressing the lack of precision in the First Congress's formulation on party organization, he offered the rules worked out at the Bund's Fifth Congress as "the implementation and further logical development of the principles [of 1898]."[7] Liber defended the organization of the Jewish proletariat on the plea of unique conditions, and insisted that the First Congress had placed no geographical limitations on the Bund's activities. The problems of the Jewish proletariat, though distinct, were linked to problems that affected all society, he noted. The Bund wanted the vague autonomy granted by the founding congress to be fleshed out into a form that would allow the Jewish proletariat to participate in all questions decided by Russian Social Democracy. A federated party would serve that purpose. The Bund would be in the party as the representative of the Jewish proletariat and would participate in the work of the whole society at the center. Anticipating the objections to federation, Liber argued that "the proletariat of a given nationality has centralistic tendencies only when it sees the solution of all its problems and its special national needs in particular at the center." Autonomy separated national needs from the center and from general questions, isolating the Jewish proletariat. A federation would break down that isolation and bring centralization.[8] In an attempt to persuade the centralist-minded Iskraite leaders, Liber argued for a psychological and representational centralization rather than a formal structural arrangement apart from national factors.

Concerned with the tone of the majority at this early stage of discussion, the Bundists now altered their proposals. They removed the paragraph declaring the Bund a "federative part" of the party, deleted the term "contracting sides" used in a number of the original paragraphs, and eliminated the clause guaranteeing the Bund participation in all declarations made in the name of the entire proletariat in areas where the Bund was active.[9] These changes came close to reducing the resolutions of the Fifth Congress to the minimum statutes, the existence of which was as yet unknown to the Iskraites. Later, in their report on the Second Congress, the Bund delegates declared:

The fact of the matter is that already, at the first sessions and particularly during the debates on the agenda, it became evident the majority of the congress was little inclined toward concessions to the Bund. In order not to increase the hostile frame of mind toward the Bund and so as to increase the possibility of agreement, we decided to exclude from the draft statutes those points that sharply emphasized our position of principle, and in this way to shift the center of gravity of the argument somewhat toward practice.[10]

The delegates admitted they had violated the instructions of the Fifth Congress but pleaded that this was the only way they saw to forestall an immediate break.[11]

The Iskraites pressed their advantage. Martov returned to his previous arguments: the Bund sought to reverse the decisions of the First Congress, which had described the party as a single organization; its autonomy differed from the powers given other committees only in degree. Martov admitted that the First Congress had formulated only a principle of organization but argued that the intent to have unity was clear. Accordingly, he proposed that the Second Congress refuse to consider the new resolution, which had not been discussed in party organs and which brought the Bund to the congress as an independent entity.[12]

Moreover, said Martov, the Jewish proletariat did not need an independent political organization to represent its interests. It was impermissible, regardless of form, for a part of the party to represent one stratum of the proletariat or its interests, whether national or professional. National distinctions played "a subordinate role" to general class interests. One might use the difficult legal position of the Jews to argue for broader autonomy, he thought, though this had nothing in common with the principle of giving representation to national organizations, but that position could never serve as a basis for separation. The Bund's particular problems resulted from "unfortunate historical conditions," which no "heroic resolution" could set aside. In Martov's view Liber had not proved the case for centralization through federation; all he had shown was the abnormality of autonomous organization.[13]

Turning to the specifics of the Bund's proposals, Martov wondered whether the arrangements sought by the Bund might not next be extended to other groups. "What would become of us," he asked, "if each organization that entered the party operated wherever it chose? In that case the party would not even be a federation."[14] Martov drew a picture of a party Central Committee like the Polish Sejm (parliament), where a veto could hinder any resolution; and of a Bund Central Committee interposed between the party Central Committee and the local organizations blocking the lines of authority. The result would be disunity and disorganization. Consider, then, what would happen if every organization in the party asked for its own central committee. In equating the Bund with the Russian local committees, and the Jewish proletariat with national proletariats within defined territorial boundaries, Martov took a line completely opposite to Liber's, as in an earlier day.

Finally, Martov introduced his own resolution on the Bund. Federation was "an important obstacle to the fuller organizational rapprochement of the conscious proletariat of the various races, which would inevitably bring great harm to the interests of all and to those of the Jewish proletariat of Russia in particular"; hence federation was "unconditionally inadmissible between the Party and the Bund." Granting the need for special tasks because of the special conditions of language and Jewish life, the resolution named the Bund an autonomous part of the RSDWP, "the limits of whose autonomy should be fixed by the working out of general Party rules. As a plan for general party rule, the Bund's proposals were referred for consideration to the discussion of party organization.[15]

As the Bund delegates later interpreted Martov's speech in their report, Martov felt the Bund was a historical anomaly whose destruction was desirable but impossible at the moment because of the party's weakness. By rejecting everything that gave recognition to the Bund as a national organization and leaving the question of organizational limits open, he would leave the way open for the party to strengthen itself. Once it became strong, the Bund could then be destroyed without any infringement of party statutes.[16] To be sure, Martov had not said all this in so many words, as the report admitted. But the delegates in fact accurately interpreted the spirit of the congress.

The solidity of the anti-Bundist camp at the congress was immediately evident. Martov had no sooner submitted his resolution than Trotsky rose to inform the delegates that 12 Jewish comrades, all members of the RSDWP, were signing the resolution and still considered themselves representatives of the Jewish proletariat.[17] The ploy was obvious: the Iskraites were intent on showing the Bundists—and the congress—that there were Jewish Social Democrats opposed to their position. Liber shouted angrily that those who signed were representatives of a Jewish proletariat "among whom they have never worked."[18]

The debate on the Bund's proposals and Martov's resolution ran on for days, from the fifth through the eighth sessions of the congress. The speeches reflected every shade of opinion, ranging from a rare note of approval for the Bund to the mildly remonstrative mixed with condescension to outright hostility. The majority view was heavily anti-Bund.

Delegates from the Caucasus, reminding the Bundists of their own national character, criticized the Bund's demands as "nationalist, not socialist."[19] B. M. Knuniants (Rusov), a delegate from Baku, spoke proudly of the lack of separatism in the Caucasus and went so far as to insist that the First Congress had made a mistake, when it permitted the existence of a special Jewish organization; that action had perhaps been historically justified but had had undesirable consequences. Without denying the Bund's services to the Jewish proletariat, Knuniants deplored the absence of committees working in all languages in western Russia, a regrettable omission for which the Bund was fully at fault. He rejected the Bund's defense of separate organization on the plea of special needs. The argument of technical requirements was inadequate; the Jews spoke no common language, and the Bund itself argued against a territorial basis of organization. As for reasons of principle, in particular the legal discrimination against the Jews, the Jewish case was not unique; many other proletarians suffered similar disabilities. All should be removed, but meanwhile separate organizations slowed and complicated revolutionary work.[20]

Several delegates insisted on the necessity of looking after the common interests of the proletariat but were also friendly to the Bund's work. One was A. S. Pikker (Martynov), a long-time member of the Union Abroad, who defended the Bund itself while decrying its tendency toward national isolation.[21] Another was M. S. Zborovsky (Kostich), a delegate from Odessa. Zborovsky, unhappy about the divisive effects of the Bund's works in his city, felt that the Bund could be useful as an organization if it united closely with a Social Democracy that was not fighting hard enough for certain demands, thus raising the revolutionary consciousness of the whole movement.[22]

Trotsky put the question sharply for the Iskraite side. The Bund was either "the only representative of the interests of the Jewish proletariat in and before the Party" or "a special organization of the Party for agitation and propaganda among the Jewish proletariat." Which was it to be? He did not want to see the Bund's activities halted, only its demand for a special position in the party rejected.[23]

Portnoy, now joining the debate, made the issue of historical conditions raised by Martov and echoed by others the focal point of his argument. If the Bund had been formed under abnormal conditions, as conceded, were the Bundists to assume that normal conditions now obtained? Did this then mean the Bund no longer had a *raison d'être*? What criterion did Martov use to determine normal conditions? Responding to objections to the Bund's exclusive demands, Portnoy declared:

In demanding that the Bund be in the Party as the only representative of the Jewish proletariat, we by no means say that no one else may work among the Jewish workers. We are simply pointing out that the Bund is the only organization working exclusively among the Jewish proletariat, and that for this reason it should be recognized as its only representative.[24]

In any case, Portnoy noted, the Bund presented its proposals as a basis for discussion, not as an ultimatum.

The indefatigable Liber rose next to argue the necessity of an independent Jewish workers' organization. The Bund's position was the same as the stand of the distinguished Marxist Rosa Luxemburg, who had demanded that the German Social Democrats grant the Polish Social Democrats the right to concern themselves with all matters touching Polish workers living in Germany.[25] (The presence of PSD representatives at the congress probably motivated Liber to draw this comparison.) Why did the Bund's opponents dwell on the isolative effects of its work, Liber wondered, instead of recalling the solidarity of the Jewish proletariat with other proletarians?[26] Even to the point of aiding many of their representatives who sat before him, to cross the Russian frontier, he might have added.[27]

The debate on historical conditions and the construction of the party was given further dimension in the attempt to define the party itself. Again and again the same point was raised: the Bund was treating the party as one side in a contract. Martov's use of the word Rossiiskii indicated his view of the party as an Empire-wide structure.[28] His old adversary Kosovsky turned the argument around: it was Martov and his comrades who treated the Bund as a side rather than as a part of the party. The agenda had demonstrated that. Kosovsky probed Martov's consistency in claiming an all-Russian viewpoint when he would allow only Russian (Russkie) committees in the south. Jews on those committees did not represent the Jewish workers, as was their right by the Rules of 1898.[29]

Liber came at last to the fundamental point. The party must recognize the realities within which Social Democracy existed. Nationalities were a fact of Russian life and the Bund but expressing a national principle of organization. The Iskraites on the other hand sought "to create an international socialism without an international movement."[30] For the Bund, the party's claim to be all-Russian, i.e., multinational, was empty without the recognition of nationalities.

At the seventh session, on the morning of August 3 (N. S.), the Bundists again moved to a new position. Liber took the floor to offer the congress a revised set of proposals. As before, the Bund delegates attempted to avoid a complete retreat to the minimum resolutions by revising and removing various clauses that stressed federation, once more going beyond their mandate. They struck the clause that specified the representation of party organizations in the central institutions and altered the paragraph on relations between the Bund and other revolutionary organizations, eliminating the power of any party to veto a change in arrangements. The paragraph had smacked too much of a treaty and therefore of federation.[31] After Liber explained the Bund's new proposals he told the assembly: "We have done everything possible for unification; we are not in a position to go further than this. Without' the remaining points the very existence of the Bund is impossible."[32]

The hard-line Iskraites were not impressed. Having introduced a resolution rejecting federation, they were unwilling even to take up the new draft, which to Martov seemed a mixture of autonomy and federation and therefore a matter to be discussed in connection with the general organization of the party.[33] Indeed, the Iskraites stood firm on Martov's definition of autonomy in terms of agitational tasks, a freedom made necessary by peculiarities of language and custom. "From our point of view," Trotsky declared, "the autonomy of the Bund is in principle no different from the autonomy of each committee."[34] Plekhanov softened this definition by adding that the limits of technical autonomy were adjustable.[35]

The Bundists viewed the refusal to take up their revised plan as an attempt to change the agenda. They had prepared concrete proposals because the Iskraites had placed the question of the Bund first; they wanted them considered and answered now. Kosovsky charged that the question on the agenda had been changed from the place of the Bund in the party to a more basic issue, autonomy or federation. But Plekhanov contended that these were not two questions but one and the same thing. Kosovsky also argued that Martov's resolution limited the autonomy granted by the First Congress, which spoke in terms of all questions specifically touching the Jewish proletariat.[36] The Bund's concessions brought no adjustments from the Iskraites.

Appreciating the extent of their difficulties, the Bundists staked their position on basic guarantees. Liber proposed a point-by-point consideration of the Bund's second draft. But against the possibility that these proposals would fail, he decided also to ask the congress to amend Martov's resolution so that it "in no way eliminates independence in all questions that touch specifically the Jewish proletariat as granted to the Bund by the First Congress of the RSDWP."[37] The Bund now found itself clinging desperately to that weak reed autonomy, the status that had seemed so ill-defined and objectionable at the beginning of the congress.

The balloting on the proposals before the congress shattered any remaining hopes the Bundists had. Liber's proposed amendment of the Martov resolution drew the first ballot and the first defeat. The vote, 13 in favor, 26 opposed, reflected some wavering on the part of the non-Bundist delegates. But when Martov's resolution was put to the test they were once again solid in their opposition to the Bund; the vote was 41 for, five—the Bund delegates—opposed. Next came Liber's motion for immediate consideration of the Bund's second set of proposals, and again the delegates stood solidly against the Bund, rejecting the motion by the same 41-to-five vote.[38]

At the conclusion of the balloting the Bund delegation violated its instructions from the Fifth Congress for the third time. Since Martov's resolution made the Bund an autonomous part of the party, and only technically autonomous at that, the Bundists should have departed at that point. Instead, as they explained later in their report, "we decided . . . to wait, since the party congress had not expressed its opinion of our rules (in their changed form)."[39]

The next fateful stage for the Bund began at the fourteenth session, on the morning of August 11, when the sixth point on the agenda, the organization of the party, came to the floor.[40] Lenin presented his plan for a highly centralized party structure, which was discussed by a number of speakers. It was then proposed that the list of speakers be closed. Liber and Medem jumped to their feet, objecting heatedly, reminding the delegates that when the congress had accepted Martov's resolution at the outset, it had agreed to consider the Bund's rules under the paragraph on organization.[41] The Iskraites, with Martov again at the fore, spoke for separate consideration, arguing that Lenin's plan gave general instructions, not details of interparty relations. The Bundists should not excite themselves unnecessarily, Martov advised, "as if the congress wanted to set a trap against them."[42] The debate was closed over the protests of the Bund delegation, which immediately introduced a declaration noting the congress's failure to abide by its own decision.[43]

The Bundists saw that their cause was doomed. Blocked in their first effort to have their rules discussed, they had now been maneuvered into a situation that made genuine consideration of their proposals impossible. Lenin's organization plan, which gave the central institutions of the party enormous powers, and the procedure of the congress would ensure that. Yet the Bund delegates continued to push their case. Liber, recalling Trotsky's description of the Bund's draft rules as "formulated mistrust," termed Lenin's work "organized mistrust."[44] The able Medem now added his voice. The Bund did not reject centralism in principle—did not its Central Committee maintain strong controls over the local organizations?—but Lenin's idea of centralization was something "monstrous," a power so great that it could destroy local organizations rather than guide them. What could such a proposal mean for the Bund? Brushing aside Martov's soothing disclaimer of a "trap," Medem declared that Lenin wanted the prior acceptance of his plan so the position of the Bund would be determined from his principles. The Bund's proposals were thus being ruled out without consideration. Turning to Lenin, Medem bluntly asked him if he did not see his plan as ruling out the possibility of the Bund's proposals being accepted, and as giving the Central Committee of the party "the right to alter the composition of the Central Committee of the Bund, to dissolve it, to repeal the decisions of Bund congresses, etc.?" Medem reminded the delegates of the seriousness of the moment: "If our proposals, which represent the minimal conditions for the continued existence of the Bund, are rejected, then the question of the Bund's departure from the Party will have been decided."[45]

Liber followed Medem's lead. Without even examining the paragraph on national organizations, the congress had made a decision. Perhaps the Bund would not be destroyed immediately, but the path to destruction of Martov's "historical abnormality" would have been laid. Would not *Iskra*'s editors walk out if their organizational principles were rejected and a so-called democratic organization was accepted?

Liber's speech then took on a different tone, as if to admit further discussion was fruitless and the time had come for spirited demonstration:

Are you really so naïve, Comrades, as to suppose for one minute that we could remain in the Party in the face of the acceptance of such a rule? That we would willingly sign our own death warrant? No, that will never be. We are not gathering to die! On the contrary, we feel the surge of fresh power! And we are certain that if our comrades will but look at all this from the point of view of the actual interests of the all-Russian Social Democratic movement as against some phantom organization of generals without an army, they will understand our actions and our attitude toward the proposed new rule.[46]

Lenin put off his reply until his plan came out of the commission processing it. His rules came to the floor again at the twenty-second session, on the morning of August 15. The Iskraites immediately introduced a preface to them making them binding for all parts of the party with certain unspecified exceptions, which would appear as appendixes. The congress agreed. The Bundists again protested, insisting that they should know what the exceptions were before they adopted general rules, and that they were entitled to present their own rules for consideration before others were accepted on the basis of procedures established by the congress itself.[47] Martov, harking back to his

resolution, replied that the congress had adopted the principle of centralization, and that in the process of point-by-point examination of the clauses, the
Bundists would have an opportunity to clarify their position.[48] Defending the
congress's procedure, Trotsky argued that "the Bund is for the Party, not
the Party for the Bund."[49] Liber denied the Bund was placing itself beyond the
control of the party; it merely wanted its rules considered. In the end the
Bundists agreed to participate in the discussion of Lenin's draft, though they
reserved the right to discuss exceptions that touched the Bund.[50]

The day before the vote was to be taken, Martov and Lenin invited the
Bundists to discuss their proposals before the commission studying the party
rules. As it turned out, Martov did not come to the meeting and Lenin appeared briefly, then excused himself. Deciding that there was now no point
to the meeting, the remaining commission members adjourned the session.
The Bundists saw this as further proof that the Bund's status had been decided, and that the party leaders had no desire to come to any agreement.[51]
But other explanations are possible, beginning with the growing differences
between Lenin and Martov over party organization, a circumstance that
placed the Bund in a rare strategic position.[52]

The final confrontation came August 18, at the twenty-seventh session. As
soon as the discussion moved to national organizations, and specifically the
Bund, Martov brought up the second paragraph of the Bund's rules. The
description of the Bund as a nonregional organization of the Jewish proletariat and its sole representative bore "a sharply expressed stamp of federalism," he asserted, and was thus to be dismissed, the congress having already
addressed itself to that point. Adding salt to the wound, he introduced a letter
from a comrade in Riga purporting to expose the evil effects of a federated
arrangement in that city. Then he proposed the paragraph be eliminated
without any replacement. As to the area of the Bund's activity, it was to remain undefined, since it was impossible to fix.[53]

Again it was Liber who carried the Bund's case. Despite the view of many
present, the Bund had not become nationalist and separatist since its Fourth
Congress, had not in fact changed at all. Liber recommended to Martov his
own speech of 1895 upholding the need for a special Jewish workers' organization. Noting the similarity between the Russian attacks and those of the PPS
in 1898, when the Bund was tasked for a lack of solidarity with the Poles and
Lithuanians against the Russian state, Liber pointed out that those vintage
arguments had not prevented the creation of a strong Social Democratic movement among the Jewish workers in Poland. Moreover, the Bund's reply to
the Poles had been carried in *Rabotnik* without any objection when Plekhanov
himself had been the editor. What had then been considered natural and legal,
Liber maintained, was now considered nationalistic. The Bund's credo, published in the same journal in 1898, had described the need for an independent

organization of the Jewish proletariat. Once again—the Bund had not changed its views.[54]

In fact it was the Russians who had changed, Liber charged. Otherwise, why had the Russian comrades not noticed these "harmful" views until recently? The truth was the Bund had grown in Poland and Lithuania without the help of the Russians. Now, with the rapid development of the movement and the need to unite Social Democratic forces, the Russians were denying the right of the Bund to exist. Said Liber: "Let our Russian comrades not forget that if this question of the Bund is for them the first page of history, for us, who have lived through almost the same struggle with the PPS, the struggle with the Russian comrades is the second page of our history."[55] After castigating the Russians for their own ignorance of the Bund's activities and, indeed, for their ingratitude in the face of the Bund's contributions to the movement, Liber concluded by defending categorically the position outlined in the second paragraph.[56]

There was little discussion. The delegates considered the two crucial points —the claim of unlimited territorial rights and the claim of sole representation of the Jewish proletariat—separately. Both were rejected by the same margin, 39 to five; the Bund stood alone. The whole paragraph was then voted down by a vote of 41 to five with five abstentions.*

After the final tally, Liber spoke again:

In the name of the whole delegation of the Bund, I declare that in view of the fact the Congress by its last vote rejected the principal paragraph of the statutes we proposed, the acceptance of which our Fifth Congress recognized as a necessary condition for the Bund's affiliation with the Party, we, in accordance with the decision of the Fifth Congress of the Bund, are leaving the Congress of the Party and declare that the Bund is withdrawing from the RSDWP. We will present a written declaration of justification to the Second Congress separately.[57]

Medem recorded his feelings of the moment: "We left. It had happened.... It even made a heavy impression on our opponents, but it was harder for us.... We took our step with heavy heart. It was a real catastrophe.... We felt much as if a piece of flesh was being torn from a living body."[58]

Though the Bundists failed to advance their own cause, they played an important role at the congress. They not only influenced decisions on national rights issues in the party program (despite their inability to agree on an acceptable principle of their own at the Fifth Congress), but also made their weight felt by voting as a bloc. Their five votes, along with those of other non-

---

* *Vtoroi ocherednoi*, p. 289. Akimov and Pikker (Martynov) of the Union Abroad, L. P. Makhnovets (Bruker) of the St. Petersburg Workers' Organization, and D. P. Kalafati (Makhov) of the Nikolaev Committee abstained from voting on the second paragraph altogether. Kalafati had two votes.

Iskraites, represented the swing votes in a sometimes closely divided congress. More important, the absence of their votes and those of the other dissidents who left the congress made a critical difference when the Iskraite camp finally ruptured.

In contrast to their isolation during the debate on the Bund's place in the party, the Bundists found friends and allies among the delegates on questions concerning nationality. When the commission on the party program finished its work and returned the program to the congress floor at the fifteenth session, Iskraite solidarity began to fade. Izenshtat, a member of the commission, introduced a change calling for "broad local and regional self-rule." Lenin objected to the word regional as too vague and subject to the interpretation that Social Democracy favored the division of the state into small regions; but Martov, looking at the expanse of Russia rather than the direct question of principle, offered amendments allowing not only local self-rule but also regional self-rule where "conditions of life and composition of population" differed markedly from the purely Russian localities.[59] Martov's view prevailed by a considerable margin; and though his was not as broad a statement as Izenshtat's, it carried enough regional freight to displease Lenin and to give national groups a definition of their future responsibilities not found in the original Iskraite version.[60] It is possible that the Bundists, who gained no direct advantage from this addition, saw in it a lever for support in other matters of nationality still to be considered.[61]

Shortly after, a paragraph guaranteeing freedom of "conscience, speech, press, assembly, strikes, and unions" came up for discussion. Liber proposed the insertion of "language" after the word "press,"[62] a suggestion that brought laughter from the delegates at first but serious discussion after. Liber declared that he was not arguing *for* the use of any language, but for the *right* to use a language other than the state's. This question brought some of the closest balloting of the congress. Eventually the majority agreed on the right of the individual to an education in his native tongue and the equality of languages in local state institutions; both were incorporated into the program of the RSDWP.[63]

The Bund's efforts to follow up these gains by expanding a general statement on self-determination to include all nationalities in the Empire did not meet similar sympathy. Medem proposed the creation of institutions guaranteeing "full freedom of cultural development" for peoples whose residence had no specific territorial association.[64] The sense of those who spoke against the proposal was that the Bund asked for institutions to support nationalism. "To us, as Social Democrats," declared E. Ia. Levin of *Iuzhnyi rabochii,* "it is of no concern whether this or that nationality as such will develop. That is a matter of spontaneous process."[65] In the view of B. A. Ginzburg (Kol'tsov), the Bundists were demanding "purely aggressive measures for the support of even those nationalities that are becoming extinct."[66] Liber attempted to convince the congress that failing such guarantees, nationalities wishing to remain in Russia might be led to emigrate, but to no avail. In the vote against the Medem proposal we see the same chasm between the Bund and the overwhelming majority that greeted every suggestion specifically affecting the Bund and, in this case, the Jews.[67]

The Bund's voting power was at its greatest when a bitter quarrel between Martov and Lenin erupted over the definition of party membership. Martov wanted the party open to members of any organization that accepted the party's leadership, whereas Lenin wanted it open only to members of one of the party organizations. The Bund stood with Martov, and Lenin's definition was narrowly defeated by a vote of 28 to 23. The five votes of the Bund, plus the two cast by the Union Abroad, provided the margin of victory as the Iskraite machine broke apart.[68]

Lenin had been haunted by the specter "that the Bund plus *Rabochee delo*, i.e., the Union Abroad, could *determine the fate* of any issue by supporting the minority of the Iskraites."[69] Shortly after the congress he expressed mystification at the Bundists' departure when "they were actually masters of the situation" and could have gained much by staying. He guessed, correctly, that they had binding instructions.[70] Bertram Wolfe, in his brilliant study of Lenin, believes that Lenin, himself a master at seizing the quick chance, simply could not comprehend how the defeated Bundists could fail to make the best of a bad situation by using their votes opportunistically.[71] The Bundists' support of Martov was not reciprocated, and they left before the deliberations on party organization were over. When the delegates of the Union Abroad withdrew shortly after, the Martov forces lost the voting edge that had produced their earlier marginal victories.

The Bundists were extremely bitter about congress's patent bias against the Bund. In their report they pointed out a particularly egregious example of unequal treatment: the congress had given its blessing to a proposal of the Polish Social Democrats (who had been invited to the congress under special rules) for "institutions guaranteeing full freedom of cultural development to all nationalities belonging to the state" but had rejected a Bundist amendment to the paragraph on self-determination containing almost identical language, and worse, had scolded the Bund for its nationalism.[72] The Bundists considered this a purely personal reaction.

The victory over the Bund at the congress marked the high point of success for the two-and-a-half-year-old Iskraite organization. The Bundists stood virtually alone in their aspiration to be a full-fledged national proletarian party within the RSDWP, drawing at most a few sympathetic votes on procedural matters and abstentions by those who, remembering the Bund's services to the movement, did not have the heart to vote against it.

The first published version of the proceedings of the Second Congress, which appeared in 1904, did not include the resolution adopted on the Bund. Later editions carried a statement to the effect that with the growth of the movement differences were certain to disappear, bringing about "the necessary complete amalgamation of the proletariat of all nationalities into one RSDWP in the interests of the liberation struggle of the working class."[73]

The Bundists' declaration did appear in the first edition of the proceedings, however. Displaying considerable hurt, it charged that from the first the congress had sought to liquidate the Bund and had refused even to discuss its proposals. Experience would prove, the departing delegates asserted, "the bankruptcy of the tendency of suppressing and leveling, which has found such clear expression in the organizational statute accepted by the Second Congress of the Russian Party at the very moment when there is a real possibility of bringing about solid unification."[74] Ironically, the hopes of both sides for the future were soon to prove false with the irreparable split in the Russian Social Democratic forces.

The Second Congress ended with the Bund and the party even further apart than before on the question of the Bund's place in the party. The new party rules conceded no more than that all party organizations had the right to manage exclusively those activities for which they had been created. This interpretation not only fell far short of the broadened aims the Bundists had evolved since 1898; it was an extremely narrow view of the First Congress's ruling. Had the original provision been so interpreted, the Bund would not have been able to grow as it had to this point. Moreover, the climate that had helped push its growth in the first place had not worsened, which might have provided some justification for retrenchment, but was on the contrary even more favorable. The political awareness of the Jewish population had both broadened and deepened, making it more necessary than ever, as the Bund saw it, to strengthen the Bund's influence among Jewish workers and intellectuals. In any case, the national character of western Russia generally and of the Jewish community itself left the Bundists little choice. The Kishinev pogrom of April 1903, an upheaval in Jewish life that was almost totally ignored at the Second Congress, was to increase the Bund's already considerable role in Jewish affairs.

17. The Bund and the State, 1903-1905

The Bundists were still feeling the emotional impact of the Lekert affair when an anti-Jewish pogrom erupted in Czestochowa, Poland, in August 1902. This new violence immediately stirred them to take up the matter of the Bund's responsibilities to the Jewish population. The Central Committee's reaction to the bloody episode was measured. *Di Arbeter Shtime* absolved the Polish people as such of guilt and even minimized the significance of the act by pointing to the peculiarly fanatical character of Czestochowa, an important religious center for Polish Catholics, thus localizing the blame. Traditional class arguments explained the behavior of the pogromists. They were a socially backward, weakly developed element; the workers among them were simply enraged and misled men who followed their spiritual and material masters blindly. The Bund placed the burden of guilt on the government, which incited one people against another for its own purposes. The entire pogrom was, in this light, the fruit of the exceptional laws, which created an atmosphere that made violence against the Jews permissible. Furthermore, the state tolerated an anti-Semitic press that openly encouraged violence.[1]

Di Arbeter Shtime made a point of praising the Polish workers who had been willing to stand up against the pogromists. At the same time, it regretted that the Polish socialists had not done more to educate their masses. "It is really a joke," one contributor noted bitterly, "that until now there is no socialist brochure against anti-Semitism in Polish."[2] The belief that the Polish movement had serious shortcomings and much revolutionary work to do comes through clearly.

On the crucial question of reacting to a pogrom, the Bund's central organ took two views. In the long run, the problem would solve itself; socialism would make the masses friends. As for now, the immediate danger required an immediate response:

We must handle ourselves like people with human dignity. Violence, no matter from where it stems, must not be glossed over. When we are attacked . . . it would be criminal on our part to bear it without resistance. In such instances we must come out with arms in hand, organize ourselves, and fight until our last drop of blood; only when we show strength will we force everyone to respect our honor.[3]

Di Arbeter Shtime's short-term answer was an unequivocal call for armed resistance.

For the Bund, the circumstances of 1902 made the development of a mass response to violence absolutely necessary. The Bundists saw no Social Democratic counterargument here as in the case of terror. Nor were they prepared to argue for restraint, as they had done in the 1890's when faced with the problem of Christian strikebreakers. The Bund's mood was too militant and its consciousness of nationality too deep for theoretical arguments to prevail. The fundamentals of working-class solidarity and of revolutionary enlightenment as a means of bringing about that solidarity were useful ideological guideposts, but they provided no practical solution to the threat to life and limb. Thus, though the Bund continued to explain the causes of the pogrom in abstract class terms, it nevertheless turned to self-defense as an immediate response. In 1902 the Bund began projecting on a national scale a policy it had only recently decreed for itself: defending demonstrations was justified; defending oneself against such arbitrary violence as a pogrom was even more justified.

The Bund's call to resist the assaults of *pogromshchiki* had little immediate effect. The Czestochowa pogrom, while drawing a quick reaction, was taken as an isolated incident in a fanatically religious town. The Bund, entrenched in the northwest provinces, had no direct experience with pogroms, a feature of southern Russian life. It was the next shock—the Kishinev pogrom of April 1903—that raised the problem of defense to the national level.

The grisly statistics of the Kishinev pogrom pale before the subsequent history of barbaric massacre; the casualties (dead and injured) ran only into the hundreds. At the time, however, the bloody incident was internationally remarked and protested. For the Jews, Kishinev was a traumatic experience, a turning point, the yardstick by which all later adversity was measured. "It burst upon the Jewish proletariat like a clap of thunder," *Di Arbeter Shtime* commented, "and left no doubt in any heart."[4]

The degree of governmental guilt is difficult to assess. Officials close to Plehve, Minister of the Interior, deny his foreknowledge or sanction of the pogrom.[5] But the local officials do not come off so well. Raaben, the governor of Bessarabia, who was dismissed shortly after the pogrom, apparently left it up to the local military to put a stop to the bloodshed.[6] As his successor, Prince S. D. Urussov, a fairly liberal man, prepared to depart for Bessarabia, Plehve told him: "Please let us have less speech-making and less philo-Semitism."[7] Urussov made a partial investigation and absolved Raaben and

Plehve of deliberate plotting. All the same, they bore some responsibility for the government's policy, the principal cause of the disorders in Urussov's view. Because of the exceptional laws, the Christian population assumed Jews were beyond the protection of the law and a danger to the state. Urussov also condemned the state by implication in ascribing blame to an anti-Semitic press that was not halted by censorship.[8] On the whole, Urussov and the Bundists were agreed on the question of responsibility.

Having no organization to speak of in Kishinev, and so not directly involved, the Bund nevertheless was deeply shaken by the pogrom and tried to grapple with its widespread implications. A host of leaflets, pamphlets, and articles followed. One of the earliest, a Central Committee leaflet, sought to draw attention, as in the Czestochowa pogrom, to the underlying and general causes: the competition between capitalists of different nationalities; the capitalists' fear of a united proletariat, leading to efforts to distract the proletariat from its true interests; and the government's pitting of one nationality against another to bolster its own position. Wherever ignorance existed among the people these campaigns succeeded.[9]

The leaflet addressed itself directly to the Zionist answers of the middle-class Jewish press, which reacted to the pogrom by bemoaning the fate of the Jews in the world. "Only one ray of light remains in Jewish life," said *Der Fraind* (The Friend) of St. Petersburg, the first legal Yiddish daily in Russia. "That is Zionism, which calls the people to their old home."[10] The Central Committee heatedly protested such tears and passivity; that was the response of slaves; free men must be ready to defend their rights.[11] Nevertheless, a certain pessimism invaded the ranks of the Bund, too. A dispirited Hillel Katz-Blum, one of the oldest pioneers, told Kremer he was unable to work with the same enthusiasm "when I see that every step of the Russian revolution moves over streams of Jewish blood." Kremer understood his feelings, Blum says.[12]

The Bund saw great danger to its revolutionary aims in Russia in the pogrom. It feared that the Jewish masses, gripped by the feeling of hopelessness expressed in *Der Fraind*, would recoil to a greater isolation than before, and accordingly stressed the guilt of the government and the inappropriateness of despair to boost the flagging spirit of the Jewish community.

The Bundists also rejected *Der Fraind*'s unqualified call for Jewish unity ("Now all the Jews of the world, without difference of opinion and party, must unite to defend themselves against their enemies"), an appeal that was echoed in other papers as well.[13] Class differences had told in Kishinev, they pointed out. Rich Jews had escaped harm by hiring others to defend them, but the poor had been left defenseless. Wealthy Jews had sent deputations to the government to beg for mercy, pleading that *they*, the rich, are good and religious, and the Jewish *worker-socialists* are guilty of everything."[14] These were the same people, *Di Arbeter Shtime* urged its readers to remem-

ber, who exploited the workers and handed them over to the police in economic conflicts. Talk of unity was simply a means of clouding the consciousness of the workers. All Jews suffered, but not equally.[15]

The Bund's call for self-defense required it to appeal to the unity and dignity
of the Jewish masses without creating a wave of national feeling that would
join the Zionist current. To forestall that possibility the Bund sought to put
itself at the head of the defense efforts. "Let the local committees of the Bund
take on the organization of the resistance. Let our organized people stand
in the first ranks," one commentary urged, at the same time exhorting the
Zionists to join the fighting proletariat.[16]

The Bundists also tried to show that pogroms were an anti-revolutionary
instrument, a task made somewhat easier by the police, who blamed the
pogrom on the socialists and threatened new outbreaks if demonstrations took
place.[17] If the violence was a function of class warfare, then it was the duty
of all proletarians to join the fight against it. At the Fifth Congress, two
months after Kishinev, the Bund resolved that,

of all the strata of the Jewish population, only the proletariat fighting under the
flag of Social Democracy represents a force capable of undertaking effective resistance to the mob that the government sets on the Jews.

The Congress . . . expresses its conviction that only the common struggle of the
proletariat of all nationalities will destroy at the root those conditions that give
rise to such events as Kishinev.[18]

By placing the fight against pogroms on a class basis, the Bund hoped to
downplay the national aspect of these outbursts and soften the effects of
aroused national feeling. To bolster its position, it called on Russian Social
Democracy to take a more active role in this respect by acquainting the Russian workers with the Jewish movement, by fighting anti-Semitism directly,
and by appealing to the Russian workers to unite with their Jewish brothers
in armed resistance during times of danger.[19]

The Bund's position was a difficult one, which placed an enormous burden
on its shoulders, for it not only wanted to assume the leadership of the armed
conflict against the government-backed, or at least government-tolerated, violence, but wanted at the same time to mute the national note in an effort that
rested on pride in national identity. The Bundists were bound to ask the support of other Social Democrats, but they could not have been surprised when
the Russians who so bitterly opposed the Bund's national and organizational
aspirations insisted that Kishinev was just one more argument for closer
organizational unity.[20]

Kishinev had lasting effects on the Jews of Russia. In the next 18 months,
down to the revolutionary days of 1905, there were numerous outbreaks, constantly refreshing the terrors of the past and conjuring up new ones, for who

could predict when an incident might spread to the proportions of a major disaster? The rumor of a pogrom was often enough to set a whole community aquiver.

With the outbreak of the Russo-Japanese war in January 1904, the state became interested in promoting internal harmony. Nevertheless, the violence continued. Local anti-Semites now used patriotic appeals to foment pogroms. In addition to their traditional accusations of ritual murder, they spread rumors that Jews were purchasing weapons for the Japanese, and even that the Jews had brought the war on the Russians in revenge for Kishinev.[21] The police found the threat of pogrom an effective weapon against revolutionary activity, for Jewish revolutionaries could not take such threats lightly. The pogrom thus became a constant in the Bund's consideration of its revolutionary work.

Eventually, the war contributed its own brand of pogrom. Reservists called to active duty frequently became difficult to handle at mobilization points, and violence often attended their presence in a town. In such circumstances, the police found it convenient to convert an ugly situation into an anti-Jewish demonstration.

The Bund's call to self-defense was an integrated and advanced expression of conscious national proletarian solidarity, the genesis of which long predated the pogroms. The notion of self-defense was not especially revolutionary, but it certainly contributed to the psychological and organizational capabilities for revolution. The Bund's intent, however, was not rebellion. It asked merely that the Jewish community and others of good will meet force with force in case of attack.

The moral basis for such a call to arms lay deep in the Bundist experience. Human dignity had been a consistent theme since pioneer days, dating back at least to Martov's insistence in 1895 that the Jewish workers had to fight for their own freedom, a direct appeal to pride and backbone that had become the psychological cornerstone of the Bund's rationale. With the call for national rights at the Fourth Congress, the concept of dignity was expanded; the Jewish worker was now held to be entitled to dignity not only as a man, but as a Jew.

As we have seen, early on in the Bund's history the leaders had rejected economic and political violence alike. On both ideological and practical grounds they had disavowed terror as dangerous for the development of true mass consciousness, potentially harmful to relations with neighboring national populations, and destructive of organizational discipline. Nevertheless, economic terror had a long history in the movement, even receiving at times the tacit approval of local committees. Political terror, in the form of organized revenge, was a more difficult problem, reflecting as it did the Jewish worker-revolutionaries' desire to assert their human dignity in the face of state violence; but it too had been rejected by the leaders after a period of hesitation. It was the decision to use force to defend demonstrations that finally opened the way to a new position on the issue of violence.

The Bund's Fifth Congress completed the official stand on self-defense, and in the following resolution legitimized the use of force: "The Congress, pointing out the necessity of the most energetic resistance to violence by thugs, recognizes that the committees and other organizations of the Bund should take all measures to see to it that at the first signs of an impending pogrom they are in a position to organize armed resistance."[22] The Bund had taken the first step toward authorizing a paramilitary arm in its attempt to protect demonstrations. Now it went all the way and placed itself on a war footing against the elements in the greater society that would assault the Jewish community.

There was little question of the Bund's ability to mount such a campaign. The Jewish community, despite its traditional air of passivity, included those to whom violence was no stranger. Carpenters, locksmiths, and others similarly engaged in crafts requiring great physical strength were often combative men and likely recruits for defense forces. Other candidates were to be found among the same lawless element that in the past often fought workers, either at the behest of employers or on their own initiative; indeed some number of these men had already joined the terrorists, particularly in the earlier days of the movement.[23] Many of these lusty and violent types had banded together into unofficial battle squads (*boevie otriady*, or BO), which obtained arms, fought police to free arrested comrades, and clashed with gangs protecting strikebreakers.[24] The chief participants, in many cases, served as leaders and organizers of the new self-defense units.

Once the authorization came down from the Central Committee, the local committee gave official sanction and specific instructions to members of these strongarm squads. Mendel Daich, an experienced streetfighter, describes the formation of the self-defense unit in Dvinsk. When rumors of a pogrom began circulating in a neighboring village of Old Believers, "an order came from the committee to accept in the self-defense only strong and aggressive members of the organization, and to separate the self-defense from agitation and propaganda work. There were about 80 men in the Dvinsk self-defense group."[25] The group was divided into squads called "tens," each with its own leader who was responsible for rallying the unit in emergencies, supplying it with weapons, and seeing to its quarters. The commander of the whole force was one Shloime Parkai; Daich served as his second.[26]

The Dvinsk self-defense group received its baptism of fire during the Easter-Passover season of 1903. For this sensitive period, when pogroms were easily fomented, the unit mobilized about 200 men. They were armed with "cold" and "hot" weapons: knives, clubs, and axes in the one instance, bombs (sometimes referred to as *knaidlekh*, or dumplings) and revolvers in the other. Two "tens" of butchers carried meat cleavers. A gymnasium student manufactured the bombs. The unit had perhaps 18 revolvers all told. But when a fight broke out on market day, that was enough to end the affair quickly: the peasants took to their heels. The police apparently found it convenient not to become involved, and a potential pogrom was thwarted.[27]

Once the immediate threat was ended, the Dvinsk Committee ordered the armed "tens" disbanded. Its instructions were resisted, however; the self-defense leaders, breathing a spirit of independence, insisted on maintaining an armed contingent of 55 men. The Dvinsk experience was repeated in its essential details in a number of towns in the Pale and Poland.[28]

The BO units, first authorized by the Bund in 1902 for the protection of demonstrations, now became a fixed part of the organization with an increased scope of activity. They acted as security patrols to protect meetings in the woods, stood guard at synagogue doors when Bund spokesmen gave "sermons" (sometimes against the wishes of the audience), and formed the core groups for expanded self-defense forces during pogroms.[29]

The first earnest test of the effectiveness of the self-defense forces came in the late summer of 1903 in Gomel. They gave a good account of themselves, to the great gratification of the Bundists, many of whom had been wracked by a sense of shame and impotence after Kishinev. How was it possible, a Bund brochure had asked back then, that pogromists could operate without hindrance for two days in a city where nearly half the population was Jewish?[30] Gomel was a different story altogether, "*a new page* in the history of the Jews of Russia," as *Di Arbeter Shtime* jubilantly entitled one of its articles.[31] Even the censored *Der Fraind* chortled quietly, "What occurred . . . was a fight rather than a pogrom."[32]

The state played an important and highly questionable role in the Gomel pogrom. The simple knowledge that Jewish youths had been arming themselves for some time did not prevent violence, which broke out on Friday, August 29, after a minor incident. The Russian participants were defeated, causing the official indictment that was handed down later to describe the fight as a "Russian pogrom."[33] On Monday, September 1, when new violence erupted, troops were on hand—called out, according to the indictment, because rumor had it that the railroad workers were going to attack the Jews in revenge for the events of Friday.[34]

The state and the Bund took completely different views of the role of the military in this new and worse round of violence, but one thing is clear: despite the presence of several companies of armed men, hundreds of Jewish homes and shops were vandalized.* As the indictment makes plain, the troops were called out to prevent the pogrom from reaching the center of town,

---

* *Der Fraind*, 201 (Sept. 20/7, 1903): 1, col. 2. The newspaper reported some 200 shops and homes destroyed, but the final figure was much higher, in the neighborhood of 700.

where the wealthier Jewish shops and homes were located.[35] That part of town was indeed kept clear, but the story was different in other Jewish quarters. The only other activity of the soldiers, by their own reports and by the Bund's, was fighting the self-defense units.

The differences between the Bund and the state over what actually happened are irreconcilable. The government firmly insisted that the only damage occurred where there were no troops; the Bund just as firmly insisted that the troops kept the self-defense forces at bay, allowing the rampaging railroad workers to do as they wanted behind a protective military cordon.[36] The government also claimed that the military prevented fights between the Christian workers and the Jews.[37] Later, in a report based on the accounts of self-defense participants, the Bund acknowledged that all resistance to the troops came from Jews—but again, only because the military appeared to be doing its best to protect the pogromists.[38] In light of the havoc wrought, it does not appear too harsh to suggest that the Bund view is closer to the truth, that the military did indeed serve as cover for the mob by holding off the self-defense units.

Despite the new and frustrating element of military intervention—the last and greatest weapon available to the Tsarist regime against its revolutionary opponents—the Bundists were ecstatic to the point of exaltation over their own part in the Gomel pogrom. The contrast with Kishinev was obvious. Where the self-defenders and pogromshchiki had met without the state's armed forces nearby, the Jewish forces had dispersed the Russian forces. The Bundists felt confident enough to report that if it had not been for the troops, no Jews would have been hurt.[39] It was too much to expect that the self-defense forces could cope with the army. Still, the 200-man group, buoyed by its showing and successes, decided on Monday evening that if fresh incursions were made on Tuesday, they would attack the troops.[40]

The Bund interpreted the spirit displayed at Gomel as a new stage in the revolutionary and social history of the Jewish people and a vindication of its principle that the Jews could and should defend themselves. The Bund proclaimed itself the progenitor of Jewish self-defense and pointed out that the Jewish proletariat represented the only power in the streets.* Gomel made it clear, the Bundists held, that far from being the defender of the Jews, as some bourgeois Jews contended, the government was their greatest enemy.

The continuing fear and reality of pogroms sparked a corresponding growth

---

* *Di Arbeter Shtime*, 35 (Oct. 1903): 10–11. The Zionist ideologue Ber Borokhov challenges the Bund on this point (*In baginen*, Tel Aviv, 1948, p. 82). He claims that the labor Zionists organized a self-defense force three and a half years before Gomel, and that he disclosed this information as early as 1907. If he is correct, the effort would have been a feeble one at best. Some sources raise doubt that a self-defense action actually took place. See J. Hertz, "Ber Borokhov un zaine mfrishim," *Unzer tsait*, Feb.–March 1971: 27–28.

in self-defense. The Jewish cause attracted not only Bundists, but also labor Zionists and Christian volunteers. Indeed, the Gomel self-defense group was of a mixed national and political composition including, among others, some 30 Christians.[41] Besides gaining a certain amount of support in Gomel itself, the Bundists won the approval of the Kharkov and Tiflis committees of the RSDWP, which sent their regards to the Gomel Committee after the pogrom.

The policy of self-defense was greeted with mixed emotions by the Jewish community. Some viewed it with sheer horror. Others, particularly the liberal and often nationalist-minded middle-class Jews, saw value in the enterprise, approved its purpose, and enjoyed its successes.[42] Outside of the community, the policy certainly gave a few would-be pogromists pause, especially after the forces became well organized. Where the cry that the Jews were arming might have provoked an outbreak of violence in the early days of the new wave of pogroms, once it became known that the Jews had defended themselves and might do so again, the self-defense policy served as no small deterrent.[43] A tradition of a fighting Jewish proletariat, with the Bund playing a major and often the only role, was established in 1903–4.

The Bund's constant fight with the police also took on greater force in this period, largely as a result of Plehve's stringent efforts to stem the fast-rising liberal and revolutionary tide of protest during his tenure as Minister of the Interior (April 1902 to July 15, 1904, the date of his assassination).[44] The tough government policy shows up in the jump in arrests in these years. By the Bund's own reckoning, 2,180 comrades were arrested between April 1901 and June 1903.[45] In the period June 1903–July 1904, 4,467 Bundists were taken, more than double the number in half the time.[46]

To the Bundists it seemed the police had dropped any pretense of restraint. By early 1904 a Vilna correspondent was reporting that 200 houses had been searched in an attempt to ferret out meetings; reports of similar police thoroughness came from Warsaw.[47] An innocuous act like smoking on Saturday, the Jewish Sabbath, could lead to detention, the suspicious police feeling certain that such irreverence clearly marked off the radical from the law-abiding Jew.[48] Landlords were penalized for allowing meetings on their property, and watchmen were ordered to report all such gatherings.[49] The state used every means of spying it could think of in the effort to suppress the revolutionary activity.

The incidence of violence against revolutionaries or suspected revolutionaries also took a marked upward turn under Plehve's guidance, and remained at high pitch after his assassination. Demonstrations brought both threats of pogrom and actual retaliation.[50] Meetings were attacked with a ferocity unknown in earlier days. One gathering in the woods outside Belostok was surrounded and fired on without any warning.[51] Where a BO was on station, though, the police often found it politic to make arrests only after a meeting or demonstration had broken up.[52] The policy of self-defense added to these troubles. For instance, the Mogilev police refused to defend streets in the Jewish quarter against mob action, sarcastically advising those seeking protection to go to the democrat-Jews for help.* The obvious intent here and elsewhere was to divide the Jewish community by blaming its problems on the revolutionaries—a justification of sorts of the violence against the Jews. Recognizing the ploy, the Bund press took pains to point out that the pogrom mobs were led by the police, and that most of them were made up of the dregs of society rather than workers.[53]

The furious police activity inevitably hindered the Bund in its work. It was difficult in the best of circumstances to get the workers to stand together; now, in the economic downslide that accompanied the Russo-Japanese war the loyalty of workers to labor solidarity was severely tested. In this situation, the added fact of intemperate police action, which led to the frequent suspension or postponement of demonstrations and meetings, was a serious setback.[54] To the extent that Plevhe and his successor, Prince P. D. Sviatopolk-Mirsky, managed to curtail the outward expression of revolutionary work, their policies were successful. At the same time, each success of the revolutionaries against such odds hardened them, chiseling a tougher and more determined movement.

For the Bund the outbreak of hostilities between Russia and Japan in January 1904 was the most dramatic political event between Kishinev and the Revolution of 1905. The war was a natural target for Social Democrats everywhere, and the Bundists joined the chorus. In their terms, the conflict grew out of a self-interested capitalist competition for markets and sources of raw materials, which was supported by a government needing the capitalists' wealth to sustain itself internally and new lands to bolster its credit and image abroad. "The entire blame for the war," said the Bund Central Committee shortly after the outbreak of hostilities, "falls on the shoulders of the governments that brought it about."[55] By virtue of broken promises in Manchuria and robbery in the post-Shimonoseki period, the Tsarist state came off a little worse than the Japanese in the Bundists' assessment of guilt.[56]

The economic dislocations, mobilization, and heightened nationalism of the war had painful repercussions in the Bund. Labor solidarity melted under the onslaught of economic crisis, throwing the Bund on the defensive. The Bundists tried to remind the workers that the new wave of unemployment was the result of the credit and transportation restrictions made necessary by military operations,[57] but despite their best efforts their influence weakened.

Mobilization posed two questions for the Bund: what should it advise re-

---

* *Posledniia izvestiia*, 201 (Nov. 26/13, 1904): 2. Governor Klingenberg went even further, telling a deputation of Mogilev Jews to let those who carried red flags help them (*Der Bund*, 5 [Oct. 1904]: 12).

serves and recruits to do when they were called up, and how could it avert pogroms at the hands of the newly assembled military forces. Mobilization was a painful, infuriating, and heart-breaking experience for the recruits and their families. The Bund took its Social Democratic task to be enlightening the recruits about the meaning of the war. In July 1904 the Central Committee addressed a leaflet to the Russian proletariat urging it not to play the government's "dangerous game."[58] Proletarians had nothing to lose: "The Japanese will shoot them if they go, and the Russian soldiers will if they do not." The Bund cautiously avoided counseling individual action, advising instead "mass rejection ... whenever possible" to "give the government to understand that if it undertakes a war harmful to the people without asking them, it cannot count on the people." In short, the proletariat's one recourse was protest.

The Bund's early response to mobilization thus stopped well short of open mass rebellion. Unlike the PPS, which suggested flight to avoid service—a reaction the Bund felt was more likely to be espoused by the minorities than the Russians—it argued that running away did not solve the problem of oppression, and could not, until such time as the reserves en masse refused to join the army. Still, flight was admissible and even desirable in special circumstances: "We can advise flight from the army only for those who leave the Tsarist army in order to join *our army*, our *revolutionary ranks*." Failing that, joint demonstrations of reservists and workers were the proper form of protest.[59] In the fall of the year the Bund suggested that recruits refuse to listen to the oath binding them to defend their country's honor; if the conflict was capitalist-inspired, the issue of national honor was clearly spurious.[60]

The plain fact is, the Bund was in an uncomfortable position with respect to the war. Its reluctance to call for desertion or insurrection can be explained at least in part by its fear that this would bring the charge of high treason down on the whole Jewish population. Could the Bund risk what it could not defend? Self-defense, effective and heartening as it was, was an insufficient response in the face of the combined forces of the police and the army; any attempt to meet them head-on would certainly lead to tragedy.

In fact the Bund, like other revolutionary organizations, had begun agitating among soldiers before the war.[61] In mid-1902, as the problem of defending demonstrations was being discussed, the suggestion was made that leaflets be distributed to soldiers and officers, explaining the issues and soliciting their participation.[62] The Bundists also hoped to penetrate the army from within. The value of having class-conscious soldiers in the army—agitators in uniform—was obvious. The lot of the Russian recruit was sad at best and that of the Jew in the Russian army worse, but some workers, made of hardy stuff, accepted or even sought military duty in service to the revolutionary cause.[63]

Between 1903 and 1904 the Bund intensified its revolutionary activities among the military. The Central Committee, in its report of June 1903 sum-

ming up the work since the Fourth Congress, noted the existence of organized groups among the soldiers and the appearance of leaflets signed by a
Military Revolutionary Group.[64] A year later, in July 1904, the Bund reported
to the Socialist International Congress at Amsterdam that despite a paucity
of statistics, great headway had been made in influencing new recruits through
meetings, leaflets, and demonstrations. Further, the organized circles in the
army were continuing to do good work in the dissemination of literature.[65]

This increase in activity did not escape the notice of military authorities.
Although agitation was not a monopoly of the Bund, Jewish soldiers became
a special target as early as January 1903, when Minister of War A. N. Kuropatkin issued a secret circular cautioning commanding officers to keep a close
check on Jewish soldiers and their belongings.[66] This was followed by another secret circular in March 1904 ordering that letters sent to the lower
ranks be read, "particularly from those who are Jews," and that Jewish soldiers "be forbidden to receive letters written in Hebrew. . . . Any privates in
whose possession letters in the Hebrew language are discovered shall be visited
by severe penalties."* All letters in any language but Russian were first to be
routed to special officers. Shortly after came yet another secret document, this
one noting that "the disseminators of criminal ideas [are] proving to be for
the most part Jewish privates, some of them being volunteers," and requesting
"the most rigorous supervision over the privates . . . and particularly over the
Jews and Letts."[67] The leaking of these secret messages, and their subsequent
publication in the foreign as well as the revolutionary press, merely deepened
the troubles of an increasingly hard-pressed regime.[68]

Despite the dark shadow raised by the war, the Bundists saw in it great
possibilities for the future of the movement. The Foreign Committee's early
reaction was a restrained warning against underestimating the staying power
of the regime. In its view revolution as a result of the war was possible but
not desirable; a revolutionary regime could easily fail in such circumstances.
Instead, said the Foreign Committee, now was the time to force the regime to
give up its prerogatives by concentrating on its internal weaknesses. Caught
in the pincers between the Japanese armies and the revolutionary movement,
the Autocracy would have to yield.[69]

But the Bundists in Russia saw more than a beleaguered, pliant Autocracy.
The belief there was strong that the war must topple the regime. In February
1904 the Bund Central Committee was certain "the war will add the last drop
to overflow the cup of suffering the Autocracy gives to all the people of Russia
and especially the proletariat."[70] The subsequent course of events buttressed
this belief. Besides Russia's economic woes, the reverses of her armies and
fleet, which to the Bundists simply reflected the failings of Russian life, gave

* "Revolutionary Propaganda." It is not clear whether Kuropatkin intended to make
any distinction between Yiddish and Hebrew, which use the same alphabet.

weight to the thesis of the impending fall of the regime. "Can our soldiers lead an equal struggle against the more educated, independent Japanese, who have already gained a taste of political freedom?" the Bund asked.[71] In the Bundists' view, the will and ability to fight were intimately linked to democracy. If Japan was not exactly a shining example of political democracy, she was far ahead of Russia in this respect in their eyes; hence the Russian armies were doomed. Moreover, the hard fact of Russia's limited rail capacity, making it impossible to maintain an adequate flow of men and matériel, strengthened their expectations.[72] Finally, the Bundists shared the view of many foreign observers that the highest circles of the Russian military were made up of sycophants and incompetents.[73] There was a touch of satisfaction in the Central Committee's finding that "the military might of Russia is not really so great and brilliant as was imagined"; and more than a touch of sarcasm in its recollection of how the Russian army had proved itself during peasant uprisings and strikes, to say nothing of "how it 'defended' the Jews from pogroms in Kishinev and Gomel."[74] Out of a combination of deep desire and objective evidence the firm conviction grew among the Central Committee members that the regime was finished: it was losing the war and could not avoid the defeat that would be the *coup de grace* for the Autocracy.

Meanwhile the dangerous strains within Russian society were also becoming obvious to the highest levels of the state. Following the assassination of Plehve in July, the regime began to reverse some of the policies associated with his name. With the appointment of the moderate Sviatopolk-Mirsky as his successor, liberals in Russia universally rejoiced at the prospect of a new political "Spring." The Bundists, for their part, limited their rejoicing to the death of Plehve, that "authentic new Haman of Jewish history" whose name was synonymous with "the wild system of police repression," with "the memory of all those ceaseless hard blows inflicted on the revolutionary movement one after another for the past two years."[75]

The Bund had foreseen the possibility of a new turn in government policy even before Mirsky's appointment. Its new theoretical Russian-language journal, *Vestnik Bunda* (The Bund Courier), felt that of two alternatives open to the government, maintaining the same level of repression or choosing a new course of concession, the second would be the more fruitful for the state because it could undermine the revolutionary movement. The state could flirt with liberalism and give the appearance of softening without yielding in any significant way, attempting in a word a "political *Zubatovshchina*." Expectations were rising all over Russia, creating a "passive excitement" over the prospect of reform from the top, a mood that boded ill for the expansion of the revolutionary movement. Indeed, rather than expansion, the movement could be seriously damaged if government concesssions brought increased anti-revolutionary sentiment.[76]

Mirsky's "Spring" moved partially along the expected lines. The new Minister of Interior at least tried to distinguish avowed revolutionaries from liberal reformers.[77] He dismissed some of Plehve's official entourage, including General Wahl, the target of Hirsh Lekert's shot; relaxed restrictions against the Zemstvos, the elected organs of local government run largely by landed gentry, even allowing a meeting of Zemstvo workers in St. Petersburg in November 1904; and eased the censorship of the press.

The change of government tone was felt in the Jewish community as well. Even before Plehve's demise, in the spring of 1904, the government had temporarily ceased expelling Jews from places where they resided illegally, in the hope of allaying their dissatisfaction in the midst of the not-too-promising war. On August 11, 1904, the Tsar signed an order providing some relief to the Jews, mostly in the way of eased residence requirements, pending a general examination of all legislation on the Jews.

These conciliatory acts drew a quick response from the Bund, which reaffirmed its unswerving enmity to the regime and disavowed the concessions. The change of ministers was of little consequence, the Bund insisted, for neither Plehve's nor Mirsky's policies truly reflected their own views. It was the Autocracy that was the real policy-maker, thus genuine change was impossible under the existing conditions. The ministers had to protect the Autocracy as best they could—*that* was the permanent policy—otherwise they would be dismissed.[78]

The Bund discounted the new policy toward the Jews. The Central Committee first published a special leaflet in both Russian and Yiddish scorning the "Jewish Manifesto" of August 11, then followed up with a more detailed analysis in *Vestnik Bunda*.[79] Because the new order affected only the residence of two groups, Jewish soldiers who had distinguished themselves in the Russo-Japanese war and the Jewish bourgeoisie, the Bund's journal saw little change in policy, and only a limited practical meaning in a few of the document's clauses.[80]

The motives behind the state's generosity appeared clear to the Bundists. The first and most general reason was the regime's internal and external difficulties; it always simulated reform at moments of crisis. But why Jewish reform? By the Bundists' reckoning, because the Jewish question took a central place in government policies, and "the position of the Jew serves as a barometer of the legal condition of the country, so that it (the government) quite naturally begins its 'reformatory' activity with 'the bringing in of changes in the legal position of the Jews.'"[81] The Bundists also credited the revolutionary ferment among the Jews with forcing the government "to calm this restless people somehow."[82]

Many in Russia, particularly those on the far right, failed to see anything praiseworthy about the struggle of the Jewish proletariat. Far from being heroic, as the Bund would have it, the Jews were "infinitely more dangerous than the Tartars." That was the feeling of M. O. Menchikoff, editor of the conservative *Novoe vremia,* who saw the central authorities as "feeling themselves too weak to tackle the problem," i.e., the Jews, and feared for the future of the regime.[83] Where the Bund saw heroism, the Russian conservative saw destruction and base cunning—but both placed the Jew at the center of Russian problems.

Even as the reforms trickled in, the state's continuing enmity toward the Jews was apparent. In an interview with Western reporters, Mirsky acknowledged the diffiicult position of the poorer Jews in Russia and the need for change; yet, as he suggested to one correspondent, there was not the remotest possibility of giving them the same rights as the Orthodox population.[84] Moreover, "Jewish Manifesto" or no, the pogroms continued. It was difficult, said the Bund, to substantiate the government's direct hand in these outbreaks; nevertheless, the state had not only prepared the groundwork for them, but also failed to halt them, except where for reasons of its own it wanted them ended. "Pogroms exist," the Bundists continued to assert, "only where the government wants them."[85]

In mid-1904 the Bund found the state far from real reform despite its conciliatory motions.[86] Nevertheless, the Bundists were now highly optimistic. The continuing defeats on the battlefield, the growing unrest, and the indecisiveness of governmental action—all indicated that the regime was extremely shaky.[87] Its concessions appeared to be an appeal for help from society—a sure sign of weakness and a bright hope for revolution.

18. The Bund and Jewish Society, 1903-1905

By 1903 the Bund was no longer a young organization by revolutionary standards. At the Second Congress of the RSDWP a new generation of leaders emerged, pushed to the fore by skills that the changing circumstances demanded. Age also began to intrude itself as an important factor. Many of the younger leaders were conscious of the distinction between themselves and those who had worked through the circle and pioneer period. Kremer in particular was regarded with a certain awe, a patriarchal figure whose name "was surrounded with various legends of the revolutionary movement." "To us younger Bundists of the second generation," says Hofman, "Arkady was the father of the Bund."[1] Medem and Raphael Abramovich, too, were keenly aware of the age difference between themselves and the "old timers." Noting that Izenshtat was "over thirty-five" in 1903, Medem comments: "At that time he really seemed an old man."[2] The disparity in age groups was even more striking at the local level. The old half-intellectual Litvak must have found the youth of the Bund members astonishing, for he makes a point of reporting that it was no rarity to find sixteen-year-olds in the Bund, or even to find nineteen-year-olds on local committees.[3] Even younger children participated in strikes.

The meeting of old and young quite naturally brought its share of conflicts. The old arguments of the Opposition over tactics and educational opportunity cropped up again. "We young ones," observes Laibechke Berman, a Dvinsk activist, "used to throw it up to older members that the intellectuals had seized all power and did not permit workers into the leadership of the organization."[4] In time, of course, Berman adjusted to tradition, just as the Bund had to adjust to his generation.

One clear sign that the Bund had made its mark on Jewish society was the impact it had on mere children. From about 1903, truly young "activists," some only age ten or so, began to draw inspiration from the Jewish revolutionaries.[5] This youth movement, though clearly imitative of the Bund, arose spontaneously.[6] It developed from the same two sources that had combined to form the Bund—workers and students—only now it was a question of apprentices and lower-school children. The main magnet, as one might suppose, was the element of mystery, all those secret meetings, forbidden books and papers, rousing revolutionary songs.[7] Yankel Levin, whose revolutionary career began with the formation of a Little Bund (Klain Bund) in Gomel, describes how as a young apprentice he moved from simple curiosity to elementary studies, a development that was sparked by a student-turned-carpenter who went "to the people." By the end of 1903 Levin and his group were anxious to try out more of the adult activities, and calling themselves a BO they began participating in strike violence and other forms of economic terror. Again duplicating the experiences of the Jewish movement, they formed their own birzhe and undertook to organize to protect their interests, a step aimed not only at employers but also at journeymen, who sometimes exploited the young apprentices almost as mercilessly.[8]

These activities drew a mixed response from the adult community. The organized workers feared that association with the inexperienced children might disrupt their own illegal activities or attract the attention of the police. Local Bund committees often ignored the youngsters or dismissed their activities as childish and "non-conscious."[9] The Gomel Committee showed small interest in the Little Bund until it attained a size (some 50 members) and notoriety that could no longer be ignored.[10] At the same time the older groups were pleased and flattered by their young imitators, and once the would-be revolutionaries showed their willingness and persistence, they were given such tasks as handing out leaflets and hiding arms. The upshot was often a close working arrangement between local old and young Bunds, the one for all practical purposes a branch of the other. However, the full impact of the youth groups, or Little Bunds as they became generally known, was not felt until 1905.

The middle-school students in a number of towns were also stirred by the revolutionary impulse. Jewish students attending the Russian schools in the northwest provinces and Poland were bound not only to know of the general unrest at the universities, which was widely publicized in the early 1900's, but also to hear of the Bund, the PPS, and other socialist groups. Indeed, even before 1903 the middle-schools had shown signs of becoming a perfect political microcosm of the larger society, with every shade of current opinion embraced by one student group or another.[11]

The Bund, with its near monopoly on mass Jewish radical activity until 1904, attracted many young Jewish students. Some made no attempt to disguise their sympathies, as for example when the students at the Chemical-Technical Institute in Vilna hooted out of class one Dr. Mikhailov, a participant in the beatings that led to the Lekert affair.[12] By 1903 the Bundists of Lodz were finding the commercial school students a valuable resource. Of largely middle-class background and presumed political innocence, they hid literature, arms, and even official party stamps in their homes with fair impunity.[18] Like the working youth, the students formed groups in a number of cities; but these, like the Little Bunds, were largely discounted by the local Bundists, who in their preoccupation with building a revolutionary mass movement and concern with day-to-day activities, failed to recognize the potential of the young activists. Only after the heat of revolution proved their value did the Bund leaders fully appreciate the material they had at hand.

The Bund stepped up its efforts to reach society with a revolutionary message in 1903-4. One reflection of this emphasis is the notable increase of meetings and demonstrations after mid-1903 (as recorded in Table 4). The data are drawn from two major Bund reports of the time, one to the Second Congress of the RSDWP covering the two-year period between May 1901 (the Fourth Congress) and June 1903 (the Fifth Congress), the other to the International covering the one-year period between June 1903 and July 1904.

As we see, the second period, shorter by half than the first, saw a two-thirds increase in the number of meetings and a remarkable 100 per cent increase in the number of participants. There was an equally impressive growth in the number of demonstrations, with the same number of actions and almost three times as many participants in half the time.

The reports also show a corresponding growth in the size of the meetings.

Table 4. Growth of Public Participation in Bund-Sponsored Activities as Reflected in Meetings and Demonstrations

Period	Total no. held	No. with size noted	Total no. of participants where size noted
Meetings[a]			
May 1901–June 1903	260	224	36,900
June 1903–July 1904	429	418	74,162
Demonstrations and Manifestations[b]			
May 1901–June 1903	44	25	7,520
June 1903–July 1904	45	31	20,340

SOURCE: *Di tetigkait fun "Bund" far di letste tsvai yor* (London, Oct. 1903), p. 13; *Doklad Internatsional'nomu Sotsialisticheskomu Kongressu v Amsterdame* (Geneva, Aug. 1904), pp. 3, 5, 9.

NOTE: Both reports were compiled by the Foreign Committee on the basis of data sent from Russia. In view of the irregularity and difficulty of communications, the material cannot be taken as complete.

[a] Does not include "official" meetings, i.e., the regular meetings of agitators and Bund workers.

[b] The Bund used the category "manifestations" to distinguish small demonstrations in schools and theaters from larger ones. Fourteen of the 44 demonstrations in the first period were so classified; no breakdown was made in the second period.

Though each period saw 12 meetings attended by crowds of 1,000 or more, only three of the 12 in the first period were attended by 2,000 or more persons, as against five in the second. Further, up to June 1903 the maximum attendance achieved was 3,000; the next year two meetings each brought out crowds of 4,000.[14] The Bund's record in this respect appears all the more remarkable when one recalls the heightened police activity in the later period.

The increasing use of strikes for political purposes is another good indicator of the Bund's redoubled efforts. The first report cites 19 such strikes, with a total of 10,550 strikers participating in 12 of them.[15] The second cites 35 political strikes in connection with May Day alone, 41 all told, and a total participation of 23,035 persons in 31 strikes.[16] Though these strikes formed only a fraction of the total strike effort, their growing numbers were a signpost of things to come. The political strike was to have great importance in the revolutionary days of 1905, when the strike and the demonstration often merged into one form of action.

The Bund's efforts to reach into society led it to alter and strengthen its literary output. Local newspapers, which were characteristic of the 1890's and continued to represent a significant quantity of the literature in the years 1901-3 (32 issues, totaling 40,650 copies), virtually disappeared in 1904. In its report to the International, the Bund attributed this development to the increased output of the Central and Foreign committees, which had been strengthened in this regard to permit more effective use of literary resources.[17]

Although the usefulness of the leaflet had begun to be widely recognized in the period 1901-3, it was overwhelmingly the favorite form of the local committees in 1903-4 and showed signs of becoming a favorite of the Central Committee as well. In 1901-3 the local committees issued 83 leaflets and the Central Committee 18 (nine in Russian), for a total of 347,150 pieces, the Central Committee's leaflets accounting for half this total.[18] By the end of the later, one-year period the Bund had printed leaflets in excess of 686,000 pieces.[19]

Despite all this increased activity, the Bund's membership appears to have remained fairly stable. In both reports the Bundists were cautious about the total size of the organization, which was equated with the number of organized workers. Both reports cited the figure 30,000 and considered it conservative.[20] The same figure was subsequently picked up in a local leaflet, which noted that "the Jewish Workers' Bund has a mighty organization; 30,000 Jewish workers in Lithuania, Poland, and Russia now fight under its banner."[21] The Zionists of socialist bent, by comparison, estimated their numbers at 16,000 in December 1905—after a year of the most revolutionary times in the experience of the Russian Jews.[22]

There are several possible explanations for the apparent stabilization of the Bund's membership in a period of growing unrest and dissatisfaction all over

Russia. Certainly the fact that the Bund all but ceased to move into other areas is partly responsible. Between the Fourth and Fifth congresses the Bund expanded not only within its old Lithuanian-Polish-Belorussian base, but also into southern Russia, establishing itself by mid-1903 in Zhitomir, Berdichev, Odessa, and Kiev and its environs, as well as in the province of Volynia.[23] But by the time the Bund was ready to report to the Amsterdam Congress, it had little to say about geographical gains; the 1904 report merely noted that the region of the Bund took in all places where there were sizable numbers of Jewish workers, and the accompanying list of organized towns revealed few changes.* By and large, the Bund had little hope of expanding beyond the bounds of Jewish working-class residence, though there were some relatively small groups of students and intellectuals in certain university centers.

The change in the character of the Bund itself, which led to a different method of reckoning membership, also may have affected the membership figures. At the time the report to the Second Congress of the RSDWP was prepared, the Bund had only just converted itself into a political party. That change brought new criteria for membership: regular reading of Bund literature; direct aid to the movement in the form of technical help and financial contributions (dues to political kases); and participation in the circles.[24] Plainly more demanding of the individual than simply banding together with fellow workers, these new requirements may have made entry into counted membership more difficult. Certainly they prevented the type of mass increase that characterized earlier periods of Bund history.

The special hardships of 1903–4 probably also account for the lack of new members. Organizational activity was difficult in the best of circumstances with a police force on the constant lookout. To this was added the shaky economic situation of the war years, which presumably caused the base for recruitment—at least of capable local personnel—to shrink under the pressures of unemployment and competition for jobs. As it was, the Bund must have had difficulty holding its ranks firm.

Despite the Bund's slowed growth, its influence among the Jewish workers increased. More and more workers attended its demonstrations and meetings and heeded its calls to action. The May Day celebrations continued to bring out numbers of workers, the repressive measures of the regime and fear of pogroms notwithstanding; they also brought more clashes with the police and more red flags. The Bund's proudest day may have come in 1904 when 700

---

* Bund biblio.: *Doklad*, pp. 3–4. Some southern Bund groups had achieved new status. The group in Odessa, for instance, had become a full-fledged committee (Mikhalevich, *Zikhroinos*, 2: 133). There was a unique situation in Dvinsk, where no new members were accepted for a time in 1904 because the organization was already doing as much work as its resources and facilities would allow (Berman, pp. 4–5).

workers participated in an open demonstration in Gomel, where the wounds of the pogrom were still fresh and where the Christian population was decidedly hostile.[25] The rising revolutionary mood and concern with political life that gripped Russia in this troubled period benefited the Bund, as it did other political parties.

The painful events that wracked the Jewish community had important international consequences for the Bund. Immigration from Russia to the United States, a steady and heavy stream before Kishinev, jumped sharply. In 1902, 37,846 Russian Jews entered the United States; the figure rose to 47,889 in 1903, to 77,544 in 1904, and to 92,388 in 1905, more than double the number in 1902.[26] How many of these immigrants were Bundists is impossible to say, but the dramatic growth of immigrant societies in New York in these years, particularly the Workmen's Circle, with its strong labor fraternal impulse, suggests that considerable numbers of the newcomers brought with them some acquaintance with the labor and radical organizations of the homeland.[27] The membership of the Workmen's Circle rose from 1,042 in 1902 to 1,883 in 1903, 4,352 in 1904, and 6,776 in 1905.[28] This group, like the landsmanshaften, was strongly Bundist in its sympathies. Even the labor Zionists in America aided the Bund until 1905.[29]

In late November 1903 the work in the United States on behalf of the Bund received an official stamp of approval with the visit of the most prominent Bundist of them all, Arkady Kremer. He was accompanied by Ezra Rozen (Berg). Kremer occupied himself with organization work and some writing, Rozen with public contact and speech-making.[30] Their primary objective was to spur the immigrants from Russia to greater financial support of the Bund, but they also tried to clarify for their sympathizers the Bund's position in regard to the RSDWP. Kremer stayed eight months, an indication of the importance the Bund placed on American support. The visitors were doubtless pleased by the well-organized effort on the Bund's behalf, managed through an executive office—the Central Union of Bund Organizations in the United States.[31] The Bund also received solid support from other organizations, notably the *Forward* Association, which published the most important Yiddish paper in the United States, and the Friends of the Bund.[32] Funds were to flow to the Bund in even greater quantity during the Revolution of 1905, when aid from the United States achieved its peak.

The Bund's ability to find the needed funds to carry on its publishing and self-defense campaigns attests to its vitality and influence. Besides members' dues and the monies earned through sale of literature, it received large contributions from people of real wealth, beginning with John Mill's friend, the Polish aristocrat who had provided the funds for the foreign press. There were also a few Bundists of considerable means.

In the immediate years before the Revolution of 1905, a number of wealthy backers provided substantial support. One of them was A. B. Sapotnitsky, a millionaire's son whose privileged background included graduation from a gymnasium in Tsarskoe Selo, a residence of the Tsars. Sapotnitsky moved into Bundist activity in his student years at the Polytechnicum of Riga. In 1902–4, thanks to his connections, that city became the financial capital of the Bund in Russia.[33] Another important supporter was David Michnik (Chekh), son of a wealthy Kishinev family, who joined a Bund group in Leipzig when he took up his studies there in 1901. When his father died in 1902, young Michnik inherited about 80,000 rubles, which he pledged to the Bund. Most of his inheritance was held in the estate for some years, so that the promised funds were not forthcoming until 1906 and after, but in the interim young Michnik provided money to the Bund from time to time through his older brothers and sisters, who also were involved in the revolutionary movement.[34]

Jewish liberals also discovered value in the Bund, particularly after it began promoting the idea of self-defense. In late 1904 the Central Committee sent Abramovich to St. Petersburg to obtain money from the liberal Jewish community there. He was given a warm reception. Self-defense, after all, was a matter of importance for all Jews, not merely for the Bund or the Jewish worker. M. M. Vinaver, one of the best known Jews in the capital and a lawyer in the suit against the governor after the Kishinev pogrom, all but gave Abramovich a blank check, saying at one point, "What do you want? We are all, in fact, Bundists."[35]

The first results of the Abramovich trip were made public in a financial statement published by the Central Committee shortly after the outbreak of the Revolution of 1905. Between October 1, 1904, and February 15, 1905, the new St. Petersburg Group of the Bund collected 1,967 rubles. That sum, together with the additional 600 rubles it forwarded to the Central Committee, proved even greater than the unusually large amount (1,798 rubles) credited to Foreign Committee contributions in the same statement.[36]

The liberals of the Pale of Settlement, though not on the whole sympathetic to the Bund's goals, did support its self-defense effort, particularly after Sviatopolk-Mirsky showed himself willing to tolerate a certain amount of liberal activity. According to Berman, local Bund leaders in Zhitomir were sometimes invited to banquets, where they were given information and funds.[37] Such fund-raising events were common in some areas but were by no means universal.[38]

The financial reports of the Central Committee tell us something, but not all, about the Bund's financial condition in this period. We find, for instance, that from the Kishinev pogrom to the outbreak of the Revolution of 1905 the committee received a little less than a third of its total published income from the local committees, which contributed as much as 46 per cent in one year and as little as 24 per cent in another.[39] The Foreign Committee contributions

Table 5. *Annual Income of the Central Committee*
(*in rubles*)

Income	1901[a]	1902	1903	1904	1905[b]
Total	3,378	7,423	13,612	16,514	2,325
Monthly average	307	618	1,134	1,376	
Peak-period average	501	1,323	1,997	2,325	

SOURCE: *Di Arbeter Shtime*, nos. 25-33, 35-39.

NOTE: The amounts received in November and December (October–December in the case of 1904) were substantially larger than the sums collected in any of the other months. It is possible that seasonal work in certain trades made these months the best time to solicit funds.

[a] Eleven months only.

[b] One month (January) only.

ranged from 1 per cent to 15 per cent. The remainder, somewhat over half, came from individuals, other unidentified organizations (presumably liberal or socialist circles), open meetings, and groups in towns without formal Bund organizations. The sources were usually disguised in the published reports, except in the case of actual committees. In some instances funds were earmarked by purpose, e.g., "For the new organ," "For arrested bristle workers," "From Lodz for the Belostok strike"; in other instances, symbols, code names, or initials identified the source, e.g., "K.," "Six," "* * *"; and in still others, the name of the place where the funds were gathered was the device used, e.g., "At a wedding through Kh," "At a gathering," "At a speech in Dvinsk."[40] Local committees published financial statements sporadically, sometimes citing expenses as well as income. The Central Committee limited its reports to income. The Foreign Committee also frequently published financial statements in its journals.

In a short span of years the Central Committee's income almost tripled. In the 28-month period February 1901–May 1903 (i.e., just prior to the Fourth Congress to just after Kishinev) its gross income was 14,327 rubles. This compares with a gross income of 31,113 rubles in the 21-month period May 1903–February 1905.* The monthly revenue was far from regular, as is clear in the dramatic differences between the monthly averages and the peak-period averages shown in Table 5.

The Central Committee received increasing support from the Foreign Committee in 1903-4, both in monies and services. By 1905 the Bundists abroad had doubled their numbers from five to ten,[41] and had been given many

* *Di Arbeter Shtime*, nos. 25-33 and 35-39. To give the point of income growth the greatest possible latitude, I have counted the report in *DAS*, no. 33, which falls in both periods (i.e., May 1903), into the earlier period.

assignments, among them the publishing of the Bund's new theoretical Rus-sian-language journal, *Vestnik Bunda*. As ever, most of the ideological con-troversies raged abroad; neither the Kishinev pogrom nor the split in the RSDWP changed that.

In the free environment of Western Europe the Foreign Committee could do all those things the home organization needed done but dared not under-take. Purchasing weapons, for instance, became an important new duty. The committee continued to publish large quantities of literature for distribution in Russia, producing in 1904-5 alone 39 pamphlets and 59 issues of papers and journals, for a total of 808,000 copies.[42] In addition to its normal liaison duties with all other socialist parties (a dangerous assignment the Central Commit-tee could scarcely carry out), the Foreign Committee served as a clearing-house and Mill as a self-described "Foreign Minister" to forward to the Cen-tral Committee complaints and suggestions from small towns in Russia, which could not easily contact the center in Russia itself.[43]

The Foreign Committee also continued to play the extremely important role of fund raiser, giving Mill yet another portfolio—that of "Finance Min-ister."[44] The Bund's connections with the United States were handled through his office. The mass migration of Russian Jews to the United States provided fresh sources of funds. Many times the new Americans requested that their contributions be used for specific purposes: for the local committee in their native town, in support of strikes, to help arrested comrades, and the like.[45]

The Central Committe relied heavily on the financial aid gathered by the Foreign Committee, which usually equaled and sometimes exceeded the amounts collected in Russia. Between January 1903 and July 1904, for ex-ample, the Foreign Committee took in 75,743 francs, as against the equivalent of 47,830 francs (19,132 rubles) collected by the Central Committee between March 1903 and July 1904.[46] Of this facet of the Foreign Committee's work, Mill comments: "Thanks to the great popularity of the Bund and the moving sympathy it aroused, every appeal for help was always crowned with success. The response to my appeals was ready and selfless, and at that time we never had any special worry because of financial difficulty or need."*

Judging by Mill's observation, the Bund was in a remarkable and enviable position as far as the money situation was concerned. But there were other reasons for a certain self-satisfaction as well. In these years the Bund operated with the smoothness of a well-functioning machine. It was not wracked by internal conflicts as were the Russian Social Democrats. Even its departure from the RSDWP and the unsettled problem of a formal adoption of a na-tional plank did not lead to anything approaching fragmentation. This solid-

---

* Mill, *Pionern*, 2: 179. It is not altogether clear what Mill means by "at that time." The surrounding material suggests he is referring to the whole 1902-4 period.

ity was at least in part the result of the extraordinary sense of identification that grew up with the organization.

To many, the strongest attribute of the Bund was its organizational cohesiveness, a quality that Litvak lays to the pattern of Jewish economic life: there was little likelihood of spontaneity in the confined atmosphere of a small shop. Says Litvak:

History so formed [the Jewish worker] that he was insufficiently primitive and seldom allowed himself to be led purely by instinct. . . . How could any action arise spontaneously among Jewish shoemakers . . . who worked in small shops and for whom an enterprise employing ten workers was a rarity . . . ? Without organization they could not move. The smallest step could be taken only if agreed on, planned, organized. One had to work very hard for that organization.[47]

This was, in large part, the charm the Bund had for the Jewish workers, among whom "a cult of organization grew up." For them, says Litvak, "the Central Committee became a kind of holy of holies" and the words "the organization has decided" a commandment.[48]

A strong feeling of community dominated all the Bund's operations. The heavy emphasis on organizational activity in Russia fostered anonymity and may have strengthened the sense of belonging. There was no "star system" in the Bund of the type seen in many of the other movements in Russia. Often the most important Bundists were the least visible (or audible). Kremer and Kosovsky relied heavily on self-effacement both for security reasons and for reasons of personal preference. And throughout Portnoy's tenure as the chief leader of the Bund in Russia, he remained an obscure figure for many. Litvak relates:

As far as I can recall, there was never a single leader in the Bund . . . who looked on himself as the boss of the party and was so regarded by others. The leadership of the Bund was always a collegial one. . . . Superficially, one might suppose that the leaders were Medem, Liber, Abramovich—the orators. . . . In truth, others who the masses scarcely knew stood on the same level with them. . . . One had an idea, others seized on it, added to it. . . . When it finally became a decision, it lost its individual character and became a collective work. It was no longer the creature of one person, but belonged to all.[49]

All facets of decision-making reflected this same collective approach. The Central Committee did not dictate decisions, but instead referred important problems to conferences. Their advice, and that of the Foreign Committee, was carefully heeded by the leaders at the center. To Litvak it seeemd that the Bund "attempted to draw as many people as possible to the leadership, so that the voice of the masses could be heard as clearly as possible."[50]

The Bund's solidity was expressed in the continuity of its leadership. In all, just 12 men sat on the Central Committee in the years up to 1905. Almost all of them were veterans of the pioneer days, and four of the 12 (Mutnikovich, Kremer, Kosovsky, and David Katz) had participated in the founding congress. Considering the high possibility of arrest, the losses among this top leadership were amazingly few. Thus, though there was consistently more work than workers to do it, particularly in the two years after the arrests of 1898, the Central Committee, which never had more than three members at any given time, was always able to be manned by experienced personnel.

Another source of strength and cohesion was the organization's ability to make full use of the many valuable members who were forced to flee Russia. The capable and dedicated Kremer and Kosovsky could be used effectively abroad (the Foreign Committee was composed, to a considerable extent, of ex-Central Committee members) until such time as they could return to Russia. When that time came, in 1905, both easily reassumed their Central Committee seats.

Around the Central Committee stood a cohort of skilled revolutionaries ready to back up its orders: writers who could be entrusted with important leaflets and the editing of a newspaper; debaters and speakers; organizers to perform the all-important tasks of troubleshooting and liaison; technicians capable of making or operating a secret press. These essential second-level members were expected to devote their lives to the demands of the movement. Among them were some of the best-known names in the Bund—Mark Liber, Raphael Abramovich, Yoina Koigan, Moissaye Olgin (real name Moishe J. Novomaisky), and David Zaslavsky.[51] Many members of this group participated in the Bund conferences, and so were largely responsible for policymaking. They moved about from town to town, their lives forming part of the lore of the Bund.*

As for the social character of the Bund, generally speaking the higher the level of organization, the higher the percentage of intellectuals. The majority of the Central Committee members in the period studied had some university or gymnasium education. Those who did not were, for the most part, the men and women who took hold in the dark days at the end of the century. It was essential to choose leaders who were at home not only in the Yiddish culture but also in the Russian world, since contact with the RSDWP was an overwhelming concern. Even extending the leadership group to include the Foreign Committee members and conference participants, the incidence of secularly educated persons was high. From all available information, about two-thirds of the Bund leaders can be counted as intellectuals.[52] At the same time, the fact that there were also a fair number of people without higher

* Franz Kursky reports an amusing situation in which he was mistaken for an inspector for the Equitable Life Assurance Society while he was carrying out a Central Committee assignment ("Bletlekh," p. 750).

education at the head of the movement indicates both a lack of exclusiveness and an eye to practical necessities.

Among the second echelon of movement members, those who worked on local committees and attended congresses, the ratio of intellectuals drops off considerably; only about one-third of this group should be so classified.[53] The importance of the non-intellectual element in the organization indicates how closely integrated the Bund was despite the great social differences implied by the level and kind of education.

Yet, however unified the Bund and however pervasive its influence, it still controlled only a fairly small portion of the potential political resources of society. This was true even where it was the largest, and often the best, revolutionary organization in an area. Its chief handicap was the lack of organization among non-Jewish workers. Indeed, the Bund's very strength among Jewish workers allowed the police to describe the revolutionary movement as being led by the "democrats"—the Jews. On a number of occasions the police substituted the word *bunt*, meaning rebellion or riot, for Bund in order to create fear and antagonism in the public mind.[54] The greater the crisis of the Tsarist regime, the greater the Bund's need to respond to the pressure to carry its message into areas where other revolutionary parties had not taken root.

As these pressures increased, deficiencies in the Bund's internal operations became evident, though it gave a good account of itself in the last months before the Revolution of 1905. When police fired on a workers' meeting outside Belostok in the late summer of 1904, the Central Committee ordered retaliatory protests throughout the Bund's sphere of operations.[55] "We must answer force with force," *Di Arbeter Shtime* declared. Though the appeal led to manifestations in a dozen cities, it also exposed the Bund's limited effectiveness: in some areas, like Mogilev, the demonstration was so small that the police did not even trouble themselves to stop it; in others, most notably Warsaw, no action could even be undertaken because of the state of police readiness.[56]

The unevenness of results on the local level was something the Central Committee could do little to correct. As in earlier days, it could offer only literature, money, speakers, and when there was time, advice. It was left to local committees to evaluate and respond to specific events as best they could. This meant dealing with situations with whatever resources they could muster, their own or those of local allies, if any. In the circumstances, it is not surprising to find an appeal for widespread action failing.

In some cases the failure was one of local leadership. Laib Blekhman, who served on the Minsk Committee in 1904, describes his chagrin at seeing a meeting broken up by a single police officer. It almost shook his faith in the movement. But he adds, "it did not take long for me to recover from my pessimism. The customary daily routine work swallowed me up little by little."[57]

Spontaneous outbursts also became a problem. The increasing number of manifestations and the growing confidence of the workers led them to a militancy that exceeded the Bundists' expectations. One demonstration in Dvinsk moved beyond Bund control, leading a Bund report to deplore a state of affairs in which, once again, "the organizations appeared at the tail of the movement."[58] Similarly, the Riga protest against the Belostok massacre developed into open demonstrations that went well beyond the intent of the local Bund committee.[59] By the end of 1904 spontaneous action of this sort was occurring with distressing frequency, showing that the traditional practices were not going to keep the lid on much longer; the revolutionary fervor was beginning to boil over.

The Kishinev pogrom evoked sharply different theories in the Jewish community about the proper response, intensifying the existing antagonisms between the various Jewish movements. The reaction of the general Zionists, who followed the lead of Theodore Herzl and rejected both socialism and political action of any sort in Russia, was completely in character. Where the Bund called for self-defense in the short term and the destruction of the regime in the longer one, the general Zionists sought to deal with the government. Herzl himself came to Russia from Vienna to speak with Plehve (this despite the fact that, in the public mind at least, the Minister of the Interior had a hand in fomenting the pogrom).

In an interview with the noted Russian-Jewish revolutionary Chaim Zhitlovsky (who Herzl mistakenly took to be a leader of the Bund), Herzl revealed the gist of his discussions with Plehve: "I have just come from von Plehve. I have an absolutely binding promise from him that he will procure a charter for Palestine for us in 15 years at the outside. There is one condition, however: the revolutionaries must stop their struggle against the Russian government. If at the end of 15 years von Plehve has not obtained the charter, [the revolutionaries] will then be free to do whatever they deem necessary."* Herzl wanted Zhitlovsky to arrange meetings with the Bund to carry out Plehve's plan. Zhitlovsky, who at first could scarcely control his anger at the shameful suggestion of dealing with Plehve, finally decided that Herzl, the idolized leader of political Zionism, was as naïve as a child about Russian affairs. He convinced Herzl that what Plehve recommended was impossible and, further, that it would do the Zionists no good and very possibly would do them harm. Herzl accordingly dropped his plan to contact the Bund.[60]

* Zhitlovsky, p. 12. Zhitlovsky did not publish this interview until 1915 in keeping with an agreement with Herzl to keep the subject of their discussions secret for the time being.

Plehve's insinuation that the Jewish revolutionaries were in large part responsible for the troubles of the Jews in Russia was a source of irreconcilable conflict between the Bund and the general Zionists—for on the whole, the Zionists, whose general rule was obedience and proper behavior, agreed with Plehve. In the words of one Odessa Zionist, the Bund "and its pernicious activities bear the blame if so much blood is needlessly spilled in Russia and if the government has worked its suspicion of the Jews up to the point of persecution."[61] He doubly damned the Bund for defending the pogromists, the Russian workers, as class allies. "In Kishinev," he charged, "the Russian workers showed us what the Jews have to expect from their [the Russians'] control."[62]

For the Bundists, the reaction of the general Zionists was entirely predictable, and their charges against the Jewish socialists only what one would expect of a bourgeois movement. On their side, they charged that the road Herzl and his followers proposed, with its emphasis on the need to live quietly in Russia, would lead to an increasingly slavish Jewish population. This attitude was not unnatural, the Bund insisted, since the Zionists were bent on inculcating much the same view in the exploited workers of the new Zion, "the utopia of the Jewish bourgeoisie."[63]

If the Bundists felt secure in the rightness of their stand, they were nevertheless deeply worried after Kishinev that out of fear and revulsion many Jews would turn to Zionism, that their feeling of isolation from the surrounding population would grow and their image of themselves as aliens who should do nothing but beg would be restored.[64] Moreover, the labor and socialist Zionists now began to pose a real threat. If anything, their shock at the bloody events in Kishinev was even greater than the Bundists'. Writes Moishe Zilberfarb, one of labor Zionism's early activists:

The Kishinev pogrom ... tore open our eyes and forced us to look around at what was happening in the world. Those of us who held that labor Zionism must not take up the revolutionary struggle against the Autocracy so as not to dissipate the national energy, which had to be saved and conserved for the realization of the national ideal, received a lesson from the Kishinev pogrom, namely, that national energy is not "saved and conserved" by a people's acceptance, with bent back, of the bloody blows of the pogrom regime.[65]

Like the general Zionists, the socialist and labor Zionists clung to the ideal of a future Jewish homeland as the final answer to the Jewish question; but unlike the general Zionists, they tried to contend with the added problem of the here and now, to devise a formula for the working classes that was consonant with human dignity and self-preservation.

The issue of whether or not to engage in the struggle in Russia was a crucial one for all Zionists, and it heightened the already important differences among Zionist groups. The divisions grew still deeper when, in August

1903, the Zionists' Sixth Congress split over the emotion-laden issue of an alternate homeland, a charter in Palestine being apparently out of the question for the time being. The very broaching of the subject was so painful that even Bundist spectators had tears in their eyes.[66] The controversy over these two issues, along with a few less important ones, such as the use of Hebrew or Yiddish, gave rise to a host of groups representing every possible shade of Zionist opinion.[67]

The Bundists and the socialist-oriented Zionists were in a paradoxical situation after Kishinev. On the one hand, both accepted the principle of Jewish self-defense, while on the other, they advocated radically different solutions to the problems of the Jews and competed for the allegiance of the same group. The charged atmosphere in Jewish society benefited both to some degree. There is no doubt that, as the Bund feared, some workers were driven away from active political work.[68] Yet there is also no doubt that the impossibility of acquiring a homeland in the foreseeable future led the labor and socialist Zionists to reexamine the question of current action and to take new account of the Bund. Zilberfarb tells of a Zionist meeting in late 1903 at which one speaker argued that political reality suggested a struggle for cultural autonomy where there was a significant Jewish minority and for territorial autonomy where the Jews could build a majority. It was a clear attempt to synthesize the Bundist and Zionist national views.[69] Though few of those in attendance agreed with the speaker, rejecting his position as far more Bundist than Zionist, the crossing of ideological lines was indicative of the temper of the times. The socialist-minded Zionists were pushed into considering contemporary issues in Russia and, thus, into the Bund's area of activity.

For the Bundists, so gloomy after Kishinev, the split at the Zionists' Sixth Congress was a promising and hopeful sign. "One can say," Medem wrote after Basel, "that from the last Congress on, Zionism no longer exists."[70] But he was much too optimistic. Labor Zionist circles and groups in fact proliferated in 1903 and 1904. Their adjustment to the immediate situation, including in many cases a new emphasis on the need for a revolutionary struggle for territory, made their movement an increasingly important consideration for the local Bund committees.[71] At the same time, many of the new circles were merely small study groups whose thrust was theoretical rather than practical.

Nor were all the Bundists as sure as Medem that Zionism was fatally flawed. A stream of articles and literature from late 1903 through 1904 attests to an unremitting Bundist concern with the new threat, at the center as well as at the local level. Judging from the correspondence in various papers from the time of the Kishinev pogrom to 1905, the problem of Zionism in general drew even more attention at meetings than the Bund's withdrawal from the RSDWP. In the spring of 1904 the Borisov correspondent noted that "we have to discuss Zionism frequently, thanks to the struggle we have to wage constantly with labor Zionism."[72] Moreover, in denying any notable success to the work of the Zionists, the Bundists seemed to protest too much. A report from Dvinsk spoke sarcastically about the "new socialists," and noted that only 15 Bundists had gone over to them—all of them, it carefully explained, clerks, the most bourgeois of workers.[73] The Grodno Zionists apparently attempted to call a work stoppage and a rally on the first day of their Sixth Congress; according to a Bund report only 25 to 30 workers showed up, along with some 50 Social Democrats. A Social Democrat addressed the crowd.[74] The Bund's report to the International in August 1904 described Zionism as "the most evil enemy of the organized Jewish proletariat fighting under the Social Democratic flag of the Bund," then confusingly announced that the new tendencies, masked under the names of Zionist socialism and labor Zionism, had no success among the Jewish workers, who were already too conscious to be taken in by the old bourgeois content. To be sure, said the report, small groups had been planted in some towns and had begun to play the game of revolution, but these were of little consequence, consisting as they did of nationalist-minded half-intellectuals and a few score non-conscious workers.[75] Despite the Bundists' disdain for their Zionist opponents, the threat from that direction was never underestimated.

Possibly the Zionist argument that most discomfited the Bundists concerned the split with the RSDWP, which the Zionists held up as yet another example of anti-Semitism. By their reasoning, the Russian Social Democrats had thought to use the Jewish workers to their own advantage, the Jews had refused to go along, and the Russians had therefore ousted them.[76] The charge was a frequent one, and a real embarrassment for the Bundists. In fact, the labor Zionists went so far as to predict that as a result of the separation the Bund would be drawn to their views.[77]

Up to 1903 the state had virtually forbidden the publication of Yiddish newspapers in Russia, finding them hard to censor (Jewish censors were not considered trustworthy by the Ministry of the Interior).[78] For the first few years after the Bund was formed, there was no legal Yiddish news organ. Six illegal publications attempted to appear regularly, five of them the work of Bund groups, the sixth the effort of the PPS.[79] A non-socialist Yiddish journal entered the field in 1899, when the Zionist-oriented *Der Yud* (The Jew) began publication in Poland (it was printed in Cracow but edited in Warsaw). This brought the total number of Yiddish publications at this point to nine, of which seven belonged to the Bund. The situation remained unchanged until 1903.

In that year Plehve gave his blessing to the publication of a Yiddish daily newspaper. The publisher of the new legal paper, *Der Fraind*, was Saul Ginzburg, who apparently had friends in the Ministry of the Interior.[80] In Ginzburg's judgment, Plehve's motive for granting him a permit to publish was to see a paper established that would agitate for Jewish emigration from Russia,[81] a plausible explanation, given Plehve's attitude toward Zionism (which was legally tolerated in early 1903) and the Zionist tone of *Der Fraind*.*

But the Bund interpreted the largesse of the state from its own revolutionary point of view. It regarded the newspaper with deep suspicion. Any paper permitted by the state, it argued, could not be inimical to the state. The truth was, the Bundists suggested, the state so feared the increasingly revolutionary Jewish proletariat that it now sought to encourage Zionism and to cloud class consciousness.[82] Several years earlier, when *Der Yud* had first appeared, Kremer had charged that "the development of the Bund forced the government to give permission for the paper to be shipped [from Cracow] ... in order to draw the workers away from the Bund."[83] To the Bundists, this interpretation seemed even more compelling in 1903: "The ever-growing influence of the Jewish proletariat of the Bund," *Di Arbeter Shtime* stated flatly, "drove the Russian government to allow the daily newspaper in jargon."[84]

Meanwhile, an illegal labor Zionist press was also beginning to bloom. (I use the term press here, as I do in the case of the Bundist media, to refer to irregular journals of a highly interpretive nature as against strictly news-bearing papers.) More than half a dozen publications authored by various Zionist groups appeared in 1903-4. Though the Bund still heavily dominated the political literary scene, its near monopoly in the Pale was broken.

The state also began to allow the publication of journals of a general educational nature during this period, and numbers of them appeared. Of 34 known titles for 1903-4, 16 were issued by the Bund. (They were all illegal.)[85] The demand for Yiddish literature on all aspects of life was seemingly insatiable, and the publishing community simply unable to satisfy it. The growing appeal of Zionist material accounted in good part for the increased demand.

The development of labor Zionism ensured a continuing concern with the national question. The Zionists' arguments raised Bundist emotions to fever pitch, at least at the local level, occasioning impassioned outbursts that contrasted rather sharply with the relatively restrained tone of the Bund leaders. Thus, we find one local Bund commitee exploding, in reaction to the theme that the Jews were aliens and should "speak softly, like a beggar at the door": "We are not strangers here and not guests, even though the Russian government considers us as such.... The richness of the land is soaked through with our blood ... ; we demand and fight for that which belongs to us—for human, civil, and political rights."[86] The case for the Russian homeland was put more

---

* In an open letter to Herzl Plehve noted that the government tolerated Zionism "as long as its goal was to create an independent state in Palestine and it promised to organize the emigration of a certain number of Russia's Jewish subjects." *Die Welt*, Aug. 25, 1903 (special issue no. 1): 1.

fully in the first issue of a new popular organ, *Der Bund*, which appeared in 1904. Pointing out that Zionists and anti-Semites alike argued in terms of property rights, *Der Bund* charged:

If our ancestors had come with swords ..., then the land would have been their "own." ... But since our ancestors came as peaceful dwellers, and in the course of a thousand years, together with the surrounding population, aided in the cultural development of the land, watering it with their sweat, soaking it with their blood, and covering it with their bones, now the Jews are "not in their home." As "aliens" can we, the proletarians, accept that point of view? No! The land where we have been living for many hundreds of years and to which we are bound by thousands of threads—this land is our home. It belongs to us just as it belongs to the Poles and Lithuanians, and all other peoples who inhabit it.[87]

Never before had the Bund so strongly argued the Jews' historical attachment to the "territory" of Russia.

Violently as the Bundists reacted to the Zionist cry for territory, they did not feel much need to develop or defend their own national views in response; their chief opponents in this regard remained the other Social Democrats. So far as the Zionists were concerned, the Bundists were confident that their own approach to the national question was culturally solid, economically just, and, in the long run, politically fruitful. They concentrated, therefore, on what they considered to be the false basis of the new Zionist ideologies.

A favorite target was the Minsk labor Zionists, the oldest and most conservative group of proletarian bent. The Bundists attacked them constantly, returning again and again to the theme of bourgeois error. How could it be otherwise, for in regarding themselves as aliens, the Zionists denied the possibility of a socialist struggle in Russia where the Jews had no ruling class and no national property.[88] But the existence of a Jewish bourgeoisie in Russia, the exploitation of the Jewish workers, the doctrine of proletarian unity— all made the struggle for socialism in Russia both possible and necessary, the Bundists insisted. The bourgeois character of the Minsk Zionists and the fact that they had not split with the general Zionists convinced the Bundists that labor Zionists merely served the purposes of the bourgeoisie. For that matter, why did they even find it necessary to form a separate party?[89]

A new Zionist current that flowed out of the Sixth Congress was represented by the so-called territorialists, those who, with the dream of Palestine apparently shattered, turned to the ultimate goal of finding territory (still considered a requisite for a healthy Jewish community) elsewhere. Meanwhile, like the labor Zionists, they found it necessary to wrestle with the awkward problem of how to behave in the present. In their earliest formulations the territorialists were prepared to admit only the necessity of defensive struggle; their politics, thus, was one of reaction to immediate circumstances.[90] In March

1904 they introduced a journal called *Vozrozhdenie* (Rebirth) to clarify their views, which were still in their infancy. Their organizational plans were even less developed than their theories and were not to receive form until after the stormy events of the Revolution of 1905.

In the Bundists' eyes the territorialists were as wrongheaded as the labor Zionists, perhaps more so, since the Vozrozhdentsy themselves at least recognized the bourgeois and unprogressive character of the old Zionism.[91] What, they asked, was the ideal of national rebirth through the acquisition of territory, whether now or later, whether in Palestine or Russia, but Zionism all over again? "Zionism is dead! hail Zionism!" proclaimed *Vestnik Bunda.*[92] As the Bundists saw it, the new brand of Zionists, like the Russian liberals, had arrived too late. The proletariat was already too revolutionary to find their promises appealing. Therefore, the newcomers had to dress themselves in revolutionary clothing, a disguise, *Di Arbeter Shtime* assured its readers, that must surely call forth only laughter and contempt.[93] The attack of the Bundists apparently shook the Vozrozhdentsy—but not enough to stop them.[94]

There were to be more serious conflicts between the Bundists and the new groups in the supercharged political atmosphere of the year 1905. In any case, the most radical forms of Zionism had their greatest following abroad and in the south, outside the strongholds of the Bund.[95]

Another new, if minor, contender for Jewish sympathies began to concern the Bundists after 1903. This was the liberal movement, which had great appeal for a small but influential segment of the Jewish community, most notably the highly educated and articulate Jews of St. Petersburg. Their concern with the Jewish condition stretched back a number of years. In 1900, for instance, a group of important Jewish lawyers there had formed an illegal Defense Bureau to protect Jewish defendants against patently unjust laws and unfair courts.* They had worked hard in behalf of the Gomel self-defense group, and also had defended a number of Jews accused of ritual murder.† Many of these men stood close to Russians of liberal political convictions, particularly as expressed in the journal *Osvobozhdenie* (Liberation), founded in 1902 under the editorship of the former Marxist P. B. Struve. In 1904 some

---

* J. Frumkin et al., pp. 32–33. Among the bureau members were G. B. Sliozberg, M. M. Vinaver, Iu. D. Brutskus, Leonti M. Bramson, and Jacob Frumkin himself.

† M. Krol, one of the defense attorneys at Gomel, has written of the unfairness of the judges, prosecutors, and procedures at the trial. He movingly relates how, after numerous violations of court procedure, the accused workers said to him: "You should leave. . . . Do not be troubled that you are leaving us without defense. We shall show the court that we shall remain without defenders rather than allow you to be insulted with impunity." ("Der Homler pogrom protses," p. 539.) The ancient myth that Jews needed Christian blood to make unleavened bread for Passover was broadcast widely from 1900 on, culminating in the notorious Mendel Beilis case on the eve of World War I.

of the St. Petersburg intelligentsia, led by Leonti M. Bramson, formed the Jewish Democratic Group, linking the cause of political democracy for Jews to Russian liberalism. The organization called for national rights for Jews in Russia.[96]

The St. Petersburg activists did not endorse the Bund's work in full. They were angered, for instance, by reports of the Bundists flouting religious custom and taking over synagogues for agitation. Yet they recognized the great importance of the Bund and were loath to attack it.[97] Indeed, many held it and the Jewish workers in the highest regard.

Political liberalism did not make much impression on the Jewish society of the Pale until late 1904. For the Bundists what few liberals there were belonged to the same group as the Zionists—the bourgeoisie. Ironically, though the Bundists made little distinction between Zionist and Jewish liberal, they frequently drew a comparison between the non-Jewish bourgeoisie and the Jewish bourgeoisie of the Pale, the second being in their opinion clearly inferior to the first. Shortly before Kishinev, the Bund pointedly contrasted the slavishness of the Jewish middle class to the state with the awakening of other parts of Russia's middle class.[98] That many members of the Jewish middle class echoed the government's charge that the revolutionaries were responsible for the pogroms only increased the Bund's anger and contempt. Doubtless many agreed with the judgment of a *Di Arbeter Shtime* correspondent that the Jewish bourgeoisie was hopeless as far as the struggle against the Autocracy was concerned.[99]

Nevertheless, the Bundists were not above seeking the support of the bourgeoisie. They had been earnestly seeking to gain the ear of the Jewish intelligentsia for several years and continued to do so. Typical of these efforts was a campaign to recruit Jewish teachers to the cause, which had fair success, the teachers perhaps being persuaded by fiery exhortations like this: "Jewish teachers! In your hands is the mightiest propaganda weapon of all—the school. In your hands rests the education of hundreds of thousands of our people. . . . Organize circles among yourselves, spread revolutionary literature, join hands with the Jewish workers' movement. Don't be afraid of jails, Siberia."[100] As we have seen, the Bundists were sometimes warmly received in local liberal bourgeois circles, participating in their discussions and benefiting from their fund-raising banquets.[101] No doubt the prospect of financial aid and the chance of airing their own point of view encouraged the Bundists to maintain such contacts.

With the coming of Mirsky's "Spring," political liberalism became something of a force in the Pale. The Jewish liberals' expressions of gratitude and loyalty to Mirsky for his encouraging words about the future of Jewry in Russia infuriated the Bund.[102] Whatever reforms he might make, it warned, would not be enough for the proletariat.[103] The Bundists, like their Social

Democratic counterparts elsewhere, saw in the liberal forces a bourgeoisie hungering for political power. The Western experience taught, they believed, that the liberals would only seek those political freedoms they found useful. Being neither poor nor hungry, they would lose their revolutionary spirit once they acquired power. Under the mask of protecting the political rights of all, the Russian bourgeoisie would exploit the population just as the bourgeoisie of the West did.[104]

Though the Jewish liberals' advocacy of equal national rights was to be lauded, said the Bund, the workers should be warned: the liberals would never join in the struggle of the proletariat. They contended that there were few class differences among Jews, and that the Jewish workers should give up their separate fight in order to pursue the national struggle. Despite the general weakness of political liberalism, *Der Bund* predicted a national-liberal party would eventually be formed.[105]

The Bund's continuing emphasis on class struggle over national struggle is manifest in its evaluation of liberalism. Said *Der Bund*: "Specific acquaintance with liberalism shows us clearly that there is a deep chasm between it and Social Democracy. The liberals are the representatives of the bourgeoisie; Social Democracy is the representative of the proletariat. The antagonism dividing the two classes also divides the two parties."[106] The fight of Social Democracy against capitalism ruled out the possibility of a common future with the middle class. The culmination of the bourgeoisie's aims was political success. That was but a first stage for the Social Democrats who, once political liberation was achieved, would move forward to economic liberation.

Nevertheless, the Bundists were prepared to support any movement that aspired to wrest greater freedom from the existing political order. So long as the tasks of both groups were the same, class divisions did not preclude cooperation, though, cautioned *Der Bund*, the extent of agreement had to be well-defined.[107] Like the other Social Democrats, the Bundists tried to weigh both the benefits and the dangers of an alliance with the liberals in the rapidly heating atmosphere of Russian political life.

Following the Kishinev pogrom the Bund met increased antagonism from still another of its traditional enemies—the religious establishment. Though it is impossible to say how deeply the resistance to the workers' movement penetrated the clergy, it is indisputable that some religious leaders took extraordinary steps against the revolutionaries, fearing that the Christians and the state would vent their wrath on the entire Jewish community. Shortly after Kishinev a meeting of rabbis in Cracow bitterly criticized the Bund, in one breath belittling the Bundists (whose "activity amounted to nothing and to every intelligent person they appeared crazy") and crediting them with the power to bring harm to the Jewish people.[108] The Cracow meeting passed a resolution calling for a denunciation of the Bundists: they were to be shunned, for their acts were against all Israel, against the holy Torah, "which has told us to obey its laws and the decrees of the government where we reside."[109] The religious establishment hoped to put as much moral distance as possible between itself and the Bundists.

On the local level, the anger of the religious leaders often led to extreme measures. In Mezhirichi, a town west of Kiev, one rabbi outdid Zubatov, forming an association of porters and cabmen to hunt out the meeting places of the young radicals and report them to the police. (This was an achievement of sorts, for as a rule men in these occupations were boisterous and rough types who were difficult to organize.) One rabbi actually visited manufacturers, drew up lists of troublemakers—those who broke the fast on Yom Kippur, for instance—and had them fired.[110] In Vilna, Grodno, and Odessa, rabbis launched attacks against the Bundists, "the democrats," and the youth and workers who espoused socialism.[111] The more radical Zionist groups also received their share of abuse.

Though a good portion of the community applauded this determined campaign, the rabbis never had the wholehearted support of their congregations—or even of their colleagues. And the Bundists, of course, fought back in their accustomed manner. The Grodno Committee distributed a leaflet attacking the clergy in general, Russian as well as Jewish, for defending the forces of reaction rather than the poor and oppressed.[112] A Vilna rabbi who blamed Jewish youth for the presence of police at synagogue doors was whistled down.[113]

If the revolutionary wave could not sweep away tradition, neither could tradition prevail. The revolutionary vitality of the Jewish community, insofar as it was represented by the Bund, had proved itself and, indeed, would become even more apparent in 1904. The clergy could do little in the circumstances. The repressive actions of the state, the secularization of the Jewish community, and even the appeal for simple justice, if not the Bund's appeal for socialism, had irreversibly changed Jewish life in Russia.

All of these changes took place amidst trying times. The Jewish population, particularly the working class, was beset by the twin horrors of pogrom and poverty. The war was a relentless drain on the Russian economy, and the workers paid most of the cost. In Odessa, for example, where in the best of times there was an oversupply of workers, port trade with the Far East fell, bringing widespread unemployment and unrelieved misery.[114] Impoverished inhabitants attacked food carts and invaded bakeries, and robberies and burglaries became all too frequent.[115] In mid-1904 the *Der Bund* correspondent in Lodz reported that 450 of the city's 900 tailors and 425 of its 600 coatmakers were unemployed.[116] In a partial survey of various local enterprises, the Belostok organization found that the number of employees had dropped from 3,300 to 1,200.[117] This was in late August 1904, at which time, according to the correspondent there, "whole trades are disappearing. Thus, out of 400–500 carpenters, locksmiths, tinsmiths, painters . . . , scarcely 150 can be counted now."[118]

The crisis severely tested the economic organizations of the Bund. A Lodz correspondent reported: "A large number of our organized members have departed, and more leave every day. Often many of our members cannot carry out their work . . . because they have nothing to wear."[119] The economic struggle was bound to suffer setbacks. It was no longer a question of pressing for new gains but of holding on to those achieved in an earlier, better day. Labor discipline was difficult to maintain, with some workers willing to accept lower standards and others insisting that they would not. The strike movement among the Jewish workers fell off sharply; both the number of strikes and the number of strikers reached their lowest point since 1898. Withal, the proportion of victories remained fairly high,[120] doubtless reflecting the hardness the movement had achieved by late 1904.

The economic crisis did not prevent political growth, however. On the contrary, thanks to the war the revolutionaries of Russia were able to tie economic agitation to political agitation. And the breakdown of discipline had its brighter side: by the end of 1904 those who responded to the Bund's call represented a militant core undeterred by adversity, men and women who could be relied on to stand fast in any situation that might arise.

19. The Competing Forces of Revolution, 1903-1905

The split with the RSDWP left the Bund standing alone. It now had to present itself to the Jewish proletariat divorced from the formal structure of the All-Russian Social Democratic community; the tie that had long provided it with an image of international strength and hope for the future was broken. Worse yet, the Bund soon found the Iskraites competing for the allegiance of workers in provinces where it once had been the most powerful, and often the only, organized Social Democratic force. Like many fraternal struggles, the conflict became increasingly bitter; indeed, the preliminaries had been acrid enough.

The Bundists abroad had been more prepared for a split than their comrades in Russia. Polemics had been open in the West, with *Posledniia izvestiia* and *Iskra* arguing back and forth, their differences laid bare for every reader to see. But even with this forewarning, the relatively well-informed circles of Western Europe were surprised and stricken. As Raphael Abramovich puts it: "The Bundists abroad ... were psychologically prepared for a fight. Nevertheless, no one believed that it would come to a real 'divorce.'"[1] To Mill the split was "a deep painful tragedy" and "a colossal catastrophe."[2] Some of the participants openly wept as they reported the circumstances to Bundist groups. According to Mill, "Noikh's [Portnoy] report in Berne ... was given in an atmosphere of extraordinary depression among the Bundists present," and Medem's presentation to a Zurich group met a similar response.[3] Of all the Bundists, the "first generation" perhaps felt the most anguish.

In Russia the split evoked astonishment and consternation in the general membership. The articles *Di Arbeter Shtime* had carried on the disputes between the Iskraites and the Bund had not reflected the depth of disagreement between the two sides. As a result, the rank and file was caught by complete surprise. Even most of the local leaders were only dimly aware of the rising controversy. Sholom Levin, who contributed so much to the operation of the secret press over the years, reports the general reaction:

The Bund's exit from the Party made an enormous impression on the organizations. It came suddenly and unexpectedly, and the members of the Bund were not prepared for it. The polemic with *Iskra* before the Congress had not reached the members. Even the members of the local skhodkas read little of *Iskra*. We were too taken up with the local, practical daily problems. Relations with the Party was to us "high politics" and the business of the Central Committee.[4]

Worried about how the news would be received in the ranks, the Bund leaders set about informing the membership of the course of events and their own position. This task fell largely to the spokesmen of the younger generation—to Medem and Abramovich abroad, to Liber in the homeland.[5]

The campaign to explain and defend the Bund's actions at the Second Congress moved into high gear in December 1903, when the Central Committee published a special leaflet in Yiddish on the subject.[6] The committee's main argument was that there had been little choice: it was either leave the congress or face extinction. The congress had considered the Bund an anomaly, harmful, nationalistic, and bourgeois, an astonishing assessment, in the committee's view, given the solidity of the Bund and its long and fruitful history. The congress not only had proved its ignorance about the Bund, but had exposed its immaturity in the lightness with which it took the Bund's proposals. The delegates did not understand that only an organization springing directly from the Jewish environment was capable of leading and developing the revolutionary potential of the Jewish workers. The utopian centralism so dear to the congress grew out of a false understanding of the basis on which a true socialist revolutionary movement should be built and an inadequate comprehension of international socialism, which did not mean cosmopolitanism.[7]

The leaflet insisted that the Bund could not remain at the congress without sacrificing the interests of the Jewish proletariat. "The suicide of the Bund would have meant the suicide of the Jewish labor movement, and the international proletarian family would have lost one of its most active and energetic members." The committee reiterated the Bund's firm belief in revolutionary Marxism and the desirability of achieving a true unity of revolutionary forces. It hoped that with the growth of the Jewish movement and greater experience among the Russian Social Democrats, that goal would be achieved.[8]

The Bund leaders carried their explanation to the local organizations directly, assigning speakers to address groups of agitators and others. These meetings ran more or less to a pattern: a resumé of the events, a discussion, and at the end, a proposed resolution in support of the Bund's action. These efforts received heavy coverage in the Bund press. The first report came from the Berdichev Committee, which indicated its meeting had been marked by long debates with Iskraites, who had obstructed the proceedings. No vote on a resolution of support was mentioned.[9] Other early reports also indicated considerable difference of opinion and no clear-cut decisions. In Smolensk, which was outside the Pale, some 20 intellectuals, the majority of them Iskra-ites, discussed the matter—rather weakly in the Bund correspondent's view.[10] In Vitebsk a group of 25, including some Iskraites, agreed rather curiously that the Bund should be the sole representative of the Jewish workers in the party; the real issue was not debated.[11] The ins and outs of the problem seem to have been too confusing for some gatherings to take decisive action.

But the situation soon changed. Within a few short weeks, the Central Committee began to receive the votes of confidence it sought. By March 1904 *Posledniia izvestiia* had reported the passage of favorable resolutions in Ber-dichev, Odessa, Lodz, Gomel, Minsk, Bobruisk, Mogilev, Warsaw, Vilna, and a host of smaller towns.[12] In most cases the votes were unanimous; in only a few were debates and dissent of any significance reported. Most of the meet-ings were aimed at the agitators, that is, the Bund's activist elements. The largest, in Vilna, was attended by 99 persons; the smallest was reported to be a Berdichev gathering of 19. A few meetings were held for workers, with as many as 200 in attendance.[13] By mid-1904 the Bund had organized 42 meet-ings of agitators, with a total attendance of over 2,100. "All meetings without exception in the Bund region," the Bund leaders reported, "approved the be-havior of the Bund delegation ... and recognized that it did everything pos-sible to avoid a split."[14] The claim was a bit exaggerated but substantially correct.

The local organizations thus stood strongly behind the Bund. All of them showed by their resolutions that they unequivocally endorsed the concept of a special Jewish workers' organization. Some also reprimanded the Second Congress for its treatment of the Bund, usually with an appropriate expres-sion of hope that the future would convince the Russian comrades of their mistake and open the way for new unity.[15] The Bund-trained cadres were not easily shaken, despite the pain of separation.

Up to the Second RSDWP Congress only two Social Democratic organiza-tions played any real role in the northwest provinces, the Bund and the Polish Social Democrats. The Iskraites had some groups there dating back to 1901, but all were tiny, isolated, and informal.[16] After the split, the Iskraites set out to gather strength from all possible sources, including the Jews of the Pale. There the Iskraite groups were composed mainly of Jewish workers and intel-lectuals who did not approve of the Bund's actions at the Second Congress. This early swing to the Iskraite cause seems to have been largely spontaneous rather than the result of outside effort. In Minsk, for example, seven or eight workers who were dissatisfied with the Bund's organizational arrangements came together in the fall of 1903. After a series of meetings they were joined by some 30 others. They established ties with Social Democratic intellectuals in the city and then with the Central Committee of the RSDWP, calling themselves the Minsk Group.[17] At about the same time a Bobruisk Bundist, G. L. Shklovsky, returned to that city after a short prison term and reestablished his contacts with the local organization in order to get leads to workers who might go over to the Iskraites. He later established an organization on his own initiative in Borisov that was almost exclusively Russian in composition.[18] The party also managed to recruit a few workers and intellectuals in Berdichev and Zhitomir.[19]

According to a party report, by November 1904 the Iskraites had gained 970 new members in the northwest provinces: 875 workers, 575 of whom were Jewish, plus 75 peasants.[20] That the *Iskra* groups, at least in the northern portions of the Pale, gained many more Jewish workers than Christian workers indicates the general backwardness of revolutionary consciousness in the non-Jewish population, particularly the Russians. Apparently only a few of the Jewish party members actually defected from the Bund. Most seem to have been at the periphery of the Bund rather than in it.[21]

In 1904 the party established two regional organizations in the Pale. The Northwest Committee (Severo-Zapadnyi Komitet), formed in May and based in Vilna, was the more significant as far as the Bund was concerned. The Polessien Committee, formed somewhat earlier, operated out of Gomel. The Northwest Committee saw itself as a corrective force. In its declaration of intent it asserted that the peculiar conditions of the region, whose main characteristic was the separate development of diverse national cultures, had provided a rich soil for nationalist tendencies. Even the Polish Social Democratic Party had not succeeded in creating a strong and steadfast organization in a territory where the Poles were the overwhelming majority. The Jewish workers seemed ready to listen to socialist ideas, but their leaders, including the Bund, were unfortunately permeated by national views. The essential task of the Northwest Committee, therefore, was "to expose for the proletariat living here by Social Democratic criticism the nationalistic tendencies that are alien to it, and in this way to purge the workers' organization of the extraneous elements that are clinging to it, stressing and pointing out the necessity of the closest unification into a single political proletarian party."[22]

The committee's main target was the Bund, which in its view had irreparably damaged itself by attempting to absorb all its opponents. In its battles with the Zionists and nationalists the Bund had become infected with their spirit, dulling the edge of its Social Democratic principles. This accounted for its departure from the congress, a fatal step that the party had been unable to prevent. In brief, the committee's purpose was to turn conscious elements away from the false path chosen by the Bund to the flag of the RSDWP.[23]

When the Bund counterattacked, it directed its fire at the RSDWP rather than the Northwest Committee. Laying the woes of Social Democracy at the door of the party's centralism, Bundist spokesmen insisted yet again that only a party springing out of a national proletariat could effectively lead that proletariat in the general class struggle. In time the incorrect views of the Russian Social Democrats would be rejected and "serious unification" would occur. Meanwhile, since the party's efforts in the northwest hindered socialist work, "the duty of all conscious Social Democrats of our region is not only not to be under the flag of this 'party,' ... but to endeavor to eject [it] from our region."[24] The Bund would not brook nonsense on its "territory."

The relationship between the local Bund committees and the new groups of the RSDWP was an uneasy and generally unpleasant one. Ie. Belenky (Sergei), one of the members of the Minsk Group, stated flatly that the RSDWP challenged the Bund for the allegiance of the Jewish proletariat.[25] The Minsk Committee of the Bund agreed: the Northwest Committee considered "its main task to be the struggle with the Bund," which could bring "nothing but harm to the cause of the proletariat."[26] So bitter was the competition in Minsk that Belenky took a peculiar pride in his arrest in the summer of 1904, the first of an Iskraite there. To that point, "the political prisoners [had] consisted almost completely of Bundists." To Belenky the fact that by the end of 1904 the Iskraites could compete with the Bundists for a cell in the Minsk jail was a good measure of the Iskraite effort.[27]

Violence and hypocrisy were no strangers in the competition—on either side. Shklovsky tells of Bundists breaking up a meeting when his party group seemed to be gaining sympathy. Yet he himself frankly admits that he worked in the Bund in order "to establish ties with the masses," since "it was impossible to build a party organization without the help of the Bundists."[28] The Bund press recorded the constant friction between the two groups: there were numerous reports of the disruption of meetings and harassment of speakers, of "untrue" accounts of events in *Iskra*, of attempts to persuade workers that the Bundists and the Zionists were the same.[29] The Bundists were just as eager to undermine the opposition, making capital, for instance, of the lack of worker solidarity among the Iskraites of Minsk after the Belostok massacre. When the Central Committee called for strikes and protest meetings, said *Posledniia izvestiia*, "only the workers who belonged to the *Iskra* organization refused to join the strike and stayed in the shops."[30] Even Zionists had turned out.

In Vilna the situation was almost as bad. One party member reported that the summer of 1904 there passed "under the sign of desperate fights with the Bundists."[31] The St. Petersburg RSDWP organization sent Boris Stolpner, an Iskraite who had earned the nickname "The Bund-Devourer" (Der Bundfresser), to Vilna to bolster the opposition.[32] Still, most of these "fights" were verbal, and neither side emerged victorious; as might be expected, both sides routinely claimed to have won each debate.

Despite the bitterness, there were moderate notes. The Polessien Committee, which took in the more southwesterly regions of the Pale, was less antagonistic in its relations with the Bund than its northwestern counterpart. Though founded in January 1904, it did not announce itself in print until September of that year. It was less hungry for Bund defectors, aiming only "to create a movement among the Russian working class of our district, since the powerfully developed Jewish movement here has influenced the general struggle of the all-Russian proletariat alongside it only weakly."[33] This did not, to be sure, suggest all efforts to gain support among Jewish workers would be dropped; but the change of emphasis plainly contributed to a more or less peaceful coexistence in the southwest.

Thus says A. Bailin, an Iskraite of Mstislavl who worked very hard in the birzhe to woo workers from the Bund, though the Bundists called the Iskraites traitors and assimilators, "we got along among ourselves."[34] This meant in some cases celebrating May 1 together, in others the funding of certain Iskraite projects by the Bund, and even on occasion a local understanding that the RSDWP groups would work only among the Christians and the Bund only among the Jews. In fact, in considerable contrast to the strain and tension elsewhere in the northwest, understandings of this sort were also reached in both Mogilev and Gomel, indicating the differences of behavior that were possible locally.[35]

The RSDWP committees in the Pale had their share of difficulties. In November 1904 the Northwest Committee spoke proudly of its work among all nationalities and its firm adherence to party principles, but acknowledged that it had problems. Most of the urban workers in the area were Jews, who were organized in the main by the Bund. Pointing out that the lack of Yiddish literature was a serious handicap, the committee appealed to the central institutions of the RSDWP to produce some.[36]

At the so-called Third Congress of the RSDWP, held in April–May 1905 and attended only by the Bolsheviks, the evaluations of the two regional committees of their own work and of the Bund reflected their difficulties. Shklovsky noted: "If by far the greater part of the Bundists still belong to the Bund, that can be explained by the fact that our Northwest Committee, unfortunately, is far from accomplishing its tasks. . . . It is enough to point out as characteristic of this committee that up to now it has not put out one printed leaflet in Yiddish."[37] D. S. Postolovsky, who represented the Northwest Committee at the congress, also pointed to the lack of Yiddish materials as the greatest hindrance to agitation and propaganda. So long as that situation persisted, he concluded, "it is impossible to compete with the Bund."[38] By its own admission the Northwest Committee, almost two years after the split with the Bund, had been unable to shake its competitors. The weakness of its technical apparatus was clear—and all the more serious since the majority of the workers it recruited, at least until late in 1904, were Jews.

The report of the Polessien Committee's representative, M. K. Vladimirov (Konstantinov), further attested to the RSDWP's relative weakness. Suggesting that the Bund would not disappear quickly, Vladimirov commented: "Nowhere is there such discipline as in the Bund. The Bund has a solid periphery, which has developed such a passionate organizational patriotism that Bundists rise to defend the views of the Bund simply because they are Bund decisions, even if they personally disagree with the decisions."[39] He criticized the hard line of the Northwest Committee, which embittered the Bundists. Better relations with workers existed where the Bund was not treated harshly. Holding that "the strength of the Bund is in our weakness," he argued that the best way to combat Bund nationalism was through joint activity, which would give the Bundist workers an opportunity to see the work of other organizations.[40] Vladimirov even went so far as to suggest that the RSDWP use the Bund's literature for its own purposes. But that suggestion brought cries of "And the national question?" and was promptly rejected.[41]

Bund sources verify the picture of modest achievement reported by the RSDWP groups. On the whole the Bund workers remained loyal to their organization. The policies of the RSDWP were a matter of concern to the Bund, but defection was not. Even in Minsk, where the Bund had encountered so many problems in the past and where the RSDWP group was of some size, the Bundists airily excused their failure to consult the Iskraites before a protest because they were "of such microscopic size that they are in no position to augment the strength or significance of any revolutionary undertaking."[42] Mikhalevich, who was in prison in Minsk but had led the organization there for a time and received reports on conditions from the outside, evaluated the situation as solidly in favor of the Bund "with the exception of a few intellectuals and followers," and Pavel Berman reports the RSDWP group in Dvinsk had little influence there, even among the Christian workers.[43] In sum, the gains made among the Jewish workers by the RSDWP by the end of 1904 did not seriously threaten the Bund's organization or following.

The increasingly sharp differences between the Bolsheviks and the Mensheviks in 1904 had little effect on the relationship of either group with the Bund on the local level. Lenin and Martov had seen eye to eye on the organizational and national questions as they related to the Bund, and their local followers continued to agree on these points in principle. For its part, the Bund saw no appreciable difference in the behavior of the Menshevik and Bolshevik members of the local and regional party groups. Indeed, Belenky was perturbed because the Bundists continued to lump them together as Iskraites even after *Iskra* became a Menshevist organ.[44] But the Bund was not so far off the mark, for later even Soviet historians acknowledged that the RSDWP committees were not homogeneous, often including both Bolsheviks and Mensheviks.[45]

Neither the Bund nor the RSDWP changed its position much after the Second Congress. And though war, internal crisis, and the rise of liberal political activity in Russia suggested the need for the closing of revolutionary ranks, the existence of formalized camps within Social Democracy instead produced new tensions. The Bundists, now officially outsiders, openly criticized the Russian Social Democrats—as indeed they were psychologically and morally bound to do, else the drastic step of severing ties with the party would have been taken in vain.

As the details of the preparations for the Second Congress and its proceedings became publicly known, the respective positions of the two camps hardened, worsening rather than improving the relations between them. Lenin, as we have seen, became furious when he learned that the Bundists had brought with them a minimum set of conditions for remaining in the party. The Bundists, in turn, reported bitterly on a voting representation that gave the entire Bund in Russia the same number of votes as *Iskra* alone—three.[46] (Plus, of course, two votes for the Foreign Committee.) While the Iskraites congratulated themselves on the solidity of their victory, claiming they had achieved "unity in basic questions of party program and tactics," the Bundists described the congress as a captive of the Iskraite forces and cautioned that a victory celebration was premature.[47] Time would prove them correct.

The Second Congress's failure to unify the Social Democratic forces was even more complete than the Bundists had supposed. The disputes between the Leninist "hards" and the Martovite "softs" became an ever greater wound within Russian Social Democracy, and before the year was out Lenin divorced himself from the editorial board of *Iskra*. No charge of "separatism" leveled against the Bund could cloak the much more serious harm to the movement resulting from the internecine struggle of the Russian comrades. Time and again the Bundists pointed out the disastrous effects of the Bolshevik-Menshevik disputes.[48]

For the Bund the heart of the evil lay in the Leninist organizational scheme brought to life at the Second Congress. The real obstacle to unity was "blind bureaucratic centralism," which left no room in the party for organizations that developed naturally out of special environmental and cultural conditions.[49] The Bund found rising support for its position after the congress. Other national Social Democratic organizations, notably in Latvia and Armenia, took virtually the same line on party organization, and Proletariat, the Polish socialist party, adopted roughly the same position.[50]

The Bundists examined centralism through the perspective of Russian revolutionary history. The "literary group" *Iskra* had moved onto the historical stage between an independent workers' movement almost without political coloration and a democratic movement stimulated by the working masses. The Iskraites, Social Democratic intellectuals, showed themselves incapable of appreciating the significance of the chasm between the intelligentsia and the masses, a cardinal sin of the Russian revolutionary movement. They assumed, out of long Russian custom, that they, the intelligentsia, were the source of light, the sole channel of political truths. They judged that any action developing out of the masses must be barren because of the weak political consciousness of the masses. This view, the Bundists felt, prevented the Iskraites from recognizing the value of economic activity and its one very strong point—the breaching of the wall between the intellectual and the worker.[51]

The Bundists reasoned that the "literary group," seeing that the growing democratic movement threatened to capture the "politically immature working class" as a purely physical force, set itself two tasks: to hold the intellectuals who might slip out of the Social Democratic ranks and to assume leadership of the democratic movement. In the Bundists' view these tasks were at once utopian and inevitably determined by the historical direction of Russian Social Democracy. The tactics the Iskraites adopted to achieve their aims were dangerous and their methods often miserable. To take the democratic movement into their hands they made room for democratic elements whose chief interest was the political struggle. Accordingly, the Iskraites pushed all other facets of the workers' struggle into the background in favor of political discussion. To hold the intelligentsia they not only sought to spread the ideas of socialism, but also felt it necessary to arouse their fears by using such "bugbear" words as "nationalist" and "primitive," and to reduce the arguments of opponents to absurdity by going to the other extreme. Whenever possible they defamed and expelled Social Democratic groups to maintain their point of view.

What kind of party was it that had no connection with workers, the Bundists asked. For intellectuals, apparently all one needed was a simple plan: a newspaper with correspondents, distributors, and propagandists, together with circles to study the material on its pages. From that an army was supposed to grow. The "party" was in fact nothing but a "literary group" that equated itself with the movement as a whole. The workers' struggle was only one aspect of the whole movement and essentially cut off from it.

But the fatal weakness of the Iskraites' plan was exposed when they tried to convert theory to practice, the Bundists argued. The organizational rule adopted by the Second Congress was "nothing but the logical development of the abstract idea of centralism ... thought up inside the four walls of a study without any attention to the needs of life, which ... are pushed into the background by the ... 'plan.'"[52] In *Iskra*'s organizational policy, the existing groups were artificial, destructible cells, whose live "atoms" could be used to build new units. This deliberate dismantling of the workers' organizations was one of the most harmful tactics in the Iskraite package. *Iskra*'s policies toward the national organizations were a further indication of its isolation from the masses.[53]

In attacking Iskraite centralism the Bund did not condemn centralization

as such. It was, after all, itself a centralized organization, and it did not support "democratism" in Russia under present conditions.[54] But there were
clear distinctions between Iskraite and Bundist centralization. The Bund's
social composition and emphasis on practical work minimized the dichotomy
between intellectual and worker, made organic, historic, mass organizations
an important element in its structure, and suggested the full support of the
workers' struggle, on the economic front as well as the political front. Despite
the strong formal powers of the Central Committee, the Bund relied heavily
on trust and practical needs for revolutionary discipline. A centralism so
based guaranteed sufficient freedom for informed and effective action on the
local level. Bundism implied a mass base, Iskraism did not. Bundism had
strong proletarian roots, Iskraism held only a proletarian ideology.

After the Second Congress the Lenin-led Bolsheviks and the Bundists had
little new to say to each other concerning organization. In various articles
after the summer of 1903, Lenin attacked the Bund's appeal for inclusion in
the party on the basis of its historically established position as "the sheerest
opportunism, 'tailism' of the worst kind."* The Bundists, he charged, sought
to raise the disunity that had existed between the First and Second congresses
to the level of principle. He ridiculed the Bund's attempt to portray federation as a closer form of unity than autonomy, contrasting the direct relationship of the center and the local organizations with the indirect ties in a federated organization.[55] The fact that the Bund itself was highly centralized,
said Lenin, merely gave weight to his own argument.[56]

Lenin's major concern with the Bund in 1904, not a great one, lay in
attempting to link it with the Mensheviks. Internal party problems of organization overrode all else for him. In his detailed, all-consuming analysis of
the voting at the Second Congress, Lenin placed great significance on the
support Martov had received from the Bund. Their common cause, he felt,
spelled opportunism, the Mensheviks thus being stricken with the same disease from which the Bund suffered.[57] The Bundists, on their side, spent
little time analyzing Lenin's complaint, for in large part his remarks were
attacks aimed at Martov rather than the Bund.

The Mensheviks' capture of *Iskra* gave them an important advantage for
developing their position on organization. Their attempts to establish their
views, however, made them a ready target. They were confronted with the
Bolsheviks on the one hand and the Bundists on the other (Lenin's attempt
to link them notwithstanding); for the Bundists showed as little sympathy
for the Mensheviks' views as the Mensheviks showed for theirs.

The Bundists and Mensheviks in fact wrangled frequently. In connection

---

* *Polnoe*, 5th ed., 8: 72–73. "Tailism" is Lenin's characterization of those who follow
the masses instead of leading them, notably the Economists.

with the disputes on organization at the Second Congress, for example, the Mensheviks complained that the Bund had refused to influence the formulation of party rules. The Bundists retorted that they had supported Martov's important proposal on party membership. If they had said little on other party rules, it was because the discussions had dealt only with the relations between the central institutions of the party, not with relations between those institutions and organizations like the Bund. If the Mensheviks would recall, they themselves had taken no position on that subject.[58]

The Mensheviks worked diligently to hammer out their views in the months following the Second Congress. In an important article in early 1904 Akselrod reexamined the course of Social Democratic history for the new *Iskra* with a critical eye.[59] Though proletarian in theory and program, Russian Social Democracy was far from that in actual composition and character, he wrote. Rather it was little more than a group of revolutionary intelligentsia striving to be the political organization of the working masses. Part of the difficulty, he opined, lay in the contradiction between Russian Social Democracy's historical position and its Social Democratic task. In the past Russian conditions had not suggested a specifically proletarian revolution; they had pointed rather toward a struggle to free the whole population from political slavery, i.e., toward a bourgeois revolution. But the concern of Social Democracy was precisely the proletarian revolution; hence its task was to turn the impending liquidation of the Autocracy into a prologue to the proletarian class struggle.[60] With the spontaneous growth of a purely workers' movement in Russia, the crucial question centered around the future guidance of the proletariat. The Social Democrats had to come out not only as the political leader of the workers against absolutism, but also as their chief defender against internal dangers, such as Economism, in order to prevent the movement from being diverted into non–Social Democratic channels. The drive for unity and centralization had arisen, to some degree, out of the need to protect the proletariat. But in the emphasis on that fight, the positive task of the party, "to broaden and deepen the content of party activity in the spirit of revolutionary Marxism," had been pushed into the background.[61]

The Second Congress marked the end of the misplaced emphasis of the earlier period, Akselrod argued. However, the central institutions and program created by the congress did not spell the end of all problems. The victory of centralism had appeared to the majority as some kind of "all-redeeming miracle, a creative talisman." The party, in its concern to struggle against anti-Marxist tendencies, had paid little attention to developing the class consciousness or the political independence of the proletariat, hardly moving beyond the notion of a bourgeois revolution. How were the principles of revolutionary Marxism to be translated into party practice? The behavior of Lenin's Bolsheviks, those fetishists of centralization, Akselrod felt, would lead to Jacobin clubs, which is to say, to revolutionary democratic elements of the bourgeoisie dragging loosely in their train peripheral popular societies and some activist sections of the proletariat.[62]

To end the contradiction was not the business of a few intellectuals. Activists from the factories who had gained political consciousness must play an important role—as they could not under a bureaucratic party regime.[63] It was the party's duty to develop class consciousness in the working masses, that they might achieve independence under Social Democracy.[64]

The Bundists greeted the new Menshevik line with an almost fierce joy. Recognition of the role of the workers was, to them, elementary and basic, and they could not forget that only recently such thoughts had been heretical in Iskraite circles.[65] But what did the new line mean in practice? In fact, not much; for all the Mensheviks' words, there was little positive evidence of any real ties with the masses. What few gains were made, it seemed to the Bundists, came largely at their own expense, and they saw the Menshevik purpose as ultimately destructive to the Bund itself. Still, the Menshevik efforts were insignificant as measured against their own, which had led to a proletarian party praised by the highest figures of European socialism, Plekhanov included, as one of the strongest workers' organizations in Russia in 1904.[66] Nor did the Menshevik position improve noticeably in this respect; their ties remained very weak in the period up to 1905.[67]

Menshevik-Bundist clashes on organization were not over practical successes, an area in which there was no real contest. For the Bundists, the Mensheviks' search for a new course was important in itself. And it was with some distress that they saw in the Menshevik writings a strong continuity with the old *Iskra*. In Martov's continuing stress on a correct program and consistent tactics (still in the process of being worked out), they saw the old process of separation of intellectual and worker at work. A program could give only the most general guidance, they insisted, and consistent tactics could come only from constant and close ties with the masses.[68]

The Mensheviks, in turn, moved beyond the practical level to a critique of the theoretical basis for the Bund's claim to partyship. They charged the Bund with deviating from Marxist principles, both in the past and in the present; moreover, the Bund could not pretend to be a political party, for the Jewish proletariat did not have the necessary qualities to permit political consolidation. A party had to have its own character, its own political tasks. That the Bundists had not devised their own program proved that they could not do so without coming into conflict with Marxism itself.[69]

The Mensheviks, plagued by their own difficulties, found the Bund's self-confidence irritating in the extreme. *Iskra* lashed out at the Bundists as parochial sectarians who placed magic significance on the word "Bund" and regarded their organization, not as a historical product, but as the very embodiment of truth.[70] On the contrary, said the journal, Russian Social Democracy and the Bund grew out of the same soil and had a common political culture and literature. Further, *Iskra* pointed to the backward industrial development of the Pale of Settlement, the lack of urban development, and the exceptional laws against the Jews as factors that tainted the Jewish proletariat with petit-bourgeois predilections—and as evidence of the backwardness of the Jewish proletariat and the Bund. Where were the Bund's theoretical works to show the party how to proceed toward a political class movement, *Iskra* wanted to know. The truth was the Bundists had learned everything from the party they now criticized; all they had managed to do was popularize what others had written.*

The Mensheviks' pique simply gave force to the Bund's argument in the dispute over organization. Jewish and Russian Social Democrats had similar intellectual roots, agreed; but their masses shared no such common background, economically or culturally. The Bund grew out of a recognition of the gap between general theory and the facts of Jewish life in Russia, and was in practice an excellent accommodation of both factors, considering the difficulties involved. But how could the intellectual and internationalist Mensheviks accept an organization not based on their own concepts? In assuming their intellectual foundations to be the most general and truest approach to organization, they were bound to regard the national and, therefore, narrower path of the Bund as faulty, regardless of past successes.

The Bund, in fact, had never abandoned the effort to reconcile the hard realities of practical necessity with Marxist ideology—so unsatisfactory on matters of nationality in general and the problems of the Jews in particular. Its continuing success amidst heightened political activity merely emphasized the need for concrete answers. The Mensheviks were completely wrong in arguing that the Bund did not regard itself as a historical product. It was precisely the Bund's profound belief in its organic development from the masses that had made it the effective organization it was. If the Bundists made much of their organization it was because it served as a reliable focal point for their activities and, for many, as a way of life.

The national question, the other major issue that divided the Bund and the RSDWP, had two facets for the Bundists. First they had to settle the matter within their own ranks, and then, as a natural extension of the organizational question, to convince the Russian Social Democrats of the importance of finding a solution for all Russian Social Democracy.

Though the Fifth Congress of the Bund failed to add a national plank to

* "Noveishaia polemika 'Bunda,'" *Iskra*, 73 (Sept. 1, 1904): 3–4. The author of this article ignored the important work of the pioneer era, *On Agitation*, an oversight the Bundists were quick to point out ("Fantaziia i deistvitel'nost'," *Vestnik Bunda*, 5 [Nov. 1904]: 22). Getzler attributes the *Iskra* article to Martov (*Martov*, p. 59), but I find it hard to believe that Martov could have forgotten Kremer's work, and indeed his own editorial contribution, in something under ten years.

the Bund's program, it did provide for continuing discussion. *Vestnik Bunda* was expressly founded to publish arguments on the national question in the hope of clarifying the Bund's program and tactics so that the gulf between intellectual and worker might be bridged and other nationalities be made aware of the Jewish workers' movement.[71]

The Bund's chief spokesman after mid-1903 was Vladimir Medem. The usually articulate Kosovsky abdicated to him on this issue; finding Medem's Neutralism distasteful, he chose not to defend it.[72] Medem himself had certain doubts about his position in 1903 but felt the search for a socialist answer to the national question had to go on.[73]

With the Bund's internal position uncertain and the continuing criticism of *Iskra* before him, Medem set out to prove that the Jews were a distinct national group. In the first issue of *Vestnik Bunda* he addressed himself to a number of Lenin's broadsides in *Iskra* attacking that concept. In one article, for instance, Lenin had stated categorically that the idea of Jewish nationality was "absolutely false and essentially reactionary."[74] Territory and language were the principal criteria of nationhood, he argued, and the Jews had neither. Lenin also denied the criterion of race as a means of identification. The history of the Jew in Western Europe, he held, showed that political liberty and the political emancipation of the Jews went hand in hand and led toward assimilation. To seek an exception in Russia was totally reactionary. The Jewish problem could be settled in only one of two ways—"assimilation or isolation."[75] In expounding the idea of Jewish nationality the Bund was committing a grave error, for it thus legitimized isolation. There was no escape from this path but fusion with the greater movement.[76]

Medem rejected Lenin's definition of nationality. Admittedly, the Jews did not fit Lenin's territorial criterion, he argued, but then neither did many other groups, especially in Eastern Europe. As to the second major criterion, language, consider the case of the English-speaking Irish people in this regard. Moreover, even if there was a connection between language and national identity, Medem declared, the Jews could not be disqualified, for the criticism of Yiddish had turned on its being relatively undeveloped, not nonexistent.[77]

Elsewhere Medem examined the argument that industrial development led to assimilation. In the West, he said, capitalism had emerged against a background of almost completely formed large nations, strengthening the already predominant ruling ethnic groups. But in Eastern Europe it was developing in multinational states whose ruling groups were bent on pushing "foreigners" from the market to gain a monopoly. At the same time, they were also intent on destroying national characteristics, particularly language, which interfered with trade. These interests coincided with those of the state, which saw cultural differences as destructive of power and internal harmony. Thus, the government and the ruling nationality pursued essentially the same goals.[78]

For Medem, to link national identity with territory was unconsciously to identify a ruling nationality with the territory it controlled. *Iskra*'s theory, based on Western history, was, in Lenin's words, "tailism" of the worst sort.[79]

But if capitalism was conducive to denationalization, Medem said, there were other elements pulling in the opposite direction, namely the masses' aspiration for political freedom and development of their own national literature. Borrowing from Kautsky, Medem took as a case in point the Jewish experience in Russia since the emancipation of the serfs, which saw the parallel development of a serious literature in Yiddish and the revolutionary movement among the Jewish workers. That new literature, evidencing the "great creative and stimulative power" of the masses, worked against the assimilative trend of capitalism. Democratization had a similar effect. In sum, Medem was satisfied that the Jews' sense of belonging to one social organism, common racial and psychological traits, and net of interclass relationships qualified them as a separate nationality, despite Lenin's assertions to the contrary.[80]

In a later article, Medem turned to search out the roots of assimilationism. The Iskraite attitude could be traced back, he felt, to the arguments of nineteenth-century thinkers, notably to the two socialist greats, Marx and Kautsky, and even further back to Marx's Hegelian friend and teacher, Bruno Bauer, who had linked the German Jews' search for civil rights and political emancipation in the early 1840's to religion. Bauer had argued that the one path to emancipation was for the Jews and the Germans to give up their respective religions and fight for freedom together as Germans, that is, as human beings.[81]

Marx himself had rejected Bauer's proposition, though not the notion of assimilation, arguing that Bauer had merely separated church and state. In his own view, the emancipation of the Jews was a necessary consequence of the development of the contemporary state, and the question not a theological one, but a matter of the economic role the Jews played in society. The modern Jew's world was material gain and his god, money. Marx saw usury and money as the twin evils of his time and reasoned that if they were abolished the Jew as such would cease to exist. By working for the abolition of his own materialistic nature, the Jew would be working for simple emancipation.[82]

Medem saw the assimilationist at work in both men. Bauer had concentrated on the specific signs of individuality in the Jews and compared them with another national group, one he considered higher. The Jew had to work for German liberty; he was not to demand anything for himself as a Jew, for that made his emancipation impossible. The rejection of Christianity did not cost the German his nationality—German was to be equated with human being. But not so in the case of the Jew; national characteristics and religion were intertwined in him, and the whole had to disappear.

Marx's assimilationism resembled Bauer's, Medem argued. He sought some

Jewish "essence," a remnant of the idealism of his younger days. Said Medem: "The assimilationist does not examine Jewish nationality in its historical development; for him Jewish society is not a living, developing organism with an internal structure like any other . . . that obeys the laws of change. For him the Jews are a social fossil . . . hardly influenced by their times."[83] If the assimilationists had examined Jewish society, he argued, they would have found development. But instead they had looked for so-called essences and were satisfied that they found them, whether in religion, in the ancient Hebrew culture, in the passivity that eschewed revolution, or in the spirit of gain. If Jewish essence was built into the capitalist order, the Jew must disappear with the end of capitalism.

Though much had changed since Marx made these pronouncements, some 60 years before, wrote Medem, they were being repeated in the twentieth century. Kautsky, for instance, still exhorted alien populations to assimilate with their neighbors in order to end national conflicts.[84] Indeed he even suggested that the anti-Semitism of a Kishinev pogrom was to be explained by the primitive, ignorant character of the Russian people. But that argument was weak, said Medem, for what was specifically Russian about ignorance, which was prevalent in many societies? Moreover, instead of faulting the "native" population, Kautsky defended assimilation by turning on the Jews themselves. Like his ideological forbears, he saw the Jews as reactionary by nature and incapable of development. He, who suggested federation for the Austrian nationalities, did not propose such a solution for the Jews. He was able to arrive at this position merely by postulating that Jewry was dead, and so could be absorbed even into a backward, ignorant population, which would become cultured in the future.[85] The "essential" point of his case was that the Jewish national culture formed some 2,000 years before had been raised to a dogma, which was negative to all culture and science and had consequently remained isolated from all social and political life. Nor was education a possible solution; it might help non-Jews, even lead them to tolerance, but Jewry itself was hopeless.[86]

Medem insisted that the new stage of Jewish history had to be studied, something the assimilationists failed to do. The essence of Judaism Kautsky referred to was past history. Further, those who depicted the Jewish workers' movement as a contradiction of the Jewish national point of view and a result of assimilation were also wrong.[87] True, proletarian movements did emancipate themselves from religious prejudices and narrow nationalism—an assimilation of sorts—but such action presented no specific solution to the Jewish question. Moreover, to recommend assimilation to the Jews, who had moved onto the proletarian path long before others, seemed superfluous.

It was worth looking at who in fact favored assimilation, Medem suggested. Arguments to the contrary, the Autocracy did not prevent assimilation. Reactionaries always accepted assimilation; what they would not accept was national development. The call for assimilation had nothing in common with Social Democracy and was inadmissible from the point of view of the proletarian class struggle, the touchstone in all issues. No one could predict the future of the Jews, including the Bund.[88]

The Social Democrats, Medem held, had seriously neglected the national question, allowing it to be preempted by the bourgeoisie. And wrongly so, it seemed. Social Democrats must ask themselves what meaning nationality could have for their ideology, which "is guided by one basic principle—the proletarian class struggle."[89] National culture, he suggested, did not exist "as something independent, as a closed circle with peculiar content." "What is national is only that peculiar *form* into which general human content is poured."[90]

How, then, should Social Democrats react to such forms? Here Medem returned to the neutralist prescription he had adopted in mid-1903. It was not the business of Social Democrats to take a stand one way or the other. They should be neither nationalists nor assimilationists, for the proletarian class struggle was the overriding issue, and what difference did language, psychology, or skin color make there? Nationalists and assimilationists made the same error, said Medem; they mistook results for goals. If the Jews did become assimilated—and there was nothing intrinsically wrong with that—it should come about through a process of evolution, not because it had been pressed as a Social Democratic goal. "We are not against *assimilation*," he cautioned, "we are against *assimilationism*." What if Jewish national culture flourished? Medem's answer was that Social Democrats had to be against nationalists and should have no interest in planting culture; but they were "not against the *national character* of culture," only against "nationalistic policy."[91]

The argument for absolute neutrality, however, did not end the issue for Medem. Though Social Democracy rejected all forms of a bourgeois character, it had clear obligations toward existing cultures, and the Bund could not be indifferent to these obligations. A nationality must be allowed to develop freely. Every oppression had to be shunted aside. "Only the internal needs of a people should play a role in the working out of cultural forms, only those internal needs have the right of expression in the competition between 'our' and 'alien' forms of national life.... Free from external pressure, the folk organism itself in the course of its development, determines its own fate."[92]

Insofar as the national question arose in the context of repression, it required a Social Democratic answer. When people sought simple emancipation their struggle was progressive, and the proletariat had to include that struggle in its own struggle for liberation. The proletarian felt the full weight of national oppression. It choked him off from the larger society, for he knew only his own language and literature—"the only window through which he can join cultural life, develop his consciousness, broaden his horizon."[93] National oppression, moreover, welded the oppressed together, implanting the psychology of an inferior being, which seriously hindered the development of a true classless society and even had harmful effects on the ruling nationality.[94]

The duty of Social Democracy, then, was not only to recognize the existence of the national question, but also to guarantee the free working out of the problem. Admittedly, a capitalist society could not work out national guarantees, just as it could not work out other social and political problems. The minimum demands the socialists made of the bourgeois world were but palliatives. Indeed, Social Democrats must be wary of putting their own national program forth as a panacea so long as capitalism existed. At the same time, dodging the issue as of minor consequence could prove harmful; besides, Social Democrats were obliged to fulfill as many of their aims as possible before the revolution.[95]

There were two possible answers to the national question, said Medem: political independence or full national rights within a multinational state. It was the second answer that the Social Democrats had failed to explore. Equal civil rights, the only answer offered thus far, simply meant eliminating the inequalities established by the ruling nationality, thereby eliminating civil and political distinctions. But though Social Democracy had no cultural preferences, it did have the task of fighting national oppression in a positive as well as a negative sense, that is, it had to guarantee national freedom, just as it had to guarantee personal freedom. The collective functions of a state, education in particular, were active rather than passive, and the realization of rights depended on how these functions were exercised. Freedom for nationalities meant the state would have to provide schools that would not grant advantages to the majority.[96] This could be managed through national self-rule or autonomy in all matters touching national life, i.e., cultural matters. For the present, though, equal civil rights remained the paramount issue, as the Fourth Congress of the Bund had resolved.[97]

Medem's arguments appeared over a ten-month period, from February to November 1904. But the problem of nationality as such continued to be of little concern to the RSDWP leaders. Martov, for instance, found Medem's arguments on assimilation strange and distracting. What difference did they make—outside of their instructive value? The problem had no political significance, since its solution must await the workers' victory. Under the circumstances such discussions were politically fruitless and introduced no new ideas. Indeed, the Bund's Fourth Congress had declared that the demand for national autonomy was premature. The Bund had hesitated, Martov contended, because it wished to avoid direct conflict with Marxist theory. Moreover, by attacking the motives of the Marxist theoreticians as assimilationist and nationalist when it could not put its own special program in a Social Democratic context, the Bund was corrupting itself. Its spokesmen were forced into becoming apologists for an ideologically unsound position. Once again Martov asserted that nationalities unquestionably had a right to self-determination, but that for now the socialists must fight separatist tendencies in the party of the proletariat.[98] The RSDWP was content to brush aside the assimilation argument as a disruptive factor rather than come to grips with the substantive issues involved.

The Iskraites also disparaged Medem's attempt to set some kind of Social Democratic position on the national question. They argued that this was a new twist: until now the Bund had only sought recognition as the sole representative of the Jewish proletariat—"hardly a valuable contribution to the ideological treasure of international Social Democracy."[99] Nor were the Iskraites taken with the notion of national cultural autonomy as a form of national self-rule and as a political demand. The only kind of self-rule that suited the party's political program was a "self-rule" that saw state functions transferred into the hands of the people. Self-rule demanded an administrative structure, local legal control, and territorial limits. Plainly, then, the fragmentation into national groups would represent "a reactionary restoration of medieval legal relations."[100] The Bund knew full well, the Iskraites pointed out, that the needs of the whole population within a given territory had to be served without reference to nationality. The Bund, however, would see special national interests institutionalized and incorporated into Social Democracy. National cultural autonomy was not a political concept. The state's sole obligation to a national culture was to see that it had the opportunity to exist and develop. It was under no obligation, indeed had no right, to create a compulsory cultural union and invest it with state power. Any such union was voluntary, and a political program could do no more than demand that a cultural union be given the same broad rights as any democratic party. Thus, the Bund's "first independent political demand," insofar as it was political, was already embodied in all democratic programs; the Bund made no new demands based on the specific interests of the Jewish proletariat and therefore its efforts bore no results. "The attempt to tie nationalist utopias organically to proletarian interests ended as it had to, with a brilliant failure."[101]

The Bundists and the Iskraites remained as far apart at the end of 1904 as they had been at the Second Congress. No matter how deep the Bund might have considered its discussion—Medem himself owned that he had enormous trouble grounding the national question on socialist principles—the Social Democrats were bound to find it difficult to examine the issues of nationality at a time when unity was so important to the movement.[102] Insofar as the Iskraites commented on national cultural autonomy, they begged the issue by insisting that institutionalized power must rest with the whole of the population of a given territory, making national considerations irrelevant. Although both sides recognized general rights, the Bundists insisted that populations had specific cultural characteristics that needed consideration. The Iskraites' description of the Bund's scheme as coercive, moreover, did not fit the facts. But the times were not ripe for a resolution of the issue. The nationality issue was still remote for the Russians, if not for the Bund. In any event, the upheaval of 1905 soon superseded all other preoccupations in both parties.

The split in the Social Democratic forces in Russia led to a bitter dispute over representation at the Amsterdam Congress of the Socialist International in September 1904. In 1900 the Bundists had attended the congress at Paris as part of the Russian delegation, but now they claimed seats as an unaffiliated Jewish party. Eight delegates came armed with 27 mandates from 17 committees, 10 organizations of lesser status, and 60 groups.*

The International had begun to face problems of representation at the Paris congress. Its rules granted each nationality, i.e., country, two votes at congresses and in the permanent bureau, its executive arm. It had adopted this two-vote formula as a way of contending with the problem of disagreements within a party or the split of one group into two separate parties. But that formula could not hope to cover the confused situation in Russia, which saw not only the split in the RSDWP but also the creation of a number of new parties.

The International Socialist Bureau met on the eve of the Amsterdam Congress to consider representation questions and to verify mandates. The new complexities did not lead it to alter the formula of two votes per country shared by the strongest parties, with other parties left to vote with the recognized sections. But the mandates of various groups were recognized by organization rather than by country, thus creating a confusing situation in which groups were recognized as organizationally independent but were not allowed to vote independently.†

Once the congress began the Bundists sought to gain one of the two votes allotted to each country. The Russian delegation, they argued, was not a unit

---

* "Vopros o predstavitel'stve . . . ," *Vestnik Bunda*, 5 (Nov. 1904): 2. Medem's recollection is that there were only seven delegates (*Fun main leben*, 2: 57); but the report to the congress (the article here cited) and the multiauthor work *Di geshikhte fun Bund* both say eight. However, the last-named work identifies only seven: Liber, Kosovsky, Mill, Kremer, E. Rozen, Max Oguz (Maximov), and Medem. (See J. S. Hertz et al., 2: 119.)

† *Vestnik Bunda*, 5 (Nov. 1904): 3–4. The Empire's nationalities were represented at the Amsterdam Congress as follows: the RSDWP, seven delegates; the Bund, eight delegates; the Latvian Social Democratic Workers' Party and the Revolutionary Ukrainian Party, one delegate each; and the Socialist Revolutionary Party, 12 delegates. The PSD and Proletariat formed one section with one vote, the PPS a second section with one vote.

but consisted of independent delegations that could not be expected to agree on the issues.[103] The bureau met to discuss the knotty problem of dividing two votes among three parties—the RSDWP, the Socialist Revolutionaries, and the Bund. Victor Adler, a prominent Austrian Social Democrat, favored a vote for the Bund on the basis of its organization and service. But others backed the SR's as representing a different viewpoint from that of the Social Democratic Bund and RSDWP, and their arguments prevailed; the SR's received one vote and the RSDWP the other.[104]

Forced to express their vote in concert with the RSDWP, the Bund delegates sought to meet with the Russian delegation but were informed that they would not be accepted into its midst, since they outnumbered the RSDWP delegates and could outvote them. The Bundists, feeling that they were being deprived of their vote, took their case to the bureau, which was now caught in the contradiction it had itself created. The bureau rejected the Bund's arguments, but fearing that the affair would be brought to the floor of the congress, Rosa Luxemburg and Karl Kautsky sought a compromise. As a temporary solution they awarded the bureau seat to the RSDWP and one vote each, or neutralization, to it and the Bund if they differed on any issue. The Bund accepted the scheme but protested the bureau's decision to establish a common Social Democratic section for the Empire. The Bund delegates did not wish to participate in votes arrived at by others. The matter obviously needed further consideration.[105]

After the Amsterdam Congress Plekhanov and the Bundists argued publicly about what had transpired. Plekhanov, describing the refusal of the bureau to grant a seat at the congress to the Bund, assigned the Bundists' difficulties to their nationalist tendencies. He pointed particularly to the arguments of the English Social Democrat H. M. Hyndman, who felt that the granting of bureau membership to the Bund would be construed as support for nationalism. The Bund had to return to the party to gain its place.[106]

Plekhanov's account infuriated the Bundists. They went directly to the bureau to find out why they had not received a seat. Their inquiries drew responses from Kautsky and Hyndman, as well as the Dutch socialist H. H. Van Kol and the secretary of the bureau, Victor Serwy. Van Kol denied that national tendencies played a role, as did Serwy, who insisted that the bureau based its decision on the ideological affinity of the Bund and the RSDWP.[107] Kautsky took much the same line, claiming that the SR's were given one of the two votes because they differed in principle from the Social Democrats while the Bund was but a separate Social Democratic organization.[108] Hyndman, in his reply, expressed his displeasure over the Russian Jews wanting a separate delegation and vote. He had felt, he added, that in excluding the SR's the bureau would have deprived a powerful segment of the Russian proletariat of a vote. The Bundists recognized his preference for the SR's, but they refused to see in his reply any grounds for Plekhanov's charge that their "nationalism" had led to the bureau's decision.[109]

When, after some delay, Plekhanov responded to the Bund's criticism of his interpretation, he did so with considerable spite. He was late in answering, he wrote, because the Bundists, or those Zionists as he termed them, were scarcely deserving of a reply. The Bund had misinterpreted his words to suggest that the debates had centered around nationalism, an example of how important it considered itself. The letters published by the Bund indicated there had been little talk of nationalism; Hyndman's one indication of the Bund's nationalist aspiration had been enough to decide the issue.[110]

Plekhanov's venom toward the Bund was almost the last straw for the Bundists. Kosovsky broke off all ties with Plekhanov, and saw Lenin as little as possible. Martov, still regarded by the Bundists as an honest man, apparently believed that Plekhanov was wrong, but he made no public statement to that effect.[111]

Despite the painful incidents surrounding representation, the Bundists derived considerable satisfaction from the congress. They were particularly gratified when their resolution censuring the anti-Jewish policy of the Tsarist government was adopted, all the more so since they had mourned their failure to introduce such a motion in 1900.[112] The recognition of the Bund as the first independent Jewish party in the International was also a great source of satisfaction.[113]

The conflicts between the Bund and the RSDWP gained ever wider notoriety among the student and émigré circles in the West. The size of the Jewish student population in the Russian colonies ensured a large audience for each discussion. In Hofman's view, there was even more interest in this ideological battle than in the Bolshevik-Menshevik fight.* The debates also moved onto the pages of Yiddish journals in the United States, to the point where Kremer found it necessary during his stay there to defend the Bund's position.†

But enemies or no, the two sides were compelled by the political problems of Russian society and the growth of the non-Marxist opposition to explore the possibilities of joint action. Nevertheless, neither was prepared to reassess

---

* Hofman, *Far 50 yor*, p. 262. Hofman tells of debates with Trotsky who, he says, knew next to nothing about the Jewish workers' movement and was just beginning to realize how unprepared he was to discuss Bund affairs.

† *Di Zukunft*, a major Yiddish journal in New York, carried a series of articles in 1903 on the Bund and its opponents authored by a longtime Foreign Committee activist, Blumstein (K. Frumin). While in New York in 1904 Kremer submitted a two-part article to the journal ("Nokh a kritiker fun Bund," *DZ*, 9: 30–35 and 10: 39–46) answering the criticisms of Jacob Milkh carried earlier that year ("Di natsionale programe fun 'Bund,'" *DZ*, 5: 26–32).

the organizational problem so soon after the split, seriously impeding the effort to stake out areas of cooperation. In June 1904 the Bundists suggested that though the current disunity was lamentable, "it is impossible to think about unification with the party again in the near future because of the great differences in organizational principle on which we stand and on which the party stands. We can speak only of a *temporary* alliance for a special *temporary* task."[114] The RSDWP, for its part, felt the weakness of its position. Martov, for example, opposed a meeting of Social Democratic organizations, as suggested by the Bundists, fearing that the Bund might unite the parties favoring federation under its hegemony and reopen the organizational question.[115] In the circumstances the RSDWP was understandably cautious.

Nevertheless, various efforts continued among the revolutionary parties to come together in order to take full advantage of popular discontent with the war and the economic crisis. The Bund's old rival, the PPS, for instance, invited it to join with other socialist organizations of oppressed nationalities seeking political federalism to work out forms of protest against the centralism of the Tsarist regime; the Bund rejected the invitation.[116] At about the same time, in May 1904, the Bundists, acting in concert with the Latvian Social Democrats, invited the RSDWP, the PSD, the PPS, Proletariat, the Lithuanian Social Democrats, the Armenian Social Democratic Workers' Organization, and the Revolutionary Ukrainian Party to a meeting to discuss joint action.[117]

The next month the RSDWP Council, faced with this and other proposals for consultation, agreed that some action was called for. Here, as at Belostok in 1902, the recurrent weakness of the leaders of Russian Social Democracy was exposed; again they were forced to react to proposals made by others instead of holding the initiative themselves. "It would be better to take that initiative upon ourselves," said Martov of the Bund's proposal, a remark that reveals much about the insecurity within the RSDWP.[118] The Russians finally decided that a preliminary conference of Social Democratic organizations should meet before considering joint action with other political elements of the opposition. They suggested a meeting with the Bund, the PSD, Proletariat, and the Latvian Social Democrats. Their message reached the Bundists in late July.[119]

In strongly supporting joint action the Bund hoped to heal some of the wounds in the movement after the split. It stood for revolutionary, if not organizational, unity among the Social Democrats. Once it found agreement with a number of Social Democratic parties, it would feel less isolated from the rest of the revolutionary community, and the conflict with the RSDWP might be eased. Since there was no hope of immediate federation at the top levels of the movement, cooperation seemed a good practical alternative for the time being.

When the Bundists met with party representatives in the late summer (they were gathering for the Amsterdam Congress) the RSDWP refused to consider the Bund's proposal to bring together all parties opposed to the Tsarist regime. The only thing to be discussed, the party delegates insisted, was the Social Democrats' reaction to a proposal of the Finnish revolutionaries for a conference of revolutionary and opposition parties. The Bund was told bluntly that its suggestion had no bearing on this question.[120] There the matter rested until November, when the Bund once more pushed for a meeting of the Social Democrats. This new initiative came amidst the seething excitement of Mirsky's "Spring" and the stirrings of political life in Russia. The Bundists drew up an agenda and sent out invitations, asking the invited organizations to reply. The majority of organizations agreed that further delay would be unfortunate.

The RSDWP Council was among those responding—but only to introduce its own proposals. The party wanted the conference to deal with the question of full unity and the meeting to be held abroad. The Bund rejected both suggestions, either of which would have changed the character of the conference and forced postponement.[121] By the time the conference finally convened, Bloody Sunday, the starting point of the Revolution of 1905, had already taken place.

Still, with all their conflicts, the Bundists and the RSDWP members were Social Democrats, and so continued to find many areas of agreement. A notable example of the sameness of their orientation to problems was their common rejection of the Finns' invitation to participate in a joint conference of all parties in Russia opposed to the regime. Indeed, they worked together to prepare an explanation of their decision.[122] And both eyed with deep suspicion the Paris Bloc that emerged from the non-Marxist gathering in the fall of 1904.

The Bund's rejection of the invitation to the Paris meeting—each party sent its own answer—was based on the Central Committee's judgment that the views of the participants were too contradictory to permit effective work. Some elements, the committee noted, even leaned to adventurism—a veiled reference to the Finnish revolutionaries' acceptance of arms and money from Japanese agents.[123] At the moment, it said, fruitful action was possible only on the basis of the class struggle without national distinctions.[124]

The resolutions of the Paris Bloc confirmed the Central Committee's suspicions. The Bloc called for a democratic republic on the basis of "general voting," a proposal that seemed distressingly vague to the Bundists, who like other Social Democrats endorsed the "four-tailed" formula of a "general, direct, equal, and secret electoral law."[125] The Bundists were equally dismayed by the tactics of the Bloc parties; it seemed to them the Bloc was adopting an opportunist line that could only feed the flabbiness of political liberalism. The

Central Committee thus dissociated itself from the Paris program; however, it welcomed the idea of coordinated work with other elements of the opposition, provided the Bund maintained its own course of revolutionary action.[126] The Bundists were prepared to *getrennt marschiern, vereint schlagen* (march separately, fight together).*

The need to contain the growth of political liberalism in Russia was another subject the Social Democrats could agree on. The Russians were more threatened by the rise of the liberal movement than the Bundists, for the Jewish liberals lacked organization and were estranged culturally and physically from the Jewish working masses, whereas the Russian liberals, recruited from the free professions and the Zemstvos, were dangerous competitors for the Russian Social Democrats.† Still, the potential danger of political liberalism for all Social Democrats was clear, and they were put in the paradoxical position of welcoming the awakening of a new political consciousness on the one hand and fearing it on the other.

Thus, despite the range of differences that troubled the Bundists and their Russian Social Democratic comrades, their shared ideological principles allowed them to take a common view of important political problems. Even at the Amsterdam Congress they voted together against Revisionism.[127] The test of their ideological solidarity was to come in 1905. The effort to join hands then would not require ideological reunification; the two sides would be able to come together then simply as Social Democrats.

Though it was undoubtedly the RSDWP that occupied most of the Bundists' time and energy, they also maintained close contact with other revolutionary parties. In 1903 and 1904 the most friendly and cooperative of these groups was the Latvian Social Democrats. In fact, the Bund and the Latvians had worked well together, mainly in Riga, since well before the Second Congress. Indeed, when Martov wished to give a precise example of the evils of federation, he had read to the congress a letter from a Russian Social Democrat in Riga describing the failures of the joint work of the Social Democrats of three nationalities—Latvian, Jewish, and Russian—over a two-year period.[128] Several months later a former Bund delegate to the United Committee in Riga responded to his complaint. He agreed that there were difficulties but claimed that they were purely technical problems, which had

---

* *Posledniia izvestiia*, 202 (Dec. 6/Nov. 23, 1904): 1. As a measure of how close the Social Democrats were in many ways, Plekhanov used the same slogan (Samuel Baron, "Plekhanov and Revolution," in Curtiss, *Essays*, p. 137).

† The Jews and the other nationalities did not have Zemstvos. Sidney Harcave implies that the liberal movement had greater influence among the Jews than Social Democracy had ("Jewish Political Parties," p. 39). His case might be stronger if it was not so all-inclusive; that is, if he limited the argument to the middle class and the educated.

nothing to do with the fact of federation.[129] Moreover, the Russian's letter suggested nothing but good relations between the Bundists and the Latvian Social Democrats; it appeared to be the Russian Social Democrats who were disgruntled.

When the Latvians established a formal Social Democratic party in 1904, their program closely matched the Bund's, ensuring continued cooperation between the two groups. The Latvians placed a high premium on the work of the national parties; favored equal cultural rights; rejected regional limits on their activity; maintained their internal organizational independence; and, in answer to a request from the Bund's Central Committee, recognized the Bund as the sole representative of the Jewish proletariat, claiming the same right for themselves with respect to Latvian workers.[130] The two parties thus not only cooperated in the streets, but also supported and comforted each other in a common stand against the RSDWP. Later, they acted together to try to unify the ranks of Russian Social Democracy and, eventually, in January 1905, Riga served as the site for a meeting of the Social Democratic parties. Down to that time, the two parties issued joint leaflets and maintained a federated committee; all in all, they had perhaps the happiest relationship of any two parties in Russia up to the Revolution of 1905, thanks no doubt to their willingness to recognize each other's claim to exclusive representation of a national group, certainly the major source of friction in the Bund's relations with the centralist and internationalist Russian Marxists and the nationalist PPS.

The Bund had only limited contact with the Socialist Revolutionaries in 1903 and 1904. Virtually their only work in common was putting a stop to the pogroms that struck again and again after Kishinev. The SR's agreed on the necessity of halting the pogromists but were unwilling to acknowledge that the Jews as such were their target. In the tense Easter-Passover season of 1904, one SR correspondent observed that though one could not stand idly by while the Jewish poor were slaughtered, there was no justification for automatically protecting the entire Jewish community. Suggesting that the pogromists were but unfortunate workers, driven mad by hunger and misery, who would find self-defense forces, police, and troops arrayed against them, he asked: "Is it possible that we socialists will fight our brothers, however blind, hand in hand with the police and ... the Jewish bourgeoisie armed in defense of its property?"[131] *Iskra*, too, wondered whether the new wave of pogroms was specifically anti-Jewish and belittled the attack on Jewish property.[132]

The Bundists challenged these views, charging that the SR's had already forgotten Kishinev and Gomel. Had not the socialists found it necessary to fight the police in those instances? The SR correspondent's statement, the Bundists felt, showed how empty content could be made to appear as radicalism by these "knights of the revolution."[133] As for their fellow Social Democrats, who asked how it was that Social Democracy defended the property of the Jews, the Bundists countered with a question of their own: "What if mass attacks begin against the property of Christians? Do you take them under your protection or not?" The Bundists assumed the answer must be no, else the Social Democrats' position in regard to Jewish property could not be logically supported. But it was not even a question of logic. Christian property was well defended by the state. It was only Jewish property that was unprotected by the law. In the circumstances it had to be defended. The Bundists argued that, in any case, when Jewish property was attacked, it was always the meager property of the Jewish poor, that the attacks invariably turned into personal ones, and that it was necessary to destroy the notion that Jews could be attacked with impunity whenever Christians wished to unburden themselves along the lines of least resistance. Uninformed SR's and Social Democrats were playing into the hands of the Zionists, reinforcing their claim of indifference to the Jewish condition.[134] The lack of sensitivity displayed by the Russians could not but cause anguish to the Bundists, whose efforts to protect themselves had just begun to bear political and psychological fruit.

Of all the national minorities whose lives touched the Jews, the Bund had its most constant and fullest contacts with the Poles. The PPS remained the most important group in the Polish revolutionary movement, with a widespread following among the Polish workers ever since its inception in 1892. A fair number of Jewish intellectuals and workers also belonged to the party. Divided on several issues since pioneer days, both organizations continued to hold to their positions in the late 1890's. In December 1899 the Bund's Third Congress announced its intention to fight the PPS, which sought "to weaken the independence and existence" of the Bund. It also resolved to open discussion on the question of Polish independence, a matter of utmost importance to the PPS, in connection with the Bund's own examination of the national question.[135] The Jewish workers figured as an increasingly important consideration in the PPS's plans, as evidenced by the decision of its Fourth Congress, in December 1898, to publish a Yiddish newspaper. But despite Der Arbeter's announced intention of showing Jewish workers that they and their Christian brothers were "children of one land," bound by the same chains of tyranny, the publication appeared only spasmodically for several years.[136] The Bundists, still wrestling with their own position on the national question, were unable or unwilling to formulate a new policy on the Polish issue. Their Social Democratic ideology and attraction to the Russians, as well as their convictions about organizational independence, kept them apart from the Polish ideology and leadership.

The situation between the two parties changed little between the Third and Fourth congresses of the Bund, the Fourth Congress contenting itself with reaffirming the resolution taken by its predecessor on the PPS. But the Fourth Congress's position on the national question in general angered the Poles. As will be recalled, the Bundists rejected territorial solutions, disavowed the changing of frontiers as a Social Democratic task, and called for a "federation of nationalities" in the future—in effect neither ruling out Polish independence nor supporting it.[137] This solution was attacked by the PPS, which interpreted it as a denial of Polish independence, a continuing preference for the Russians, and a lack of concern for the Poles.[138]

The significant number of Jewish workers in Poland (the Jews represented about 15 per cent of the total population and a much higher percentage in the cities) and the success of the Bund made the Jewish question a major issue at the Sixth Congress of the PPS, in June 1902. To improve the PPS's position among the Jewish workers the congress authorized the creation of a special committee on Jewish affairs under the leadership of Felix Zaks. Zaks, a Polish Jew who knew Yiddish well, both expanded the output of Yiddish literature and raised its quality.[139] But apart from this move, the Sixth Congress contented itself with reaffirming the party's traditional position: the minorities in Poland should unite under a common flag to fight for Polish independence and a democratic republic, in which all would have full rights as citizens.[140]

By late 1902 neither side had budged much from its position. For the Bundists the cardinal organizational objective of the PPS, revolutionary unification under its control, was unacceptable; and its political objective, Polish independence, an open question. The Bund's broad political commitment continued to be to an international proletarian revolution, and that commitment established its primary posture in relation to the PPS. Nevertheless, the Bund's shift from a universalist and equal civil rights position to an emphasis on national proletarianism affected its attitude toward the Polish party, as was clearly reflected in its analysis of the resolution of the PPS's Sixth Congress. The Bundists contended, with less than complete accuracy, that the PPS had learned nothing from its failures among the Jewish proletariat. It had forgotten that "*only* [the Bund] carries on the liberation struggle of the Jewish proletariat," and that the Jewish workers had the right to make their own demands rather than aspire only to the goals the PPS proclaimed for the Polish and Lithuanian proletariat. Moreover, said the Bund, since Jewish workers suffered hardships all over the Empire, not just in Poland, they had to unite independently to work together with the parties of the peoples among whom they dwelt. If they did not, they would become fragmented and would be forced to follow the non-Jewish parties, an extremely unfortunate development that could not lead to real rights for the Jews.[141]

These arguments were forged of the Bund's traditional internationalism and its new national concerns. At the end of 1902 the Bundists could stress their growing strength and challenge what they considered the cavalier nationalism of the PPS by pointing out that in some towns the so-called indigenous populations were minorities living among the Jews.[142] Although by this time the Bund's national orientation was well known, the Bundists could still quite properly argue their own international position as against the national priorities of the Poles. In addition, the recent pogrom at Czestochowa had released the hostile feelings that lurked just beneath the surface of Jewish-Christian relations, prompting *Di Arbeter Shtime* to say with passion: "When we Jews have to endure various assaults from the government...we treat it as a common, customary matter.... [At Czestochowa, however] we were insulted and assaulted by persons...as impoverished and rightless as ourselves. That could deceive many of us workers, conceal the true reasons for this event, and raise hostile feelings."[143]

When the PPS responded to the Bundists, it took cognizance of their strengthened national point of view. Zaks viewed that trend as vindication of his party's national position and as evidence of the unsatisfactory answer of the Social Democrats to the national question, even though the Bundists had not yet recognized the principle of Polish independence. The investigation of the national question in the Bundist journals abroad was added proof of the direction in which they were moving.[144] Meanwhile, Zaks indicated, the Bund's indecision was inexcusable. Why did it not speak out on such an important matter as Polish independence? Its endless hesitation demonstrated a negative attitude. Indeed, all its arguments leaned toward the negative; it favored other Polish parties over the PPS, and it ignored the culture and conditions of the people among whom it worked. For that matter the Bundists showed more sympathy for the Finns than they did for either the Poles or the Lithuanians. Zaks dwelt at length on the alleged unfair treatment of the Poles by the Bund.[145]

The PPS's criticism raised disturbing questions. The Bund's indecision was difficult to explain. Lenin, for instance, found the Fourth Congress's "it's-none-of-my-business" position with respect to the Polish frontiers a matter of taking the line of least resistance rather than a stand on principle.[146] The PPS itself sensed (correctly perhaps) one reason for the Bund's reactions: "The majority of Lithuanian Jews do not like Poles in general. The memories of the old days, when every Polish nobleman...could oppress and humiliate the Jews, still lives among them."[147] The historical antagonism of the two cultures was not so readily overcome. The Bundists may indeed have found it easier to praise the distant Finns than their close neighbors, though the Bund journals contained a goodly share of news about Polish activities. Certainly, the imperious tone of the PPS and its insistence on its own demands, together with its stated lack of regard for the Bund, did nothing to heal the old wounds.

In any event the Bundists were in a good ideological position to attack the

PPS on the familiar Social Democratic grounds of opposition to nationalism, or "social patriotism." To the Poles' charge that the Bund discriminated against them by not approving a Polish democratic republic while upholding a Russian one,[148] the Bundists countered with the argument that their position was an international one; the Russian Social Democrats considered themselves to be internationalists, despite an unconscious Great Russian emphasis at times. A Russian democratic republic involved all the peoples of the Empire and a successful struggle against the Autocracy. A Polish democratic republic merely involved the peoples of historic Poland and suggested a struggle against the Russians as well as the Autocracy. The Bund's arguments on this point were not affected by the split with the RSDWP, since the question of the ultimate goal of a Russian republic was never at issue.

The Bund's national and organizational aims also worked against unity with the Poles. It would retain its unity in an unfragmented Russia, and the Jewish proletariat would be the stronger as a consequence. For the RSDWP the class war came first; all decisions on national and territorial divisions had to be postponed until the defeat of the Russian state.[149] The Bundists did not disagree with that view. In the end, after long discussions, they did not adopt a national point in their program before the Second RSDWP Congress, despite their desire for organizational independence and equality within the party on a national basis. With all their arguments with the Russians, the Bundists stood together with them in giving the class war priority over their own national goals. They thus saw the PPS as divisive and nationalist.

Though no major changes occurred in the stands of the two parties in 1903–4, the strength of the Bund and the relatively unsuccessful effort of the PPS to attract Jewish workers, plus the heating up of the political situation in Russia, led some in the PPS to rethink their position on the Bund. Pilsudski considered Zaks's concessions to the Bund too extensive: he tied its existence to its acceptance of the PPS program, in effect recognizing the Bundists.[150] Admitting the high quality of the Bund's organization,[151] Pilsudski suggested that the PPS response should be to clean its own house. In November 1903 he called on the PPS to improve relations with the Jewish workers by fighting anti-Semitism.[152]

The outbreak of the Russo-Japanese war prompted the PPS, like the Bund, to seek ways of increasing the strength of the revolutionary forces in the Empire through cooperation. As we have seen, the Bundists refused to participate in a PPS-sponsored meeting of all the national parties, instead inviting the PPS to meet with Social Democratic organizations to discuss joint work. But if the Poles were unable to entice the Bund to join their effort because of the nationalist character of their proposed conference, the Bundists were no more successful in interesting the PPS in their proposal because of political conflicts within the Polish revolutionary movement. As for the Bundists' refusal to participate with the PPS and other parties in the Paris meeting, the non-Marxist nature of that gathering had precluded any chance for direct involvement for the Social Democrats. Barriers between the various organizations were not easily bridged, even when conditions warranted rapprochement.

On the personal and local levels, relations between the Bund and the PPS were not always so bad as the generally hostile formal statements issued by both sides would indicate. As late as 1902 we find Pilsudski, one of the most militant and national-minded of the PPS leaders, meeting on friendly terms with his old acquaintance Kremer in London.[153] In some cases the Bundist and the Pepesovets made little distinction between their respective organizations and overlooked or were unaware of the differences in political program.[154]

Though there are instances of attempted and even successful cooperation at the local level in demonstrations and joint leaflets, there are also instances of flat refusal to act together.[155] All in all, the story was one of missed opportunities. Considering what might have been accomplished in Warsaw and other areas, the half-hearted attempts at cooperation yielded pitifully few rewards.

The fact is, there were other revolutionary parties in Poland that were ideologically closer to the Bund than the PPS. One was the party Proletariat, formed in 1900 (the third to bear that name). Like the PPS, it saw Polish independence as a worthy goal, but it disagreed with the PPS on the possibility of achieving independence in the near future. Consequently, Proletariat accepted the minimum demands of the Social Democrats—a constituent assembly and provisions for broad self-rule—which allowed it to work with both the Russian and the national Social Democratic organizations, including the Bund.* Unlike the PPS, Proletariat recognized the Bund as an independent organization. But compared with the PPS, it mustered few forces: its major influence was confined to Warsaw, where it slowly gained a following among Polish intellectuals over a period of years.[156]

The Bundists welcomed the new Polish party, though they disagreed with its acceptance of terror as a tactic.[157] But the two groups began to draw apart after the Second Congress of the RSDWP. At a conference in October 1903 the Polish party adopted certain resolutions that took the Bund by surprise. Though it accepted the Bund's views on program and organization, it moved toward *Iskra*'s views on the national question, which the Bund judged to be

* M. Mazovetsky, "Pis'ma iz Russkoi Pol'shi," *Vestnik Bunda*, 5 (Nov. 1904): 14. Mazovetsky (Mazowiecki) was the pseudonym of Ludwig Kulczycki, a member of Proletariat and a historian of the socialist movement in Poland. Sympathetic to the Bund, he wrote articles for its Polish-language journal, *Glos Bundu*, which were then translated into Russian for *Vestnik Bunda* (Mill, *Pionern*, 2: 144–45).

assimilatory.[158] Nevertheless, the accommodations of the moment were more significant than the vague aims of the future, and the support the two organizations gave one another was surely psychologically valuable to both, if meaningless in any practical sense.

When the Bundists and the Latvians began their efforts to draw the revolutionaries together in the spring of 1904, Proletariat was invited to participate. Later that year the party discussed its willingness to enter the RSDWP with the Russians. Plekhanov reported his conversation with Ludwig Kulczycki to that effect to the Council of the RSDWP.[159] Nothing resulted from their discussions. When the Bund-Latvian effort to arrange a meeting recommenced in late 1904 conflicts in the Polish revolutionary movement were a serious impediment. The PPS, finding its own invitation rejected, now laid down conditions for attendance, one of which was that Proletariat not be allowed to participate. Although the invitation to the PPS was withdrawn, no representatives of Proletariat attended the Riga meeting in January 1905.[160]

The Bund's relations with the Polish Social Democrats, close allies for a number of years, also began to worsen in 1903. The Social Democratic Party of the Kingdom of Poland (Socjaldemokracja Krolestwa Polskiego, SDKP or, more generally, PSD) had broken off from the PPS to become an independent entity in 1893 and had held its first congress the following year. The new party adopted the minimum program of the socialists in Russia, a liberal constitution with autonomy for Poland, and stressed close cooperation with the Russian movement. It rejected independence for Poland as a goal, a stand that brought it into head-on conflict with the PPS.[161]

Most of the ideological leaders of the PSD lived abroad, and it was largely with these émigrés that the Bund had ties in the 1890's (these dated back to the earliest pioneer days, Lev Jogiches serving as the primary link between the two movements). There was little opportunity for coordinated activity within the Empire, since few Polish Social Democrats were active at the local level in this period.[162] In late 1899 some Lithuanian Social Democrats under the leadership of Feliks Dzierżyński, who was close to the Bundists at the time, fused with the SDKP, which amended its name accordingly to the SDKPiL ("iL" standing for "and Lithuania"). Though the Polish Social Democrats did not achieve great numbers, they assumed an important place in the revolutionary movement in the Empire, particularly their intellectual forces. The Bund's Fourth Congress recognized the SDKPiL as an official Social Democratic party, with which the Bund might federate. In contrast, the Bundists were content merely to extend the hand of friendship to Proletariat as they would to any revolutionary socialist organization.[163]

At the turn of the century the Polish Social Democrats, especially those in Russia, held positions close to those expressed by the Bundists. In early 1901 they called for guarantees of full national self-determination within a democratic constitution. Further, they accepted the principle of federation for the all-Russian party.[164] At their Third Congress, in the summer of that year, they reasserted these demands and specifically endorsed the principle of a federated relationship with the Russian, Jewish, and Lithuanian proletarian organizations.[165] These actions brought cries from dissident PSD members of undue Bund influence within the organization.[166]

Heavily committed to internationalism, the SDKPiL leaders began to take a more negative line on the Bund in 1903. In this they were strongly influenced by the Iskraites, who were then in the process of preparing for the Second RSDWP Congress.* The Iskraites approached the PSD early in 1903 about participating in the forthcoming congress. They hoped to use the Polish party to break down the national and organizational positions of the Bund by robbing it of its status as the only non-Russian member group in the party and by demonstrating that other national Social Democratic organizations did not agree with the Bund.[167] The Polish leaders abroad showed increasing hostility toward the Bund as the year went along.[168] Liber reported to the Foreign Committee a conversation he had early in 1903 with Dzierżyński in which the Pole indicated the PSD was strongly against the Bund. The party would probably oppose federation if it was invited to the congress, he said.[169]

The Fourth Congress of the SDKPiL, which met in Berlin in July 1903 to decide what to do about the upcoming RSDWP congress, reversed several of its own congresses. Expressing their basic desire for a common Social Democratic organization for the whole Russian state, the delegates declared the problem of organizational form to be secondary and still open. But having so stated, they then proceeded to lay down conditions for the continued existence of their party that virtually duplicated the Bund's stand, though they carefully avoided using the word federation in their resolutions. The PSD sought full independence in matters involving agitation and organization in Poland and Lithuania, and wanted its own congresses, committees, name, and literature. It also demanded the right to absorb any other Polish socialist organization desiring to enter the RSDWP. These terms were presented as a *sine qua non* for uniting with the RSDWP.[170]

At the Second RSDWP Congress the Bundists, aware that the PSD was being used as an instrument against them, fought unsuccessfully to hold the Iskraites to their rules for admission to the congress. But Portnoy's motion calling for a declaration from the SDKPiL Congress specifying the Polish party's relationship to the RSDWP was overwhelmingly rejected (35 to eight, with five abstentions).[171] The Second Congress then approved (37 to six,

* Nettl, *Rosa Luxemburg*, 1: 272-73. The arrest in 1902 of Stanislaw Trusiewicz (K. Zalewski), who firmly opposed the extreme anti-national faction in the party, probably had something to do with the PSD's new position. *Ibid.*, p. 266; Krzhizhanovsky, p. 107.

with three abstentions) a motion of its commission to make the Poles invited guests, with a right to speak but no vote.[172]

As it turned out, the presence of the PSD delegates did not prove important or even harmful to the Bund. The Poles' terms were presented to the congress and referred to a commission for consideration over the objections of the Bundists, who wanted them discussed openly. Given the nature of the PSD conditions, the Bundists stood to gain from an open debate and the Iskraites to lose.[173]

In the end it was not the organizational problem but the national question that alienated the Poles from the RSDWP. The seventh point of the RSDWP draft program, which called for self-determination for all nationalities in the Empire, ran directly counter to the PSD's rejection of Polish independence as an immediate goal, a position it had adopted at its Fourth Congress in the hope of eroding the PPS's strength.[174] The SDKPiL had adopted a substitute formulation that would make "nationalistic" interpretations impossible. But the Polish delegates had hardly left their congress for the RSDWP meeting when Lenin published an article in which he held out the possibility of an independent Poland at some future time.[175] Rosa Luxemburg dispatched a letter (in the form of a declaration) asking that the point on self-determination be changed to a demand for "institutions guaranteeing full freedom of cultural development for all nationalities in the state."[176] The RSDWP would not accept it.

The Polish formulation of the national point pleased the Bundists, Medem in particular. He solicited the support of Adolph Warszawski (Warski), one of the two Polish delegates, for an amended motion combining "self-determination" and "institutions," but Warszawski refused. The PSD would brook no compromise, and its delegation soon departed. Medem's amended formula was later rejected by the congress.[177]

By its actions the PSD revealed its purpose at the meeting. It hoped to use the congress as a weapon against the PPS, not to serve as the RSDWP's weapon against the Bund. The Poles remained aloof from the Bund's problems, and later reproved the Bundists for not regarding the national point as crucial, as they did. In answer to that criticism Medem, recalling the fate of the national question at the Bund's Fifth Congress and his anguish at his inability to do more, writes: "We could only place our fate on those points in which we were certain the whole organization would back us like steel and iron."[178]

Though the PSD did not become an effective lever against the Bund, as the Iskraites had hoped, the decisions of the Poles' Fourth Congress and their increasingly hostile attitude disturbed the Bundists greatly. It seemed to them that the PSD's departure from the concept of federation endorsed at its previous congress indicated a deterioration of relations that could only be harmful to both organizations, a development the admittedly weak PSD could scarcely afford.[179]

Relations between the two groups remained strained after the Second Congress despite the similarity of many of their positions in fact if not in name.[180] Published accounts of what happened at the Second Congress only added to the growing antagonism. From Warszawski's report in the PSD press the Bundists learned how deeply the Poles resented the Bund's attempt to block both their access to the congress and their unification with the RSDWP. The Bundists returned the fire by pointing out the kinds of tactics *Iskra* had resorted to, attempting to gain entry for the PSD alone, while they themselves had tried to get other national Social Democratic parties invited as well. More painful to the Bundists, perhaps, was Warszawski's opinion that the Bund overvalued its political role in the "general economy of revolutionary forces."[181] This downgrading of their organization, it seemed to them, was in line with the attitude of the Russians, who were willing to make exceptions for the PSD because it was geographically separated from their area of work and did not attract forces from the Russian movement as the Bund did.*

As might be expected, the local PSD groups did not all take the same hard line as their intellectual leaders. The PSD did not compete with the Bund for the allegiance of Jewish workers, as the PPS and the RSDWP did; and the Bundists organized Polish workers only where the Polish revolutionaries left a vacuum that threatened their own activities.[182] At most the competition centered around the assimilated Polish-Jewish intellectuals, many of whom were PSD leaders. There was an occasional crossing over of lines, as in the case of Jakub Hanecki, a former Bundist who represented the PSD at the Second Congress, and in the other direction, Franz Kursky, who was once close to the Polish party.[183]

Cooperation between the Polish Social Democrats and the Bundists did not cease after the Second Congress. May 1, 1904, saw the banners of the Bund, the SDKPiL, and Proletariat raised together in Warsaw.[184] But it is all too clear from each group's hostile evaluations of the other's work that the relationship was on the whole an uneasy one.[185]

Mutual antagonism did not, however, prevent the Bundists from including the PSD in their effort to draw the revolutionary forces together in May 1904. The first attempt at contact came in July 1904. Then came a delay for the Social Democratic talks at Amsterdam. Finally, in December, the PSD responded to the new Bund-Latvian initiative. It objected to the invitation of the PPS, though it was willing to accept the PPS's presence if it left the Paris Bloc. Ultimately, the PSD rejected the invitation on grounds that it doubted

* Bund biblio.: *Vtoroi s''ezd*, pp. 53–54. Though Dimanshtein finds the PSD demands similar to the Bund's in many ways, he holds that the territorial factor made them qualitatively different (*Natsionale frage*, p. 48).

anything useful could be accomplished by groups with such antithetical aims and tactical views and, like the RSDWP, left the question of its attendance vague.[186] Its relations with the Bund were not at issue.

Despite the Bund's widespread contacts with the non-Jewish revolutionary parties after the Second Congress, little cooperation resulted. That strained relations over ideological points prevented practical working relationships indicates the fundamental weakness of the total movement, despite its vitality, and emphasizes the isolation of the Bund from the non-Jewish parties. Only the PPS and the RSDWP made a distinct effort to gain headway among the Jewish workers, and they did badly in this respect, whereas the Bund continued to grow. The Bund was in a good position to defend its work and purpose under the circumstances, the weakness of its opponents in its own region merely reaffirming its position. Unification would have had little effect on the Bund's position among the Jewish workers. From the Bund's point of view, closer ties with other parties would have done little more than salve some of its feeling of isolation and raise its hopes.

20. The Revolution of 1905

On Sunday, January 9, 1905, the workers of the Putilov plant in St. Petersburg, led by the Orthodox priest Father G. A. Gapon, approached the Tsar's Winter Palace to present a petition of their grievances.* Instead of a royal audience, they were met with gunfire from the troops guarding the palace. Bloody Sunday, as the event became known, initiated a wave of strikes and protests that marked the opening phase of the Revolution of 1905. Spreading throughout the country, the unrest gave way to bolder demonstrations and finally to a social and political revolt that cracked the foundations of autocratic Russia.

The crisis forced the revolutionaries to review their positions. They had to evaluate their own strength and their relationship to the aroused social forces they hoped to guide and control; and to weigh their chances of fulfilling their aims against the risk of failure. Heady at the prospect of realizing their dreams, they greeted the new challenges with enormous enthusiasm and vigor. Small wonder, then, that when the Revolution was over and their goals had not been met, many of them were exhausted for years, or completely burned out.

The news of the events in St. Petersburg spread quickly. The turn-out of scores of thousands of Russian workers on the streets of the capital had no precedent in the history of the Russian revolutionary movement. The radicals were overwhelmed, certain that a cataclysm was imminent, that the moment for which they had lived and dreamed for so many years was at hand.

The mood among the Bund leaders was electric. Abramovich, who had left St. Petersburg several days before Bloody Sunday for a meeting with the Central Committee in Dvinsk, had there described the preparations for the Sunday demonstration, which had been no secret. The committee commissioned him to write a leaflet immediately.[1] Abramovich took a tone well suited to the high drama of the moment. Beginning with a ringing salutation ("Comrades! On the streets of St. Petersburg the first barricades have been

---

* Gapon had been organizing the St. Petersburg workers for several years with the knowledge of the government.

built. Three hundred thousand workers have gone into the streets to demand freedom, to fight for freedom, and to die for freedom"), he continued:

We have fought in the name of socialism for many years, and we have fought against the power of capital for many years, and we have for many years not ceased to lead the struggle against the autocracy, which has answered all our demands with whippings, bullets, pogroms, and massacres. We have flooded the earth of Russia with our blood, and now freedom is blooming from this earth.

The great day has come! *The revolution has come!* It began in St. Petersburg and will set the whole country on fire with its flame. Either we will gain our freedom or we will die!...Comrades in all towns, take up the battle! Throw down your work in the shops, in the factories....Let everyone go into the street and unfurl the red flag!

Attack the stores where arms are sold! Everyone get a gun, a revolver, a sword, an ax, a knife! Arm yourselves! If you are attacked by the Tsar's soldiers you will be able to defend yourselves like soldiers of the revolution.

Remember that life in prison is harder than dying in battle!

Let every street become a battlefield!...Let us give up the blood of our hearts and receive the rights of human beings![2]

The Foreign Committee, trying to convey the delirium of the moment, published part of an emotional letter from a young woman worker in Dvinsk in *Posledniia izvestiia*: "I don't know where to begin....Oh, if I could meet with you...I could then die in peace—I would die with the knowledge that we met at the most important moment of life....But that is impossible.... If I remain among the living, good; if not—goodbye, be well!"[3] Here was the spirit of a crusader prepared to do battle in a holy war. There was no sense of a minor skirmish in either document, but rather the emotion surrounding a supreme effort in the revolutionary struggle and the desire to offer a final sacrifice to win.

The local Bund committees, no less enthusiastic, hastened to make as much capital as possible of the events in St. Petersburg. Within days, either alone or with other revolutionary parties, they organized meetings, demonstrations, and strikes, and issued leaflets calling for general protest.

As always, the ability to mobilize the workers varied greatly from committee to committee. The most dramatic effort came in Riga, where what began as a general strike called on January 11 by the Bund and other revolutionary organizations ended in bloodshed. On January 12, the first day of the strike, some 20,000 demonstrators heeded the call of the Federated Committee. The next day the number rose to an estimated 50,000–60,000, including 7,000–8,000 Jews, though Riga was outside the Pale. A special strike commission was chosen by the Latvian party and the Bund, which the RSDWP organization joined on January 15.[4]

The first objective of the strike was to bring everything to a halt. Striking workers moved from factory to factory to see that all work stopped. But the activists went further. Attempts were made to acquire arms—there was even talk of attacks on police stations—and violence ensued. Although the figures of the police and the Bund on the dead and wounded do not agree, both sets of statistics indicate the grim determination of the strikers. By the Bund's reckoning, on the second day of the strike, January 13, government troops killed over 30 workers and badly wounded 70 others.*

Local officials were thoroughly alarmed. But the strike did not signal an all-out insurrection. On January 20, the Riga strike commission decided to end the political strike and to concentrate on economic issues, demanding an eight-hour day, higher pay, and wages for days missed through strikes. The Bundists were well satisfied with the results of this decision, for many shopowners acceded in some part to the demands. Indeed, certain government officials stepped in to persuade the employers to make concessions.[5]

Events in the small town of Krinki, in the province of Grodno, followed a different course. There, the Bund leaders formed a committee with the Polish Social Democrats, which decided to halt all work and to attack government offices. On January 17, the federated committee mobilized a meeting of 1,500 workers, a remarkable number in so small a town. Moving into the center of town with their fight groups at the fore, the demonstrators captured the post office, cut all communications with the outside world, and wrecked the police station and its records. They then helped themselves to arms and supplies, leaving the town, as the Bundists expressed it, "clean." The police promptly disappeared. The Bundists seem to have been reluctant to touch the funds in the post office, but the local anarchists apparently had no such qualms and helped themselves liberally. In the end, the Bundists gave in and took 80 rubles.[6]

The following day troops arrived, retook the town without a fight, and arrested several hundred persons. The governor of the province, A. V. Lastochkin, acknowledged the seriousness of the situation in Krinki, reporting that it was the only major disturbance in the whole province.[7] In contrast to Riga, where the burden of prosecuting the strike fell on Latvian shoulders, the Bund here played the principal role. If the Krinki activists, whether out of a sense of being away from the center of events or merely in an awareness of the futility of engaging government troops, surrendered the gains of the previous day without a struggle, they had nevertheless exhibited a new daring and willingness to go beyond a simple demonstration, though the time for a do-or-die battle had plainly not arrived.

* *Di Arbeter Shtime*, supplement to 39 (March 1905): 8. According to the police report, 22 demonstrators were killed and 60 were wounded, 20 of them mortally. On the other side there were eight soldiers wounded, two of whom eventually died. *Revoliutsiia: Ianvar'-Mart*, pp. 496–97.

The Riga and Krinki cases were great successes compared with the activities elsewhere. In Warsaw, an old center of revolution, the various groups were unable to mobilize their forces in a like effort. The news of Bloody Sunday arrived there January 10. By January 12 a leaflet had been distributed, and the day after the revolutionary organizations discussed a unified effort. But the Polish Social Democrats could not bring themselves to work with the PPS, whose membership in the Paris Bloc had further exacerbated relations between the two camps. Thus, though the moment was one of enormous revolutionary significance, cooperation was restricted to Warsaw's Social Democrats; and even then the special commission set up by the Bund and the PSD did not work.

December 1904 had been a month of crisis in Warsaw, so that by January 12 the Jewish workers were in a revolutionary mood. The Bund, anxious to retain its control over them, felt it had to respond quickly with a general strike. But the commission could not agree on when the strike was to be called and also differed over the distribution of a leaflet. The Bundists felt their participation was useless, and their representative left. Nevertheless, the organizations, including the PPS, were aware of each other's plans. The strike began on the fourteenth, a Friday. In the familiar pattern, groups of workers went from shop to shop, closing down those that were still operating. Sunday, it was hoped, would be the greatest day of the "revolt." All the organizations agreed to hold a demonstration. But the presence of a considerable body of troops, in addition to the police, made large gatherings impossible. The workers were unable to build barricades and mostly demonstrated without any real leadership. The Bundists held several meetings of 200–300 workers, but these too were set upon by the troops. Few workers were armed, and those who looked for guns had small success.[8]

The frustration of the Warsaw Committee of the Bund at the dismal outcome of the day of "revolt" comes through clearly in the words of the report it filed the next day: "What does one do? All the material was present by which great revolutionary acts are carried out; the masses are there, ready to make the greatest sacrifices, the mood is there, the consciousness is there. And yet it is not possible to do anything."[9] In the following days, though the workers' spirits remained high, the situation began to quiet down. The committee had nothing new to report. The authorities, for their part, assigned great importance to the course of events in Warsaw, attributing the lack of serious disorder to their preparedness.[10]

The first outburst of revolution lasted only a few weeks. According to the reports of 35 Bund organizations in *Di Arbeter Shtime*, all of the major general strikes called in protest of Bloody Sunday were over or were ending by the last week of January. At the same time, it was evident to many of the Bund groups that the crisis was not over, for new strikes were beginning. The unrest thus had to be considered by the revolutionary organizations as part of a continuing confrontation.

Exactly what the Bund expected in the train of the January events is not clear. The Central Committee's first leaflet suggests it saw an immediate fight to the finish. In it the Bund leaders demanded a democratic republic with a constituent assembly and universal suffrage, civil and national rights, an eight-hour day, an end to the war with Japan, and the freeing of all political and religious prisoners.[11] But many local organizations did not (and could not) interpret the leaflet as instructions to initiate an all-out insurrection. The Zhitomir Committee, for example, observed in its report that the Central Committee had ordered "a general strike with the aim of protesting the Peters-burg events," that is, a political strike merely to show mass dissatisfaction.[12] The organization at Krinki probably interpreted the Central Committee's instructions in much the same way, even though the demonstrators went further and seized government buildings. Despite the unparalleled call to action in the committee's fiery leaflet, the demands made were more in the nature of an immediate reflex than a deliberate plan of insurrection. No one knew how far events might go in the days after January 9, and the Bund, with all its splendid spirit and organization, would scarcely have considered leading an insurrection on its own.

The performance of the Bund throughout the entire revolutionary year of 1905 must be judged in the context of the geographic region in which it operated. The varying fortunes of local committees were naturally tied to the revolutionary and popular resources at hand. Suicidal adventures were not the Bund's way, and revolutionary conflict in 1905 was based largely on local resources, even when the issues were national in scope.

Revolutionary action in the western provinces of Russia, the Bund's region, was well organized and zealous. The Polish, Latvian, and Jewish revolution-aries did not lag behind the Russians in their fervor and determination. Over 400,000 workers struck in Russia during January; of this total, the Polish province of Petrokow (and its major city, Lodz) contributed some 100,000, Warsaw over 47,000, and Latvia over 43,000. In Petrokow province some 650 plants were struck, in Warsaw 417, and in Latvia about 275, mostly in Riga. In Moscow, by contrast, only 134 plants were shut down.[13]

Though St. Petersburg was undeniably the initiating point for the Revolu-tion, its workers and leaders were distinctly less rebellious than those in the west. V. N. Kokovtsov, the Minister of Finance, summed up the general situation for the Tsar a week after Bloody Sunday. The St. Petersburg work-ers were calming down, he noted; and in Moscow the strikes were neither especially large (he estimated the number of strikers there at 20,000) nor especially stubborn. Less happily, he found, "the state of affairs in the western regions of the Empire appears far more serious, particularly in the Baltic

and the western region of the Vistula." The situation there was one of determined resistance and armed clashes. Kokovtsov singled out for special
mention the strikes in Lodz and Warsaw, the result, it seemed to him, of
"highly developed social revolutionary propaganda." At the time of his report,
January 16, he saw no signs of abatement in the mood of the workers there.[14]
On the Social Democratic leadership in the Empire, the Bund report on the
immediate response to January 9 noted pointedly: "The provinces are distinguishing themselves with their consciousness and discipline, being in this
respect far ahead of the chief cities. In the provinces the most important role
in the movement is being played by the borderlands (especially in the west),
where the masses are heeding the voices of Social Democracy."[15] In the center
of Russia, the Bundists judged, it seemed to be a case of either legal organizations or a movement without leadership. Why was it a Father Gapon who
rallied the St. Petersburg workers and wrote their petition to the Tsar?
Where were the St. Petersburg organizations, Menshevik or Bolshevik?

The Bundists were delighted with the quality of their work in January
in comparison to that of the Russians. They contended that the Jewish
workers had displayed a good revolutionary education and, indeed, that they
had come so far as to merit recognition as an independent political movement
—which had developed, the Bundists were careful to add, "under the flag
of the Bund." Holding up their own achievements against the Russian Social
Democrats' claims of control, the Bundists pointed out that "not only did
Social Democratic ideas rule the workers' heads, but Social Democracy itself
...as a real live *organization* was at one with the masses on the streets and
in the shops."[16] The Bundists believed the past days had proved that organizations having "a strong organic tie with the daily life and the struggle of
the masses" alone could gain "a permanent influence" and lead the proletariat.
Had not the Bund been able to both call workers out on strike and send them
back to work?[17]

All the same, the Bund leaders recognized that this was no time for
complacency, and promptly called a conference to reexamine their immediate
goals and tactics in light of the new developments. This was the Sixth Conference, which met in Dvinsk from February 11 through February 17 and
comprised 25 persons.[18]

Unlike all previous conferences, the Sixth Conference included elected delegates,* reflecting the Central Committee's trust in the local committees in this
most urgent of moments. Additional evidence of the close interaction between
the center and the local bodies is found in the Central Committee's preparations for the discussions. Before making any decision, it wanted a report from

---

* Mikhalevich, *Zikhroinos*, 2: 128. Since Abramovich was an invited participant, the
committee apparently did not follow uniform procedures in the selection of delegates.

each committee on the past weeks' accomplishments. Specifically, it wanted to know what action each committee had taken, approximately how many Jewish and non-Jewish workers had participated, what had been done to win over the non-Jewish workers, and what mistakes had been made.[19]

The discussions at the conference centered on three questions:[20] what was the meaning of the January events; what political line should be adopted "to give the masses...slogans that would tie them to the general political developments in the country";[21] and what procedures would permit the broadest possible organization for the future. The continuing strikes and high spirit of the workers kept the focus of the Sixth Conference on tasks related to a renewed outbreak of hostilities.

This time the weaknesses of the organization, which had been recognized but largely left undealt with by earlier Bund meetings, could not be ignored. As *Di Arbeter Shtime* put it: "It became obvious that they [the organizations] were not well suited enough for the leadership of a proletarian movement that began spontaneously; that they were unable to make use of mighty expression of revolutionary zeal." To acquire the strength necessary for what seemed to be the last fight with absolutism, the Bund had to attract the broadest possible support within the Jewish community.

On a tactical level, the conference spelled out some of the methods for success. Local institutions had to be strengthened, and leadership talent had to be spread out more equally among the organizations. Apparently the range of response from success to failure made its impression on the delegates. The conference was aware of the relatively narrow emphasis on which previous work had been based and noted that some leading activists had to be freed to deal with the unorganized masses. Finally, the number of meetings and armed demonstrations had to be increased.

The conference also took cognizance of the possibility of open insurrection. It suggested that the local organizations obtain arms, teach their members to use them, and urge them to resist not only the police, but even the military. As in the past, it advocated the building of special forces to lead the resistance.

The Bund's lack of solid links with the non-Jewish population disturbed the conferees. The January events had demonstrated that the revolutionary movement had failed to reach its full potential because of "the revolutionary passivity of the broad masses of the non-Jewish proletariat and the fact that [the Bund had] no permanent ties with them." The Bundists assigned the blame for this failure to the other Social Democratic organizations, which had no influence among the masses, and felt that the extraordinary moment called for extraordinary measures. What properly should be handled by separate organizations in normal time the Bund was now prepared to take on. The conference proposed that groups of non-Jewish workers be organized "under the control of the committees," for the purpose of "spreading literature among the non-Jewish proletariat" and "establishing permanent ties with these working masses." The revolutionary moment was pushing the Bund out of the narrow role of leader of a national proletariat into the role of regional leader where necessary.

The same techniques for drawing the masses into the streets were to be used, but now every revolutionary manifestation was to be pushed to its limit. The most suitable instrument for broad participation was the general strike, a potent weapon that must surely weaken the industrial and cultural life of the Empire. When the opportunity arose, the conference insisted, "we must demonstrate, attack the administrative and governmental institutions and also the representatives of the administration and military if the removal of these representatives might be useful for the success of the revolutionary manifestation."[22] The special groups that were to lead these attacks were to be under the control of the committees but to be given as much independence as possible. Unity with other organizations, "except those that aim at disorganizing the Jewish proletariat," was altogether desirable. Nevertheless, all organizations had to remain independent, their unity being achieved through special joint committees of the type formed for the January strike action. Before mobilizing a mass protest, the committees must discuss their plans with Social Democratic groups that had influence among the non-Jewish workers. Agreements were to be made with non–Social Democratic organizations only in the case of a planned open demonstration, only if they had standing in the non-Jewish community, and only if they too called for a constituent assembly based on a democratic election.

Anticipating the possibility of government concessions in the form of special commissions to consider the needs of the workers, the conference recommended that the workers participate only on condition the state guaranteed both their personal safety and their right to vote. It regarded elections for such commissions as an opportunity for Social Democratic workers to agitate and put forth their minimum program, a democratic government. When the commissions failed, as they surely must, since they would undertake only half-measures, the workers would be shown once again that legal reform was impossible under the existing political system.

The Bund looked forward to a long period of unrest after January, the first stage of the revolution. The Central Committee's report on the conference rhapsodized: "Such a feeling was not awakened by the Rostov [strike of November 1902], nor the strikes in southern Russia. We felt immediately a storm had risen [in St. Petersburg] that was matchless in its fury."[23] The final reckoning with the Autocracy looked to be at hand.

The Empire-wide explosion that followed Bloody Sunday shook the Russian state as no other event since the assassination of Alexander II in 1881. Sviatopolk-Mirsky was one of its first political victims. His political "Spring," which had "begun as an idyl, was ending in a bloody tragedy."[24] Mirsky was dismissed on January 15, to be replaced by A. G. Bulygin, an administrator of exceedingly modest talent.[25]

The government, quite typically, dealt with the grievances that had flared up so dramatically with simultaneous sternness and conciliation. High-ranking officials made improving the conditions of the urban worker their first order of business. Zubatov's former superior, General D. F. Trepov, now the newly appointed governor-general of St. Petersburg and a favorite of the Tsar, tried to get the monarch to step in directly to calm the workers; and a special commission, which included elected workers from St. Petersburg, was set up under Senator N. V. Shidlovsky to deal with labor problems.

On a broader political stage, the Tsar issued two documents that made clear the ambivalent mood of the state. In a manifesto issued on February 18 he asked the Russian people to stand firm behind the throne. Later the same day he released a rescript to Interior Minister Bulygin, directing him to draft a plan that would allow popularly elected (and deserving) representatives to participate in the preparation of laws. This simultaneous call for support of the Autocracy and some form of popular representation produced considerable confusion. As Gurko points out, it permitted the supporters of the throne to emphasize the message of the manifesto and the regime's opponents to hail the Tsar's rescript as a first, if limited, step toward a government of the people.[26]

The publication of the rescript to Bulygin marked the beginning of a new political stage in the Revolution of 1905. Talk of a Duma, or parliament, dominated the political life of Russia until the disclosure of Bulygin's plan on August 6, 1905. The question was discussed quite freely at every level, though the government had probably not intended any such reaction. Political groups of every shade of opinion arose to take the fullest possible advantage of the relative freedom.

The Russian Social Democrats entered the Revolution of 1905 with their immediate political goals set. At the conference of Social Democratic organizations held in January 1905 in Riga, the participants named as their immediate aim a constituent assembly elected on the basis of the four-tailed formula of a universal, equal, direct, and secret vote; an end to the war; the freeing of all political and religious prisoners; and an eight-hour workday. In addition, the Social Democrats gave notice that they would demand of the constituent assembly a democratic republic; guarantees ensuring personal safety; the basic freedoms of speech, assembly, conscience, and press; the right to organize and strike; the end of all exceptional laws against nationalities; the right of nationalities to be educated in their own languages; the election of judges; a popular army; and the separation of church and state. These demands were endorsed by the RSDWP, the Bund, the Latvian Social Democratic Workers' Party, and the Revolutionary Ukrainian Party.[27]

Given this kind of minimum program, the timid first steps of the belea-guered regime could scarcely satisfy the Social Democrats. The Bund's Central Committee issued a leaflet denouncing the Tsar's rescript as a ruse to quiet the populace in a time of great crisis; the appeal to the "best people," the advisory character of the proposed assembly, and the absence of any sense of urgency showed how little significance there was in the Tsar's actions. The Bundists pointed out that the Tsar himself had said the foundations of the Empire had to remain untouched. The state was only playing a game.[28]

It was not a game for revolutionaries, however. Standing firm on the de-mand for a constituent assembly, the Central Committee insisted that even this would not "make peace between the Tsar and the people." The people's representatives must then "liquidate the old order completely and work out new forms."[29] The future looked bright to the Bundists, for who would have supposed a year earlier that the Tsar would make such concessions, trifling though they were. But in truth his concessions were altogether irrelevant. "We don't need a Tsar at all," the committee concluded. "We need a demo-cratic republic."[30]

When Bulygin's plan was released, the Bund's worse suspicions were con-firmed. Not only did he propose to restrict the franchise largely to the prop-ertied and the wealthy, but he wanted also to exclude those who did not speak Russian. And Poland, along with other areas, was to have special rules for the election. The Tsar's authority was to remain fixed in law, and the Duma to be merely "a special consultative legislative establishment."[31] It seemed clear to the Bundists that "Nicholas the Last" had only allowed this limited Duma to protect himself. He plainly had no intention of granting any real freedom, and the masses could expect nothing from his Duma.[32]

But the lack of positive content in the Bulygin plan did not end the matter for the Bund. The Duma's very existence threatened the workers' struggle, for even these paltry concessions might be tempting to those who might bene-fit from them, namely, the industrial bourgeoisie and the liberals. The in-dustrial leaders were bound to be pleased at the thought of an end to labor unrest. And some liberals might consider the project a useful first step, a device with which they could "steal a constitutional regime in such a way that Tsarism would not notice."[33] Through this small gift the government could pacify these groups, defeat the proletariat, and then disperse the Duma at its pleasure.

What, then, was to be done about Bulygin's Duma? Since such a feeble instrument was of no use to the forces of revolution, the election of the Duma representatives had to be stopped. Only through continuing revolutionary activity would the workers' demands be met, the Bundists argued; hence revolutionaries had to fight anything that would help restore peace and order at this moment. Liberals who accepted the Bulygin proposal must be treated as traitors and defenders of Tsarism; and those who did not must be pushed "further to the left." The broadest segments of the population, the petit bourgeoisie and the peasants, must be made to see the emptiness of the "victory." The revolutionary workers must not only employ established methods of protest, but attend all election assemblies—break in if necessary. They had to boycott the elections actively, which meant using "all means allowed us by Social Democratic tactics in order to stop the elections from taking place." Finally, they must prepare for "an armed people's uprising," should it come to that.[34]

The Bundists saw certain useful by-products in the anti-Duma campaign. The greater the pressure brought to bear against the Bulygin plan, they reasoned, the less enthusiastic the wealthy would be about supporting it. And where it did gain the support of the rich, its nature would be all the more clear to the people. An active boycott would awaken self-reliance among the masses, heightening their revolutionary mood and class consciousness. If the Duma could be destroyed, the people would once again be brought face to face with the regime, and revolution would again be a real possibility. In the last analysis, resistance to the Bulygin Duma promised the quickest and greatest amount of change.[35]

The Bund now accepted the revolutionary situation in terms of the minimum Social Democratic political goals of a constituent assembly and a democratic republic. Shifting from a distant apocalyptic expectation to a present possibility, the Bundists intensified every form of work known to them after January. But the problem was how to take advantage of the enhanced opportunities of the post-January period. The Sixth Conference declared that revolution required action on a broad scale, necessitating a coordinated effort beyond accepted organizational boundaries. Operationally, this meant coordination at every level: inside the Bund, among the various parties, and most important, with the unorganized masses—the single force capable of bringing off the revolution. To reach and radicalize these masses—"to maintain a constant condition of stormy anger"—all efforts were now directed to this goal.[36]

Popular unrest did not die out after January. The strike continued to be the most important expression of dissatisfaction, providing both a broad-based form of action and a powerful springboard for escalation. Between February and October the Empire was shaken by successive waves of strikes. February was a month of high activity, though the level was considerably below that of January. After a further decline in strikes in March, the level of activity rose again in April, reached a sharp peak in May, then fell in the summer months, reaching a low point in September. But this was the proverbial calm before the storm, for in October close to half a million workers went out on strike.[37]

Two facts attest to a new political mood among the urban workers. One is that over half the strikers in the entire January–October period engaged in political rather than economic strikes. The second is the coincidence of political strikes with the highest levels of strike activity (in January, April, May, and October), and the coincidence of economic strikes with the lowest levels (in March, July, and September).[38]

As in January the provinces where the Bund was strongest were the scenes of massive strikes. Lodz, Riga, Vilna, and Belostok were all in the forefront of the strike movement, along with the two border centers of Baku and Tiflis.[39] Petrokow province, incorporating the city of Lodz, led the Empire in number of strikes (2,316 as compared with St. Petersburg's 1,861), and was second only to Latvia in percentage of workers participating (95.1 per cent against 97 per cent in Latvia).[40] In the other provinces of the northwest the percentage of workers who joined in was as follows: Kovno, 82.1; Vilna, 81.4; Grodno, 79.9; Minsk, 66.2; Vitebsk, 54.3; Mogilev, 47.5; and Warsaw, 40.7.[41]

Strikes among Jewish workers reflected the general pattern. The Bund press carried a steady stream of reports of new outbreaks in town after town.[42] Workers often lashed out on their own initiative, fired with new confidence in their own power, which was further fueled by the authorities' hesitancy to act. In the first few months after Bloody Sunday the government sought rapprochement with the workers and persuaded a number of employers to settle with their workers or at least to get the strikers to the bargaining table with factory inspectors and the police, a situation reminiscent of the Zubatov days.[43] The Bundists attempted to counter this "soft" approach by trying to convince the workers of the compromising nature of the state's tactics.

In the early days of the Revolution some of the Bundists, their eyes fixed on a higher revolutionary goal, questioned the value of economic strikes, feeling that they depleted energies vital to the political conflict. Most changed their view, however, when it became apparent that economic action produced the mood for political action.[44] Taking advantage of that mood, Bund agitators attended every strike meeting and were usually able to dominate the proceedings. The unprecedented scale of worker involvement gave the Bundists the access to the masses they had dreamed of so long.

From February to October the Bund gradually achieved the peak of its influence among the Jewish workers, who had to be impressed with its ability to organize meetings and provide illegal literature, its disciplined cadres prepared to lead or guide militant protests, and not least its paramilitary defense groups ready to protect such actions and help prevent reprisals in the Jewish community. Along with other organizations, the Bund also helped the striking workers financially. In January a meeting of revolutionary organizations in Vilna allotted the Bund Committee 150 rubles a day for strikes, double the amount granted the other four parties together.[45] In Warsaw, in the heated days of October, the local organization obtained tax records and imposed levies on Jewish taxpayers in behalf of striking workers. The Bund even had its own facilities for distributing food at that point.[46]

The Bundists penetrated new shops, reaching workers who had once been inaccessible. At times the agitators were invited in by workers who had heard of the Bund and wished it to lead or organize their strikes. By some reports the very invocation of the Bund's name influenced the outcome of strikes, forcing concessions from employers.[47] The Bund's use of the boycott against uncooperative shopowners proved a potent tool, as this apology from one Warsaw employer attests: "Recognizing that the boycott placed on me by the Bund as a result of my disgraceful behavior toward the workers (beating and even turning several of them over to the police) is fully deserved; ... and wanting to remove that ugly stain, I turn to the Warsaw Committee of the Bund with a request to remove the boycott, and I give my approval in advance to whatever demands the Bund may make."[48] Taking advantage of the economic strike, the Bund now extended its real power to the limits of the strike movement itself.

Withal, the Bundists never lost sight of their political goals, and they tried to turn each meeting and demonstration, regardless of its origin, to political purpose. Every effort was made to convert public gatherings for funerals, holiday celebrations, and the like into political manifestations. With the new level of public participation the Bund had opportunities to push its political goals as never before. Where once the purpose of meetings and demonstrations had been to educate the masses to issues and discipline, they were now called "to square accounts" with Tsarism. By May the Bundists were claiming that "the greater part of our work is carried out in the open."[49]

The birzhe continued to be an important outlet for Bund activity. The street markets grew in size and significance, some becoming almost a territorial base under BO protection. At countless birzhe meetings (some with as many as 1,000 participants) the Bund distributed its literature and rallied the gathered workers to one form of protest or another.[50] Through the early months of 1905 the police took little action against these street throngs, fearing to intrude, and the military was indifferent or at least passive. But once the state began to take a firmer stand against acts of rebellion in the summer months, the birzhes came under strong attack. These onslaughts met armed resistance and even on occasion hastily thrown-up barricades.[51]

The political manifestations growing out of these clashes form the most dramatic page in the Bund's history as a revolutionary organization. Neither the pioneer period, with its mystery of underground origin and anonymity, nor the subsequent period of economic work among the Jewish workers, with all its small victories, can match the glamor of the turbulent months of 1905. For thousands of Bundists and Bund sympathizers, the exhilaration of political revolution, open and visible, and the personal participation in a heroic struggle made those few short months their moment in history.

In contrast to the feverish activity that followed each sudden turn of events, the Bund's May Day plans were carefully laid out well in advance. The Bund leaders had no thought of making the celebration a signal for an uprising, but chose merely to use it to explain where matters stood. The Central Committee's traditional leaflet reviewed the year's events, pointing out the current weakness of Tsarism as compared with a year earlier. "The coming year," it predicted, "will put an end to political slavery," with the working class leading the way. "We have written a golden page in the history of the Jewish workers' movement," the committee proclaimed, calling for a celebration in which "we will all leave our factories [and] come forth under our red proletarian flags. Our workers' holiday will be a holiday of struggle."[52]

Preparations began more than a month before May 1 (April 18, O.S.). Looking back some days after the event, the Bund leaders decided that they had to work still harder—even though their efforts and the general revolutionary consciousness were clearly greater than in previous years.[53] This was a simple acknowledgment that the vast growth of the stage on which the revolution was playing itself out had stretched their technical and manpower resources to the limit. Moreover, as we shall see, the state and conservative forces launched a counterattack aimed particularly at the Jews and the Bund, creating problems of unprecedented gravity.

Despite the Bundists' own rather harsh assessment of their May Day accomplishments, they had a certain success. Meetings of 20,000 and more workers took place in half a dozen cities of the Pale, these in addition to the activities in the birzhes. Scores of meetings were held in the streets, in many cases the first celebrations not held secretly in the woods; scores of others were held in synagogues and factories.[54] There were in fact too many and the organizations too busy to report them all.

May 1 was one of the revolutionary peaks of 1905. Nevertheless, the workers did not try or expect to own the streets. Indeed, before the holiday the Central Committee suggested to the local organizations that celebration by general strike, which is to say, absence from the streets, would be sufficient if local conditions did not warrant open demonstration. It also suggested that the Bundists hold off their demonstrations until after Easter to reduce the chances of a pogrom.[55]

The Bund press carried reports from some 80 towns and cities detailing the day's events.[56] There were disappointments, to be sure, but also pleasant surprises. The leaders were extremely proud, for example, that thanks to strikes "literally all Warsaw came to a halt."[57] Lodz, less fortunately, was the scene of demonstrations marked by considerable violence. Kovno had both strikes and demonstrations.[58] The stories of the events in each city would fill volumes in their own right; suffice it to say that the Bund accomplished its general purpose—to demonstrate the solidarity of the working class under difficult conditions. The May Day preparations had been aimed specifically at a limited manifestation, and the succeeding weeks saw a decline in total activity, though not to the pre-May level for some months.

The rapidly growing influence of the Bund turned it into something of a state within a state. Its activists were well known in their communities, and in fact began to be called on for advice on matters far out of their field. "Divorce, dowries, a falling-out between business partners, a swindled speculator, a shamed girl, a family dispute, the complaints of a servant girl about her employer—all sorts of matters were brought there [to the birzhe], and it was impossible to refuse help, to say that it would be better to go to the rabbi."[59] In Gomel and other cities Little Bund groups now fought the police with all the ferocity of their elders, took casualties, and became firmly linked with the adult Bund.[60] Says Litvak:

The authority of the Bund in Warsaw and in all Poland [in 1905] was very great, not only among the workers but among the great mass of the petit bourgeoisie and intelligentsia. It was regarded as some kind of mystical being, with fear and hope. It could achieve everything, reach everyone.... The word of the Bund was law; its stamp worked like hypnosis. Wherever an injustice, wherever an insult, even when it had no relation to the workers' movement, ... one came to the Bund as to the highest tribunal. . . . It was legendary. But there was something mighty in the history of the Bund in those years that aroused and fed the legend; and the legend, for its part, doubled the power of the Bund.[61]

These are the words of a dedicated Bundist, of course; there were certainly Jews in the Pale who were untouched by revolutionary events, and others who adhered to rival parties and even fought the Bund. But Litvak was a fairly sensitive observer, and we can suppose there is a core of truth here. Furthermore, he is not alone in making this claim. Hear Raphael Abramovich, for example: "When I went into one of our [Bund] towns, I used to feel like the representative of a great power that was well-loved and supported by the working masses and the intelligentsia alike."[62] By demonstrating its willingness and ability to act at a time when traditional agencies broke down, the Bund gained a standing in the Jewish community that no other organization could match.

Hardly had the post-May wave of political activity begun to subside when the news of the Bulygin Duma broke, introducing another, more intense round of political discussion. The Bund immediately took its case against the Duma to the people, exhorting them in leaflets and at meetings to reject the empty gesture. This campaign prompted wide discussion of the subject throughout the Pale, notably in Warsaw, Belostok, Gomel, Dvinsk, and

Kovno, and in a number of cities Bund meetings led to declarations of support for the organization's position.[63]

In October a new crisis arose in the form of the greatest wave of strikes yet, following the announcement of the ratification of the Treaty of Portsmouth on the third. In Gurko's opinion that announcement, which officially ended the Russo-Japanese war, also ended any sense of patriotic moral obligation the war may have imposed on the Russians.[64] Strikes broke out in St. Petersburg on October 4 and quickly took on a political cast. The whole country was soon ignited. The chief instigators were the railroad workers, who held "the veins of capitalism" in their hands. The hostile Gurko presents this picture of the state of affairs in the capital. "Slowly but surely they [the strikes] affected nearly every public utility service.... By October 10 nearly all the working population of St. Petersburg was on strike.... The striking workers crowded the central parts of the city and organized noisy meetings. The Cossack patrols and the mounted police were powerless to prevent such gatherings."[65]

Meanwhile, the rest of the country had begun to churn. Again from Gurko: "News from the *gubernias* [provinces] told tales of similar occurrences in many other cities.... The railroad strike, in accord with orders from St. Petersburg, spread ... over the entire network and paralyzed the economic life of the country."[66] In Moscow all the factories were on strike by October 15, and there was no electricity or transportation. Other Muscovites soon went out: "The zemstvo and city employees ... actors of the Imperial theater, druggists, physicians, and the students of secondary schools all joined the strike."[67] By one estimate just under a half million people went into the streets, three-fourths of them in support of political demands.[68]

For the Bundists the October wave of strikes was the long-expected revolutionary impulse, the fruition of all their hopes and dreams. The actions of the Russian workers infused the entire revolutionary movement with new energy just when the months of strife seemed to have exhausted even the most dedicated radicals—September had marked the low point of strike activity in 1905.[69] Revitalized, the Bund organizations helped mobilize general strikes in a host of towns.

As in other periods of crisis the October strikes brought varying degrees of local success. Though no single party (or even the revolutionary parties taken as a body) could claim full responsibility for October's victory, the efforts of the Bundists in their own area of work plainly reached a high point during this crisis. It is important to note, too, that October was still only a general strike, a form of heavy pressure designed to extort reforms from the Tsarist regime, not an outright insurrection aimed at the seizure of power. Furthermore, even in the face of the most unified action yet on the part of its opponents, the Tsarist regime, eager as it was to calm the storm, was not prepared to give up the streets except where it was forced to do so by local circumstance.

Local success or failure depended on a number of factors. Plainly, the complete shutdown of factories and retail outlets for any period of time created serious problems. In Vilna, where the general strike started relatively early, food supplies soon ran short, and the local organization was forced to let the bakery workers break their strike so the hungry could be fed. With the daily life of the city at a virtual standstill workers gathered together or strolled the streets in what was an almost euphoric atmosphere. Still, military patrols were around and about, and desultory clashes between workers and soldiers brought casualties, more meetings, funerals, and the probability of further clashes. In Vilna the food shortage finally led to a halt of the strike on October 12, though the organizations there immediately began planning new action.[70] However potent a weapon, the general strike was of limited usefulness over the long haul.

In Vitebsk the Bund and the RSDWP called a general strike rather later than most—for October 17—and in a joint leaflet made it plain they were after not just a political strike, but a revolt. The police and the military moved to create a pogrom mood in order to forestall the strikers, using reservists as their weapon; and the revolutionary organizations then began mounting a self-defense campaign. Fortunately for all concerned the strike had no sooner begun that it was interrupted by news of the October Manifesto. An ugly situation at once turned into a victory celebration, with thousands of workers massed in the street to listen to the editor of the local newspaper read the manifesto.[71]

What must have been one of the most heartwarming experiences of the Bundists occurred in Gomel. In a strike that began there on October 13 the railroad workers moved independently of the Jewish workers, with the RSDWP organization able to do little about the matter. Violence broke out when government forces moved in. Both the SR's and the Bundists battled back with bombs. Just as the strike showed signs of collapsing because of the refusal of Christian shopkeepers to stay closed on Saturday, news of the manifesto arrived, and an open meeting of 3,000 workers gathered. Shortly thereafter the railroad workers began pouring into town, and Jews and Christians rejoiced together in mass meetings, some including as many as 5,000 people. It seems altogether fitting to find a unified group in this once so bitterly divided community attending the words of a Bundist orator, the more so since the occasion was the appearance of a manifesto that, symbolically at least, marked the end of the old era.[72]

The Bund's years of work as a revolutionary organization culminated in October. At the very least it was the strongest revolutionary force among the Jewish workers; but it was often much more. It became not only the most important protector of the Jewish community, but also the sole link and sometime leader in the concerted work of the revolutionary organizations. The

Manifesto of October 17 fell far short of the Bundists' hopes, but the Bund's work in October, its blending of action and political purpose, brought it to a peak of popular appeal in which its desires and those of a broad segment of the population merged. That was perhaps as much as any revolutionary organization in Russia could achieve in 1905. For Litvak, anyway, "red 1905" seemed "the brightest light of the Jewish proletariat."[73]

The state and its conservative supporters soon regrouped for a counter-attack. Force was a potent answer to the impatient revolutionaries. The police, who were charged with handling most local disturbances, received heavy military support to quell the continuing unrest and violence. There may have been as many as 300,000 troops in Poland from the summer months on.[74]

Just as the regime's obvious weaknesses spurred its opponents of the left and center to a new effort, so doubts about the state's ability to preserve itself frightened conservatives into organizing themselves.[75] Both the use of armed force and the formation of a political right had special meaning for the Jewish population and for the Bund; each vigorous step in the process of revolutionary escalation elicited an equally vigorous response against the Jewish community.

Anti-Jewish attitudes in the government were no secret. S. Iu. Witte, then chairman of the Committee of Ministers, flatly asserts that the Tsar blamed the pogroms on the Jews; somewhat more cautiously he says that Trepov had no objection to pogroms.[76] Prince Urussov, who had shown himself relatively kindly disposed to the Jews during his investigation of the Kishinev pogrom, characterized Trepov more boldly as "a sergeant-major by education and a pogromist by conviction."[77] The police department, one of Trepov's preserves, eventually became directly involved in turning out anti-Jewish leaflets.[78]

The anti-Semites leveled the most general charge possible at the Jews: they were to blame for all of Russia's woes. In 1905 private or police-aided societies, identified by the general name Black Hundreds, sprang up to give new voice and virulence to this charge.[79] Their inflammatory leaflets and speakers flooded the Pale. "Soon, soon a new time will come, friends, when there will be no Jews. The root of all evil, the root of all our misfortunes is the Jews." So read a typical leaflet, distributed in several cities.[80] The Jews were variously denounced as seekers of power, enemies of the Tsar, and antichrists. In Kiev they were accused of the murder of the Grand Duke Sergei, whose "innocent blood" was spilled "only because his whole life was dedicated to the defense of the Russian people against the conceited Jews."[81] Jews were often charged with plotting to destroy neighborhood churches;[82] were accused of being in the pay of the Japanese; were condemned as bloodsuckers and corrupters of the students, who were in turn attacked for having "sold the soul of the poor people to the rich Yid."[83] In Kishinev a leaflet warned: "Brothers, Russian workers! ... We have learned that they are inciting you to meet on Saturday, February 19, and to go to the governor to demand work. Beware, comrades! This is the handiwork of the socialist-Jews."[84] The charges were all-inclusive—all Jews were socialists, all were rich.[85] There was no easy way for the Bund or the Jews as a group to defend themselves against these attacks and an aroused Christian population.

Yet it was easy enough to plant the charge of Jewish revolution in the Pale in 1905. The very success of the Bundists, which sometimes left them the only or the most important revolutionary element in a town, gave substance to the argument. A Russian general told his officers that most of the propaganda against the state was the work of the Jews, "who have organized the so-called Bund among themselves. The Bund is a strong organization in which all are united to a man in their convictions; it possesses large sums of money and has already succeeded in drawing a mass of people into its ranks. [It is] a deep ulcer for our government."* The Bundists themselves recognized the tragic and complementary duality of their position.[86]

The anti-Semitic campaigns of the new reactionary movement reached their peak during the Easter season, a period when the tensions between Jews and Christians always increased, and in the weeks before May 1, with its predictable rallies and unrest. But the Black Hundreds and local authorities used every occasion to foment anti-Jewish activity. No sooner had the Manifesto of February 18 appeared than a rash of pogrom rumors followed in Kishinev, Kreslavka, and Polotsk.[87] The mutterings of February were translated into action in the period between Passover and May 1. Cossacks, peasants, criminal elements—some acting on their own, others prodded by the police or the military—were the shock troops. The worst of the spring pogroms occurred in late April in Zhitomir, where scores were killed and wounded. In the late spring and early summer new outbursts followed each Russian military defeat, with the army playing an important role in the atrocities.[88]

The mood of violence forced self-defense activity among the Jews to new heights—and the Bund continued to lead in the development and deployment of the defense forces. Dedicated revolutionaries and non-revolutionaries, Jews and non-Jews—the fight against pogroms was often a common effort. The tradition of sacrifice for the cause, for humanity, and for simple self-preservation produced heroes and martyrs. It seemed to Litvak that "the more dangerous the work, the greater the zeal with which it was accepted.... That was

---

* *Posledniia izvestiia*, 249 (Sept. 18/5, 1905): 6; and 227 (April 20/7, 1905): 5. Count Aloys Lexa Aehrenthal, the Austrian ambassador to Petersburg at the time of the Revolution, saw a link between the Bund's prominent position in the revolutionary movement and the alleged refusal of Jewish bankers to support their Christian counterparts in a loan to the Russian state. See Hans Heilbronner, "Count Aehrenthal and Russian Jewry, 1903–1907," *Journal of Modern History*, 1966, no. 4, p. 401.

the strength of the revolution, which...raised even the weak and the dis-pirited."[89] The pre-Revolutionary self-defense experience was of great value in 1905: no Kishinev-type surprises occurred, though the self-defenders were often unsuccessful in their efforts to turn back the pogromists.

The Sixth Conference expanded the self-defense program, calling for the building of special armed groups and for the arming and training of workers. The search for arms began in earnest, and money for their purchase was so-licited from the Jews of the United States as well as those in Russia. One ap-peal aimed chiefly at the American Jewish community read:

The path of revolution has set Jewish Social Democracy the task of arming the Jewish proletariat. We must prepare not only for pogroms, but also for the last attack on absolutism, when all the workers of Russia will . . . break the chains of political coercion.

The revolution is near. Help our struggle in the one way you can help...with the means to buy arms.[90]

The favorite weapon of the armed units was the revolver. Particularly popu-lar was the Browning, which was purchased at the plant in Liége and smug-gled into Russia by professional smugglers or hardy individuals willing to take the risk, or by bribing shipping agents to falsify shipping documents.[91] Wom-en were sometimes used to run guns, since they were not apt to be suspected by the police. Raphael Abramovich's sister Sonya, who was a Bundist before he was, participated in this activity.[92]

Bombs became an important weapon for the Bund only after the threat to the Jewish population increased sharply in the summer of 1905.[93] Many Bund-ists, Mikhalevich among them, had deep misgivings about explosives on the purely technical ground that dynamite was difficult to handle and hide, and had only limited usefulness.[94] Chemists, students, and others with some knowledge of the art made the first crude weapons. Abramovich alleges that one rabbi turned out excellent bombs.[95] Later the Bund developed bomb-makers in its own ranks. The very possession of arms came to have a romantic aura in those violent times. "Among the broad masses," Litvak notes, "...everyone dreamed of having a revolver."[96] Abramovich adds, with considerable justice: "The peaceful Jewish population of Russia was strongly militarized in the year 1905."[97]

The BO units continued to be the permanent core of the Bund's defense forces, responsible for the protection of meetings, demonstrations, birzhes, and the like. Reserve and volunteer forces were grafted onto them at critical mo-ments. It was BO members who took on the task of instructing workers in the use of small arms, as ordered by the Sixth Conference. The Bund's plans before a mass demonstration or strike became more elaborate as time went on. Eventually it even set up hospital facilities (manned by *feldshers*, or medical aides) to care for wounded demonstrators and BO members.[98]

The BO units were also responsible for seeing that shops and businesses closed down during strikes, a task that kept them especially busy in 1905. The police and sometimes the military were usually just as bent on keeping the shops open, but in many cases shopkeepers, faced with ultimatums from both sides, gave in to the BO. "The threats of the police," says Mendel Daich, "had no effect, because the owners feared us more than they did the police."[99]

The total BO force was never of great size. In answer to a Central Committee questionnaire sent out in early 1906, ten local organizations reported a total force of 520 men and a total arsenal of 563 revolvers.[100] Though all of the groups that responded were important ones, they still represented only a fraction of the 17 committees, 10 groups, and 60 smaller organizations that sent mandates to the delegates to the Amsterdam Congress. An 1,100-man permanent force in 1905 is probably an extremely conservative estimate. The responses to the questionnaire were based, in all likelihood, on the size of the permanent squads.*

The greatest test of the self-defense forces came during the Zhitomir pogrom. The Bundists believed they detected a shift in government strategy in that battle. Previously, they held, the state had valued the pogrom as a way of diverting popular anger from itself and, perhaps, as a way of demonstrating that the people were unprepared for political freedom and needed the forces the regime could muster. But that was not the case in late April, the Bundists claimed, for the government had no hope of popular support by then; it was completely isolated and indeed in a worse position than an army of occupation. Only the Black Hundreds—those "hooligans" of the underworld—and a few fanatical newspapers stood with the state and its armed forces. The hooligans had everything to gain from siding with the police, who could arm

---

* Mark that my 1,100 figure is simply an estimate. I have arrived at it by using the reporting committees' 52-man average for the other five committees (the Central and Foreign committees, two of the 17 mentioned in the report to the Amsterdam Congress, did not have defense units); by arbitrarily allotting half that average to the ten groups; and by allowing several dozen men for the small groups.

Cahan's figures differ radically from those reported to the Central Committee (see his "Tsu der geshikhte," pp. 16–18). The Vilna Committee, for example, claimed a BO force of 75 (not counting reserves), whereas Cahan gives the figure 300 (also supposedly not counting reserves) for Vilna. Likewise, the Minsk and Vitebsk committees reported 60 and 55 men, respectively, whereas he puts their respective forces at 230 and 200. And so on down the line. Though Cahan indicates he does not include in these figures the reserve forces, which he estimates to have been about three times as great as the regular forces, he appears to have done just that. He refers, to be sure, to a different period, the spring of 1905, but that could surely not account for the wide discrepancy between his figures and those in the Central Committee's questionnaire, for it is unreasonable to suppose the Bundists would have so drastically reduced their defense forces at a time when the danger of pogroms was just as great. I find the lower limit of Cahan's total figure (8,000–10,000) about right; but only for a force consisting of reserves as well as standing units.

them and give them protective cover as they looted and rampaged to their heart's content. In turning these rowdies loose, the police had a specific end in view: drawing the forces of the revolution out into the open, where they could be destroyed. This hope of engaging and eliminating the revolutionaries, the Bundists insisted, accounted in large part for the enormous agitation preceding the pogrom. The truth was, Zhitomir was simply "a conflict of organized hooligans against the organized revolutionary forces."[101]

Painful as the Zhitomir pogrom was for the Bund and the other forces that fought the armed mob, it did not accomplish its purpose for two reasons. In the first place, the Christian population proved relatively indifferent. More important, the act of self-defense in a real sense and especially in a psychological sense prevented the pogrom from becoming a second Kishinev.[102]

The expectation of further conflict with the state after January made the issue of armed insurrection a vital consideration throughout 1905. At the Sixth Conference the Bundists agreed that attacking government buildings during an uprising would be useful. The stormy days of January had shown that state offices could be seized. Attacks of this sort, however, were to be left to special groups, which could best control and lead a mob at such critical moments.[103] The published record of the Sixth Conference goes no further than this; for security reasons all other discussions of armed revolt were kept secret.

By March the Bundists were discussing the question of open revolution on a more practical level. Proceeding beyond the Sixth Conference's concern with immediate military objectives and leadership, they began looking at the hard questions of logistics, capabilities, and tactics. Once the tide of feverish activity ebbed, excitement gave way to a more somber but fuller picture of what was entailed in full-blown revolt. The Foreign Committee began to stress the political and moral meaning of revolt. Not that technical and military considerations were felt to be unimportant; the Bundists abroad simply sought to strike some kind of balance, to offset what they saw as an undue emphasis in some quarters on such matters.[104] Though it was certainly necessary to arm as many people as possible, said the Bund leaders, at best the revolutionary organizations could stock only small caches of arms; they could never supply in advance the arms needed for tens of thousands of people. Without those arms immediately at hand there could not be a successful armed attack; partly armed, undisciplined masses could not fight a regular army. Thus, mass arming must await the start of the decisive storm against the Autocracy, "when the seizure of arsenals and weapons stores appears psychologically possible."[105]

A more important consideration for the Bundists was the political and social outcome of the revolution. The results would depend on the preliminary work of revolutionizing the masses and "the gradual disorganization of the state machinery" rather than the form of "the last decisive struggle." The proletariat's consciousness and organization would determine how well it played its role, not arms or the seizure of state banks. The Bund leaders, plainly somewhat fearful of their own armed units, insisted that the flag of revolt must be raised by a broad organization with the flexibility to orient itself to changing political circumstances. In a situation of constant need for and increasing reliance on the BO units, the possibility arose that the Bund's armed groups might assume the independence of the SR squads and be persuaded to the same terrorist frame of mind.[106]

One of the bloodiest and most memorable weeks of the Revolution came in late June. Following a battle between Cossacks and Polish and Jewish demonstrators in Lodz, new, more militant demonstrations were held, with calls for the seizure of arms stores. On June 23 the workers built barricades in various quarters of the city, attacked the police and their agents, and armed themselves with guns wrested from the government troops. Over 1,500 people were wounded or killed as a direct or indirect result of this outbreak.[107]

The Lodz affair prompted a new round of discussion of military tactics in Bundist circles. Soon after, the Bund press began to print articles on the proper construction of barricades,[108] the erecting of which signaled an important step toward real war. But even at that difficult moment, when defeat was taken as the beginning of eventual victory, the Bundists insisted that workers at the barricades were no match for the standing army of the Autocracy. At a certain point they hoped that the sight of workers prepared to fight and die for freedom would affect the soldiers themselves. Hence, the longer the workers held out, the better the chance of a breakdown in military discipline. This was no forlorn hope, for the army showed evidence of cracking under the same strains in Russian society that prompted the workers' movement.[109] In fact, during the military action in Lodz the troop commanders were impelled to send Jewish and Polish soldiers out of the city lest they join the rebels.[110]

The Bund argued that the revolutionary organizations, with strong discipline and firm control, must lead the final revolt. Experienced and armed, their cadres would provide the leadership needed to push the action to the highest level of intensity, until at last the army itself, that cornerstone of state power, crumbled in face of the heroism and determination of the masses and their leading organizations. The Bundists, looking back on their past efforts, rejected the idea of a popular revolt succeeding on its own.

A logical tactic was to try to weaken the morale of the armed forces. The revolutionaries pushed the same propaganda line as before, attempting to convince soldiers that they must not fight the common people in support of a corrupt regime. This effort often transcended party lines. Special military revolutionary groups were set up and worked with ever-greater intensity as the number of clashes between soldiers and workers increased.

The campaign to win over the common soldier did not produce anything so sensational as mass desertion or its equivalent in the Pale. Nevertheless, the work of the Bundists and others worried the regime, and the constant agitation did its damage. The officers of one regiment were ordered to be on the lookout for Jewish soldiers in civilian dress participating in anti-government meetings and agitation among their fellow soldiers; many had been spotted by the local police.[111] In Grodno the revolutionaries suceeded in organizing meetings and circles of soldiers.[112] But bringing the soldiers together in more than a physical sense was difficult, especially when commanders tried to forestall cooperation, as they did in Poland, by attempting to stir the Russian soldiers against the alien Jews and Poles.[113] During the turbulent days of October the Central Committee put out a leaflet to dissuade recruits from taking the oath of duty, which would pledge them to war on their own people. "Swear another oath—a holy oath to the people," the leaflet instructed them. "And on the day when you are taken into the street against the masses, attack and kill your officers, and join the people with your weapons and strengthen their ranks."[114] At that crucial stage, such propaganda was considered vital for the success of the Revolution.

Among the Jews of the Pale the Bund's militant response to the revolutionary developments was second to none. But others acted too to take advantage of the new political current, sometimes at cross-purposes with the Bundists, sometimes for the same goals. The Jewish liberals stood to gain the most from the immediate course of political events. Under the quasi-legal conditions prevailing after January they were able to meet and make their views known to the government and the Jewish people.[115] They relied heavily, at least at first, on mass petitions demanding (in moderate language, to be sure) equal rights for Jews. "We expect equal rights as human beings in whom the feeling of human dignity is alive," went one, "as conscious citizens of the modern state."[116]

In late March representatives of both the liberals and the Zionists met in Vilna to form a League for the Attainment of Full Rights for the Jewish People of Russia. The new group did not pretend to be a political party, incorporating as it did those of widely varied political persuasions, but sought merely to bind those of every possible point of view within the Jewish population for a common struggle for Jewish emancipation. Going beyond the first demands of the petitions, the league asked for full civil and political rights, as well as national cultural self-determination. It also called for universal suffrage in the forthcoming Duma elections and even asked that the appointed Jewish aldermen in municipal Dumas resign their posts.[117]

At their Sixth Conference the Bundists considered the problem of dealing with the non-proletarian Jewish population, and more specifically, how best to maximize the influence of the Social Democratic movement as represented by the Bund.[118] As always, they faced the dilemma of working with a liberal bourgeoisie whose support would be helpful in the short term but whose ultimate goals were far from their own, and indeed a threat to the Social Democratic future.

With the commencement of the political campaign of the liberal Jews, the

Bund began to counterattack. The early petitions, which had asked for no more than equal rights, irked the Bundists, revealing only that "the slaves of yesterday cannot give up their slavish psychology."[119] The unrevolutionary character of the demands added to their contempt. To ask for equal rights in Tsarist Russia was but to seek the "equality of rightlessness."[120] The Bundists labeled the liberals hypocrites who stepped forth only after having taken courage from the blows the proletariat had dealt the state; they sought the rewards for which the working class and its revolutionary partners had fought so valiantly, and now tried to divert the workers to a political party under their control, only to exploit them the more. All the same, the Bundists felt that for the Jewish bourgeoisie even these first modest petitions were a long step forward.[121]

When a newly formed Jewish Democratic Group called for the creation of a democratic party in March, the Bundists, in a long commentary, praised the act as progressive. Actually, in issuing its appeal the Group was careful not to alienate the Bund. On the contrary, it paid homage to the organization that had singlehandedly fostered the spirit of protest over the years. But, the Group held, since the Bund could organize only one portion of the Jewish population, the workers, it had done all it could. The new party would address itself to the broadest levels of the population and would work with other parties in pursuit of general democratic demands and the opportunity for Judaism to realize itself.[122]

"Progressive" or not, the Jewish Democratic Group's announced goals displeased the Bundists as much as the petitions had. They found the appeal to all Jews as "a single organized whole" both vague and presumptuous. The Group, the Bundists protested, did not raise the question of who would rebuild Russia, a constitutional monarch or a constituent assembly. Further, the absence of social demands in its program was disturbing. Even the call for national cultural and religious self-determination, which the Group considered two facets of one thing, dissatisfied the Bundists because the matter was left to private initiative. The Bund held that national equality demanded positive action from the state. The Bundists saw the liberal assimilationist at work— willing to abandon the discredited assimilationist slogans, to be sure, but clearly of that persuasion in declining to attach political significance to the principle of cultural self-determination. The whole proposal was "a miserable moderately liberal program" geared to the moment.[123]

The Bundists would not allow the liberals to rest with halfway measures. After the League for the Attainment of Rights was formed in late March along the lines suggested by the Jewish Democratic Group, they continued their attack. Nothing could be expected from such a loose association. What would it do? "Words and more words! The new League will only talk." Would it fight? No. It would merely "attain"—with empty words.[124]

Many, though by no means all, Jewish liberals greeted the announcement of the Bulygin Duma with enthusiasm. The liberal Russian-Jewish weekly *Voskhod* (Ascent), which represented the opinion of the league,[125] found the Duma on balance worthwhile, only a first small step toward justice, admittedly, but of real value nevertheless. "The great thing," a lead article noted, "is recognition of the principle of Jewish representation on a level with Christians." Having achieved equality at the top, the Jews could now set about erasing the inequalities that remained.[126] The liberal journal thus accepted the tactical line of gradualism, insisting that fundamental reform could never be gained by a direct course.[127] So much for the revolution.

The liberals' reaction to the Bulygin plan convinced the Bundists of the correctness of their own stand. Contemptuously, they chided the Jewish liberals for leaving the opposition at the first chance, satisfied with a farcical Duma in which they saw "new bright times . . . for the Jews."[128] The Bundists concluded that the only way to impress the liberals, who alone stood to gain from cooperation with the government, was to criticize them, to refuse to adjust to their position, and to demonstrate strength.[129] There was plainly little room for compromise and rapprochement between the two camps.

On the local level, interaction between Bundists and Jewish liberals varied widely, ranging from temporary cooperation to aloofness and enmity. To the Jewish middle class, the Bund's long political hegemony had been trying, and the liberals welcomed the opportunity to express themselves in the relatively open atmosphere available to them. In Zhitomir, as liberals met in a synagogue to discuss the founding of a Jewish Liberal Party, the Bundists tried to prevent people from signing their petitions for equal rights.[130] In Grodno, the Bundists invited themselves to a meeting of liberals and debated the question of political activity with them. The liberal reporter present did not write up an account of the meeting, fearing that liberal legality might be compromised.[131] In Dvinsk, when Jewish "society" met to choose representatives for the league's founding convention in Vilna, Bund speakers were sent to challenge the right of the liberals to speak in the name of the whole Jewish people.[132] Even as the Bundists admitted the possibilities in liberal political activity, they fought it as hard as they could.

Self-defense afforded a special area of cooperation in 1905, but even here there were difficulties. Questions of control and politics were crucial. In Bobruisk, for example, the Bundists adamantly refused to form joint forces with the bourgeoisie. Self-defense action was political, they held, and consequently unity with the liberals was unthinkable.[133] Similarly, in Zhitomir a liberal attempt to unite all Jews in a "national self-defense" was rejected as a sign of the liberals' desire for hegemony over the workers' movement and a signal that "the war on two fronts"—against the Autocracy and the liberals—"is beginning right now."[134]

Shortly after the Zhitomir pogrom the Bundists had looked closely at the problem of self-defense and the liberals. Self-defense had not been so popular with some liberals a few weeks earlier, the Bundists pointed out; now all of a sudden the Jewish revolutionaries were heroes. But the liberal view of self-defense was politically shortsighted, for it assumed that self-defense was a fight against the underworld. It was no such thing, the Bundists insisted; it was a part of the political struggle, just as pogroms were part of the government's policy to save itself. For all Jews to join together in a fight on the spot, to join with those who merely wanted to protect their property and who rejected political struggle at other times, was not enough. Only a revolutionary party acting openly against the autocratic order at all times could wage a real fight against the Tsar. The Jews were not one in class terms, and a loss of class consciousness by the Jewish proletariat under such conditions would cost it its strength. The proletariat had to fight in the ranks of "the one party that advances on its victorious path—in the ranks of the Bund."[135]

Possibly the best relations between liberals and Bundists existed in St. Petersburg, where the Bundists were a relatively small group and the absence of competition for mass support permitted less abrasive discussion. The Bund sent Abramovich to St. Petersburg again in February 1905. As in 1904 he addressed meetings of liberal professional unions (actually political clubs), familiarizing them with the Bund and its goals. He found there a warm reception for the call for equal rights but little understanding of or enthusiasm for national cultural autonomy.[136] In the more heated political atmosphere of the Pale the meeting of Bundist and Jewish liberal sometimes bordered on violence. Here the Bund had the additional muscle of the BO unit to take charge of events, allowing, for instance, the Bundists to break up liberal meetings after the Bund began to boycott the Bulygin Duma.[137]

As the Bundists sought to forestall defections to the liberal movement, they were forced to fight the same battle on another front—against the attractions of proletarian Zionism, which was also on the rise. The relations between Bundists and Zionists did not change appreciably after January; hostility and suspicion continued to separate them.

The Bund's Sixth Conference, viewing the immediate future as a preparatory period for further revolution, laid down rules for cooperation with non–Social Democratic parties, resolving that close ties could be established when necessary. By its proposed arrangement, each organization would remain independent, merely associating itself with other groups on ad hoc committees working toward specific goals. The Sixth Conference ruled out any working arrangement with parties that did not demand a democratically elected constituent assembly, and also with any group that aimed at the disorganization of the Jewish proletariat.[138] The Bundists did not specify which parties they had in mind, but we can assume the second exclusion was aimed at the Zionists, who had long been considered a disruptive force.

Still, the two movements did come together at times in the self-defense effort, and to good effect in Odessa, Mogilev, and Dvinsk.[139] Other areas, though equally under the threat of pogroms, saw less happy results. At Brest and Ekaterinoslav the two sides differed over the disposition of weapons, and at Berdichev they could not agree on a plan of action. Moreover, the Bundists would have no part of the various attempts to build a "national self-defense," considering such actions Zionist-inspired.[140]

Fault-finding, quick accusation, and even violence marked the Bund-Zionist relationship. The Bund press reported the failures of the labor Zionists with an air of long-suffering annoyance and showed a singular lack of enthusiasm for their successes. Speaking of the agitation for May 1, the Bund correspondent from Plock sourly admitted that, "unfortunately," the labor Zionists had the strongest influence among the Jews.[141] When the Zionists of Riga began an independent search for self-defense funds the Bundists accused them of giving donors the impression their money would go to the Bund.[142]

The two groups also met (and frequently clashed) in the bid for leadership of the economic struggle. The labor Zionists made some headway in organizing new groups of workers, notably among the clerks. But though by rights the Bundists should have welcomed the entrance of new elements into the workers' struggle, they were instead deeply annoyed at this evidence of growing Zionist strength in the relatively open atmosphere of 1905. Bund correspondents reported Zionist organizing work in Lodz, Bobruisk, Borisov, Pinsk, Ekaterinoslav, Mogilev, Zhitomir, Rovno, Belostok, and Kishinev between January and October.[143] Cooperation being less urgent in economic work than in the self-defense effort, the two groups were less inclined to mask their antagonism in the competition for the allegiance of the Jewish workers. Numerous reports show that neither side was willing to help or support the other.

The most significant development in the labor Zionist movement in 1905, apart from its continuing growth, was its clarification of ideology and first steps toward party organization. The revolutionary situation contributed to this process, as it did in the case of other parties. The territorialists, whose first official words had been heard at the Sixth Zionist Congress in 1903, formally organized as the Zionist-Socialist Workers' Party (SS) in February 1905.* The labor wing of Zionism continued to break into other camps, with some groups insisting on Palestine (Poale Zionists) and others suggesting the possibility of parliamentary reform in Russia and Poland (Seimists), though none achieved the formal status of the SS until after October. The most important

---

* Gutman, "Tsu der forgeshikhte," pp. 171–73. The name, which was later sharply criticized, was chosen for tactical reasons. Zionist (Sionist in Russian) was adopted simply to allow the party to join in the forthcoming Seventh Zionist Congress, for its members did not seek a Jewish homeland in Palestine. Socialist was chosen over Social Democratic because of SR influence and also for brevity.

Zionist event of the year was the Seventh Zionist Congress at Basel, in the summer of 1905, where the territorialists formally left the Zionist movement.

The Bundists viewed all the developments within Zionism (which appeared "like fungus after rain" in the train of the January events, in the words of one Bund correspondent) with a mixture of apprehension and disdain.[144] At the same time they found the general trend in the movement heartening and even took some credit for the labor Zionists' evolution from a strike or labor orientation to a socialist orientation. The further step of playing with the idea of a general strike and a democratic republic was a favorable sign, they thought. Zionist slogans or no, to the Bundists it seemed that "the time is not far off when Zionism with all its national attributes . . . would be found an open fig leaf" and "a purely Jewish Social Democratic party" would be announced.[145]

The Bundists pinned their hopes on the revolution as the moment of truth. They saw a certain promise in the liberal movement, but none at all in Zionism; the time for fruitless dreams had long since passed for the Jewish people.[146] The split at the Seventh Zionist Congress strengthened their view that Zionism was ending in a fiasco. Uninterested in the general Zionists, the Bundists turned to the SS. How could the SS, which disagreed with the other Zionist groups on the issue of Palestine, not disagree with them on the matter of the class struggle? Zionism was a voluntary union, and those of socialist bent who stayed in it and worked with nonsocialists were traitors to the revolution. There could be no accommodation within Zionism, which sought to avoid the class struggle. Either one gave up the socialist struggle or one gave up Zionist work.[147] In fact, the revolutionary events of 1905 scarcely touched the general Zionists, as the discussions at the Seventh Congress revealed. Medem, who attended the congress and the subsequent meeting of the dissident SS, saw in the confusion and seeming helplessness of the proceedings "a still-born child."[148]

The Bundists were quite content to see increasing ideological argument tear the Zionists apart. Moreover, they felt that the Revolution was advancing, and that its victories would eliminate at least some of the problems which had given impetus to Zionism in the first place (the Bundists were willing to admit there were material reasons for Zionism's birth and temporary growth).[149] Measuring the seemingly hopeless goal of the Zionists against the now very real possibility of advance in Russia, the Bundists saw the whole issue of Zionism as contrived—and as an obstacle to the further fulfillment of the obvious tasks at hand.

The Bund and indeed the whole of the revolutionary community in Russia recognized the urgent need for cooperation and coordinated action in the critical weeks after January. To the Bundists this meant, above all, unity in the Social Democratic camp. But however eager the various parties were to capitalize on the revolutionary fever in the Empire, they could not just forgive and forget; despite their common interests and shared perceptions, the heritage of dispute and fragmentation was too strong to be dispelled at a crack. Indeed, only with great difficulty did the Bund and the Latvian Social Democrats persuade several parties to come together in January to discuss policy, tactics, and organization.

The Riga Conference provided solid evidence of the continuing divisions in the Social Democratic camp. The initiators, the Bundists and the Latvians, had no far-reaching organizational changes in mind; they suggested no more than that the assembled representatives set policy on future relations with the liberals, the Paris Bloc, and other non–Social Democratic political organizations; work out the mechanics of further cooperation among their own organizations; and issue a joint declaration.[150] But the RSDWP representative balked at even so mild an undertaking, seeking to minimize the significance of the conference in favor of RSDWP efforts abroad to arrange a meeting through the good offices of the International. The Bundists, who were hearing this proposal for the first time, felt the organizations in Russia could achieve unity more effectively than the theoreticians abroad.[151] Despite their high hopes, however, little was achieved at Riga. None of the resolutions passed was binding, and the only step toward coordination was a decision to hold conferences on tactics and joint action at least every six weeks.[152] The Mensheviks, who attended the conference, wanted these follow-up meetings limited to an exchange of views and also insisted on the exclusion of several organizations, with the result that the whole plan was soon dropped, dimming all hope of a strong Social Democratic bloc.[153]

In any case each organization reserved the right to set its own line on such crucial policy matters as the proper relations between the Social Democrats and the bourgeoisie, the correct action in a revolutionary situation, and the degree of cooperation, if any, with a government of bourgeois character. These questions continued to preoccupy all the Social Democratic organizations throughout the revolutionary era.

For Russian Social Democracy the beginnings of the Revolution heralded the long-awaited bourgeois-democratic stage of history that Plekhanov had forecast a generation before.[154] This was the view of the Riga Conference, with its demand for a democratic republic, and one the Bund wholeheartedly supported. Accordingly, the conference accepted without question the tactical necessity of working with bourgeois liberals under certain conditions.[155] The so-called Third Congress of the RSDWP, which was actually attended only by the Bolsheviks, generally endorsed that point of view as well.

But when it came to the question of how to precipitate the bourgeois-democratic revolution the Social Democratic organizations parted company. The Bolsheviks, taking the hard view, emphasized the need for special fighting units to spearhead the masses, an emphasis the Bundists considered dangerous as a possible distraction from the more important political tasks. The Bolsheviks' error, the Bundists claimed, stemmed from their attempt to run the Revolution from abroad. They overestimated the power of the special organizations and their ability to arm the masses.[156] The Bundists also feared the independent position the paramilitary units might be tempted to take. As the days passed nothing happened to change their minds. In late summer *Di Arbeter Shtime*, commenting on the Bolshevik dream of creating an armed uprising, rejected the tactic as hopelessly mistaken. Experience had taught the Bundists, the journal said, that though they could lead the workers into the streets, they could not "create anger"; they could do no more than put the workers' anger to use once it arose, a development that came about only through education.[157]

The Bundists agreed heartily with the Bolsheviks, however, on the Social Democratic position on the Bulygin Duma. In September a conference of Social Democratic organizations, attended by the Latvian Social Democratic Party, the Revolutionary Ukrainian Party, the Mensheviks, the Bolsheviks, and the Bund, declared the Bulygin proposal "a great falsification of popular representation." A majority at the conference endorsed the policy of sabotaging the plan by an active boycott, including if necessary the forcible prevention of meetings.[158] The Bundists softened their attitude toward violence, but they along with the Bolsheviks remained staunch defenders of the boycott policy to the end—right down to the seating of the First Duma.

This was but one of a whole series of points on which the Mensheviks differed with the Bundists. Menshevism came into its own in 1905. The Mensheviks took the view that the time was propitious for a popular uprising, and accordingly Social Democracy had to be transformed into a mass movement. But the broad masses, whose work it was to bring about the revolution, could not be united under the flag of a single party, Menshevik or otherwise, they held. Consequently, they saw their role as being one of influencing and giving political direction to the masses, rather than providing official leadership.[159] On the path toward democratization, they wanted to see broad-based, nonparty unions established. Later, in October, when workers' councils (soviets) were formed, the Mensheviks enthusiastically supported them.

The tendency of a large segment of the Menshevik leadership to downgrade the role of party organization upset the Bundists. They attributed the trend to the Social Democrats' failure to lead the Russian proletariat in January. Pointing to their own experiences, they continued to insist that the awakening of the Russian workers would enable the Russian Social Democrats to lead those workers just as the Bund was able to lead the Jewish workers. Organization, it seemed to them, had to avoid both lifeless doctrinairism and unprincipled casting about.[160]

When the issue of the Bulygin Duma arose, the Mensheviks, with Martov leading the way, argued that the workers had to play an independent role in the bourgeois-democratic revolution. To boycott passively meant keeping the masses dispersed; to boycott actively meant pushing liberal democratic elements into the camp of the reactionaries.[161] Workers had to enter the election campaign, the Mensheviks held, but the victors must not go to the Duma. Instead they must establish a revolutionary people's assembly to function alongside the legally elected one. That body could then assert pressure against the state Duma and could provide a framework for a future revolutionary government. The Bundists would abide no argument in favor of the elections or the Duma. They saw no use in the proposed Duma for the workers.

The Bundists thus often stood somewhere between the Bolsheviks and the Mensheviks. In their revolutionary spirit and readiness for action, and in their faith in organization, they stood closer to the Bolsheviks than the Mensheviks, but they moved to the other side of the scale in their emphasis on the spontaneous action of the masses, the Menshevik dream. The Bundists constantly insisted that their practical experience led them to their tactics. They could rely on their workers, many of whom were organized, and were prepared to provide leadership when the proper time came. That experience probably kept the Bund from the more extreme positions of the two RSDWP factions. Attuned to the streets of the Pale, the Bundists accepted both the need for caution and the need for local freedom of action to permit full use of the revolutionary forces of the Pale. They were aware of the power they could unleash in the large centers there, but they were also aware that without the Russian workers the revolution they wanted could not succeed.

In point of fact, all these high-level arguments had relatively small impact in the Pale between February and October. Party leaders, Bundist as well as Menshevik and Bolshevik, could only watch events and analyze their success afterwards. Their views dictated the mood and actions of their respective local organizations only sporadically, and then only on issues of vast significance, such as the Duma elections (which in any case did not receive major attention until after October).

The local Social Democratic organizations carried out their work as best they could, sometimes competing bitterly, sometimes working smoothly together. To some extent the new revolutionary vistas led to a breakdown of old hostilities, though a reservoir of ill-will remained. Generally speaking, the Bund's relationship with the Latvian Social Democrats was the only one that could be called excellent, and it was extremely limited in its effect.

The Bund's Sixth Conference, following the recommendations of the Riga Conference, placed coordinated action and agitation high on the list of Bund priorities.[162] The chief instrument to this end was the commission, of which there were two types: a standing, federated body binding Social Democratic organizations together and a temporary working arrangement with non–

Social Democratic parties to help coordinate strikes, demonstrations, and self-defense efforts.

The Bund press records scores of instances of cooperation between the RSDWP groups and the local organizations up to October 1905. It took almost every imaginable form: parades in which the red standards of all parties floated side by side were reported from Dvinsk, coordinated political strikes from Vilna, united self-defense actions from Mogilev, joint meetings and demonstrations from Smorgon and Gomel.[163]

There is also ample evidence of continuing discord among local groups. The relative weakness of the Iskraites in the Bund strongholds (local Bundists rarely drew distinctions between Bolshevik and Menshevik, even in 1905) drew the complaints and scorn of the Bundists. Thus, the disappointed Bundists grumbled and sniped at their fellow Social Democrats for being able to muster the services of only a few "ex-Bundists" instead of the expected Russian masses during a strike in Polotsk. Similarly, the Iskraites' inability to draw large numbers of workers into strikes in Kiev, where the Bundists did well despite the fact that Jewish residence in the area was limited, prompted a few choice Bundist remarks.[164] Where the RSDWP had hampered the Bund's organizational efforts, particularly in Odessa, the Bundists blamed the weakness of the movement among Jewish workers on the party.[165] In Ekaterinoslav, where the Bund had begun to organize much later than the RSDWP, the Bundists accused the party of still refusing to cooperate with them, even though it had not reached the Jewish masses itself.[166] Occasionally the recriminations turned into full-scale verbal battles. In Riga, where there were sharp differences of long standing, angry outbursts over alleged direct interference found their way into the Bund press.[167]

The same mixed picture of cooperation and complaint appears in the Bolshevik publications Vpered (Forward) and Proletarii (Proletarian). The Vpered correspondent in Odessa reported, at the end of January, that temporary agreement with the Bund was unavoidable, and Piatnitsky, then active in the city, recalls the efforts of the Bundists to bring the Social Democrats together.[168] In Minsk the RSDWP Committee complained that the Bund had informed it only at the last minute of a decision to strike.[169] There was dangerous in-fighting at times, as when the RSDWP, trying to force the Bund to take the party into account, asked its own workers not to go out on a Bund-called strike, so it would become a purely Jewish affair that would evoke national antagonisms.[170] The Bolshevik press also carries several reports of local cooperation, largely of the kind related in the Bund press.[171]

The major difference in the reports of the Bundists and the Bolsheviks is more a matter of interpretation than of fact. Though the Iskraites accepted the Bund as the larger and stronger organization, they charged it with divisiveness and narrowness in its work[172]—a proper conclusion from the anti-national point of view of the RSDWP. The Bund's major complaint, apart from the disastrous weakness of the other's groups, was the RSDWP's intrusion into the organization of Jewish workers. The Bundists insisted that the party organize Russian rather than Jewish workers, arguing that otherwise it largely wasted its efforts, drawing few workers from the Bund and leaving its own work virtually untouched. By and large the Bund's complaint was exaggerated, for the party did in fact move toward the Russian workers in 1905, leaving the Jewish proletariat to the Bund.

The Mensheviks' reports are of much the same nature as those of the Bundists, though of consistently less belligerent tone than the reports in both the Bolshevik and the Bundist press. As a Menshevik reporter in Odessa noted, the two wings of the party had more trouble with each other than they had with the Bund.[173] Another Menshevik correspondent reported that a Bundist was sent to speak for the Social Democrats at a liberal banquet in Vitebsk.[174] Bundist complaints specifically naming the Mensheviks are rare, there being so little distinction between the party factions in the minds of the local Bundists.

The local relations between the Bundists and the non–Social Democratic Russian revolutionaries were somewhat worse than the relations within the Social Democratic camp. Though the militancy of the SR's had a certain appeal to some Bundists and to the public at large in a time so ripe for open conflict, a deep ideological gulf still separated the Bund from the Socialist Revolutionary movement and worked against any kind of close relationship.

A common readiness to face fire drew the SR's and the Bundists together for self-defense efforts and general strikes. In some cases they actually worked hand in hand, in others they merely kept one another informed of their plans.[175] The methods of the SR's tended to reflect their terrorist emphasis. At rumors of a pogrom, for instance, they often warned the local administration they would hold it responsible for any disorders, a warning that at once heartened the Jews and worried the authorities.[176]

The most serious disputes between the SR's and the Bundists occurred in Belostok, where an anti-intellectual and terrorist element badgered the Bundists and even threatened their lives. The result was a barrage of leaflets from both sides baring the hostility between them, as well as several attempts to disrupt strikes.[177] Elsewhere the relationship was at best an uneasy one. The SR's, aware of their small numbers in the Bundist centers, were sometimes resentful at the Bund's insistence on controlling self-defense forces and strikes when their own contribution was significant.[178] But SR resentment did not particularly trouble the Bundists. The fact is, the SR's played a minor role in the local history of the Bund and among the Jews.

The Anarchists, who had established small groups before 1905, expanded their activities in the troubled days of the Revolution. They were able to attract a certain number of Jewish workers who had become disillusioned with the Bund's Social Democratic ideology and were bent on destroying the existing order as quickly as possible.[179] The Bund found the Anarchists' direct action annoying, especially after the workers took to the streets and violence became increasingly widespread. In Belostok, where Anarchism became a force to conjure with,[180] its adherents organized strikes, attacked the police—sometimes with bombs—and generally pushed for violence at every opportunity. The Bundists, sticking to their Social Democratic tactics, argued with them frequently. Following the arrest of some Bundists in the spring, the Belostok Anarchists went so far as to spread rumors that the Bund had ceased to exist.[181]

In May the SR's of Belostok joined the Anarchists to form a significant segment of the revolutionary movement there. Their violence reached a peak of sorts in their "expropriations," a nice term for outright robbery and extortion. Moreover, they used the Bund's name in the process of their work. The furious Bundists found them little better than hooligans.[182] But the Anarchists had even less impact on the Bund than the SR's; and they began to lose their appeal shortly after October.

Of greater importance to the Bund in 1905 than both the SR's and the Anarchists were the Polish socialist parties. The clarification of procedures that took place in Riga, as well as tradition, placed the Bund squarely alongside the SDKPiL, though the PPS had greater influence among the Polish workers in most places. The Bund and the PSD stressed their unity with the revolutionary workers of Russia.

The PPS underwent considerable internal strain as a result of the Revolution. Was the party to maintain its strong plank of Polish independence and armed uprising, or was solidarity with the Russians and the national minorities to take precedence? At the regular conference of the PPS Central Committee in March 1905, the "young ones," dissidents, took the latter view. Their stand led to a compromise. Converting the conference into a party congress, the Seventh, the PPS replaced the plank on Polish independence with a demand for a constituent assembly for Warsaw. For the Bundists, a measure of rapprochement resulted from the proceedings. The PPS agreed to reach an understanding with the Bund in practical matters, provided the Bund recognized the party's new plank.[183]

When the Polish proletariat took to the streets in 1905, the Bund was in an awkward position vis-à-vis the two parties. Its prior obligation to the PSD angered the PPS, and joint work among the three was often difficult to arrange. In July the Bund and the PSD sat down in conference in an attempt to iron out their difficulties. They agreed on the use of native languages for agitation and for the purpose of maintaining special organizations. They also agreed to consult each other before entering any agreement with other parties that might affect their respective work. The PSD was seeking support against the PPS, the Bund support against the proletarian Zionists. Indeed, the conferees explicitly stated that the Bundists were to support the PSD position on the participation of Polish organizations at international conferences while the Polish Social Democrats supported the Bund against other Jewish parties.[184]

The Bund's ties with the PSD resulted in a fair degree of cooperation. The number of Polish Social Democrats grew impressively in the course of the year, rising from a few hundred at the start of 1905 to about 30,000 in early 1906.[185] As with other parties, the Bundists joined with the PSD in strikes and demonstrations, sitting with its representatives on both federated and associated commissions. Their collaboration in Lodz was particularly fruitful.[186]

Despite the softening of the PPS's attitude toward the Bund, cooperation between the two was hard to arrange. A real effort was made in the larger towns, resulting in constant joint or parallel manifestations and a clearly higher level of solidarity than before. Yet there was also a good deal of unpleasantness, with charges flowing back and forth to the effect that each group was working only in the interests of its own constituency. More painful to the Bundists were the occasions when the anti-Jewish temper of the times led the PPS to heap verbal abuse on its own Jewish sections.[187] In all fairness, though, it should be noted that even the PSD fell into this frame of mind, asking the Bund to hold separate meetings of Jewish workers; and that at the September conference of the Social Democratic parties no less a body than the Central Committee of the RSDWP requested the Bundists to sign the simple name "Bund" to all documents instead of identifying their organization as Jewish.[188] Small wonder that the Bundists remained a little suspicious of their revolutionary colleagues.

The generally increased activities of the other revolutionary parties did not impair the Bund's work. Though it lost its monopoly in many towns and some number of workers to the terrorists, it continued to grow and to maintain its status. It remained the leading party of the Jewish workers. Many centers were unarguably "Bund towns," Dvinsk, Vilna, and to some degree Minsk among them. In other centers, particularly the important Polish cities of Warsaw and Lodz, which were in no sense of the word "Bund towns," it was nevertheless able to mobilize powerful forces. The total picture in the Russia of 1905 is one of an enormous expansion of revolutionary forces, a process that affected the Bund no less than the other members of the revolutionary community. In short, in the area of local revolutionary activity, the Bund proudly held its own.

The publication of Bulygin's draft, which raised the political temperature of all Russia, galvanized the Bundists into action. The Central Committee immediately held a council, which made two important decisions: to boycott the elections to the Duma and to convene a regular congress to chart the Bund's course in the current crisis.[189] Zurich was set as the site of the congress, the Sixth, Russia being judged too dangerous for such a gathering. Abramovich went abroad to make the arrangements after discussing the agenda with the local organizations.[190] While enroute, the delegates learned of the growing conflict between the railroad workers and the government and of the preparations for a general strike. A few of the delegates, Litvak and Rozen among them, excused themselves, informing the Zurich meeting that the seriousness of the moment made it impossible for them to join the delegates already abroad; but 30 delegates, representing 12 committees, 6 organizations, and the Central Committee assembled. Among the missing were the delegates from Warsaw, Riga, Gomel, and the Regional Committee of Poland.[191]

The outbreak of the new disturbances in Russia raised havoc with the plans of the Sixth Congress, which began its work on October 13. News of the fast-moving events in Russia produced confusion and anxiety among the delegates. Here were many of the Bund leaders far from their organizations during the greatest revolutionary crisis of their time. Kosovsky scolded the delegates: "It isn't seemly that a Bund Congress act like schoolchildren."[192]

The new developments forced reconsideration of the agenda. Questions involving tactics were dropped, for as Medem observes, "it would have been idle to pass any kind of tactical directives" under the circumstances.[193] A number of other items were also dropped, including discussion of the Duma, organizational problems, and most of the points that did not require answers of principle. As amended, the agenda provided for discussion of the national and Polish questions, of territorial principles, and of the Zionist movement, along with the regular reports and routine business of every congress.[194] What had been envisioned as a full-scale review of tactics and unsettled questions of principle ended in hurried resolutions. The delegates were bent on getting back to Russia; that mattered above all else at the moment.[195]

Yet the congress made its own history, passing a resolution that marked the end of a long journey. Though some delegates held to earlier positions on the national question, the great majority endorsed the principle of national cultural autonomy as originally defined in 1901.[196] Their resolution demanded full equal and civil rights for Jews, state guarantees of the Jews' right to use their own language in their dealings with state institutions, and Jewish autonomy in cultural questions (provided these concerned the Jews alone and had no general significance).[197]

The other resolutions of the Sixth Congress changed little. The Bund's answer to the Polish question remained the same: it would not accept Polish independence as part of a Social Democratic program, for that could only mislead the Polish proletariat, whose real interests would be served in a democratic Russian state "with broad territorial self-rule."[198] The Bund remained solidly Social Democratic in its approach to the Polish question, rejecting as well the compromise solution of a separate constituent assembly for the Poles. Such demands, the Bundists maintained, were not in the interests of a proletariat whose forces needed to be concentrated to fight off counterrevolution.[199]

In point of fact, the Sixth Congress's endorsement of national cultural autonomy was not as dramatic a step as one might think. That principle, unofficially defended since the Fourth Congress, had been pressed for openly by the Central Committee well before the Sixth Congress, in a leaflet distributed in December 1904.[200] Medem surmises that the committee was impelled to take such action (which was technically illegal) only because it sensed how much the sentiment for full national rights had grown since the Fifth Congress.[201] The Bund leaders plainly expected ratification of their actions without serious opposition. The chief importance of the congress, therefore, was symbolic. It marked the completion of the Bund's ideology at the very moment when the government seemed almost certain to collapse.

21. Epilogue

The Manifesto of October 17 was the crowning political event of the Revolution of 1905. The Tsar, acting on the advice of Witte, reacted to the widespread disorders and strikes by conceding broad rights to the people of the Empire, including personal inviolability and freedom of conscience, speech, assembly, and association. The manifesto reaffirmed the principle of a Duma as a major participant in the legislative process and spoke of extending the franchise to classes not covered in earlier decrees.[1]

Ever cautious about drastic overt action and perhaps still somewhat numb from the sensational events, many of the leading Bundists, and especially those returning to Russia from the Sixth Congress, found it difficult to believe that a serious change had taken place. Izenshtat took the manifesto to be a trick of the police to bring the revolutionaries out into the open, a view that was expressed by others when the Central Committee met in late October.[2] Yet the Bundists could not ignore the weakness of the government, which became all too plain in the "free days" following the announcement, when the still-vague rights granted in the manifesto were interpreted in the streets. From a practical standpoint, the first task was to determine what to take of the new and what to retain of the old. That there was any discussion at all of what should be altered, and of how and how much, in itself indicated a major turn in Russian history, even if the direction was far from clear.

Both the manifesto and the current political situation suggested what changes might take place. If certain things were now legal, many others clearly remained illegal. The most dangerous step of all, obviously, was for the Bund to reveal itself, and the organization decided to remain secret. Its important weapons, too, had to be retained and protected, which is to say, the BO's, the illegal presses, the journals, and the Foreign Committee.[3] Meanwhile, the Bund meant to test the new freedom by creating other instruments conforming to the spirit of the times and the manifesto.

The press was bound to be one of the easiest ways of scouting the government's intentions. The Central Committee almost immediately undertook to start a Yiddish daily in Vilna, *Der Veker*, as well as a Russian-language week-ly, *Yevreiskii rabochii* (The Jewish Worker). The sheer enormity of the task, involving the solution of great technical and literary problems (censorship still existed and the permission of the regime still had to be obtained), was altogether new to the Bund's experience. The Central Committee, which felt this work should have priority over everything else, had to mobilize literally "all members who could hold pens in their hands."[4]

Despite the Central Committee's intentions, the old organs began to dis-appear. *Di Arbeter Shtime* never resumed publication, its last issue appearing in September 1905; the very symbol of the Bund's underground press in Rus-sia, its demise symbolized the end of an era. *Der Bund* ceased publication in November 1905 and *Posledniia izvestiia* in January 1906. The illegal presses were the next to go; each was shut down and its equipment packed away.[5]

One of the most urgent and important new problems was deciding what tack to take on the workers' organizations. With the right to form trade unions came the possibility of organizing workers on a grand scale, and the obvious advantage of an organization able to finance itself through a large membership seemed a fitting reward for the workers who had struck so val-iantly during the first ten months of the year. But the Bundists and their fel-low revolutionaries had serious reservations about endorsing the trade union movement. As the Bund saw it, the difficulty would come in retaining the loyalty of the masses so that revolutionary work could continue until the final goal, a socialist society, was reached. Though political work and economic work were differentiated in the Bund to a significant degree after 1902, there was no such clear distinction in personnel, and many of those engaging in one form of activity also engaged in the other.[6]

To the revolutionary parties the choice seemed to be between the neutral trade union, an organization that had no political ties and that accepted mem-bers without regard to their political views, and a union that was tied both ideologically and organizationally to a given party. In the northwest prov-inces the RSDWP, the socialist Zionists, and the PPS all supported the de-velopment of neutral trade unions.[7] But the Bund did not.

The majority of Bundists, and eventually, in late 1905, the Central Commit-tee, opted for party unions for historical, ideological, and tactical reasons. They argued that the economic and political development of the Jewish movement had been a parallel process. To a Social Democrat economic struggle was only part of the all-important class struggle that alone would lead to the full liber-ation of the working class. The Bundists insisted that trade unionism would lead to "professional egoism," to the workers' concentration on narrow trade interests and neglect of the great tasks of the future.[8]

On a more practical level, the Bundists argued that party-directed unions were a tactical necessity. They insisted that since Russia was in transition and there were still no political guarantees, the Social Democrats did not yet have the power to carry on their political struggle openly. Consequently, to support independent trade unions was to give the bourgeois democrats the opportunity to draw workers into their net.[9] The Bundists, in short, regarded the victory of October as unfinished business and, as with their technical apparatus, they were not prepared to endanger their gains by voluntarily relinquishing control to the enemy. In their view, if the situation in Russia calmed down for any appreciable period, neutral unions would lose their class consciousness and become purely trade unionist; but if the stormy days continued (and the streets were still seething in December), the unions would be pushed into a political struggle by force of circumstances, which would almost certainly be fought under bourgeois democratic influence. There was no such thing as a non-party political struggle, the Bund insisted; all political action must ultimately come under the lead of some party or other.[10] The party union alone was acceptable.

The Bund's organization was also soon altered to fit the new conditions. In a move to democratize controls through mass participation and, to some degree, to decentralize, the Seventh Conference (March–April 1906) granted substantial power to the rank and file. The selection of local committees, until then the prerogative of the Central Committee, was left to general meetings of skhodkas and local intellectual centers, which were also given the right to name delegates to the upcoming Seventh Congress.[11] These moves indicate the Bundists admitted at least some improvement in the political situation, for they would never have risked such changes under the conditions prevailing before October.

Even some of the underground personnel responded to the new times. Many felt that the need for their particular services had ended—that the time of speakers and talented party leaders had begun. Indeed, Laibechke Berman's wife left the movement altogether, though she returned with the success of the counterrevolution in 1907.[12] Medem's description of the mood of those days rings true: "One thing was clear: this time it was not simply a storm, not merely a repulsed attack.... A new [era] was beginning, either a whole or a half-revolution but a revolution nonetheless."[13]

The regime, however, was more resilient than the revolutionaries had supposed, and the Bundists were soon grappling with the problems of counterrevolution. For the Jews the announcement of the October Manifesto brought a new set of horrors, triggering a wave of pogroms the day after that surpassed all previous violence perpetrated against them. The southern areas of the country and Odessa in particular were hard-hit.[14] The complicity of the state in these actions was later proved beyond any reasonable doubt.[15]

As the delegates to the Sixth Congress were making their way home they met refugees from pogroms in Ekaterinoslav and Odessa, and their joy abruptly cooled at what they saw.[16] Like many, Medem was torn between elation and sorrow: "For many years [we Jewish socialists] had awaited the great day, and when it came it was being drenched in a torrent of Jewish blood."[17] The doubts were reminiscent of the post-Kishinev period. Isaac Devenishski (Aaron, Vaiter), an important member of the Vilna Committee in the days following the announcement of the manifesto, began to lose his faith in "the people."[18] These circumstances alone were enough to raise doubts about the meaning of legality. There, plain for all to see, were the Black Hundreds, organizing themselves as never before, bolder and more ambitious in their actions after October. Some Bundists were bound to ask themselves if this did not bode ill for the future despite the words of the manifesto, if in fact it did not signal the beginning of the counterrevolution.

Yet many revolutionaries, the Bundists among them, were convinced that the victory of October was simply a beginning, that the government was losing control. Though the pogroms brought sadness, the "free days" were the headiest of the whole Revolution. In Warsaw, writes Litvak, "people kissed in the streets."[19] Catholics held religious processions, and numbers of political prisoners were forcibly freed from jails (little knowing, of course, that political prisoners would be granted amnesty a few weeks later). The Bund reached the height of its glory, with both the organization and individual members achieving brief power but enduring fame. Devenishski began to be called "police chief" around Vilna and even negotiated with the governor over the stationing of troops in the city.[20] Another who gained a measure of fame was Shmeun Klevansky, whose flowery oratory completely won over a hostile crowd of thousands of railroad workers in Riga. So much so that though he began his speech to catcalls and the insulting epithet "Yid," he ended up being adopted as their "Maksim," their hero.[21] In that time of revolutionary passion, such events kept the Bund's hopes high.

The continuation of strikes after the manifesto was issued contributed to the belief that new victories awaited the hardy. Though the number of strikers fell off in November, some 350,000 workers were still in the streets; and in the next month the number swelled to over 400,000. This figure was below October's, but included more political strikers than the number it had taken to force the manifesto.[22] The eventful two and a half months saw uprisings among the sailors at Kronstadt and other bases, peasant revolts, the declaration of martial law in Poland (where the strikes hardly ceased), and the formation of the St. Petersburg Soviet, or Workers' Council. Each new event spurred fresh optimism among the Bundists.[23]

The Bundists labored incessantly to infuse the Jewish workers with the enthusiasm needed for the conflict that was sure to come. "We have already breathed the air of freedom," the Central Committee proclaimed in October, "and what has cost us thousands of victims we will not let go."[24] In an assessment of the post-October events, *Der Bund* mused that "a general uprising is not a dream but a reality that could become a fact at any moment." The manifesto amounted only to a "constitutional autocracy." The goal of the proletariat and the Social Democrats remained a constituent assembly and a democratic republic, and that required an armed uprising.[25]

The high point of revolutionary action after October came in December, which saw a mass uprising in Moscow. This was to be the last major outbreak of urban violence of the Revolution. The Bundists attempted to respond to the new revolutionary call, the third of the year, but this time their efforts fell short of those of January and October. Abramovich, looking back at the period, suggests three reasons for the Bund's reduced effectiveness: the pogroms, the sheer fatigue of continuous revolutionary action, and a feeling among the Bund leaders that the Jewish workers were no longer in the vanguard, as they had been for so many years, that leadership was now passing to the Russian workers.[26] The first two reasons seem sound enough, but the third may say more about Abramovich, then the Bund's representative to the St. Petersburg Soviet, than it does about the Bundists. Of greater importance was the fact that the government had gradually regrouped its forces and rallied support for its actions. In October the populace had largely sympathized with the strikers, but that sympathy tended to melt away as the workers' demands grew more radical.

The Bundists had no way of knowing, of course, that the tide of revolution would recede after the failure of the Moscow uprising, and they continued to pin their hopes on armed revolt. The first issue of *Der Veker* (which was still under the constraints of censorship) spoke of the government shooting its last bullets at the proletariat. It pictured a beleaguered and even defunct Autocracy, and insisted the only remaining question was "what kind of order will be founded in its place. A limited monarchy with limited . . . rights" or "a true democratic order with broad unlimited . . . rights." The proletariat had to arm if a truly democratic system was to be established.[27] Far from discouraging the Bundists, the Moscow revolt strengthened their conviction that success through armed uprising was possible.[28]

Accepting as axiomatic the continuing strength of the Revolution, the Bundists had little reason to accept the Duma on Witte's terms. The new broadened electoral law announced on December 11 still excluded from the franchise, among others, those who worked in enterprises with fewer than 50 male employees,[29] a restriction that ensured the exclusion of large numbers of Jewish workers. In the continuing absence of guarantees that might lead to a constituent assembly on a truly democratic basis, the Bundists held to the course of boycotting the Duma. Nothing had occurred, they maintained, to warrant a change of tactics.[30] The Seventh Conference of the Bund, which met a few days prior to the April 27 convocation of the Duma, reaffirmed the policy of active boycott on the grounds that the contradiction between social forces in

Russia and the existing political order could not be resolved, and that the existence of a Duma would in itself hinder the revolutionary struggle.[31]

Unlike the extreme-left parties (with the exception of the Mensheviks), the liberal camp accepted the October Manifesto, albeit with some hesitation. The Jewish liberals backed the newly formed Constitutional Democratic Party (Kadets). Many were unhappy with the provisions of the December 11 electoral law but argued that, once elected, the Duma representatives could extend the franchise to those who were presently excluded. The ultimate hope was "to discredit the government and its allies ... in order to summon a Duma on the basis of a universal electoral law."[32]

The unity of the opponents of the regime now began to crumble from the political center outward. The Bundists refused to believe that the liberals could or would change the Duma from within. In any case, if the liberals were to be taken at their word, they meant to deal only with the issue of the electoral law. In *Der Veker*'s opinion, the liberals would be drawn into schemes and counterschemes, and in the end would simply give what would inevitably be a reactionary body a sheen of popular representation, to the profit of the regime. If the liberals were serious, they would back the boycott, the paper concluded; but they were not to be trusted.[33]

The composition of the First Duma brought surprises for both the left and the right. Twelve Jews, several Mensheviks, and a considerable number of leftists (soon to be known as the Trudoviks) gained seats. The liberal Kadets, the single largest party in the Duma, were able to exercise a majority with some help from the left and the moderate right.[34]

Weak as it was, the Duma was plainly a going concern. Recognizing that fact, as well as the unexpectedly liberal character of the assembly, the Bundists now abandoned the tactic of complete boycott and began to advocate the use of public persuasion to influence deputies to work for radical changes. They believed that the basic contradiction between the Duma's impotence and the increasing demands for fundamental change would ignite the revolutionary spark, which they saw as still very much alive. Boycott had been justified at the time it was advocated, they maintained, but now practicality demanded that the Duma be used to revolutionary purpose.[35]

The temper of the Duma led the government to dissolve it on July 8, 1906, less than three months after its convocation. The wide support in the Duma for agrarian reform through expropriation, and the delegates' demands for an official accounting on a number of issues, including the government's treatment of the Jews, provided the state with its excuse. On the same day, the Tsar fixed February 20, 1907, for the convocation of the Second Duma.

The existence of the First Duma had persuaded the Bundists that they had to make use of it for their own ends. Having come to that position, they quite naturally felt that participation in the elections to the new Duma might prove useful. At the Seventh Congress, in September 1906, the Bund lined up with a number of other revolutionary parties, including the Bolsheviks, to end the boycott and take advantage of the new conditions in the land. Temporarily, at least, legal activity was to supersede armed revolution on the political agenda.

The cessation of the boycott signified a qualified acceptance of the settlement of October 1905. The limited freedoms of 1906 replaced the revolutionary optimism of 1905. In 1907 new state actions would partially destroy the October settlement and again push the Bundists underground. But those days properly belong in another period of the Bund's history.*

By October 1905 the Bund had established a formidable reputation both in the Jewish community and in the revolutionary camp of the Russian Empire. It had gained that position by its determined search for answers to the key problems troubling not only the Jewish population but all the peoples of the Empire. The broadest problem facing the Jews toward the end of the nineteenth century was how to accommodate themselves to a society beginning to undergo rapid economic modernization and developing a new political consciousness while retaining their own identity. Although the Bund held common ground with other Jewish movements and with important segments of the revolutionary movement, its answers to that problem distinguished it to one degree or another from all other groups.

Passionate Marxists but residents of Jewish Russia, the Bundists selected the Jewish worker as the focal point of the modernization they hoped to achieve. They placed him in a dual relationship to the problem. On the one hand they saw him as linked by class interests to the entire working class of the Empire and viewed his struggle as part of a general class struggle for the realization of socialism; on the other hand they saw his cultural identity as a vital element in his life, in need of modernization but nevertheless containing the ingredients out of which his new identity would be constructed. In short, the Bund at the same time tied the Jewish workers to a larger community of class within the Empire and insisted on their distinctiveness from other ethnic groups, while seeking an identity for them suited to both these aspects of their existence.

The Bund was the first organization in the Empire to single out the Jewish working class as worthy of attention and to organize it into a force capable of acting in its own behalf. By concentrating on the workers and insisting on the

---

* The Bund continued to be active in Russia until the early 1920's, when it vanished as a formal organization, the victim of internal fragmentation and Soviet pressure. In Poland, which gained its independence in the aftermath of the Revolution, the Bund survived, and continues to play a role in the political life of the country and the cultural life of its Jewish population. For a recent study of the Bund in Poland, see Bernard K. Johnpoll, *The Politics of Futility: The General Jewish Workers' Bund of Poland, 1917–1943* (Ithaca, N.Y., 1967).

importance of the class struggle, the Bundists broke with the dominant concept of identity among the Jews—that they were one people regardless of all other distinctions. That focus brought them into conflict with most other Jewish organizations, not only on the crucial point of identity but on the equally crucial point of accommodation to society. To the Zionists, the upholders of a united national and territorial ideal, the Bundists seemed to make the interests of the Jews as a whole subordinate to class interests. To the Jewish liberals, the intellectual and bourgeois segment of Jewish society, the Bund seemed not only to be destroying the unity of the Jews but also to be offering democratic values that were only partially acceptable and proletarian and socialist values that were totally unacceptable.

Only the socialist or proletarian-oriented Zionists, a weak movement until 1905, took the Bundist view that the Jewish working class was the major agent of modernization. But the great differences between the two groups on the nature of Jewish identity and the definition of nationality in territorial terms placed them far apart and made them competitors.

Among the traditionally nonpolitical elements within Jewish society, the Bund appeared as heretic to the religious, as lawbreaker to the would-be loyal subject, as bearer of great woe to those who feared the wrath of the regime would be visited against all Jews for the Bund's actions, and as social radical to those who accepted the traditional values of the social structure. The Bund broke more completely with Jewish society than any other Jewish organization, for it called for nothing less than a radical transformation of that society.

Nevertheless, in successfully instilling the values of dignity and self-assertion into the Jewish worker the Bundists achieved a position of leadership in times of stress that no other part of the society could claim. The Bund was the unquestioned leader of self-defense when the Jewish community was under constant threat of attack, and many segments of the Jewish community had to thank it for that. Further, it helped produce a social and political consciousness that became a useful part of the heritage of the Jews. However grudgingly, both labor Zionists and liberals recognized the Bund's positive role as teacher and fighter, and paid it due respect even as they criticized it for its "mistaken" aspirations.

It was the Bundists' acceptance of the existing environment as the proper arena for the struggle of the Jewish worker that gave their organization its peculiar strength. By tying their revolutionary doctrine and organization to the changing economic and political life of the Empire, and the future identity of the Jewish worker to the existing cultural base, they offered an approach to his immediate and long-range problems with which he could readily identify. The workers did not have to reject themselves as they were, nor did they have to take it on faith that a territory would appear for them in the Near East or in some other distant area of the world at some future date. The Bund offered them a direct struggle and the chance to play a meaningful part in their own liberation. By projecting a role of leadership for the Jewish workers in which they could participate immediately, the Bund wedded them to action on their own behalf and to pride in themselves despite all existing disabilities.

The Bund's intimate connection with the life of the Jewish workers gave the movement enormous cohesion. The institutions of the workers' movement became extensions of the Jewish workers' life, infused with a new spirit and organization. The workers understood and responded to these institutions, and the Bundists rarely moved so far ahead of their constituents that they lost touch with them.

That intimacy had some drawbacks, however. Conscious of their strengths and weaknesses, the Bund leaders undertook only a limited struggle against economic and political foes. They were aware that their adherents, few in number compared with the total Russian proletariat, could not initiate and carry great events through to a successful conclusion, that the mass power of the Jewish working class could not make the revolution alone. Indeed, the very success of the Bund in its local conflicts often heightened the loneliness of the movement—a fact that revolutionaries of other nationalities, Zionists, and officials of the Tsarist regime noticed and used against the Bund, each group in its own way. After the first years the Bundists even had to take care not to destroy some of the weaker elements of the craft economy among the Jews.

The Bund had little or no support among the other Jewish organizations working for change in Russia, a fact that plainly helped to reduce its effectiveness. Controlling only a small portion of the potentially revolutionary masses, the Bund necessarily had to depend on other, greater forces to achieve the maximum results; and the Bundists were accordingly charged with having given up their independence of action. The Zionists in particular were quick to attack the Bundists on this point, and unfortunately for the Bundists the actions of the Russian and Polish revolutionaries sometimes reinforced the Zionist interpretation. The Zionists, like the Russians and Poles, could envision themselves as independent revolutionary organisms; the Bund could do so only to a lesser extent.

Nor did the Bundists' Marxist ideology answer the question of national identity satisfactorily in the eyes of the other organizations. The Bund's national cultural autonomy was exceedingly pale compared with the Zionists' territorial and cultural vision. Moreover, the autonomy the Bund held out for was vague. Outright territorial solutions were easily articulated and readily understood in light of existing political experience. To many the Bundist solution to identity rested heavily on uncertain faith, whereas the Zionist solution was clear, if distant in terms of actual fulfillment.

The most difficult problem for the Bundists was the problem of the economic and political position of the Jewish worker in Russia. The economic life of the Jew was declining, and the Jewish worker, seeking access to the benefits of the new industrial society, ran into a wall of legal and cultural restrictions and hostility that made the Bund's view of the future hard to believe. Emigration indicated the Jews' lack of faith in a future in Russia, even when there was sympathy for the Bund and its work. The ever-present threat of pogroms assuredly did not speak well of the Jewish worker's acceptance as an equal partner. Under the circumstances, the Bundists could only reject the Zionist argument that the problem of anti-Semitism defied solution and insist on the beneficial long-range effects of education and socialism.

The Bund also found it hard to muster support in the general revolutionary movement. Insofar as the Bund accepted the task of organizing and revolutionizing the Jewish workers of the Empire, it was at one with the major thrust of Social Democracy in Russia. But its desire to retain its organizational identity and to claim for the Jewish workers a future identity as Jews deeply disturbed the centralists and internationalists among the Russian Social Democrats. They had just begun the process of unifying themselves and regarded that unity as the most important aspect of their work. Moreover, they doubted that the Jews had a national identity worth maintaining in the future. How to deal with the Bund without defining the future identity of the Jews became a difficult problem for the RSDWP, raising national, organizational, and cultural issues of major importance. More than any other party within Russian Social Democracy in these early years, the Bund sought an equitable resolution of the problem of national identity, one that would answer the needs of its own workers as well as those of other nationalities, and yet keep Social Democracy as closely knit as it had to be in order to accomplish its ends. Thanks to the major part the Bund had played in the development of Russian Social Democracy, it was able to play the role of gadfly to remind the Russians of their obligations to the nationalities—and it played that role to the hilt in the years between 1901 and 1905, even if its suggestions and demands were usually ignored.

More than any other Social Democratic group in Russia up to October 1905, the Bund was an organization resting on a mass base; and for this it was admired and studied, even by its sharpest critics. To be sure, the admiration was often reluctant, for the strength of the Bund could not be explained away in terms of some extraordinary mechanical principle of organization; it was impossible to ignore the national-cultural aspects of cohesion—that extra dimension of hatred toward the regime and desire to preserve one's identity that gave many of the national revolutionary parties a greater unity than that achieved by the Russians.

The Bund's will to fight to change the world was an altogether new phenomenon for the Jews of Russia. For scores of thousands of them it served as a pioneer of democracy and socialism, as an organizer of modern life, as the symbol of a bright tomorrow. Above all, it created a generation of Jews unwilling to bend under the double yoke of class and ethnic origin. For that alone, the Bund would be given its page in the history of revolutionary movements of the modern world.

Reference Matter

Biographical Notes

Listed here are brief histories of the post-1905 careers of most of the important Bundists of the period studied. Regrettably, the list is not as complete or as detailed as I would like, for in the chaotic years of war and revolution, Soviet purge and Nazi occupation, many of the men and women mentioned in the text simply dropped from sight—or at least largely from the written record. For earlier information on the Bundists listed below, consult the Index.

ABRAM DER TATE, *see* BLEKHMAN.

ABRAMOVICH, RAPHAEL (RAPHAEL REIN), 1880–1963. Served briefly as the Bund's representative in the St. Petersburg Soviet in 1905. Selected as the Bund and RSDWP candidate for the Second Duma in Vitebsk and Kovno in 1906. Edited various Bund journals in 1908–9 and also taught school. Arrested and exiled in 1910–11. Broke exile and fled to Western Europe. Returned to Russia as a leader of the internationalist wing of the Bund and of the Mensheviks in 1917. Went to Berlin in 1920 to become a leading figure in the Menshevik publication *Sotsialisticheskii vestnik*. Also contributed heavily to Yiddish publications. Lived in the United States after 1940, continuing his journalistic activities until his death.

BANEVUR, BORIS (KUPETS), c. 1872– ? Gave the Bund financial help after 1905. Apparently politically inactive after World War I. Probably died during World War II.

BERMAN, L., *see* LIBKIND.

BERMAN, PAVEL, 1873–1922. Completed his studies at the polytechnicum at Karlsruhe, Germany, in 1903. Returned to Russia after the 1905 Revolution but was not politically active. Worked as an engineer and in 1917 helped form a metal workers' union in Petrograd. Killed in an accident.

BERNSTEIN, LEON, 1877–1962. Remained abroad during the 1905 Revolution. Lived in France for many years, earning his living after 1906 as a professional journalist. Left off active political work but continued to help the Bund groups abroad. Worked for a time as secretary to Vladimir Burtsev (the founder and publisher of *Byloe*) after the February Revolution. Active in the French underground during World War II.

BLEKHMAN, LAIB (ABRAM DER TATE), 1874–1962. Continued to be an important figure in the tanners' union until 1909 or 1910, then moved to the United States. Took an active part in the socialist movement among American Jews. Returned to Russia in 1917 and worked briefly for the Bund. Returned to the United States after the Bolsheviks came to power and worked as a dental technician. Participated in the Workmen's Circle school program for a time, then became more or less politically inactive for a period of years. Became active again in Bund organizations in the United States after World War II.

BLUM, *see* HILLEL KATZ.

BORISOV, *see* RAFES.

CHEMERISKY, ALEXANDER (SASHA), c. 1880– ? Arrested in 1908 and exiled to eastern Siberia until 1910. Worked for the Bund press. Attended the Eighth Conference in 1910. Worked abroad for the Bund for a time, then returned to Russia and was arrested and jailed until 1917. Joined the Communist Party after the October Revolution. Served as Secretary of the Central Bureau of the Jewish Section of the Party Central Committee. Contributed heavily to the Yiddish-language equivalent of *Pravda*, the Moscow *Emes*. Concerned himself with the organization and industrialization of Russian Jewry and wrote on themes dealing with the Communist Party and the Russian Jews in the 1920's. Arrested around 1930 for his Zubatovite activities before 1905 and given a life sentence. Fate unknown.

DAICH, MENDEL, 1885– ? Joined the Russian Communist Party after the October Revolution and served in the Cheka. Arrested in 1937 or 1938 during the purge trials. Fate unknown.

DEVENISHSKI, ISAAC MEIER (ARON; VAITER), 1878–1919. Extremely active in the Bund in 1905–6, then went to Galicia and became a full-time writer. Served on the editorial board of a Bund weekly in 1907, then dropped all his Bund activities. Wrote plays and concerned himself with cultural work until 1912, then, disheartened by the current situation, gave himself up to the Tsarist police. Exiled to Siberia until 1917. Returned to Vilna in 1918 and again involved himself in literary work. Shot and killed by a Polish soldier in Vilna.

FRUMKIN, BORIS, 1872– ? Worked for the Bund press after 1905. Left Russia in 1907 to work with the Foreign Committee and remained abroad for many years. Wrote for Russian journals on historical themes and collaborated with Franz Kursky on a collection of documents on the Bund and the 1905 Revolution, which was published in 1913. Went with the Communist Bund when the Bund split after the Bolshevik Revolution. Lived in Moscow until the early 1930's. Fate unknown.

GOLDMAN, MIKHEL (MARK LIBER), 1880–1937. Joined the Bund Central Committee in October 1905 and served as its representative in the St. Petersburg Soviet for a time. Became the Bund's representative to the RSDWP in August 1906. Gained legal status in Russia in 1908 but remained active in the Social Democratic movement. Arrested in 1910 and fled abroad. Returned to Russia in 1914; re-arrested in 1915. Returned from exile in 1917 to become the Bund's representative in the Petrograd Soviet and a strong supporter of the Provisional Government. Also devoted some of his energies to the Mensheviks and in 1918 was in the top rank of both parties. Became involved in underground Menshevik work in the Soviet Union in 1922–23. Later arrested and imprisoned; still later executed by the Soviet authorities.

GOZHANSKY, SAMUEL (LONU), c. 1867– ? Attended the Bund's conferences and congresses in 1905 and 1906, then left active political work. Began contributing to the Bund press again in 1917. Joined the Communist Party after the October Revolution. Worked in the union movement and served on the editorial board of the Yiddish edition of Lenin's works. Apparently arrested during the purges of 1936–38 and exiled. Fate unknown.

GURVICH, EVGENIIA (ZHENIA), 1861–1940. Worked for the RSDWP in Minsk but never cut her ties with the Bund. Elected to the Minsk City Council in 1917. Arrested in 1922 for her membership in the Bund but released on the intercession of D. B. Riazanov. Though not a member of the Communist Party, worked in the Marx-Lenin-Engels Institute, probably until 1931, when Riazanov, the head of the institute, was dismissed as a Menshevik. Died in Moscow.

HELFAND, KHAIM YANKEL (A. LITVAK), 1874–1932. Continued to be an important literary figure in the Bund after 1905, and attended its conferences and congresses through 1912. Arrested and jailed briefly in 1907. Visited the United States in 1908. Worked abroad with the Bund's Foreign Committee from 1912 to the outbreak of World War I, then left for the United States, arriving in 1915. Lectured and wrote (for the organ of the Jewish Socialist Federation and other journals) for two years. Returned to Russia in 1917 and resumed literary work for the Bund. Edited a number of newspapers and published several volumes in southern Russia in 1918–20; and served on the Central Committee of the special Social Democratic Bund formed there. Returned to Vilna in the early 1920's, again editing Bund journals and also engaging in Yiddish educational work. Moved permanently to the United States in 1925 and continued to write prolifically on literature, socialism, cultural history, and the Jewish labor movement until his death.

HELLER, ANNA, *see* MRS. PINAI ROSENTHAL.

HOFMAN, BEN-TSION (ZIVION), 1874–1954. Continued to be an important writer for the Bund press in 1905–6. Went abroad in late 1906 and took a doctorate at Berne. Moved to the United States in 1908, to serve as a journalist and an active member of Jewish socialist circles. Sympathetic to the Communists for a time after 1917 but parted company with them in 1922. Served as editor of *Justice*, publication of the International Ladies Garment Workers' Union, and headed the Education Department of the Workmen's Circle. Was close to the Bund organizations in the United States until his death. Was also an important Yiddish literary figure through these years.

HURVICH, TSIVIA, 1874– ? Arrested in late 1905, released, then re-arrested in August 1906 and exiled to Astrakhan province. Broke exile in May 1907 and returned to Vilna. Became active in the Russian labor movement in St. Petersburg, working for the RSDWP. Caught and exiled to Archangel but managed to escape during World War I. Became secretary of the Social Democratic Duma Fraction. Worked for the Menshevik-Internationalists in 1917. Fate unknown.

IZBITSKY, JOSEPH (BAINISH MIKHALEVICH), 1876–1928. Arrested and exiled to the far north in 1906 but managed to escape. Participated in the election campaign for the Second Duma, wrote for the Bund press, and served as a delegate to the London Congress of the RSDWP in 1907. Re-arrested in 1909 and exiled to Archangel. Permitted to leave Russia for reasons of health in 1912 but soon returned to work on the Bund press. Worked for the Bund in German-occupied Vilna during World War I. Active from 1918 on in the Polish Bund, especially in educational and cultural work.

IZENSHTAT, ISAIAH (VITALI; UDIN), 1867–1937. Became one of the most important figures in the Bund after Portnoy's arrest in 1905. Served as chief editor of the Bund's first legal daily from 1906 to 1912. Arrested during the election campaign for the Fourth Duma and exiled to Astrakhan province; involved in cooperative work there. Joined the Central Committee of the Bund in 1917. Opposed the Bolsheviks after the October Revolution. Arrested in 1921 but permitted to leave Russia in 1922. Member of the Menshevik Delegation Abroad in Berlin. On the demise of the Social Democratic Bund, devoted himself to Menshevism but maintained contact with the Bundists and the Bund Archives. Both the Bundists and the Mensheviks celebrated his seventieth birthday in 1937. Died soon after in Paris. His wife, Liuba, a Bund pioneer, died in 1903 in New York.

KAHAN, BARUKH MORDECAI (VIRGILI), 1883–1936. Attended various Bund and RSDWP meetings and wrote for the Bund press in 1906–7. Participated in the labor movement in Vilna in 1908, then drifted out of active work until World War I. Served as a Bund delegate to the Petrograd Soviet in 1917 and worked on the Bund journal in Petrograd,

Yevreiskii rabochii. Worked from the 1920's on to set up a secular Yiddish school system and helped create the Yiddish Scientific Institute in Vilna. Member of the Vilna Committee of the Bund in these years.

KAPLINSKY, ISRAEL MIKHEL, ? –1919? Worked for the Bund in Warsaw and Vilna after 1905. Exposed as a provocateur in 1909. Apparently lived in Saratov thereafter. Executed by the Soviet authorities for his activities on behalf of the Tsarist police.

KATZ, DAVID (TARAS), 1876– ? Continued to be active in the Bund until 1909, then moved to the Caucasus. At the end of the 1920's he and his wife were living in Moscow. Later career and fate unknown.

KATZ, MRS. DAVID (*née* MARYA ZHALUDSKY), 1875– ? Served on the Dvinsk Committee. Politically inactive after 1908.

KATZ, HILLEL (BLUM; KATZ-BLUM), 1863-1943. Lived in the United States from 1904 until his death. Active in the American socialist movement throughout his lifetime.

KATZ, SAMUEL (SHMUEL THE DARK ONE). Moved to Germany before 1905 and worked as a typesetter. Emigrated to the United States and probably died before World War I. Presumably politically inactive after he left Russia.

KISIN, ABRAHAM, ? –1905. Killed in a demonstration in Vilna in October 1905.

KLEVANSKY, SHMEUN (MAKSIM), 1878–? Freed by the amnesty of 1905. Sent to the United States in 1906 on behalf of the Bund but apparently became inactive after 1907. Returned to Russia in 1917 and worked for the International Bank. Turned to journalistic work after the October Revolution. Briefly opposed the Communists, then reportedly worked for a state economic agency during the NEP period. Later career and fate unknown.

KOIGAN, FISHL (YOINA), c. 1870-1923. Remained on the Bund Central Committee until 1910. Continued to be a major Bund activist in southern Russia until 1907. Represented the Bund at RSDWP and International Socialist congresses before World War I. Lived abroad after 1910, a considerable part of the time in tuberculosis sanitoria. Worked as a dentist in Geneva during World War I. Returned to Russia after the 1917 revolution and joined the Communist Party in 1918. Member of the Soviet diplomatic mission to Berlin in the early 1920's and served the Soviet government in various other capacities until his death.

KOPELSON, TSEMAKH (GRISHIN; TIMOFEI), 1869-1933. Headed the Bund publishing house in Vilna until 1908, then left Russia for a time, living in Western Europe and the United States. Remained active in Russian Social Democratic and Bund publications. Returned to Russia after the 1917 Revolution and joined the Communist Party. Worked for Gosizdat, the state publishing agency. Died in an automobile accident.

KOSOVSKY, VLADIMIR, *see* NAHUM LEVINSON.

KREMER, AARON (ALEXANDER; ARKADY), 1865-1935. Continued to play an important role in the Bund until his arrest in 1907. Ceased to be a party professional on his release in 1908 but continued to serve the Bund in many capacities. Went to France in 1912 and took an engineering degree in 1914. Worked as an engineer in France until 1921, then returned to Vilna. Taught mathematics and played an active role in the Bund there until his death.

KREMER, MRS. AARON (*née* MATLE SREDNITSKY; PATI), 1867-1943. Accompanied her husband in his travels after 1908. Active in Bund organizations in Vilna in the 1920's, though not in a leadership role. Died in the Vilna ghetto.

LAPSERDAK, ALTER (EZRA ROZEN; BERG). Played an important role in the Bund in Warsaw and served as an editor of the local Bund organ until 1906, then worked for the Bund in Odessa. Active in the election campaigns for the Second and Third Dumas. Member of the Central Committee for a time in 1906. Found employment in St. Petersburg after 1908 but maintained contact with his old comrades. Worked in economic institutions and the state bank after the October Revolution. Worked in the Soviet bank in Paris for a time. Later career and fate unknown.

LEVIN, SHOLOM, 1877–1970. Worked in the legal Bund press in 1906–7. Arrested and exiled to Siberia in 1910. Made his way to the United States in 1912. Was closely oriented to the Communists in the United States from 1917 on.

LEVIN, YANKEL, 1888–1941? Worked for the Bund Central Committee in Warsaw in 1913–14, in the Ukraine in 1915–16, and in Belorussia in 1917. Wrote occasional articles for the Bund press. Became a member of the Central Committee in 1919. Stayed with the left wing when the Bund split in 1920, then moved over to the Communist Party. Worked on Jewish colonization projects in the Crimea and Birobidjian. Served as secretary of the Regional Committee of the Communist Party in Birobidjian in 1929. Journalistically active through the 1920's and 1930's. Arrested and accused of being a Japanese spy in the late 1930's. Probably executed by the Soviet authorities in 1941.

LEVINSON, NAHUM MENDEL (VLADIMIR KOSOVSKY), 1867–1941. Continued to be an important writer and editor for the Bund. Also wrote for Menshevik journals in the years 1910–13. Went abroad in 1907 and refused to return to Russia through Germany in 1917. Lived in Berlin from 1920 to 1930 and there continued to write for the Bund and other Jewish journals. Returned to Warsaw in 1930 and was active in the central circles of the Bund there for several years, contributing to the main Bund paper, *Folkstsaitung*. Made his way to the United States in 1941 and resumed Bundist activities just before his death.

LEVIT, ROSA. Edited a paper for needleworkers in Vilna in 1907, then worked for the Bund in Lodz for a time. Arrested in 1908. Worked for the Central Committee in 1914. Member of Bundist and Menshevik circles in 1917 and worked with the Soviet in Petrograd. Continued her work in Moscow in 1918. Arrested in 1921 and imprisoned until the early 1930's, then exiled to Suzdal. Fate unknown.

LIBER, MARK, *see* MIKHEL GOLDMAN.

LIBKIND, LAIB (BERMAN; LAIBECHKE), 1882–1960. Continued to work for the Bund's self-defense groups and newspapers after 1905. Made a member of the Central Committee in 1917. Migrated from Russia to Poland in 1922 and there ran a trade school for furniture-makers. Later moved to the United States and worked as a carpenter. Remained a staunch Bund loyalist to the end.

LITVAK, A., *see* KHAIM HELFAND.

MEDEM, VLADIMIR, 1879–1923. Took the "soft" line in 1906, welcoming the reunification of the Bund with the RSDWP. Edited various Bund newspapers up to World War I and wrote extensively on the national question. Arrested in 1913; released in 1915. Played an important role in the Bund in German-occupied Poland during World War I and helped build a Jewish school system there. Broke politically with the Bund leadership in 1921 and lived his life out in the United States.

MICHNIK, DAVID (CHEKH), c. 1881–1905. Committed suicide in February 1905.

MIKHALEVICH, BAINISH, *see* JOSEPH IZBITSKY.

MILL, JOSEPH (JOHN), 1870–1952. Continued to work abroad for the Foreign Committee until 1915. Lived the rest of his life in the United States, working as a dental technician. Active in the Jewish socialist movement in the United States and wrote for a number of Yiddish journals and newspapers. Remained close to the Bundist movement in the United States.

MUTNIKOVICH, ABRAM (GLEB; MUTNIK), 1868–1930. Recalled from abroad in 1906 by the Central Committee and thereafter performed various editorial tasks for the Bund. Was a principal in interrogating Kaplinsky, the provocateur, in 1909. Left active political work soon after and lived in Sweden during World War I. Was in contact with and helping the Central Committee and Bund activists in a number of cities in 1917. Moved to Berlin after the war and remained close to the Bund group there until his death.

NEMANSKY, *see* ZELDOV.

NOVOMAISKY, MOISHE JOSEPH (MOISSAYE OLGIN), 1878–1939. A major contributor to the legal press in 1906. Studied in Heidelberg in 1907–9, then returned to Russia. Active in adult education work and also wrote literary criticism for the Bund press. Went abroad to work for a Bund publication in 1913. Unable to make his way back to Russia at the outbreak of war, he moved to the United States. Worked for the Yiddish daily *Forverts* in New York. Received a Ph.D. from Columbia University in 1918 and joined the faculty of the New School for Social Research the next year. Became editor of the Yiddish newspaper *Fraihait* and worked on a number of publications close to the Communist movement. From 1932 on was the New York correspondent for *Pravda*.

OLGIN, MOISSAYE, *see preceding entry*.

PORTNOY, JEKUTHIEL (NOIKH), 1872–1941. Given amnesty in 1905 after a short imprisonment. Resumed his seat on the Central Committee and remained on it for a number of years. Helped form the Committee of Bund Organizations in Poland in 1914 and was an important figure there during the German occupation in World War I. Served as chairman of the Central Committee of the Polish Bund after the war. Made his way to New York via the USSR and Japan in 1941. Died shortly after his arrival.

RAFES, MOISHE (BORISOV), 1883–1942. Continued to be active in Gomel and Vilna after 1905. Attended Bund Conferences in 1910 and 1912. Arrested in 1916 for his Bund activities in Petrograd and released in 1917. Served as secretary to the Bund Central Committee and as a member of the Executive Committee of the Petrograd Soviet. Moved to the left in 1919, joining the Communist Bund and later the Communist Party. Was a leading figure in the Workers' Soviet in Moscow. Subsequently played a role in the formation of Soviet China policy and was active in the movie industry. Arrested in 1942 and died the same year.

REIN, RAPHAEL, *see* RAPHAEL ABRAMOVICH.

ROSENTHAL, DR. PINAI (AN-MAN; PAVEL), 1872–1924. Released from prison in the amnesty of October 1905. Served on the editorial board of the Bund's legal paper, *Der Veker*, and its successors for the next several years. Returned to medical work as a bacteriologist in 1908 but continued to write articles for Bund journals. Active also in adult education work. Served in the army in World War I. Resumed Bund activity in 1917. Remobilized into the Red Army in 1919. Returned to Vilna in 1921 and there worked for the Bund in an unofficial capacity, contributing articles to a number of its journals.

ROSENTHAL, MRS. PINAI (*née* ANNA HELLER), 1872– ? Released from exile in 1905. Attended the Bund's Seventh Conference in 1906. Member of the Vilna Committee and active in cultural work there during the years of reaction. Dropped out of political work during the war, then renewed her activities in 1917 as secretary of the Central Committee. Returned to Vilna with her husband in 1921. Remained tied with the Social Democratic Bund. Active in evening educational work. Wrote a number of memoir pieces and worked for the Vilna Committee and children's and women's organizations after her husband's death in 1924. Arrested by the NKVD after the Nazi-Soviet pact and died in a Soviet prison.

ROZEN, EZRA, *see* ALTER LAPSERDAK.

SAPOTNITSKY, ALBERT, ? –1908. Left Riga at the end of 1905 and entered law school at St. Petersburg University. Simultaneously served as a revolutionary agitator for a Social

Democratic organization active among the military. Arrested in the summer of 1907 and sentenced to four years of hard labor. Committed suicide after brutal treatment.

SHADOVSKY, ISRAEL KHAIM (VICTOR SHULMAN), 1876–1951. Amnestied from Siberian exile in 1905. Resumed work for the Central Committee. Arrested several times in 1906–8 and went abroad at the end of 1909 after release from exile. Continued to work for the Bund and attended its Eighth Conference in 1910. Returned to Warsaw in 1914 to become a central figure in the Bund organization there. Active in organizing legal unions during the German occupation in World War I. Was a leading member of the Bund in Poland after October 1917, working for its daily newspaper, *Folkstsaitung*. In the late 1920's wrote a history of the Bund. Escaped to the United States in 1941 and helped to represent the Bund in America until his death.

SHULMAN, VICTOR, *see preceding entry.*

SOROKA, HIRSH, 1873–1909. Left Russia and apparently wandered around Europe for several years. Died in New York.

SREDNITSKY, MATLE, *see* MRS. AARON KREMER.

WEINSTEIN, AARON (RAKHMIEL), 1877–1938. Served on the Bund's Central Committee after 1905 and represented the Bund at various RSDWP conferences before World War I. Arrested in 1915 and exiled to Siberia until 1917. Served in the Minsk City Council and was a leading political figure in the city from 1917 to 1920. Adhered to the right wing of the Bund until 1919 but shifted sharply to the left in that year and led a Bund faction into the Communist Party in 1921. Member of the Central Executive Committee of the Belorussian Soviet and of the Central Committee of the local Communist Party. Also active in Jewish colonization work. Denounced as a Bundist-nationalist and arrested in 1937. Committed suicide in prison.

ZASLAVSKY, DAVID, 1879–1965. Worked as a writer and speaker for the Bund in 1905–6. Began writing also for non-Bundist newspapers in Kiev in 1907. Served as a Bund representative in the Petrograd Soviet in 1917. Halted his political activity for a time after 1919, writing on historical themes about the revolutionary movement. Joined the Communist Party in 1925 and began to write for *Pravda* and *Izvestiia*. Also continued to do some writing for Yiddish newspapers.

ZELDOV, SENDOR (SERGEI NEMANSKY), 1873–1924. Worked abroad with Bund groups until mid-1906, then returned to Vilna and worked as an editor in the Bund publishing house. Went to St. Petersburg in 1908 but continued to write occasional articles for the Bund, especially on trade unions. Returned to active work in 1917, taking up editorial duties on the Bund's central organ. His wife, the former Taibechke Oshmiansky, remained a faithful Bundist until her death in 1935.

ZHALUDSKY, MARYA, *see* MRS. DAVID KATZ.

ZIVION, *see* HOFMAN.

Notes

Complete authors' names, titles, and publication data are given in the Bibliography, pp. 385–96. Full data for the citations preceded by the words "Bund biblio." can be found in the separate Bund Bibliography on page 395. The following abbreviations are used in the notes:

DAS	Di Arbeter Shtime	PI	Posledniia izvestiia
DYA	Der Yidisher Arbeter	PR	Proletarskaia revoliutsiia
KIS	Katorga i ssylka	VB	Vestnik Bunda
LS	Leninskii sbornik		

Chapter One

1. Dubnow, *History*, 2: 35–36.

2. *Ibid.*, p. 63. One *verst* = 0.6629 miles.

3. *Ibid.*, pp. 64–65.

4. *Ibid.*, p. 14.

5. *Ibid.*, 1: 315–16.

6. Zborowski and Herzog, pp. 76–79.

7. Salo Baron, 1: 348–73, contains a general description of these institutions. See also S. Rabinowitsch.

8. *Sbornik*, 1: xx-xxii, xxxiii.

9. Lestchinsky, "The Jews," pp. 62, 64.

10. *Sbornik*, 2, table 4.

11. J. Raisin, p. 12.

12. Schechter, p. 1.

13. Levitats, pp. 83–84; J. Raisin, pp. 174–77.

14. Dubnow, *History*, 2: 366–67.

15. *Sbornik*, 2: 233.

Chapter Two

1. Mill, *Pionern*, 1: 79.

2. The personal data on the Bundists come from the memoirs and biographies of a number of close acquaintances and relatives. The major biographical collections are J. S. Hertz, *Doires Bundistn*; Z. Raizen, *Leksikon fun der yidisher literatur, prese, un filologie*; and S. Niger and J. Shatski, *Leksikon fun der naier yidisher literatur*.

3. Mill, *Pionern*, 1: 86; Gozhansky, "Yevreiskoe," pp. 86–87.

4. Mill, *Pionern*, 1: 18–19.

5. *Arkady*, pp. 25–26.

6. Hertz, *Doires, Bundistn*, 1: 158. The contributor, Dina Blond, knew the Rosenthal family well.

7. Mutnik, 2: 66.

8. Mill, *Pionern*, 1: 45–46.

9. I. Gurvich, p. 66; E. Gurvich, "Yevreiskoe," pp. 48–49. Isaac Gurvich was an important circle leader in Minsk.

10. Plekhanov, 4: 54; 2: 349–50.   11. E. Gurvich, "Yevreiskoe," p. 48.

12. *Ibid.*; I. Gurvich, p. 66.   13. E. Gurvich, "Yevreiskoe," p. 61.

14. Kopelson, "Ershte," p. 52; Aksel'rod-Ortodoks, p. 31.

15. Kopelson, "Ershte," pp. 50–52; E. Gurvich, "Yevreiskoe," p. 49.

16. I. Gurvich, p. 66.   17. E. Gurvich, "Yevreiskoe," p. 38.

18. I. Gurvich, pp. 67–70.   19. Kopelson, "Yevreiskoe," pp. 71–72.

20. *Ibid.*, p. 71.   21. *Arkady*, p. 395.

22. Mill, *Pionern*, 1: 49–47; Kopelson, "Ershte," p. 59.

23. E. Gurvich, "Yevreiskoe," p. 50.

24. I. Il'iashevich, "Chto delat' yevreiam v Rossii?" *Vestnik Narodnoi Voli* (Geneva), 1886, 5: 123–24.

25. Deutsch, "Ershter," p. 677.

26. Cherikover, "Yidn-revolutsionern, p. 113.

27. Kirzhnits, "Nachalo," pp. 208–9.   28. Deutsch, "Ershter," p. 680.

29. Kirzhnits, "Nachalo," p. 214.   30. *Materialy* (1906), pp. 19–21.

31. E. Gurvich, "Yevreiskoe," p. 48; Kirzhnits, "Nachalo," p. 208.

32. Peskin, p. 548.

33. Kopelson, "Ershte," p. 66.

34. Liuba Aksel'rod-Ortodoks among them. See her article, pp. 23–24.

35. I. Gurvich, p. 68; E. Gurvich, "Ershte," p. 3.

36. Cited in Sh. Rabinovich, pp. 335–36.   37. Menes, "Yidishe arbeter," p. 48.

38. Ainzaft, p. 252.   39. Sh. Rabinovich, p. 318.

40. Menes, "Yidishe arbeter," p. 3. The social place of such behavior is described in Zborowski and Herzog, p. 217.

41. Menes, "Yidishe arbeter," p. 16; Ainzaft, p. 253; Sh. Rabinovich, p. 318.

42. E. Gurvich, "Yevreiskoe," pp. 40–42; I. Gurvich, p. 73; Kopelson, "Yevreiskoe," pp. 71, 73; Sh. Rabinovich, p. 319.

43. E. Gurvich, "Yevreiskoe," p. 42; Kopelson, "Yevreiskoe," p. 71; I. Gurvich, p. 66.

44. E. Gurvich, "Yevreiskoe," p. 50.

45. Blum, p. 76. Although Blum's memoirs were not published until 1940, he wrote them some forty years earlier; he read them at a meeting in Switzerland in 1901.

46. *Ibid.*, p. 23.   47. *Ibid.*, p. 28.

48. *Ibid.*, p. 32.   49. *Ibid.*, pp. 29–30.

50. *Ibid.*, pp. 13–14.

51. E. Gurvich, "Yevreiskoe," p. 43; *Arkady*, p. 180.

52. Menes, "Yidishe arbeter," pp. 53–54.

53. E. Gurvich, "Yevreiskoe," p. 42; Kopelson, "Yevreiskoe," p. 73, and "Ershte," pp. 66–67.

Chapter Three

1. Kopelson, "Yevreiskoe," p. 70; *Arkady*, p. 114.

2. Mill, *Pionern*, 1: 59.

3. *Ibid.*, pp. 79–80.

4. Kopelson, "Yevreiskoe," p. 74.

5. The characteristics that made Vilna peculiarly suitable as a home for the Bund are described in Iuditsky, "Durum," pp. 3–4; and in *Arkady*, p. 357.

6. Gozhansky, "Yevreiskoe," p. 83. See also Izenshtat, p. 2.

7. Mill, *Pionern*, 1: 38.

8. Kopelson, "Yevreiskoe," p. 74. See also Pipes, pp. 57–60.

9. Gozhansky, "Ershte," p. 8.   10. Mill, *Pionern*, 1: 81.

11. Kopelson, "Yevreiskoe," p. 70.   12. Kopelson, "Ershte," pp. 55–56.

13. Kopelson, "Yevreiskoe," p. 73.

14. *Arkady*, p. 115; Kopelson, "Yevreiskoe," pp. 70–71.

15. Peskin, p. 548.   16. Mill, *Pionern*, 1: 67.

17. Syromiatnikov, p. 164.   18. Mill, *Pionern*, 1: 95–97.

19. *Pervoe Maia 1892*, p. 5.

20. Gozhansky, "Yevreiskoe," p. 86; *Arkady*, pp. 396–97.

21. Gozhansky, "Yevreiskoe," p. 86; Peskin, p. 552; *Arkady*, pp. 397–98.

22. Gozhansky, "A briv," p. 641.

23. Kremer, *Ob agitatsii*, p. 7.

24. Peskin, p. 552; Gozhansky, "Yevreiskoe," p. 84; *Arkady*, p. 180.

25. Gozhansky, "A briv," pp. 636, 645.

26. Bund biblio.: *Di geshikhte fun der yidisher arbeter bevegung*, pp. 52–53.

27. Blum, p. 33.

28. Mikhalevich, *Zikhroinos*, 1: 32; Blum, p. 34.

29. Odinetz et al., p. 51.   30. Mikhalevich, *Zikhroinos*, 1: 32.

31. Gordon, cols. 16–19, 21.   32. Mill, *Pionern*, 1: 98.

33. *Ibid.*, p. 99; *Arkady*, p. 53; Martov, *Zapiski*, pp. 227, 230.

34. Bernstein, *Ershte*, p. 159.   35. Gordon, cols. 45–46.

36. *Ibid.*   37. Peskin, p. 553.

38. Bernstein, *Ershte*, p. 156.   39. Gozhansky, "Yevreiskoe," p. 89.

40. Mill, *Pionern*, 1: 91.   41. *Pervoe Maia 1892*, pp. 7–15.

42. *Ibid.*, pp. 26–27.   43. Kopelson, "Yevreiskoe," p. 71.

44. Kopelson, "Ershte," pp. 66–67; Sh. Rabinovich, p. 337; Cherikover, "Onhaibn," p. 579.

45. Mill, *Pionern*, 1: 103–4. See also *Arkady*, pp. 53–54.

46. Mill, *Pionern*, 1: 106; Litvak, "Zhargonishe komitetn," p. 8.

47. Litvak, "Zhargonishe komitetn," p. 8.

48. *Ibid.*, p. 6.

49. *Ibid.*, pp. 9–13. For a brief description of the history of Yiddish literature during these years, see Niger, "Yiddish Literature," pp. 165–219.

50. Litvak, "Zhargonishe komitetn," p. 13.

Chapter Four

1. "Statut," p. 90.

2. Akimov, p. 16.

3. Zeldov, "Vozniknovenie 'Arbeter Shtime,' " p. 266.

4. Blum, pp. 39–40.

5. B. Frumkin, "Ocherki," p. 260. See also Peskin, p. 554; Shkliar, col. 207.

6. Kremer, *Ob agitatsii*, p. 17.

7. Kopelson, "Ob opozitsie."

8. Litvak, "Zhargonishe komitetn," pp. 6–7.

9. Alter Bekanter, "Perets," pp. 9–10.

10. Litvak, "Zhargonishe komitetn," p. 19.

11. *Ibid.*, pp. 20, 22, 26.

12. Gozhansky, "A briv," p. 632.

13. *Ibid.*, p. 642. See also Kremer, *Ob agitatsii*, p. 13.

14. Bund biblio.: *Istoriia*, 1901, p. 72. This, the Russian version of the report to the Congress, slightly differs from the Yiddish version published earlier (Bund biblio.: *Di geshikhte fur der yidisher . . .* , March 1900).

15. Dubnow-Erlich provides the most complete study of the organizing of the bristle and tanning workers.

16. Bund biblio.: *Istoriia*, 1901, p. 67.

17. Mill, "Geburt," p. 14, col. 1.

18. Dubnow-Erlich, pp. 18, 191–93; Sintovsky, pp. 27–28.

19. Agursky, *Sotsialistishe literatur*, p. 32.

20. Mutnikovich, "Materialy," p. 4.

21. *DYA*, 1 (Dec. 1896): 18–23, 41–50.

22. Mutnikovich, "Materialy," p. 11; Agursky, *Sotsialistishe literatur*, p. 29.

23. Mutnikovich, "Materialy," pp. 5, 13, 16.

24. Borokhov, p. 66.   25. S. Levin, pp. 100–101.

26. Mutnikovich, "Materialy," p. 8.   27. Blum, p. 145.

28. Mutnikovich, "Materialy," p. 5; Agursky, *Sotsialistishe literatur*, p. 30.

29. Mutnikovich, "Materialy," p. 4; Agursky, *Sotsialistishe literatur*, p. 31.

30. Mill, *Pionern*, 1: 216. Mill attended the meeting.

31. *Arkady*, p. 160.

32. D. Katz, "Pervyi s"ezd," p. 133; Blum, p. 134.

33. *Arkady*, pp. 159–60.   34. Dushkan, p. 240.

35. Gozhansky, *Shtot magid*, p. 5.   36. *Ibid.*, pp. 12–14.

37. S. Levin, p. 121.   38. Mikhalevich, *Zikhroinos*, 1: 16.

39. *DYA*, 2–3 (Feb. 1897): 42; Agursky, *Sotsialistishe literatur*, pp. 30, 35.

40. Mikhalevich, *Zikhroinos*, 1: 23; *DAS*, 1 (Aug. 1897): col. 3.

41. Agursky, *Sotsialistishe literatur*, pp. 35, 362.

42. *Rabochee*, 4, 1 (1961): 803.

43. *Der Minsker Arbeter*, 2 (Jan. 1901): 3; *Istoriia*, 1901, p. 58.

44. *DYA*, 10 (1900): 70. This issue is devoted to the report the local committees of the Bund delivered at the International Socialist Congress at Paris in 1900.

45. Blekhman, p. 30.

46. Agursky, *Sotsialistishe literatur*, p. 313.

47. *Ibid.*, p. 370.

48. Cited in *Listok "Rabotnika"* (Geneva), (Nov. 1897): 18.

49. *Ibid.*, p. 20.

50. Blum, p. 23. See also Raitshuk, p. 1. I have heard many similar stories from contemporaries of Blum and Raitshuk.

51. A. Rosenthal, "Froien-geshtaltn," p. 60.

52. Litvak, "Zhargonishe komitetn," p. 23. See also Zborowski and Herzog, pp. 124–26.

53. Bernstein, *Ershte*, p. 77; Bok, p. 6.

54. Bernstein, *Ershte*, p. 77.

55. *Ibid.*, p. 147; Blum, pp. 67–68.

56. *Arkady*, p. 189; Bernstein, *Ershte*, p. 38.

57. Blum, pp. 67–68.

58. Blum, p. 120; Mikhalevich, *Zikhroinos*, 1: 3; B. Kahan-Virgili, pp. 84–85.

59. Cherikover, "Onhaibn," pp. 594–96; Menes, "Yidishe arbeter," pp. 55–57; S. Levin, pp. 128–29.

60. Menes, "Yidishe arbeter," pp. 58–59; Ab-E, p. 28.

61. *Arkady*, pp. 398–99.

62. Gozhansky, "A vikuakh," p. 694. Gozhansky later placed the date of the brochure at 1893 or 1894 ("Yevreiskoe," pp. 85–86). The printed version appeared in 1896 or early 1897.

63. Litvak, "Zhargonishe komitetn," p. 19; S. Levin, p. 115.

64. Dushkan, p. 242.

65. Mutnikovich, "Tsu der geshikhte," p. 13; Kirzhnits, "Nachalo," pp. 220–21.

66. Shvarts, *Juzef Pilsudski*, pp. 124–25.

67. "Fun di redaktsion," *DYA*, 1 (Dec. 1896): 1–2.

68. Sh. Rabinovich, p. 340.

Chapter Five

1. Kremer, *Ob agitatsii*, p. 7.

2. *Ibid.*, p. 6.

3. *Ibid.*, p. 9.

4. *Pervoe Maia 1892*, p. 9.

5. *Ibid.*, pp. v–vi.

6. *Ibid.*, pp. 20–21.

7. Gozhansky, "A vikuakh," pp. 630–31.

8. Mill, *Pionern*, 1: 107. The Il'iashevich article appeared in *Vestnik Narodnoi Voli*, 5 (1886): 83–126.

9. *Vestnik Narodnoi Voli*, 5 (1886): 101, 110, 122, 124–25.

10. Gozhansky, "Yevreiskoe," p. 83.

11. *Ibid.*, p. 89.

12. Drobner, p. 111.

13. Translated into Yiddish from *Przedświt*, no. 4, April 1893; cited in Shvarts, *Juzef Pilsudski*, p. 258.

14. Mill, *Pionern*, 1: 116–17.

15. *Ibid.*, p. 117.

16. Pinsker, pp. 5–6, 9, 22.

17. Asher Ginzberg, pp. 258, 289–90, 293.

18. *Pervoe Maia 1892*, pp. 24–26.

19. Mill, *Pionern*, 1: 107–8.

20. *Arkady*, p. 395; Gozhansky, "Ershte kraizlekh," p. 7; Kopelson, "Yevreiskoe," p. 71.

21. Gozhansky, "Yevreiskoe," p. 82.

22. Bund biblio.: *Geshikhte fun der yidisher arbeter bevegung* (1900), pp. 59–60.

23. Mill, *Pionern*, 1: 216.

24. *Ibid.*

25. *Ibid.*

26. Bund biblio.: *Di naie epokhe*, pp. 9–10.

27. *Ibid.*, pp. 9–11.

28. Rafes, *Kapitlen*, pp. 28, 32–33.

29. Mill, *Pionern*, 1: 229.

30. Martov, *Zapiski*, p. 245.

31. *Ibid.*, p. 246.

32. Liesin, "Main ershte," p. 305.

33. Liesin, *Zikhroinos*, p. 283.

34. Mikhalevich, *Zikhroinos*, 1: 26; B. Frumkin, "Ocherki," p. 121; A. M. Ginzburg, p. 109.

35. "K istorii" (1896), p. 55; *DYA*, 2-3 (Feb. 1897): 39. Although the name of the town is not mentioned, the number of participants, the approximate locations, and the description of the proceedings leave no doubt that the city is Vilna.

36. Bund biblio.: *Istoriia*, 1901, p. 71.

37. *DYA*, 4-5 (Nov. 1897): 17.

38. "Tsu di lezer," *ibid.*, 1 (Dec. 1896): 9.

Chapter Six

1. Samuel Baron, *Plekhanov, Father of Marxism*, p. 127.

2. *Doklad predstavlennyi*, p. 19.

3. Meshcheriakov, pp. 21–22.

4. Akimov-Makhnovets, pp. 129–30.

5. Mill, *Pionern*, 1: 202.

6. Dushkan, pp. 240–42.

7. [Mutnikovich], "Bund," *Zhizn'* (London), 2 (1902): 99. Signed G. Ya.

8. Dushkan, p. 239.

9. *Doklad predstavlennyi*, pp. 18–19.

10. Peskin, p. 555.

11. Mill, *Pionern*, 1: 159; *Arkady*, p. 367; Martov, *Zapiski*, p. 175.

12. Lenin, *Sochineniia*, 2d ed., 28: 7; Meshcheriakov, p. 23; B. Nikolaevsky, "V. I. Ulianov-Lenin," pp. 89–90.

13. *DYA*, 1 (Dec. 1896): 51; *DYA*, 4–5 (Nov. 1897): 46.

14. Mill, *Pionern*, 1: 270–71.   15. D. Katz, "Pervyi s"ezd," p. 138.

16. *DYA*, 1 (Dec. 1896): 13.   17. Perazich, p. 256; *Arkady*, p. 155.

18. Akimov-Makhnovets makes this argument, p. 131. See also Martov, *Zapiski*, pp. 246–47.

19. *DYA*, 1 (Dec. 1896): 2.   20. *Arkady*, pp. 358–60.

21. *Ibid.*, p. 86; Peskin, p. 555.   22. D. Katz, "Pervyi s"ezd," p. 136.

23. Mutnikovich, "Ershter," p. 4; D. Katz, "Pervyi s"ezd," p. 137.

24. D. Katz, "Pervyi s"ezd," p. 138.

25. "Der onfang . . . ," *DYA*, 10 (1900): 31.

26. "Materialy" (1907), pp. 3, 9.

27. *Ibid.*, pp. 7–8. The original of this document bore a note from the PPS leaders to the effect that the Jewish question must be discussed and that the lack of literature created specifically for the Jews was a great danger.

28. *Ibid.*, pp. 13–17.

29. "Der onfang . . . ," *DYA*, 10 (1900): 35.

30. Mill, *Pionern*, 1: 267–68.   31. *DAS*, 6 (1897): col. 1.

32. D. Katz, "Pervyi s"ezd," p. 141.   33. Mill, *Pionern*, 1: 269–70.

34. D. Katz, "Pervyi s"ezd," pp. 138–40.

35. *Ibid.*, p. 139; Mill, *Pionern*, 1: 275; Mutnikovich, "Ershter," p. 3, col. 3.

36. *DAS*, 6 (1897): cols. 1–2.

37. *Ibid.*, col. 4; D. Katz, "Pervyi s"ezd," p. 137.

38. D. Katz, "Pervyi s"ezd," p. 141; *DAS*, 6 (1897): col. 4.

39. *Arkady*, p. 165.

40. D. Katz, "Pervyi s"ezd," p. 146; *Arkady*, p. 165.

41. *DAS*, 6 (1897): cols. 5–6.   42. *Arkady*, p. 165.

43. *DAS*, 6 (1897): col. 6.   44. D. Katz, "Pervyi s"ezd," p. 148.

45. *Ibid.*, p. 147; *DAS*, 6 (1897): col. 4; Mill, *Pionern*, 1: 276.

46. *DAS*, 6 (1897): col. 4; Mutnikovich, "Ershter," p. 3, cols. 3–4.

47. *DAS*, 6 (1897), cols. 4–5; *Arkady*, pp. 166–67.

48. D. Katz, "Pervyi s"ezd," p. 146.

Chaper Seven

1. *Arkady*, pp. 185, 385; D. Katz, "Mezhdu," p. 149.

2. *Arkady*, pp. 186–87, 385–86; D. Katz, "Mezhdu," p. 172.

3. Mill, *Pionern*, 1: 301.

4. *Arkady*, pp. 386–87.

5. Mutnikovich, "Ershter," p. 3, col. 4. See also Rosenbaum, 1: 91.

6. S. Levin, p. 108.   7. D. Katz, "Mezhdu," pp. 151–52.

8. *Otchet.*   9. S. Levin, pp. 146–47.

10. "Czarty zjazd P.P.S. . . . ," *Przedświt*, 3 (March 1898): 19. Trans. from Polish by Hillel Kempinski.

11. "Sprawa Proletaryatu Żydowskiego," *ibid.* (April 1898): 1–5.

12. *Arkady*, pp. 188–89.

13. Bund biblio.: *Di milkhoma* (1898), pp. 6, 10–11.

14. *Ibid.*, pp. 25–26.   15. *Ibid.*, p. 14.

16. *Ibid.*, pp. 29–31.   17. *Ibid.*, pp. 32–36.

18. *Ibid.*, p. 46.   19. *Ibid.*, pp. 49–53.

20. *Ibid.*, p. 15.   21. Eidelman, "K istorii," p. 32.

22. *Ibid.*, p. 31; Akimov-Makhnovets, p. 135.

23. Eidelman, "K istorii," p. 31.

24. *Ibid.*, p. 32.

25. Akimov-Makhnovets, pp. 135–36, 144. According to Perazich (p. 261), Mutnikovich and others felt that the Kievans were pushing too far too fast.

26. Eidelman, "Po povodu," p. 68. Eidelman denies that Kremer was empowered to speak for the Kievans, as Akimov asserts (Akimov-Makhnovets, p. 133). Kremer himself does not say one way or the other.

27. *Arkady*, p. 364.

28. Moysnski, p. 168.

29. Eidelman, "K istorii," p. 52.

30. Tuchapsky, p. 68; Eidelman, "Po povodu," p. 81.

31. Eidelman, "Po povodu," p. 78; "Dokumenty" (1923), pp. 390–91; Tuchapsky, p. 62.

32. Eidelman, "K istorii," pp. 46–47, 52, 64.

33. Tuchapsky, p. 68.

34. D. Katz, "Mezhdu," pp. 155–56.

35. Tuchapsky, p. 69; Akimov-Makhnovets, p. 155.

36. Eidelman, "K istorii," pp. 53, 64.

37. *Ibid.*, pp. 54, 61–62.

38. *Pervyi s"ezd RSDRP*, p. 83; Akimov-Makhnovets, p. 155; D. Katz, "Mezhdu," p. 151.

39. Eidelman, "K istorii," p. 61.

40. *Iz perezhitogo*, p. 66.

41. *Pervyi s"ezd RSDRP*, p. 83.

42. Even Eidelman defends the Bund against the charge of *force majeure* ("Ob ekonomicheskikh," p. 143).

43. Men'shchikov, 1: 33.

44. *Arkady*, pp. 382–83; Men'shchikov, 2: 108. Menshchikov defected from the Okhrana in 1909 (Bukhbinder, "Razgrom," p. 147).

45. Struve, p. 75.

46. *Arkady*, p. 365.

47. D. Katz, "Mezhdu," p. 159; Bukhbinder, "Razgrom," p. 161.

48. Men'shchikov, 2: 163–64.

49. My account of the investigation is drawn mainly from Men'shchikov, 2: 108–12. I have checked his material against information in the memoirs of Mill, Kremer, Kosovsky, and David Katz.

50. *Arkady*, p. 189.

51. Men'shchikov, 2: 32–33.

52. D. Katz, "Mezhdu," p. 154.

53. Bukhbinder, "Razgrom," p. 168. David Katz was told to make himself scarce even before May 1 ("Mezhdu," p. 154).

54. Men'shchikov, 2: 186; D. Katz, "Mezhdu," p. 154.

55. *Arkady*, p. 194.   56. *Ibid.*, p. 389.

57. B. Frumkin, "Zubatovshchina," p. 200. 58. Men'shchikov, 2: 13.

59. *DAS*, 11 (Dec. 1898): 5.   60. *Ibid.*, pp. 5–6.

Chapter Eight

1. Bukhbinder, "Razgrom," pp. 149–50.
2. Mikhalevich, *Zikhroinos*, 1: 54.
3. Bernstein, "David Katz," p. 20; D. Katz, "Mezhdu," pp. 161–62.
4. Bernstein, "David Katz," p. 20; *Arkady*, p. 225.
5. "Unzer Tsvaiter Tsuzamenfor . . . ," *DAS*, 11 (Dec. 1898): 1.
6. *Ibid.*, p. 1; D. Katz, "Mezhdu," p. 165. Katz mentions that no record of the number of organized workers was kept until after the Third Congress.
7. *DAS*, 11 (Dec. 1898): 1–2.
8. *Ibid.*, p. 2.
9. D. Katz, "Mezhdu," p. 171.
10. See Gaselnik, pp. 175–77. Gaselnik was chosen to publish cheap editions of scientific works in Yiddish.

11. *DAS*, 11 (Dec. 1898): 2.	12. Bernstein, *Ershte*, p. 103.
13. D. Katz, "Mezhdu," pp. 167–68.	14. *Ibid.*, p. 166.
15. *DAS*, 11 (Dec. 1898): 3.	16. D. Katz, "Mezhdu," p. 172.
17. *Ibid.*, p. 173.	18. *Ibid.*, pp. 173–74.
19. *Ibid.*, p. 162.	20. *Ibid.*, pp. 162, 172; Mill, *Pionern*, 2: 4.
21. D. Katz, "Mezhdu," p. 162.	22. *Ibid.*, pp. 176–77.

23. Deutsch, *Gruppa*, 6: 220.
24. Mill, *Pionern*, 1: 301–2; Mill, "Tsvantsig," 1: 594.

25. Bernstein, *Ershte*, p. 127.	26. Mill, *Pionern*, 2: 7.
27. *Ibid.*, p. 13.	28. *Ibid.*, p. 6.
29. *Ibid.*, p. 8.	30. *Ibid.*
31. *Ibid.*, p. 47.	32. *DYA*, 6 (March 1899): 1.
33. Mill, *Pionern*, 1: 139.	34. *DAS*, 12 (March 1899): 1.

35. Mill, *Pionern*, 2: 33. On the activities in Berne, see Kursky, *Gezamelte*, pp. 206–8.
36. Bund biblio.: *Istoriia*, 1901, pp. 114, 117.
37. Mill, *Pionern*, 2: 32.
38. Bund biblio.: *Istoriia*, 1901, p. 114.
39. *DYA*, 6 (March 1899): 62; *DYA*, 7 (Aug. 1899): 50; *DYA*, 8 (Dec. 1899): 41.
40. *DYA*, 7 (Aug. 1899): 40.

Chapter Nine

1. Mill, *Pionern*, 1: 278.
2. Epshtein, p. 7, col. 1.
3. *Arkady*, p. 381.
4. "Gomel'skoe rabochee dvizhenie," in Agursky, *Sotsialistishe literatur*, p. 358. The police managed to obtain a copy of the document cited (*Arkady*, p. 161).
5. Lev, "Pervye," pp. 269–70, 272–73; *DYA*, 10 (1900): 65–66.
6. Hofman, "Vi azoi," pp. 59–61.
7. Alter Bekanter, "Onhaib," pp. 159–63.
8. Bukhbinder, "Yevreiskoe," pp. 131–32. Bukhbinder relies heavily on the reports of police agents.
9. *DAS*, 16 (March 1900): 2.
10. *DYA*, 9 (1900): 2, 8.
11. A. M. Ginzburg, p. 113; Mikhalevich, *Zikhroinos*, 1: 58.
12. S. Levin, pp. 138–39.
13. *Ibid.*, p. 144.

14. Shulman, *Baginen*, p. 51; Shkliar, col. 191.
15. "Der I Mai 1809...," *DYA*, 7 (Aug. 1899): 17.
16. Bund biblio.: *Istoriia*, 1901, pp. 102–6.
17. Lev, "Pervye," p. 271; A. M. Ginzburg, p. 122.
18. Borokhov, p. 99.
19. "Unzer 8-ter Tsuzamenfor," *Der Veker*, 3 (Jan. 1900): 1.
20. Bund biblio.: *Istoriia*, 1901, p. 85.
21. Der Belostoker Komitet, *DYA*, 10 (1900): 63; Mikhalevich, *Zikhroinos*, 1: 58.
22. Grodno Sots. Dem. Kom., *DYA*, 10 (1900): 65; Alter Bekanter, "Onhaib," pp. 159, 163.
23. "Di arbeter bevegung...," *DAS*, 14 (Aug. 1899): 4.
24. Shkliar, cols. 193, 220.
25. S. Levin, p. 147.
26. Medem, 1: 199.
27. A. M. Ginzburg, p. 112; Berman, p. 165.
28. Lev, "Pervye," p. 273. On the birzhe, see also Shkliar, col. 199; *25 yor*, pp. 102–5; and Bernstein, *Ershte*, pp. 33–35.
29. Dubnow-Erlich, pp. 203–4; *DAS*, 15 (Dec. 1899): 13.
30. Bund biblio.: *Istoriia*, 1901, p. 108.
31. Bernstein, *Ershte*, p. 129; *Der Varshaver Arbeter*, 2 (1899): 7; *Der Belostoker Arbeter*, 1 (April 1899): 45.
32. Borokhov, p. 66.
33. *Der Belostoker Arbeter*, 1 (April 1899): 31.
34. "Vos hert zikh...," *DAS*, 14 (Aug. 1899): 12, 16.
35. Shkliar, col. 197; *Der Belostoker Arbeter*, 1 (April 1899): 36; *Der Veker*, 3 (Jan. 1900): 2; *DAS*, 1 (Aug. 1897), col. 2.
36. *Der Veker*, 3 (Jan. 1900): 1–3.
37. Aronson "Lebnsveg," p. 19; *25 yor*, p. 82; Mikhalevich, *Zikhroinos*, 1: 145.

Chapter Ten

1. P. Rosenthal, "Bialystoker," p. 53; Mill, "Natsionale frage," p. 117.
2. "Tsionizmus...," *DYA*, 6 (March 1899): 3–14.
3. *Ibid.*, pp. 5–12.
4. *Ibid.*, p. 11; Mill, *Pionern*, 2: 55.
5. Mill, *Pionern*, 2: 51–56.
6. "Unzer Dritter Tsuzamenfor," *DAS*, 16 (March 1900): 3–4.
7. *Ibid.*
8. Mill, *Pionern*, 2: 66.
9. *Ibid.*, p. 67.
10. *DAS*, 16 (March 1900): 4.
11. D. Katz, "Mezhdu," p. 178. Hillel Katz-Blum confirms that Mill's demand was a new one (Blum, p. 184).
12. Mill, *Pionern*, 2: 53.
13. Mill, "Tsvantsig," 2: 50.
14. Mill, *Pionern*, 2: 46. See also Weizmann, 1: 51.
15. Mill, *Pionern*, 2: 35–36.
16. "Der kamf...," *DYA*, 8 (Dec. 1899): 9.
17. *Ibid.*, p. 12.
18. See Samuel Baron, *Plekhanov, Father of Marxism*, pp. 186–207, and Keep, pp. 54–66, for two views of the meaning and importance of Economism.
19. Samuel Baron, *Plekhanov, Father of Marxism*, pp. 186–98, describes the relations between the two generations.

20. Mill, *Pionern*, 2: 27–28.
21. *Ibid.*, pp. 30–31.
22. *Ibid.*, 1: 176–78, 202–3, 206.
23. Kremer, *Ob agitatsii*, pp. 37–43.
24. *Ibid.*, pp. 30, 34.
25. B. N-sky, p. 141.
26. *DYA*, 7 (Aug. 1899): 5.
27. *DAS*, 16 (March 1900): 4.
28. Lenin, *Sochineniia*, 3d ed., 4: 385.
29. See Pipes for a full description of the St. Petersburg movement.
30. Lenin, *Sochineniia*, 2d ed., 2: 611–12.
31. Lenin, *Rabochee delo*, 4-5 (Sept.-Dec. 1899): 16–18.
32. *Ibid.*, pp. 24–27.
33. D. Katz, "Mezhdu," p. 177.
34. *Ibid.*, p. 178.
35. *Ibid.*; P. Rosenthal, "Bialystoker," p. 54.
36. *DAS*, 16 (March 1900): 3.

Chapter Eleven

1. Shulman, "Ershter," p. 17, col. 6; Homel SD Komitet, *DYA*, 11 (1901): 47.
2. *Sbornik*, 1: xxiv.
3. Lestchinsky, p. 28.
4. *Sbornik*, 1: xxxiii.
5. *1905 yor*, p. 68.
6. Zaslavsky, "Tsu der geshikhte," p. 75.
7. Garvi, pp. 23, 47. See also Martov, *Istoriia*, 3d ed., p. 58; Iuditsky, "Yidishe arbeter," p. 56.
8. Rubach, p. 150.
9. *Ibid.*, pp. 150–51; Bernstein, "Ershte," p. 141.
10. Bund biblio.: *Chetvertyi s"ezd*, p. 18.
11. *Pervyi s"ezd RSDRP*, p. 82.
12. Zaslavsky, "Tsu der geshikhte," p. 76.
13. Kursky, "Ver zenen," p. 13, col. 2.
14. "Vegen unzer nonste oifgabe," *DAS*, 18 (July 1900): 1–3.
15. *Ibid.*, pp. 2–3.
16. *DAS*, 23 (April 1901): 7.
17. "Der ershter mai . . . ," *DAS*, 18 (July 1900): 4.
18. "Tsu der frage . . . ," *DAS*, 19 (Sept. 1900): 5.
19. Zubatov, pp. 161–62; Gurko, p. 115; Koz'min, p. 64.
20. Zubatov, p. 160.
21. Bukhbinder, "Yevreiskoe," p. 129. Bukhbinder cites one of Zubatov's documents in the police archives where Bukhbinder did much of his work (B. Frumkin, "Zubatovshchina," p. 202).
22. *Arkady*, p. 207; "Tsarskii listok," *Byloe*, 7 (1908): 96.
23. Bukhbinder, "Razgrom," p. 193.
24. B. Frumkin, "Zubatovshchina," p. 207.
25. Piontkovsky, p. 292.
26. See *Arkady*, pp. 203–7, 391–92; and Bukhbinder, "Razgrom," pp. 151–52.
27. "Vide fun Kaplinsky," p. 12.
28. B. Frumkin, "Zubatovshchina," p. 205.
29. Chemerisky et al., pp. 315–17.
30. B. Frumkin, "Zubatovshchina," pp. 208–9; Shulman, "Baginen," p. 54; Mikhalevich, *Zikhroinos*, 2: 5–9.
31. B. Frumkin, "Zubatovshchina," pp. 209–10.
32. "Di arbeter bevegung . . . ," *DAS*, 15 (Dec. 1899): 2, 7.
33. Chemerisky et al., p. 317.

34. *25 yor*, p. 166.

35. *Ibid.*, p. 167.

36. "Zubatov ...," *DAS*, 19 (Sept. 1900): 1–4.

37. *Ibid.*, p. 4.

38. "Tsu der frage ...," *ibid.*, pp. 4–6.

39. *25 yor*, p. 167.

40. "Di 'faterlikhe zorg' ...," *DAS*, 7 (Nov. 27/Dec. 9, 1897): 1.

41. Medem, 1: 225.

42. *Der Minsker Arbeter*, 1 (Dec. 1900): 8.

43. Bernstein, *Ershte*, p. 187.

44. Zaslavsky, "Zubatov," p. 114.

45. Chemerisky et al., p. 31. See also B. Frumkin, "Zubatovshchina," p. 210.

46. B. Frumkin, "Zubatovshchina," p. 207; Mikhalevich, *Zikhroinos*, 2: 9; Zubatov, p. 167; "Zubatov ...," *DAS*, 19 (Sept. 1900): 3.

47. Dubnow-Erlich, pp. 211, 215.

48. Bund biblio.: *Chetvertyi s"ezd*, p. 15.

49. *DAS*, 4–5 (Sept. 1897): col. 6; *DAS*, 11 (Dec. 1898): 7–8; *Der Belostoker Arbeter*, 1 (April 1899): 3; *Der Kamf*, 1 (Sept. 1900): 11. Examples are legion.

50. "Vos villen mir," *Der Belostoker Arbeter*, 1 (April 1899): 2–3; "Vos villen mir," *Der Kamf*, 1 (Sept. 1900): 10–14; *DAS*, 21 (Jan. 1901): 12b.

51. *DYA*, 6 (March 1899): 6–7; Marie Syrkin, p. 239.

52. B. Borokhov, "Tsu der geshikhte fun der Poa" Ts. bevegung," *Yidisher arbeter pinkos*, 1 (1927): 48–49.

53. Gutman, pp. 153–54.

54. *Ibid.*, p. 154.

55. S. Levin, pp. 158–59; Zaslavsky, "Tsu der geshikhte," pp. 71–72; Mikhalevich, *Zikhroinos*, 1: 72.

56. *DAS*, 23 (April 1901): 5–6.

57. "Der Fierter Tsionistishen Kongress," *DAS*, 21 (Jan. 1901): 4–7.

58. Gutman, pp. 155–56; N. Syrkin, p. 13; Kivin, p. 31.

59. Litvak, "Minsk," pp. 466–67.

60. *Der Minsker Arbeter*, 1 (Dec. 1900): 8.

61. Zaslavsky, "Zubatov," pp. 119–21.

62. *Ibid.*, p. 123.

63. Lev, "Pervye," p. 276; Zaslavsky, "Zubatov," p. 115; Bukhbinder, "Nezavisimaia," pp. 214–15, 217.

64. Bund biblio.: *Chetvertyi s"ezd*, p. 15.

65. Kursky, *Gezamelte*, pp. 263–67.

66. *LS*, 3: 134.

67. *Ibid.*, p. 222.

68. "Unzer Dritter Tsuzamenfor," *DAS*, 16 (March 1900): 4.

69. "Der Internatsionaler Sotsialistisher Kongress," *DYA*, 8 (Dec. 1899): 1–2.

70. *Ibid.*, 11 (1901): 6. See also Mendelsohn, pp. 135–36.

71. Bund biblio.: *Di geshikhte*, March 1900, pp. 1–2.

72. *Ibid.*, pp. 1–2.

73. *LS*, 3: 83.

74. Samuel Baron, *Plekhanov, Father of Marxism*, pp. 201–7; Keep, pp. 57–58.

75. Deutsch, *Gruppa*, 4: 220.

76. Steklov, p. 211.

77. "Fun der presse," *DYA*, 9 (1900): 75–76.

78. *Ibid.*, p. 76.
79. Martov, *Zapiski*, p. 412.
80. Lenin, *Sochineniia*, 3d ed., 2: 494.
81. *Ibid.*, pp. 500, 503.
82. *Ibid.*, p. 498.
83. *Ibid.*, 4: 12.
84. *Ibid.*, pp. 39–40.
85. *Ibid.*, p. 10.
86. *LS*, 4: 51–52; Nikolaevsky, 1: 10–12; Meshcheriakov, p. 26; P. Rosenthal, "Bialystoker," pp. 66–67; Rubach, pp. 156–59.
87. *LS*, 4: 53–55.
88. Lenin, *Sochineniia*, 3d ed., 4: 5.
89. *Ibid.*, p. 30.
90. *LS*, 1: 56.
91. D. Katz, "Mezhdu," pp. 157–60; Martov, *Zapiski*, p. 397; Lenin, *Sochineniia*, 3d ed., 4: 385.
92. Lenin, *Sochineniia*, 5th ed. (Moscow, 1960), 4: 338–39.
93. "Novye druz'ia . . . ," *Iskra*, 1 (Dec. 1900): 3.
94. *LS*, 3: 98.
95. *LS*, 8: 133; L. Gol'dman, pp. 13–14.
96. Zakharova-Tsederbaum, pp. 52–54.
97. P. Rosenthal, "Bialystoker," p. 55.
98. *Ibid.*, pp. 55–56.
99. Kosovsky, "Martov," p. 176.
100. *DYA*, 6 (March 1899): 11–13.
101. "Di natsionale frage . . . ," *DYA*, 8 (Dec. 1899): 23–27.
102. Mill, "Natsionale frage," p. 117.
103. At that there were only two discussions written by Bundists in the journal around the time of the Fourth Congress (Mill, *Pionern*, 2: 80).
104. Mill, "Natsionale frage," p. 117.
105. Mill, *Pionern*, 2: 81–82.
106. *Ibid.*, p. 82.
107. *Arkady*, p. 326.
108. *Ibid.*
109. P. Rosenthal, "Bialystoker," p. 55.
110. Hofman, "Vi azoi," p. 63.
111. Kursky, *Gezamelte*, p. 209.
112. Mill, *Pionern*, 2: 72–73; Kursky, *Gezamelte*, pp. 206–10.
113. *Arkady*, pp. 332–33.
114. *Ibid.*, p. 108.

Chapter Twelve

1. Bund biblio.: *Chetvertyi s"ezd*, pp. 5–6.
2. *Ibid.*, p. 5.
3. *Ibid.*
4. Bund biblio.: *Di tetigkait*, pp. 3–4, 14.
5. *Ibid.*, p. 14.
6. *Ibid.*
7. *Ibid.*, p. 16.
8. *DAS*, 16 (March 1900): 3.
9. B. Frumkin, "Zubatovshchina," p. 212.
10. Bund biblio.: *Chetvertyi s"ezd*, p. 9.
11. *Ibid.*, p. 10.
12. "Vos hot uns gegeben . . . ," *DAS*, 24 (Aug. 1901): 1.
13. Supplement to *Der Minsker Arbeter*, 3 (June 1901).
14. Bukhbinder, "Nezavisimaia," p. 242.
15. *Ibid.*, pp. 242–43.
16. *Ibid.*, p. 243.
17. *Ibid.*
18. *DAS*, 25 (Oct. 1901): 22–24.
19. *Der Minsker Arbeter*, 4 (Nov. 1901): 1–5.
20. B. Frumkin, "Zubatovshchina," pp. 225–26.
21. Rafes, *Kapitlen*, p. 58.
22. In Frumkin's opinion this was the Bundists' most effective argument ("Zubatovshchina," pp. 225–26).
23. Bukhbinder, "Nezavisimaia," p. 221.
24. B. Frumkin, "Zubatovshchina," p. 220.
25. Piontkovsky, p. 295; Bukhbinder, "Nezavisimaia," p. 220.

26. *Der Minsker Arbeter*, 4 (Nov. 1901): 13; *DAS*, 26 (Jan. 1902): 23–24.

27. Reprinted in *Posledniia izvestiia*, the Bund's Russian-language news sheet (64 [April 10, 1902]: 3).

28. Vilner Gruppe YUAP, pp. 4–6.

29. *Ibid.*, pp. 2–3.

30. Bund biblio.: *Tsu ale Vilner arbeter*.

31. Piontkovsky, p. 298.

32. *Ibid.*, pp. 299–300, 305.

33. YUAP (Feb. 5, 1903).

34. *PI*, 56 (Feb. 14, 1902): 1.

35. B. Frumkin, "Zubatovshchina," p. 222; Bukhbinder, "Nezavisimaia," p. 210.

36. Bukhbinder, "Nezavisimaia," pp. 221–22; *PI*, 102 (Jan. 1, 1903/Dec. 19, 1902): 1; *PI*, 113 (March 20/March 7, 1903): 2–3.

37. YUAP (July 6, 1903), pp. 1–2.

38. "M'lekhaim umi lemuvis," *DAS*, 35 (Oct. 1903): 15–16.

39. Bukhbinder, "Nezavisimaia," p. 229.

40. Zaslavsky, "Zubatov," pp. 119–21.

41. Gutman, p. 155.

42. Piontkovsky, pp. 296–97.

43. *Der Arbeter Tsionist* (Minsk), 2 (1903): col. 23.

44. *Ibid.*, cols. 5–6.

45. "K istorii" (1917), p. 93.

46. *DAS*, 26 (Jan. 1902): 23–24.

47. "Vasiliev . . . ," *DAS*, 29 (Sept. 1902): 14.

48. Mikhalevich, *Zikhroinos*, 2: 17.

49. Bund biblio.: *Chetvertyi s"ezd*, p. 6.

50. *Ibid.*, p. 7.

51. *Ibid.*

52. *Ibid.*, pp. 9–10.

53. *Ibid.*

54. *Ibid.*, p. 8.

55. Bund biblio.: *Di tetigkait*, pp. 13–14.

56. [J. Martov], "Novye druz'ia Russkago proletariata," *Iskra*, 1 (Dec. 1900): 3.

57. *DAS*, 24 (Aug. 1901): 13–17.

58. Pertsev et al., p. 377; "Fershtarkte shmirah," *Der Klasen-Kamf* (Vilna), 6 (Dec. 1901): pp. 6–7.

59. *PI*, 65 (April 17, 1902): 1.

60. Gurko, p. 191. Gurko was a high-ranking official in the Ministry of the Interior.

61. *PI*, 46 (Dec. 1901): 1.

62. For information provided by those arrested, see "Politseiskii razboi . . . ," *PI*, 70 (May 29, 1902); and "Di shendlikhe beshtrofung," *DAS*, 27 (June 1902). For a detailed secondary account of the affair (in Yiddish), see Hertz, *Hirsh Lekert*.

63. "Der rakhe nehmer," supplement 1 to *Der Klasen-Kamf* (Vilna), 4 (May 1901): 1.

64. *Tovarishchi rabochie!*, May 1902. The version printed in *PI*, 70 (May 29, 1902), adds the words "for all time" at the end (p. 3).

65. Bund biblio.: *Girsh Lekert*, pp. 2–5.

66. *Ibid.*, p. 1.

67. See Hertz, *Hirsh Lekert*, pp. 92–105, for a list of the literature written in dedication to the martyr.

68. Bund biblio.: *Girsh Lekert*, pp. 1–2.

69. "Vi darf . . . ," *DAS*, 27 (June 1902): 11.

70. *Ibid.*, pp. 11–12.

71. *Ibid.*, p. 11.

72. *Hirsh Lekert*, p. 20.

73. "Demonstratsionen . . . ," *DAS*, 27 (June 1902): 2.

74. *Ibid.*

75. "Der V-ter Konferents . . . ," *DAS*, 29 (Sept. 1902): 3.

76. *Ibid.*

77. *Ibid.*, pp. 2–3.

78. "Vi darfen . . . ," *ibid.*, p. 4.

79. "Demonstratsionen . . . ," *DAS*, 27 (June 1902): 4.

80. *DAS*, 29 (Sept. 1902): 6.

81. "Tsu di frage . . . ," *DYA*, 14 (Oct. 1902): 162–67; also (in Russian) *PI*, 88 (Oct. 4, 1902): 2–5.

82. *Ibid.*　　　　　　　　　　　　　83. *PI*, 88 (Oct. 4, 1902): 1.

84. *PI*, 85 (Sept. 11, 1902): 1.　　　　85. *PI*, 90 (Oct. 16, 1902): 4.

86. Bund biblio.: *Piatyi s"ezd*, pp. 29–30.

87. F. Frumkina, pp. 11–12; Mikhalevich, *Zikhroinos*, 2: 86–87.

88. Shtupler, p. 53; Mikhalevich, *Zikhroinos*, 1: 149.

89. *Revoliutsionnaia Rossiia* (London), 7 (June 1902): 1–2.

90. Chernov, pp. 164–65.

91. "Piataia Konferentsiia 'Bunda'," *Revoliutsionnaia Rossiia*, 13 (Nov. 1902): 6.

92. Bund biblio.: *K voprosu o terrorizme*, p. 26.

93. "Poslednee slovo obviniaemago, *Iskra*, 26 (Oct. 15, 1902): 2.

94. Plekhanov, 23: 279.

95. "Unzere nonste . . . ," *DAS*, 28 (Aug. 1902): 1–3.

96. *Ibid.*, p. 2.　　　　　　　　　　97. *Ibid.*

98. *Ibid.*, pp. 2–3.　　　　　　　　99. *DAS*, 29 (Sept. 1902): 2.

100. *Hirsh Lekert*, p. 35.　　　　　101. *PI*, 88 (Oct. 4, 1902): 3.

102. Zheleznikov and Liov, pp. 140–41.

103. *Ibid.*, pp. 142–45; Mikhalevich, *Zikhroinos*, 2: 66–69.

104. P. Rosenthal, "Bialystoker," pp. 46–47.

105. G. Ia. [Mutnikovich], *Zhizn'* (London), 2 (May 1902): 104–5.

106. Bund biblio.: *Piatyi s"ezd*, pp. 33–34.

107. Akimov, pp. 22–24.

108. Bund biblio.: *Istoriia*, 1901, p. 114, and *Di tetigkait*, p. 15.

109. Bund biblio.: *Di tetigkait*, p. 5.

110. Bund biblio.: *Vozzvanie*, pp. 2–3.

111. *Ibid.*, pp. 13–25.

Chapter Thirteen

1. The report was compiled by Portnoy and Rosenthal. Rosenthal wrote the section on the national question (see his "Bialystoker," p. 59).

2. Bund biblio.: *Chetvertyi s"ezd*, p. 10.

3. *Ibid.*

4. *Ibid.*, pp. 10–11.

5. *Ibid.*, p. 11. Although this formulation was accepted, a small group of delegates came out for the territorial breakup of the Empire first (Blekhman, p. 106).

6. Bund biblio: *Chetvertyi s"ezd*, pp. 11–12.

7. *Ibid.*, p. 12.

8. P. Rosenthal, "Bialystoker," p. 60.

9. Bund biblio.: *Chetvertyi s"ezd*, pp. 12–13.

10. P. Rosenthal, "Bialystoker," p. 60.　　11. Bund biblio.: *Chetvertyi s"ezd*, p. 13.

12. *Ibid.*　　　　　　　　　　　　　　13. *Ibid.*

14. *Ibid.*, p. 14.　　　　　　　　　　15. *Ibid.*, p. 5.

16. *Ibid.*, p. 15.　　　　　　　　　　17. *Ibid.*

18. *Ibid.*, p. 14.

19. "Di oislendishe organizatsie fun 'Bund,' " in Kursky, *Gezamelte*, pp. 211–20.

20. Bund biblio.: *K voprosu o natsional'noi avtonomii* . . . . The Central Committee made a few changes in the text before publishing the pamphlet.

21. *Ibid.*, p. 6.

22. *Ibid.*, pp. 7–9, 14.

23. Kursky, *Gezamelte*, pp. 217–19.

24. Abramovich, 1: 110–11.

25. *Ibid.*

26. Blekhman, pp. 154, 158; *25 yor*, p. 116.

27. "Diskusies," parts 1 and 2; "Debate." Franz Kursky, the Bund archivist, has confirmed the loss of the resolution (Abramovich, 1: 111).

28. "Diskusies," 1: 92–93.

29. *Ibid.*, pp. 93–94.

30. *Ibid.*

31. *Ibid.*, p. 90.

32. *Ibid.*, p. 95.

33. *Ibid.*, p. 90; "Debate," p. 87.

34. "Debate," p. 87; "Diskusies," 1: 96.

35. "Diskusies," 1: 95.

36. *Ibid.*, 2: 90–91.

37. "Debate," p. 87.

38. "Diskusies," 2: 83–84.

39. *Ibid.*, p. 85.

40. "Debate," pp. 83, 92.

41. S. Levin, p. 225.

42. "Iz Partii," *Iskra*, 7 (Aug. 1901): 6.

43. *Ibid.*

44. *Ibid.*, 8 (Sept. 10, 1901): 6.

45. *Ibid.*, 7 (Aug. 1901): 5.

46. *Zaria* (Stuttgart), 4 (Aug. 1902): 40–54.

47. Kursky, *Gezamelte*, p. 204; Mill, *Pionern*, 2: 45.

48. *Zaria*, 4 (Aug. 1902): 47.

49. *Ibid.*, pp. 49–51.

50. "Iz Partii," *Iskra*, 33 (Feb. 1, 1903): 7–8.

51. "Natsional'nyi vopros . . . ," *Iskra*, 44 (July 15, 1903): 1.

52. Marie Syrkin, p. 303.

53. *Ibid.*, pp. 294–97.

54. *Ibid.*, pp. 296–97.

55. *Ibid.*, pp. 299–302.

56. "Der Tsionizm un der 'Bund,'" *Der Hamoin* (Berlin), 1 (1903): 57.

57. *Programmnyia pis'ma*, p. 12.

58. Asher Ginzberg, pp. 280–83.

59. *Der Arbeter Tsionist* (Minsk), 2 (1903): cols. 11–14. See also Kivin, pp. 32–33.

60. "Poale Tsion . . . ," *DAS*, 33 (May 1903): 5–8.

61. Marie Syrkin, p. 35.

Chapter Fourteen

1. *Iskra*, 7 (Aug. 1901): 6.

2. *Ibid.*

3. *Ibid.*, 8 (Sept. 10, 1901): 6.

4. *Ibid.*

5. *Ibid.*

6. *LS*, 8: 142–43.

7. *LS*, 3: 183, 185.

8. *LS*, 3: 162.

9. *LS*, 8: 151.

10. *LS*, 3: 173.

11. *LS*, 3: 177.

12. "Martov tsu Aleksander."

13. Kosovsky, "Martov," p. 177.

14. Zakharova-Tsederbaum, p. 19.

15. Steklov, pp. 235–36.

16. Martynov, pp. 19–20.

17. *Pis'ma P. B. Aksel'roda*, p. 46.

18. Mill, *Pionern*, 2: 102–3.

19. Zakharova-Tsederbaum, pp. 57–58; *Pis'ma P. B. Aksel'roda*, p. 46.

20. Piatnitsky, p. 18.

21. B. Gol'dman, "Pered," p. 46. See also Kursky, "Moisai Gurevich," p. 30.

22. *Arkady*, pp. 338–39.

23. *Ibid.* The "historical turning point" is a reference to Martov's speech of 1895.

24. Rubach, p. 149; Nikolaevsky, "Iz epokhy," 1: 12. Even Iskraites fell prey to this notion. See Lenin to S. O. Tsederbaum, *LS*, 8: 183; and Krupskaia to L. I. Goldman and S. O. Tsederbaum, *LS*, 8: 196.

25. Some sources speak of an initiative by the Union Abroad as well as the Bund. See, for example, Volkovicher, "V. I. Lenin," p. 63; and Valk, pp. 131–32.

26. P. Rosenthal, "Bialystoker," p. 66.

27. *Ibid.*, p. 67.   28. *LS*, 3: 46.

29. *PR*, 6 (1930): 141.   30. *LS*, 3: 290.

31. *LS*, 8: 214–15; Lenin, *Sochineniia*, 3d ed., 5: 66–70.

32. Valk, pp. 136–37; P. Rosenthal, "Bialystoker," p. 68; *LS*, 8: 225–26.

33. "Zametki Aleksandra Kremera o Belostokskoi Konferentsii R.S.D.R.P. Mart 1902" (Bund Archives). The material in this document is essentially the same as that found in the police notes of April 1902 ("Materialy" [1902]). Also P. Rosenthal, "Bialystoker," p. 68; and Yermansky, p. 58.

34. Valk, p. 139.

35. Though Yermansky states that Rosenthal (An-man) was on the O.C. (p. 59), Rosenthal himself confirms that Portnoy was the Bund representative ("Bialystoker," p. 69).

36. *Vtoroi ocherednoi*, p. 20.

37. For discussions in English of the steps leading to the reconstitution of the O.C., see Shukman; Wildman; and Tobias, "Bund and Lenin."

38. *Arkady*, pp. 370–71.

39. *LS*, 13: 136.

40. *LS*, 8: 238. References to the Iskraites gaining control of the congress begin earlier: *LS*, 8: 232.

41. *LS*, 8: 239.   42. *LS*, 8: 244–45.

43. *LS*, 8: 257–58.   44. *LS*, 8: 247–49.

45. "Soiuz Russkikh Sotsialdemokratov."   46. *LS*, 8: 294.

47. *Vtoroi ocherednoi*, p. 25.   48. *LS*, 8: 244.

49. *LS*, 8: 272.   50. Lepeshinsky, p. 147.

51. *LS*, 8: 296.

52. *Vtoroi ocherednoi*, p. 21. Krasikov, it should be noted, was abroad until mid-October (*LS*, 8: 293).

53. "Izveshchenie . . . ," *Iskra*, 32 (Jan. 15, 1903): 1.

54. *PI*, 106 (Feb. 3/Jan. 21, 1903): 1.

55. "Iz Partii," *Iskra*, 33 (Feb. 1, 1903): 7; "Po povodu . . . ," *ibid.*, p. 4. The Pskov delegates drafted a letter to the groups abroad stating that the announcement of the O.C.'s existence was to be released after the Bund signed it. For the text, see Lepeshinsky, pp. 147–48. See also Kirzhnits, "Bund un RSDAP," p. 62.

56. Predstavitel' Tsentral'nago.

57. Bobrovskaia, pp. 137–38; *LS*, 8: 322–23. V. N. Rozanov, who was active in the south and later joined the O.C., defends the Bund and states that his organization also received a late invitation (pp. 36–37).

58. *Vtoroi ocherednoi*, p. 21.

59. *Ibid.*; Bobrovskaia, p. 173.

60. *Vtoroi ocherednoi*, p. 21.

61. "Iz Partii," *Iskra*, 37 (April 1, 1903): 8.

Chapter Fifteen

1. *PI*, 106 (Feb. 3/Jan. 21, 1903): 1–2.

2. "Po povodu . . . ," *Iskra*, 33 (Feb. 1, 1903): 4.

3. *Ibid.*

4. *Ibid.*

5. "Iskra o Bunde," *PI*, 109 (Feb. 26/13, 1903): 1–2.

6. *Ibid.*, p. 2.

7. *Ibid.*, pp. 2–3.

8. *Ibid.*, p. 3.

9. Kosovsky's reference was to a note of Lenin's on the Manifesto of the Armenian Social Democrats, which appeared in *Iskra*, 33 (Feb. 1, 1903): 7–8.

10. *PI*, 109 (Feb. 26/13, 1903): 3–4.

11. "Po povodu...," *PI*, 105 (Jan. 28/15, 1903): 1–2. See also Rubach, pp. 354–55.

12. *PI*, 105 (Jan. 28/15, 1903): 1.

13. *Ibid.*, pp. 1–2.

14. "Nuzhna...," *Iskra*, 34 (Feb. 15, 1903): 2.

15. *Ibid.*

16. *Ibid.*

17. *Ibid.*

18. "Serditoe bezsilie," *PI*, 112 (March 14/1, 1903): 1.

19. *Ibid.*

20. *Ibid.*, p. 2.

21. *Ibid.*

22. "Yedinaia Russkaia sotsialdemokratiia...," *Iskra*, 36 (March 15, 1903): 2–4.

23. *Ibid.* Getzler, pp. 56–59, discusses Martov's change of position on the Jewish movement and its tasks.

24. Bund biblio.: *Avtonomiia.*

25. *Ibid.*, p. 6.

26. *Ibid.*, p. 13.

27. *Ibid.*, pp. 14–15.

28. *Ibid.*, p. 16.

29. *Ibid.*, p. 19.

30. *Ibid.*, pp. 20–21.

31. *Iskra*, 34 (Feb. 15, 1903): 2.

32. Bund biblio.: *Avtonomiia*, p. 22.

33. *Ibid.*, pp. 23–24.

34. *Ibid.*, pp. 25–27.

35. *LS*, 8: 298. Undated; no earlier than Dec. 11, 1902.

36. *LS*, 8: 337.

37. *LS*, 8: 355–56.

38. *LS*, 4: 219.

39. *LS*, 8: 350.

40. Among her targets was B. I. Goldman. *PR*, 6–7 (1928): 132.

41. B. Gol'dman, "Pered," p. 54.

42. Kirzhnits, "Bund un RSDAP," p. 67.

43. *Ibid.*, pp. 67–68.

44. B. Gol'dman, "Pered," pp. 54–55.

45. Portnoy's proposal appeared in *PI* several weeks before the Orel meeting (106, Jan. 21, 1903). The O.C. report (*Vtoroi ocherednoi*) mentions only the invitation of national organizations (p. 22).

46. *Vtoroi ocherednoi*, pp. 383–84.

47. *Ibid.*, p. 379.

48. "Bund delegate to Foreign Committee."

49. *Vtoroi ocherednoi*, p. 384.

50. "Bund delegate to Foreign Committee."

51. *PR*, 6–7 (1928): 173.

52. *Ibid.*

53. E. M. Aleksandrova to Lenin et al., *LS*, 8: 350. Undated; no later than May 19, 1903.

54. *Ibid.*

55. Bund biblio.: *Otvet "Iskre,"* p. 4.

56. *LS*, 8: 351.

57. *Ibid.*

58. *Pis'ma P. B. Aksel'roda*, p. 84. Blekhman, who worked among the tanners, found some support for Lenin's views on organization there in 1902 (*Bleter*, pp. 149–50).

59. *PI*, 105 (Jan. 28/15, 1903): 2.

60. "Bund un RSDAP," *DAS*, 32 (March 1903): 5.

61. Kirzhnits, "Bund un RSDAP," pp. 70–77.

62. *Ibid.*, p. 70.

63. *Ibid.*, pp. 72–73.

64. *Ibid.*

65. *Ibid.*, pp. 74–75.

66. *Ibid.*, pp. 75–76.

67. *Ibid.*, p. 77.

68. Abramovich, 1: 115.
69. *Piatyi s"ezd*, p. 6.
70. "V Tsuzamenfor," supplement to *DAS*, 34 (June 1903).
71. *Piatyi s"ezd*, p. 8.
72. *Ibid.*, p. 10.
73. *Ibid.*, pp. 10–11.
74. *Ibid.*, p. 12.
75. *Ibid.*, p. 14.
76. *Ibid.*
77. *Ibid.*, p. 16.
78. *Ibid.*, p. 17.
79. *Ibid.*, p. 20.
80. *Ibid.*, p. 18.
81. Kirzhnits, "Bund un RSDAP," pp. 84–85.
82. *Ibid.*, p. 84.
83. *Piatyi s"ezd*, p. 24.
84. *Ibid.*, p. 26.
85. Kirzhnits, "Bund un RSDAP," pp. 86–87.
86. *Iskra*, 49 (Oct. 1, 1903): 3–4.
87. *Ibid.*, p. 3.
88. S. Levin, p. 229. See also Blekhman, p. 159; and Medem, 2: 21–22.
89. Medem, 2: 23; Kosovsky, "VI. Medem," p. 156.

Chapter Sixteen

1. *LS*, 6: 50–51.
2. *LS*, 6: 56–57; *Vtoroi ocherednoi*, pp. 31–33.
3. *Vtoroi ocherednoi*, p. 31.
4. *Ibid.*, p. 32.
5. *Ibid.*, pp. 31–32.
6. *LS*, 6: 186.
7. *Vtoroi ocherednoi*, pp. 56–57.
8. *Ibid.*, pp. 57–59.
9. *Ibid.*, p. 56; Bund biblio.: *Vtoroi s"ezd*, pp. 7–8.
10. Bund biblio.: *Vtoroi s"ezd*, p. 7.
11. *Ibid.*
12. *Vtoroi ocherednoi*, pp. 60–61.
13. *Ibid.*, p. 61.
14. *Ibid.*
15. *Ibid.*, p. 62.
16. Bund biblio.: *Vtoroi s"ezd*, p. 9.
17. *Ibid.*, p. 10.
18. *Vtoroi ocherednoi*, p. 63.
19. *Ibid.*, p. 65.
20. *Ibid.*, pp. 66–67.
21. *Ibid.*, p. 69.
22. *Ibid.*, pp. 67–68.
23. *Ibid.*, p. 75.
24. *Ibid.*, p. 70.
25. *Ibid.*, p. 74.
26. *Ibid.*
27. I. N. Mosynski (Iuz. Konarsky), "Iz epokhi II-go s"ezda (1900–1904 gg.)," *KIS*, 8–9 (1928): 19.
28. *Vtoroi ocherednoi*, p. 84.
29. *Ibid.*, pp. 87–88.
30. *Ibid.*, p. 93.
31. *Ibid.*, pp. 97–98.
32. *Ibid.*, p. 98.
33. *Ibid.*, p. 99.
34. *Ibid.*, p. 101.
35. *Ibid.*, p. 102.
36. *Ibid.*, p. 101.
37. *Ibid.*, p. 107.
38. *Ibid.*, pp. 107–8.
39. Bund biblio.: *Vtoroi s"ezd*, p. 23.
40. *Vtoroi ocherednoi*, p. 153.
41. *Ibid.*, p. 158.
42. *Ibid.*
43. *Ibid.*, p. 159.
44. *Ibid.*, p. 156.
45. *Ibid.*, pp. 160–61.
46. *Ibid.*, p. 162.
47. *Ibid.*, p. 236; Bund biblio.: *Vtoroi s"ezd*, p. 36.
48. *Vtoroi ocherednoi*, p. 236.
49. *Ibid.*, p. 237.
50. *Ibid.*, p. 238.
51. Bund biblio.: *Vtoroi s"ezd*, p. 44.
52. Shukman, p. 246.
53. *Vtoroi ocherednoi*, p. 285.
54. *Ibid.*, pp. 285–87.
55. *Ibid.*, p. 288.
56. *Ibid.*
57. *Ibid.*, p. 289.

58. Medem, 2: 31.
60. Shukman, pp. 229–30.
62. *Vtoroi ocherednoi*, p. 171.
64. *Ibid.*, pp. 175–76.
66. *Ibid.*, p. 176.
68. *Ibid.*, pp. 253–54.
70. Lenin, *Polnoe*, 5th ed., 8: 49.
71. Wolfe, p. 243.
72. *Vtoroi ocherednoi*, pp. 176–77; Bund biblio.: *Vtoroi s"ezd*, p. 31.
73. *Vtoroi s"ezd RSDRP: Protokoly*, p. 440.
74. *Ibid.*, p. 717.

59. *Vtoroi ocherednoi*, p. 170.
61. *Ibid.*, p. 233.
63. *Ibid.*
65. *Ibid.*
67. *Ibid.*, p. 177.
69. *LS*, 6: 228.

Chapter Seventeen

1. "Der rabinek (pogrom) ...," *DAS*, 29 (Sept. 1902): 11.
2. "Felieton," *DAS*, 30 (Oct. 1902): 9.
3. *Ibid.*
4. "Mai khronik," *DAS*, 33 (May 1903): 16.
5. Gurko, pp. 246–49; Lopukhin, pp. 14–16. Lopukhin was the director of the police department under Plehve.
6. Gurko, p. 248.
7. Urussov, p. 9.
8. *Ibid.*, pp. 79–81.
9. Bund biblio.: *Tsu ale yidishe arbeter*. The date on this document, 1902, is obviously incorrect; it should be dated April 1903.
10. *Der Fraind*, 80 (April 26/13, 1903): 2, col. 3.
11. Bund biblio.: *Tsu ale yidishe arbeter*.
12. Blum, pp. 92–93.
13. *Der Fraind*, 87 (May 4/April 21, 1903): 1, col. 4; *Yidishe Folkstsaitung* (Cracow) May 13, 1903, p. 3, col. 1.
14. "Der pogrom ...," *DAS*, 33 (May 1903): 1–2.
15. *Ibid.*
16. Bund biblio.: *Kishinever hariga*, pp. 3, 6.
17. *Ibid.*, pp. 15, 47–49.
18. *Piatyi s"ezd*, pp. 32–33.
19. Bund biblio.: *Kishinever hariga*, p. 7.
20. See [Iu. Martov], "Mobilizatsiia ...," *Iskra*, 41 (June 1, 1903): 1–2.
21. "Fun yidishen leben," *Der Bund*, 3 (April 1904): 11; Bund biblio.: *Yevreiskie pogromy*.
22. *Piatyi s"ezd*, p. 33.
23. Litvak, "Lobuzes," pp. 123–24.
24. Daich, pp. 2–3; Berman, pp. 139–42; *Hirsh Lekert*, p. 9.
25. Daich, pp. 7–8.   26. *Ibid.*
27. *Ibid.*   28. See *Hirsh Lekert*, p. 13.
29. Berman, pp. 216–22; Motolski, pp. 36–37; Litvak, *Geklibene*, p. 181; Vinocur.
30. Bund biblio.: *Kishinever hariga*, p. 3.
31. *DAS*, 35 (Oct. 1903): 10.
32. *Der Fraind*, 201 (Sept. 20/7, 1903): 1, col. 4.
33. "Obvinitel'nyi Akt," pp. 1–2.   34. *Ibid.*, pp. 2–3.
35. *Ibid.*, p. 3.   36. Bund biblio.: *Pogrom v Gomele*.
37. *Der Fraind*, 201 (Sept. 20/7, 1903): 1, col. 4; "Obvinitel'nyi Akt," p. 4.

38. "Etlikhe verter . . . ," *DAS*, 36 (Feb. 1904): 5. According to Kursky, this article was written by Max Rabinovich, one of the self-defense organizers in the city ("Fargesene," p. 590).

39. "A naie blat," *DAS,* 35 (Oct. 1903): 11.

40. *DAS*, 36 (Feb. 1904): 8.

41. Bund biblio.: *Doklad*, p. 7; Aronson, "Homler 'birzhe,' " p. 10.

42. Vinocur, pp. 4–5.

43. Bund biblio.: *Doklad*, p. 8; *DAS*, 38 (Sept. 1904): 19.

44. See Gurko, p. 227.

45. Bund biblio.: *Di tetigkait*, p. 16.

46. Bund biblio.: *Doklad*, p. 10.

47. *Der Bund*, 1 (Jan. 1904): 11, 14.

48. *DAS*, 38 (Sept. 1904): 20.

49. *Der Bund*, 3 (April 1904): 17.

50. *PI*, 199 (Nov. 14/1, 1904): 1.

51. Bund biblio.: *Tsu ale Belostoker arbeter.*

52. *PI*, 197 (Oct. 29/16, 1904): 1.

53. Bund biblio.: *Tsu ale Dvinsker ainvoner.*

54. *Der Bund*, 3 (April 1904): 18; *DAS*, 38 (Sept. 1904): 18–19.

55. Bund biblio.: *Di milkhoma un di zelbsthershung*, p. 2.

56. *Ibid.*, p. 1. See also "Di milkhoma," *DAS*, 36 (Feb. 1904): 17.

57. "Di milkhoma . . . ," *DAS*, 37 (June 1904): 1–2; *Der Bund*, 2 (March 1904): 10; "Arbetslozigkait un hunger," *Der Bund*, 3 (April 1904): 1.

58. Bund biblio.: *Po povodu mobilizatsii*, pp. 1–2.

59. "Unzer entfer . . . ," *Der Bund*, 4 (July 1904): 1–2.

60. Bund biblio.: *Brider-rekruten.*

61. See Shvarts, "Revolutsionere," pp. 121–42.

62. "Demonstratsionen . . . ," *DAS*, 27 (June 1902): 2.

63. Shvarts, "Revolutsionere," p. 130. See also "Revolutionary Propaganda."

64. Bund biblio.: *Di tetigkait*, p. 11.

65. Bund biblio.: *Doklad*, p. 8.

66. *PI*, 148 (Oct. 15/2, 1903): 2–3.

67. "Revolutionary Propaganda."

68. *Ibid.*; *PI*, 161 (Jan. 5, 1905/Dec. 23, 1904): 4.

69. "K voprosu . . . ," *VB*, 1-2 (Jan.-Feb. 1904): 26–28.

70. Bund biblio.: *Di milkhoma un di zelbsthershung*, p. 2.

71. "Di milkhoma," *Der Bund*, 5 (Oct. 1904): 11.

72. *Ibid.*, p. 9.

73. "Khronik . . . ," *DAS*, 38 (Sept. 1904): 11.

74. Bund biblio.: *Vegen der mobilizatsie*; "Der militarizmus . . . ," *Der Bund*, 4 (July 1904): 6.

75. "Beglyia zametki," *VB*, 4 (July 1904): 24.

76. *Ibid.*, pp. 25–26.

77. Gurko, p. 311.

78. "Falshe hofnungen," *DAS*, 38 (Sept. 1904): 6–7.

79. Bund biblio.: *Di tsarishe*; "Tsarskaia milosti . . . ," *VB*, 5 (Nov. 1904): 1–6.

80. "Tsarskaia milosti . . . ," *VB*, 5 (Nov. 1904): 1–2.

81. *Ibid.*, pp. 3–4.

82. *Ibid.*, p. 4.

83. Menchikoff, pp. 91, 94.

84. "Tsarskaia milosti . . . ," *VB* 5 (Nov. 1904): 4. The *New York Times* confirmed this statement (Sept. 12, 1904, p. 4, col. 3).

85. "Tsarskaia milosti . . . ," *VB*, 5 (Nov. 1904): 5.

86. "Beglyia zametki," *VB*, 4 (July 1904): 26.

87. "Sotsialdemokratie . . . ," *DAS*, 39 (Jan. 1905): 1–2. On the indecisiveness of the regime, see Gurko, pp. 309–22.

Chapter Eighteen

1. Hofman, *Far 50 yor*, p. 275. See also Berman, p. 323.
2. Medem, 2: 16, 19; Abramovich, 1: 109–11.
3. Litvak, *Vos geven*, pp. 212–13.
4. Berman, p. 164. See also *Hirsh Lekert*, p. 27.
5. Litvak, *Vos geven*, pp. 212–14.
6. Hertz, *Geshikhte*, p. 9; Vainer, p. 13. Hertz's work is the fullest examination of the Bundist youth groups I have found.
7. Y. Levin, p. 15.
8. *Ibid.*, pp. 15–29.
9. *Ibid.*, p. 22; Litvak, *Vos geven*, p. 212.
10. Levin, *Vos geven*, pp. 21–22.
11. For an account of such a development in a Polish gymnasium, see "Bronislav," pp. 84–86.
12. *DAS*, 27 (June 1902): 15.
13. Wolf-Jasny, pp. 305–6.
14. Bund biblio.: *Doklad*, pp. 5, 9, and *Di tetigkait*, p. 14.
15. Bund biblio.: *Di tetigkait*, p. 14.
16. Bund biblio.: *Doklad*, p. 5.
17. *Ibid.*, p. 11.
18. Bund biblio.: *Di tetigkait*, p. 15.
19. Bund biblio.: *Doklad*, p. 11. The total for 241 alone was 686,785.
20. Bund biblio.: *ibid.*, p. 14, and *Di tetigkait*, p. 16.
21. Bund biblio.: *Tsu ale arbeter . . . fun Shereshevsky's fabrik*.
22. Cited in *In baginen*, p. 81.
23. Bund biblio.: *Di tetigkait*, pp. 3–4.
24. *Ibid.*, pp. 5–6.
25. Bund biblio.: *Doklad*, p. 6.
26. Epstein, 1: 349.
27. *Ibid.*, pp. 298–305.
28. *Ibid.*, p. 304.
29. Shpizman, 1: 117.
30. *Arkady*, pp. 230–31.
31. Kursky, *Gezamelte*, p. 266.
32. M. Gurevich, p. 566. Gurevich became the Bund's permanent delegate in the United States in 1905.
33. "K biografii A. B. Sapotnitskogo," *KIS*, 3 (1925): 219–21.
34. Kursky, "David Michnik," pp. 25–28.
35. Abramovich, 1: 189–90.
36. *DAS*, 39 (Jan. 1905): 17.
37. Berman, pp. 257–59.
38. See *Der Bund*, 4 (July 1904): 19.
39. *DAS*, 33–39 (May 1903–Jan. 1905).
40. *Ibid.*
41. Mill, *Pionern*, 2: 173.
42. *Ibid.*, p. 171. He does not cite specific dates.
43. *Ibid.*, pp. 179–80.
44. *Ibid.*, p. 179.
45. *Ibid.*, pp. 171, 179.
46. Bund biblio.: *Doklad*, p. 12.
47. Litvak, *Vos geven*, pp. 117–18.
48. *Ibid.*, p. 119.
49. Litvak, *Geklibene*, p. 169.
50. *Ibid.*
51. Abramovich, 1: 137; Mikhalevich, *Zikhroinos*, 2: 142; Zaslavsky, "Tsu der geshikhte," pp. 78–79; Kursky, "Bletlekh," 1: 594.
52. Henry J. Tobias and Charles E. Woodhouse, "The Leadership of the Jewish Bund" (unpublished paper presented at the YIVO Research Conference on Jewish Participation in Movements Devoted to the Cause of Social Progress, September 1964), p. 8.
53. *Ibid.*
54. See *PI*, 166 (Feb. 9/Jan. 27, 1904).
55. *PI*, 197 (Oct. 29/16, 1904): 1; "Der Belostok hariga," *DAS*, 38 (Sept. 1904): 22.
56. *DAS*, 38 (Sept. 1904): 22; *PI*, 199 (Nov. 14/1, 1904): 4.
57. Blekhman, pp. 171–72.
58. *PI*, 198 (Nov. 5/Oct. 23, 1904): 3.
59. *Ibid.*, pp. 1–2.
60. Zhitlovsky, pp. 13–17.
61. "Zwei Berichte," *Die Welt* (Vienna), June 12, 1903, p. 5. For other charges in the same vein, see *Vilner Flugblat*, 4 (Jan. 1904): 5; and *DAS*, 33 (May 1903): 15.

62. *Die Welt*, June 12, 1903, p. 5, col. 2.

63. "Poale Tsion . . . ," *DAS*, 33 (May 1903): 5.

64. Bund biblio.: *Kishinever hariga*, p. 1.   65. Zilberfarb, p. 116.

66. Zhitlovsky, p. 25.   67. *In baginen*, pp. 87–92.

68. *DAS*, 34 (Aug. 1903): 10.   69. Zilberfarb, pp. 120–21.

70. "Der sakh hakel . . . ," *DAS*, 35 (Oct. 1903): 1.

71. Zilberfarb, p. 123.   72. *PI*, 179 (May 5/April 22, 1904): 2.

73. *DAS*, 34 (Aug. 1903): 10.   74. *DAS*, 35 (Oct. 1903): 17–18.

75. Bund biblio.: *Doklad*, pp. 14–15.

76. *PI*, 177 (April 25/12, 1904): 8; *PI*, 179 (May 5/April 22, 1904): 2; *PI*, 200 (Nov. 19/6, 1904): 2.

77. "Iskra . . . ," *VB*, 3 (June 1904): 21.   78. Saul Ginzburg, p. 185.

79. See Kirzhnits, *Yidishe prese*.   80. Saul Ginzburg, pp. 186–90.

81. *Ibid.*, p. 186.

82. "Der Fraind," *DAS*, 33 (May 1903): 9–11.

83. *Arkady*, p. 328. Kremer's charge is echoed in the police reports of late 1901. See Piontkovsky, p. 294.

84. *DAS*, 33 (May 1903): 9.

85. Kirzhnits, *Yidishe prese*, pp. 18–21.

86. Bund biblio.: "Mit vos zainen," pp. 2–3.

87. "Der 'Bund' un di onfirer . . . ," *Der Bund*, 1 (Jan. 1904): 3.

88. "Di Poale Tsion . . . ," *DAS*, 37 (June 1904): 5–6.

89. *Ibid.*, pp. 6–9.

90. Zilberfarb, pp. 122–23.

91. "Sotsial-Revoliutsionizm . . . ," *VB*, 3 (June 1904): 13.

92. *Ibid.*, pp. 14–15.

93. *Ibid.*, p. 15.

94. Zilberfarb, p. 124.

95. See Gutman, pp. 162–63, 168, on the areas of new Zionist strength.

96. J. Frumkin et al., p. 35; Aronson, *Rusish-yidishe inteligents*, p. 10; "Zhizn' i deiatel'nost' . . . ," *Yevreiskii mir* (New York), 1944, p. 9. Bramson, who was active in a number of Jewish causes, was elected to the First Duma.

97. Sliozberg, pp. 136–38.

98. *DAS*, 31 (Jan. 1903): 10.

99. *DAS*, 34 (Aug. 1903): 11–13.

100. Bund biblio.: *Ko vsem yevreiskim narodnym uchiteliam*.

101. Berman, pp. 258–59.

102. "Di burzhuazie troimt," *Der Bund*, 5 (Oct. 1904): 1–2.

103. *Ibid.*, p. 2.   104. "Di liberalen . . . ," *ibid.*, pp. 5–9.

105. *Ibid.*, p. 9.   106. *Ibid.*

107. *Ibid.*   108. Lev, *Klerikalizm*, p. 38.

109. *Ibid.*, p. 39.

110. "Der proletarisher . . . ," *DAS*, 35 (Oct. 1903): 16–17.

111. *Ibid.*; *PI*, 160 (Dec. 24/11, 1903): 4. *PI*, 162 (Jan. 13/Dec. 31, 1904): 3 refers to similar events in Kiev.

112. Bund biblio.: *Po povodu s"ezda ravvinov*.

113. *DAS*, 35 (Oct. 1903): 17.

114. *Der Bund*, 2 (March 1904): 10.

115. "Arbaitslozigkait un hunger," *ibid.*, 3 (April 1904): 1; *ibid.*, 4 (July 1904): 14.

116. *Ibid.*, 4 (July 1904): 14.

117. *Ibid.*, p. 20.

119. *Ibid.*

118. *PI*, 190 (Aug. 29/16, 1904): 3.

120. Borokhov, pp. 29, 44, 68, 99, 107.

Chapter Nineteen

1. Abramovich, 1: 124.

3. *Ibid.*

5. Medem, 2: 41; Abramovich, 1: 124.

7. *Ibid.*

9. *PI*, 157 (Dec. 7/Nov. 24, 1903): 4.

2. Mill, *Pionern*, 2: 119.

4. S. Levin, p. 232.

6. Bund biblio.: *Vegen der aroistretung.*

8. *Ibid.*

10. *PI*, 158 (Dec. 12/Nov. 29, 1903): 4; *PI,* 159 (Dec. 17/4, 1903): 3.

11. *PI*, 159: 3.

12. *PI*, 159, 161, 162–67, and 169–70 (Dec. 17/4, 1903–Feb. 25/March 9, 1904); "Fun unzer partai leben," *DAS*, 36 (Feb. 1904): 19–21.

13. *PI*, 175 (April 11/March 29, 1904): 3.

14. Bund biblio.: *Doklad*, p. 9.

15. See *PI*, nos. 159–61, for examples of these resolutions.

16. Iurenev, p. 164.

18. *Ibid.*, pp. 72–75.

20. "Otchet o partiinoi . . . ," *Iskra*, 78 (Nov. 20, 1904): 7.

17. Agursky, *1905*, pp. 1–4.

19. *1905 yor*, pp. 69–70.

21. Pokrovsky, p. 40; Agursky, *1905*, pp. 73–76, 144; Aronson, "Revoliutsionnaia," pp. 16–17; Aronson et al., p. 316; Mikhalevich, *Zikhroinos*, 2: 62.

22. Reprinted in Russian in *VB*, 4 (July 1904): 22–23; and in Yiddish in Kirzhnits, *Yidisher arbeter*, pp. 40–44.

23. *VB*, 4 (July 1904): 23.

24. *Ibid.*, p. 24.

25. Agursky, *1905*, p. 5.

26. "Novoiavlenie . . . ," *PI*, 190 (Aug. 29/16, 1904): 6–7.

27. Agursky, *1905*, p. 22.

29. *PI*, nos. 151, 157, 160, 192.

28. *Ibid.*, pp. 74–75.

30. *PI*, 199 (Nov. 14/1, 1904): 3.

31. Iurenev, p. 166. In this article, Iurenev made use of the oral reports of members of the RSDWP.

32. Blekhman, p. 176.

34. Agursky, *1905*, p. 144.

36. *Iskra*, 78 (Nov. 20, 1904): 8.

33. Pokrovsky, Appendix 1, p. 341.

35. *Ibid.*; *Tretii*, pp. 365, 369–70.

37. *Tretii*, p. 368. Shklovsky's pseudonym at the congress was Dedushkin.

38. *Ibid.*, p. 394.

40. *Ibid.*

39. *Ibid.*, p. 369.

41. *Ibid.*, p. 396.

42. *PI*, 199 (Nov. 14/1, 1904): 3.

43. Mikhalevich, *Zikhroinos*, 2: 62; Berman, p. 279.

44. Agursky, *1905*, p. 6.

45. See, for example, Agursky, *Revoliutsionere*, p. 101.

46. "Der Tsvaiter Partai-Tsuzamenfor," *DAS*, 36 (Feb. 1904): 1.

47. *Ibid.*, p. 2; "Nash s"ezd," *Iskra*, 53 (Nov. 25, 1903): 2.

48. *DAS*, 37 (June 1904): 3; Bund biblio.: *Doklad,* p. 9.

49. *DAS*, 36 (Feb. 1904): 7.

50. "Unzere Armenishe . . . ," *DAS*, 38 (Sept. 1904): 10; "Iz revoliutsionnago . . . ," *VB*, 1-2 (Jan.-Feb. 1904): 21.

51. "Iskrizm," *VB*, 5 (Nov. 1904): 17–18.

53. *Ibid.*

55. Lenin, *Polnoe*, 5th ed., 8: 67.

52. *Ibid.*, p. 19.

54. *Vtoroi ocherednoi*, p. 150.

56. *Ibid.*, p. 235.

57. *Ibid.*, pp. 330, 354–55.

58. "Iskra do i posle 'reformy,' " *VB*, 1–2 (Jan.-Feb. 1904): 10.

59. "Ob"edinenie . . . ," *Iskra*, 55 (Dec. 15, 1903): 2–5.

60. *Ibid.*, p. 2.   61. *Ibid.*, pp. 3–4.

62. *Ibid.*, p. 5.   63. *Ibid.*

64. "Ob"edinenie . . . ," *Iskra*, 57 (Jan. 15, 1904): 2.

65. "Iskrizm," *VB*, 5 (Nov. 1904): 19.

66. "Chleny . . . ," *ibid.*, p. 28; "V Amsterdame," *Iskra*, 74 (Sept. 20, 1904): 5. As late as mid-1904 Martov still had words of praise for the Bund's habit of discussing matters with workers (supplement to *Iskra*, 69 [July 10, 1904]).

67. Schwarz, "Men'shevizm," p. 30.

68. "Iskrizm," *VB*, 5 (Nov. 1904): 20–21.

69. "Na ocheredi," *Iskra*, 69 (July 10, 1904): 3.

70. "Noveishaia polemika 'Bunda,' " *Iskra*, 73 (Sept. 1, 1904): 3.

71. Editors' note, *VB*, 1-2 (Jan.-Feb. 1904): 1.

72. Kosovsky, "Vl. Medem," pp. 156–57.

73. Medem, 2: 55–56.

74. "Polozhenie Bunda v Partii," *Sochineniia*, 5th ed. (Moscow, 1960), 8: 72.

75. *Ibid.*, p. 74. Lenin ignored Marx's work on the Jews in his citations.

76. *Ibid.*, p. 76.

77. "Natsional'nost' i assimilatsiia," *VB*, 1–2 (Jan.-Feb. 1904): 3–6.

78. *Ibid.*, pp. 4–5.   79. *Ibid.*, p. 8.

80. *Ibid.*   81. *Ibid.*, VB, 3 (June 1904): 1–2.

82. *Ibid.*, pp. 2–3; Runes, p. 37. See also Hofman, *Far 50 yor*, p. 84.

83. "Natsional'nost' i assimilatsiia," *VB*, 3 (June 1904): 3.

84. *Ibid.*, p. 4.

85. *Ibid.*, pp. 4–5.

86. *Ibid.*

87. *Ibid.*, p. 5; "Neskol'ko slov . . . ," supplement to *Iskra*, 58 (Jan. 25, 1904).

88. "Natsional'nost' i assimilatsiia," *VB*, 3 (June 1904): 6.

89. "Sotsialdemokratiia . . . ," *VB*, 4 (July 1904): 6.

90. *Ibid.*, p. 7.   91. *Ibid.*, pp. 7–8.

92. *Ibid.*, p. 8.   93. *Ibid.*

94. *Ibid.*, pp. 8–9.   95. *Ibid., VB*, 5 (Nov. 1904): 7–8.

96. *Ibid.*, p. 10.   97. *Ibid.*, pp. 12–14.

98. "Na ocheredi," *Iskra*, 69 (July 10, 1904): 2–4.

99. "Ob odnoi . . . ," *Iskra*, 82 (Jan. 1, 1905): 2.

100. *Ibid.*   101. *Ibid.*

102. Medem, 2: 54–55.   103. *VB*, 5 (Nov. 1904): 4–5.

104. *Ibid.*, p. 5; Medem, 2: 67.   105. *VB*, 5 (Nov. 1904): 5–7.

106. "Chleny . . . ," *ibid.*, p. 27; "V Amsterdame," *Iskra*, 74 (Sept. 20, 1904): 5.

107. *VB*, 5 (Nov. 1904): 28.   108. *Ibid.*, pp. 27–28.

109. *Ibid.*   110. "Iz Partii," *Iskra*, 82 (Jan. 1, 1905): 6.

111. Kosovsky, "Martov," pp. 178–79.   112. Mill, *Pionern*, 2: 164–65.

113. Mendelsohn, p. 137.

114. "Di milkhoma un di sotsialdemokratie," *DAS*, 37 (June 1904): 4.

115. Nikolaevsky, "R.S.-D.R.P.," pp. 59–65.

116. "Ein Dokument."   117. *Ibid.*

118. Nikolaevsky, "R.S.-D.R.P.," p. 60.   119. *Ibid.*, p. 65; "Ein Dokument."

120. "Ein Dokument."   121. *Ibid.*

122. Volkovicher, "Partiia," pp. 119–20.

123. "Otvet na priglashenie," *PI*, 204 (Dec. 22/9, 1904): 1; Martov, *Istoriia*, 2d ed. (Moscow, 1923), p. 92.

124. *PI*, 204 (Dec. 22/9, 1904): 1.

125. "Otvet Tsentral'nago Komiteta Bunda," *PI*, 202 (Dec. 6/Nov. 23, 1904): 1.

126. *Ibid.*

127. "Vopros o predstavitel'stve . . . ," *VB*, 5 (Nov. 1904): 2.

128. *Vtoroi ocherednoi*, pp. 378–79.

129. "Neskol'ko slov . . . ," *VB*, 1-2 (Jan.-Feb. 1904): 18–20.

130. "I-yi s"ezd . . . ," *VB*, 5 (Nov. 1904): 24.

131. *Revoliutsionnaia Rossiia*, 46 (May 5, 1904): 16–17.

132. "Yeshche o mobilizatsii," *Iskra*, 76 (Oct. 20, 1904): 6.

133. "Sots.-rev. i yevreiskie pogromy," *VB*, 3 (June 1904): 22.

134. "Tsarskaia milosti i pogromy," *VB*, 5 (Nov. 1904): 5–7.

135. *DAS*, 16 (March 1900): 4.

136. *Der Arbeter*, 1 (Dec. 1898): 1.

137. Bund biblio.: *Chetvertyi s"ezd*, pp. 11–14.

138. "Bund . . . ," *Robotnik*, 41 (Sept. 17, 1901): 1–2. Trans. by H. Kempinski.

139. Shvarts, *Pilsudski*, pp. 194–96, 201.

140. "Szósty szazd P.P.S.," *Robotnik*, 46 (Aug. 5, 1902): 1. Trans. by H. Kempinski.

141. "P.P.S. vegen . . . ," *DAS*, 30 (Oct. 1902): 1–5.

142. *Ibid.*, p. 2.   143. *DAS*, 29 (Sept. 1902): 11.

144. Zaks, p. 5; Shvarts, *Pilsudski*, p. 202.   145. Zaks, pp. 5–12.

146. Lenin, *Sochineniia*, 3d ed., 5: 344.   147. Zaks, p. 14.

148. *Ibid.*, p. 17.   149. Lenin, *Sochineniia*, 3d ed., 5: 341–44.

150. Shvarts, *Pilsudski*, pp. 204–5; Zaks, p. 19.

151. Pilsudski, p. 80.   152. Shvarts, *Pilsudski*, p. 286.

153. *Ibid.*, pp. 194–95.   154. Stern, pp. 19–20.

155. A few cases are cited in Hertz et al., 2: 136–37. See also *Iskra*, 39 (May 1, 1903): 5; "Der mai faier . . . ," *Der Bund*, 3 (April 1904): 16; and *DAS*, 32 (March 1903): 15.

156. Mazovetsky, *VB*, 5 (Nov. 1904): 14–15.

157. *DAS*, 19 (Sept. 1900): 14; Bund biblio.: *Chetvertyi s"ezd*, p. 16.

158. "Iz revoliutsionnago . . . ," *VB*, 1-2 (Jan.-Feb. 1904): 21.

159. *LS*, 15: 59–60.

160. M. Rafes, "Primiritel'nye," pp. 170–71. The information in this article duplicates and supplements the material in the document printed in the *St. Louis Arbeiter Zeitung* (see "Ein Dokument").

161. Nettl, 1: 75–77; Mazovetsky, *VB*, 5 (Nov. 1904): 15.

162. Mill, *Pionern,* 1: 181; Kursky, *Gezamelte*, pp. 170–72, 323–24.

163. Bund biblio.: *Chetvertyi s"ezd*, p. 16.

164. "Iz Partii," *Iskra*, 7 (Aug. 1901): 5.

165. Krzhizhanovsky, p. 107.

166. *Ibid.*

167. *Ibid.*, p. 111; *LS*, 8: 337; Kirzhnits, "Bund un RSDAP," p. 72; Nettl, 1: 272–73.

168. Nettl cites a number of letters among the Poles bitterly criticizing the Bund (1: 272–73).

169. Kirzhnits, "Bund un RSDAP," p. 72.

170. Ganetsky, pp. 189–90; *VB*, 1-2 (Jan.-Feb. 1904): 20; *Vtoroi ocherednoi*, 134–36.

171. *Vtoroi ocherednoi*, pp. 48–49, 54.

172. *Ibid.*, pp. 47, 53–54.

173. *Ibid.*, pp. 134–37. See Shukman, pp. 280–86, for an account of PSD-Bund relations.

174. *Vtoroi s"ezd, RSDRP: Protokoly*, Appendix 12, p. 721.

175. Lenin, *Sochineniia*, 3d ed., 5: 341–42.

176. Krzhizhanovsky, p. 121; *Vtoroi ocherednoi,* Appendix 9, p. 390.

177. Medem, 2: 28.

178. *Ibid.*, pp. 28–29.

179. *VB*, 1-2 (Jan.-Feb. 1904): 20–21; Krzhizhanovsky, pp. 120–21.

180. [Portnoy], "Di sotsialdemokratie . . . ," *DAS*, 37 (June 1904): 21–23.

181. Cited in "Delegatsiia Pol'skoi . . . ,"*VB*, 3 (June 1904): 22–23.

182. Mikhalevich, *Zikhroinos*, 1: 149.

183. Kursky, *Gezamelte*, pp. 323–24; Hertz et al., 2: 141.

184. *Der Bund*, 3 (April 1904): 16. On ties in 1903, see Berman, pp. 216–23.

185. *VB*, 1-2 (Jan.-Feb. 1904): 2.

186. Rafes, "Primiritel'nye," pp. 169–72.

Chapter Twenty

Unless otherwise noted, articles cited by journal name in this chapter were published in 1905.

1. Abramovich, 1: 190–92.

2. Bund biblio.: *Tsum kamf!*

3. *PI*, 212 (Feb. 1/Jan. 19): 1.

4. "Di revolutsionere . . . ," *DAS*, supplement to 39 (March): 7–8.

5. *Ibid.* For the report of a factory inspector who stressed the need to meet workers' demands, see *Revoliutsiia: Ianvar'-Mart*, p. 504.

6. *DAS*, supplement to 39 (March): 17.

7. *Revoliutsiia: Ianvar'-Mart*, p. 507.

8. *DAS*, supplement to 39 (March): 10–12.

9. *Ibid.*, p. 12.   10. *Revoliutsionnoe*, pp. 28–29.

11. Bund biblio.: *Tsum kamf!*   12. *DAS*, supplement to 39 (March): 29.

13. *Revoliutsiia: Ianvar'-Mart*, p. 711. 14. Romanov, p. 8.

15. *DAS*, supplement to 39 (March): 1.   16. *Ibid.*, pp. 2–4.

17. *Ibid.*

18. "Di VI Konferents fun Bund," *ibid.*, p. 31.

19. *DAS*, supplement to 39 (March): 30.

20. My discussion of the conference proceedings in the text is based on the *DAS* supplement cited in the previous note, pp. 31–32.

21. Abramovich prepared the material for the discussion on this question. *In tsvai revolutsies*, 1: 194–95.

22. The text of the resolution breaks off at this point with ellipses and the words "secret clauses."

23. *DAS*, supplement to 39 (March): 1.   24. Gurko, p. 350.

25. *Ibid.*, pp. 355–56.   26. *Ibid.*, p. 372.

27. "Tsum proletariat . . . ," *DAS*, 39 (Jan.): 14–15.

28. Bund biblio.: *Tsar's konstitutsie.*

29. *Ibid.*

30. *Ibid.*

31. "All-Highest Manifesto on the Establishment of a State Duma," cited in Raeff, pp. 141–53.

32. Bund biblio.: *A folksfertretung.*

33. "Di gosudarstvenaia duma," *DAS*, 40 (Sept.): 2.

34. *Ibid.*, p. 4.

35. "Di sotsialdemokratie . . . ," *Der Bund*, 9 (Oct.): 1–4.

36. Litvak, *Geklibene*, p. 178.   37. Varzar, p. 6.

38. *Ibid.*   39. *Ibid.*, p. 15.

40. *Ibid.*, pp. 9, 103.   41. *Ibid.*, p. 103.

42. See, for instance, every issue of *PI* from no. 219 through no. 246.

43. *PI*, 219 (March 7/Feb. 22): 3; *PI*, 227 (April 20/7): 3; *PI*, 229 (May 5/April 22): 3; *PI*, 232 (May 23/10): 2–3.

44. Litvak, *Geklibene*, p. 178.

45. The Lithuanian Social Democrats received 50 rubles, the PPS 15, the RSDWP 7, and the SR's 3 (*PI*, 221 [March 15/2]: 1). See also Mitskevich-Kapsukas, p. 57.

46. Litvak, *Geklibene*, p. 186.

47. *PI*, 220 (March 11/Feb. 26): 3; *PI*, 229 (May 5/April 22): 4; *PI*, 238 (June 27/14): 3; *DAS*, 40 (Sept.): 24.

48. *Der Bund in 1905–1906*, p. 76.

49. "Vi zolen . . . ," *Der Bund*, 6 (May): 1.

50. Litvak, *Geklibene*, pp. 178–79; *PI*, 227 (April 20/7): 1–2; *PI*, 228 (April 26/13): 1.

51. Litvak, *Geklibene*, p. 179; Y. Levin, pp. 30–31; *PI*, 246 (Aug. 22/9): 5.

52. Bund biblio.: *Der ershter Mai*. Some of the copies were printed in red.

53. "Der ershter Mai . . . ," *Di Letste Pasirungen*, 10 (June 21/8): 1.

54. *Ibid.*   55. *Ibid.*

56. *Der Bund in 1905–1906*, p. 70.   57. Litvak, *Geklibene*, p. 185.

58. *PI*, 232 (May 23/10): 2; *PI*, 234 (June 7/May 25): 1.

59. Chemerisky, "In Lodz," p. 1. See also *PI*, 230 (May 11/April 28): 6.

60. Y. Levin, pp. 30–33; Rozen, pp. 31–32.

61. Litvak, *Geklibene*, p. 180.

62. Abramovich, 1: 222.

63. *DAS*, 40 (Sept.): 26–39; *PI*, 245 (Aug. 9/July 27): 1.

64. Gurko, p. 393.   65. *Ibid.*, pp. 393–94.

66. *Ibid.*, p. 394.   67. *Ibid.*

68. Varzar, p. 6. In all likelihood Varzar's estimates are low (see p. 1). Harcave, for one, would more than double Varzar's figures (*First Blood*, p. 186).

69. Varzar, p. 6.   70. *Der Bund*, 10 (Nov. 22/9): 7.

71. *Ibid.*, p. 8.   72. *Ibid.*, pp. 10–11.

73. Litvak, *Geklibene*, p. 191.   74. Harcave, *First Blood*, p. 155.

75. See Rogger, "Russian Fascism," pp. 398–99, and "Formation of the Right," pp. 66–67.

76. Witte, 2: 351.

77. *Ibid.*, pp. 350–51.

78. *Ibid.*, pp. 351–52; Lopukhin, p. 88. See Factory Inspector A. V. Varentsov's report to the Minister of Finance, in *Revoliutsiia: Ianvar'-Mart*, p. 528.

79. The Black Hundreds were never a party as such, but rather were separate groups of a similar mood and political style. See Rogger, "Russian Fascism," p. 399.

80. *PI*, 220 (March 11/Feb. 26): 6.   81. *PI*, 225 (April 6/March 24): 6.

82. *PI*, nos. 230–32.   83. *PI*, 222 (March 20/7): 6.

84. *PI*, 223 (March 23/10): 4.   85. *PI*, 244 (Aug. 5/July 23): 4.

86. Vinocur, "Pogroma." An edited version of this work appears in *Der Bund in 1905–1906*, pp. 51–67.

87. *PI*, nos. 221, 223, 227.

88. For a short summary of pogrom activity in 1905, see Dubnow, 3: 113–20.

89. Litvak, *Geklibene*, p. 181.

90. Bund biblio.: *Di pogromen*, pp. 1–2.

91. Berman, p. 304.

92. Abramovich, 1: 202.

93. Berman, p. 295.

94. Mikhalevich, *Zikhroinos*, 2: 152–53.

95. Abramovich, 1: 202–3.

96. Litvak, *Geklibene*, p. 180.

97. Abramovich, 1: 202–3.

98. Litvak, *Geklibene*, p. 181.

99. Daich, p. 16.

100. "Statisticheskiia."

101. "Der emese geshtalt . . . ," *Der Bund*, 7 (May): 2–6.

102. *PI*, 231 (May 18/5): 2.

103. *DAS*, supplement to 39 (March): 32.

104. "Tekhnicheskiia . . . ," *PI*, 222 (March 20/7): 1–2.

105. *Ibid.*, p. 2.

106. *Ibid.*, p. 3. Laibechke Berman, who joined a central commission on self-defense formed in January 1906, holds that the Bund rejected any elaborate plan involving the self-defense units (pp. 299–303).

107. "Krovavaia nedelia . . . ," *PI*, 238 (June 27/14): 1–3.

108. "Voennyia zametki," *PI*, 242 (July 25/12): 1–2.

109. "Lodz un Odes," *Der Bund*, 8 (July): 15.

110. *PI*, 241 (July 17/4): 3–4.

111. *PI*, 229 (May 5/April 22): 7.

112. *PI*, 252 (Oct. 10/Sept. 27): 9.

113. Litvak, *Geklibene*, p. 182.

114. Bund biblio.: *Tsu ale rekruten*.

115. J. Frumkin et al., p. 36.

116. Reprinted from *Der Fraind* in *PI*, 224 (March 30/17): 4. *Der Fraind* reported that it bore 7,000 signatures. Excerpts from this and similar petitions appear in Dubnow, 3: 108–9.

117. Dubnow, 3: 111–12. Dubnow was a member of the league's Central Bureau.

118. *DAS*, supplement to 39 (March): 31.

119. Bund biblio.: *Mir un zai*.

120. *Ibid.*

121. *Ibid.*

122. "Prizyv . . . ," *PI*, 225 (April 6/March 24): 2–3.

123. "Narozhdenie . . . ," *ibid.*, pp. 1–2.

124. "Fun yidishen leben," *Der Bund*, 6 (May): 13.

125. Harcave, "Jewish Political Parties," pp. 58–59.

126. "Gosudarstvennaia Duma," *Voskhod*, 32 (Aug. 11): cols. 1–5.

127. "K vyboram . . . ," *Voskhod*, 37 (Sept. 16): col. 2.

128. *DAS*, 40 (Sept.): 23.

129. "Di sotsialdemokratie . . . ," *Der Bund*, 9 (Oct.): 1–2.

130. *PI*, 227 (April 20/7): 6.

131. *PI*, 229 (May 5/April 22): 5.

132. *PI*, 232 (May 23/10): 3.

133. *PI*, 239 (July 4/June 21): 3.

134. *PI*, 245 (Aug. 9/July 27): 4.

135. "Zelbst-shuts . . . ," *Der Bund*, 7 (May 1905): 1–2.

136. Abramovich, 1: 203–11; *PI*, 233 (May 31/18): 7.

137. Berman, p. 171.

138. *DAS*, supplement to 39 (March): 32.

139. *PI*, nos. 220, 233, 243; *DAS*, 40 (Sept.).

140. *PI*, 239 (July 4/June 21): 3; *PI*, 245 (Aug. 9/July 27): 4.

141. *PI*, 230 (May 11/April 28): 4.

142. *PI*, 232 (May 23/10): 4.

143. *PI*, nos. 224, 227, 229, 230, 233, 236, 237, 244; *DAS*, 40 (Sept.): 27, 28, 32.

144. *PI*, 225 (April 6/March 24): 5.

145. "Narozhdenie . . . ," *ibid.*, p. 1.

146. "Fun yidishen leben," *Der Bund*, 6 (May): 12.

147. "Der klain-burgerlikher sotsializmus . . . ," *DAS*, 40 (Sept.): 14–16.

148. Medem, 2: 80–83.

149. *DAS*, 40 (Sept.): 16.

150. Rafes, "Primiritel'nye," pp. 171–72.

151. *Ibid.*, pp. 172–73.

152. *Ibid.*, pp. 175, 179.

153. "Mezhdupartiinyia," pp. 11–12. An edited version of this material appears in *Der Bund in 1905–1906*, pp. 92–107.

154. Samuel Baron, "Plekhanov and Revolution," pp. 134–35.

155. *DAS*, 39 (Jan.): 15–16.

156. *PI*, 222 (March 20/7): 1–3. The Bundists singled out a discussion of current tactics by Anatole Lunacharsky ("Tverdyi kurs," *Vpered*, 5 [Feb. 7/Jan. 25]: 1–2) that strongly recommended disruptive actions, and Lenin's article "Novyia zadachi i novyia sily," *ibid.*, 9 (March 8/Feb. 23).

157. "Revolutsionere tsait-fragen," *DAS*, 40 (Sept.): 5–6.

158. "Di konferents . . . ," *Di Letste Pasirungen*, 22 (Oct. 21/8): 1–2.

159. Martov, *Istoriia*, 3d ed., pp. 110–11.

160. "Yevreiskii proletariat . . . ," *PI*, 226 (April 12/March 30): 1–2.

161. Martov, *Istoriia*, 3d ed., pp. 126–27.

162. *DAS*, supplement to 39 (March): 32.

163. *PI*, nos. 219, 220, 232, 233, 237, 239, 246.

164. *PI*, 221 (March 15/2): 3; *PI*, 220 (March 11/Feb. 26): 5.

165. *PI*, 240 (July 10/June 27): 1.

166. *PI*, 236 (June 16/3): 6.

167. *PI*, 228 (April 26/13): 5.

168. "Iz rabochego dvizheniia," *Vpered*, 9 (March 8/Feb. 23): 17; Piatnitsky, pp. 75–76.

169. *Vpered*, 7 (Feb. 21/8): 9.

170. For an interesting general description of local relations between the Bolsheviks and the Bund, see Dimanshtein, "Di revolutsionere," pp. 17–23.

171. See, for example, *Proletarii*, nos. 5 (June 26/13); 7 (July 10/June 27); and 15 (Sept. 5/Aug. 23).

172. See, for example, Iurenev, p. 176. Gorelik estimates the Bund membership in Bobruisk at 1,000 and the party's at no more than 150 (Agursky, *1905*, p. 89). See also Aronson, "Revoliutsionnaia," p. 32.

173. *Iskra*, 101 (June 1): 6.

174. *Iskra*, 93 (March 10): 5.

175. *PI*, nos. 220, 223, 235, 243.

176. *Revoliutsionnaia Rossiia*, 62 (March 25): 11; and 68 (June 1): 13; also Aronson et al., *Vitebsk*, pp. 357–60.

177. *PI*, 237 (June 21/8): 3–4; *PI*, 242 (July 25/12): 5–6.

178. *Revoliutsionnaia Rossiia*, 59 (Feb. 10): 17.

179. Frank, pp. 389–91; Avrich, pp. 17–20, 42–49.

180. Frank, pp. 393–401.

181. *Der Bund*, 7 (May): 9.

182. *PI*, 242 (July 25/12): 5–6.

183. Shvarts, *Juzef Pilsudski*, pp. 223–25; Pestkovsky, p. 40.

184. Rafes, "Primiritel'nye," pp. 184–86.

185. Nettl, 1: 337.

186. *PI*, nos. 219, 220, 230, 232, 235, 243.

187. *PI*, 240 (July 10/June 27): 5.

188. *PI*, 227 (April 20/7): 2; Rafes, "Primiritel'nye," p. 197.

189. Abramovich, 1: 223; Mikhalevich, *Zikhroinos*, 2: 155–57.

190. Abramovich, 1: 223.

191. "Der VI-ter Tsuzamenfor . . . ," *Der Veker*, 1 (Jan. 3, 1906/Dec. 25): 4; Mikhalevich, *Zikhroinos*, 2: 157–58. *Der Veker* was the Bund's first legal daily in Russia.

192. Mikhalevich, *Zikhroinos*, 2: 159.
193. Medem, 2: 90.
194. *Der Veker*, 1 (Jan. 3, 1906/Dec. 25): 4.
195. Medem, 2: 96.
196. *Ibid.*, pp. 90–93.
197. *Der Veker*, 1 (Jan. 3, 1906/Dec. 25): 4.
198. *Ibid.*
200. *Vos mir darfen.*
199. *Ibid.*; Medem, 2: 93–94.
201. Medem, 2: 91–92.

Chapter Twenty-one

1. For the text, see Spector, pp. 237–38.
2. Abramovich, 1: 227–28.
3. *Ibid.*, p. 228.
4. *25 yor*, p. 69.
5. S. Levin, p. 283.
6. "Di profesionele ferainen," *Der Bund*, 11 (Dec. 1905): 5; *25 yor*, p. 83.
7. "Di profesionele ferainen," *Der Bund*, 11 (Dec. 1905): 5; Kirzhnits, *Profbevegung,* p. 7.
8. Kirzhnits, *Profbevegung*, pp. 5–6.
9. *Ibid.*, p. 6.
10. *Ibid.*
11. Bund biblio.: *Sed'maia Konferentsiia Bunda*.
12. Berman, pp. 269, 364–65.
13. Medem, 2: 86.
14. Dubnow, *History*, 3: 127–31.
15. Lopukhin, pp. 86–87.
16. Mikhalevich, *Zikhroinos*, 2: 160–62.
17. Medem, 2: 94–95.
18. Niger and Raizen, p. 90.
19. Litvak, *Geklibene*, p. 186.
20. Abramovich, 1: 227; Niger and Raizen, p. 84; Medem, 2: 85–88.
21. Hofman, *Far 50 yor*, pp. 306–8; Abramovich, 1: 216.
22. Varzar, p. 6.
23. "Fun gezelshaftlikhen leben," *Der Bund*, 11 (Dec. 1/Nov. 18, 1905): 6–7. A chronology of the events of late 1905 is included in *Revoliutsiia: Noiabr'-Dekabr'*, part 4: 913–21.
24. Bund biblio.: *Tsu ale fraie birger.*
25. "Di Oktober teg," *Der Bund*, 10 (Nov. 22/9, 1905): 1–2.
26. Abramovich, 1: 241.
27. "Di gezelshaftlikhe klasen . . . ," *Der Veker* (Jan. 3, 1906/Dec. 25, 1905): 1–2.
28. Olgin, "Vos bevaizt . . . ," *ibid.*, p. 2.
29. M. N. [Olgin?], "Naie lates . . . ," *ibid.*, p. 3.
30. M. N. [Olgin?], "Boikot," *Der Veker*, 4 (Jan. 10, 1906/Dec. 28, 1905): 1.
31. Bund biblio.: *Sed'maia Konferentsiia Bunda*
32. M. Pritykin, "Novyi izbiratel'nyi zakon," *Voskhod*, 2 (Jan. 13, 1906): col. 18.
33. N. [Olgin], "Di konstitutsionalistn-demokraten . . . ," *Der Veker*, 21 (Feb. 1/Jan. 19, 1906): 4.
34. Miliukov, pp. 96–97.
35. P. Rosenthal (An-man), "Tsu iz rikhtig . . . ," *Folkstsaitung* (Vilna), 61 (May 22/9, 1906): 1–2; Kirzhnits, *Yidisher arbeter*, part 2: 135–39.

Bibliography

Publications issued by the Central Committee, the Foreign Committee, and various local committees of the Bund are listed separately on pages 395–96. The following abbreviations are used in the Bibliography:

DAS	Di Arbeter Shtime		PI	Posledniia izvestiia
DYA	Der Yidisher Arbeter		PR	Proletarskaia revoliutsiia
DZ	Di Zukunft		UT	Unzer tsait
KIS	Katorga i ssylka		YHS	YIVO historishe shriften, Vol. 3, 1939
KL	Krasnaia letopis'		VB	Vestnik Bunda
LS	Leninskii sbornik			

I. GENERAL WORKS

Ab–E. "Kamf-bilder fun amol," *Yugent veker* (Warsaw), no. 20, Oct. 20, 1927.

Abram der Tate, *see* Blekhman.

Abramovich, R. *In tsvai revolutsies.* 2 vols. New York, 1944.

Agursky, Sh. (S.) *Di revolutsionere bevegung in Vaisrusland, 1863–1917.* Moscow-Kharkov-Minsk, 1931.

———. *Di sotsialistishe literatur oif yidish in 1875–1897.* vol. 2. Minsk, 1935.

———, ed. *1905 in Vaisrusland.* Minsk, 1925.

Ahad Ha'am, *see* Asher Ginzberg.

Ainzaft, S. "Ekonomicheskaia bor'ba Belostokskikh tekstil'shchikov v 80-kh i 90-kh godakh," in Sh. Dimanshtein, *Revoliutsionnoe,* listed below.

Akimov, Vl. *Materialy dlia kharakteristiki razvitiia Rossiiskoi Sotsial Demokraticheskoi Rabochei Partii.* Geneva, 1904.

Akimov-Makhnovets, Vl. "Pervyi s"ezd Rossiiskoi S.-DR Partii," *Minuvshie gody* (St. Petersburg), 1908, no. 2.

Aksel'rod-Ortodoks, L. "Iz moikh vospominanii," *KIS,* 1930, no. 2.

Alter Bekanter. "Der onhaib fun der yidisher arbeter bevegung in Lodz," *Roiter pinkos,* vol. 2 (1924).

———. "Perets un di arbeter-bevegung," *Di Arbeter Shtime* (Petrograd), no. 45 (Sept. 27, 1917).

An-man, *see* P. Rosenthal.

Arkady: Zamlbukh tsum andenk fun Arkady Kremer. New York, 1942.

Aronson, Grigory. "Di Homler 'birzhe' un di Homler zelbstshuts," *Der Wecker* (New York), April 1, 1955.

———. "Der lebsveg fun John Mill," *UT* (New York), 1952, no. 11.

———. "Revoliutsionnaia iunost', Vospominaniia, 1903–1917," Paper no. 6, Inter-University Project on the History of the Menshevik Movement. New York, Aug. 1961.

———. *Rusish-yidishe inteligents.* Buenos Aires, 1962.

———, Jakov Leshchinsky, and Abraham Kin, eds. *Vitebsk amol.* New York, 1956.

Avrich, Paul. *The Russian Anarchists.* Princeton, N.J., 1967.

B. Kahan-Virgili: Zamlbukh tsu zain biografie un kharakteristik. Vilna, 1938.

Baron, Salo. *The Jewish Community.* 3 vols. New York, 1942.

Baron, Samuel H. "Plekhanov and the Revolution of 1905," in John Shelton Curtiss, ed., *Essays in Russian and Soviet History.* New York, 1963.

———. *Plekhanov, the Father of Russian Marxism.* Stanford, Calif., 1963.

Berman, L. [Laibechke]. *In loif fun yorn: Zikhroinos fun a yidishen arbeter.* New York, 1945.

Bernstein, Leon. "David Katz (Taras) un der Tsvaiter Tsuzamenfor fun 'Bund,'" *UT* (New York), 1954, no. 10.

———. *Ershte shprotsungen.* Buenos Aires, 1956.

Blekhman, Laib [Abram der Tate]. *Bleter fun main yugent: Zikhroinos fun a Bundist.* New York, 1959.

Blum, *see* H. Katz.

Bobrovskaia, Ts. S., comp. "Iz perepiski 'Iskry' s mestnymi organizatsiiami," *PR,* 1928, no. 6–7.

Bok, M. "In baginen fun der yidisher arbeter bevegung," *Fraie Arbeter Shtime* (New York), July 25, 1947.

Borokhov, B. *Di yidishe arbeter bevegung in tsifern.* Berlin, 1923.

"Bronislav Groser's avtobiografie," *Roiter pinkos,* vol. 1 (1921).

Brutskus, Boris Davidovich. *Professional'nyi sostav yevreiskago naseleniia Rossii.* St. Petersburg, 1908.

Bukhbinder, N. A. *Istoriia yevreiskogo rabochego dvizheniia v Rossii po neizdannym arkhivnym materialam.* Leningrad, 1925.

———. "Nezavisimaia yevreiskaia rabochaia partiia," *KL,* no. 2–3 (1922).

———. "Razgrom yevreiskogo rabochego dvizheniia v 1898 g. (po neizdannym arkhivnym materialam)," *KL,* no. 4 (1922).

———. "Yevreiskoe rabochee dvizhenie v Minske (1893–1905)," *KL,* no. 5 (1923).

Bund. Official publications are listed separately on pp. 395–96.

"Bund Delegate at Orel to Foreign Committee." [February 1903?] Letter in Bund Archives, New York.

Der 'Bund' in der revolutsie fun 1905–1906: Loit di materialn fun Bundisher arkhiv. Warsaw, 1930.

Cahan, A. "Tsu der geshikhte fun der Bundistisher zelbstshuts," *UT* (New York), 1953, no. 12.

Chemerisky, A. "In Lodz in 1905," *Roite bleter,* book 1, 1929.

———, M. Rafes, and M. [Esther] Frumkina. "Vospominaniia ob 'Yevreiskoi nezavisimoi rabochei partii'," *Krasnyi arkhiv,* 1922, vol. 1.

Cherikover, A. "Di onhaibn fun der umlegaler literatur in yidish," *YHS.*

———. "Yidn-revolutsionern in di 60er un 70er yorn," *YHS.*

Chernov, V. M. *Pered burei.* New York, 1953.

Daich, M. "Vegn main revolutsionerer arbet," *Roite bleter,* book 1, 1929.

"Di debate vegn der natsionaler frage oifn V Tsuzamenfor fun 'Bund,'" *UT* (Warsaw), 1928, no. 1.

Deutsch, Lev. "Der ershter yidisher-sotsialistisher propagandist," *DZ,* 1916, no. 8.

———, ed. *Gruppa "Osvobozhdenie Truda."* 6 vols. Moscow-Leningrad, 1924–28.

Dimanshtein, Sh. *Di natsionale frage ofn Tsvaitn Tsuzamenfor fun der partei*. Moscow, 1934.

———. "Di revolutsionere bevegung tsvishn di yidishe masn in der revolutsie fun 1905," *Roite bleter*, book 1, 1929.

———, ed. *Revoliutsionnoe dvizhenie sredi yevreev*. Moscow, 1930. Miscellany 1.

"Di diskusies vegn der natsionaler frage oifn V Tsuzamenfor fun 'Bund,' Iuni, 1903 in Zurich" (2 parts), *UT* (Warsaw), 1927, nos. 2 and 3.

"Doklad organizatsii 'Iskry' II s"ezdu RSDRP v 1903 g. (s predisoloviem N. K. Krupskoi)," *PR*, 1928, no. 1(72).

Doklad predstavlennyi delegatsiei Russkikh sotsial'demokratov Mezhdunarodnomu rabochemu sotsialisticheskomu Kongressu v Londone v 1896 g. Geneva, 1896.

"Ein Dokument der russischen Revolution (bisher unveröffentlicht)," *St. Louis Arbeiter-Zeitung*, April 10, 1909. Copy in Bund Archives, New York.

"Dokumenty o I s"ezde R.S.D.R.P.," *KL*, 1923, no. 7.

Dokumenty "Ob"edinitel'nago" s"ezda. Geneva, Dec. 1901.

"Donosy tsariu o russkoi emigratsii," *Byloe*, 1909, no. 11–12.

Drobner, Boleslaw, ed. *Ocherki po istorii sotsialisticheskago dvizheniia v Russkoi Pol'she*. Lvov, 1904.

Dubnow, Semen Markovich. *History of the Jews in Russia and Poland*. Translated by I. Friedlaender. 3 vols. Philadelphia, 1916–20.

———. *Nationalism and History*. Edited by Koppel S. Pinson. Cleveland, 1961. Paperback.

Dubnow-Erlich, Sophie. *Garber Bund un bershter Bund*. Warsaw, 1937.

Dushkan, M. N. "Minskaia konferentsiia 1895 goda," in Sh. Dimanshtein, *Revoliutsionnoe*, listed above.

Eidelman, B. "K istorii vozniknoveniia Rossiiskoi Sots.-Dem. Rabochei Partii," *PR*, 1921, no. 1.

———. "Ob 'ekonomicheskikh' tendentsiiakh na I s"ezde RSDRP," *PR*, 1928, no. 10.

———. "Otvet kritiku," *PR*, 1927, no. 6.

———. "Po povodu stat'i Akimova," *PR*, 1921, no. 1.

Epshtein, A. "Vi der 'Bund' hot geholfen di Rusishe Sotsial-Demokraten," *Der Tog* (New York), Nov. 14, 1937.

Epstein, Melech. *Jewish Labor in U.S.A.* 2 vols. New York, 1950–53.

Frank, Herman. *Geklibene shriftn*. New York, 1954.

Frumkin, B. M. "Ocherki iz istorii yevreiskago rabochago dvizheniia v Rossii (1885–1897)," *Yevreiskaia starina*, 1913, no. 1.

———. "Zubatovshchina i yevreiskoe rabochee dvizhenie," *Perezhitoe*, vol. 3, 1911.

Frumkin, Jacob, Gregory Aronson, and Alexis Goldenweiser, eds. *Russian Jewry* (1860–1917). Translated by Mirra Ginsburg. New York, 1966.

F. Frumkina [Minchanka]. "Pis'ma F. Frumkinoi," *Byloe*, 1908, no. 8.

25 yor (1897–1922): Zamlbukh. Warsaw, 1922.

Ganetsky, Ia. "Delegatsiia SDKPiL na s"ezde RSDRP," *PR*, 1933, no. 2.

Garvi, P. A. *Vospominaniia sotsialdemokrata*. New York, 1946.

Gaselnik, A. "A. Gaselnik's oisgaben," *YIVO* bleter, 1939, vol. 14.

Getzler, Israel. *Martov: A Political Biography of a Russian Social Democrat*. Cambridge, Eng., 1967.

Ginzberg, Asher [Ahad Ha'am]. *Selected Essays*. Translated and edited by Leon Simon. Philadelphia, 1912.

Ginzburg, A. M. [Naumov]. "Nachal'nye shagi Vitebskogo rabochego dvizheniia," in Sh. Dimanshtein, *Revoliutsionnoe*, listed above.

Ginzburg, Saul. *Amolike Peterburg: Forshungen un zikhroinos vegn yidishn lebn in der rezidents-shtot fun tsarishn Rusland.* New York, 1944.

Gol'dman, B. I. [Gorev]. "Marksizm i rabochee dvizhenie v Peterburge chetvert' veka nazad (vospominaniia)," *Krasnaia nov',* 1921, no. 3.

———. "Pered vtorym s"ezdom (vospominaniia)," *KIS,* 1924, no. 1.

Gol'dman, L. "Organizatsiia i tipografiia 'Iskry' v Rossii (iz lichnykh vospominanii)," *KIS,* 1925, no. 17(4).

Gordon, Abram [Rezhchik]. *In friling fun Vilner yidisher arbeter-bevegung.* Vilna, 1926.

Gorin, B. "Di naie zhargonishe literatur in Rusland," *DZ,* 1894, no. 11.

Gozhansky, Sh. "A vikuakh vegn mazel," *YHS.*

———. "Yevreiskoe rabochee dvizhenie nachala 90-kh godov," in Sh. Dimanshtein, *Revoliutsionnoe,* listed above.

———. [Lonu]. "A briv tsu agitatoren," *YHS.*

———. "Erinerungen fun a papirosen-makherke" (3 parts), *UT* (Warsaw), 1928, nos. 7, 8–9, and 10.

———. "Di ershte propagandistishe kraizlekh," *DAS* (Petrograd), no. 45 (Sept. 27, 1917).

[Gozhansky, Sh.]. *Der shtot magid.* Vilna, 1897.

Gruppa Sionistov-sotsialistov. *Vozzvanie k yevreiskoi molodezhi.* London, May 1901.

Gurko, V. I. *Features and Figures of the Past: Government and Opinion in the Reign of Nicholas II.* Translated by Laura Matveev. Edited by J. E. Wallace Sterling, Xenia Joukoff-Eudin, and H. H. Fisher. Stanford, Calif., 1939.

Gurevich, M. "Der 'Bund' in Amerike," *DZ,* 1937, no. 10.

Gurvich, E. A. "O pervim s"ezde R.S.-D.R.P.," *KIS,* 1928, no. 40.

———. "Yevreiskoe rabochee dvizhenie v Minske v 80-kh g.," in Sh. Dimanshtein, ed., *Revoliutsionnoe,* listed above.

——— [Zhenia Hurvich]. "Di ershte propagandistishe kraizn," *Roite bleter,* book 1, 1929.

Gurvich, I. "Pervye yevreiskie rabochie kruzhki," *Byloe,* 1907, no. 6.

Gutman, M. "Tsu der forgeshikhte fun S.S.," *Roiter pinkos,* vol. 1 (1921).

Harcave, Sidney. *First Blood: The Russian Revolution of 1905.* New York, 1964.

———. "Jewish Political Parties and Groups and the Russian State Dumas from 1905 to 1907." Unpub. Ph.D. diss., Univ. of Chicago, March 1943.

Hertz, J. S. "A farshvartster ponem" (2 parts), *UT,* 1967, nos. 6 and 7–8.

———. *Di geshikhte fun a yugent: Der Klainer Bund–Yugent Bund Zukunft in Poiln.* New York, 1946.

———. *Hirsh Lekert.* New York, 1952.

———, ed. *Doires Bundistn.* 3 vols. New York, 1956–68.

———, G. Aronson, S. Dubnow-Erlich, et al. *Di geshikhte fun Bund.* 3 vols. to date. New York, 1960–.

Hirsh Lekert:tsum 20-tn yortog fun zain kepung. Moscow, 1922.

Hofman, B. [Zivion]. *Far 50 yor: Geklibene shriftn.* New York, 1948.

———. "Vi azoi ikh bin gekumen tsum 'Bund,' " *UT* (New York), 1945, no. 3.

In baginen. Tel Aviv, March 1948.

Iuditsky, A. "Durum un Lite in der geshikhte fun 'Bund,' " *Folkstsaitung* (Kiev), no. 5 (Sept. 20, 1917).

———. "Di yidishe arbeter bevegung oif Ukraine," *Di roite velt,* 1926, no. 4.

Iurenev, I. "Rabota R.S.-D.R.P. v Severo-Zapadnom Krae (Vil'na) (1903–1913 gg.)," *PR,* 1924, no. 8–9.

Izenshtat, Isaiah [Vitali]. "Plekhanov un di yidishe arbeter bevegung," *Der Veker* (Minsk), July 4, 1918.

"K istorii yevreiskago rabochago dvizheniia." Vilna, 1896. Typewritten copy in Bund Archives, New York.

"K istorii Zubatovshchiny," *Byloe*, 1917, no. 1(23).

Kahan-Virgili, *see* B. *Kahan-Virgili in B entries*.

Katz, D. [Taras]. "K voprosu ob uchastii delegatsii 'Bunda' na I s"ezde R.S.-D.R.P.," *KL*, 1923, no. 7.

———— [V. Tsoglin]. "Mehzdu pervym i tret'im s"ezdami Bunda," in Sh. Dimanshtein, *Revoliutsionnoe*, listed above.

————. "Pervyi s"ezd Bunda," in Sh. Dimanshtein, *Revoliutsionnoe*, listed above.

Katz, Hillel [Blum]. *Zikhroinos fun a Bundist*. New York, 1940.

Keep, J. L. H. *The Rise of Social Democracy in Russia*. Oxford, Eng., 1963.

Khaifets, S. Ia. "K biografii Al'berta Borisovicha Sapotnitskogo," *KIS*, 1925, no. 3.

Kirzhnits, A. "Bund un RSDAP erev dem Tsvaiten Partai Tsuzamenfor," *Visenshaftlekhe yorbikher*, 1929, vol. 1.

————. "Nachalo sotsialisticheskoi pechati na yevreiskom iazyke v Rossii," in Sh. Dimanshtein, *Revoliutsionnoe*, listed above.

————. *Di profbevegung tsvishn di yidishe arbeter in di yorn fun der ershter revolutsie*. Moscow, 1926.

————. *Di yidishe prese in der gevezener ruslendisher imperie (1823-1916)*. Moscow-Kharkov-Minsk, 1930.

————, comp. *Der yidisher arbeter*. Edited by M. Rafes. vol. 2. Moscow, 1925.

Kivin, Sh. "Bam vigele fun der partai," *Yidisher arbeter pinkos*, 1927, vol. 1.

Kokovtsov, Count V. N. *Out of My Past: Memoirs of Count Kokovtsov*. Edited by H. H. Fisher. Translated by Laura Matveev. Stanford, Calif., 1935.

Kopelson, T. "Evreiskoe rabochee dvizhenie kontsa 80-kh i nachala 90-kh godov," in Sh. Dimanshtein, *Revoliutsionnoe*, listed above.

————. "Ob 'opozitsie' 1893 g." 1907. Manuscript in Bund Archives, New York.

———— [Timofei]. "Di ershte shprotsungen (zikhroinos fun di yorn 1887–1890)," *Arbeter-luakh* (Warsaw), 1922 (3d year).

Kosovsky, V. "Martov un di Russishe Sotsial Demokratie," *DZ*, 1924, no. 3.

————. "Vl. Medem un di natsionale frage (a kapitel zikhroinos)," *DZ*, 1928, no. 3.

Koz'min, B. P. *S. V. Zubatov i yego korrespondenty*. Moscow-Leningrad, 1928.

Kremer, Aleksandr. "Zametki Aleksandra Kremera o Belostokskoi konf. R.S.-D.R.P." March 1902. Typewritten manuscript in Bund Archives, New York.

[Kremer, Aleksandr]. *Ob agitatsii*. Geneva, 1896.

Krol, M. "Der Homler pogrom-protses," *DZ*, 1937, no. 9.

Krzhizhanovsky, S. "Pol'skaia Sotsialdemokratiia i II s"ezd RSDRP," *PR*, 1933, no. 2.

Kursky, Franz. "Bletlekh zikhroinos" (2 parts), *DZ*, 1934, nos. 10 and 11.

————. "David Michnik ('Chekh'): dem ondenk fun a khaver un fraint," *DZ*, 1935, no. 1.

————. *Gezamelte shriftn*. New York, 1952.

————. "Moisai Gurevich ('Matvei,' 'Misha')," *UT* (New York), 1945, no. 2.

————. "Ver zenen geven di grinder fun 'Bund'?," *Naie Folkstsaitung* (Warsaw), Nov. 19, 1937.

———— [Sh. K. Frants]. "Fargesene nemen," *DZ*, 1922, no. 10.

Kuskova, E. D. "Istoricheskaia bibliografiia," *Byloe*, 1906, no. 10.

Leikowicz, Ch., ed. *Lite*. vol. 2. Tel Aviv, 1965.

Lenin, V. I. *Polnoe sobranie sochinenii*. 5th ed. 55 vols. Moscow, 1958–65.

————. *Sochineniia*. 2d ed. 30 vols. Moscow-Leningrad, 1927–32.

————. *Sochineniia*. 3d ed. 30 vols. Moscow, 1928–37.

Leninskii sbornik. Edited by L. B. Kamenev. 35 vols. Moscow-Leningrad, 1924–45.

Lepeshinsky, P. *Na povorote.* 3d ed. Moscow, 1935.

Lestchinsky, Jacob. "The Jews in the Cities of the Republic of Poland," *YIVO Annual of Jewish Social Science.* vol. 1. New York, 1946.

———. *Der yidisher arbeter.* Vilna, 1906.

Lev, A. "Pervye shagi yevreiskogo rabochego dvizheniia v g. Grodno," in Sh. Diman-shtein, *Revoliutsionnoe,* listed above.

———, ed. *Der klerikalizm in kamf kegn der arbeter-bevegung.* 3d ed. Moscow, 1934.

Levin, Sholom. *Untererdishe kemfer.* New York, 1946.

Levin, Yankel. *Fun yene yorn: "Klain Bund."* Minsk, 1924.

Levitats, Isaac. *The Jewish Community in Russia, 1772–1844.* New York, 1943.

Liesin, Abraham. "Main ershte bagegenish mit David Pinsky," *DZ,* 1922, no. 5.

———. *Zikhroinos un bilder.* New York, 1954.

Litvak, A. *Geklibene shrijtn.* New York, 1945.

———. "Lobuzes, genovim un kombinatorn (a kapitel zikhroinos), *Roiter pinkos,* vol. 2 (1924).

———. "Minsk un di Minsker," *DZ,* 1933, no. 8.

———. *Vos geven: Etiudn un zikhroinos.* Vilna, 1925.

———. "Di 'zhargonishe komitetn,' " *Roiter pinkos,* vol. 1 (1921).

Lopukhin, A. A. *Otryvki iz vospominanii (po povodu vospominanii Gr. S. Iu. Witte).* Moscow-Leningrad, 1923.

Martov, L. *Istoriia Rossiiskoi Sotsial-Demokratii.* 3d ed. Petrograd-Moscow, 1923.

———. *Zapiski sotsial-demokrata.* vol. 1. Berlin, 1922.

"Martov tsu Aleksander." June 7, 1901. Letter in Bund Archives, New York.

[Martynov, A. S.] *Dva s"ezda: III'i ocherednoi s"ezd soiuza i ob"edinitel'nyi s"ezd.* Geneva, 1901.

"Materialy do Historii P.P.S. i ruchu revolucyjnego w zaborze rosyjskim od r. 1893–1904." vol. 1. Warsaw, 1907. Typewritten copy in Bund Archives, New York.

Materialy k istorii yevreiskago rabochago dvizheniia. vol. 1. St. Petersburg, 1906.

"Materialy o Belostokskoi konferentsii R.S.-D.R.P., Mart, 1902," *PR,* 1922, no. 9.

Medem, V. *Fun main leben.* 2 vols. New York, 1923.

Medesh, Vadim. "The First Party Congress and Its Place in History," *The Russian Review,* 1963, no. 2.

Menchikoff, M. O. "The Jewish Peril in Russia," *Monthly Review* (London), Feb. 1904.

Mendelsohn, Ezra. "The Jewish Socialist Movement and the Second International, 1889–1914: The Struggle for Recognition," *Jewish Social Studies,* 1964, no. 3.

Menes, Abraham. "The Jewish Socialist Movement in Russia and Poland," in *The Jewish People: Past and Present,* vol. 2. New York, 1948.

———. "Di yidishe arbeter bevegung in Rusland fun onhaib 70er bizn suf 90er yorn," *YHS.*

Men'shchikov, L. *Okhrana i revoliutsiia.* 4 vols. Moscow, 1925–32.

"Mezhdupartiinyia otnosheniia i ob"edinenie s RSDRP." Manuscript in Bund Archives, New York.

Mikhalevich, B. "Erev 'Bund,' " *Roiter pinkos,* vol. 1 (1921).

———. *Zikhroinos fun a yidishen sotsialist.* 3 vols. Warsaw, 1921–29.

[Mikhalevich, B.] "Gehaime drukeraien," *Arbeter-luakh* (Warsaw), 1922 (3d year). Signed B. M.

Miliukov, Paul. *Political Memoirs.* Translated by Carl Goldberg. Edited by Arthur P. Mendel. Ann Arbor, Mich., 1967.

Mill, John. "Di geburt fun Bund." *Naie Folkstsaitung* (Warsaw), Nov. 19, 1937.

———. "Di natsionale frage un der 'Bund,'" *DZ*, 1918, no. 2.

———. *Pionern un boier.* 2 vols. New York, 1946–49.

———. "Tsvantsig yor 'Bund'" (2 parts), *DZ*, 1917, no. 10, and 1918, no. 1.

Minchanka, *see* F. Frumkina.

"Mit vos zainen besheftigt di Kovner 'tsionisten,'" *Flug-blettel*, Oct. 1903.

Mitskevich-Kapsukas, V. "1905 g. v Litve," *PR*, 1922, no. 11.

Mosynski, I. N. [Iuz. Konarsky]. *Na putiakh k 1-mu s"ezdu R.S.-D.R.P.* Moscow, 1928.

Motolski, Elie. "1-ter Mai 1903 in Varshe (a bletl zikhroinos), *UT* (New York), 1945, no. 7.

[Mutnikovich, A.] "Bletlekh fun main leben" (2 parts), *DZ*, 1933, nos. 11 and 12. Signed Abram Mutnik.

———. "Der Ershter Tsuzamenfor fun Bund," *Di Hofnung* (Vilna), Sept. 15/Oct. 8, 1907. Signed G-b.

———. "Tsu der geshikhte fun der entviklung fun zhargonisher umlegaler politishe presse in Rusland," *DAS*, no. 25 (Oct. 1901). Signed A.G.

———. "Materialy dlia kharakterishtiki rabochego dvizheniia nashego goroda za poslednie 4-5 let/sobrany v 1896 godu." Typewritten manuscript in Bund Archives, New York.

Nettl, J. P. *Rosa Luxemburg.* 2 vols. London, 1966.

Niger, Samuel. "Yiddish Literature in the Past Two Hundred Years," in *The Jewish People: Past and Present*, vol. 3. New York, 1952.

———, and Z. Raizen, eds. *Vaiter-bukh.* Vilna, 1920.

———, and Jacob Shatski, eds. *Leksikon fun der naier yidisher literatur.* 7 vols. to date. New York, 1956–   .

Nikolaevsky, B. "V. I. Ulianov-Lenin v Berline v 1895 godu," *Letopisi marksizma* (Moscow-Leningrad), 1926, vol. 1.

———, ed. "R.S.-D.R.P. o soglasheniiakh s oppozisionnymi i revoliutsionnymi partiiami v 1904 godu," *KIS*, 1927, no. 3.

[Nikolaevsky, B.] "Iz epokhy 'Iskry' i 'Zari'" (2 parts), *KIS,* 1927, nos. 6 and 7. Signed B. N.

———. "Pis'mo G. V. Plekhanova v redaktsiiu 'Rabochei gazety,'" *Letopis' revoliutsii* (Berlin), book 1, 1923. Signed B. N-sky.

1905 yor in Berdichev: Notitsen un zikhroinos. Kiev, 1925.

"Obvinitel'nyi Akt po delu Shmae Borukhov Gorelike . . . i drugikh," May 4, 1904. Official copy in Bund Archives, New York.

Odinetz, D. M. et al. *Russian Schools and Universities in the World War.* New Haven, Conn., 1929.

Otchet Mezdunarodnomu sotsialisticheskomu biuro o Vseobshchem Yevreiskom Rabochem Soiuze v Litve, Pol'she i Rossii (Bund). December, 1902. Mimeographed copy in Bund Archives, New York.

Perazich, S. V. "Iz vospominanii S. V. Perazicha (S. V. Pomerants)," *KL*, 1923, no. 7.

Pertsev, V. N. et al., eds. *Dokumenty i materialy po istorii Belorussii (1900–1917).* vol. 3. Minsk, 1953.

Pervoe Maia 1892 goda: Chetyre rechi yevreskikh rabochikh s predisloviem. Geneva, 1893.

Pervyi s"ezd RSDRP Mart 1898 goda: Dokumenty i materialy. Moscow, 1958.

Peskin, Jacob. "Di 'Grupe Yidishe Sotsial-Demokraten' in Rusland un Arkady Kremer," *YHS.*

Pestkovsky, S. "Bor'ba Partii v rabochem dvizhenii v Pol'she v 1905–1907 gg.," *PR*, 1922, no. 8.

Piatnitsky, O. *Zapiski Bol'shevika.* 5th ed. Moscow, 1956.

Pilsudski, Joseph. *Joseph Pilsudski: The Memories of a Polish Revolutionary and Soldier.* Translated and edited by D. R. Gillie. London, 1931.

Pinsker, Lev Semenovich. *Auto-emancipation.* New York, 1935.

Piontkovsky, S. "Novoe o Zubatovshchine," *Krasnyi arkhiv,* 1922, vol. 1.

Pipes, Richard. *Social Democracy and the St. Petersburg Labor Movement, 1885–1897.* Cambridge, Mass., 1963.

Pis'ma P. B. Aksel'roda i Iu. O. Martova, 1901–1916. Edited by F. Dan, B. Nikolaevsky, and L. Tsederbaum-Dan. Berlin, 1924.

Plekhanov, G. V. *Sochineniia.* Edited by D. Riazanov. 2d ed. 24 vols. Moscow, 1923–27.

Pobedonostev, Constantin. *L'Autocratie Russe.* Paris, 1927.

Pokrovsky, M. N., general ed. *1905: Yevreiskoe rabochee dvizhenie.* Compiled by A. D. Kirzhnits. Edited by M. Rafes. Moscow-Leningrad, 1928.

"Predstavitel' Tsentral'nago Komiteta Bunda—Pis'mo k redaktsii." Feb. 1903. Letter in Bund Archives, New York.

Programmnyia pis'ma. no. 1, London, July 1902.

Rabinovich, Sh. "Mit 50 yor tsurik," *YHS.*

Rabinowitsch, S. *Die Organizationen des jüdisches Proletariat in Russland.* Karlsruhe, 1903.

Rabochee dvizhenie v Rossii v XIX veke: Sbornik dokumentov i materialov. vol. 4. 1961–63.

Radek, Karl. *Portraits and Pamphlets.* New York, n.d.

Raeff, Marc, ed. *Plans for Political Reform, 1730–1905.* Englewood Cliffs, N.J., 1966.

Rafes, M. *Kapitlen geshikhte fun "Bund."* Kiev, 1929.

———. *Ocherki po istorii Bunda.* Moscow, 1923.

———, comp. "Primiritel'nye popytki 'Bunda' v 1905 goda," *PR,* 1922, no. 11.

Raisin, Jacob S. *The Haskalah Movement in Russia.* Philadelphia, 1913.

Raitshuk, Elie. "Fun vaitn oiver," *Roite bleter,* book 1, 1929.

Raizen, Z., ed. *Leksikon fun der yidisher literatur, prese, un filologie.* 4 vols. Vilna, 1928–30.

Revoliutsiia 1905–1907 v Rossii: Dokumenty i materialy. Nachalo pervoi Russkoi revoliutsii: Ianvar'–Mart 1905. Edited by N. S. Trusova. Moscow, 1955.

Revoliutsiia 1905–1907 v Rossii: Dokumenty i materialy Vysshii pod"em Revoliutsii 1905–1907 gg.: Vooruzhennye vostaniia: Noiabr'–Dekabr' 1905 goda: Chast' chetvertaia. Edited by A. L. Sidorov. Moscow, 1957.

Revoliutsionnoe dvizhenie v Belorussii 1905–1907. Edited by A. I. Azarov, E. P. Luk'ianov, and V. N. Zhigalov. Minsk, 1955.

"Revolutionary Propaganda in the Army of the Czar," *New York Times,* Sept. 4, 1904.

Rogger, Hans. "The Formation of the Russian Right, 1900–1906," *California Slavic Studies* (Berkeley, Calif.), vol. 3, 1964.

———. "Was There a Russian Fascism?" *Journal of Modern History,* 1964, no. 4.

Romanov, B. A., ed. "Nachalo proletarskoi revoliutsii v Rossii," *Krasnyi arkhiv,* 1926, vol. 11–12.

Rosenbaum, M. M. *Erinerungen fun a sotsialist-revoliutsioner.* 2 vols. New York, 1921.

Rosenthal, Anna. "Bletlekh fun a lebens-geshikhte (Vilna)," *YHS.*

———. "Froien-geshtaltn in 'Bund,'" *UT* (New York), 1947, no. 3–4.

Rosenthal, Pinai [Pavel]. "Der ershter onhoib," *Roiter pinkos,* vol. 2 (1924).

——— [An-man]. "Der Bialystoker period in leben fun Ts. K. fun 'Bund,'" *Roiter pinkos,* vol. 1 (1921).

[Rozanov, V. N.] "Iz partiinago proshlago (po lichnym vospominaniiam), *Nasha zaria* (St. Petersburg), 1913, no. 6. Signed Vl. R-v.

Rozen, Nathan. "Iberlebungen fun a 'Klainem-Bundist' (derinerungen fun Vilne, Vitebsk, un Polotsk)," *UT* (New York), 1943, no. 12.

Rubach, M. A., ed. *Istoriia Yekaterinoslavskoi Sotsial-Demokraticheskoi organizatsii, 1889–1903.* Ekaterinoslav, 1923.

Runes, Dagobert D., ed. *A World Without Jews.* 4th ed. New York, 1960.

Sbornik materialov ob ekonomicheskom polozhenii yevreev v Rossii. 2 vols. St. Petersburg, 1904.

Schechter, Solomon. "The Chassidim," in *Studies in Judaism.* 1st series. Philadelphia, 1945.

Schwarz, Solomon. "Men'shevizm i Bol'shevizm v ikh otnoshenii k massovomu rabochemu dvizheniiu." Inter-University Project on the History of the Menshevik Movement. New York. Mimeographed.

———. *The Russian Revolution of 1905.* Chicago, 1967.

Shkliar, H. "Onhaib fun der yidisher arbeter bevegung in Lite," in Leikowicz, listed above.

Shpizman, L. *Geshikhte fun der Tsionistisher arbeter bevegung in Tsufn Amerike.* 2 vols. New York, 1955.

Shtupler, B. "Tsvai pionern fun der revoliutsionerer arbeter-bevegung in Bialystok," in Herman Frank et al., eds., *Natsionale un politishe bevegungen bai jidn in Bialystok.* vol. 1. New York, 1951.

Shukman, H. "The Relations Between the Jewish Bund and the RSDRP, 1897–1903." Unpub. D.Phil. diss. Oxford University, 1961.

Shulman, V. "Baginen," *UT* (New York) 1945, no. 3.

———. *Bletlekh geshikhte fun der yidisher arbeter bevegung.* part 1. Warsaw, 1929.

———. "Der ershter forposten in durum," *Naie Folkstsaitung* (Warsaw), Oct. 17, 1927.

———. "Der pionern-period fun der yidisher sotsialistisher bevegung in Rusland," *YIVO bleter,* 1946.

Shvarts, P. *Juzef Pilsudski: zain batsiung tsu der yidnfrage un zain kamf kegn 'Bund.'* Warsaw, 1936.

———. "Revolutsionere arbet fun 'Bund' in der tsarisher armai," *YIVO bleter,* 1962.

Sintovsky, Elijah. "Der bershter Bund," *UT* (New York), 1941, no. 7.

Sliozberg, G. B. *Dela minuvshikh dnei: Zapiski Russkago Yevreia.* vol. 3. Paris, 1934.

"Soiuz Russkikh Sotsialdemokratov—Zagranichnomu Komitetu Bunda." February 2, 1903. Letter in Bund Archives, New York.

Spector, Ivar and Marion, eds. *Readings in Russian History and Culture.* Boston, 1965.

"Statisticheskiia dannyia o B.O." [1906?] Manuscript in Bund Archives, New York.

"Der statut fun der kase un bailage vegn der noitikait aintsuordnen bibliotekn, Vilna, 1894," *UT* (Warsaw), 1928, no. 2.

Steklov, Iu. "V ssylke i v emigratsii (ideinye konflikty)," *PR,* 1923, no. 5.

Stern, Beryl. *Zikhroinos fun shturmishe yorn: (Bielsk, 1898–1907).* Newark, N.J., 1954.

Struve, Peter. "My Contacts and Conflicts with Lenin," *Slavonic and East European Review* (London), 1934, no. 37.

Syrkin, Marie. *Nachman Syrkin, Socialist Zionist: A Biographical Memoir.* New York, 1961.

Syrkin, N. "Tsu der geshikhte fun sotsialistishen tsionizm," *Der Yidisher Kemfer* (New York), vol. 15, no. 146 (Dec. 20, 1935).

Syromiatnikov, M. "Pervoe Maia v tsarskoi Rossii," *Krasnyi arkhiv,* 1937, vol. 82.

Tobias, Henry J. "The Bund and the First Congress of the RSDWP: An Addendum," *The Russian Review*, 1965, no. 4.

———. "The Bund and Lenin Until 1903," *The Russian Review*, 1961, no. 4.

Toiznt yor Pinsk. Edited by Dr. B. Hofman [Zivion]. New York, 1941.

Tretii s"ezd RSDRP: Aprel'–Mai 1905: Protokoly. Moscow, 1959.

"Tsarskii listok," *Byloe*, 1908, no. 7.

Tsoglin, V., *see* D. Katz.

Tuchapsky, P. L. *Iz perezhitogo*. Odessa, 1923.

Urussov, Prince Serge Dmitriyevich. *Memoirs of a Russian Governor*. Translated by Herman Rosenthal. New York, 1908.

Vainer, A. [Abrashe]. "Der Klainer Bund," *Yugent Veker* (Warsaw), no. 24 (Nov. 1, 1937).

Valk, S. "K istorii Belostokskoi Konferentsii 1902 goda," *PR*, 1930, no. 6.

Varzar, V. E., comp. *Statistika stachek rabochikh na fabrikakh i zabodakh za 1905 g.* St. Petersburg, 1908.

Vestnik Narodnoi Voli. Geneva, 1886.

"Di vide fun provokator Kaplinsky," *Roite bleter*, book 1, 1929.

Vilner Gruppe fun der Y.U.A.P. *Flug-blettel*. Sept. 1902.

[M. Vinocur?]. Pogroma i samooborona." [1906?] Manuscript in Bund Archives, New York. Signed M. V.

Vohliner, A., ed. *Yidisher arbeter yor-bukh un almanakh*. New York, 1927.

Volkovicher, I. "Partiia i Russko-Iaponskaia Voina," *PR*, 1924, no. 12.

———. "V. I. Lenin i sobiranie partii vokrug staroi 'Iskry' (po neizdannym materialam Zhenevskogo partiinogo arkhiva)," *PR*, 1924, no. 3.

Vtoroi ocherednoi s"ezd Ross. Sots.-Dem. Rabochei Partii: Polnyi tekst protokolov. Geneva, 1904.

Vtoroi s"ezd RSDRP: Protokoly. Moscow, 1959.

Weizmann, Chaim. *Trial and Error*. 2 vols. Philadelphia, 1949.

Wildman, Allen K. "Lenin's Battle with Kustarnichestvo: The Iskra Organization in Russia," *Slavic Review*, 1964, no. 3.

Witte, S. Iu. *Vospominaniia*. 3 vols. Moscow, 1960.

Wolf-Jasny, A. *Geshikhte fun der yidisher arbeter bevegung in Lodz*. Lodz, 1937.

Wolfe, Bertram D. *Three Who Made a Revolution*. New York, 1948.

Woodhouse, Charles E., and Henry J. Tobias. "Primordial Ties and Political Process in Pre-Revolutionary Russia: The Case of the Jewish Bund," *Comparative Studies in Society and History*, 1966, no 3.

Yermansky, O. A. *Iz perezhitogo (1887–1921 gg.)*. Moscow-Leningrad, 1927.

Y.U.A.P., Der Komitet fun der. *Tsu ale yidishe arbeter un arbeterinen*. July 6, 1903.

———. *Tsu unzere partei genossen*. Feb. 1903.

Zakharova-Tsederbaum, K. I., and S. I. Tsederbaum. *Iz epokhi "Iskry" (1900–1905 gg.)*. Moscow-Leningrad, 1926.

[Zaks, F.]. *A klarer entfer*. London, 1904. First appeared as an appendix to *Der Arbeter*, 1903, no. 8.

Zaslavsky, D. "Tsu der geshikhte fun 'Bund' in Kiev," *Roiter pinkos*, vol. 1 (1921).

———. "Zubatov i Mania Vil'bushevich," *Byloe*, 1918, no. 3.

Zborowski, Mark, and Elizabeth Herzog. *Life Is with People: The Culture of the Shtetl*. New York, 1962.

[Zeldov, S.]. "Vi azoi iz tsuzamengeshtelt un opgedrukt gevoren der ershter numer 'Arbeter Shtime,' " *Di Hofnung* (Vilna), Sept. 25/Oct. 8, 1907. Signed Z.

———. "Vozniknovenie 'Arbeter Shtime,' " *Perezhitoe*, 1908, vol. 1.

Zheleznikov, Jacob, and Shmuel Liov, "Epizodn un mentshen in der Pinsker Bundisher bevegung," in B. Hofman [Zivion], ed., *Toiznt yor Pinsk*. New York, 1941.

Zhitlovsky, Chaim. *Gezamelte shriften*. vol. 9. New York, 1919.

Zilberfarb, M. "Di grupe 'Vozrozhdenie,' " *Roiter pinkos*, vol. 1 (1921).

Zivion, *see* Hofman.

Zubatov, S. V. "Zubatovshchina," *Byloe*, 1917, no. 4.

2. BUND PUBLICATIONS

A. Books, Pamphlets, and Leaflets

Avtonomiia ili federatsiia. London, April 1903.

Brider rekruten. Oct. 1904. Central Committee. 35,000 copies.

Chetvertyi s"ezd Vseobshchago Yevreiskago Rabochago Soiuza v Litve, Pol'she, i Rossii. Geneva, 1901.

Doklad Internatsional'nomu Sotsialisticheskomu Kongressu v Amsterdame. Geneva, Aug. 1904.

Der ershter mai. April 1905. Central Committee. 130,000 copies.

A folksfertretung on dem folk. Aug. 1905. Central Committee. 130,000 copies.

Di geshikhte fun der yidisher arbeter bevegung in Rusland un Poilen. Geneva, March 1900.

Di geshikhte fun yidisher arbeter-Bund. Vilna, 1906.

Girsh Lekert i yego protsess. July 1902.

Istoriia yevreiskago rabochago dvizheniia v Rossii i Pol'she. Geneva, 1901.

K voprosu o natsional'noi avtonomii i preobrazovanii Ros. Sots.-Demok. Rabochei Partii na federativnykh nachalakh. London, Feb. 1902.

K voprosu o terrorizme. London, Feb. 1903.

Di Kishinever hariga: Materialen un dokumenten. London, 1903.

Ko vsem yevreiskim narodnym uchiteliam. Aug. 1903.

Di milkhoma fun der Poilisher Partai gegn dem Yidishn Arbeter Bund. July 1898.

Di milkhoma un di zelbsthershung. Feb. 1904.

Mir un zai (vegen der yidisher liberaler bevegung). March 1905. Central Committee. 60,000 copies.

"Mit vos zainen basheftigt di Kovner tsionisten," *Flug-blettel*, Oct. 1903. Kovno Committee.

Di naie epokhe in der yidisher arbeter bevegung. Geneva, 1900.

Otvet "Iskre." March 1903. Central Committee.

Piatyi s"ezd Vseobshchago Yevreiskago Rabochago Soiuza v Litve, Pol'she, i Rossii. London, Oct. 1903.

Po povodu mobilizatsii. July 1904. Central Committee. 10,000 copies.

Po povodu s"ezda ravvinov v Grodne. Nov. 1903. Grodno Committee.

Pogrom v Gomele. Sept. 1903.

Di pogromen in Rusland un di zelbstfertaidigung. April 16–20, 1905.

Sed'maia Konferentsiia Bunda. Geneva, 1906.

Di tetigkait fun "Bund" far di letste tsvai yor. London, Oct. 1903.

Tovarishchi rabochie! May 1902.

Di tsarishe nadove far yiden. Sept. 1904. Central Committee. 18,000 copies in Russian, 48,000 in Yiddish.

Dem tsar's konstitutsie. March 1905.

Tsu ale arbeter un arbeterinen fun Shereshevsky's fabrik. Nov. 1904. 1,000 copies.

Tsu ale Belostoker arbeter un arbeterinen. Nov. 1904.

Tsu ale Dvinsker ainvoner. Aug. 1903.

Tsu ale fraie birger. Nov. 8 (Oct. 26), 1905.

Tsu ale rekruten. Oct. 1905. Central Committee. 77,000 copies in Yiddish, 30,000 in Russian, 10,000 in Polish.

Tsu ale Vilner arbeter un arbeterinen. July 1902.

Tsu ale yidishe arbeter un arbeterinen. April 1902 [sic].

Tsum kamf! Jan. 1905. Central Committee. 115,000 copies in Yiddish, 100,000 in Russian.

Vegen der aroistretung fun "Bund" fun der Ruslander Sotsial-Demokratisher Arbeter Partai. Dec. 1903. Central Committee. 20,000 copies.

Vegen der mobilizatsie. July 1904. Central Committee. 48,000 copies.

Vos mir darfen. Dec. 1904.

Vozzvanie k yevreiskoi intelligentsii. 3d ed. London, Feb. 1903.

Vtoroi s"ezd Rossiiskoi S.-D.R. Partii. Otchet delegatsii Bunda. London, 1903.

Yevreiskie pogromy i organizantsiia proletariata: K russkim tovarishcham. April 1904.

B. Newspapers and Journals

Di Arbeter Shtime (Vilna-Bobruisk-Warsaw), 1897–1905.

Der Belostoker Arbeter, 1899–1902.

Der Bund, 1904–5.

Der Kamf (Gomel), 1900–1901.

Der Klasen-Kamf (Vilna), 1900–1901.

Di Letste Pasirungen in raion fun Bund, 1904–6.

Der Minsker Arbeter, 1900–1905.

Posledniia izvestiia (London-Geneva), 1901–6.

Der Varshaver Arbeter, 1899–1905.

Der Veker [publication of the bristle workers], 1898–1903.

Der Veker (Vilna), 1905–6.

Vestnik Bunda (Geneva), 1904.

Der Yidisher Arbeter (Pressburg-Geneva-London), 1896–1904.

Index

Index